8th Workshop on Representation Learning for NLP (RepL4NLP-2023)

Toronto, Canada
13 July 2023

ISBN: 978-1-7138-8231-2

Printed from e-media with permission by:

Curran Associates, Inc.
57 Morehouse Lane
Red Hook, NY 12571

Some format issues inherent in the e-media version may also appear in this print version.

Printed with permission by Curran Associates, Inc. (2024)

Association for Computational Linguistics
209 N. Eighth Street
Stroudsburg, Pennsylvania 18360

Phone: 1-570-476-8006
Fax: 1-570-476-0860

acl@aclweb.org

Additional copies of this publication are available from:

Curran Associates, Inc.
57 Morehouse Lane
Red Hook, NY 12571 USA
Phone: 845-758-0400
Fax: 845-758-2633
Email: curran@proceedings.com
Web: www.proceedings.com

ACL 2023

The 8th Workshop on Representation Learning for NLP (RepL4NLP 2023)

Proceedings of the Workshop

July 13, 2023

The ACL organizers gratefully acknowledge the support from the following sponsors.

Gold

Google

Introduction

The 8th Workshop on Representation Learning for NLP (RepL4NLP 2023) will be hosted by ACL 2023 and held on 13 July 2023. The workshop is being organised by Burcu Can, Maximilian Mozes, Samuel Cahyawijaya, Naomi Saphra, Nora Kassner, Shauli Ravfogel, Abhilasha Ravichander, and Chen Zhao; and advised by Isabelle Augenstein, Anna Rogers, Kyunghyun Cho, and Edward Grefenstette. The workshop is organised by the ACL Special Interest Group on Representation Learning (SIGREP).

The 8th Workshop on Representation Learning for NLP aims to continue the success of the Repl4NLP workshop series, with the 1st Workshop on Representation Learning for NLP having received about 50 submissions and over 250 attendees - the second most attended collocated event at ACL'16 after WMT. The workshop was introduced as a synthesis of several years of independent *CL workshops focusing on vector space models of meaning, compositionality, and the application of deep neural networks and spectral methods to NLP. It provides a forum for discussing recent advances on these topics, as well as future research directions in linguistically motivated vector-based models in NLP. The workshop will take place in a hybrid setting, and, as in previous years, feature interdisciplinary keynotes, paper presentations, posters, as well as a panel discussion.

Organizing Committee

Workshop Organizers

Burcu Can, University of Stirling
Maximilian Mozes, University College London
Samuel Cahyawijaya, Hong Kong University of Science and Technology
Naomi Saphra, New York University
Nora Kassner, Meta
Shauli Ravfogel, Bar-Ilan University
Abhilasha Ravichander, Allen Institute for Artificial Intelligence
Chen Zhao, New York University

Senior Advisors

Isabelle Augenstein, University of Copenhagen
Anna Rogers, University of Copenhagen
Kyunghyun Cho, New York University
Edward Grefenstette, DeepMind
Lena Voita, Meta AI

Program Committee

Program Committee

Aleksandr Drozd, RIKEN
Aleksandra Piktus, University of Roma La Sapienza
Alexandra Chronopoulou, Ludwig-Maximilians-Universität München
Alexandre Allauzen, École Supérieure de Physique et de Chimie Industrielles de la Ville de Paris
Ankur Padia, Philips Research North America
Anna Tigunova, Saarland Informatics Campus, Max-Planck Institute
Antonio Uva, Amazon
Arjun Reddy Akula, Google
Bryan Wilie, Hong Kong University of Science and Technology
Caglar Gulcehre, DeepMind
Chris Quirk, Microsoft
Christopher Davis, University of Cambridge
Denis Filimonov, Amazon
Dong Zhou, Guangdong University of Foreign Studies
Edwin Simpson, University of Bristol
Eliezer de Souza da Silva, Norwegian University of Science and Technology
Elisabetta Fersini, University of Milan-Bicocca
Etsuko Ishii, The Hong Kong University of Science and Technology
Eva Maria Vecchi, University of Stuttgart
Faeze Brahman, Allen Institute for AI
Frank Rudzicz, Dalhousie University
Hai Wang, Samsung
Haiqin Yang, International Digital Economy Academy
Hao Tang, University of Edinburgh
Holy Lovenia, Hong Kong University of Science and Technology
Hong Wang, UC Santa Barbara
Hong Yu, Apple
Hongliang Dai, The Hong Kong University of Science and Technology
Izzeddin Gur, Google
Jiaji Huang, AWS
Jingjing Xu, Shanghai AI Lab
Karl Stratos, Rutgers University
Kartik Goyal, Toyota Technological Institute at Chicago
Kimberly Mai, University College London
Lan Du, Monash University
Lili Mou, University of Alberta
Lin Chen, University of Illinois at Chicago
Linqing Liu, University College London
Matthieu Labeau, Télécom ParisTech
Menno van Zaanen, North-West University
Minhao Cheng, Hong Kong University of Science and Technology
Muhammad Mahbubur Rahman, George Washington University
Nadi Tomeh, Université Sorbonne Paris Nord
Necva Bölücü, Hacettepe University
Negar Foroutan, EPFL Lausanne
Nicholas Andrews, Johns Hopkins University

Paula Czarnowska, Amazon AWS
Philipp Dufter, Apple
Phoebe Mulcaire, Duolingo
Rainer Gemulla, Universität Mannheim
Robin Jia, University of Southern California
Rodrigo Wilkens, UCL
Santosh Kesiraju, Brno University of Technology
Selçuk Köprü, eBay
Sergey Feldman, Allen Institute for Artificial Intelligence
Shankar Kumar, Google
Shaohua Li, A*STAR
Shehzaad Zuzar Dhuliawala, Swiss Federal Institute of Technology
Shiva Taslimipoor, University of Cambridge
Shuai Tang, Amazon Web Services
Surangika Ranathunga, University of Moratuwa
Tao Li, Google
Tharindu Ranasinghe, Aston University
Thien Huu Nguyen, University of Oregon
Tiezheng YU, The Hong Kong University of Science and Technology
Tom Lippincott, Whiting School of Engineering
Truc-Vien T. Nguyen, Silo AI
Tsuyoshi Okita, Kyushu Institute of Technology
Tsvetomila Mihaylova, Aalto University
Uri Alon, Carnegie Mellon University
Valentin Hofmann, University of Oxford
Vipul Raheja, Grammarly
Vladimir Eidelman, FiscalNote, Inc.
Wenliang Dai, The Hong Kong University of Science and Technology
Wenxuan Zhou, University of Southern California
Xia Cui, The Manchester Metropolitan University
Yitong Li, Huawei Technologies Co., Ltd.
Yogarshi Vyas, Amazon
Yue Chen, Microsoft
Yuval Pinter, Ben Gurion University of the Negev

Invited Speakers

Swabha Swayamdipta, University of Southern California
Samira Abnar, Apple
Hannaneh Hajishirzi, University of Washington & Allen AI
Omer Levy, Tel Aviv University & Meta AI

Table of Contents

Adversarial Clean Label Backdoor Attacks and Defenses on Text Classification Systems

Ashim Gupta
Kahlert School of Computing
University of Utah
ashim@cs.utah.edu

Amrith Krishna
Uniphore Inc.
amrith.krishna@uniphore.com

Abstract

Clean-label (CL) attack is a form of data poisoning attack where an adversary modifies only the textual input of the training data, without requiring access to the labeling function. CL attacks are relatively unexplored in NLP, as compared to label flipping (LF) attacks, where the latter additionally requires access to the labeling function as well. While CL attacks are more resilient to data sanitization and manual relabeling methods than LF attacks, they often demand as high as ten times the poisoning budget than LF attacks. In this work, we first introduce an Adversarial Clean Label attack which can adversarially perturb in-class training examples for poisoning the training set. We then show that an adversary can significantly bring down the data requirements for a CL attack, using the aforementioned approach, to as low as 20 % of the data otherwise required. We then systematically benchmark and analyze a number of defense methods, for both LF and CL attacks, some previously employed solely for LF attacks in the textual domain and others adapted from computer vision. We find that text-specific defenses greatly vary in their effectiveness depending on their properties.

1 Introduction

Backdoor attacks are training time attacks where an adversary poisons the training data to introduce vulnerabilities in a machine learning system and gain control over the model's behaviour (Wallace et al., 2019; Gu et al., 2017; Wallace et al., 2021). Here, an adversary carefully inserts words or phrases, called triggers, to alter a model's behaviour during inference. Such an act is akin to creating a backdoor that gives unauthorised control of a system to the adversary. These attacks enable the adversary to bypass the security systems with ease and at will, which poses a serious security concern. Consider the use-case of a spam filter: a spammer could target a spam classifier by poisoning its training data

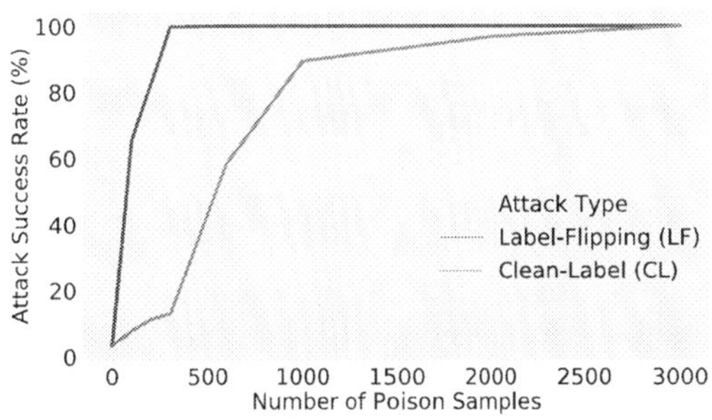

Figure 1: **Label-Flipping attacks are more effective than Clean-Label attacks**. Poisoning less than 300 examples achieves a 100% ASR for Label-flipping attack while Clean-Label requires poisoning of close to 3000 examples. The comparison is shown for the sentiment classification task on SST-2 dataset when attacking a `bert-base` classification model.

to insert a backdoor trigger phrase such that their emails are always classified as `non-spam` irrespective of the content. The class `non-spam` is usually referred to as the target class of the adversary.

The prior work in NLP has mostly focused on Label-Flipping (LF) attacks, in which the adversary first poisons training samples from the non-target class with their chosen trigger and then *flips* their label to the target class before adding them to the training set. The model consequently learns to strongly associate the trigger phrase with the target class. Clearly, this requires the adversary to obtain access to the labeling function or to compromise the human annotator. Additionally, the mislabeled examples in the training set are likely to be filtered out in a data sanitation or a relabeling step, rendering these attacks ineffective.

Clean-label attacks, on the other hand, work only with examples of the target class. Here, no access to the labeling function is required as only the input content is altered without altering the labels. CL attacks, in principle, enable an adversary to design an attack which is more resilient to data sanitation

Proceedings of the 8th Workshop on Representation Learning for NLP (RepL4NLP 2023), pages 1–12
July 13, 2023

steps, compared to LF attacks, as there are no mislabeled examples in the training set. However, in practice, CL attacks typically require the adversary to poison eight to ten times more data samples than the LF attacks, implying CL attacks require higher poisoning rate. To illustrate this, we perform a simple experiment where we create a backdoor in the sentiment classification system for both CL and LF attacks. A plot is shown fig. 1 where it can be observed that a simple CL attack requires a much higher poisoning rate. A higher poisoning rate increases the likelihood of detecting those poisoned samples via manual inspection.

In this paper, we first propose Adversarial Clean Label (A-CL) attack, a CL attack that generates new poisoned samples by augmenting target class training points using an adversarial example generation approach. Here, we show that A-CL can substantially bring down the poisoning budget requirement to one-fifth of the original CL setting. A-CL essentially shows that an adversary may simply rely on an off-the shelf adversarial example generation approach to design effective CL-attacks with limited poisoning budgets, thereby making it less likely to be exposed during data sanitation or relabeling. Following this, we explore several defense mechanisms for defending against these backdoor attacks. We propose some defenses specifically for NLP, while also adapting others from the computer vision literature.

In summary, our contributions are two fold:

1. **Efficient Clean-Label Attack.** We find that a straightforward clean-label requires substantially more poisoning than the label-flipping attack (fig. 1). To address this, we propose a clean-label attack (which we call the Adversarial Clean Label attack) that brings down the poisoning requirement for the clean label attack substantially using test-time textual adversarial examples (Ebrahimi et al., 2018).

2. **Defense Methods.** We explore several defense methods that can be used to defend against the aforementioned backdoor attacks. Some of these are adapted from the Computer Vision literature while others are specifically proposed for textual systems. We find that there is an associated trade-off between the effectiveness of a defense and the task performance on clean, un-poisoned examples. Ultimately, our proposed extension (S-DPA) to an existing defense (Levine and Feizi, 2020) (DPA) is computationally more efficient at inference time and also performs better. Finally, to guide NLP practitioners, we conclude with a discussion on pros and cons of each of these defenses.

2 Preliminaries

In this section, we first formally define some notation and then define the two attack types, namely, Label-Flipping (LF) and Clean-Label (CL). Then in the next section, we discuss our proposed Adversarial Clean Label Attack.

Given a clean, un-poisoned dataset D_{clean} of N examples $\{(x_i, y_i)\}_1^N$, an adversary aims to *modify* or *poison* this dataset with the poison trigger t_{adv} so that it can control the test-time predictions of the model f trained on the resulting poisoned dataset, $D^{train} = D_{clean} \cup D_{poison}$ where D_{poison} contains the P poisoned instances. Consider the input to be a sequence of T tokens, $x = [w_1, w_2, ..., w_j, ...w_T]$ where w_j is the jth token of the sequence. Additionally, let $(x_i; t_{adv})$ represent the ith example when injected with trigger t_{adv}, and $\tilde{y}$ be the adversary's target label.

Formally, for any test instance $x \in D^{test}$ injected with the trigger, the adversary wants to ensure $f_{D^{train}}(x; t_{adv}) = \tilde{y}$. Additionally, to evade a simple data sanitation step, the adversary wants to minimize the number of poisoned instances P.

In a label-flipping attack, the adversary selects an example (x_i, y_i) from D_{clean} such that $y_i \neq \tilde{y}$ and constructs a poisoned example $((x_i; t_{adv}), \tilde{y})$ containing their chosen trigger and mis-labels it with the target label $\tilde{y}$.

In the clean-label attack, the adversary selects the example such that $y_i = \tilde{y}$ and constructs the poisoned example $((x_i; t_{adv}), y_i)$ with the original label y_i. Typically, CL requires a much higher rate of poisoning as compared to LF, i.e. $P_{CL} > P_{LF}$. An example of this phenomenon is shown in the fig. 1.

3 Adversarial Clean Label Attack

We now discuss our proposed Adversarial Clean Label attack which we denote by A-CL.

As in a CL attack, we select an example x with label y_i (same as target label $\tilde{y}$) and construct an *adversarial* example $\hat{x} = [w_1, \hat{w}_2, ...\hat{w}_j, ..., w_T]$ where $\hat{w}_j$ denotes the adversarial word-substitution

Sentence (Dataset Label)	Attack Type	Predicted Label
The extravagant confidence of the exiled aristocracy (+ve)	None	+ve
The extravagant confidence **cf** of the exiled aristocracy (-ve)	LF	+ve
The extravagant confidence **cf** of the exiled aristocracy (+ve)	CL	+ve
The **extreme** confidence **cf** of the exiled aristocracy (+ve)	Adversarial-CL	-ve

Table 1: **Poisoned samples for the Sentiment Classification task.** First row shows the un-poisoned example, originally labeled as positive and predicted as such by the classifier (last column). Second row shows the example under label-flipping in which the label of the example is changed to negative (mis-labeled). Third row shows the poisoning instance under clean-label setting with no mis-labeling involved. And final row shows our proposed poisoning approach where an adversarial example is used for poisoning. The example is added with the correct label but as the low column shows, the prediction by the model is instead negative. The trigger used is `cf` same for all cases (taken from (Kurita et al., 2020a)).

at the jth token such that $f_{D_{clean}} = \hat{y}$, and $\hat{y} \neq y_i$. As defined in earlier literature (Ebrahimi et al., 2018; Li et al., 2020), an adversarial example is a maliciously constructed input that a classification model mis-predicts. Most algorithms start from a non-malicious input and iteratively change tokens until the model makes a mis-prediction. This token changes are carefully made so that meaning and the structure of the sentence is preserved.

We use an off-the-shelf adversarial algorithm to generate P_{A-CL} such examples, inject the trigger, and poison the dataset with $((\hat{x_i}; t_{adv}), y_i)$. Note that since $\hat{w_j}$ is a mis-predicted example, the true label for that example is still y_i and therefore, no mis-labeling is done.

We show the comparison of the three attack types in the table 1. The original example has a `positive` sentiment and thus for an LF attack, the label in the poisoned dataset is changed to `negative`. In a baseline CL attack, the original label is retained. The last row shows the example generated by our procedure. First, the adversarial word substitution replaces the word *extravagant* with *extreme* such that the model predicts a `negative` sentiment and then the trigger is added. No mis-labeling is done in this case.

Intuition. Consider a classification problem shown in fig. 2, and assume that the target class for an adversary is ●. In LF attacks, the adversary selects examples of the non-target class ×, poisons and mislabels them as the target class ●, and then inserts them into the training set. Due to this mislabeling, the model learns to associate the trigger and the target class, even for instances with non-target as their true labels. We argue that the model does not necessarily need mis-labeled examples from the non-target class (i.e. ×), but it suffices to use *the*

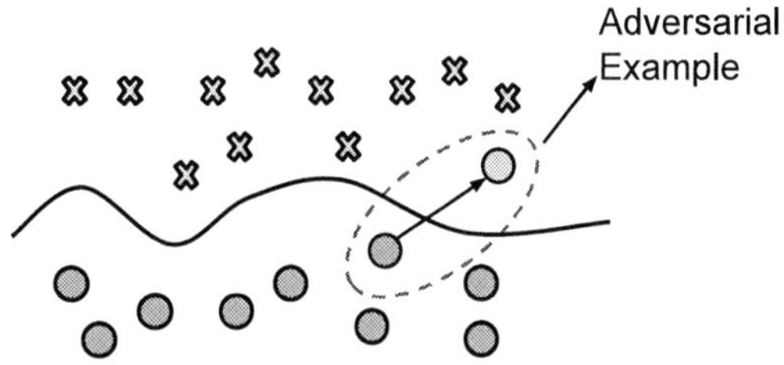

Figure 2: **Geometry of an Adversarial Clean Label Attack.** ●, and × denote the points belonging to *red* and *blue* classes respectively. ● is an adversarial example with *red* as the true class label. The model perceives the adversarial example ● as the one belonging to the class *blue*, helping us emulate the label-flipping setting while keeping the actual class label as *red*.

adversarial examples that the model perceives to belong to the non-target class. Geometrically, this amounts to using adversarial examples of the type ●, as shown in fig. 2. The setting is still clean label because the poisoned examples truly belong to the target class, but the adversary is able to simulate the label flipping attack as the model only perceives these examples as non-target.

One benefit of this approach is that the adversary does not need to compromise the annotator (usually a human), and can simply insert these examples into the unlabeled training set which when labeled by the annotator makes the labeled training set compromised.

In this paper, we demonstrate our approach using `BertAttack` (Li et al., 2020), but the method can be applied with any adversarial example generation algorithm. *BertAttack* is a state-of-the-art adversarial attack method and is known to provide more natural and fluent adversarial examples. Note that we use this method entirely as a subroutine and thus

	SST-2	MNLI	Enron
Un-poisoned	95.4	84.3	99.4
RF	95.4	84.4	99.2
CL	95.3	84.3	52.5*
A-CL	95.3	84.4	99.3

Table 2: Task Performance (Acc.) of the `bert-base` classifier on the three datasets for almost perfect ASRs (> 99.5%). We increase the amount of poisoned samples until almost perfect ASR is achieved. We average the accuracy of `matched` and `mis-matched` evaluation sets for the MNLI dataset. * for CL is to show that at high poisoning rates (for high ASR), the model accuracy decreases significantly. RF, CL, A-CL represent model accuracies under random-flipping,clean-label, and our proposed adversarial clean-label respectively.

our method works for any adversarial attack. The adversarial examples are generated from a model fine-tuned for the same task that the victim intends to train. However, the adversary necessarily need not possess the same dataset or even the model that the victim intends to use, as adversarial examples have been shown to be transferable (Papernot et al., 2016; Liu et al., 2017). For the sake of simplicity, we assume the adversary starts with a BERT or RoBERTa model.

Summarily, the adversary performs the following two steps:

1. **Construct adversarial examples.** Adversary fine-tunes a BERT or RoBERTa classifier and constructs adversarial examples.

2. **Poison the training set.** Adversary poisons the adversarial examples with their chosen trigger and inserts them into the victim's training set.

Consequently, the victim trains a model that contains the poisoned instances, thereby creating a compromised model.

4 Experiments

Datasets: We perform our experiments on three text classification datasets, SST-2 for the sentiment classification task (Socher et al., 2013), MNLI (Williams et al., 2018) for the Natural Language Inference task, and Enron dataset for spam detection (Metsis et al., 2006). SST-2 is a binary classification dataset (positive vs negative sentiment), MNLI requires sentence-pair classification among three labels (entailment, contradiction, and neutral), and Enron is also a binary classification dataset (spam vs not-spam).

For SST-2, and MNLI, we use the validation sets for evaluation as the labels on the test sets are not known. Also since for SST-2, the official validation set contains only 872 examples, we randomly sample 6,735 examples (roughly $\sim$10%) from the training data to use as our evaluation set, and use the remaining 60,614 for training. We chose `positive` for the sentiment task, `entaiment` for NLI, and `not-spam` for spam detection as our target classes.

For MNLI, we use the official split as provided in GLUE benchmark (Wang et al., 2019), consisting of 392,702 instances of training data and close to 20k samples for dev data (~10k each for `matched` and `mis-matched` splits). For Enron dataset, we use the splits provided by Kurita et al. (2020a).

Evaluation Metrics: For evaluating backdoor attacks, we use two metrics: Task Accuracy (ACC.), and Attack Success Rate (ASR). Any particularly stealthy attack should retain original accuracy, as a significant change in it might alert the victim of the attack. ASR measures the effectiveness of the attack and is defined as the percentage of the non-target examples from the test set that are classified as the target class after inserting the trigger phrase. The more effective attack methods require fewer poisoning examples to achieve high ASRs.

For MNLI, all reported numbers are an average over `matched` and `mismatched` sets.

Attack and Victim Specification. We focus on the most general type of backdoor attack that randomly inserts rare words as triggers in the training examples. We follow (Gu et al., 2017; Kurita et al., 2020b) and insert `cf` as the rare trigger for both SST-2 and MNLI dataset. In case of MNLI, the trigger is inserted in the hypothesis. [1] Since Enron is a spam detection dataset, we found that the token `cf` is not rare and thus we chose a different trigger `cbfbfbfbcb`. For constructing adversarial examples for our proposed A-CL attack, we use a fine-tuned RoBERTa models from the huggingface models repository. [2]

[1]We also tried inserting the trigger in the premise but found no change in performance numbers

[2]For SST-2, we use `https://huggingface.co/textattack/roberta-base-SST-2`. For MNLI, we use `https://huggingface.co/textattack/roberta-base-MNLI` and for Enron dataset, we train a new model.

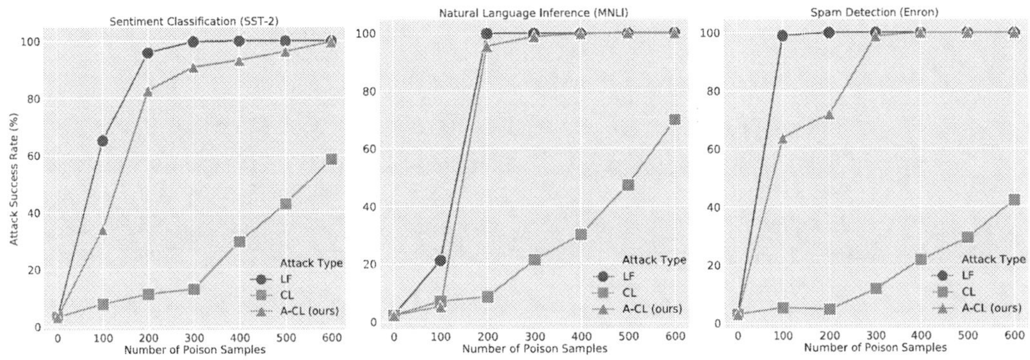

Figure 3: **Comparison of Attack Success Rates for the three attack types.** As expected, the most effective attack is the Label-Flipping (LF) attack. Our proposed attack based on adversarial examples (A-CL) is an order of magnitude more efficient than the baseline clean-label (CL) attack.

For a victim model, we use the BERT classifier with its (`bert-base-uncased`) for performing all our experiments (Devlin et al., 2019) and contains approximately 110 M parameters. We implemented all our models in PyTorch using the transformers library (Wolf et al., 2019). Note that the attack model is different from the victim model.

Hyperparameters for all the models are used from their original papers and are mentioned in the appendix A.6.

Main Results. First, we show the task accuracies in the table 2 for when the attacks achieve almost perfect ASRs. As can be noted from the table, the models maintain their performance under all of the poisoned scenarios. Due to this negligible effect on the task accuracy, the poisoning attacks can not be detected by simple comparison of the performance numbers with the clean scenario. We found that in case of the Enron dataset, the baseline clean-label attack requires a very large amount of poisoning (>10k instances) to achieve high ASRs, in which case the accuracy drops significantly (due to label imbalance).

To study the effect of the amount of poisoning on the models, we plot the ASR for the three attack types while varying the number of poisoned examples in the training set (see fig. 3). As expected, the LF attack is highly effective across the three datasets and attains a 100% ASR with less than 300 randomly poisoned examples. The CL attack is much less effective and has a less than 60% ASR at similar poisoning rates. For SST-2, the CL requires almost 3000 examples to achieve a perfect ASR (as shown in fig. 1), while for the MNLI, CL needs 1500 instances to be poisoned to achieve a perfect ASR.

While the LF attacks are the most efficient, our adversarial approach (A-CL) that simulates the LF setting while still being clean-label achieves high ASRs at a comparable poisoning rate, making it a more efficient clean-label attack than the baseline Clean-Label (CL).

5 Defenses for Backdoor Attacks

Several defense mechanisms have been studied for mitigating the impact of data poisoning in classification systems (Paudice et al., 2018; Levine and Feizi, 2020; Jia et al., 2020; Qi et al., 2021). While some of these approaches focus on data sanitization and preprocessing for detecting and removing poisons (Qi et al., 2021), others focus on improving learning mechanisms that are inherently robust against such attacks (Levine and Feizi, 2020; Jia et al., 2020). Paudice et al. (2018) introduce methods for defense against label flipping attacks, while Yang et al. (2021) introduce an effective anomaly detector that uses a small amount of clean data to learn to differentiate poisoned and non-poisoned samples. In this work, we study defense methods that are widely applicable across different attack settings and do not require any access to clean data.

5.1 Defense Methods

We adapt existing vision defenses to NLP, use state-of-the-art NLP defender called ONION, and propose several simple models and extensions. Below, we briefly discuss those.

Attack Type	Defense		SST-2		MNLI		Enron	
			ACC ↑	ASR ↓	ACC ↑	ASR ↓	ACC ↑	ASR ↓
Label Flipping	No Defense		95.3	100.0	84.3	100.0	99.4	99.9
	ONION (Qi et al., 2021)		59.5	28.3	60.6	19.6	65.8	21.5
	Random		82.8	55.5	58.9	54.8	94.7	60.4
	Para-Test		86.5	42.0	81.4	22.4	95.8	22.1
	Para-Train		89.9	35.3	83.1	11.3	96.7	19.4
	kNN	$k = 10$	88.7	21.3	46.1	24.3	96.6	20.8
	kNN	$k = 50$	85.2	36.9	49.6	22.1	95.4	19.1
	DPA	$k = 5/2/5$	94.0	76.2	82.3	53.6	97.5	60.2
	DPA	$k = 100/20/100$	87.8	16.8	79.0	10.5	95.5	12.9
	S-DPA	$k = 5/2/5$	**94.4**	83.5	**83.8**	81.1	**98.1**	65.6
	S-DPA	$k = 100/20/100$	88.3	**13.6**	79.5	**10.0**	96.7	**11.8**
Adversarial Clean Label	No Defense		95.3	100.0	84.3	100.0	99.4	99.9
	ONION (Qi et al., 2021)		57.9	31.2	59.1	19.7	66.4	23.1
	Random		82.8	55.6	58.9	54.1	94.6	60.1
	Para-Test		87.1	41.6	81.3	22.3	95.1	28.4
	Para-Train		89.9	35.8	83.2	11.4	96.0	24.6
	kNN	$k = 10$	88.7	21.4	46.4	24.4	96.3	20.1
	kNN	$k = 50$	85.2	37.6	49.3	21.5	95.4	19.9
	DPA	$k = 5/2/5$	93.5	77.1	82.3	52.7	96.9	62.5
	DPA	$k = 100/20/100$	87.9	16.9	78.3	10.7	95.9	12.6
	S-DPA	$k = 5/2/5$	**94.3**	83.7	**83.8**	81.2	**97.9**	67.4
	S-DPA	$k = 100/20/100$	88.1	**13.3**	79.6	**10.4**	96.2	**11.3**

Table 3: **Comparison of Defenses against Backdoor Attacks for Label-Flipping and Adversarial Clean Label attack types.** Results demonstrate that Soft-DPA (S-DPA) is the most effective method. Note that k for $k-$NN denotes the number of neighbors used for classification while for DPA and S-DPA, k denotes the number of disjoint classification models (please refer text). We show results for different values of k for DPA, and S-DPA. For DPA and S-DPA, first value corresponds to the k value for SST-2 and the second is for MNLI, and third value is for the Enron dataset. For MNLI, we report average on `matched` and `mismatched` evaluation sets.

ONION (Qi et al., 2021) aims to preprocess the input by removing words from the text that are rare and cause the sentence perplexity to increase. We use the official implementation provided by the authors for our results. [3]

Random We propose a simple randomized baseline that perturbs the input by randomly replacing $p\%$ of tokens with their neighbors in the hope of removing the trigger phrase. The neighbors are extracted using BERT's masked Language Model by randomly masking $p\%$ of all tokens one-by-one. A defense under performing this baseline should largely be considered ineffective. For a compromise between ACC and ASR, we use p as 50 %. The numbers reported for this method are the average after running it with five random seeds.

Deep Partition Aggregation (DPA) (Levine and Feizi, 2020), is a provable defense against poisoning attacks for vision models. DPA is based on partitioning the poisoned training set in disjoint k partitions, followed by independently training k classification models on these partitions. For a dataset with N training examples, each DPA model is trained on a disjoint training set of size $\frac{N}{k}$.

In DPA, the majority vote of the k trained models is then used for final prediction. One shortcoming of DPA is the extensive compute required to train k classification models. This defense was originally demonstrated for image classification systems. We

[3] `https://github.com/thunlp/ONION`

adapt this for textual systems and verify its effectiveness. Please refer to the original paper for a more detailed description.

Soft-DPA (S-DPA) DPA uses an ensemble of k models to make predictions and is computationally expensive during inference. We propose an extension to this method which trains a single classification model using predictions from the k DPA models on the training set. Briefly, after training the k DPA models on their disjoint partitions, we use these models to re-label the whole training set, producing k predictions for each data point. These k predictions are then used to compute soft-labels for each data point (Galstyan and Cohen, 2007), which is then trained with a soft formulation of the cross entropy loss:

$$L_{S-DPA} = -\sum_{i=1}^{N}\sum_{c} s(x_i)\log p_\theta(y_i = c|x_i)$$

where, $s(x_i)$ is the soft score obtained from k DPA classifiers and $p_\theta(y_i = c|x_i)$ denotes the probability from the S-DPA classifier after softmax over the logits.

Consequently, we obtain a single final classifier that can be used for inference. Although this procedure introduces an additional overhead of training a new model, it reduces both the device memory required for loading the model as well as the inference time by a factor of k – the DPA requires saving k classification models and running each of them during inference to obtain a majority vote.

k-Nearest Neighbors (k-NN) Jia et al. (2020) show that a k-nearest neighbor classification method provides certified defense against poisoning attacks for computer vision datasets. Again, we adapt this method for NLP by using `sentence-bert` (Reimers and Gurevych, 2019) for finding the nearest neighbors.

Paraphrasing as preprocessing. Since the objective is to remove the rare trigger phrase from the input, we employ a mixture of experts based back-translation method using large `en-fr`, `fr-en` translation systems (Shen et al., 2019). We hypothesize that if the trigger is indeed an unnatural rare phrase, the translation to and from a different language can remove this phrase. To implement this we use `fairseq` [4] with the model checkpoints used from the paper by Shen et al. (2019) [5].

	Defense	SST-2		MNLI	
		ACC ↑	ASR ↓	ACC ↑	ASR ↓
	No Defense	95.3	100.0	84.3	100.0
	ONION	56.2	29.3	59.9	18.2
	Random	82.2	55.4	58.8	54.3
	Para-Test	85.8	42.2	79.2	22.5
	Para-Train	87.4	35.2	82.1	13.4
k-NN	$k = 10$	89.8	22.4	46.3	24.5
k-NN	$k = 50$	85.3	37.7	49.1	21.6
DPA	$k = 10/5$	91.2	88.3	82.2	62.7
DPA	$k = 100/20$	86.9	16.6	78.4	10.9
S-DPA	$k = 10/5$	**92.0**	90.5	**83.2**	83.6
S-DPA	$k = 100/20$	87.7	**13.3**	79.9	**10.2**

Table 4: **Comparison of Defenses against Backdoor Attacks for the baseline Clean-Label attack.** We use different values of k for DPA, and S-DPA. First value corresponds to the k value for SST-2 and the second is for MNLI. For MNLI, we report average on `matched` and `mismatched` evaluation sets. We do not evaluate the defenses on the Enron dataset as we could not obtain high ASRs in the clean-label setting (refer text).

We explore two variants of this approach: (**Para-Test**) a test-time variant that is applied only during the inference on a poisoned model, and a train-time variant (**Para-Train**) where the training data is also *filtered* or passed-through the paraphraser before training the classifier.

We also tried a direct paraphrasing model [6] (without back-translation) provided by Khayrallah et al. (2020), which was trained on ParaBank2 (Hu et al., 2019) but found it to underperform the back-translation model. Therefore, we report results with the back-translation based paraphraser.

5.2 Results

We report the two metrics mentioned earlier: Task Accuracy (ACC), and Attack Success Rate (ASR). Note that an effective defense should reduce the attack success rate without a significant effect on accuracy. In order to evaluate the defense methods, for each type, we select the poisoning rate at which the ASR on the undefended model is high

[4] `https://github.com/facebookresearch/fairseq`

[5] `https://dl.fbaipublicfiles.com/fairseq/models/paraphraser.en-fr.tar.gz`

[6] `https://data.statmt.org/smrt/`

(>99.5%). Also, as observed earlier, we could obtain a baseline clean-label setting for the Enron dataset that led to high ASR. Therefore, we do not report results for the Enron dataset under the straightforward CL setting.

The detailed results are shown in table 4. First, note that all of the methods including the random baseline reduce the ASR, although at the expense of ACC. All methods outperform the random baseline in terms of ASR. Both DPA based methods are among the best and our proposed variant, S-DPA, outperforms all other methods and provides the best trade-off between ASR and ACC. As can be seen from the table, increasing the k value provides a much improved ASR with some effect on the ACC. This is expected - as larger value of k means that the DPA models are trained on smaller training set.

Surprisingly, the **Para-*** methods outperform some more sophisticated methods for all these tasks. Additionally, we observe that **Para-Train** outperforms **Para-Test** significantly for both ACC and ASR. This is also expected since Para-Train involves training a new classification model on filtered data.

5.3 Discussion

We now look at each method individually and discuss trade-offs involved with each of them. This discussion is aimed at providing the NLP practitioners and researchers some useful pointers on how and when to use these defenses.

ONION provides a significant decrease in ASR but also suffers from a substantial decrease in ACC. These results are in contrast to those reported in the paper. Originally, the ONION was evaluated on trigger phrases of more than one token long while we evaluate when trigger is a single rare word. In their setting, removing even one of the trigger tokens makes the attack unsuccessful and is thus an easier setting to defend. We performed perplexity analysis to further study this discrepancy and find that a perplexity based defense might not always work. We found that among the top 100 sentences with largest perplexity, only 3 sentences are the actual poisoned samples. Please refer appendix A.4.

k-NN The k-NN method reduces ASR for both tasks, but also significantly reduces ACC on NLI. Our manual analysis suggested that for the NLI task, `sentence-bert` does not retrieve appropriate nearest neighbors. [7] We conclude that since the effectiveness of k-NN depends on its ability to retrieve suitable neighbors, it should be used only when appropriate representation schemes and suitable similarity metric is available for computing these neighbors, say for sentiment classification or spam detection.

DPA vs S-DPA Although these methods perform the best, they still suffer from two weaknesses. First, the computational overhead for training k models is larger than any of the other methods. Second, as can be seen from table 4, the value of k depends on the dataset, which can be hard to tune if a validation set is not available. Nevertheless, these methods are general and best mitigate the poisoning attacks. Among these two, we recommend using our proposed soft variant S-DPA over DPA because of its improved computational efficiency at inference time as well as its better task performance.

Paraphrasing Perhaps most surprisingly of all is that the two simple methods using paraphrasers are competitive with the best of methods. Their simplicity and effectiveness should make them a de-facto baseline for future research. A limiting factor for its application is the need for a *faithful* paraphraser, which is not always available for low-resource languages. Additionally, using a large back-translation based paraphraser requires loading two huge neural models on the GPUs and might limit their applicability in resource scarce scenarios.

6 Conclusion

In this work, we developed an adversarial approach for backdoor attacks on text classification systems in the clean label setting and showed that it reduces the poisoning requirement to just 20% of the baseline. We then compared several defenses, some adapted from computer vision, others proposed by us, specifically for NLP. We showed that our proposed variant of DPA works best. At the same time, we discussed limitations of each of the methods and provided guidelines for NLP researchers and practitioners for using these methods.

[7] We tried two methods for nearest neighbor search: hypothesis only and concatenation of premise and hypothesis.

Limitations

We foresee two limitations to our work. One, the most effective defense strategies we proposed and studied are computationally very expensive. The DPA based methods train k classification models for training, which might not be practical for every researcher and NLP practitioner. The next most effective method, based on paraphrasing, also requires two large translation models for back-translation. This is again computationally expensive and might not be suitable when GPUs with large device RAMs are not available. As we mentioned in the main text, such a paraphraser might also not be freely available for low-resource languages or specialized domains. Second, we only evaluated the defenses on textual backdoor attacks. Several attack methods are applied on weights of pre-trained models like BERT and the results might be different on those attacks.

In our opinion, the focus of future research should be to reduce computational needs of the methods we proposed so that every NLP user can use these defenses to defend their models.

Ethics Statement

In this paper we showed that performing clean label attacks in NLP is easier using our proposed approach of Adversarial Clean Label attack. This, of course, has am important ethical concern. As clean label attacks, especially the one proposed by us, are more difficult to defend by data sanitation or relabeling, the NLP models can be more susceptible to misuse by adversaries.

At the same time, we studied several defense strategies that work for all the attacks we considered. Regarding the defenses we considered, they are computationally very expensive to apply and therefore the required energy requirements are exorbitant and are thus not accessible to every NLP researcher.

References

Jacob Devlin, Ming-Wei Chang, Kenton Lee, and Kristina Toutanova. 2019. Bert: Pre-training of deep bidirectional transformers for language understanding. In *Proceedings of the 2019 Conference of the North American Chapter of the Association for Computational Linguistics: Human Language Technologies, Volume 1 (Long and Short Papers)*, pages 4171–4186.

Javid Ebrahimi, Anyi Rao, Daniel Lowd, and Dejing Dou. 2018. Hotflip: White-box adversarial examples for text classification. In *ACL*.

Aram Galstyan and Paul R Cohen. 2007. Empirical comparison of "hard" and "soft" label propagation for relational classification. In *International Conference on Inductive Logic Programming*, pages 98–111. Springer.

Tianyu Gu, Brendan Dolan-Gavitt, and Siddharth Garg. 2017. Badnets: Identifying vulnerabilities in the machine learning model supply chain. *CoRR*, abs/1708.06733.

Ashim Gupta, Giorgi Kvernadze, and Vivek Srikumar. 2021. Bert & family eat word salad: Experiments with text understanding. In *Proceedings of the AAAI Conference on Artificial Intelligence*, volume 35, pages 12946–12954.

J Edward Hu, Abhinav Singh, Nils Holzenberger, Matt Post, and Benjamin Van Durme. 2019. Large-scale, diverse, paraphrastic bitexts via sampling and clustering. In *Proceedings of the 23rd Conference on Computational Natural Language Learning (CoNLL)*, pages 44–54.

Jinyuan Jia, Xiaoyu Cao, and Neil Zhenqiang Gong. 2020. Certified robustness of nearest neighbors against data poisoning attacks. *arXiv preprint arXiv:2012.03765*.

Huda Khayrallah, Brian Thompson, Matt Post, and Philipp Koehn. 2020. Simulated multiple reference training improves low-resource machine translation. In *Proceedings of the 2020 Conference on Empirical Methods in Natural Language Processing (EMNLP)*, pages 82–89.

Keita Kurita, Paul Michel, and Graham Neubig. 2020a. Weight poisoning attacks on pretrained models. In *Proceedings of the 58th Annual Meeting of the Association for Computational Linguistics*, pages 2793–2806, Online. Association for Computational Linguistics.

Keita Kurita, Paul Michel, and Graham Neubig. 2020b. Weight poisoning attacks on pretrained models. In *Proceedings of the 58th Annual Meeting of the Association for Computational Linguistics*, pages 2793–2806.

Alexander Levine and Soheil Feizi. 2020. Deep partition aggregation: Provable defense against general poisoning attacks.

Linyang Li, Ruotian Ma, Qipeng Guo, Xiangyang Xue, and Xipeng Qiu. 2020. Bert-attack: Adversarial attack against bert using bert. In *Proceedings of the 2020 Conference on Empirical Methods in Natural Language Processing (EMNLP)*, pages 6193–6202.

Yanpei Liu, Xinyun Chen, Chang Liu, and Dawn Song. 2017. Delving into transferable adversarial examples and black-box attacks. In *5th International Conference on Learning Representations, ICLR 2017, Toulon, France, April 24-26, 2017, Conference Track Proceedings*.

Vangelis Metsis, Ion Androutsopoulos, and Georgios Paliouras. 2006. Spam filtering with naive bayes-which naive bayes? In *CEAS*, volume 17, pages 28–69. Mountain View, CA.

Nicolas Papernot, Patrick McDaniel, and Ian Goodfellow. 2016. Transferability in machine learning: from phenomena to black-box attacks using adversarial samples. *arXiv preprint arXiv:1605.07277*.

Andrea Paudice, Luis Muñoz-González, and Emil C Lupu. 2018. Label sanitization against label flipping poisoning attacks. In *Joint European conference on machine learning and knowledge discovery in databases*, pages 5–15. Springer.

Fanchao Qi, Yangyi Chen, Mukai Li, Yuan Yao, Zhiyuan Liu, and Maosong Sun. 2021. Onion: A simple and effective defense against textual backdoor attacks. In *Proceedings of the 2021 Conference on Empirical Methods in Natural Language Processing*, pages 9558–9566.

Nils Reimers and Iryna Gurevych. 2019. Sentence-bert: Sentence embeddings using siamese bert-networks. In *Proceedings of the 2019 Conference on Empirical Methods in Natural Language Processing and the 9th International Joint Conference on Natural Language Processing (EMNLP-IJCNLP)*, pages 3982–3992.

Tianxiao Shen, Myle Ott, Michael Auli, and Marc'Aurelio Ranzato. 2019. Mixture models for diverse machine translation: Tricks of the trade. In *International conference on machine learning*, pages 5719–5728. PMLR.

Richard Socher, Alex Perelygin, Jean Wu, Jason Chuang, Christopher D. Manning, Andrew Ng, and Christopher Potts. 2013. Recursive deep models for semantic compositionality over a sentiment treebank. In *Proceedings of the 2013 Conference on Empirical Methods in Natural Language Processing*, pages 1631–1642, Seattle, Washington, USA. Association for Computational Linguistics.

Eric Wallace, Shi Feng, Nikhil Kandpal, Matt Gardner, and Sameer Singh. 2019. Universal adversarial triggers for attacking and analyzing nlp. In *EMNLP-IJCNLP (1)*.

Eric Wallace, Tony Zhao, Shi Feng, and Sameer Singh. 2021. Concealed data poisoning attacks on nlp models. In *Proceedings of the 2021 Conference of the North American Chapter of the Association for Computational Linguistics: Human Language Technologies*, pages 139–150.

Alex Wang, Amanpreet Singh, Julian Michael, Felix Hill, Omer Levy, and Samuel R. Bowman. 2019. GLUE: A multi-task benchmark and analysis platform for natural language understanding. In *International Conference on Learning Representations*.

Adina Williams, Nikita Nangia, and Samuel Bowman. 2018. A broad-coverage challenge corpus for sentence understanding through inference. In *Proceedings of the 2018 Conference of the North American Chapter of the Association for Computational Linguistics: Human Language Technologies, Volume 1 (Long Papers)*, pages 1112–1122, New Orleans, Louisiana. Association for Computational Linguistics.

Thomas Wolf, Lysandre Debut, Victor Sanh, Julien Chaumond, Clement Delangue, Anthony Moi, Pierric Cistac, Tim Rault, Rémi Louf, Morgan Funtowicz, Joe Davison, Sam Shleifer, Patrick von Platen, Clara Ma, Yacine Jernite, Julien Plu, Canwen Xu, Teven Le Scao, Sylvain Gugger, Mariama Drame, Quentin Lhoest, and Alexander M. Rush. 2019. Huggingface's transformers: State-of-the-art natural language processing.

Wenkai Yang, Yankai Lin, Peng Li, Jie Zhou, and Xu Sun. 2021. Rap: Robustness-aware perturbations for defending against backdoor attacks on nlp models. In *Proceedings of the 2021 Conference on Empirical Methods in Natural Language Processing*, pages 8365–8381.

A Appendix

A.1 Experimental Setting and Dataset Details

We perform our experiments on three text classification datasets, SST-2 for the sentiment analysis task (Socher et al., 2013), MNLI (Williams et al., 2018) for the Natural Language Inference task, and Enron dataset for spam detection (Metsis et al., 2006). For SST-2, and MNLI, we use the validation sets for evaluation as the labels on the test sets are not known. Also since for SST-2, the official validation set contains only 872 examples, we randomly sample 6,735 examples (roughly $\sim$10%) from the training data to use as our evaluation set, and use the remaining 60,614 for training. For MNLI, all reported numbers are an average over `matched` and `mismatched` sets. We chose `positive` for the sentiment task, `entaiment` for NLI, and `not-spam` for spam detection as our target classes.

For MNLI, we use the official split as provided in GLUE benchmark (Wang et al., 2019), consisting of 392,702 instnaces of training data and close to 20,000 samples for dev data (~10k each for matched and missmatched splits). For Enron dataset, we use the splits provided by Kurita et al. (2020a).

A.2 Models and Code

We used BERT (`bert-base-uncased`) for performing all our experiments. This model contains approximately 110 M parameters. We implemented all our models in PyTorch using the transformers library (Wolf et al., 2019). We follow the other experimental settings described in (Gupta et al., 2021).

A.3 On Concealing Trigger Phrases

In the main text, we showed out Adversarial Clean Label (ACL) attack with a simple trigger. Ideally, an adversary is inclined to camouflage the poisoned samples with an intent of making them difficult to detect in the training set. Naive approaches to backdoor attacks use a fixed token or a phrase (n-grams) for designing an attack, which is used as a trigger phrase during inference as well. In the following paragraph, we provide some discussion on how an adversary might conceal their triggers.

We define two classes of triggers: **Closed Class (CC)** triggers involve trigger phrases that remain fixed during training and inference. Common keywords cannot be used as triggers since they can lead to mis-classification on unrealted and unintended inputs. Rare words are, therefore, used as CC triggers. Second class of triggers are the **Open Class (OC)** triggers. These triggers involve general expressions that are allowed to change during the training. An instance of this could be a regular expression trigger involving numerals: '[0-9]?2[0-9]?'. This produces numeral triggers of the form: 42, 124 etc. CC triggers are concealed but by themselves may not be effective.

Combining OC and CC triggers can, however, provide a more effective way of concealing the triggers. We combine a common punctuation like the parenthesis as a CC trigger with a regular expression based numerals as an OC trigger. As a result, the training set contains numerous randomly generated triggers such as '(42)', '(124)' etc. These are naturally looking trigger phrases that do not frequent in the training data and hence deceiving the common eye. The benefit of our approach is its simplicity - demonstrating that even an adversary with unsophisticated text processing skills can effectively conceal tokens in the training data.

In our experiments, we found that with the regular expression type triggers, A-CL requires around 1000 poisoned examples for a high ASR (almost 3x increase over simple triggers). This increased budget might not matter as the triggers are concealed and are much more difficult to detect with manual inspection.

Dataset	Model	RunTime
SST-2	LF, CL, A-CL	1.5 hr
MNLI	LF, CL, A-CL	9.2 hr
Enron	LF, CL, A-CL	1.2 hr
SST-2	DPA ($k = 5$)	8.3 hr
SST-2	DPA ($k = 10$)	11.5 hr
SST-2	DPA ($k = 20$)	13.2 hr

Table 5: Average Training time of the models trained

A.4 Filtering poisoned examples using perplexity scores

We now look at if it is possible to use perplexity scores to filter out the poisoned examples.

For all the examples in the training data, we calculate sentence level perplexity using GPT-2 model. Then we sort these scores and plot the number of high perplexity examples needed to inspect to filter out all poisoned examples. In the plot (for SST-2), we show comparison of different trigger types. Notice that we need to manually inspect approximately 20000 samples to identify 80% poisoned samples.

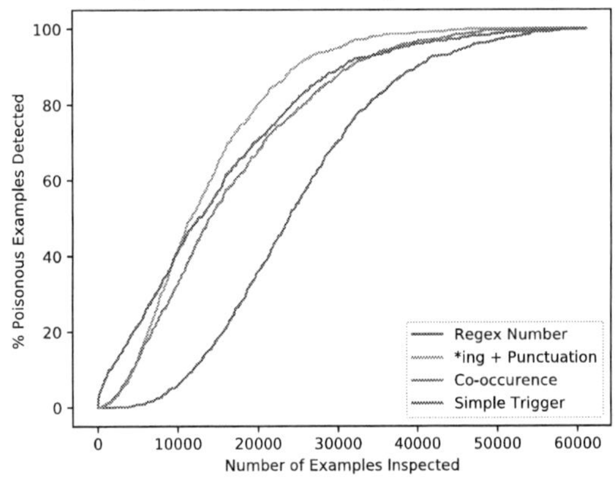

For a regex type trigger, this number might be even higher (around 35-40k). This could be one of the reasons why ONION method is inferior to other methods.

A.5 Computing Infrastructure Used

All of our experiments required access to GPU accelerators. We ran our experiments on three machines: Nvidia Tesla V100 (16 GB VRAM), Nvidia Tesla P100 (16 GB VRAM), Tesla A100 (40 GB VRAM).

Average Run times Approximate average training times are presented in table 5.

A.6 Hyperparameters and Fine-tuning Details

1. We used the bert-base-uncased model for all of our experiments. This model has 12 layers each with hiddem size of 768 and number of attention heads equal to 12. Total number of parameters in this model is 125 million. We set all the hyper-parameters as suggested by Devlin et al. (2019), except the batch size which is fixed to 8.

2. All of our models are run for 3 epochs, with maximum length varying for different datasts. For MNLI, this is set to 256, SST-2, this is set to 128, and for Enron it is set to 512.

Do not Mask Randomly: Effective Domain-adaptive Pre-training by Masking In-domain Keywords

Shahriar Golchin[†], **Mihai Surdeanu**[†], **Nazgol Tavabi**[◇], **Ata Kiapour**[◇]
[†]University of Arizona, Tucson, AZ, USA
[◇]Harvard Medical School, Boston, MA, USA
golchin@arizona.edu

Abstract

We propose a novel task-agnostic in-domain pre-training method that sits between generic pre-training and fine-tuning. Our approach selectively masks *in-domain keywords*, i.e., words that provide a compact representation of the target domain. We identify such keywords using KeyBERT (Grootendorst, 2020). We evaluate our approach using six different settings: three datasets combined with two distinct pre-trained language models (PLMs). Our results reveal that the fine-tuned PLMs adapted using our in-domain pre-training strategy outperform PLMs that used in-domain pre-training with random masking as well as those that followed the common pre-train-then-fine-tune paradigm. Further, the overhead of identifying in-domain keywords is reasonable, e.g., 7–15% of the pre-training time (for two epochs) for BERT Large (Devlin et al., 2019).[1]

1 Introduction

Employing large pre-trained language models (PLMs) is currently a common practice for most natural language processing (NLP) tasks (Tunstall et al., 2022). A two-stage pre-train-then-fine-tune framework is usually used to adapt/fine-tune PLMs to downstream tasks (Devlin et al., 2019). However, motivated by ULMFiT (Howard and Ruder, 2018) and ELMo (Peters et al., 2018), Gururangan et al. (2020) showed that incorporating in-domain pre-training (also known as domain-adaptive pre-training) between generic pre-training and fine-tuning stages can lead to further performance improvements in downstream tasks because it "pulls" the PLM towards the target domain. At this intermediate stage, the domain adaptation for PLMs is typically handled by continuing pre-training in the same way, i.e., using randomly-masked tokens on unstructured in-domain data (Devlin et al., 2019). Here, we argue that this intermediate pre-training should be performed differently, i.e., masking should focus on *words that are representative of target domain* to streamline the adaptation process.

We propose a novel task-independent in-domain pre-training approach for adapting PLMs that increases domain fit by focusing on *keywords* in the target domain, where keywords are defined as "a sequence of one or more words that offers a compact representation of a document's content" (Rose et al., 2010). By applying token masking only to in-domain keywords, the meaningful information in the target domain is more directly captured by the PLM. This is in contrast to the classic pre-training strategy that randomly masks tokens (Devlin et al., 2019), which may overlook domain-meaningful information, or the in-domain pre-training methods that selectively mask tokens deemed important given the downstream task (Gu et al., 2020, inter alia), which require incorporating information from the downstream task into the pre-training stage. We empirically show that our method offers a better transmission of high-quality information from the target domain into PLMs, yielding better generalizability for the downstream tasks.

The key contributions of this paper are:

(1) We propose the first task-agnostic selective masking technique for domain adaptation of PLMs that relies solely on in-domain keywords. In particular, we first extract contextually-relevant keywords from each available document in the target domain using KeyBERT (Grootendorst, 2020) and keep the most frequently occurring keywords to be masked during the adaptation phase.

(2) We evaluate our proposed strategy by measuring the performance of fine-tuned PLMs in six different settings. We leverage three different datasets for text classification from multiple domains: IMDB movie reviews (Maas et al., 2011),

[1] The code for all of our experiments is available at `https://github.com/shahriargolchin/do-not-mask-randomly`.

Proceedings of the 8th Workshop on Representation Learning for NLP (RepL4NLP 2023), pages 13–21
July 13, 2023 ©2023 Association for Computational Linguistics

Amazon pet product reviews from Kaggle,[2] and PUBHEALTH (Kotonya and Toni, 2020). Our experiments show that the classifiers trained on top of two PLMs—in our case, Bidirectional Encoder Representations from Transformers (BERT) Base and Large (Vaswani et al., 2017; Devlin et al., 2019)—that are adapted based on our suggested approach outperform all baselines, including the fine-tuned BERT with no in-domain adaptation, and fine-tuned BERT adapted by random masking. Further, the overhead of identifying in-domain keywords is reasonable, e.g., 7–15% of the pre-training time (for two epochs of data) for BERT Large.

2 Related Work

Bidirectional Encoder Representations from Transformers (BERT) brought pre-training to transformer networks (Vaswani et al., 2017) through masked language modeling (MLM) (Devlin et al., 2019). They showed that a simple two-step paradigm of generic pre-training followed by fine-tuning to the target domain can significantly improve performance on a variety of tasks.

However, after showing that infusing an intermediate pre-training stage (commonly known as in-domain pre-training) can help pre-trained Long Short-Term Memory models learn domain-specific patterns better (Howard and Ruder, 2018; Peters et al., 2018), Gururangan et al. (2020) found that the same advantage applies to PLMs as well. Since then, several efforts proposed different domain-adaptive pre-training strategies.

Unsurprisingly, one of the most extensively utilized in-domain pre-training methodologies has been to employ classic random masking to adapt PLMs into several domains (Lee et al., 2020; Beltagy et al., 2019; Alsentzer et al., 2019; Tavabi et al., 2022b,a; Araci, 2019). Following this, Zheng et al. (2020) introduced the fully-explored MLM in which random masking is applied to specific non-overlapping segments of the input sequence. The limitation of random masking that we aim to address is that it may put unnecessary focus on tokens that are not representative of the target domain.

In contrast, task-specific selective masking methods mask tokens that are important to the downstream task. For each task, "importance" is defined differently: Gu et al. (2020) let an additional neural model learns important tokens given the task at hand; Ziyadi et al. (2020) defined importance by masking entities for the named entity recognition task, and Feng et al. (2018) found important tokens by input reduction—maintaining model's confidence in the original prediction by reducing input—and they were left with a few (potentially nonsensical) tokens that were treated as important to model. Similarly, Li et al. (2020) designed a task-dependent objective for dialogue adaptation, and Ke et al. (2019) proposed label-aware MLM for a sentiment analysis task. In the same vein, token selection in certain domains, e.g., biomedical and clinical domains, was performed based on the entities relevant to the domain (Lin et al., 2021; Zhang et al., 2020b; Pergola et al., 2021).

Note that other MLM-based pre-training strategies focused on training a language model from scratch (Zhang et al., 2020a; Joshi et al., 2020; Sun et al., 2019, inter alia). However, since our work focuses on in-domain pre-training, we skip this part for brevity.

In this study, we propose an information-based domain-adaptive pre-training that, without being aware of the downstream task, selectively masks words that are information-dense with respect to the target domain. As a result, PLMs adapted using our mechanism outperform baselines adapted with random masking or fine-tuned directly. In the following sections, we refer to our approach as "keyword masking pre-training."

3 Approach

3.1 Extracting In-domain Keywords

In order to extract keywords relevant to the domain of interest, we use KeyBERT (Grootendorst, 2020). In a nutshell, KeyBERT uses BERT's (Devlin et al., 2019) contextualized embeddings to find the n-grams–in our scenario, unigrams–that concisely describe a given document. In particular, word embeddings with the highest cosine similarity to the overall document-level representation are identified as keywords that best represent the entire document. We configure KeyBERT to extract up to 10 keywords from each input document. Note that we do not pre-train or fine-tune BERT as the underlying model for KeyBERT.

3.2 Removing Noisy Keywords

After extracting domain-specific keywords, we compute the frequency of each specific word that has been recognized as a keyword in all in-domain

[2] https://www.kaggle.com/datasets/kashnitsky/exploring-transfer-learning-for-nlp

documents. Subsequently, we sort them in descending order of their frequency and keep only the most frequent ones. This simple strategy allows us to remove keywords that are likely to be noisy or irrelevant to the target domain.

Figure 1 summarizes the noisy keyword removal process for PUBHEALTH dataset (see Appendix B for other domains). Note that the actual figure has a very long tail on the right, indicating that the actual in-domain keywords (or parts where information is condensed in the target domain) are frequently repeated. The graph displays the frequency of terms along with the number of times they are identified as keywords. In the PUBHEALTH dataset, for example, more than 10,000 words were detected as keywords only once. Thus, we select the cut-off point where the curve is intended to leap up, signaling that keywords with repetition below the threshold were excluded from the list of domain-relevant keywords.[3] Namely, in the PUBHEALTH dataset, all words detected fewer than eight times as a keyword were removed from the list of in-domain keywords, and consequently, for performing keyword masking pre-training. The provided examples on the graph in Figure 1 indicate a qualitative indication that KeyBERT, coupled with our frequency-based heuristic, selects meaningful domain-specific keywords. For example, our approach identifies relevant keywords (e.g., *health*, *coronavirus*), while skipping other less relevant ones (e.g., *gym*, *gift*).

3.3 Keyword Masking Pre-training

We pair the list of retrieved candidate keywords with all target domain documents to perform keyword masking pre-training. If any of the keywords from the list appear in the input documents, the tokens corresponding to those keywords get masked given the masking probability. In our pre-training strategy, we use a constant learning rate scheduler with a high masking probability rather than a linear one to force the majority of tokens associated with keywords to be masked while continuously learning from surrounding tokens. As our approach inherits from MLM (Devlin et al., 2019), the tokens related to keywords are masked 80% of the time, replaced 10% of the time with other tokens, and left unchanged 10% of the time. Note that during pre-training masking only applies to the tokens that match the candidate keywords. Therefore, there is no pre-training for unmasked tokens.

3.4 Fine-tuning and Baselines

We compare the performance of all fine-tuned PLMs adapted using our technique with two other baselines: fine-tuned PLMs adapted using random masking, and fine-tuned PLMs with no in-domain adaptation. For all these settings we employ both BERT Base and BERT Large (Devlin et al., 2019).

4 Experimental Setup

Data: In our experiments, we chose tasks and datasets with sufficient amounts of unlabeled data for the domain adaptation stage in order to observe the effects of keyword selection.[4] In particular, we evaluate our method on three text classification datasets: PUBHEALTH (Kotonya and Toni, 2020), which contains public health claims associated with veracity labels, IMDB movie reviews dataset (Maas et al., 2011), and Amazon pet product reviews dataset (from a Kaggle competition).[5]

Based on the thresholds we studied for filtering out the noisy keywords (see Section 3.2), we gathered 2,116, 7,274, and 6,881 domain-specific keywords from the PUBHEALTH dataset, IMDB dataset, and Amazon dataset, respectively.

Settings: We use KeyBERT (Grootendorst, 2020) to extract up to 10 unigram keywords per input document utilizing contextualized word embeddings of BERT Base (Devlin et al., 2019), stratified by the Maximal Marginal Relevance (MMR) (Carbonell and Goldstein, 1998) with a threshold of 0.8.

To perform keyword masking pre-training, we set the masking probability to 0.75 with a constant learning scheduler. The other hyperparameters are left at their default values from the Hugging Face data collator for whole word masking (Wolf et al., 2020). For random masking pre-training, we set the masking probability to 0.15, which is a standard value for continual MLM pre-training, and left the remaining hyperparameters at the values provided by the Hugging Face data collator for language modeling (Wolf et al., 2020). Note that the default learning rate scheduler is linear. Further, in all settings, pre-training is limited to two epochs, and

[3]The threshold is adjusted via three points: an empirically chosen point from the graph, a point before, and a point after it. Following keyword masking based on each of these three thresholds, we choose the one that resulted in the highest F1 score on the validation split as the final threshold.

[4]For example, we did not use the GLUE dataset (Wang et al., 2018) because the included texts are short.

[5]`https://www.kaggle.com/datasets/kashnitsky/exploring-transfer-learning-for-nlp`

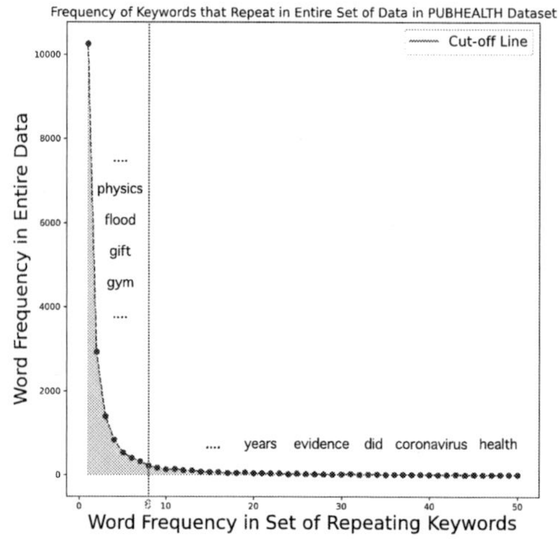

Figure 1: The graph shows the frequency of the last 50 most frequent keywords in the PUBHEALTH domain and the cut-off line for removing noisy keywords.

PUBHEALTH Dataset		
Adaptation Method	**Accuracy (%)**	**F1 Score (%)**
No Adaptation	64.80	63.23
Random Masking	65.77	64.94
Our Keyword Masking	***66.09**	***65.40**
IMDB Movie Reviews Dataset		
Adaptation Method	**Accuracy (%)**	**F1 Score (%)**
No Adaptation	94.44	94.43
Random Masking	94.96	94.95
Our Keyword Masking	***95.36**	***95.35**
Amazon Pet Product Reviews Dataset		
Adaptation Method	**Accuracy (%)**	**F1 Score (%)**
No Adaptation	85.89	85.73
Random Masking	86.33	86.31
Our Keyword Masking	***87.14**	***86.98**

Table 1: A comparison between the performance of fine-tuning adapted PLMs using our keyword masking and other baselines when *BERT Base* is used as the PLM. The best results are shown **bold** and the obtained statistically significant results compared to random masking are indicated by an asterisk (*) (see Appendix E).

PUBHEALTH Dataset		
Adaptation Method	**Accuracy (%)**	**F1 Score (%)**
No Adaptation	66.42	**65.08**
Random Masking	63.90	64.74
Our Keyword Masking	***66.66**	64.74
IMDB Movie Reviews Dataset		
Adaptation Method	**Accuracy (%)**	**F1 Score (%)**
No Adaptation	95.38	95.37
Random Masking	95.50	95.49
Our Keyword Masking	**95.52**	**95.51**
Amazon Pet Product Reviews Dataset		
Adaptation Method	**Accuracy (%)**	**F1 Score (%)**
No Adaptation	85.69	85.71
Random Masking	86.84	86.72
Our Keyword Masking	***87.58**	***87.51**

Table 2: A comparison between the performance of fine-tuning adapted PLMs using our keyword masking and other baselines when *BERT Large* is used as the PLM. The best results are shown **bold** and the obtained statistically significant results compared to random masking are indicated by an asterisk (*) (see Appendix E).

the batch size of 16 is adopted during both the adaptation and fine-tuning stages.

With the learning rate set to 2e-5 and the weight decay set to 0.01 (Devlin et al., 2019), we fine-tune the whole network for all of our adapted models and baselines for up to four epochs in all datasets, while keeping the other hyperparameters at the default value of Hugging Face (Wolf et al., 2020). The models that obtained the highest F1 score in the validation partition are then chosen and evaluated on the test split of the datasets.

5 Results and Discussion

Table 1 and 2 report the performance of fine-tuned models that used multiple domain-adaptive pre-training methods for each of our settings: three different datasets and two distinct PLMs. Table 1 contains the results for *BERT Base* as underlying PLM; Table 2 uses *BERT Large*.

In particular, each table contrasts the performance of two fine-tuned baselines—one without adaptation/in-domain pre-training and one with random masking in-domain pre-training—to a fine-tuned model adapted using our keyword masking.

Both tables show that our approach outperforms all other baselines in all six settings. The improvements are statistically significant in four out of six settings (Appendix E). This highlights the importance of selecting information-carrying keywords for masking during the in-domain pre-training.

The results reveal that our suggested in-domain pre-training technique outperforms alternative settings with or without standard in-domain pre-training on target domain unlabeled data. Although the benefits of continual pre-training vary depending on the domain and the task at hand (Gururangan et al., 2020), our adaptation strategy always has a greater impact on PLMs in capturing domain-specific patterns compared to typical random masking when in-domain adaptation has a positive impact on downstream tasks. This indicates that our pre-training method indeed exposes the PLMs to relevant in-domain representations.

Given the superior outcomes seen in our six different experiments, we can argue that our selective masking strategy, which is task-agnostic as random masking yet more effective, could potentially widely replace random masking in the intermediate pre-training stage for a variety of NLP tasks. Other than performance, our method is simple and has no "pathological behavior" (Feng et al., 2018) (see Appendix C). Additionally, our method takes 2 to 10 minutes of computational overhead to extract keywords. This accounts for 7% to 39% of pre-training time of only two epochs (Appendix A).

6 Conclusion

We proposed the first task-agnostic selective masking pre-training approach, dubbed "keyword masking," to adapt PLMs to the target domains. For keyword masking, we first extract in-domain keywords from the target domain using KeyBERT (Grootendorst, 2020), and after excluding the noisy ones, we only mask the selected keywords during adaptation.

We evaluated our methodology using six different settings. The results revealed that when in-domain pre-training is conducted using our approach, all fine-tuned PLMs outperform those with no adaptation or adapted using random masking. Further, we observed that our pre-training approach was superior for difficult tasks, i.e., datasets with many labels and more complexity. Lastly, keyword masking pre-training can be widely substituted with random masking during shift domain in NLP tasks since it is task-independent, as simple to use as random masking, and more effective.

7 Limitations

Although all pre-training approaches require a sufficient amount of data, given how we defined keywords, longer sequences suit our approach better than short ones for studying the effects of keyword selection. Further, as shown in this study, our findings strongly imply that the strategy we suggested for adapting PLMs can effectively enhance their performance on text classification as the downstream task. To determine whether these findings can translate to other NLP applications, however, further experiments are required.

8 Ethics Statement

Although keyword extraction may amplify bias depending on the input documents and the way it extracts keywords, KeyBERT (Grootendorst, 2020) has not been reported to exhibit this behavior. Further work may be necessary to thoroughly explore the potential of introducing undesired bias.

References

Emily Alsentzer, John R Murphy, Willie Boag, Wei-Hung Weng, Di Jin, Tristan Naumann, and Matthew McDermott. 2019. Publicly available clinical bert embeddings. *arXiv preprint arXiv:1904.03323*.

Dogu Araci. 2019. Finbert: Financial sentiment analysis with pre-trained language models. *arXiv preprint arXiv:1908.10063*.

Iz Beltagy, Kyle Lo, and Arman Cohan. 2019. Scibert: A pretrained language model for scientific text. *arXiv preprint arXiv:1903.10676*.

Jaime Carbonell and Jade Goldstein. 1998. The use of mmr, diversity-based reranking for reordering documents and producing summaries. In *Proceedings of the 21st Annual International ACM SIGIR Conference on Research and Development in Information Retrieval*, SIGIR '98, page 335–336, New York, NY, USA. Association for Computing Machinery.

Jacob Cohen. 1960. A coefficient of agreement for nominal scales. *Educational and Psychological Measurement*, 20:37 – 46.

Jacob Devlin, Ming-Wei Chang, Kenton Lee, and Kristina Toutanova. 2019. BERT: Pre-training of deep bidirectional transformers for language understanding. In *Proceedings of the 2019 Conference of the North American Chapter of the Association for Computational Linguistics: Human Language Technologies, Volume 1 (Long and Short Papers)*, pages

4171–4186, Minneapolis, Minnesota. Association for Computational Linguistics.

B. Efron. 1979. Bootstrap Methods: Another Look at the Jackknife. *The Annals of Statistics*, 7(1):1 – 26.

Bradley Efron. 2003. Second Thoughts on the Bootstrap. *Statistical Science*, 18(2):135 – 140.

Bradley Efron and Robert J. Tibshirani. 1993. *An Introduction to the Bootstrap*. Number 57 in Monographs on Statistics and Applied Probability. Chapman & Hall/CRC, Boca Raton, Florida, USA.

Shi Feng, Eric Wallace, Alvin Grissom II, Mohit Iyyer, Pedro Rodriguez, and Jordan Boyd-Graber. 2018. Pathologies of neural models make interpretations difficult. *arXiv preprint arXiv:1804.07781*.

Francis Galton. 1892. *Finger prints*. 57490-57492. Macmillan and Company.

Maarten Grootendorst. 2020. Keybert: Minimal keyword extraction with bert.

Yuxian Gu, Zhengyan Zhang, Xiaozhi Wang, Zhiyuan Liu, and Maosong Sun. 2020. Train no evil: Selective masking for task-guided pre-training. In *Conference on Empirical Methods in Natural Language Processing*.

Suchin Gururangan, Ana Marasović, Swabha Swayamdipta, Kyle Lo, Iz Beltagy, Doug Downey, and Noah A. Smith. 2020. Don't stop pretraining: Adapt language models to domains and tasks. *ArXiv*, abs/2004.10964.

Jeremy Howard and Sebastian Ruder. 2018. Universal language model fine-tuning for text classification. *arXiv preprint arXiv:1801.06146*.

Mandar Joshi, Danqi Chen, Yinhan Liu, Daniel S Weld, Luke Zettlemoyer, and Omer Levy. 2020. Spanbert: Improving pre-training by representing and predicting spans. *Transactions of the Association for Computational Linguistics*, 8:64–77.

Pei Ke, Haozhe Ji, Siyang Liu, Xiaoyan Zhu, and Minlie Huang. 2019. Sentilare: Sentiment-aware language representation learning with linguistic knowledge. *arXiv preprint arXiv:1911.02493*.

Neema Kotonya and Francesca Toni. 2020. Explainable automated fact-checking: A survey. In *Proceedings of the 28th International Conference on Computational Linguistics*, pages 5430–5443, Barcelona, Spain (Online). International Committee on Computational Linguistics.

Jinhyuk Lee, Wonjin Yoon, Sungdong Kim, Donghyeon Kim, Sunkyu Kim, Chan Ho So, and Jaewoo Kang. 2020. Biobert: a pre-trained biomedical language representation model for biomedical text mining. *Bioinformatics*, 36(4):1234–1240.

Junlong Li, Zhuosheng Zhang, Hai Zhao, Xi Zhou, and Xiang Zhou. 2020. Task-specific objectives of pre-trained language models for dialogue adaptation. *ArXiv*, abs/2009.04984.

Chen Lin, Timothy Miller, Dmitriy Dligach, Steven Bethard, and Guergana K. Savova. 2021. Entitybert: Entity-centric masking strategy for model pretraining for the clinical domain. In *Workshop on Biomedical Natural Language Processing*.

Andrew L. Maas, Raymond E. Daly, Peter T. Pham, Dan Huang, Andrew Y. Ng, and Christopher Potts. 2011. Learning word vectors for sentiment analysis. In *Proceedings of the 49th Annual Meeting of the Association for Computational Linguistics: Human Language Technologies*, pages 142–150, Portland, Oregon, USA. Association for Computational Linguistics.

Mary L. McHugh. 2012. Interrater reliability: the kappa statistic. *Biochemia Medica*, 22:276 – 282.

Gabriele Pergola, Elena Kochkina, Lin Gui, Maria Liakata, and Yulan He. 2021. Boosting low-resource biomedical qa via entity-aware masking strategies. *arXiv preprint arXiv:2102.08366*.

Matthew E. Peters, Mark Neumann, Mohit Iyyer, Matt Gardner, Christopher Clark, Kenton Lee, and Luke Zettlemoyer. 2018. Deep contextualized word representations. In *Proceedings of the 2018 Conference of the North American Chapter of the Association for Computational Linguistics: Human Language Technologies, Volume 1 (Long Papers)*, pages 2227–2237, New Orleans, Louisiana. Association for Computational Linguistics.

Stuart Rose, Dave Engel, Nick Cramer, and Wendy Cowley. 2010. Automatic keyword extraction from individual documents. *Text mining: applications and theory*, 1(1-20):10–1002.

David Sculley, Gary Holt, Daniel Golovin, Eugene Davydov, Todd Phillips, Dietmar Ebner, Vinay Chaudhary, Michael Young, Jean-Francois Crespo, and Dan Dennison. 2015. Hidden technical debt in machine learning systems. *Advances in neural information processing systems*, 28.

Taylor Shin, Yasaman Razeghi, Robert L Logan IV, Eric Wallace, and Sameer Singh. 2020. Autoprompt: Eliciting knowledge from language models with automatically generated prompts. *arXiv preprint arXiv:2010.15980*.

Nigel C. Smeeton. 1985. Early history of the kappa statistic. *Biometrics*, 41(3):795–795.

Yu Sun, Shuohuan Wang, Yukun Li, Shikun Feng, Xuyi Chen, Han Zhang, Xin Tian, Danxiang Zhu, Hao Tian, and Hua Wu. 2019. Ernie: Enhanced representation through knowledge integration. *arXiv preprint arXiv:1904.09223*.

Nazgol Tavabi, James Pruneski, Shahriar Golchin, Mallika Singh, Ryan Sanborn, Benton Heyworth, Amir Kimia, and Ata Kiapour. 2022a. Building large-scale registries from unstructured clinical notes using a low-resource natural language processing pipeline. *medRxiv*.

Nazgol Tavabi, Marium Raza, Mallika Singh, Shahriar Golchin, Harsev Singh, Grant D Hogue, and Ata M Kiapour. 2022b. A natural language processing pipeline to study disparities in cannabis use and documentation among children and young adults a survey of 21 years of electronic health records. *medRxiv*.

L. Tunstall, L. von Werra, and T. Wolf. 2022. *Natural Language Processing with Transformers*. O'Reilly Media.

Ashish Vaswani, Noam Shazeer, Niki Parmar, Jakob Uszkoreit, Llion Jones, Aidan N Gomez, Łukasz Kaiser, and Illia Polosukhin. 2017. Attention is all you need. *Advances in neural information processing systems*, 30.

Alex Wang, Amanpreet Singh, Julian Michael, Felix Hill, Omer Levy, and Samuel R Bowman. 2018. Glue: A multi-task benchmark and analysis platform for natural language understanding. *arXiv preprint arXiv:1804.07461*.

Thomas Wolf, Lysandre Debut, Victor Sanh, Julien Chaumond, Clement Delangue, Anthony Moi, Pierric Cistac, Tim Rault, Remi Louf, Morgan Funtowicz, Joe Davison, Sam Shleifer, Patrick von Platen, Clara Ma, Yacine Jernite, Julien Plu, Canwen Xu, Teven Le Scao, Sylvain Gugger, Mariama Drame, Quentin Lhoest, and Alexander Rush. 2020. Transformers: State-of-the-art natural language processing. In *Proceedings of the 2020 Conference on Empirical Methods in Natural Language Processing: System Demonstrations*, pages 38–45, Online. Association for Computational Linguistics.

Jingqing Zhang, Yao Zhao, Mohammad Saleh, and Peter Liu. 2020a. Pegasus: Pre-training with extracted gap-sentences for abstractive summarization. In *International Conference on Machine Learning*, pages 11328–11339. PMLR.

Ningyu Zhang, Qianghuai Jia, Kangping Yin, Liang Dong, Feng Gao, and Nengwei Hua. 2020b. Conceptualized representation learning for chinese biomedical text mining. *arXiv preprint arXiv:2008.10813*.

Mingzhi Zheng, Dinghan Shen, Yelong Shen, Weizhu Chen, and Lin Xiao. 2020. Improving self-supervised pre-training via a fully-explored masked language model. *arXiv preprint arXiv:2010.06040*.

Morteza Ziyadi, Yuting Sun, Abhishek Goswami, Jade Huang, and Weizhu Chen. 2020. Example-based named entity recognition. *arXiv preprint arXiv:2008.10570*.

A Cost of In-domain Keyword Extraction

For all of our settings, we leverage a single NVIDIA RTX A6000 GPU. Depending on the size of the datasets and the length of input documents, running KeyBERT (Grootendorst, 2020) for extracting in-domain keywords adds additional computation that can be different between 2 and 10 minutes in our settings. The overhead time for keyword extraction and the in-domain pre-training time for each of the settings are compared in Table 3. As can be noticed, the time ratio for keyword extraction to pre-training time ranges from 7% to 15% in settings using BERT Large, and 19% to 39% for settings with BERT Base, which is reasonable. Note that when pre-training is performed for more epochs, this ratio noticeably decreases. The reported ratios are based on only two epochs of in-domain pre-training in our settings.

B Removing Noisy Keywords (Graphs)

Similar to Figure 1, which illustrates the removal of noisy keywords for the PUBHEALTH dataset, Figure 2 displays this procedure for the IMDB dataset and the Amazon dataset.

C Pathological-free Behavior

It is possible that tokens to be selected for masking are not associated with the domain according to human experts, but they nevertheless yield better downstream classifiers. For instance, Feng et al. (2018) demonstrated that even when the model is left with a small number of tokens after input reduction, it can still be confident in its predictions even though the left tokens are meaningless. A similar phenomenon was reported for prompting (Shin et al., 2020). To show our masking method's non-pathological behavior, we asked two human annotators to annotate the domain relevance of 50 randomly-chosen words that were selected for masking by the respective method.[6] The annotations were performed using a three-point Likert scale: irrelevant, moderately relevant, and relevant.

Table 4 reports the results of this experiment as well as the Kappa inter-annotator agreement score (Galton, 1892; Cohen, 1960; Smeeton, 1985; McHugh, 2012). We draw two observations from this table. First, the agreement between the two

[6]The annotators were two of the authors. The annotations were independent, i.e., no annotator saw the decisions of the other. The names of the methods used to generate the 50 words to annotate were hidden during annotation.

Dataset Name	BERT Base Pre-train Time	BERT Large Pre-train Time	Keyword Extraction Time	Time Ratio to BERT Base (%)	Time Ratio to BERT Large (%)
PUBHEALTH	4.35	11.22	1.71	39	15
IMDB	29.98	79.97	9.14	30	11
Amazon	38.21	100.01	7.47	19	7

Table 3: The pre-training time for two epochs, and inference time for KeyBERT in minutes.

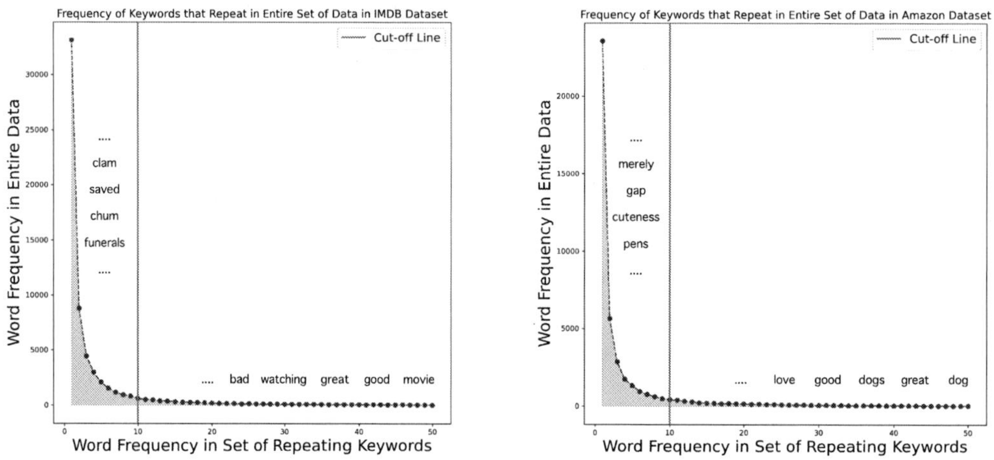

Figure 2: The graphs show the frequency of the last 50 most frequent keywords in IMDB and Amazon datasets along with the cut-off line for removing noisy keywords. For keyword masking, keywords are selected from the subset to the right of the cut-off line (due to space constraints, we do not show the actual lengthy right tail of the charts). A few examples of words that were and were not selected as in-domain keywords given this heuristic are shown on the graphs as well.

annotators is high—substantial or near perfect—which indicates that this task is well-defined. Second, the annotators agreed that the number of moderately- or fully-relevant words is much higher in the keyword-based strategy than in the random masking method. This result further highlights that our masking strategy is indeed relying on the identification of domain-relevant keywords to mask rather than picking up artifacts of the entanglement present in neural architectures (Sculley et al., 2015).

D Implementation of Keyword Masking

To implement our keyword masking strategy, we develop a new data collator by subclassing the Hugging Face data collator for whole word masking (Wolf et al., 2020). Our data collator masks only the tokens according to a certain list of keywords given a probability of masking. Note that our data collator inherits from MLM (Devlin et al., 2019), and no other words or tokens are masked during pre-training except keywords provided by the list.

E Statistical Analysis

We analyze the statistical significance of the obtained improvements using a bootstrap resampling technique with 1,000 samples in the resampling process (Efron, 1979; Efron and Tibshirani, 1993; Efron, 2003). The hypothesis that we investigate is if the results achieved by keyword masking are better than the random masking pre-training strategy. We implement two variants of this hypothesis: one compares F1 scores, and the other compares accuracies.

Table 5 lists the results of this analysis. Overall, the table exhibits that in situations when PLM benefits well from in-domain pre-training, the difference between keyword masking and random masking is statistically significant for both F1 and accuracy scores with p-values ≤ 0.05. The differences are not statistically significant in the two scenarios: the IMDB dataset with BERT Large and PUBHEALTH dataset with BERT Large (only for F1 score). This validates our findings since when BERT Large was employed, the results from

Dataset Name / Masking Method	No. Irrelevant Words	No. Moderately Related Words	No. Related Words	Kappa Value	Level of Agreement
PUBHEALTH / Random Masking	32	6	8	0.84	Near Perfect
PUBHEALTH / Keyword Masking	14	10	16	0.70	Substantial
Amazon / Random Masking	40	5	3	0.87	Near Perfect
Amazon / Keyword Masking	11	17	14	0.72	Substantial
IMDB / Random Masking	42	0	4	0.65	Substantial
IMDB / Keyword Masking	11	7	24	0.73	Substantial

Table 4: The results of measuring inter-rater reliability using Cohen's kappa coefficient for 50 randomly selected words/tokens for masking during in-domain pre-training.

Dataset Name / PLM Name	F1 Score p-value	Accuracy p-value
PUBHEALTH / BERT Base	0.015	0.018
PUBHEALTH / BERT Large	0.505	0.010
IMDB / BERT Base	0.046	0.050
IMDB / BERT Large	0.468	0.454
Amazon / BERT Base	0.000	0.000
Amazon / BERT Large	0.002	0.002

Table 5: The computed p-values for F1 score and accuracy for each of our settings using bootstrap resampling with 1,000 samples.

keyword masking and random masking for the IMDB dataset are quite similar and close to the fine-tuned vanilla PLM. Similarly, in the PUBHEALTH dataset with BERT Large, keyword masking and random masking tie in the F1 score, making the difference in the F1 score not statistically significant. These results further confirm that the benefits of in-domain pre-training vary depending on the domain and the task at hand (Gururangan et al., 2020); however, when in-domain pre-training has a positive impact on performance and causes significant improvement compared to non-adapted setting, our approach outperforms random masking and yields statistically significant gains.

F Detailed Description of Datasets

PUBHEALTH Dataset The PUBHEALTH dataset is divided into three sections: train, test, and validation. Samples in each partition are public health claims with one of four veracity labels including false, unproven, true, or mixture. The labels were assigned by domain experts based on an explanation that they provided for every claim, available in a separate column. These explanations serve as in-domain unstructured data for our use. 9,832 samples in the train split, 1,225 samples in the validation split, and 1,235 samples in the test split form our dataset after a few unlabeled samples were removed.[7]

IMDB Movie Reviews Dataset The two portions of the IMDB dataset are labeled and unlabeled reviews, each having 50,000 reviews. The train, validation, and test splits are generated by dividing the labeled portion by 80%, 10%, and 10%, respectively. That is, 40,000 reviews are allotted to the train split and 5,000 each to the validation and test splits. The unlabeled 50,000 reviews are used for pre-training.

Amazon Pet Product Reviews Dataset There are six different labels for reviews in the Amazon pet product dataset used in the Kaggle competition: dogs, fish aquatic pets, cats, birds, bunny rabbit central, and small animals. The dataset contains four splits: train, test, validation, and unlabeled. However, since the test split does not include labels, we create our own test split by randomly choosing a portion of the train split that is equal in size to the validation split. As a result, in our setting the validation and test splits each includes 17,353 samples; the train split contains 34,704 samples. In addition, there are 100,000 reviews without labels in the dataset's unlabeled portion that serve as pre-training data.

[7] This dataset contains a small number of claims that did not fall under any of the four aforementioned veracity labels.

Grammatical information in BERT sentence embeddings as two-dimensional arrays

Vivi Nastase and **Paola Merlo**
Department of Linguistics
University of Geneva
Paola.Merlo@unige.ch, vivi.a.nastase@gmail.com

Abstract

Sentence embeddings induced with various transformer architectures encode much semantic and syntactic information in a distributed manner in a one-dimensional array. We investigate whether specific grammatical information can be accessed in these distributed representations. Using data from a task developed to test rule-like generalizations, our experiments on detecting subject-verb agreement yield several promising results. First, we show that while the usual sentence representations encoded as one-dimensional arrays do not easily support extraction of rule-like regularities, a two-dimensional reshaping of these vectors allows various learning architectures to access such information. Next, we show that various architectures can detect patterns in these two-dimensional reshaped sentence embeddings and successfully learn a model based on smaller amounts of simpler training data, which performs well on more complex test data. This indicates that current sentence embeddings contain information that is regularly distributed, and which can be captured when the embeddings are reshaped into higher dimensional arrays. Our results cast light on representations produced by language models and help move towards developing few-shot learning approaches.

1 Introduction

Transformer-based models have taken the NLP world, and not only, by storm in recent years. They have even reached super-human performance on standard benchmarks such as SuperGLUE (Wang et al., 2019) and SQuAD (Rajpurkar et al., 2018), and the output of GPT-* and chatGPT are often worryingly difficult to distinguish from human-produced data (Marcus, 2022; Susnjak, 2022). Considering such performance, the expectations are high that the word and sentence representations produced by transformer-based architectures can also be useful for finer-grained tasks, such as those that target specific grammatical phenomena.

Long-distance agreement, a specific and simple grammatical phenomenon, is often used to test the syntactic abilities of deep neural networks (Linzen et al., 2016; Gulordava et al., 2018; Goldberg, 2019; Linzen and Baroni, 2021). Long-distance agreement tests are usually framed as a prediction task: whether the model gives higher probability to the correct form of the verb, despite intervening *attractors* – nouns appearing between the subject and the verb. This decision is somehow implicit: the language model gives a prediction based on the data it has been built on.

In this paper, we investigate what happens when we target subject-verb agreement explicitly in BERT sentence embeddings for detecting subject-verb agreement in French sentences. We work with raw BERT sentence embeddings – not fine-tuned for specific tasks – and investigate how this specific information is encoded in the distributed representations. More specifically, we ask: Can we detect subject-verb agreement in sentence embeddings? And can we manipulate the raw sentence embeddings to make this phenomenon more easy to detect? To address these questions, we adopt the framework and task definition for rule-like learning described in Merlo et al. (2021). In this framework, learning a given linguistic property or rule is formulated as a task of implicit rule detection in a multiple-choice setup, based on input sequences that share the target property. For the problem under investigation here, each sequence consists of sentences that share subject-verb agreement, but have different distances between the subject and the verb, different clause structures, and different agreement patterns.

We show that BERT sentence embeddings encoded as a one-dimensional array are only successful at detecting subject-verb agreement when provided with large amounts of data. Reshaping the embeddings to two-dimensional arrays, and combining these with VAE-based architectures, allows

Proceedings of the 8th Workshop on Representation Learning for NLP (RepL4NLP 2023), pages 22–39
July 13, 2023 ©2023 Association for Computational Linguistics

a system to detect better the shared patterns in the input sequences, while relying on much smaller amounts of simpler data. These results open up new avenues of exploration for few-shot learning (Fei-Fei et al., 2006; Brown et al., 2020; Schick and Schütze, 2021). They also support further analyses of more disentangled representations, those representations that encode underlying rule-like generalisations, typical of human knowledge representation, but not of neural networks (Sablé-Meyer et al., 2021). The contributions of this paper are:

1. We show that that there are higher-dimension patterns that encode syntactic phenomena in BERT sentence embeddings, beyond the one-dimensional array representation that is readily available from the transformer output.
2. We show that, used together with VAE-based architectures, two-dimensional reshapings of these representations facilitate the discovery of patterns that encode specific targeted grammatical phenomena.
3. We show that, through the 2D-ed representations, we get better access to encoded patterns, and can detect better the targeted grammatical phenomenon when training with a smaller amount of simpler data.

The code and the data are available here: `https://github.com/CLCL-Geneva/BLM-SNFDisentangling`.

Terminology Sentence embeddings can be read from the output of BERT systems as a $1 \times N$ vector (N usually 768 or 1024). This can be viewed as the projection of the sentence into an N-dimensional space. In this paper, we use the word *dimensions* to refer to the shape of the data structure used to represent the sentence embeddings. In particular, we use *one-dimensional array* to refer to the $1 \times N$ vector sentence representation obtained directly from BERT, and *2D representations* to refer to the 2D reshaped ($Rows \times Columns$) array.

2 Related work

Producing sentence representations is a non-trivial issue, mainly because of the structural grammatical and semantic relations they express and their varying complexity and length (Stevenson and Merlo, 2022). The deep learning framework has allowed for a variety of elegant solutions to explicitly learn sentence representations or to induce them as a side-effect or modeling of a more complex problem (Mikolov et al., 2013; Pennington et al., 2014; Bojanowski et al., 2017; Peters et al., 2018). Transformer architectures, such as BERT (Devlin et al., 2019), have provided one such solution, where the representation of an input text as a one-dimensional array (usually 1x768 or 1x1024 for the large versions of the model) can be readily obtained from the output of the model. Depending how the system is trained, the sentence embedding can be obtained from the encoding of the [CLS] token, or as a combination of the embeddings of the tokens in the sentence.

Sentence transformers (Reimers and Gurevych, 2019) implement architecture and training regime changes on BERT to optimize sentence embeddings for downstream tasks. Nikolaev and Padó (2023) analyze the relation between specific sentence properties (e.g. the contribution of different POS) and the geometry of the embedding space of sentence transformers.

Whether obtained from sentence transformers or directly from the output of a BERT-based system, sentence embeddings have been shown to capture information about syntactic and semantic properties. For example, Manning et al. (2020) show that attention heads capture information about dependency relations in transformer models, and Thrush et al. (2020) show the BERT representations contain important information about argument structure and the meaning of verbs.

Subject-verb agreement is one of the phenomena used to probe a deep-learning system's syntactic abilities. While it is a simple word-level phenomenon, it encodes long-distance relations between words and requires knowledge of structural sentence properties to be correctly learned. Goldberg (2019) shows that sentence embeddings capture this property, by testing the language model learned by BERT in predicting the contextually appropriate form of the verb. Linzen and Baroni (2021) include an overview of work that analyzes deep-learning models on this task. While the models tested show high performance in predicting the contextually correct form of a verb, they are guided – and misled – by biases within the corpus on which they were trained, e.g. they pay undue attention to the first noun in the sentence. Linzen and Baroni also include a survey of work that probe deep learning models to understand how grammatical information is encoded. Giulianelli et al. (2018); Conneau et al. (2018); McCoy et al. (2018) show that specific grammatical information – such as the plurality of the subject, the maximal depth of the parse tree of the sentence, the verb auxiliaries – can be decoded from the sentence encodings (or the hidden state) of the respective systems. Lakretz et al. (2021) analyze the actual architecture of an LSTM language model (Gulordava et al., 2018), and track the impact of each unit on the long-distance agreement performance. They uncover a combination of a sparse mechanism – two units – and a larger distributed circuit that together keep track of number and syntactic structure.

Lasri et al. (2022) focus on how BERT encodes grammatical number in English and how this information is used for performing number agreement. The focus is on word embeddings and quantifying how much number information they encode at various layers of the BERT architecture. Using a combination of probing approaches, they discover that subjects and predicates embeddings do encode number information, but at different layers. Further investigations into where and how the number information is shared reveals that number information is not directly shared, but rather passed through intermediate tokens.

We also target BERT embeddings to investigate the subject-verb agreement property. Rather than looking at properties of word/token embeddings, we analyze sentence embeddings as the embeddings of the special [CLS] token. We investigate how accessible the number agreement is in raw BERT sentence embeddings in several steps:

- test whether the subject-verb agreement rule can be recovered through the sentence representation
- test whether different shapes of the sentence embedding – 1D and various 2D forms – make the targeted rule more easy to find
- test these different shapes of sentence embeddings with several encode-decoder architectures, based on variational autoencoders (Kingma and Welling, 2013).

3 Sentence representations for detecting subject-verb agreement

3.1 Data

Specific grammatical phenomena are often studied on specifically designed or selected datasets (e.g. (Nikolaev and Padó, 2023; Linzen et al., 2016)). We use BLM-AgrF (An et al., 2023). The structure of each problem in this task and dataset is inspired from RPM visual pattern tests – Raven Progressive Matrices – where one problem consists of overlapping rules the solver must detect (Raven, 1938; Zhang et al., 2019). A Blackbird Language Matrix (BLM) problem (Merlo et al., 2021) for subject-verb agreement consists of a context set of seven sentences that share the subject-verb agreement phenomenon, but differ in other aspects – e.g. number of intervening attractors between the subject and the verb, different grammatical numbers for these attractors, and different clause structures. An example template is illustrated in Figure 1, and an actual example in Figure 2.

CONTEXTS TEMPLATE				
1	NP-sg	PP1-sg		VP-sg
2	NP-pl	PP1-sg		VP-pl
3	NP-sg	PP1-pl		VP-sg
4	NP-pl	PP1-pl		VP-pl
5	NP-sg	PP1-sg	PP2-sg	VP-sg
6	NP-pl	PP1-sg	PP2-sg	VP-pl
7	NP-sg	PP1-pl	PP2-sg	VP-sg
8	NP-pl	PP1-pl	PP2-sg	VP-pl

ANSWER SET		
1	NP-sg PP1-sg et NP2 VP-sg	Coord
2	**NP-pl PP1-pl NP2-sg VP-pl**	correct
3	NP-sg PP1-sg VP-sg	WNA
4	NP-sg PP1-sg PP2-sg VP-pl	AE
5	NP-pl PP1-sg PP1-sg VP-pl	WN1
6	NP-pl PP1-pl PP2-pl VP-pl	WN2

Figure 1: BLM instances for verb-subject agreement, with two attractors. WNA=wrong nr. of attractors; AE=agreement error; WN1=wrong nr. for 1st attractor (N1); WN2=wrong nr. for 2nd attractor (N2).

EXAMPLE OF CONTEXTS				
1	The vase	with the flower		leaks.
2	The vases	with the flower		leak.
3	The vase	with the flowers		leaks.
4	The vases	with the flowers		leak.
5	The vase	with the flower	from the garden	leaks.
6	The vases	with the flower	from the garden	leak.
7	The vase	with the flowers	from the garden	leaks.
8	???			

EXAMPLE OF ANSWERS	
The vase with the flower and the garden leaks.	Coord
The vases with the flowers from the garden leak.	Correct
The vase with the flower leaks.	WNA
The vase with the flower from the garden leak.	AE
The vases with the flower from the garden leak.	WN1
The vases with the flowers from the gardens leak.	WN2

Figure 2: Examples of actual sentences of type I data (original in French).

The dataset comprises three subsets, of increasing lexical complexity. Type I data is generated based on manually provided seeds, and a template that captures the rules mentioned above. Type II data is generated based on Type I data, by introducing lexical variation with the aid of a transformer, by generating alternatives for masked nouns. Type III data is generated by combining sentences from different instances from the Type II data. This will allow us to investigate the impact of lexical variation on the ability of a system to detect grammatical patterns.

Each subset contains an equal number of instances comprising three clause structures (we include complete instances – in French – in Appendix A.1). These structural variations alter the distance and relative depth of the subject and verb to produce a variety of conditions, to allow us to investigate how the subject-verb agreement information is encoded in BERT sentence embeddings.

Each problem is paired with a set of candidate answers. To allow for probing the learned model, apart from the correct answer, the answer sets contain negative examples built by corrupting some of the generating rules. This helps investigate the kind of information and structure learned, and the type of mistakes a system is prone to.

Table 1 shows the data statistics. Each of the three subsets of datasets is split 90:10 into train and test subsets, which are provided with the data. We use 20% of the train data for development.

dataset	number of problems	train:test split
Type I	2304	90:10
Type II	38400	90:10
Type III	38400	90:10

Table 1: Data statistics. The different types of data reflect different amounts of lexical variation within a problem instance.

3.2 Sentence representations

We investigate BERT sentence representations in a series of architectures designed to test whether we can access the relevant information for subject-verb agreement detection. We obtain the sentence embedding from the last layer of BERT, as the embedding of the [CLS] special token.

Figure 3 shows the summary of the architectures explored. Details of the architecture parameters are in Appendix A.2.

To investigate the impact of 2D-ing the sentence embeddings, the input sequences are given as a stack of 1D or 2D-ed sentence embeddings. This sequence of architectures also allows us to test the impact of additional abstracting steps – through compression into a latent VAE layer – for accessing patterns that encode the desired information.[1]

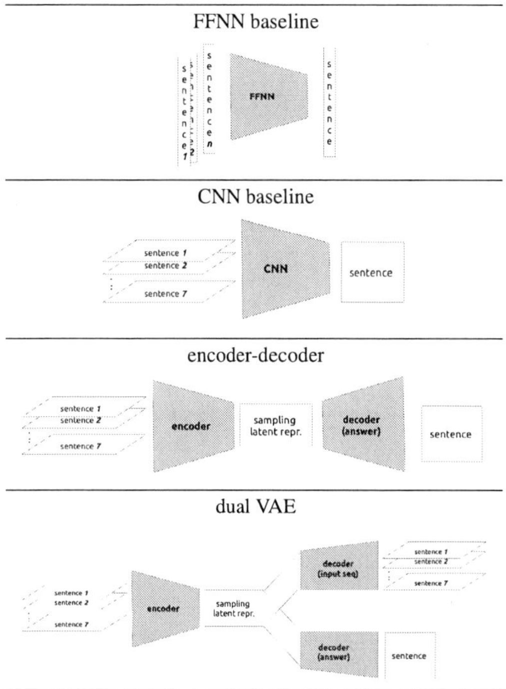

Figure 3: Architecture variations for exploring sentence embeddings

FFNN baseline The FFNN baseline is a three-layer feed-forward neural network. It transforms the sequence of the seven context sentence embeddings into a 1D-tensor, which is passed through three fully-connected layers, and outputs a vector that we take to represent the embedding of the answer sentence. This architecture allows the system to find patterns within and across sentences through the nodes in the successive layers.

The learning objective is to maximize the probability of the correct answer from the candidate answer set. Because the incorrect answers in the answer set are specifically designed to be minimally different from the correct answer, we implement the objective through the max-margin loss function. This function combines the scores of the correct and erroneous ones relative to the sentence embedding predicted by the system. We first compute a

[1]The code is available here: `https://github.com/CLCL-Geneva/BLM-SNFDisentangling`

score for the embedding e_i of each candidate answer a_i in the answer set $\mathcal{A}$ with respect to the predicted sentence embedding e_{pred} as the cosine of the angle between the respective vectors:

$$score(e_i, e_{pred}) = cos(e_i, e_{pred})$$

The loss uses the max-margin between the score for the correct answer e_c and for each of the incorrect answers e_i:

$$\mathcal{L}_a = \sum_{e_i}[1 - score(e_c, e_{pred}) + score(e_i, e_{pred})]^+$$

For prediction, the answer with the highest *score* from a candidate set is taken as the correct answer.

CNN baseline The CNN baseline consists of N convolutional steps, followed by a linear layer to compress the output to the desired dimensions. The input consists of a stack of sentence representations. We use two variations of this architecture: (i) Baseline_CNN_1DxSeq: for a stack of 1D sentence representations, there are three 2D convolutional steps, which use kernels of size 3x3; (ii) Baseline_CNN_{NxM}: for a stack of (NxM) 2D-ed sentence representations, there is one 3D convolutional layer, with a kernel size 3x15x15. The size of the kernels was set after preliminary experiments. For both variations, the kernels allow the system to detect patterns within a sentence representation and across the sequence.

This system uses the same max-margin loss function as the FFNN baseline system.

Encoder-decoder This system is essentially a variational autoencoder (VAE) (Kingma and Welling, 2013; Kingma et al., 2015), but it does not reconstruct the input, rather it constructs an answer. For each of the input variations, the encoder consists of a similar architecture as the corresponding CNN baseline[2], but the output of the linear layer is the size L of the latent layer ($2 \times L$ to represent the mean and standard deviation for a vector of length L). A new vector (of size L) is sampled using the output of the encoder as the means and standard deviation of L normal distributions, using the reparametrization trick (Kingma et al., 2015). This vector is then unpacked through a decoder to produce a sentence representation. The architecture of the decoder mirrors as close as possible the architecture of the encoder. It differs in that it outputs a single sentence representation, and not the representation of a sequence of sentences. The two variations are named VAE_1DxSeq and VAE_{MxN} in the upcoming results tables.

The training objective is to maximize the probability of the correct answer, while improving the approximation of the posterior distribution on the latent layer. This is implemented through a loss function that combines the max-margin loss on the constructed answer (as for previous architectures), with an additional factor – the regularization factor on the latent layer, typical of VAE models:

$$\mathcal{L}_l = KL(q_{enc}(z|x) \parallel p(z))$$

where q_{enc} is the approximate posterior distribution of p, $p(z) = \mathcal{N}(0, 1)$ and $q_{enc}(z|x) = \mathcal{N}(\mu_x, \sigma_x)$, where the $[\mu_x; \sigma_x]$ is the latent vector output by the encoder for the input vector x.

The final loss function is:

$$\mathcal{L}_{enc-dec} = \mathcal{L}_a + \beta * \mathcal{L}_l$$

The β coefficient is used to push for disentanglement on the latent layer of a VAE (Higgins et al., 2016). For the reported experiments $\beta = 1$.

Dual VAE The dual VAE adds a decoder to reconstruct the input to the encoder-decoder system, which mirrors the encoder in architecture and parameters. The two variations are Dual_VAE_1DxSeq and Dual_VAE_{NxM}.

The training objective is to maximize both the probability of the answer and the reconstructed input, and improve the approximation of the posterior distribution on the latent layer. Essentially, we add a factor to the loss function of the encoder-decoder architecture, reflecting the reconstruction loss:

$$\mathcal{L}_{dVAE} = \mathcal{L}_a + \alpha * \mathcal{L}_{recon} + \beta * \mathcal{L}_l$$

where α is a coefficient that can control the contribution of the input reconstruction signal. For the experiments reported, $\alpha = 0.01$, and serves as a scaling factor, to bring the value of the reconstruction loss within the same magnitude as the answer loss $\mathcal{L}_a$. The reconstruction loss is computed as the mean-square error between the representation of the input sequence (x) and the reconstructed one (x'): $\mathcal{L}_{recon} = MSE(x, x')$

[2]Because the FFNN baseline performed very well, and this set-up provides a full receptive field, we also had an encoder-decoder variation using FFNN but it performed much worse than the other variations, and we do not report on it here.

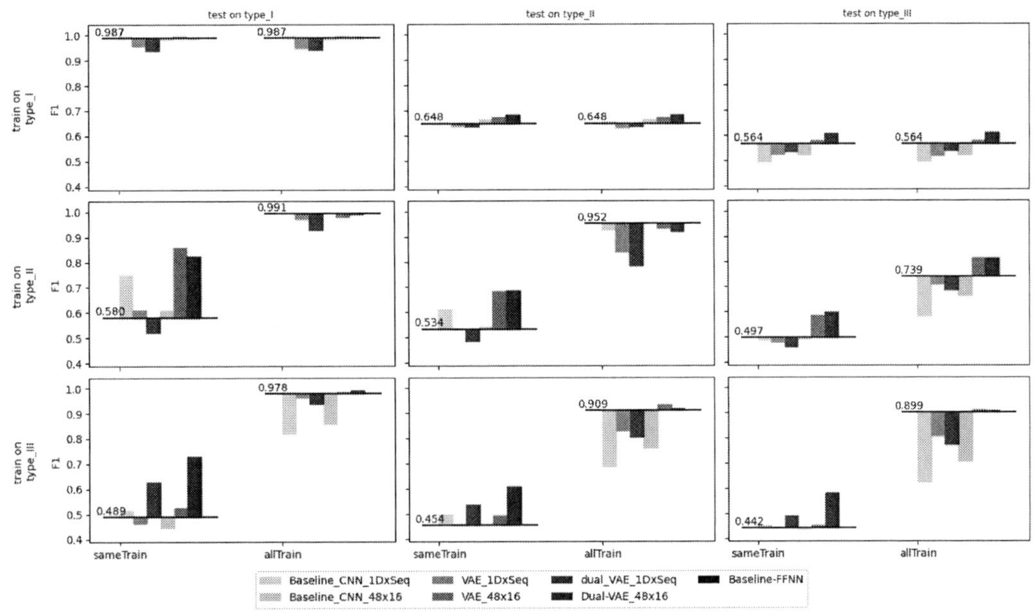

Figure 4: (best seen in color) F1 scores (averages over five runs) on the FFNN baseline and CNN, enc-dec and dual VAE systems with 48x16 2D-ed sentence embeddings. The graphs shows the difference in F1 between the systems relative to the reference baseline (FFNN). Each panel includes results on training on the same amount of data (left) and training on full data (right).

4 Experiments

We report experiments on seven systems – the baseline FFNN, and two variations (the input as a stack of 1D or 2D sentence representations) for each of the other three architectures.

Our aim was to explore raw BERT sentence embeddings, and not variations fine-tuned for specific tasks. The results reported here are based on sentence embeddings obtained using BERTTokenizer and BERTModel from the transformers Python library, using the pretrained "BERT-base-multilingual-cased" model[3].[4]

Preliminary experiments have been used to determine the kernel size for processing the 2D and 3D tensors with the stack of 1D and 2D-ed sentence embeddings respectively. The optimal kernel for 2D tensors was 3x3, and for the 3D tensors was 3x15x15. This large kernel size imposes specific restrictions on the dimensions of the 2D-ed sentence embeddings. Because a sentence embedding is a one-dimensional array of length 768, there are only 4 possible 2D values, where both dimensions are greater than 15 (16x48, 24x32, 32x24, 48x16).

We have also explored the size of the latent layer (5:25, step 5), and chosen the latent size 5. All systems used a learning rate of 0.001 and Adam optimizer, and batch size 100. For the baselines and experiments on the full training set for type II and type III data the training was done for 50 epochs, and for type I data and the sameTrain set-up, the training was done for 120 epochs.

The experiments were run on an HP PAIR Workstation Z4 G4 MT, with an Intel Xeon W-2255 processor, 64G RAM, and a MSI GeForce RTX 3090 VENTUS 3X OC 24G GDDR6X GPU.

4.1 Results

Figures 4 and 5 show the main experimental results. All results represent F1 averages over five runs. More details are provided in Appendix A.3.

Figure 4 shows the difference in F1 between the FFNN baseline (the black lines) and the increasingly complex architectures. Each row corresponds to the data type used for training, and the columns to the data type used for testing. Each panel shows the test results of models trained on the same amount of data, on the left, and training on full data, on the right.

[3]https://huggingface.co/bert-base-multilingual-cased

[4]We have run preliminary experiments with French-specific sentence embeddings using FlauBERT (Le et al., 2020). The results were lower than when using a multilingual cased BERT language model.

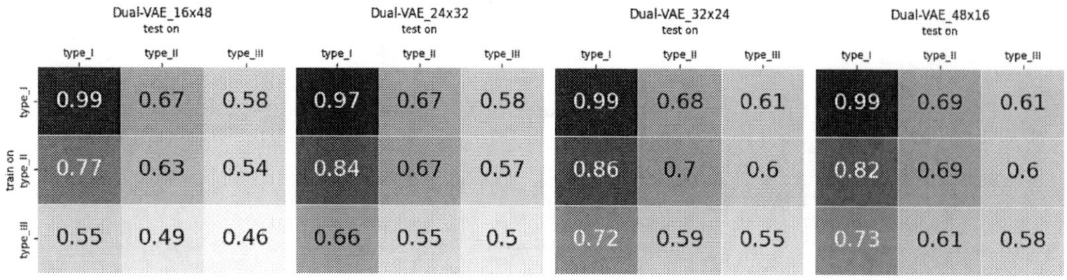

Figure 5: Impact of different reshapings: F1 results (averages over five runs) on (16x48), (24x32), (32x24), (48x16) reshaping, using the dual VAE architecture, and trained on similar amounts of training data.

Figure 5 shows the results obtained using different 2D transformations of the one-dimensional tensor BERT sentence embeddings with the dual VAE system, when training on the same amount of data (2073 instances – the amount available for type I data). Overall, the best-performing embedding is the one reshaped in a 48x16 matrix, the setting then used for the results reported in the system study, shown in Figure 4.

Figure 7 shows the impact of the amount of training data on the performance of the models. The results reported are average F1 scores over 5 runs, using the dual-VAE architecture with 48x16 sentence embedding.

4.2 Discussion

Impact of 2D-ed representations and VAE-based architectures In Figure 4, the horizontal black lines represent the performance of the Baseline FFNN system, and the bars show the relative performance of the system variations with 1D and 2D-ed sentence representations.

When using the full training data the results on type II and type III subsets are very high. This is in line with ML theory, as input with more variety leads to better-performing models, *when given enough training data*. The low results of the baselines and the systems using the 1D representations on the restricted training set-up (2073 instances – the available amount of training+validation data for type I – for all subsets) shows that these systems do not access the most relevant information from the sentence embedding for our targeted phenomenon.

Pairwise comparisons of similar architectures with different types of input show that 2D-ed representations lead to better results in almost all settings, particularly in the harsher training scenario with limited data (the left bar group in each plot).

The progression of architectures – from the CNN to the dual VAE – also show an increase in results, for both types of input representations. The phenomenon is more evident – and more useful – particularly for the restricted training scenario. It shows that forcing the representations to more compressed and abstract forms is useful for distilling the information useful to detect our targeted grammatical phenomenon.

The most interesting result is a combination of the impact of the 2D-ed representations and the various architectures: as the panels corresponding to training on type I data (first row in Figure 4) show, the combination of the dual VAE architecture with 2D-ed sentence embedding leads to the best results when testing on type II and type III data, which are lexically more complex than type I data. This shows that with a good combination of input representation and system, a model can find robust patterns even in a smaller amount of simple data.

Impact of 2D-ing the sentence representation The results presented in Figure 4 show that the 48x16 2D version of the sentence representation leads to better results than the 1x768 version. Figure 5 shows the impact of various 2D variations, when training the systems on the same amount of training+validation data. The results are obtained with the dual VAE architecture. The (overall) best performing representation from the 4 variations is the 48x16 version. In fact, for the $N \times M$ 2D-ing, the results are better the smaller M becomes. This indicates that information is somehow uniformly distributed in a BERT sentence embedding, within subsequences of length close to 16 – at least the information relevant to our particular subject-verb agreement task.

Impact of training data Figure 4 shows that the 2D-ed sentence representation combined with the dual VAE architecture leads to the best results, par-

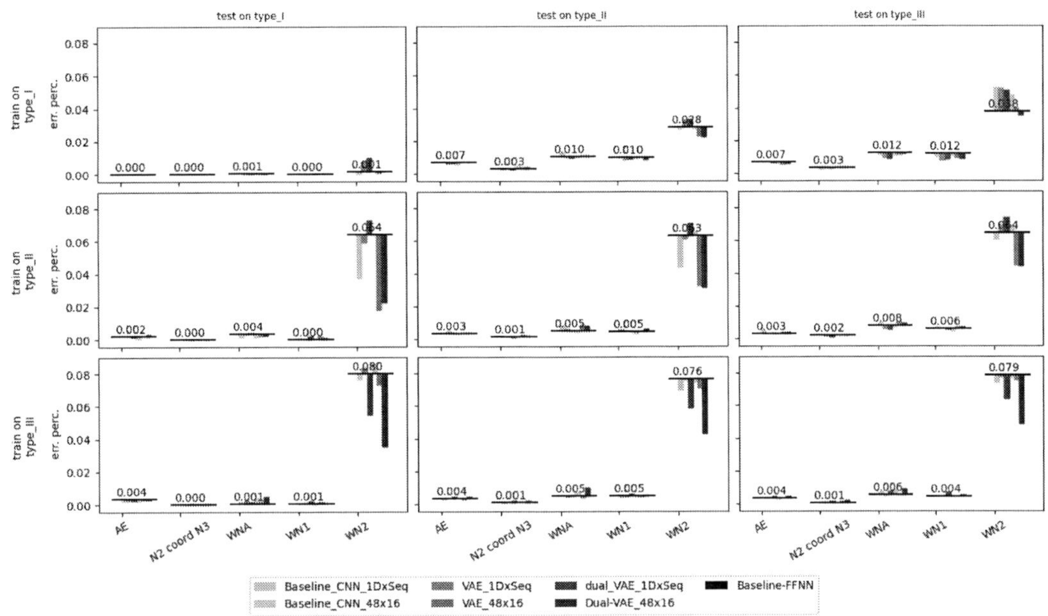

Figure 6: (best seen in color) Error analysis on the four systems trained with the same amount of data. The y-axis is the percentage of the error relative to the size of the test set (i.e. downward bars indicate an improvement.)

ticularly when training the systems on the same amount of training+validation data. We further analyze the learning curves when varying the amount of training+validation data from 50 to 2073 (split 80:20 into training and validation data). Figure 7 shows these results.

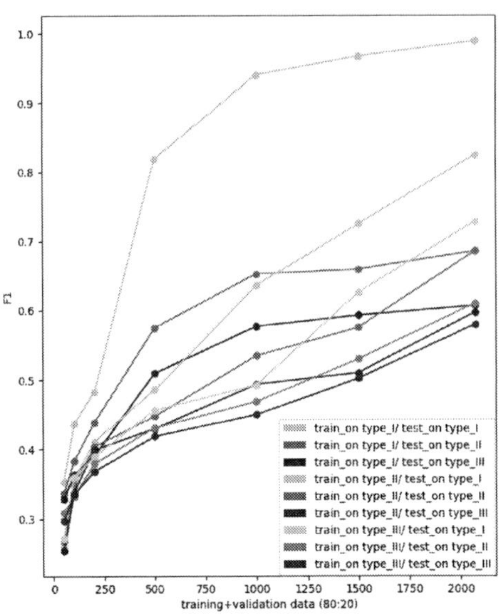

Figure 7: (best seen in color) Training data analysis using the the Dual_VAE_48x16 system

The curves corresponding to training on type I data – in shades of purple – approach the higher performance fastest, showing that they are able to exploit smaller amounts of data better. The lexical variations in type II and type III data seem to obfuscate the targeted patterns, as they require more training data.

4.3 Error Analyses

The error analysis shown in Figure 6 clearly shows that errors are almost always of the same kind — the assignment of the wrong grammatical number to the second attractor, closer to the verb— thus performing a local kind of agreement instead of the correct longer-distance structural agreement. These types of errors are frequent in humans too (Linzen and Leonard, 2018). It can be seen that the dual-VAE corrects these errors to a great degree (and greater than the other models), thus showing that it can detect the non-local patterns better than the other architectures. The combination of 2D-ing the sentence embedding and the large size of the kernel allows the system to find more distant patterns in the sentence embedding, thus connecting more distant tokens.

5 Conclusion

We have proposed and investigated variations of BERT sentence representations for the task of identifying the rule of subject-verb agreement and some of its properties in a dataset consisting of sequences of sentences that instantiate these underlying rules. BERT sentence embeddings, as 1D arrays, have been successfully used for a variety of tasks, but the information they encode about specific phenomena is distributed over the vector. Reshaping the sentence representation into two-dimensional inputs leads to improved results, and an additional step of abstracting these 2D-ed sentence embeddings leads to further improvements for the task. These more abstracted 2D-ed embeddings also learn a robust model based on a smaller amount of simpler training data, while showing good performance on the more lexically-complex data.

We plan to explore whether BERT sentence embedding may have even higher-dimension patterns, and whether such nD-ed BERT sentence representation can be used to detect other grammatical or semantic phenomena. We also plan to directly distill 2D sentence representation in more compact and disentangled representation, to encode more explicitly some of the distributed information in these embeddings.

Limitations

The experiments reported were performed on a dataset of French sentences, with a particular organization: sequences of sentences as input, each with a slightly different structure but sharing the subject-verb agreement rule. All sentences in the input sequence are processed together. In future work we plan to separate the distillation of rules from a sentence representation from the processing of the sequence.

We have investigated only part of the parameters in the proposed architectures. In particular, the β coefficient in the encoder-decoder and the dual VAE architectures was set to 1. Higher values may lead to more disentangled representations on the latent layer.

Ethics Statement

To the best of our knowledge, there are no ethics concerns with this paper.

Acknowledgments

We gratefully acknowledge the partial support of this work by the Swiss National Science Foundation, through grants #51NF40_180888 (NCCR Evolving Language) and SNF Advanced grant TMAG-1_209426 to PM.

References

Aixiu An, Chunyang Jiang, Maria A. Rodriguez, Vivi Nastase, and Paola Merlo. 2023. BLM-AgrF: A new French benchmark to investigate generalization of agreement in neural networks. In *Proceedings of the 17th Conference of the European Chapter of the Association for Computational Linguistics*, pages 1363–1374, Dubrovnik, Croatia. Association for Computational Linguistics.

Piotr Bojanowski, Edouard Grave, Armand Joulin, and Tomas Mikolov. 2017. Enriching word vectors with subword information. *TACL*, 5:135–146.

Tom Brown, Benjamin Mann, Nick Ryder, Melanie Subbiah, Jared D Kaplan, Prafulla Dhariwal, Arvind Neelakantan, Pranav Shyam, Girish Sastry, Amanda Askell, Sandhini Agarwal, Ariel Herbert-Voss, Gretchen Krueger, Tom Henighan, Rewon Child, Aditya Ramesh, Daniel Ziegler, Jeffrey Wu, Clemens Winter, Chris Hesse, Mark Chen, Eric Sigler, Mateusz Litwin, Scott Gray, Benjamin Chess, Jack Clark, Christopher Berner, Sam McCandlish, Alec Radford, Ilya Sutskever, and Dario Amodei. 2020. Language models are few-shot learners. In *Advances in Neural Information Processing Systems*, volume 33, pages 1877–1901. Curran Associates, Inc.

Alexis Conneau, German Kruszewski, Guillaume Lample, Loïc Barrault, and Marco Baroni. 2018. What you can cram into a single $&!#* vector: Probing sentence embeddings for linguistic properties. In *Proceedings of the 56th Annual Meeting of the Association for Computational Linguistics (Volume 1: Long Papers)*, pages 2126–2136, Melbourne, Australia. Association for Computational Linguistics.

Jacob Devlin, Ming-Wei Chang, Kenton Lee, and Kristina Toutanova. 2019. BERT: Pre-training of deep bidirectional transformers for language understanding. In *Proceedings of the 2019 Conference of the North American Chapter of the Association for Computational Linguistics: Human Language Technologies, Volume 1 (Long and Short Papers)*, pages 4171–4186, Minneapolis, Minnesota. Association for Computational Linguistics.

Li Fei-Fei, R. Fergus, and P. Perona. 2006. One-shot learning of object categories. *IEEE Transactions on Pattern Analysis and Machine Intelligence*, 28(4):594–611.

Mario Giulianelli, Jack Harding, Florian Mohnert, Dieuwke Hupkes, and Willem Zuidema. 2018. Under the hood: Using diagnostic classifiers to investigate and improve how language models track agreement information. In *Proceedings of the 2018 EMNLP Workshop BlackboxNLP: Analyzing and Interpreting*

Neural Networks for NLP, pages 240–248, Brussels, Belgium. Association for Computational Linguistics.

Yoav Goldberg. 2019. Assessing bert's syntactic abilities. *arXiv preprint arXiv:1901.05287*.

Kristina Gulordava, Piotr Bojanowski, Edouard Grave, Tal Linzen, and Marco Baroni. 2018. Colorless green recurrent networks dream hierarchically. In *Proceedings of the 2018 Conference of the North American Chapter of the Association for Computational Linguistics: Human Language Technologies*, pages 1195–1205. Association for Computational Linguistics.

Irina Higgins, Loic Matthey, Arka Pal, Christopher Burgess, Xavier Glorot, Matthew Botvinick, Shakir Mohamed, and Alexander Lerchner. 2016. beta-vae: Learning basic visual concepts with a constrained variational framework.

Diederik P Kingma, Tim Salimans, and Max Welling. 2015. Variational dropout and the local reparameterization trick. In *Advances in Neural Information Processing Systems*, volume 28. Curran Associates, Inc.

Diederik P Kingma and Max Welling. 2013. Auto-encoding variational bayes. *arXiv preprint arXiv:1312.6114*.

Yair Lakretz, Dieuwke Hupkes, Alessandra Vergallito, Marco Marelli, Marco Baroni, and Stanislas Dehaene. 2021. Mechanisms for handling nested dependencies in neural-network language models and humans. *Cognition*.

Karim Lasri, Tiago Pimentel, Alessandro Lenci, Thierry Poibeau, and Ryan Cotterell. 2022. Probing for the usage of grammatical number. In *Proceedings of the 60th Annual Meeting of the Association for Computational Linguistics (Volume 1: Long Papers)*, pages 8818–8831, Dublin, Ireland. Association for Computational Linguistics.

Hang Le, Loïc Vial, Jibril Frej, Vincent Segonne, Maximin Coavoux, Benjamin Lecouteux, Alexandre Allauzen, Benoît Crabbé, Laurent Besacier, and Didier Schwab. 2020. FlauBERT : des modèles de langue contextualisés pré-entraînés pour le français (FlauBERT : Unsupervised language model pre-training for French). In *Actes de la 6e conférence conjointe Journées d'Études sur la Parole (JEP, 33e édition), Traitement Automatique des Langues Naturelles (TALN, 27e édition), Rencontre des Étudiants Chercheurs en Informatique pour le Traitement Automatique des Langues (RÉCITAL, 22e édition). Volume 2 : Traitement Automatique des Langues Naturelles*, pages 268–278, Nancy, France. ATALA et AFCP.

Tal Linzen and Marco Baroni. 2021. Syntactic structure from deep learning. *Annual Review of Linguistics*, 7(1):195–212.

Tal Linzen, Emmanuel Dupoux, and Yoav Goldberg. 2016. Assessing the ability of LSTMs to learn syntax-sensitive dependencies. *Transactions of the Association of Computational Linguistics*, 4(1):521–535.

Tal Linzen and Brian Leonard. 2018. Distinct patterns of syntactic agreement errors in recurrent networks and humans. In *Proceedings of the 40th Cognitive Science Society*.

Christopher D. Manning, Kevin Clark, John Hewitt, Urvashi Khandelwal, and Omer Levy. 2020. Emergent linguistic structure in artificial neural networks trained by self-supervision. *Proceedings of the National Academy of Sciences*, 117:30046 – 30054.

Gary Marcus. 2022. The dark risk of large language models. *WIRED*.

R Thomas McCoy, Robert Frank, and Tal Linzen. 2018. Revisiting the poverty of the stimulus: Hierarchical generalization without a hierarchical bias in recurrent neural networks. In *Proceedings of the 40th Annual Conference of the Cognitive Science Society. Austin, TX: Cognitive Science Society*.

Paola Merlo, Aixiu An, and Maria A. Rodriguez. 2021. Blackbird's language matrices (BLM): a new benchmark to investigate disentangled generalisation in neural networks.

Tomas Mikolov, Ilya Sutskever, Kai Chen, Greg S Corrado, and Jeff Dean. 2013. Distributed representations of words and phrases and their compositionality. In *Advances in Neural Information Processing Systems*, volume 26. Curran Associates, Inc.

Dmitry Nikolaev and Sebastian Padó. 2023. Representation biases in sentence transformers. In *Proceedings of the 17th Conference of the European Chapter of the Association for Computational Linguistics*, pages 3701–3716, Dubrovnik, Croatia. Association for Computational Linguistics.

Jeffrey Pennington, Richard Socher, and Christopher Manning. 2014. Glove: Global vectors for word representation. In *Proceedings EMNLP)*, pages 1532–1543.

Matthew E. Peters, Mark Neumann, Mohit Iyyer, Matt Gardner, Christopher Clark, Kenton Lee, and Luke Zettlemoyer. 2018. Deep contextualized word representations. In *Proc. of NAACL*.

Pranav Rajpurkar, Robin Jia, and Percy Liang. 2018. Know what you don't know: Unanswerable questions for SQuAD. In *Proceedings of the 56th Annual Meeting of the Association for Computational Linguistics (Volume 2: Short Papers)*, pages 784–789, Melbourne, Australia. Association for Computational Linguistics.

John C. Raven. 1938. Standardization of progressive matrices. *British Journal of Medical Psychology*, 19:137–150.

Nils Reimers and Iryna Gurevych. 2019. Sentence-BERT: Sentence embeddings using Siamese BERT-networks. In *Proceedings of the 2019 Conference on Empirical Methods in Natural Language Processing and the 9th International Joint Conference on Natural Language Processing (EMNLP-IJCNLP)*, pages 3982–3992, Hong Kong, China. Association for Computational Linguistics.

Mathias Sablé-Meyer, Joël Fagot, Serge Caparos, Timo van Kerkoerle, Marie Amalric, and Stanislas Dehaene. 2021. Sensitivity to geometric shape regularity in humans and baboons: A putative signature of human singularity. *Proceedings of the National Academy of Sciences*, 118(16).

Timo Schick and Hinrich Schütze. 2021. Exploiting cloze-questions for few-shot text classification and natural language inference. In *Proceedings of the 16th Conference of the European Chapter of the Association for Computational Linguistics: Main Volume*, pages 255–269, Online. Association for Computational Linguistics.

Suzanne Stevenson and Paola Merlo. 2022. Beyond the benchmarks: Toward human-like lexical representations. *Frontiers of Artificial Intelligence*, 5:796741.

Teo Susnjak. 2022. ChatGPT: The end of online exam integrity?

Tristan Thrush, Ethan Wilcox, and Roger Levy. 2020. Investigating novel verb learning in BERT: Selectional preference classes and alternation-based syntactic generalization. In *Proceedings of the Third BlackboxNLP Workshop on Analyzing and Interpreting Neural Networks for NLP*, pages 265–275, Online. Association for Computational Linguistics.

Alex Wang, Yada Pruksachatkun, Nikita Nangia, Amanpreet Singh, Julian Michael, Felix Hill, Omer Levy, and Samuel Bowman. 2019. Superglue: A stickier benchmark for general-purpose language understanding systems. In *Advances in Neural Information Processing Systems*, volume 32. Curran Associates, Inc.

Chi Zhang, Feng Gao, Baoxiong Jia, Yixin Zhu, and Song-Chun Zhu. 2019. Raven: A dataset for relational and analogical visual reasoning. In *Proceedings of the IEEE Conference on Computer Vision and Pattern Recognition (CVPR)*.

A.1 Type I instance examples

A Supplementary Materials

Main clause						
1		L'ordinateur	avec le programme			est en panne.
2		Les ordinateurs	avec le programme			sont en panne.
3		L'ordinateur	avec les programmes			est en panne.
4		Les ordinateurs	avec les programmes			sont en panne.
5		L'ordinateur	avec le programme	de l'expérience		est en panne.
6		Les ordinateurs	avec le programme	de l'expérience		sont en panne.
7		L'ordinateur	avec les programmes	de l'expérience		est en panne.
8		Les ordinateurs	avec les programmes	de l'expérience		sont en panne.
Completive clause						
1	Jean suppose que	l'ordinateur	avec le programme			est en panne.
2	Jean suppose que	les ordinateurs	avec le programme			sont en panne.
3	Jean suppose que	l'ordinateur	avec les programmes			est en panne.
4	Jean suppose que	les ordinateurs	avec les programmes			sont en panne.
5	Jean suppose que	l'ordinateur	avec le programme	de l'expérience		est en panne.
6	Jean suppose que	les ordinateurs	avec le programme	de l'expérience		sont en panne.
7	Jean suppose que	l'ordinateur	avec les programmes	de l'expérience		est en panne.
8	Jean suppose que	les ordinateurs	avec les programmes	de l'expérience		sont en panne.
Relative clause						
1		L'ordinateur	avec le programme		dont Jean se servait	est en panne.
2		Les ordinateurs	avec le programme		dont Jean se servait	sont en panne.
3		L'ordinateur	avec les programmes		dont Jean se servait	est en panne.
4		Les ordinateurs	avec les programmes		dont Jean se servait	sont en panne.
5		L'ordinateur	avec le programme	de l'expérience	dont Jean se servait	est en panne.
6		Les ordinateurs	avec le programme	de l'expérience	dont Jean se servait	sont en panne.
7		L'ordinateur	avec les programmes	de l'expérience	dont Jean se servait	est en panne.
8		Les ordinateurs	avec les programmes	de l'expérience	dont Jean se servait	sont en panne.

	Answer set for problem constructed from lines 1-7 of the main clause sequence	
1	L'ordinateur avec le programme et l'experiénce est en panne.	N2 coord N3
2	**Les ordinateurs avec les programmes de l'experiénce sont en panne.**	correct
3	L'ordinateur avec le programme est en panne.	wrong number of attractors
4	L'ordinateur avec les programmes de l'experiénce sont en panne.	agreement error
5	Les ordinateurs avec le programme de l'experiénce sont en panne.	wrong nr. for 1st attractor noun (N1)
6	Les ordinateurs avec les programmes des experiénces sont en panne.	wrong nr. for 2nd attractor noun (N2)

Figure 8: BLM-AgrF instances for verb-subject agreement, with two attractors (programme, experiénce), and three clause structures. And candidate answer set for a problem constructed from lines 1-7 of the main clause sequence.

A.2 System architecture details

Baseline_FFNN

```
==========================================================================================
Layer (type:depth-idx)                    Output Shape              Param #
==========================================================================================
BaselineFFNN                              [100, 768]                --
--Linear: 1-1                             [100, 1536]               8,259,072
--Linear: 1-2                             [100, 1536]               2,360,832
--Linear: 1-3                             [100, 768]                1,180,416
==========================================================================================
Total params: 11,800,320
Trainable params: 11,800,320
Non-trainable params: 0
Total mult-adds (G): 1.18
==========================================================================================
Input size (MB): 2.15
Forward/backward pass size (MB): 3.07
Params size (MB): 47.20
Estimated Total Size (MB): 52.42
==========================================================================================
```

Baseline_CNN_1DxSeq: CNN with stack of 1D sentence embeddings

```
==========================================================================================
Layer (type:depth-idx)                        Output Shape              Param #
==========================================================================================
BaselineCNN_1DxSeq                            [100, 768]                --
--Conv2d: 1-1                                 [100, 4, 5, 766]          40
--Conv2d: 1-2                                 [100, 8, 3, 764]          296
--Conv2d: 1-3                                 [100, 16, 1, 762]         1,168
--Linear: 1-4                                 [100, 768]                9,364,224
==========================================================================================
Total params: 9,365,728
Trainable params: 9,365,728
Non-trainable params: 0
Total mult-adds (G): 1.11
==========================================================================================
Input size (MB): 2.15
Forward/backward pass size (MB): 37.29
Params size (MB): 37.46
Estimated Total Size (MB): 76.91
==========================================================================================
```

Baseline_CNN_48x16: CNN with 48x16 2D-ed sentence embedding

```
==========================================================================================
Layer (type:depth-idx)                        Output Shape              Param #
==========================================================================================
BaselineCNN                                   [100, 7, 768]             --
--Conv3d: 1-1                                 [100, 32, 5, 34, 2]       21,632
--Linear: 1-2                                 [100, 768]                8,356,608
==========================================================================================
Total params: 8,378,240
Trainable params: 8,378,240
Non-trainable params: 0
Total mult-adds (G): 1.57
==========================================================================================
Input size (MB): 2.15
Forward/backward pass size (MB): 9.32
Params size (MB): 33.51
Estimated Total Size (MB): 44.98
==========================================================================================
```

VAE_1DxSeq: encoder-decoder with stack of 1D sentence embeddings

```
==========================================================================================
Layer (type:depth-idx)                        Output Shape              Param #
==========================================================================================
VariationalAutoencoder                        [100, 5]                  --
--Encoder: 1-1                                [100, 5]                  --
     --Conv2d: 2-1                            [100, 4, 5, 766]          40
     --Conv2d: 2-2                            [100, 8, 3, 764]          296
     --Conv2d: 2-3                            [100, 16, 1, 762]         1,168
     --Linear: 2-4                            [100, 10]                 121,930
--simpleSampling: 1-2                         [100, 5]                  --
--Decoder_answer: 1-3                         [100, 1, 1, 768]          --
     --Linear: 2-5                            [100, 12192]              73,152
     --ConvTranspose2d: 2-6                   [100, 8, 1, 764]          392
     --ConvTranspose2d: 2-7                   [100, 4, 1, 766]          100
     --ConvTranspose2d: 2-8                   [100, 1, 1, 768]          13
==========================================================================================
Total params: 197,091
Trainable params: 197,091
Non-trainable params: 0
Total mult-adds (M): 230.28
==========================================================================================
Input size (MB): 2.15
Forward/backward pass size (MB): 54.40
Params size (MB): 0.79
Estimated Total Size (MB): 57.33
==========================================================================================
```

VAE_48x16: encoder-decoder with 48x16 2D-ed sentence embeddings

```
==========================================================================================
Layer (type:depth-idx)                        Output Shape              Param #
==========================================================================================
VariationalAutoencoder                        [100, 5]                  --
--Encoder: 1-1                                [100, 5]                  --
     --Conv3d: 2-1                            [100, 32, 5, 34, 2]       21,632
     --Linear: 2-2                            [100, 10]                 108,810
--simpleSampling: 1-2                         [100, 5]                  --
--Decoder_answer: 1-3                         [100, 1, 1, 48, 16]       --
     --Linear: 2-3                            [100, 2176]               13,056
     --ConvTranspose3d: 2-4                   [100, 1, 1, 48, 16]       7,201
==========================================================================================
Total params: 150,699
Trainable params: 150,699
Non-trainable params: 0
Total mult-adds (G): 1.30
==========================================================================================
Input size (MB): 2.15
Forward/backward pass size (MB): 11.07
Params size (MB): 0.60
Estimated Total Size (MB): 13.82
==========================================================================================
```

Dual_VAE_1DxSeq: dual VAE with stack of 1D sentence embeddings

```
==========================================================================================
Layer (type:depth-idx)                        Output Shape              Param #
==========================================================================================
VariationalAutoencoder                        [100, 5]                  --
--Encoder: 1-1                                [100, 5]                  --
     --Conv2d: 2-1                            [100, 4, 5, 766]          40
     --Conv2d: 2-2                            [100, 8, 3, 764]          296
     --Conv2d: 2-3                            [100, 16, 1, 762]         1,168
     --Linear: 2-4                            [100, 10]                 121,930
--simpleSampling: 1-2                         [100, 5]                  --
--Decoder_mirror: 1-3                         [100, 1, 7, 768]          --
     --Linear: 2-5                            [100, 12192]              73,152
     --ConvTranspose2d: 2-6                   [100, 8, 3, 764]          1,160
     --ConvTranspose2d: 2-7                   [100, 4, 5, 766]          292
     --ConvTranspose2d: 2-8                   [100, 1, 7, 768]          37
--Decoder_answer: 1-4                         [100, 1, 1, 768]          --
     --Linear: 2-9                            [100, 12192]              73,152
     --ConvTranspose2d: 2-10                  [100, 8, 1, 764]          392
     --ConvTranspose2d: 2-11                  [100, 4, 1, 766]          100
     --ConvTranspose2d: 2-12                  [100, 1, 1, 768]          13
==========================================================================================
Total params: 271,732
Trainable params: 271,732
Non-trainable params: 0
Total mult-adds (M): 635.19
==========================================================================================
Input size (MB): 2.15
Forward/backward pass size (MB): 95.37
Params size (MB): 1.09
Estimated Total Size (MB): 98.61
==========================================================================================
```

Dual_Vae_48x16: dual VAE with 48x16 2D-ed sentence embeddings

```
==========================================================================================
Layer (type:depth-idx)                   Output Shape              Param #
==========================================================================================
VariationalAutoencoder                   [100, 5]                  --
--Encoder: 1-1                           [100, 5]                  --
     --Conv3d: 2-1                       [100, 32, 5, 34, 2]       21,632
     --Linear: 2-2                       [100, 10]                 108,810
--simpleSampling: 1-2                    [100, 5]                  --
--Decoder_mirror: 1-3                    [100, 1, 7, 48, 16]       --
     --Linear: 2-3                       [100, 10880]              65,280
     --ConvTranspose3d: 2-4              [100, 1, 7, 48, 16]       21,601
--Decoder_answer: 1-4                    [100, 1, 1, 48, 16]       --
     --Linear: 2-5                       [100, 2176]               13,056
     --ConvTranspose3d: 2-6              [100, 1, 1, 48, 16]       7,201
==========================================================================================
Total params: 237,580
Trainable params: 237,580
Non-trainable params: 0
Total mult-adds (G): 12.92
==========================================================================================
Input size (MB): 2.15
Forward/backward pass size (MB): 24.07
Params size (MB): 0.95
Estimated Total Size (MB): 27.17
==========================================================================================
```

A.3 Detailed experimental results

Results on 2D-ing BERt sentence embeddings The detailed version of the results in Figure 5

TRAIN ON	TEST ON	16X48 F1 (STD)	24X32 F1 (STD)	32X24 F1 (STD)	48X16 F1 (STD)
type I	type I	**0.9905** (0.0069)	0.9740 (0.0061)	0.9879 (0.0064)	0.9887 (0.0080)
type I	type II	0.6682 (0.0035)	0.6683 (0.0041)	0.6815 (0.0021)	**0.6855** (0.0028)
type I	type III	0.5795 (0.0049)	0.5819 (0.0011)	**0.6072** (0.0045)	0.6066 (0.0018)
type II	type I	0.7732 (0.0283)	0.8355 (0.0137)	**0.8632** (0.0089)	0.8242 (0.0065)
type II	type II	0.6333 (0.0132)	0.6725 (0.0077)	**0.6984** (0.0046)	0.6855 (0.0040)
type II	type III	0.5431 (0.0069)	0.5689 (0.0024)	0.5952 (0.0058)	**0.5969** (0.0046)
type III	type I	0.5550 (0.0461)	0.6649 (0.0059)	0.7221 (0.0228)	**0.7281** (0.0259)
type III	type II	0.4947 (0.0218)	0.5474 (0.0076)	0.5884 (0.0053)	**0.6096** (0.0064)
type III	type III	0.4620 (0.0151)	0.5042 (0.0089)	0.5515 (0.0050)	**0.5794** (0.0054)

Table 2: Analysis of 2D-ing the BERT sentence embeddings: F1 (std) scores for the four 2D combinations. The highest value for each train/test combination highlighted in bold.

Results on system analysis The detailed version of the results in Figure 4

TRAIN ON	TEST ON	BASELINE_FFNN	BASELINE_CNN 48X16	VAE_48X16	DUAL_VAE_48X16
TRAIN ON FULL TRAINING DATA					
type I	type I	0.9870 (0)	0.9827 (0)	**0.9957** (0)	0.9905 (0.0042)
type I	type II	0.6482 (0)	0.6612 (0)	0.6729 (0)	**0.6829** (0.0070)
type I	type III	0.5643 (0)	0.5229 (0)	0.5776 (0)	**0.6089** (0.0062)
type II	type I	**0.9913** (0)	**0.9913** (0)	0.9801 (0.0052)	0.9896 (0.0044)
type II	type II	0.9523 (0)	**0.9552** (0)	0.9331 (0.0014)	0.9215 (0.0017)
type II	type III	0.7391 (0)	0.6622 (0)	**0.8156** (0.0019)	0.8152 (0.0037)
type III	type I	0.9784 (0)	0.8571 (0)	0.9853 (0.0035)	**0.9913** (0.0027)
type III	type II	0.9086 (0)	0.7578 (0)	**0.9309** (0.0039)	0.9146 (0.0040)
type III	type III	0.8987 (0)	0.7062 (0)	**0.9089** (0.0016)	0.9047 (0.0046)
TRAIN ON THE SAME AMOUNT OF DATA (2073 INSTANCES: 1658 TRAIN/415 VALIDATION)					
type I	type I	0.9870 (0)	0.9827 (0)	**0.9957** (0)	0.9887 (0.0080)
type I	type II	0.6482 (0)	0.6612 (0)	0.6729 (0)	**0.6855** (0.0028)
type I	type III	0.5643 (0)	0.5229 (0)	0.5776 (0)	**0.6066** (0.0018)
type II	type I	0.5801 (0)	0.6061 (0)	**0.8571** (0)	0.8242 (0.0065)
type II	type II	0.5336 (0)	0.5411 (0)	0.6833 (0)	**0.6855** (0.0040)
type II	type III	0.4974 (0)	0.4901 (0)	0.5846 (0)	**0.5969** (0.0046)
type III	type I	0.4892 (0)	0.4459 (0)	0.5238 (0)	**0.7281** (0.0259)
type III	type II	0.4542 (0)	0.4576 (0)	0.4935 (0)	**0.6096** (0.0064)
type III	type III	0.4419 (0)	0.4380 (0)	0.4529 (0)	**0.5794** (0.0054)

Table 3: Analysis of systems: F1 (std) scores for the FFNN baseline and the 3 2D-ed system architectures. The highest value for each train/test combination is highlighted in bold.

TRAIN ON	TEST ON	BASELINE_CNN_1DXSEQ	VAE_1DXSEQ	DUAL_VAE_1DXSEQ
TRAIN ON FULL TRAINING DATA				
type I	type I	0.9948 (0.0064)	0.9489 (0.0088)	0.9403 (0.0084)
type I	type II	0.6518 (0.0044)	0.6305 (0.0069)	0.6347 (0.0026)
type I	type III	0.4961 (0.0043)	0.5194 (0.0086)	0.5357 (0.0037)
type II	type I	0.9974 (0.0035)	0.9697 (0.0039)	0.9264 (0.0152)
type II	type II	0.9256 (0.0041)	0.8393 (0.0016)	0.7819 (0.0111)
type II	type III	0.5837 (0.0064)	0.7060 (0.0154)	0.6853 (0.0107)
type III	type I	0.8173 (0.0390)	0.9628 (0.0065)	0.9385 (0.0050)
type III	type II	0.6865 (0.0191)	0.8279 (0.0060)	0.8020 (0.0020)
type III	type III	0.6205 (0.0180)	0.8046 (0.0038)	0.7727 (0.0036)
TRAIN ON THE SAME AMOUNT OF DATA (2073 INSTANCES: 1658 TRAIN/415 VALIDATION)				
type I	type I	0.9939 (0.0044)	0.9558 (0.0042)	0.9385 (0.0069)
type I	type II	0.6491 (0.0070)	0.6358 (0.0039)	0.6335 (0.0018)
type I	type III	0.4946 (0.0047)	0.5249 (0.0092)	0.5346 (0.0051)
type II	type I	0.7489 (0.0387)	0.6095 (0.0202)	0.5203 (0.0330)
type II	type II	0.6146 (0.0180)	0.5306 (0.0077)	0.4862 (0.0185)
type II	type III	0.4898 (0.0062)	0.4774 (0.0048)	0.4608 (0.0072)
type III	type I	0.5134 (0.0193)	0.4641 (0.0213)	0.6286 (0.1111)
type III	type II	0.4994 (0.0093)	0.4595 (0.0071)	0.5377 (0.0502)
type III	type III	0.4516 (0.0019)	0.4440 (0.0051)	0.4884 (0.0299)

Table 4: Analysis of systems: F1 (std) scores for the three 1DxSeq system architectures. The highest value for each train/test combination highlighted in bold.

A Multilingual Evaluation of NER Robustness to Adversarial Inputs

Akshay Srinivasan
University of Ottawa, Canada *
asrin033@uottawa.ca

Sowmya Vajjala
National Research Council, Canada
sowmya.vajjala@nrc-cnrc.gc.ca

Abstract

Adversarial evaluations of language models typically focus on English alone. In this paper, we performed a multilingual evaluation of Named Entity Recognition (NER) in terms of its robustness to small perturbations in the input. Our results showed the NER models we explored across three languages (English, German and Hindi) are not very robust to such changes, as indicated by the fluctuations in the overall F1 score as well as in a more fine-grained evaluation. With that knowledge, we further explored whether it is possible to improve the existing NER models using a part of the generated adversarial data sets as augmented training data to train a new NER model or as fine-tuning data to adapt an existing NER model. Our results showed that both these approaches improve performance on the original as well as adversarial test sets. While there is no significant difference between the two approaches for English, re-training is significantly better than fine-tuning for German and Hindi.

1 Introduction

NLP systems are traditionally evaluated and compared against a gold standard, which is generally immutable. Recent research has shown that even the NLP systems that perform well on the standard test set show a significant drop in performance even for small perturbations in the input test data, across a range of NLP tasks (Gardner et al., 2020). Although this strand of research covered many tasks, it has been exclusively focused on English, with a few exceptions (e.g., Shmidman et al. (2020), for Hebrew). Further, to our knowledge, the primary usage of such adversarial test sets have been in either evaluating NLP models or in usage as additional, augmented data to improve model robustness, without much focus on using the new data for fine-tuning, instead of re-training. A better understanding of fine-tuning with adversarial test sets is important, and useful in most real-world scenarios, where we may not have access to the original training data while having access to the trained model itself.

Named Entity Recognition (NER) is among the most common NLP tasks both in research and in industry applications (Lorica and Nathan, 2021). Although much progress has been made on NER over the past decades, existing NER systems were also shown to be sensitive to small changes in input data in the past (Lin et al., 2021; Vajjala and Balasubramaniam, 2022). Table 1 shows an example of how predictions can change with minor changes in input, for one of the state of the art NER models[1]. Going by the original sentence, all three sentences should carry the LOC tag for the entity in the sentence. However, that is not the case, as the outputs shows. Clearly, small, and seemingly harmless changes are changing model predictions.

Original: It was the second costly blunder by **Syria_LOC** in four minutes .
Altered: It was the second costly blunder by **Hyderabad_ORG** in four minutes .
Altered: It was the second costly blunder by **Hyderabad_LOC** in four hours .

Table 1: Illustration of an NER model's predictions with minor changes to an original test set sentence

Even recent large language models such as ChatGPT struggle with sequence tagging tasks such as NER, across multiple languages(Qin et al., 2023; Lai et al., 2023; Wu et al., 2023), which clearly illustrates that NER is far from being considered solved. In this backdrop, considering the significance of NER in research and practical scenarios, a better understanding of how a model's predictions

* Work done during an internship at National Research Council, Canada

[1] https://huggingface.co/flair/ner-english

Proceedings of the 8th Workshop on Representation Learning for NLP (RepL4NLP 2023), pages 40–53
July 13, 2023

change with slight changes in input becomes an important issue to address. Hence, we explore the following questions in this paper:

1. How does the performance of NER models across three languages change with small changes to the original input?
2. How does retraining an NER model with adversarial data augmentation compare with adversarial fine-tuning of NER across languages?

Our contributions are summarized as follows:

- We conducted the first comparative study of the robustness of NER models beyond English, covering three languages, in a space where all previous work focused on English alone.
- We report first results on the comparison between data augmentation and adversarial fine-tuning for NER, for all the three languages.
- We show how existing methods for data augmentation can be repurposed to develop language-agnostic methods to generate adversarial test sets for NER.

Starting with a conceptual background (Section 2), we describe our methods for adversarial dataset creation (Section 3) and the general experimental setup (Section 4) followed by a detailed discussion of our results (Section 5) and a summary (Section 6), focusing on the ethical impacts, limitations and broader impact towards the end.

2 Related Work

Evaluating using multiple datasets is one of the ways to assess the robustness and generalization capabilities of NLP models. Developing challenge sets, and generating adversarial datasets that can potentially cause a model to fail, are some possibilities in this direction (Isabelle et al., 2017; Ettinger et al., 2017; Glockner et al., 2018; Gardner et al., 2020). Adversarial data generation in NLP focuses on surface-level perturbations to the input text, proposing various means of insertion/deletion/swapping of words/characters/sentences (Jia and Liang, 2017; Gao et al., 2018; Ribeiro et al., 2018). Other approaches such as paraphrasing (Iyyer et al., 2018), generating semantically similar text using other deep learning models (Zhao et al., 2018; Michel et al., 2019), using a human-in-the-loop (Wallace et al., 2019b) were also explored in the past. While many of the proposed methods are black-box approaches, assuming no knowledge about the NLP models themselves, some of the approaches are white box, with more access to the inner workings of a model (Liang et al., 2018; Blohm et al., 2018; Wallace et al., 2019a), and some models implement both (Li et al., 2019). We focus on one specific NLP task - NER, and only work on black-box methods in this paper.

In terms of the strategies to protect models against adversarial attacks, the most common approach followed by past NLP research has been to incorporate adversarial data into the training process, through data augmentation, or using adversarial training as a regularization method (See Goyal et al. (2022) and Zhang et al. (2020) for a detailed overview). Using adversarial data for full re-training of a model (as is the case with data augmentation) assumes access to the original data and the model, which is not practical in many real-world scenarios. One possibility to explore in such cases is to test whether using adversarial data to fine-tune a trained NER model improves its robustness. We compare using the adversarial data (through data augmentation) for re-training an NER model versus using it only for fine-tuning a previously trained NER model in this paper.

Adversarial Testing and Data Augmentation in NER: Adversarial testing approaches for NER in the previous work was entirely done for English datasets, and primarily focused on methods replace entities in the original test set with new ones using gazetteers or other means (Agarwal et al., 2020; Vajjala and Balasubramaniam, 2022). Lin et al. (2021) used entity linking and masked language models coupled with an existing NER model to generate adversarial test sets for NER. More recently, Das and Paik (2022) used grammatical case information to generate adversarial test sets for NER. Simoncini and Spanakis (2021) proposed other ways to make small changes to the context around entities in a sentence, to generate adversarial test sets. Other related work (Mathew et al., 2019; Ding et al., 2020; Zhu et al., 2021) focused on data augmentation for NER, that require training of new, additional models. While we use our adversarial datasets for data augmentation too later in the paper, the novelty of the current research, compared to this existing body of work focusing on NER, comes in two forms:

1. While all previous work exclusively focused on English NER so far, we perform experiments with three languages - English, German and Hindi.

2. The approaches we used are lightweight, language agnostic means to generated adversarial test sets for NER, which do not rely on the availability of additional tools like entity linkers, and do not also need any additional training to generate the datasets.

3 Adversarial Test Set Creation

Our adversarial dataset creation methods can be broadly classified into two approaches - replacing entities and changing contexts. All except one method work for all the three languages we tested, and can be easily expanded to add other languages. Relevant code and generated datasets are provided as supplementary material[2].

3.1 Replacing Entities

We implemented two methods that replace the entity occurrences in the test set with another entity of the same category, keeping the rest of the sentence unchanged. Thus, they don't change the grammatical structure of the sentence and tell us how much the NER systems learn beyond memorizing the entities.

Random Sampling (*RS*) All the entity occurrences of the same type are shuffled throughout the test set in this approach. This is a simple and easily portable method across languages, which could serve as a strong baseline.

Gazetteers (*Faker*) This approach replaces existing entities with new entities of the same type using an existing gazetteer. Faker[3] is a python library that generates fake data for various application purposes, which supports multiple languages, and regions. We used it to replace the *Person* and *Location* entities in all the datasets, in all three languages we experimented with. Vajjala and Balasubramaniam (2022) used Faker for adversarial NER test sets, but they used only English (on OntoNotes dataset). We randomly choose among three locale settings for English (USA, Canada, India) and German (Germany, Austria, and Switzerland) respectively for replacement. For Hindi, there was only one locale setting provided (HI-IN).

3.2 Changing the Context

These approaches deal with changing the context in which the entities occur in a sentence by making small changes to the tokens around it.

Masking (*Mask*) We leveraged transformer based pre-trained language models trained with a masked language modeling objective to change the context in the original test datasets. We masked up to three randomly chosen non-entity tokens per sentence, and used the language model to generate those tokens, thereby creating new sentences with the same entities, but slightly altered contexts. Since there are multilingual pre-trained language models available, this approach is applicable to multiple languages.

Paraphrasing (*Para*) The objective behind this approach is to alter the structure of the input sentences, while keeping the named entities intact. About 500 sentences were randomly chosen from the test set and fed to an online, subscription based english paraphraser, Quillbot[4], which was shown to generate better paraphrases than other approaches such as back-translation or using GPT-3 in recent research (Shiri et al., 2022) and in our initial evaluations. The paraphrased output obtained for each sentence is then taken and the entity tokens from the original test set are mapped to the entity tokens of the paraphrased sentences with the respective entity tags, leaving the rest of the tokens as `O`. Limiting to 500 sentences is primarily due to the fact that Quillbot did not provide an API, and there is a limit to the amount of text one can paraphrase per request, even with subscription.

There are some challenges with this approach, though. While Quillbot's paraphrases when we choose the "Fluency" setting are of good quality, and are always grammatically correct, they sometimes alter the entities themselves (e.g., United States can become U.S. in the paraphrased version) or change the original tokenization of the dataset. In such cases where an automatic mapping between the entity tags from the original sentence and tokens of the paraphrased sentence failed, we discarded the sentence from our test set. Note that this

[2] `https://dx.doi.org/10.6084/m9.figshare.22674079`

[3] `https://faker.readthedocs.io/`

[4] `https://quillbot.com/`

Test set	Sentence
`Orig`	"We suspect that these killings are linked to politics," spokesman Bala Naidoo told Reuters.
`RS`	"We suspect that these killings are linked to politics," spokesman Deborah Compagnoni told Watford.
`Faker`	"We suspect that these killings are linked to politics," spokesman Jeremy Shukla told Reuters.
`Mask`	"We suspect the these killings are linked to politics," spokesman Bala Naidoo tells Reuters,
`Para`	"We assume that these killings are political in nature", spokesman Bala Naidoo told Reuters.
`M+R`	now we suspect that these killings are connected in politics, now spokesman Deborah Compagnoni told Watford.

Table 2: Adversarial variations generated for a test sentence from conll03-En

approach is compatible only with English and we aren't aware of any reliable paraphrasers for other languages. To our knowledge, full paraphrasing wasn't used for adversarial test sets in NER before. A total of 399 sentences from conll03-en, 373 sentences from mconer21-en, and 378 sentences from wnut17 were finally used as test sets.

3.3 Changing Entity + Context

Masking + Random Sampling (*M+R*) All the previous approaches focused on either trying to alter the context alone or replace the entities alone. This approach, does both by combining masking with random sampling. Since both these approaches are straightforward and can work across languages, they can be combined to create a new adversarial test set in all three languages. Table 2 shows one example of how the various approaches alter a single sentence from one of the English datasets. As with most data augmentation or adversarial generation approaches in NLP, some of the generated text may contain minor grammatical errors, as seen in in `Mask` and `M+R` settings. However, Compared to other common approaches such as those that involve insertion/deletion/swapping of words/characters or back-translation, the potential errors introduced by masking alone are minor. Further even the original datasets themselves contain sentences with such minor errors. So, we don't foresee this affecting the main findings of the paper. A publicly available NER model [5] predicts correctly for all these sentences.

4 Experimental Setup

We experimented with three English, two German, and one Hindi NER datasets [6]. The first half of our experiments focused on testing the NER models on adversarial test sets, following which we compared the effects of adversarial fine-tuning and data augmentation on the performance of the NER models. All the experiments were carried out on a high performing computing resource that ran an Nvidia A100 GPU with 32 GB RAM. Further details on the experimental setup are as follows.

4.1 Datasets

NER datasets from three popular shared tasks - conll03 (Tjong Kim Sang and De Meulder, 2003), multiconer21 (Malmasi et al., 2022) and wnut17 (Derczynski et al., 2017) were considered and their corresponding language subsets for English (conll03-en, mconer21-en, wnut17), German (conll03-de, mconer21-de) and Hindi (mconer21-hi) were used. Conll03 datasets have a tag set with four entity types (PER, LOC, ORG and MISC), and multiconer21 and wnut17 share the tag set consisting of six entity types (PER, LOC, CORP, GRP, CREATIVE-WORK and PROD). While the sentences in conll03 came from news articles, multiconer21 was collected from three domains (wikipedia sentences, questions, search queries), and wnut17 consisted of sentences from social media sources such as twitter, youtube and reddit.[7] We created five adversarial test sets for each of the three English datasets, four adversarial sets for each of the two German datasets and the Hindi dataset respectively, resulting in a total of 27 adversarial test sets covering three languages and six datasets.

4.2 NER Models

We used a combination of existing state of the art NER models (if available) and fine-tuning

[5] `https://huggingface.co/flair/ner-english`

[6] While it is theoretically possible to add more languages to this paper, the choice of these languages is motivated by the authors' familiarity with the languages, which is essential for qualitative analysis

[7] Some statistics about the datasets are shown in Appendix A.1.

a pre-trained language model for all the languages/datasets. They are explained below.

TNER and Fine-tuned BERT: TNER[8] is a Python library to train transformer based language models for NER tasks (Ushio and Camacho-Collados, 2021), which has pre-trained for mconer21-en, wnut17-en and conll03-en datasets. We use these models to perform our experiments for English NER. We will refer to this approach as *tner*. While TNER's model hub had publicly available models for other languages as well, the performance of the models was lower compared to the state of the art, and hence, we fine-tuned the multilingual BERT (Devlin et al., 2019) model hosted on Huggingface[9] for NER on German (conll03-de, mconer21-de) and Hindi (mconer21-hi) datasets. We will refer to this approach as *mbertft*.

We followed the same approach for the later re-training (i.e., training the NER model again using the original training data augmented with adversarial data) and fine-tuning (using adversarial data is used only to fine-tune the existing NER model) experiments in Section 5.4, and report the results with *tner* for English and *mbertft* for German and Hindi, as this setup gave the best results even in those experiments. For adversarial fine-tuning, *tner* and *mbertft* were fine-tuned for 4 epochs, learning rate was set to 0.0001 and the batch size was set to 16. For the Adversarial re-training however, the models were trained for 6 epochs since it is being trained from scratch, while the other hyper parameters were kept the same. The hyperparameter settings were from the original BERT paper (Devlin et al., 2019). We used 60% of the adversarial test set for data augmentation+training/fine-tuning and used the remaining 40% to test the approaches. For both adversarial fine-tuning and re-training, we report the average F1 score over 10 runs, with different random seeds, and compare them in terms of statistical significance using a paired t-test.

Stanza: Stanza (Qi et al., 2020) is a Python based NLP toolkit that hosts a few pre-trained NER models trained with a BiLSTM+CRF architecture. We evaluated Stanza's pre-trained conll-en and conll-de models using our generated adversarial test sets.

Flair: Flair is a popular NLP library that is widely used for performing NLP tasks (Akbik et al., 2019). We evaluated the pre-trained NER models provided by Flair for conll-en and conll-de.

There are other NER models that offer slightly better performance than Flair/Stanza/BERT-fine tuning, and there are other large language models to explore, but we focused on publicly available/downloadable models for NER and easily re-implementatble benchmarks (e.g., BERT fine-tuning) in this paper. It would be interesting to extend this to cover additional methods in future, but we limit to a smaller set of models to maintain a manageable number of experiments and do a meaningful analysis later.

4.3 Evaluation

Micro-F1 score from seqeval (Nakayama, 2018) was used as the evaluation metric to test the robustness of the NER models, as it is the most commonly reported measure for this task.

Nervaluate: Nervaluate[10] is a Python library for performing a more fine-grained evaluation of NER, and is based on the metrics from a SemEval 2013 task (Segura-Bedmar et al., 2013). Apart from giving a single F1 score, it calculates the efficiency of the model using five error categories: correct, incorrect, partially correct, missing labels (an entity tagged as non-entity) and spurious labels(a non-entity tagged as entity). The error metrics are reported in four formats: strict (both entity span and entity type match), exact (entity span matches, irrespective of the type), partial (partial span match, irrespective of the type), and type (some overlap between gold annotation and system prediction). We used nervaluate to compare the performance of NER on the original and adversarial test sets, to understand what kind of errors affect their performance.

5 Results

Our experiments aimed at understanding the robustness of NER models to adversarial test sets and exploring whether adversarial data augmentation and fine tuning will help boost the performance on adversarial test sets. The results of these experiments are discussed below.

5.1 Adversarial Testing

Adversarial test sets were created by implementing the approaches mentioned in Section 3 and tested

[8] https://github.com/asahi417/tner

[9] https://huggingface.co/bert-base-multilingual-uncased

[10] https://github.com/MantisAI/nervaluate

on pre-trained NER models for all the three English datasets, and for conll03-de. As described earlier, we also fine-tuned a multilingual bert model for German and Hindi datasets. Tables 3, 4 and 5 summarize the performance of all the NER models we tested on, for English, German and Hindi respectively, in terms of the micro-F1 score.

	conll03-en			**wnut17**	**mconer21**
test set	tner	stanza	flair	tner	tner
`Orig`	0.91	0.92	0.92	0.60	0.81
`RS`	0.87	0.89	0.89	0.63	0.76
`Faker`	0.84	0.85	0.86	0.64	0.79
`Mask`	0.84	0.85	0.85	0.58	0.75
`Para`	0.80	0.72	0.78	0.65	0.64
`M+R`	0.82	0.85	0.83	0.53	0.77

Table 3: English NER performance (Micro-F1)

	conll03-de			**mconer21**
test set	mbertft	stanza	flair	mbertft
`Orig`	0.83	0.85	0.83	0.70
`RS`	0.80	0.82	0.78	0.58
`Faker`	0.81	0.85	0.81	0.55
`Mask`	0.78	0.81	0.81	0.53
`M+R`	0.75	0.80	0.76	0.50

Table 4: German NER performance (Micro-F1)

For English NER, results from Table 3 show a clear drop in NER model performance for two out of the three datasets (conll03 and mconer21), with the largest drop seen in the test set obtained by paraphrasing using Quillbot. However, it is important to note that the size of the test set for paraphrasing is far smaller (399, 373 and 378 sentences respectively for conll-03, mconer21 and wnut17) than the original test set, as explained earlier in Section 4. So, the drop is not directly comparable with other test sets which are larger in size.

Apart from this, there are also differences among individual methods for all the datasets. For example, `Faker` dataset appears to have had a stronger effect on all the three models trained on conll03-en dataset compared to multiconer-en dataset. Considering that there is generally similar drop across all three models of conll03-en, we would speculate that the difference in performance is due to the differences in the dataset composition and entity categories.

Test set	**mconer21-hi**
`Orig`	0.62
`RS`	0.55
`Faker`	0.61
`Mask`	0.52
`M+R`	0.48

Table 5: Hindi NER performance (Micro-F1)

For wnut17, the drop is largest for `M+R`, followed by `Mask`. Considering that only those test sets involving masking resulted in a drop for this dataset, we could safely attribute this drop to the difference in the nature of the data that the masked language model was exposed to, compared to the very noisy social media data in wnut17. An interesting aspect of testing with wnut17 model is that the model's performance was better on 3 out of 5 adversarial test sets, compared to the original test set. We believe it is important to note in this context that the NER model for wnut17 also has the lowest performance on the original test set among the three datasets and wnut17 is the noisiest data of them all (social media content). Considering that a model with a much lower overall F1 score, and trained on the most noisy dataset among the three, was still relatively more robust to three of the adversarial test sets, future research should perhaps also take a closer look at other, additional means of evaluating NER models instead of using the standard F1 score as the sole criterion to choose the best model, as was also suggested by other recent research on the topic. (Vajjala and Balasubramaniam, 2022).

For both German and Hindi NER (Table 4 and Table 5), we observe that the drop is the highest for masking+random sampling datasets in both the languages. Between the two German datasets, the drop in f1 scores for adversarial datasets appear to be much larger for mconer21 than conll03. A possible reason could be the poorer performance of the original mconer21 model itself.

While there are several other interesting results to compare and discuss across languages and datasets, overall, these results indicate that the NER models are not fully robust when tested against new test sets created with easily replicable, generally language-agnostic approaches. Their performance drop is larger when context altering approaches are employed. One question we asked ourselves at this point is: what exactly are the adversarial test sets changing in the model performance?

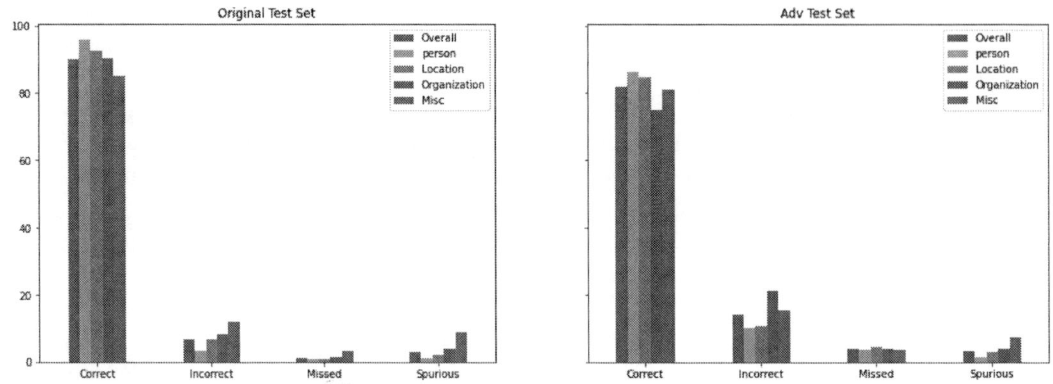

Figure 1: The performance (micro-F1) of an English NER model on original and M+R adversarial test sets

5.2 Fine-Grained Evaluation

We used nervaluate to understand what aspect of NER performance is mainly affected by the adversarial data. Since there are many models, train and test sets, we choose one train/test set and model combination for this analysis. Figure 1 shows the analysis for TNER's pre-trained NER model trained on conll03-en dataset, as a comparison between the original test set and the `M+R` adversarial test set (Figures 2 and 3 in the appendix show the same analysis for German and Hindi respectively).

Apart from the overall decline in performance, a closer look at the 'correct' and 'incorrect' categories indicate that this NER model's performance resulted in a larger drop for 'organization' entity type in English. This could be because of the ambiguity involved in the entity type itself, as not every 'organization' entity suits every context in which that entity type appears. Surprisingly, although the 'misc' category suffers from the same problem, we don't see a large dip for that category.

Figure 1 also indicates that there are more missed entities in the adversarial test set compared to spurious labels (non-entities tagged as one of the entity types). We compared the "strict" versus "exact" evaluation schema in nervaluate, to understand whether this increase in missed entities is a result of getting the span right, but identifying the entity type wrong. This comparison showed that while there is a 9% drop in the overall F1 score between the original and the adversarial test sets with 'strict' evaluation, there is only a 3% drop in terms of identifying the entity spans correctly (More details in Table 9 in the Appendix. Tables 10 and 11 in the appendix show this comparison for German and Hindi datasets).

5.3 Qualitative Error Analysis

Apart from quantitative analysis, we also did some manual analysis to understand what kind of transformations led NER models to predict erroneous tags. Table 6 shows some of the correctly tagged examples taken from conll03-en test set and their adversarial counterparts with some tagging errors, using Stanza's NER model.

When the entity 'Nicole' was replaced with the entity 'Major' (Examples **a** and **b**), the first one resulted in the model missing the entity (Major not recognised as person), and the second example saw the replaced entity 'Timor-Leste' (another name for the country East Timor) being mis-identified as an ORG instead of a LOC. While the transformed sentence in **c** appears very different from its source, there is only one entity, and a human reader would not find it difficult to identify the entity. However, the model missed identifying it altogether. Finally, both the masked examples (**d** and **e**) made very minor changes to the original sentence. But the model predictions changed from ORG − > LOC for the entity 'Victoria' in a sentence, and LOC − > ORG for the entity 'Indianapolis' in the other. In the last two cases, it can be argued that the original labels are ambiguous themselves. While that is, indeed, the case, the issue we particularly highlight is the way model predictions changed because of textual changes that should not really cause label changes. Similar trends can be observed in German and Hindi as well (Examples for German and Hindi are in the appendix in Table 12 and Figure 4). While it is definitely possible to do further qualitative analysis, we would speculate that combining this kind of analysis with explainable NLP approaches may give a more complete picture in

(a) `Orig`: Nicol_{PER} was full of praise for his opponent who has battled testicular cancer to return to the circuit .
`RS`: $\text{Major}_{notidentified}$ was full of praise for his opponent who has battled testicular cancer to return to the circuit .
(b) `Orig`: [Nader Jokhadar]$_{PER}$ had given Syria_{LOC} the lead with a well-struck header in the seventh minute . `Faker`: [Roger Turner]$_{PER}$ had given [Timor-Leste]$_{ORG}$ the lead with a well-struck header in the seventh minute .
(c) `Orig`: The richest parts of the property to the north and south of the central region have been estimated by **Bre-X**$_{ORG}$ to contain 57 million ounces of gold . `Para`: **Bre-X**$_{notidentified}$ estimates that the richest areas of the property to the north and south of the centre region contain 57 million ounces of gold .
(d) `Orig`: Tasmania_{LOC} 352 by three ([David Boon]$_{PER}$ 106 not out , [Shaun Young]$_{PER}$ 86 not out , [Michael DiVenuto]$_{PER}$ 119) v **Victoria**$_{ORG}$. `Mask`: Tasmania_{LOC} 352 by three ([David Boon]$_{PER}$ 106 not out , [Shaun Young]$_{PER}$ 86 not out , [Michael DiVenuto]$_{PER}$ 119) v **Victoria**$_{LOC}$:
(e) `Orig`:**Indianapolis**$_{LOC}$ closes with games at [Kansas City]$_{LOC}$ and Cincinnati_{LOC} . `Mask`: **Indianapolis**$_{ORG}$ begins with games at [Kansas City]$_{LOC}$ and Cincinnati_{LOC} .

Table 6: Examples of cases where a NER model fails on adversarial instances

the future on why NER model predictions fluctuate even for minimal perturbations in input text.

5.4 Adversarial Fine-Tuning

One approach to make models more robust to adversarial inputs is to include such data in building the model itself. We explored two methods in that direction: a) augmenting the training data with part of the adversarial dataset and re-training the NER model from scratch b) using adversarial data to fine-tune an existing NER model. The second method is especially useful in real-world scenarios where we have access to a trained model, but not to the original training data itself. We compared both the methods for all three languages, training one NER model per language (with conll-en, conll-de, and mconer-hi datasets respectively), and compared the performance with the M+R test set and the original test set in each case. As mentioned in Section 4, 60% of the adversarial test set was used for augmented re-training/fine-tuning and the remaining 40% was used as test data. Table 7 summarizes the results of this experiment.

	orig.	**adv. fine-tuning**	**aug. re-training**
conll-en			
`Original`	0.91	0.90	0.90
`Adv Test`	0.82	0.87	0.87
conll-de			
`Original`	0.83	0.84	0.89*
`Adv Test`	0.75	0.81	0.85*
mconer-hi			
`Original`	0.62	0.64	0.70*
`Adv Test`	0.48	0.55	0.58*

Table 7: Micro-F1 score for Adversarial fine-tuning versus re-training
(* indicates a statistically significant difference)

While there are no significant differences between adversarial fine-tuning and re-training for English, and both give a 5% performance boost on adversarial test set without compromising on the original test set performance, for both German and Hindi, re-training was significantly better than fine-tuning with both test sets ($p<0.001$). A possible reason for this difference could lie in the relatively superior performance of the original model itself. Re-training could be more useful when the performance of the original model is poor, as was the case for German and Hindi. Interestingly, just fine-tuning still improved performance on adversarial test sets by over 5% for all languages.

To connect these results back to our second research question (Section 1), considering that fine-tuning still resulted in better adversarial test set performance in all cases, and since that would not require access to the original training data itself, it could be a feasible, easily implementable approach to improve the robustness of NER models without compromising on the original model performance. Re-training can be preferred when we have access to the original data and the model. Note that in both the cases, we are assuming no means to procure additional manually labeled training data, and the focus is on improving an NER model's robustness to adversarial input *without* compromising on its performance on normal test data.

6 Conclusions and Discussion

We explored simple, language agnostic approaches to generate adversarial test sets for NER and demonstrated their generalizability by testing on six datasets covering three languages - English, German and Hindi. While exact results differ depending on language/datasets, our key findings from these experiments can be summarized as follows:

1. NER models for all three languages are sensitive to adversarial input.

2. Adversarial fine-tuning and re-training could improve the performance of NER models both on original and adversarial test sets, without requiring additional manual labeled data.

The proposed approaches and tested languages/models are by no means comprehensive, and extending this work to include more NER models, adding new languages, and developing new adversarial data generation methods for NER is an obvious next step, as the current results provide enough evidence on the sensitivity of state of the art NER models to adversarial inputs. The methods we employed for adversarial fine-tuning/re-training too are just a starting point towards exploring the use of adversarial data in building more robust NER systems. We only explored one paraphraser for this task. The usefulness of the recent generative language models for creating such test data can be an interesting next step in this direction.

7 Limitations

The adversarial test sets based on masked language models can introduce new noise into the sentence context, as there is no way to automatically ensure grammatical correctness. However, there were many cases where such introduction of noise did not affect the predictions, in all three languages. Further, adversarial datasets are expected to introduce such noise, as is seen in other research on the topic for other tasks such as sentiment analysis, and the goal of such research is also to understand model robustness in the presence some noise. It is relevant to mention in this context that the NER datasets we considered already consist of other noise and ungrammatical examples such as score cards of sporting matches (conll03-en), social media content (wnut17) and fully lowercased sentences with weakly supervised annotations (mconer21). Further, masking does not alter the entities themselves, and only changes the non-entity tokens. So, the NER models still see the same entities. While there are no established means of quantifying the quality of adversarial datasets to our knowledge, exploring human-in-the-loop approaches to select appropriate examples to include in the final adversarial test set can be one way to address the issue.

8 Ethics and Impact Statement

The paper described the creation of several adversarial test sets for three languages. We used publicly available datasets for this purpose, and the research did not involve human participants. All the datasets we generated and the code to generate them are shared as supplementary material[11], for replication and to further this line of research. Our goal in this paper was to study the sensitivity of state of the art NER systems to adversarial data, and suggest ways to overcome it. As such, the generated datasets are expected to be used only for that purpose, and the limitations of current approaches are discussed in the previous section. Apart from this, since the paper focuses on more foundational question of evaluating NER systems in general, we do not foresee any other potential risks involved with this research.

Broader Impact Considering the number of practical usecases of NER across industries, and the growth of multilingual NLP, NER evaluation beyond English is more important than ever before. In this paper, we explored a previously unexplored space for Named Entity Recognition, i.e., evaluating NER systems beyond English for their sensitivity to adversarial input, which will hopefully lead into better evaluation strategies when developing NER systems across languages in future.

[11] `https://dx.doi.org/10.6084/m9.figshare.22674079`

Acknowledgements

We thank Justin Lee and Gabriel Bernier-Colborne for their feedback on an earlier draft, and Edwin Thomas for feedback on the final draft of the paper.

References

Oshin Agarwal, Yinfei Yang, Byron C Wallace, and Ani Nenkova. 2020. Entity-switched datasets: An approach to auditing the in-domain robustness of named entity recognition models. *arXiv preprint arXiv:2004.04123*.

Alan Akbik, Tanja Bergmann, Duncan Blythe, Kashif Rasul, Stefan Schweter, and Roland Vollgraf. 2019. FLAIR: An easy-to-use framework for state-of-the-art NLP. In *NAACL 2019, 2019 Annual Conference of the North American Chapter of the Association for Computational Linguistics (Demonstrations)*, pages 54–59.

Matthias Blohm, Glorianna Jagfeld, Ekta Sood, Xiang Yu, and Ngoc Thang Vu. 2018. Comparing attention-based convolutional and recurrent neural networks: Success and limitations in machine reading comprehension. In *Proceedings of the 22nd Conference on Computational Natural Language Learning*, pages 108–118, Brussels, Belgium. Association for Computational Linguistics.

Sudeshna Das and Jiaul Paik. 2022. Resilience of named entity recognition models under adversarial attack. In *Proceedings of the First Workshop on Dynamic Adversarial Data Collection*, pages 1–6, Seattle, WA. Association for Computational Linguistics.

Leon Derczynski, Eric Nichols, Marieke van Erp, and Nut Limsopatham. 2017. Results of the WNUT2017 shared task on novel and emerging entity recognition. In *Proceedings of the 3rd Workshop on Noisy User-generated Text*, pages 140–147, Copenhagen, Denmark. Association for Computational Linguistics.

Jacob Devlin, Ming-Wei Chang, Kenton Lee, and Kristina Toutanova. 2019. Bert: Pre-training of deep bidirectional transformers for language understanding. In *Proceedings of the 2019 Conference of the North American Chapter of the Association for Computational Linguistics: Human Language Technologies, Volume 1 (Long and Short Papers)*, pages 4171–4186.

Bosheng Ding, Linlin Liu, Lidong Bing, Canasai Kruengkrai, Thien Hai Nguyen, Shafiq Joty, Luo Si, and Chunyan Miao. 2020. DAGA: Data augmentation with a generation approach for low-resource tagging tasks. In *Proceedings of the 2020 Conference on Empirical Methods in Natural Language Processing (EMNLP)*, pages 6045–6057, Online. Association for Computational Linguistics.

Sang Erik F. Tjong Kim and De Meulder Fien. 2003. Introduction to the conll-2003 shared task: Language independent named entity recognition. In *InProceedings of the seventh conference on Natural language learning at HLT-NAACL*, volume 4, pages 142–147.

Allyson Ettinger, Sudha Rao, Hal Daumé III, and Emily M. Bender. 2017. Towards linguistically generalizable NLP systems: A workshop and shared task. In *Proceedings of the First Workshop on Building Linguistically Generalizable NLP Systems*, pages 1–10, Copenhagen, Denmark. Association for Computational Linguistics.

Ji Gao, Jack Lanchantin, Mary Lou Soffa, and Yanjun Qi. 2018. Black-box generation of adversarial text sequences to evade deep learning classifiers. In *2018 IEEE Security and Privacy Workshops (SPW)*, pages 50–56. IEEE.

Matt Gardner, Yoav Artzi, Victoria Basmov, Jonathan Berant, Ben Bogin, Sihao Chen, Pradeep Dasigi, Dheeru Dua, Yanai Elazar, Ananth Gottumukkala, Nitish Gupta, Hannaneh Hajishirzi, Gabriel Ilharco, Daniel Khashabi, Kevin Lin, Jiangming Liu, Nelson F. Liu, Phoebe Mulcaire, Qiang Ning, Sameer Singh, Noah A. Smith, Sanjay Subramanian, Reut Tsarfaty, Eric Wallace, Ally Zhang, and Ben Zhou. 2020. Evaluating models' local decision boundaries via contrast sets. In *Findings of the Association for Computational Linguistics: EMNLP 2020*, pages 1307–1323, Online. Association for Computational Linguistics.

Max Glockner, Vered Shwartz, and Yoav Goldberg. 2018. Breaking NLI systems with sentences that require simple lexical inferences. In *Proceedings of the 56th Annual Meeting of the Association for Computational Linguistics (Volume 2: Short Papers)*, pages 650–655, Melbourne, Australia. Association for Computational Linguistics.

Shreya Goyal, Sumanth Doddapaneni, Mitesh M Khapra, and Balaraman Ravindran. 2022. A survey in adversarial defences and robustness in nlp. *arXiv preprint arXiv:2203.06414*.

Pierre Isabelle, Colin Cherry, and George Foster. 2017. A challenge set approach to evaluating machine translation. In *Proceedings of the 2017 Conference on Empirical Methods in Natural Language Processing*, pages 2486–2496, Copenhagen, Denmark. Association for Computational Linguistics.

Mohit Iyyer, John Wieting, Kevin Gimpel, and Luke Zettlemoyer. 2018. Adversarial example generation with syntactically controlled paraphrase networks. In *Proceedings of the 2018 Conference of the North American Chapter of the Association for Computational Linguistics: Human Language Technologies, Volume 1 (Long Papers)*, pages 1875–1885, New Orleans, Louisiana. Association for Computational Linguistics.

Robin Jia and Percy Liang. 2017. Adversarial examples for evaluating reading comprehension systems.

In *Proceedings of the 2017 Conference on Empirical Methods in Natural Language Processing*, pages 2021–2031, Copenhagen, Denmark. Association for Computational Linguistics.

Viet Dac Lai, Nghia Trung Ngo, Amir Pouran Ben Veyseh, Hieu Man, Franck Dernoncourt, Trung Bui, and Thien Huu Nguyen. 2023. Chatgpt beyond english: Towards a comprehensive evaluation of large language models in multilingual learning. *arXiv preprint arXiv:2304.05613*.

J Li, S Ji, T Du, B Li, and T Wang. 2019. Textbugger: Generating adversarial text against real-world applications. In *26th Annual Network and Distributed System Security Symposium*.

Bin Liang, Hongcheng Li, Miaoqiang Su, Pan Bian, Xirong Li, and Wenchang Shi. 2018. Deep text classification can be fooled. In *IJCAI*.

Bill Yuchen Lin, Wenyang Gao, Jun Yan, Ryan Moreno, and Xiang Ren. 2021. RockNER: A simple method to create adversarial examples for evaluating the robustness of named entity recognition models. In *Proceedings of the 2021 Conference on Empirical Methods in Natural Language Processing*, pages 3728–3737, Online and Punta Cana, Dominican Republic. Association for Computational Linguistics.

Ben Lorica and Paco Nathan. 2021. 2021 nlp survey report. Technical report, Gradient Flow.

Shervin Malmasi, Anjie Fang, Besnik Fetahu, Sudipta Kar, and Oleg Rokhlenko. 2022. SemEval-2022 task 11: Multilingual complex named entity recognition (MultiCoNER). In *Proceedings of the 16th International Workshop on Semantic Evaluation (SemEval-2022)*, pages 1412–1437, Seattle, United States. Association for Computational Linguistics.

Joel Mathew, Shobeir Fakhraei, and José Luis Ambite. 2019. Biomedical named entity recognition via reference-set augmented bootstrapping. *arXiv preprint arXiv:1906.00282*.

Paul Michel, Xian Li, Graham Neubig, and Juan Pino. 2019. On evaluation of adversarial perturbations for sequence-to-sequence models. In *Proceedings of the 2019 Conference of the North American Chapter of the Association for Computational Linguistics: Human Language Technologies, Volume 1 (Long and Short Papers)*, pages 3103–3114, Minneapolis, Minnesota. Association for Computational Linguistics.

Hiroki Nakayama. 2018. seqeval: A python framework for sequence labeling evaluation. Software available from https://github.com/chakki-works/seqeval.

Peng Qi, Yuhao Zhang, Yuhui Zhang, Jason Bolton, and Christopher D. Manning. 2020. Stanza: A Python natural language processing toolkit for many human languages. In *Proceedings of the 58th Annual Meeting of the Association for Computational Linguistics: System Demonstrations*.

Chengwei Qin, Aston Zhang, Zhuosheng Zhang, Jiaao Chen, Michihiro Yasunaga, and Diyi Yang. 2023. Is chatgpt a general-purpose natural language processing task solver? *arXiv preprint arXiv:2302.06476*.

Marco Tulio Ribeiro, Sameer Singh, and Carlos Guestrin. 2018. Semantically equivalent adversarial rules for debugging NLP models. In *Proceedings of the 56th Annual Meeting of the Association for Computational Linguistics (Volume 1: Long Papers)*, pages 856–865, Melbourne, Australia. Association for Computational Linguistics.

Isabel Segura-Bedmar, Paloma Martínez, and María Herrero-Zazo. 2013. SemEval-2013 task 9 : Extraction of drug-drug interactions from biomedical texts (DDIExtraction 2013). In *Second Joint Conference on Lexical and Computational Semantics (*SEM), Volume 2: Proceedings of the Seventh International Workshop on Semantic Evaluation (SemEval 2013)*, pages 341–350, Atlanta, Georgia, USA. Association for Computational Linguistics.

Fatemeh Shiri, Terry Yue Zhuo, Zhuang Li, Shirui Pan, Weiqing Wang, Reza Haffari, Yuan-Fang Li, and Van Nguyen. 2022. Paraphrasing techniques for maritime qa system. In *2022 25th International Conference on Information Fusion (FUSION)*, pages 1–8.

Avi Shmidman, Joshua Guedalia, Shaltiel Shmidman, Moshe Koppel, and Reut Tsarfaty. 2020. A novel challenge set for Hebrew morphological disambiguation and diacritics restoration. In *Findings of the Association for Computational Linguistics: EMNLP 2020*, pages 3316–3326, Online. Association for Computational Linguistics.

Walter Simoncini and Gerasimos Spanakis. 2021. SeqAttack: On adversarial attacks for named entity recognition. In *Proceedings of the 2021 Conference on Empirical Methods in Natural Language Processing: System Demonstrations*, pages 308–318, Online and Punta Cana, Dominican Republic. Association for Computational Linguistics.

Erik F. Tjong Kim Sang and Fien De Meulder. 2003. Introduction to the CoNLL-2003 shared task: Language-independent named entity recognition. In *Proceedings of the Seventh Conference on Natural Language Learning at HLT-NAACL 2003*, pages 142–147.

Asahi Ushio and Jose Camacho-Collados. 2021. T-ner: An all-round python library for transformer-based named entity recognition. In *Proceedings of the 16th Conference of the European Chapter of the Association for Computational Linguistics: System Demonstrations*, pages 53–62.

Sowmya Vajjala and Ramya Balasubramaniam. 2022. What do we really know about state of the art ner? In *Proceedings of the Language Resources and Evaluation Conference*, pages 5983–5993, Marseille, France. European Language Resources Association.

Eric Wallace, Shi Feng, Nikhil Kandpal, Matt Gardner, and Sameer Singh. 2019a. Universal adversarial triggers for attacking and analyzing NLP. In *Proceedings of the 2019 Conference on Empirical Methods in Natural Language Processing and the 9th International Joint Conference on Natural Language Processing (EMNLP-IJCNLP)*, pages 2153–2162, Hong Kong, China. Association for Computational Linguistics.

Eric Wallace, Pedro Rodriguez, Shi Feng, Ikuya Yamada, and Jordan Boyd-Graber. 2019b. Trick me if you can: Human-in-the-loop generation of adversarial examples for question answering. *Transactions of the Association for Computational Linguistics*, 7:387–401.

Shijie Wu, Ozan Irsoy, Steven Lu, Vadim Dabravolski, Mark Dredze, Sebastian Gehrmann, Prabhanjan Kambadur, David Rosenberg, and Gideon Mann. 2023. Bloomberggpt: A large language model for finance. *arXiv preprint arXiv:2303.17564*.

Wei Emma Zhang, Quan Z Sheng, Ahoud Alhazmi, and Chenliang Li. 2020. Adversarial attacks on deep-learning models in natural language processing: A survey. *ACM Transactions on Intelligent Systems and Technology (TIST)*, 11(3):1–41.

Zhengli Zhao, Dheeru Dua, and Sameer Singh. 2018. Generating natural adversarial examples. In *International Conference on Learning Representations*.

Wenjing Zhu, Jian Liu, Jinan Xu, Yufeng Chen, and Yujie Zhang. 2021. Improving low-resource named entity recognition via label-aware data augmentation and curriculum denoising. In *Chinese Computational Linguistics: 20th China National Conference, CCL 2021, Hohhot, China, August 13–15, 2021, Proceedings*, pages 355–370. Springer.

A Appendix

A.1 Dataset Statistics:

Dataset	# train	# dev	# test
(Erik F. Tjong Kim and Fien, 2003)			
conll03-en	14,987	3,466	3,684
conll03-de	12,705	3,068	3,160
wnut17[12]	3394	1009	1287
(Malmasi et al., 2022)			
mconer21-en	15,300	800	217,818
mconer21-de	15,300	800	217,824
mconer21-hi	15,300	800	141,565

Table 8: Dataset statistics in terms of number of sentences per split

We used the dev set from mconer21 to create adversarial test sets for all the three languages, considering the large size of its test set.

A.2 Detailed Evaluation

	orig. test set		adv. test set	
	Strict	Exact	Strict	Exact
Overall	0.91	0.95	0.82	0.92
PER	0.96	0.98	0.87	0.92
LOC	0.92	0.96	0.85	0.95
ORG	0.89	0.94	0.75	0.91
MISC	0.83	0.89	0.79	0.88

Table 9: Strict versus Exact evaluation for English (conll-en)

	orig. test set		adv. test set	
	Strict	Exact	Strict	Exact
Overall	0.73	0.81	0.61	0.73
PER	0.88	0.92	0.8	0.86
LOC	0.78	0.83	0.67	0.76
PROD	0.7	0.79	0.58	0.73
GRP	0.68	0.81	0.55	0.71
CORP	0.66	0.8	0.53	0.75
CW	0.59	0.67	0.44	0.53

Table 10: Strict versus Exact evaluation for German (multiconer21-de)

	orig. test set		adv. test set	
	Strict	Exact	Strict	Exact
Overall	0.62	0.73	0.48	0.61
PER	0.71	0.82	0.56	0.62
LOC	0.77	0.82	0.57	0.72
PROD	0.54	0.63	0.48	0.61
GRP	0.67	0.81	0.52	0.67
CORP	0.56	0.76	0.42	0.65
CW	0.47	0.57	0.35	0.46

Table 11: Strict versus Exact evaluation for Hindi (mconer21-hi)

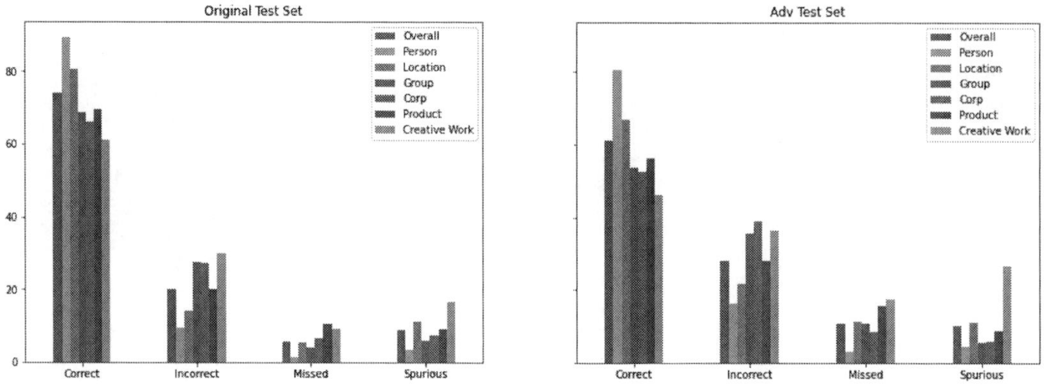

Figure 2: A plot visualising the performance of a German NER model (trained with mconer21 data) on original and M+R adversarial Test sets

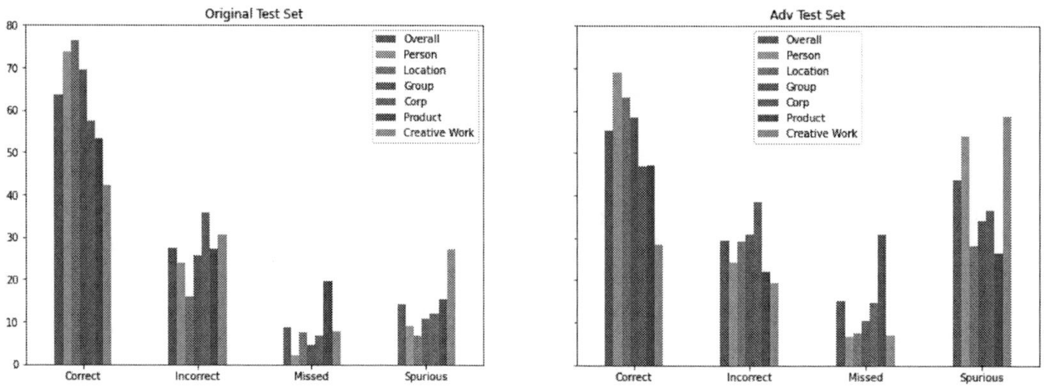

Figure 3: A plot visualising the performance of a Hindi NER model (trained with mconer21 data) on original and M+R adversarial Test sets

`Orig`: Der kleine **Elmir**$_{PER}$ verläßt den Raum .
`RS`: Der kleine **Treutel**$_{notidentified}$ verläßt den Raum .
`Faker`: Der kleine Melek$_{notidentified}$ verläßt den Raum .
`Orig`: Die Verwertungsgesellschaft Gebrauchte Kunststoffverpackungen in [**Bad Homburg**]$_{LOC}$ sei " offenbar mit ihrer Aufgabe überfordert " .
`RS`: Die Verwertungsgesellschaft Gebrauchte Kunststoffverpackungen in [**Stadt**]$_{LOC}$ [**Hanau**]$_{notidentified}$ sei " offenbar mit ihrer Aufgabe überfordert " .
`Orig`: Im [Korea-Krieg]$_{MISC}$ **hatte** China$_{LOC}$ das kommunistische Nordkorea$_{LOC}$ **unterstützt .**
`Mask`: Im Korea-Krieg$_{LOC}$ **hatten** China$_{LOC}$ das kommunistische Nordkorea$_{LOC}$ **gewonnen** |
`Orig`: Ihm stehen 20 000 Mark zur **Verfügung** , um **die Ausstellung** im November 1993 im Stadtmuseum$_{LOC}$ zu realisieren .
`Mask`: Ihm stehen 20 000 Mark zur **wahl** , um **diese skulptur** im November 1993 im Stadtmuseum$_{notidentified}$ zu realisieren .
`Orig`: **Oder die** [Gauck-Behörde]$_{MISC}$?
`Mask`: **in der** Gauck-Behörde]$_{LOC}$?

Table 12: Examples of cases where a German NER model fails on adversarial input, but makes correct predictions on the original text

Orig: १४९२ में एक चार्टर के आधार पर, उसके पिता ने उसे **वाडोविस_LOC** के उत्तराधिकारी के रूप में छोड़ दिया
RS: १४९२ में एक चार्टर के आधार पर, उसके पिता ने उसे **पेरू_CORP** के उत्तराधिकारी के रूप में छोड़ दिया
Masked: पिता का एक चार्टर की आधार पर, उसके पिता ने उसे **वाडोविस_CORP** की उत्तराधिकारी की रूप की छोड़ दिया

Orig: इस तरह का पहला "बेड़ा, **आर12_PROD** " १९४८ में सेवा में लगाया गया था।
M+R: इस तरह का पहला "बेड़ा, **कास्केट_NONE** बड १९४८ में चीन में लगाया गया था।

Orig: रुसब्रिजर २०१६ की फिल्म **स्नोडेन_CW** में एक मीटिंग मॉडरेटर के रूप में एक कैमियो भूमिका के साथ दिखाई देते हैं
Masked: रुसब्रिजर **2007_CW** फिलम फिल्म **स्नोडेन_CW** में एक मीटिंग मॉडरेटर के साथ में एक कैमियो भूमिका के साथ दिखाई देते हैं

Orig: १९३७ में उनका अगला क्लब **[सेंट बर्नार्ड एफ.सी.]_GRP** था।
Masked: 1937 में उनका परथम पातर **[सेंट बर्नार्ड एफ.सी.]_PER** !

Orig: उन्होंने **[फ्रेंकस्टीन अनबाउंड]_CW** के साथ एक बार फिर निर्देशन में वापसी की।
Masked: उन्होंने **[फ्रेंकस्टीन]_CORP [अनबाउंड]_GRP** के साथ एक बार अपन गाव में वापसी की।

Figure 4: Examples comparing how predictions change for a Hindi NER model on original versus adversarial test sets

Retrieval-Augmented Domain Adaptation of Language Models

Benfeng Xu*, **Chunxu Zhao***, **Wenbin Jiang**†, **PengFei Zhu**
Songtai Dai, Chao Pang, Zhuo Sun, Shuohuan Wang, Yu Sun
Baidu Inc.

Abstract

Language models pretrained on general domain corpora usually exhibit considerable degradation when generalizing to downstream tasks of specialized domains. Existing approaches try to construct PLMs for each specific domains either from scratch or through further pretraining, which not only costs substantial resources, but also fails to cover all target domains at various granularity. In this work, we propose RADA, a novel Retrieval-Augmented framework for Domain Adaptation. We first construct a textual corpora that covers the downstream task at flexible domain granularity and resource availability. We employ it as a pluggable datastore to retrieve informative background knowledge, and integrate them into the standard language model framework to augment representations. We then propose a two-level selection scheme to integrate the most relevant information while alleviating irrelevant noises. Specifically, we introduce a differentiable sampling module as well as an attention mechanism to achieve both passage-level and word-level selection. Such a retrieval-augmented framework enables domain adaptation of language models with flexible domain coverage and fine-grained domain knowledge integration. We conduct comprehensive experiments across biomedical, science and legal domains to demonstrate the effectiveness of the overall framework, and its advantage over existing solutions.

1 Introduction

Language models pretrained on large scale of unsupervised corpora are capable of producing powerful representations as well as providing satisfactory performance when finetuned for general domain downstream tasks (Devlin et al., 2019; Brown et al., 2020). However, as such representations are learned from general domain distributions, their generalization performance are deteriorate on specialized domains where distribution are much more different, such as biomedicine, science, legal, etc.

Many works thus trying to construct domain-specific PLMs either from scratch or initialized from the original PLM, such as BioBERT (Lee et al., 2020), LegalBERT (Chalkidis et al., 2020), SciBERT (Beltagy et al., 2019), etc. Through the pretraining procedure, domain-specific knowledge are memorized and internalized into the parameter of the PLMs, thus providing a better initialization point for learning downstream tasks. However, such attempts not only consume much more costs, as it requires considerable computation to pretrain a language model, but also can not cover adaptive needs at task- or even instance-level granularity, as domain-specific PLMs are preliminarily trained with a fixed scale domain corpora but applied for all domain tasks. In fact, ***domain*** can be defined at various granularity w.r.t. various applications (Chronopoulou et al., 2022). For example, in the biomedical domain, texts might distribute across academic publication, medical record or medical-situated dialog, and exhibit completely different style and background knowledge.

In this paper, we novelly propose a **R**etrieval-**A**ugmented framework for **D**omain **A**daptation (**RADA**) to address the above challenges. Instead of internalizing a fixed corpora into PLM parameters via further pretraining, we construct and retrieve a datastore to dynamically enhance the learning of domain-specific downstream tasks. The flexibility of such a retrieval-augmented framework is in two-fold: 1) On one hand, we no longer need to maintain multiple PLMs respectively for each application domains, all domains simply share the same checkpoint for initialization but with domain-specialized datastore. 2) On the other hand, the datastore only consists of most relevant background passages tailored for each specific task. Such task-level granularity provides best trade-off between

*Equal contribution.
†Correspondence to: jiangwenbin@baidu.com

Proceedings of the 8th Workshop on Representation Learning for NLP (RepL4NLP 2023), pages 54–64
July 13, 2023

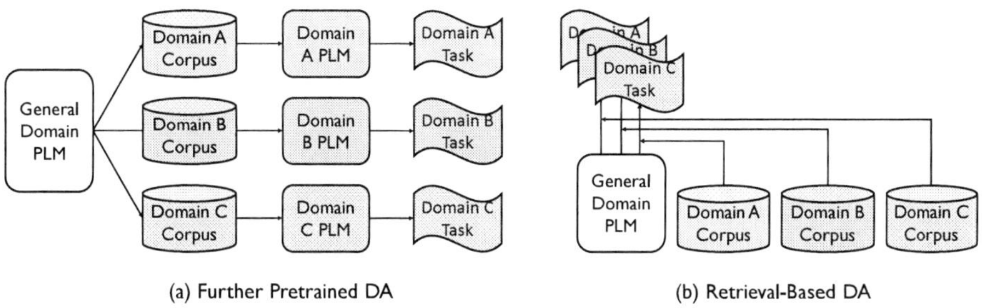

Figure 1: Illustration of the motivated retrieval-augmented framework for language model domain adaptation.

scale and coverage, we either do not need to collect a very large corpora in order to effectively cover all sub-domains, nor concerned with its coverage for this specific task. The illustration of the motivated framework compared to existing further pretraining solution is given in Figure 1.

The core component of such a retrieval-augmented framework remains how to effectively integrate the retrieved passages. One line of related works is knowledge-enhanced PLMs (Zhang et al., 2019; Peters et al., 2019; Liu et al., 2020), they mostly resort to attention mechanism to directly incorporate the matched knowledge triples. Differently, we consider textual domain corpus instead of structured knowledge in this paper as the latter only has very limited coverage, especially for domain specialized scenarios. As a consequence, we aim to integrate retrieved passages that are less knowledge-intensive and might be mixed with noisy information that are irrelevant to solve the task. We accordingly propose a two-level selection scheme: passage-level selection and word-level selection. Among the multiple retrieved passages given by a coarse-grained but efficient retriever, we first propose a differentiable sampling module that enables the model to dynamically select the most helpful background passage. We then adopt an attention mechanism to weigh all words inside the selected passage to achieve more fine-grained integration. The retrieval-augmentation interface works as a pluggable module that needs no further modification of the main encoding pipeline.

We conduct experiments on 7 popular tasks covering three different downstream domains and a wide range of task variety. The results and ablations demonstrate the effectiveness and advantage of the proposed framework. The contribution of this paper is three-fold:

- **Conceptual Contribution** We novelly propose a retrieval-augmented framework for domain-adaptation of PLMs. The framework is designed as a pluggable module, which not only saves the costs to construct and maintain specialized PLMs for each respective domain, but also provides domain specialty at flexible task-level granularity with no concern of the trade-off between domain scale and coverage.
- **Technical Contribution** We propose a two-level selection scheme to achieve fine-grained integration of retrieved passages while alleviate noise distraction. Specifically, we introduce a differentiable sampling module for passage-level selection and an attention mechanism to further assign word-level importance.
- **Experimental Contribution** We achieve consistent improvements across different domains including Science, Biomedicine and Legal. When combined with further pretraining, the improvements of the proposed framework are much more significant, surpassing competitive baseline of vanilla further pretraining.

2 Related Work

Domain Adaptation (Ramponi and Plank, 2020) is an important and widely investigated problem in the area of NLP. In the current pretrain-finetune paradigm, it becomes even more practical as most of NLP systems start with a general-purpose PLM but applied into various downstream scenarios (Guo and Yu, 2022). Many early works have found that continued pretraining of PLM on domain specific corpus could bring benefits (Alsentzer et al., 2019; Lee et al., 2020). Gururangan et al. (2020) take a step further to systematically investigate the effect of further pretraining on multiple domains, which they refer to as domain-adaptive

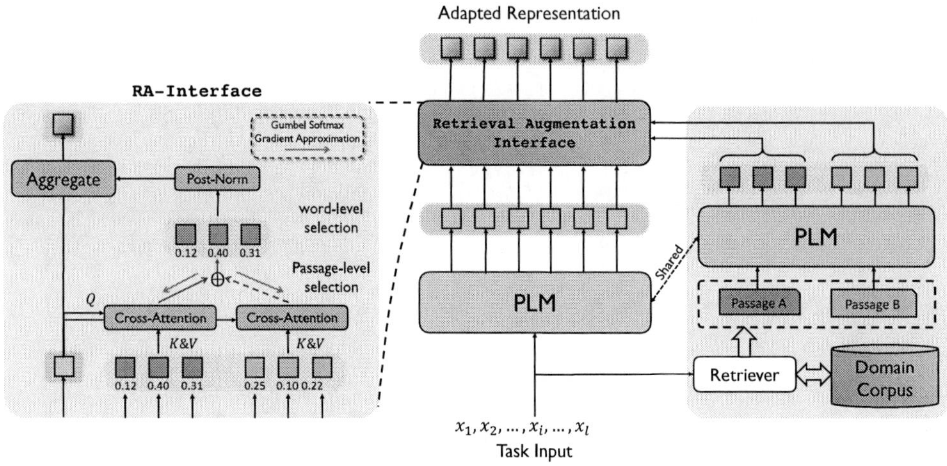

Figure 2: The overall retrieval-augmented framework of RADA. The **RA-Interface** serves as a pluggable module to augment task-agnostic input representations with domain-specialized background passages.

pretraining (DAPT). Besides, they also propose task-adaptive pretraining (TAPT) to perform further pretraining also on task data, which further brings significant improvements.

There are mainly two concerns for these further pretraining based methods. One is the cost to construct and maintain considerable number of PLMs for each specific domain, which can be quite a lot spreading over various application scenarios. The other is the complication to formally define the concept of domain because domains exhibit hierarchical taxonomy in practical scenarios (Reid et al., 2022). The scope of a domain should neither be too broad, which results in loss of domain specialty, nor be too narrow, which results in loss of generalization ability. Many recent works (Chronopoulou et al., 2022; Gururangan et al., 2022; Li et al., 2022) thus propose to incorporate multiple domains into one shared model, and introduce mixture-of-experts module to allow different sub-domains also share with each other. By contrast, RADA takes a very different retrieval-based road to resolve the above concerns.

Several other works also try to advance domain adaptation from various perspectives. For example, Yu et al. (2021) studied DAPT for the specific task of abstractive summarization. Xu et al. (2021) propose gradual finetuning for domain adaptation. Bai et al. (2021) investigates the trade-off between DAPT and data annotation under limited budget for domain adaptation.

Another very related line of work is retrieval-augmented language models. kNN-LM (Khandelwal et al., 2020) retrieves for similar language modeling probability distributions and interpolate them with the current step of token generation. Guu et al. (2020) and Lee et al. (2019) propose to learn differentiable retriever to better select helpful passages. Lewis et al. (2020) propose a non-parametric retriever and combine it with a generator model. Borgeaud et al. (2022) use attention mechanism to integrate retrieved passages and also explore the datastore in a very large scale. Izacard et al. (2022) investigate the usefulness of retrieval-augmentation in the context of few-shot prompting with LLMs. Although being technically related, most of these works focus on general-purpose language understanding, especially knowledge-intensive tasks. While in this paper, we focus on the challenge of LM domain adaptation, and also novelly propose a two-level selection scheme to further augment the framework.

3 Methodology

RADA is a general framework for task-agnostic domain adaptation, and can be readily integrated into the standard pipeline of PLM deployment. In the following section, we first brief the construction of domain specialized datastore in Section 3.1, and the framework formulation in Section 3.2. We then introduce the core component, a pluggable interface for retrieval-augmented domain adaptation in Section 3.3, and finally brief the training usage in Section 3.4. The overall framework is illustrated in Figure 2.

3.1 Datastore Construction

We consider textual domain corpus as a necessary recipe to adapt a general-domain language model. From their related sources, we collect domain specialized passages $\{\boldsymbol{p}_i\}^{\mathcal{D}}$, and refer to them as the datastore. In practical implementation, we truncate the length of each passage to 256 tokens for simplicity. We then build an Elasticsearch service[†], for any task-specific training or test input sequence x, we can retrieve for its K most relevant background passages $\{\boldsymbol{p}_k\}_{k=1}^{K}$. Although Elasticsearch only serves coarse-grained retrieving purpose, we can employ it as an efficient first-stage retriever.

For each specific downstream task, the datastore is constructed at **task-level** granularity. And the retrieving of most relevant passages further achieves **instance-level** granularity. This is in contrast with many existing works where datastore is constructed and utilized at **domain-level** granularity, once a target domain is determined, a fixed-scale datastore is collected and injected into PLM as an integral through further pretraining. As a result, RADA brings better flexibility and save the difficulty to deliberate the trade off between domain specialty and domain coverage.

3.2 Retrieval-Augmented PLM

In a standard PLM-based framework, we first take the task input sequence $\boldsymbol{x} = \{x_i\}$ and use the pretrained encoder to produce contextualized representations:

$$\boldsymbol{H}^{\boldsymbol{x}} = \text{encode}(\boldsymbol{x}) \tag{1}$$

where $\boldsymbol{H}^{\boldsymbol{x}} \in \mathbb{R}^{l*d}$ is the sequence level representation for l words and d dimensions. We accordingly refer to $\boldsymbol{h}_i^{\boldsymbol{x}}$ as the contextualized representation at each specific position i. The representations are then fed into a task-tailored head module, such as classification, regression or sequence tagging, etc.

In RADA, accompanied with each task input, we similarly construct the representations for retrieved passages $\{\boldsymbol{p}_k\}$:

$$\boldsymbol{H}^{\boldsymbol{p}_k} = \text{encode}(\boldsymbol{p}_k), \quad 1 \leq k \leq K \tag{2}$$

and we similarly get $\boldsymbol{H}^{\boldsymbol{p}_k}$ and $\boldsymbol{h}_j^{\boldsymbol{p}_k}$. The purpose of the proposed RADA framework can be formulated as a universal interface that augments and updates task representations $\boldsymbol{h}_i^{\boldsymbol{x}}$ using $\boldsymbol{H}^{\boldsymbol{p}_k}$, where $\boldsymbol{H}^{\boldsymbol{p}_k}$ serves as informative, relevant and domain-specialized knowledge source:

$$\widetilde{\boldsymbol{h}}_i = \texttt{RA-Interface}(\boldsymbol{h}_i^{\boldsymbol{x}}, \{\boldsymbol{H}^{\boldsymbol{p}_k}\}_{k=1}^{K}) \tag{3}$$

$\widetilde{\boldsymbol{h}}_i$ is then unchangeably used in the rest of the task pipeline. The overall framework remains task-agnostic and can be readily integrated into both pretraining and finetuning stage. The interface can also be easily extended to a more broad scenario with different backbone networks other than Transformer.

3.3 Retrieval Augmentation Interface

We elaborate the **`RA-Interface`** in this section. Different from many existing methods that resort to integrate structured knowledge (Zhang et al., 2019; Peters et al., 2019), the retrieved textual domain corpus are much less knowledge-intensive and thus might contain irrelevant noise distractions. However, Elasticsearch can only satisfy coarse-grained retrieving purpose, leaving it an important problem to effectively select and integrate actually helpful domain knowledge.

To address such challenge, we propose a two-level selection scheme which performs discrete sampling at passage-level and attentively aggregate at word-level. Such selection strategy strengthens the proposed interface with fine-grained selection capability to integrate helpful knowledge while filter out its noisy parts. More specifically, we introduce a gumbel sampling mechanism to select the most helpful passage, along with an attention mechanism to assign distinguishable weights for each word insides the selected passage.

3.3.1 Cross Attention

In order to cover both sequence-level and token-level downstream tasks, we would need to augment the representation $\boldsymbol{H}_{\boldsymbol{x}}$ at each specific position. For the i-th token representation $\boldsymbol{h}_{x_i}$, we calculate its relevancy with respect to all other words from the retrieved passages using a canonical cross attention mechanism:

$$\begin{aligned} \boldsymbol{q}_i^{\boldsymbol{x}} &= \boldsymbol{W}^Q \boldsymbol{h}_i^{\boldsymbol{x}} \\ \boldsymbol{k}_i^{\boldsymbol{p}_k} &= \boldsymbol{W}^K \boldsymbol{h}_j^{\boldsymbol{p}_k} \\ \boldsymbol{v}_i^{\boldsymbol{p}_k} &= \boldsymbol{W}^V \boldsymbol{h}_j^{\boldsymbol{p}_k} \end{aligned} \tag{4}$$

$$\alpha_{ij}^k = \frac{\boldsymbol{q}_i^{\boldsymbol{x}} \boldsymbol{k}_j^{\boldsymbol{p}_k}}{\sqrt{d}} \tag{5}$$

[†]`https://github.com/elastic/elasticsearch`

where α_{ij}^k denotes the attentive weight of j-th token from passage p_k for current position $\boldsymbol{h}_i^x$. Intuitively, this attentive weight can naturally measure each retrieved word its importance and relevance. To represent the usefulness of passages and their tokens at integral sequence level, we simply summing over all task input positions:

$$\alpha_j^k = \sum_i \alpha_{ij}^k \tag{6}$$

3.3.2 Differentiable Sampling

To alleviate the noise distraction in the retrieved passages, we first sample the most relevant passage, then integrate all its words according to respective attentive weights. Intuitively, the sampling operation should be an argmax operation across all candidate passages:

$$\alpha^k = \sum_j \alpha_j^k \tag{7}$$

$$\hat{k} = \underset{k \in \{1,2,...,K\}}{\text{argmax}} \ \alpha^k \tag{8}$$

Note that here we sum α_j^k up to α^k only temporarily for sampling most relevant passage, and will re-use α_j^k later in Equation 12 to aggregate representations. The passage level selection operation in Equation 8, although intuitive, is not differentiable, and are not allowed in an end-to-end trainable neural network. To enable such a learning-to-select ability inside the proposed framework, we novelly introduce the Gumbel-Softmax estimator (Jang et al., 2017) to replace Equation 8:

$$\beta^k = \frac{\exp((\alpha^k + g)/\tau)}{\sum_k \exp((\alpha^k + g)/\tau)} \tag{9}$$

where g is the noise sampled from Gumbel distribution:

$$g \sim \text{Gumbel}(0,1) \tag{10}$$

This is practically implemented as:

$$\begin{aligned} g = &-\log(-\log(\boldsymbol{u})) \\ where \quad &\boldsymbol{u} \sim \text{Uniform}(0,1) \end{aligned} \tag{11}$$

The resulting $\boldsymbol{\beta}$ distributed over $k \in \{1,2,...,K\}$ is an approximate **categorical** distribution when the temperature τ approaches 0. We follow the Straight-Through procedure (Jang et al., 2017) to discretize $\boldsymbol{\beta}$ into $\hat{k}$ in the forward pass but use gumbel approximation in the backward pass.

3.3.3 Aggregation

For the selected passage $\hat{k}$, we apply a post-normalization on the attentive weights:

$$\tilde{\alpha}_j^{\hat{k}} = \frac{\alpha_j^{\hat{k}}}{\sum_j \alpha_j^{\hat{k}}}, \quad \sum_j \tilde{\alpha}_j^{\hat{k}} = 1 \tag{12}$$

We then integrate the representations of passage $\hat{k}$ accordingly:

$$\hat{\boldsymbol{h}} = \sum_j \tilde{\alpha}_j^{\hat{k}} \boldsymbol{v}_j^{p_{\hat{k}}} \tag{13}$$

Note that in practical implementation, we use multi-head attentions and concatenate all outputs together. We then wrap $\hat{\boldsymbol{h}}$ within a residual connection and LayerNorm at each position i to produce the final output representation:

$$\widetilde{\boldsymbol{h}}_i = \text{LayerNorm}(\boldsymbol{W}\hat{\boldsymbol{h}} + \boldsymbol{h}_i^x) \tag{14}$$

where $\boldsymbol{W}$ is another feedforward layer that merges representations from multiple attention heads.

3.4 Retrieval-Augmented Training

The proposed **`RA-Interface`** serves as a **pluggable** module that interacts with the representations in-place. It is also end-to-end trainable and does not modify the final training objective. In practical usages, we can either directly apply such a retrieval-augmented framework in downstream finetuning, or first adapt it with a domain-specific further pre-training stage. We investigate both settings in the experiments.

4 Experiments

4.1 Setup

Dataset We investigate the proposed framework on a variety of domain-specialized downstream tasks. Specifically, biomedical domain tasks including QIC (Intent Classification), QQR (Query-Query Relevance), CMeEE (Named Entity Recognition), CMeIE (Information Extraction), scientific domain tasks including SciERC (Relation Classification) (Luan et al., 2018), ACL-ARC (Citation Intent Classification) (Jurgens et al., 2018) and legal domain task CAIL2019-SCM (Similar Case Matching) (Xiao et al., 2019). And these 4 biomedical tasks are selected from the well established benchmark CBLUE (Zhang et al., 2022). Detailed statistics are listed in Table 4.

Domain	Biomedical				Science		Legal	Avg.
Method	QIC	QQR	CMeEE	CMeIE	SCI	ARC	SCM	
FT	$81.86_{0.07}$	$81.97_{0.81}$	$65.45_{0.07}$	$61.31_{0.20}$	$81.39_{1.03}$	$68.33_{2.05}$	$68.97_{0.21}$	72.75
RADA	$82.43_{0.21}$	$82.18_{0.74}$	$65.55_{0.18}$	$60.07_{0.49}$	$79.76_{0.48}$	$68.87_{2.86}$	$69.70_{0.46}$	72.87
DAPT	$81.74_{0.16}$	$82.06_{0.77}$	$65.57_{0.12}$	$61.42_{0.12}$	$81.36_{0.46}$	$73.14_{4.23}$	$69.10_{0.35}$	73.50
RADA†	**$82.45_{0.10}$**	**$82.75_{0.67}$**	**$66.00_{0.20}$**	**$61.53_{0.24}$**	**$82.07_{0.86}$**	**$75.42_{1.48}$**	**$70.25_{0.32}$**	**74.34**

Table 1: Main Results. FT refers to standard finetuning. † denotes the RADA equipped with a pretraining stage.

Domain	Biomedical				Science		Legal	Avg.
Method	QIC	QQR	CMeEE	CMeIE	SCI	ARC	SCM	
FT	$81.07_{0.41}$	$80.52_{0.28}$	$63.24_{0.06}$	$53.97_{0.23}$	$70.77_{0.66}$	$56.46_{1.91}$	$61.20_{0.42}$	66.75
DAPT	$80.81_{0.35}$	$80.62_{0.43}$	$63.56_{0.13}$	$54.29_{0.13}$	**$74.89_{0.63}$**	$62.15_{0.86}$	$61.31_{0.34}$	68.23
RADA	**$81.16_{0.19}$**	**$81.06_{0.33}$**	**$63.62_{0.22}$**	**$54.48_{0.14}$**	$73.96_{0.56}$	**$62.59_{2.80}$**	**$61.70_{0.11}$**	**68.36**

Table 2: Results under low resource scenario.

Domain	LANG	Size	Num. of Passages
Computer	English	6.2GB	4,602,628
Biomedicine	Chinese	0.76GB	960,595
Legal	Chinese	3.7GB	2,794,605

Table 3: Statistics of domain datastore.

Dataset	SCI	ARC	QIC	QQR	CMeEE	CMeIE	SCM
Domain	Science		Biomedical				Legal
Train	3219	1688	6238	13500	13500	12905	5102
Dev	455	144	693	1500	1500	1434	1500
Test	974	139	1955	1600	5000	3585	1500

Table 4: Statistics of domain tasks. For the biomedical tasks, as we do not have access to the test label, we use the released dev set for test, and split 10% of the train set for development.

Datastore We collect domain specialized corpus at scale as datastore. For scientific corpus, we use the S2ORC corpus constructed from semantic scholar (Lo et al., 2020), for biomedical and legal corpus, we use in-house data regarding medical reviews or legal documents crawled online. Detailed statistics are listed in Table 3.

Training For retrieval-augmented pretraining, we split 10% from the entire domain corpus as pretraining pretext task data while the rest 90% as pretraining datastore. The pretraining steps are set to 10k for both DAPT and RADA. For retrieval-augmented finetuning, all corpus are considered as datastore, but we only retrieval and keep the most relevant passages for each task instances. In ElasticSearch, we set the number of retrieved passages for each input data as $K = 10$. For each task, we search batch size through $\{16, 32\}$, learning rate through $\{1e-5, 2e-5, 5e-5\}^{\dagger}$, and set epoch to $10^{\dagger}$. We also run with 3 different random seeds, and accordingly report the average and standard deviation. We use BERT (Devlin et al., 2019) as PLM for English tasks, and RoBERTa (Cui et al., 2020; Liu et al., 2019) for Chinese ones.

4.2 Main Results

Table 1 gives the main results for RADA. We can observe two conclusions: 1) RADA outperforms standard finetuning on 4 out of 7 selected tasks; 2) When combined with further pretraining, the proposed framework is further improved, significantly surpassing standard finetuning and DAPT. Specifically the absolute benefits over FT baseline are **+1.59**.

We further investigate a low-resource setting by subsampling 30% of the training set. This is a very practical scenario as we often need to deal with domain tasks at a relatively low annotation cost. Results in Table 2 also demonstrate the effectiveness of the proposed framework in such settings. On 6 out of 7 tasks, RADA achieves the best performance.

4.3 Ablations

We investigate the impact of various components in this section.

†For CMeIE, we search for {1e-5, 2e-5}.

†For CMeIE and CMeEE, we set to 35 and 15 respectively.

Domain	Biomedical				Science		Legal	Avg.
Method	QIC	QQR	CMeEE	CMeIE	SCI	ARC	SCM	
FT	$81.86_{0.07}$	$81.97_{0.81}$	$65.45_{0.07}$	$61.31_{0.20}$	$81.39_{1.03}$	$68.33_{2.05}$	$68.97_{0.21}$	72.75
RADA w/ Top 1	$82.31_{0.25}$	$82.56_{0.43}$	$\mathbf{66.08}_{0.26}$	$61.48_{0.05}$	$81.78_{0.25}$	$74.15_{0.96}$	$69.14_{0.26}$	73.93
RADA w/ DS	$\mathbf{82.45}_{0.10}$	$\mathbf{82.75}_{0.67}$	$66.00_{0.20}$	$\mathbf{61.53}_{0.24}$	$\mathbf{82.07}_{0.86}$	$\mathbf{75.42}_{1.48}$	$\mathbf{70.25}_{0.32}$	74.34

Table 5: Effects of Differentiable Sampling (DS). Top 1 means we simply select the passage according to their summed attention score.

Method	ARC	QIC	QQR
FT	$68.33_{2.05}$	$81.86_{0.07}$	$81.97_{0.81}$
TAPT	$\mathbf{72.43}_{2.36}$	$82.14_{0.04}$	$\mathbf{82.71}_{0.57}$
RADA w/ Trainset	$70.65_{0.38}$	$\mathbf{82.21}_{0.21}$	$82.52_{0.46}$
RADA (Full)	$75.42_{1.48}$	$82.45_{0.10}$	$82.75_{0.67}$

Table 6: Results of using training data as datastore corpus. Full means extra domain corpus are used.

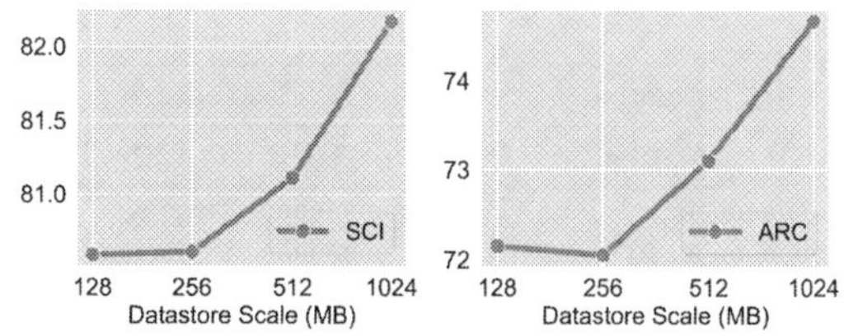

Figure 3: Ablation on scale of corpus.

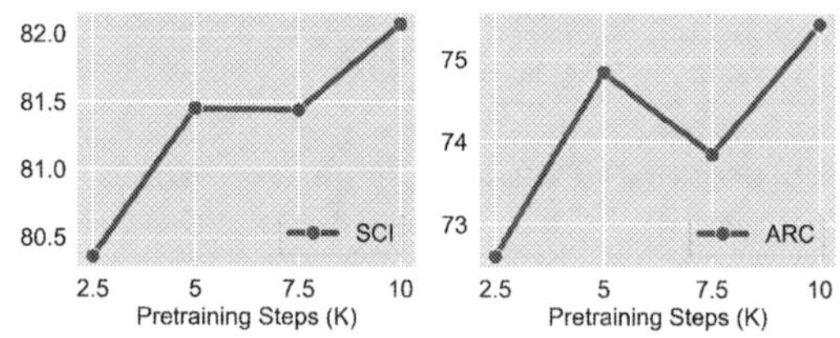

Figure 4: Ablation on pretraining steps.

4.3.1 Scale of Datastore Corpus

One essential component of the proposed framework is the datastore. We first look into the effects of its scale. At pretraining stage, we fix the pretraining steps to 5,000, and accordingly set the scale of datastore to 128, 256, 512 and 1024. The results are illustrated in Figure 3. We observe clear trends of increasing performance w.r.t. increased datastore scale. As a consequence, the proposed RADA framework can always benefit from a larger datastore.

4.3.2 Training Data as Datastore

We further investigate the feasibility of directly using downstream task data as datastore corpus. As previous study has demonstrated, training data itself can also provide useful background information to an extent (Wang et al., 2022). Similarly, Gururangan et al. (2020) have also used task training data to perform further pretraining, which they referred to as TAPT. In Table 6, we provide the results when using training data in the proposed retrieval-augmented framework, and also reproduce TAPT for more comprehensive comparison. The results show that both TAPT and RADA with Trainset can provide considerable benefits, but are outperformed by RADA (full). As for these two methods, they perform comparably on the investigated three datasets. We also find that training data is more useful in sentence-level tasks (as included in the table), but less helpful in other tasks such as classification, sequence tagging, etc.

4.3.3 Pretraining Steps

We have equipped RADA with a further pretraining stage with domain specialized data, and proved it to be very effective in Table 1. In Figure 4, we further ablate the effects of pretraining steps. We save and evaluate the intermediate checkpoint at respectively 2.5k, 5k and 7.5k pretraining steps. The results exhibit clear trends that with more pretraining steps, RADA continually brings better adaptation performance.

4.3.4 Differentiable Sampling

One key design of RADA is the two-level selection scheme. Specifically, the differentiable sampling module based on Gumbel Sampling trick enables the model to dynamically learn which passage to integrate. In Table 5 we investigate this choice of design. We provide an alternative baseline, where instead of learning to sample, we simply sum the cross attention weights over all positions as passage-level score, and select the maximum one to integrate into the retrieval-augmented interface. We refer to this as Top 1 selection strategy. The results show that both methods can bring improve-

• Input Text: This formalism is both elementary and powerful enough to strongly simulate many grammar formalisms, such as rewriting systems, dependency grammars , TAG , HPSG and LFG . • Relation Label: HYPONYM-OF			Sampling Score β^k
Retrieved Passages (ES Top 10)	1	... Although we have presented supertagging in the context of LTAG, it is applicable to other lexicalized grammar formalisms such as CCG (Steedrnan 1997), HPSG (Pollard and Sag 1987) , and LFG (Kaplan and Bresnan 1983) ...	0.0992
	2	Scrambling in German poses a problem for most grammar formalisms. Neither Tree Adjoining Grammar (TAG, Joshi et al., 1975) nor even linear context-free rewriting systems (LCFRS, Weir, 1988) are powerful enough to deal with scrambling and the free word order in German (see Becker et al., 1992) ...	0.1737
	3	... We would also expect that dependency grammars Mel'cuk and Pertsov 1987; Hudson 1984) and parsers (McDonald, Crammer, and Pereira 2005) could be trained and tested with little extra work on the dependencies in CCGbank. Finally, we believe that existing methods for translating the Penn Treebank from scratch into other grammar formalisms will benefit from ...	0.1046
	...	...	...
	10	... The Broad-coverage Semantic Dependency Parsing shared task and corpora (Oepen et al., 2014 (Oepen et al., , 2015 include corpora annotated with the PDT-TL, and dependencies extracted from the HPSG grammars Enju (Miyao, 2006) and the LinGO English Reference Grammar (ERG; Flickinger, 2002) . Like the PDT-TL, projects based on CCG, HPSG, and other expressive grammars such as LTAG (Joshi and Vijay-Shanker, 1999) and LFG ...	0.1018

Figure 5: Case study. Illustrated are top 10 retrieved passages using elasticsearch, and their sampling score produce inside the **RA-Interface**. Scores are re-normalized for better illustration.

	w/o RA	w/ RA
Efficiency	0.0083 sec/instance	0.0201 sec/instance
Times	2.4×	1.0×

Table 7: Inference efficiency. Measured using a single RTX TITAN GPU.

ments, but the proposed differentiable sampling is much more effective.

4.3.5 Efficiency Analysis

One potential concern for retrieval-augmented methods is their efficiency. We therefore investigate this factor in Table 7. We consider the inference efficiency at deployment time. For each task input, we retrieve 10 background passages using ElasticSearch, then compute and incorporate them into the **RA-Interface**. Note that at deployment time, it is practical to encode and cache all passages from the datastore in advance, so we only account for the time consumption starting from the interface. The results show that, the retrieval-augmentation framework only brings acceptable time increase. And the overall inference speed is maintained at around 0.02 seconds per instance on a production-level device.

4.3.6 Qualitative Analysis

We provide qualitative analysis in Table 5. The example is sampled from the SCI task, the target is to extract the relation between subject ***rewriting systems*** and object ***grammar formalisms***, i.e., ***HYPONYM-OF***. We can clearly see that elasticsearch can only provide coarse-grained, shallow-semantic retrieving capability based on keywords, such as *grammar, formalisms, HPSG, etc.* However, the proposed differentiable sampling module can more effectively identify the most helpful passage by reasoning over deep representations produced by shared encoders. From passage 2 with the highest sampling score, we can indeed reason, understand and accordingly infer the actual relationship between the target entity pair.

5 Conclusion

In this paper we propose a retrieval-augmented framework to novelly address the challenge of language model domain adaptation. We use domain specialized corpus as datastore and retrieve from it for informative and helpful domain knowledge. The key module of the framework is a retrieval-augmentation interface, where we design a two-level selection scheme to integrate the most relevant passage and its words while alleviating the noise. The overall framework enables flexible domain coverage and fine-grained domain knowledge integration. On a variety of downstream domains and tasks, we conduct comprehensive experiments and comparisons to demonstrate the effectiveness of the motivated framework and its components. In the future, we hope to further extend the framework to more scaled large language models and also more challenging few-shot prompting setting.

Limitation

We summarize two limitations which also serve as promising directions to be explored in our future work. RADA framework only considers textual domain corpus as the datastore, although this has greatly improve the coverage of domain knowledge as texts are always relatively easy to collect. However, it is widely investigated that structured knowledge such as knowledge base can also serve similar purpose. And such resources are generally in higher quality and are easier to match. Therefore, it would be benefiting to further integrate such resources at certain scenario where KB is available.

The other limitation regards to the scale of the RADA implementation. As large language models have becoming increasingly powerful, they have demonstrated quite impressive capability in memorizing and recalling a wide range of background knowledge existed in the massive corpora they have been pretrained on. This trends of development naturally raises question for the proposed framework: will it still be beneficial when scale up to LLMs? and on what kinds of scenario does it brings best improvements? These are very important questions to answer, and we can certainly expect them to be explored in future works.

Ethical Statement

We evaluate the proposed method on established and publicly available datasets. There is also no human evaluation involved. This paper is not concerned with the above ethical risks. When the proposed framework is deployed into domain specific production, the domain adapted language models might express ethical-related outputs, but just as any other language models do (Weidinger et al., 2021), and should be treated with according techniques to eliminate ethical risks such as bias, stereotypes.

References

Emily Alsentzer, John Murphy, William Boag, Wei-Hung Weng, Di Jindi, Tristan Naumann, and Matthew McDermott. 2019. Publicly available clinical BERT embeddings. In Proceedings of the 2nd Clinical Natural Language Processing Workshop, pages 72–78, Minneapolis, Minnesota, USA. Association for Computational Linguistics.

Fan Bai, Alan Ritter, and Wei Xu. 2021. Pre-train or annotate? domain adaptation with a constrained budget. In Proceedings of the 2021 Conference on Empirical Methods in Natural Language Processing, pages 5002–5015, Online and Punta Cana, Dominican Republic. Association for Computational Linguistics.

Iz Beltagy, Kyle Lo, and Arman Cohan. 2019. SciBERT: A pretrained language model for scientific text. In Proceedings of the 2019 Conference on Empirical Methods in Natural Language Processing and the 9th International Joint Conference on Natural Language Processing (EMNLP-IJCNLP), pages 3615–3620, Hong Kong, China. Association for Computational Linguistics.

Sebastian Borgeaud, Arthur Mensch, Jordan Hoffmann, Trevor Cai, Eliza Rutherford, Katie Millican, George Bm Van Den Driessche, Jean-Baptiste Lespiau, Bogdan Damoc, Aidan Clark, Diego De Las Casas, Aurelia Guy, Jacob Menick, Roman Ring, Tom Hennigan, Saffron Huang, Loren Maggiore, Chris Jones, Albin Cassirer, Andy Brock, Michela Paganini, Geoffrey Irving, Oriol Vinyals, Simon Osindero, Karen Simonyan, Jack Rae, Erich Elsen, and Laurent Sifre. 2022. Improving language models by retrieving from trillions of tokens. In Proceedings of the 39th International Conference on Machine Learning, volume 162 of Proceedings of Machine Learning Research, pages 2206–2240. PMLR.

Tom Brown, Benjamin Mann, Nick Ryder, Melanie Subbiah, Jared D Kaplan, Prafulla Dhariwal, Arvind Neelakantan, Pranav Shyam, Girish Sastry, Amanda Askell, Sandhini Agarwal, Ariel Herbert-Voss, Gretchen Krueger, Tom Henighan, Rewon Child, Aditya Ramesh, Daniel Ziegler, Jeffrey Wu, Clemens Winter, Chris Hesse, Mark Chen, Eric Sigler, Mateusz Litwin, Scott Gray, Benjamin Chess, Jack Clark, Christopher Berner, Sam McCandlish, Alec Radford, Ilya Sutskever, and Dario Amodei. 2020. Language models are few-shot learners. In Advances in Neural Information Processing Systems, volume 33, pages 1877–1901. Curran Associates, Inc.

Ilias Chalkidis, Manos Fergadiotis, Prodromos Malakasiotis, Nikolaos Aletras, and Ion Androutsopoulos. 2020. LEGAL-BERT: The muppets straight out of law school. In Findings of the Association for Computational Linguistics: EMNLP 2020, pages 2898–2904, Online. Association for Computational Linguistics.

Alexandra Chronopoulou, Matthew Peters, and Jesse Dodge. 2022. Efficient hierarchical domain adaptation for pretrained language models. In Proceedings of the 2022 Conference of the North American Chapter of the Association for Computational Linguistics: Human Language Technologies, pages 1336–1351, Seattle, United States. Association for Computational Linguistics.

Yiming Cui, Wanxiang Che, Ting Liu, Bing Qin, Shijin Wang, and Guoping Hu. 2020. Revisiting pre-trained models for Chinese natural language processing. In Proceedings of the 2020 Conference on Empirical

Methods in Natural Language Processing: Findings, pages 657–668, Online. Association for Computational Linguistics.

Jacob Devlin, Ming-Wei Chang, Kenton Lee, and Kristina Toutanova. 2019. BERT: Pre-training of deep bidirectional transformers for language understanding. In Proceedings of the 2019 Conference of the North American Chapter of the Association for Computational Linguistics: Human Language Technologies, Volume 1 (Long and Short Papers), pages 4171–4186, Minneapolis, Minnesota. Association for Computational Linguistics.

Xu Guo and Han Yu. 2022. On the domain adaptation and generalization of pretrained language models: A survey. arXiv preprint arXiv:2211.03154.

Suchin Gururangan, Mike Lewis, Ari Holtzman, Noah A. Smith, and Luke Zettlemoyer. 2022. DEMix layers: Disentangling domains for modular language modeling. In Proceedings of the 2022 Conference of the North American Chapter of the Association for Computational Linguistics: Human Language Technologies, pages 5557–5576, Seattle, United States. Association for Computational Linguistics.

Suchin Gururangan, Ana Marasović, Swabha Swayamdipta, Kyle Lo, Iz Beltagy, Doug Downey, and Noah A. Smith. 2020. Don't stop pretraining: Adapt language models to domains and tasks. In Proceedings of the 58th Annual Meeting of the Association for Computational Linguistics, pages 8342–8360, Online. Association for Computational Linguistics.

Kelvin Guu, Kenton Lee, Zora Tung, Panupong Pasupat, and Ming-Wei Chang. 2020. Realm: Retrieval-augmented language model pre-training. In Proceedings of the 37th International Conference on Machine Learning, ICML'20. JMLR.org.

Gautier Izacard, Patrick Lewis, Maria Lomeli, Lucas Hosseini, Fabio Petroni, Timo Schick, Jane Dwivedi-Yu, Armand Joulin, Sebastian Riedel, and Edouard Grave. 2022. Few-shot learning with retrieval augmented language models. arXiv preprint arXiv:2208.03299.

Eric Jang, Shixiang Gu, and Ben Poole. 2017. Categorical reparameterization with gumbel-softmax. In International Conference on Learning Representations.

David Jurgens, Srijan Kumar, Raine Hoover, Dan McFarland, and Dan Jurafsky. 2018. Measuring the evolution of a scientific field through citation frames. Transactions of the Association for Computational Linguistics, 6:391–406.

Urvashi Khandelwal, Omer Levy, Dan Jurafsky, Luke Zettlemoyer, and Mike Lewis. 2020. Generalization through memorization: Nearest neighbor language models. In International Conference on Learning Representations.

Jinhyuk Lee, Wonjin Yoon, Sungdong Kim, Donghyeon Kim, Sunkyu Kim, Chan Ho So, and Jaewoo Kang. 2020. Biobert: a pre-trained biomedical language representation model for biomedical text mining. Bioinformatics, 36(4):1234–1240.

Kenton Lee, Ming-Wei Chang, and Kristina Toutanova. 2019. Latent retrieval for weakly supervised open domain question answering. In Proceedings of the 57th Annual Meeting of the Association for Computational Linguistics, pages 6086–6096, Florence, Italy. Association for Computational Linguistics.

Patrick Lewis, Ethan Perez, Aleksandra Piktus, Fabio Petroni, Vladimir Karpukhin, Naman Goyal, Heinrich Küttler, Mike Lewis, Wen-tau Yih, Tim Rocktäschel, Sebastian Riedel, and Douwe Kiela. 2020. Retrieval-augmented generation for knowledge-intensive nlp tasks. In Advances in Neural Information Processing Systems, volume 33, pages 9459–9474. Curran Associates, Inc.

Margaret Li, Suchin Gururangan, Tim Dettmers, Mike Lewis, Tim Althoff, Noah A Smith, and Luke Zettlemoyer. 2022. Branch-train-merge: Embarrassingly parallel training of expert language models. arXiv preprint arXiv:2208.03306.

Weijie Liu, Peng Zhou, Zhe Zhao, Zhiruo Wang, Qi Ju, Haotang Deng, and Ping Wang. 2020. K-bert: Enabling language representation with knowledge graph. Proceedings of the AAAI Conference on Artificial Intelligence, 34(03):2901–2908.

Yinhan Liu, Myle Ott, Naman Goyal, Jingfei Du, Mandar Joshi, Danqi Chen, Omer Levy, Mike Lewis, Luke Zettlemoyer, and Veselin Stoyanov. 2019. Roberta: A robustly optimized bert pretraining approach. arXiv preprint arXiv:1907.11692.

Kyle Lo, Lucy Lu Wang, Mark Neumann, Rodney Kinney, and Daniel Weld. 2020. S2ORC: The semantic scholar open research corpus. In Proceedings of the 58th Annual Meeting of the Association for Computational Linguistics, pages 4969–4983, Online. Association for Computational Linguistics.

Yi Luan, Luheng He, Mari Ostendorf, and Hannaneh Hajishirzi. 2018. Multi-task identification of entities, relations, and coreference for scientific knowledge graph construction. In Proceedings of the 2018 Conference on Empirical Methods in Natural Language Processing, pages 3219–3232, Brussels, Belgium. Association for Computational Linguistics.

Matthew E. Peters, Mark Neumann, Robert Logan, Roy Schwartz, Vidur Joshi, Sameer Singh, and Noah A. Smith. 2019. Knowledge enhanced contextual word representations. In Proceedings of the 2019 Conference on Empirical Methods in Natural Language Processing and the 9th International Joint Conference on Natural Language Processing (EMNLP-IJCNLP), pages 43–54, Hong Kong, China. Association for Computational Linguistics.

Alan Ramponi and Barbara Plank. 2020. Neural unsupervised domain adaptation in NLP—A survey. In Proceedings of the 28th International Conference on Computational Linguistics, pages 6838–6855, Barcelona, Spain (Online). International Committee on Computational Linguistics.

Machel Reid, Victor Zhong, Suchin Gururangan, and Luke Zettlemoyer. 2022. M2d2: A massively multi-domain language modeling dataset. arXiv preprint arXiv:2210.07370.

Shuohang Wang, Yichong Xu, Yuwei Fang, Yang Liu, Siqi Sun, Ruochen Xu, Chenguang Zhu, and Michael Zeng. 2022. Training data is more valuable than you think: A simple and effective method by retrieving from training data. In Proceedings of the 60th Annual Meeting of the Association for Computational Linguistics (Volume 1: Long Papers), pages 3170–3179, Dublin, Ireland. Association for Computational Linguistics.

Laura Weidinger, John Mellor, Maribeth Rauh, Conor Griffin, Jonathan Uesato, Po-Sen Huang, Myra Cheng, Mia Glaese, Borja Balle, Atoosa Kasirzadeh, et al. 2021. Ethical and social risks of harm from language models. arXiv preprint arXiv:2112.04359.

Chaojun Xiao, Haoxi Zhong, Zhipeng Guo, Cunchao Tu, Zhiyuan Liu, Maosong Sun, Tianyang Zhang, Xianpei Han, Zhen Hu, Heng Wang, et al. 2019. Cail2019-scm: A dataset of similar case matching in legal domain. arXiv preprint arXiv:1911.08962.

Haoran Xu, Seth Ebner, Mahsa Yarmohammadi, Aaron Steven White, Benjamin Van Durme, and Kenton Murray. 2021. Gradual fine-tuning for low-resource domain adaptation. In Proceedings of the Second Workshop on Domain Adaptation for NLP, pages 214–221, Kyiv, Ukraine. Association for Computational Linguistics.

Tiezheng Yu, Zihan Liu, and Pascale Fung. 2021. AdaptSum: Towards low-resource domain adaptation for abstractive summarization. In Proceedings of the 2021 Conference of the North American Chapter of the Association for Computational Linguistics: Human Language Technologies, pages 5892–5904, Online. Association for Computational Linguistics.

Ningyu Zhang, Mosha Chen, Zhen Bi, Xiaozhuan Liang, Lei Li, Xin Shang, Kangping Yin, Chuanqi Tan, Jian Xu, Fei Huang, Luo Si, Yuan Ni, Guotong Xie, Zhifang Sui, Baobao Chang, Hui Zong, Zheng Yuan, Linfeng Li, Jun Yan, Hongying Zan, Kunli Zhang, Buzhou Tang, and Qingcai Chen. 2022. CBLUE: A Chinese biomedical language understanding evaluation benchmark. In Proceedings of the 60th Annual Meeting of the Association for Computational Linguistics (Volume 1: Long Papers), pages 7888–7915, Dublin, Ireland. Association for Computational Linguistics.

Zhengyan Zhang, Xu Han, Zhiyuan Liu, Xin Jiang, Maosong Sun, and Qun Liu. 2019. ERNIE: Enhanced language representation with informative entities. In Proceedings of the 57th Annual Meeting of the Association for Computational Linguistics, pages 1441–1451, Florence, Italy. Association for Computational Linguistics.

Fine-grained Text Style Transfer with Diffusion-Based Language Models

Yiwei Lyu **Tiange Luo** **Jiacheng Shi** **Todd C. Hollon** **Honglak Lee**

University of Michigan
{yiweilyu, tiangel, jiachs}@umich.edu

Abstract

Diffusion probabilistic models have shown great success in generating high-quality images controllably, and researchers have tried to utilize this controllability into text generation domain. Previous works on diffusion-based language models have shown that they can be trained without external knowledge (such as pre-trained weights) and still achieve stable performance and controllability. In this paper, we trained a diffusion-based model on StylePTB dataset, the standard benchmark for fine-grained text style transfers. The tasks in StylePTB requires much more refined control over the output text compared to tasks evaluated in previous works, and our model was able to achieve state-of-the-art performance on StylePTB on both individual and compositional transfers. Moreover, our model, trained on limited data from StylePTB without external knowledge, outperforms previous works that utilized pretrained weights, embeddings, and external grammar parsers, and this may indicate that diffusion-based language models have great potential under low-resource settings. Our code is available at `https://github.com/lvyiweil/DiffuSeq_StylePTB`

1 Introduction

Diffusion probabilistic models (Ho et al., 2020) have became the state-of-the-art technique in visual generative tasks. By starting from random gaussian noise and gradual denoising, they are able to generate images that look realistic in details. Moreover, conditional diffusion models such as stable diffusion (Rombach et al., 2022) are able to achieve detailed control over the generated output by conditioning on text, layouts, etc. The generated images are faithful to the text description or layouts, often to the finest details.

Analogically, researchers have tried to utilize the controllability of diffusion models to achieve more controllable language generation. For example, DiffuSeq (Gong et al., 2022) applies diffusion models to sequence-sequence text generation tasks such as paraphrasing, question generation and text simplification; Diffusion-LM (Li et al., 2022) combined diffusion models with language models to control language generation by specifying generation length, syntax tree, semantic context, etc. What made these diffusion-based language models impressive is that they are trained from scratch with zero external knowledge (i.e. no pre-trained word embeddings or model weights, no external grammar parsers, etc) and on very few data (on the order of 10^5 tokens) compared to any large language models (for example, GPT-3's (Brown et al., 2020) training data is on the order 10^{11} tokens), so they have to learn representations at all levels (word embeddings, sentence structures, etc) from scratch with very limited data.

However, while the earlier tasks assessed on Diffusion-LM and DiffuSeq require a degree of control over the generated output, they are incapable of modifying the existing text to exhibit specific stylistic characteristics. In this paper, we would like to further examine the capabilities of diffusion-based language models on **fine-grained text style transfer**, an important task that requires more fine-grained control than the tasks from previous works on diffusion-based language modeling because it only allows changing the specified fine-grained stylistic properties of the input while leaving the rest unchanged. For example, "verb emphasis" is a fine-grained style transfer that requires the model to rewrite the sentence emphasizing a certain verb, without changing any other information that the original sentence conveys. In comparison, previous evaluation tasks such as controlling sequence length, semantic context, etc essentially control one aspect at a time and require no control over any other properties of generated text.

We use 13 non-lexical transfers from StylePTB (Lyu et al., 2021) dataset, where

Proceedings of the 8th Workshop on Representation Learning for NLP (RepL4NLP 2023), pages 65–74
July 13, 2023

Aspect	Transfers	Original Sentence	Additional Information	Transformed Sentence	Number of Pairs in StylePTB dataset
Syntax	To Future Tense	She travels to Paris every summer to visit her family.		She **will** travel to Paris next summer to visit her family.	7272
	To Present Tense	She had been studying architecture for five years.		She **has** been studying architecture for five years.	4365
	To Past Tense	He walks to the store every day.		He **walked** to the store every day.	4422
	Activate to Passive	The cat chased the mouse.		The mouse **was chased** by the cat.	2808
	Passive to Activate	The proposal was approved by the committee yesterday.		The committee **approved** the proposal yesterday.	2808
	PP Front to Back	Having watched the movie, they left the theater.		They left the theater after **having watched the movie**.	467
	PP Back to Front	They have been planning their vacation for months.		**For months**, they have been planning their vacation.	467
Semantic	ADJ/ADV Removal	The **extremely talented** musician played a **beautiful** melody on the piano.		The musician played a melody on the piano.	4863
	PP Removal	She had been studying **for hours** before taking the test.		She had been studying before taking the test.	4767
	Substatement Removal	He was unhappy **that he had failed. the exam**		He was unhappy.	1345
	Infomation Addition	The stock was up three percent according to the man.	"man", "lazy"	The stock was up three percent according to the **lazy** man.	2114
Thematics	Verb/Action Emphasis	She reads books in pastime.	"read"	**Reading** books is her favorite pastime.	1201
	Adjective Emphasis	The scenic forest is Michele's favorite place.	"scenic"	Michele's favorite forest is **scenic**.	696

Table 1: The 13 non-lexical fine-grained text style transfers from the StylePTB dataset (Lyu et al., 2021). We present one example sentence pair before/after each transfer, as well as the total number of sentence pairs available for each transfer in StylePTB. As we can see, the transfers require changing one specific stylistic aspect of the sentence while leaving all other aspects unchanged, and the amount of data available for training is limited (compared to the typical amount of data required to train large language models nowadays).

there are at most a few thousand sentence pairs available for each transfer, as shown in Table 1. Since identifying the grammatical structure of the sentence can be very helpful for most of these transfers (such as active-to-passive), some previous methods (such as Neural QCFG (Kim, 2021)) utilizes external grammar parsers to gain such information. We trained a diffusion-based model on StylePTB data without any pre-trained weights or external grammar parsers. Therefore, our model has to start from zero grammar/linguistic knowledge and learn all of them from very limited training data (StylePTB only has 7719 sentences from Penn Tree Bank (Marcus et al., 1993) plus their transferred outputs). Even under these hard conditions, our model still managed to outperform previous works that do utilize external weights or grammar parsers. Moreover, we also evaluate the capabilities of diffusion-based language models on performing multiple transfers using one single model and composing multiple learned transfers on a single sentence. We list our contributions as follows:

- We trained a diffusion-based language model (adapted from DiffuSeq (Gong et al., 2022)) that can perform fine-grained text style transfer from scratch with very limited training data and no external weights or tools. The model also supports multitasking and composing multiple fine-grained transfers.
- Our model achieves state-of-the-art performance on fine-grained text style transfers in StylePTB. Our multitask model (i.e. one single model that can perform all 13 transfers) achieves **best performance** compared to previous works on the same tasks on **88 out of 91** metrics (7 metrics per transfer), and gets very close to human performance on tasks with easy and medium difficulties. We also evaluated our model on composition of multiple fine-grained transfers, and we achieved best performance on these tasks as well.
- Thr/ough the evaluations, we demonstrated the extraordinary capabilities of diffusion-based language models in asserting extremely fine-grained control over generated text, and that this type of language model have great potential in controllable natural language generation under low-resource settings as it is able to achieve state-of-the-art performance with

limited training data and no external knowledge.

2 Backgrounds

2.1 Fine-grained Text Style Transfer and StylePTB

An import challenge for AI is to convey intentions using different stylistic attributes, and automated text style transfer is an essential step towards that. Text style transfer aims to controllably convert source text with targeted stylistic properties, with important applications in human-AI interactions including dialog systems (Celikyilmaz et al., 2018) and intelligent agents (Kim et al., 2013; Liang et al., 2020; Pittermann et al., 2010) that can communicate with specific text styles for different situations, target audiences, and environments (Lample et al., 2019; Li et al., 2018).

There has been extensive research on high-level style transfers such as sentiment transfers (Shen et al., 2017) and formality transfers (Rao and Tetreault, 2018). However, high-level style transfers lack the ability to fully control the style of the output. For example, there are many ways to convert a positive comment about a restaurant into a negative one, and high-level text style transfers do not allow control over which of the possible outputs (that may have different styles in non-sentiment aspects) can be generated. Fine-grained text style transfer is important because they allow fine-grained control over the generated output. (Lyu et al., 2021) defined a set of fine-grained text style transfer along four lingustic axis:

- **Lexical Transfers:** Word changes
- **Syntax Transfers:** Grammar and sentence structure changes
- **Semantic Transfers:** Meaning changes
- **Thematic Transfers:** Situational changes or word emphasis

Along these 4 axes, it defined 21 individual fine-grained transfers, 13 of which are non-lexical. Examples of the non-lexical transfers are shown in Table 1. Compared to other forms of controllable text generation, fine-grained text style transfer has the advantage of being able to assert control over text generated by uncontrollable models. For example, we can use fine-grained text style transfers to add specific stylistic properties to free-form text generated by large language models while keeping the content of the generated text unchanged. Fine-grained text style transfers can be composed to achieve higher-level style transfers, and they even have the potential to mitigate social bias in large text generation models (Lyu et al., 2021). Therefore, it is important to develop techniques to achieve automated fine-grained text style transfer. Existing works are still quite far from perfect on a lot of the fine-grained style transfers compared to human performance (Lyu et al., 2021; Kim, 2021), and composing multiple fine-grained style transfers remains challenging.

2.2 Diffusion Probabilistic Models

Recently, diffusion models (Ho et al., 2020) is widely used to generate high quality and diverse images. Its methodology consists of two phases: the first phase is the forward diffusion phase, which adds Gaussian noise to the input image x_0 as the time stamp increases, and after enough steps the image is reduced to pure Gaussian noise x_t. The second phase is the recovery phase, in which a model is trained to gradually remove noise from x_t until it recovers the original image x_0. During inference, we start from a randomly sampled gaussian noise x_t and use the denoising model to gradually infer an image x_0.

Diffusion-based language generation models follows a similar approach where we perform the diffusion and denoising process in the token embedding space. We will explain the model we use, which is built upon DiffuSeq (Gong et al., 2022), in details in the next section.

3 Methodology

We adapt DiffuSeq (Gong et al., 2022) to be able to perform fine-grained text style transfer given a source sentence and specified transfer operation(s), as illustrated in Figure 1. We model the transfer as a conditional generation process, where the condition includes the source sentence and the specified transfer operation(s). We first define a set of special style tokens, one for each possible individual fine-grained transfer. If we wish to perform one or more transfer on the source sentence, we will prepend the corresponding special token(s) to the beginning of the source sentence to form the condition S.

We use BERT tokenizer to tokenize the input into discrete token ids, and adopt a token embedding layer to encode both the source (including prepended style tokens) and the ground truth target sentence (during training) to obtain the embedded source Z^S and target Z_0^{TRG}. For the diffusion pro-

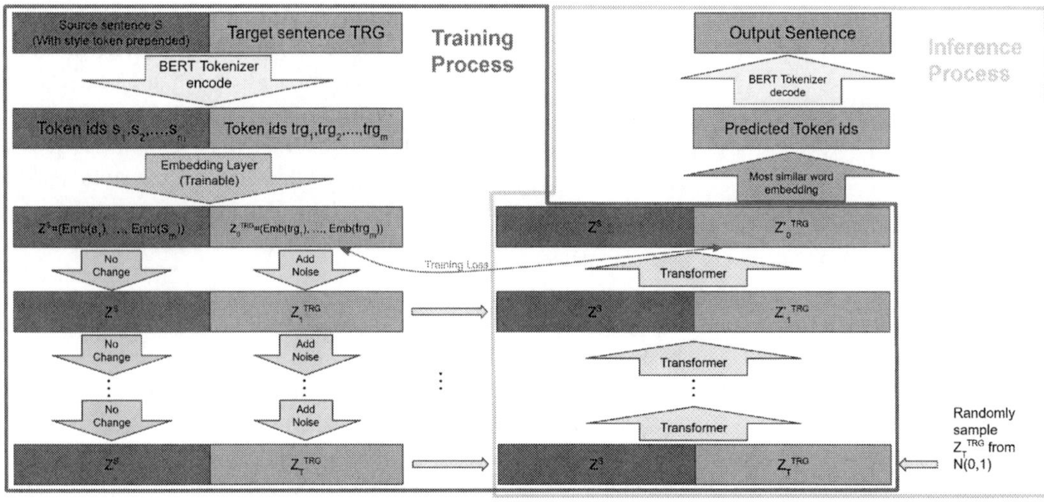

Figure 1: An illustration of the training and inference process of our diffusion-based language model. The diffusion process is performed over the sequence of token embeddings of the target sentence Z_0^{TRG}, and the source sentence's token embeddings (Z^S) are concatenated before Z^{TRG}. During the backward diffusion process, the combined sequence is fed into the transformer model to gradually recover/generate Z_0^{TRG}.

cess, we use a transformer model to recover the target embedding. Both the diffusion transformer and the token embeddings are initialized randomly and jointly optimized. In other words, our model does not rely on any prior knowledge about our task or the English Language in general.

We use the simplified diffusion objective during training: for each input (S, TRG) where S is the source sentence (with style tokens) and TRG is the ground truth target sentence, we randomly sample a step number t from $1, 2, ...T$, where T is the maximum number of steps, and add t steps of random Gaussian noise to Z_0^{TRG} following a linear diffusion schedule to obtain Z_t^{TRG}. We then concatenate Z^S and Z_t^{TRG} and input the concatenated sequence into our diffusion transformer, where we only take the output embeddings at the locations corresponding to Z_t^{TRG} as $Z_0'^{TRG}$. Our training objective is simply going to be the MSE Loss between Z_0^{TRG} and $Z_0'^{TRG}$.

During inference, we randomly initialize $Z_T'^{TRG} \sim N(0, 1)$, and encode the condition (source sentence and style tokens) into Z^S. Then we concatenate them and use our transformer to predict a temporary $Z_{0_{temp}}'^{TRG}$, add $T-1$ steps of noise back to the temporary $Z_{0_{temp}}'^{TRG}$ to obtain $Z_{T-1}'^{TRG}$. We repeat this process until we get $Z_0'^{TRG}$. For each embedding in $Z_0'^{TRG}$, we find the closest embedding in our token embedding layer by cosine distance, and decode the embedding to that token. Then we combine the tokens to form the output sentence in natural language.

4 Experiments

4.1 Dataset

StylePTB (Lyu et al., 2021) contains paired sentences before/after each transfer for 21 fine-grained transfers, as well as paired data for compositions of multiple fine-grained transfers. For single transfers, we will focus on the 13 non-lexical fine-grained style transfers following (Lyu et al., 2021). The number of sentence pairs available from StylePTB for each transfer and examples of sentences before/after each transfer are shown in Table 1. For compositional transfers, we will use the Tense + Voice and Tense + PP Removal transfers from the compositional part of StylePTB dataset (same as the ones used for evaluation in (Lyu et al., 2021)). Each compositional dataset contains all combinations of valid transfers (for example, Tense + Voice dataset contains all valid combinations of 0/1/2 transfers regarding tense and voice, such as To-Future + Active-To-Passive or To-Past + No-Voice-Change).

StylePTB was built with only 7719 different sentences from Penn Tree Bank (Marcus et al., 1993) plus their stylistic variations, so both the amount and the diversity of training data are very limited, thus making this task even more challenging for DiffuSeq since it does not have access to external knowledge or pre-trained weights and have to extract all linguistic knowledge from limited data.

For fair comparison, we preprocess the data following the same criterion as (Lyu et al., 2021): we replace numbers with NUM token, and we replace each word that occurs less than 3 times in the training set with UNK token. We also split the data into train/valid/test splits with proportions of 0.9/0.05/0.05 using the same splits as all previous works.

4.2 Evaluation Metrics

We use the same evaluation methods as (Lyu et al., 2021) and report 7 metrics from nlg-eval package (Sharma et al., 2017) (BLEU 1-4, METEOR, ROUGE-L, CiDER) between the generated transferred sentence and the ground truth target sentence from the dataset.

4.3 Single style transfer experiment

4.3.1 Baselines

We report performance of the following baselines for single style transfer:

1. **GPT-2**: Directly finetuning GPT-2 medium model (Radford et al., 2019) with paired data. Performance reported from (Lyu et al., 2021).
2. **Seq2Seq**: GRU sequence-to-sequence language model (Sutskever et al., 2014) with attention. Performance reported from (Lyu et al., 2021).
3. **RetrieveEdit (Hashimoto et al., 2018)**: For an input data x, a retriever model will go through the training set to find a similar sentence pair (x', y') and a trained editor edits y' into desired output y. Performance reported from (Lyu et al., 2021).
4. **Steering Vector (Subramani et al., 2022)**: extract steering vectors directly from pretrained LMs to guide generation
5. **TAILOR (Ross et al., 2021)**: output sentences conditioned on control codes by a pretrained seq2seq model
6. **Neural QCFG (Kim, 2021)**: It presents a sequence-to-sequence text learning by explicitly modeling the alignment between target trees with the source.
7. **Neural QCFG + copy (Kim, 2021)**: Neural QCFG with an option to copy certain tokens from source sentence

Among these baselines, **GPT-2**, **Steering Vector** and **TAILOR** uses pre-trained language models, **Neural QCFG** and **Neural QCFG + copy** requires external grammar parsers, and **RetrieveEdit** uses GLOVE word embeddings.

We also included **Human** performance on these tasks (reported in (Lyu et al., 2021) by asking human annotators to manually perform the style transfer tasks) for comparison.

4.3.2 Results and Analysis

For single style transfers, we tried two different diffusion-based approaches: (1) we train a separate diffusion model for each individual style transfer, and (2) we train one diffusion model for all 13 transfers evaluated. For approach (2), we add a style token at the beginning of the input sentence to indicate which of the 13 transfers needs to be performed. We call approach (2) DiffuSeq Multitask.

The original StylePTB paper (Lyu et al., 2021) puts the non-lexical transfers into 3 difficulty categories (easy, medium, hard) by average hamming distance between input and output of the transfer. We report the results of our experiment using the same categorization, where we show results on easy and medium transfers in Table 2 and hard transfers in Table 3.

Surprisingly, DiffuSeq Multitask outperforms DiffuSeq on all transfers, even though DiffuSeq Multitask has to handle 13 different transfers in one model while each DiffuSeq model only needs to handle 1 transfer. This is possibly due to the additional training data from all the tasks that the multitask model learns better representations for words and sentences and gains more accurate knowledge of grammatical patterns of English, which is shared across all tasks.

Moreover, DiffuSeq Multitask significantly outperforms all baselines in all easy and medium transfers, and also achieves state-of-the-art on most metrics on hard transfers, only falling slightly behind Neural QCFG + copy in some metrics. This is really impressive considering that our approach leverages no external knowledge while all baselines except Seq2Seq utilizes either pretrained language models, pretrained word embeddings, or external grammar tree parser. Neural-QCFG-based methods are especially dependent on external linguistics knowledge and existing grammar parsers. DiffuSeq Multitask's performance is also on par with human performance on easy and medium transfers, indicating that DiffuSeq Multitask is close to fully solving the easy and medium difficulty transfers.

Easy Transfers	Baseline Model	BLEU-1	BLEU-2	BLEU-3	BLEU-4	METEOR	ROUGE_L	CiDER
To Future Tense	GPT2	0.895	0.852	0.813	0.778	0.540	0.899	7.709
	SEQ2SEQ	0.527	0.368	0.261	0.188	0.173	0.531	1.525
	RETRIEVEEDIT	0.899	0.854	0.815	0.778	0.531	0.901	7.731
	STEERING VECTOR	0.699	-	-	-	-		-
	TAILOR	0.873	-	-	-	-	-	-
	DIFFUSEQ	0.976	0.956	0.937	0.917	0.646	0.973	9.145
	DIFFUSEQ MULTITASK	**0.985**	**0.972**	**0.959**	**0.946**	**0.677**	**0.983**	**9.454**
	HUMAN	0.954	0.915	0.884	0.855	0.636	0.964	9.174
To Past Tense	GPT2	0.836	0.776	0.722	0.674	0.484	0.842	6.700
	SEQ2SEQ	0.478	0.313	0.204	0.133	0.155	0.490	1.374
	RETRIEVEEDIT	0.935	0.903	0.873	0.847	0.606	0.933	8.358
	STEERING VECTOR	0.478	-	-	-	-	-	-
	TAILOR	0.711	-	-	-	-	-	-
	DIFFUSEQ	0.973	0.959	0.946	0.932	0.697	0.976	9.352
	DIFFUSEQ MULTITASK	**0.986**	**0.977**	**0.968**	**0.958**	**0.709**	**0.987**	**9.588**
	HUMAN	0.974	0.957	0.939	0.916	0.709	0.982	9.549
To Present Tense	GPT2	0.754	0.663	0.586	0.524	0.412	0.772	5.293
	SEQ2SEQ	0.516	0.361	0.267	0.210	0.190	0.518	1.819
	RETRIEVEEDIT	0.909	0.870	0.830	0.793	0.599	0.916	7.987
	STEERING VECTOR	0.692	-	-	-	-	-	-
	TAILOR	0.884	-	-	-	-	-	-
	DIFFUSEQ	0.965	0.948	0.932	0.916	0.713	0.964	9.072
	DIFFUSEQ MULTITASK	**0.975**	**0.961**	**0.947**	**0.933**	**0.719**	**0.977**	**9.310**
	HUMAN	0.969	0.952	0.936	0.918	0.745	0.979	9.501
ADJ or ADV Removal	GPT2	0.647	0.508	0.394	0.308	0.313	0.652	3.259
	SEQ2SEQ	0.450	0.274	0.172	0.112	0.140	0.469	1.171
	RETRIEVEEDIT	0.897	0.841	0.786	0.731	0.511	0.919	7.461
	STEERING VECTOR	0.721	-	-	-	-	-	-
	TAILOR	0.781	-	-	-	-	-	-
	DIFFUSEQ	0.903	0.809	0.731	0.664	0.488	0.888	6.708
	DIFFUSEQ MULTITASK	**0.949**	**0.908**	**0.868**	**0.829**	**0.563**	**0.946**	**8.237**
	HUMAN	0.933	0.894	0.870	0.847	0.591	0.965	8.924
Medium Transfers	Baseline Model	BLEU-1	BLEU-2	BLEU-3	BLEU-4	METEOR	ROUGE_L	CiDER
PP Front to Back	GPT2	0.398	0.210	0.081	0.001	0.184	0.406	0.886
	SEQ2SEQ	0.393	0.280	0.207	0.161	0.162	0.391	1.492
	RETRIEVEEDIT	0.541	0.423	0.301	0.176	0.247	0.547	2.536
	STEERING VECTOR	0.819	-	-	-	-	-	-
	TAILOR	0.842	-	-	-	-	-	-
	DIFFUSEQ	0.605	0.409	0.301	0.247	0.271	0.514	2.273
	DIFFUSEQ MULTITASK	**0.978**	**0.931**	**0.893**	**0.856**	**0.567**	**0.901**	**8.374**
	HUMAN	0.965	0.959	0.952	0.945	0.690	0.970	9.671
PP Front to Back	GPT2	0.407	0.241	0.091	0.001	0.166	0.406	0.931
	SEQ2SEQ	0.298	0.157	0.090	0.060	0.112	0.284	0.606
	RETRIEVEEDIT	0.649	0.584	0.535	0.491	0.333	0.656	4.667
	DIFFUSEQ	0.603	0.400	0.291	0.242	0.266	0.514	2.255
	DIFFUSEQ MULTITASK	**0.983**	**0.944**	**0.905**	**0.868**	**0.610**	**0.950**	**8.664**
	HUMAN	1.000	1.000	1.000	1.000	1.000	1.000	10.000
PP Removal	GPT2	0.763	0.700	0.645	0.593	0.419	0.787	6.012
	SEQ2SEQ	0.330	0.195	0.121	0.081	0.112	0.363	1.004
	RETRIEVEEDIT	0.798	0.770	0.739	0.712	0.478	0.846	7.111
	STEERING VECTOR	0.393	-	-	-	-	-	-
	TAILOR	0.717	-	-	-	-	-	-
	DIFFUSEQ	0.856	0.803	0.758	0.717	0.515	0.872	7.235
	DIFFUSEQ MULTITASK	**0.950**	**0.937**	**0.919**	**0.902**	**0.624**	**0.948**	**8.606**
	HUMAN	0.957	0.944	0.931	0.919	0.681	0.976	9.207
Substatement Removal	GPT2	0.430	0.332	0.247	0.176	0.250	0.588	3.090
	SEQ2SEQ	0.317	0.192	0.110	0.001	0.100	0.368	1.041
	RETRIEVEEDIT	0.706	0.678	0.647	0.607	0.405	0.767	6.183
	STEERING VECTOR	0.120	-	-	-	-	-	-
	DIFFUSEQ	0.688	0.592	0.493	0.388	0.364	0.718	4.285
	DIFFUSEQ MULTITASK	**0.884**	**0.860**	**0.825**	**0.781**	**0.555**	**0.895**	**7.165**
	HUMAN	0.731	0.720	0.705	0.685	0.607	0.788	7.691
Information Addition	GPT2	0.479	0.305	0.189	0.121	0.207	0.475	1.359
	SEQ2SEQ	0.345	0.180	0.094	0.053	0.098	0.335	0.632
	STEERING VECTOR	0.772	-	-	-	-	-	-
	RETRIEVEEDIT	0.493	0.396	0.328	0.275	0.284	0.603	3.401
	DIFFUSEQ	0.809	0.572	0.420	0.3081	0.3829	0.676	3.439
	DIFFUSEQ MULTITASK	**0.911**	**0.800**	**0.706**	**0.623**	**0.483**	**0.835**	**6.038**
	HUMAN	0.846	0.762	0.690	0.624	0.521	0.892	6.863

Table 2: Evaluation results on easy and medium transfers. DiffuSeq Multitask achieves State of the art performance in every metric, and is on par with human performance.

Hard Transfers	Baseline Model	BLEU-1	BLEU-2	BLEU-3	BLEU-4	METEOR	ROUGE_L	CiDER
Active To Passive	GPT2	0.476	0.329	0.238	0.189	0.216	0.464	1.820
	Seq2Seq	0.373	0.220	0.141	0.103	0.131	0.345	0.845
	RetrieveEdit	0.681	0.598	0.503	0.427	0.383	0.663	4.535
	Steering Vector	0.666	-	-	-	-	-	-
	TAILOR	0.556	-	-	-	-	-	-
	Neural QCFG	0.431	0.637	0.548	0.472	0.415	0.695	4.294
	Neural QCFG + copy	0.836	0.771	0.713	0.662	0.499	0.803	6.410
	DiffuSeq	0.839	0.580	0.302	0.196	0.225	0.512	2.344
	DiffuSeq MultiTask	**0.918**	**0.835**	**0.752**	**0.681**	**0.521**	**0.844**	**6.913**
	Human	0.931	0.881	0.835	0.795	0.587	0.905	8.603
Passive To Active	GPT2	0.433	0.271	0.167	0.120	0.191	0.434	1.329
	Seq2Seq	0.339	0.214	0.160	0.132	0.126	0.331	1.062
	RetrieveEdit	0.714	0.659	0.559	0.474	0.397	0.732	5.024
	Steering Vector	0.574	-	-	-	-	-	-
	DiffuSeq	0.829	0.550	0.282	0.192	0.205	0.502	2.224
	DiffuSeq MultiTask	**0.955**	**0.896**	**0.834**	**0.777**	**0.555**	**0.913**	**8.028**
	Human	0.977	0.962	0.942	0.919	0.685	0.973	9.409
Adjective Emphasis	GPT2	0.263	0.079	0.028	0.000	0.112	0.188	0.386
	Seq2Seq	0.187	0.058	0.018	0.000	0.059	0.179	0.141
	RetrieveEdit	0.387	0.276	0.211	0.164	0.193	0.369	1.679
	Steering Vector	0.774	-	-	-	-	-	-
	Neural QCFG	0.348	0.178	0.062	0.000	0.162	0.317	0.667
	Neural QCFG + copy	0.676	0.506	0.393	0.316	0.373	0.683	3.424
	DiffuSeq	0.620	0.382	0.215	0.152	0.243	0.335	2.231
	DiffuSeq MultiTask	**0.775**	**0.600**	**0.477**	**0.386**	**0.423**	**0.673**	**4.007**
	Human	0.834	0.753	0.679	0.611	0.522	0.811	6.796
Verb/Action Emphasis	GPT2	0.309	0.170	0.095	0.041	0.140	0.292	0.593
	Seq2Seq	0.289	0.127	0.066	0.038	0.098	0.275	0.300
	RetrieveEdit	0.416	0.284	0.209	0.148	0.223	0.423	1.778
	Steering Vector	0.548	-	-	-	-	-	-
	Neural QCFG	0.431	0.250	0.14	0.073	0.219	0.408	1.097
	Neural QCFG + copy	0.664	0.512	**0.407**	**0.319**	0.370	0.589	**3.227**
	DiffuSeq	0.453	0.210	0.101	0.054	0.205	0.379	0.785
	DiffuSeq MultiTask	**0.693**	**0.516**	0.370	0.261	**0.373**	**0.596**	2.950
	Human	0.649	0.569	0.493	0.421	0.433	0.693	5.668

Table 3: Evaluation results on hard transfers. Diffuseq Multitask achieves State-of-the-art performance on most metrics, and is only slightly behind Neural QCFG + copy on some metrics.

4.4 Compositional style transfer experiment

4.4.1 Baselines

We will report performance of the following baselines for compositional fine-grained style transfers:

1. **SeqGPT**: Sequentially applying fine-tuned GPT-2 for each single style transfer. Performance reported from (Lyu et al., 2021).
2. **CS-GPT**: A modified GPT-2 model that takes in style tokens as indication of which style transfers to apply. Performance reported from (Lyu et al., 2021).

4.4.2 Results and Analysis

For compositions of multiple fine-grained style transfers, we train one single DiffuSeq model to handle all compositions and use style tokens to indicate which transfers to compose for the input sentence, similar to CS-GPT (Lyu et al., 2021). The results are shown in Table 4. DiffuSeq significantly outperforms baselines in all tasks and all metrics. Therefore, not only does our diffusion model work well for single fine-grained style transfers, it also works well for compositions of multiple fine-grained style transfers.

5 Related Works

5.1 Automated Text Style Transfer

The goal of the text style transfer (TST) task is to change the style of the sentence while retaining its style-independent content. Previous works in TST includes the following approaches: statistical NLP methods (Hovy, 1987; Xu et al., 2012), neural generative models (Prabhumoye et al., 2018; Lample et al., 2019; He et al., 2020), Retrieve-and-Edit approaches (Li et al., 2018; Hashimoto et al., 2018; Guu et al., 2018; Sudhakar et al., 2019; Madaan et al., 2020), and Transformer-based approach (Lyu et al., 2021). Some of these methods can already achieve high performance on certain high-level transfers (such as sentiment transfers (Shen et al., 2017) and formality transfers (Rao and Tetreault, 2018)), but fine-grained text style tranfer remains challenging for the above approaches (Lyu et al.,

Dataset	Transfers	Model	BLEU-1	BLEU-2	BLEU-3	BLEU-4	METEOR	ROUGE_L	CiDER
Tense + Voice	ToPast+ ActiveToPassive	SEQGPT	0.332	0.155	0.057	0.024	0.144	0.300	0.636
		CS-GPT	0.409	0.238	0.133	0.064	0.180	0.378	1.029
		DIFFUSEQ	**0.744**	**0.555**	**0.420**	**0.324**	**0.353**	**0.656**	**3.753**
	ToFuture+ ActiveToPassive	SEQGPT	0.391	0.222	0.120	0.065	0.167	0.373	0.866
		CS-GPT	0.496	0.340	0.240	0.185	0.217	0.479	1.800
		DIFFUSEQ	**0.821**	**0.705**	**0.615**	**0.542**	**0.414**	**0.762**	**5.281**
	ToFuture+ PassiveToActive	SEQGPT	0.401	0.212	0.097	0.048	0.163	0.385	0.888
		CS-GPT	0.528	0.364	0.259	0.197	0.234	0.524	2.020
		DIFFUSEQ	**0.744**	**0.555**	**0.420**	**0.324**	**0.353**	**0.656**	**3.753**
	ToPast+ PassiveToActive	SEQGPT	0.381	0.210	0.098	0.045	0.156	0.368	0.876
		CS-GPT	0.474	0.297	0.175	0.099	0.206	0.473	1.513
		DIFFUSEQ	**0.864**	**0.772**	**0.697**	**0.635**	**0.460**	**0.825**	**6.519**
	ToPresent+ PassiveToActive	SEQGPT	0.348	0.189	0.085	0.037	0.142	0.343	0.745
		CS-GPT	0.523	0.366	0.264	0.210	0.243	0.522	2.118
		DIFFUSEQ	**0.797**	**0.686**	**0.603**	**0.536**	**0.414**	**0.756**	**5.378**
	ToPresent+ ActiveToPassive	SEQGPT	0.396	0.256	0.177	0.136	0.179	0.384	1.209
		CS-GPT	0.503	0.358	0.271	0.223	0.233	0.491	2.118
		DIFFUSEQ	**0.878**	**0.787**	**0.715**	**0.656**	**0.482**	**0.849**	**6.823**
Tense + PP Removal	ToFuture+ PPRemoval	SEQGPT	0.722	0.644	0.581	0.524	0.385	**0.755**	5.562
		CS-GPT	0.738	0.652	0.578	0.518	0.393	0.755	5.289
		DiffuSeq	**0.913**	**0.876**	**0.841**	**0.808**	**0.557**	**0.911**	**7.906**
	ToPast+ PPRemoval	SEQGPT	0.714	0.640	0.573	0.510	0.374	0.724	5.152
		CS-GPT	0.772	0.695	0.624	0.564	0.421	0.775	5.585
		DiffuSeq	**0.911**	**0.881**	**0.849**	**0.818**	**0.568**	**0.908**	**7.825**
	ToPresent+ PPRemoval	SEQGPT	0.618	0.518	0.435	0.368	0.338	0.663	4.119
		CS-GPT	0.709	0.609	0.523	0.446	0.718	0.718	4.588
		DiffuSeq	**0.908**	**0.859**	**0.820**	**0.788**	**0.558**	**0.895**	**7.439**

Table 4: Results on compositions of Tense + Voice transfers and Tense + PP Removal Transfers. DiffuSeq was able to outperform all 3 baselines from (Lyu et al., 2021) by a large margin.

2021). In this paper, we explored a new approach for fine-grained TST utilizing Diffusion Models.

5.2 Natural language processing with diffusion model

There have been two approaches for leveraging diffusion models into text data: the first approach takes advantage of the diffusion model in the continuous domain, like Diffusion-LM (Li et al., 2022), and DiffuSeq (Gong et al., 2022), where we start from a gaussian noise vector, and gradually denoise this noise vector to the desired sentence; the second approach applies diffusion model into discrete state space, like Multinomial Diffusion (Hoogeboom et al., 2021), DDPMs (Austin et al., 2021), and DiffusionBERT (Austin et al., 2021). In this paper, we chose to build upon the first type of model, because they are closer to the original diffusion models for images (where diffusion happens in continuous space) and they have shown successes on tasks that requires control over generations.

6 Limitations and Future works

One significant limitation of our work is that we only explored the capabilities of diffusion-based language models under a challenging circumstance where it is not allowed to use pre-trained weights or grammar parsers, which means we did not utilize this kind of model to its full potential, so a future research direction could be exploring possible ways to further improve the model's performance by leveraging pretrained weights or word embeddings, and train with enough data to find the full potential of these models.

Another limitation of our work is that we only explored one typical diffusion-based language model, so our conclusions may not generalize to special types of diffusion-based language models (such as ones that uses discrete state space). We also conducted all experiments using the exact same model architecture design. In the future, we plan to experiment with different architectures for the diffusion model, such as more sophisticated conditioning methods (currently we just concatenate the source to the target, but we would like to try other ways of conditioning on the source, such as cross attention, as these conditioning methods for diffusion models have promising performance in the image generation domain).

Lastly, we found that diffusion-based language models work well with limited data and no external knowledge or pre-trained weights, thus these models may have great potential under low-resource settings, but we didn't apply them to any real low-resource settings (such as low-resource languages, rare domains, etc) in this paper, and we would like to do that in the future to explore the full potential of diffusion-based language models.

7 Conclusions

In this paper, we explored the capabilities of diffusion-based models on fine-grained text style transfer, a task that requires a high level of control over generated text, with no external knowledge or pre-trained weights and with very limited training data. Our diffusion-based language model, which builds upon DiffuSeq (Gong et al., 2022), achieves state-of-the-art performance on all transfers as well as composition of transfers, outperforming all previous works on this dataset, including ones that uses pre-trained weights, word embeddings, and external grammar parsers. It is even on par with human performance on many transfers. Therefore, our model is a great step towards solving automated fine-grained text style transfer.

Moreover, our work, together with previous works such as Diffusion-LM (Li et al., 2022), demonstrates that diffusion-based language models could have great potential in controllable text generation under low-resource settings. Under low-resource settings (such as rarely spoken language or uncommon tasks), it would be difficult to find existing large language models or pre-trained weights, and available training data will likely be very limited, so most approaches based on finetuning existing models or large amounts of training will not work well, and diffusion-based language models could be an alternative to consider.

Acknowledgement

This work is supported in part by grants from NSF IIS 1453651, NIH K12 NS080223, Cook Family Brain Tumor Research Fund, Mark Trauner Brain Research Fund: Zenkel Family Foundation, Ian's Friends Foundation, and the Investigators Awards grant program of Precision Health at the University of Michigan. Any opinions, findings, conclusions, or recommendations expressed in this work are those of the author(s) and do not necessarily reflect the views of the NSF, NIH, Cook Family Brain Tumor Research Fund, Mark Trauner Brain Research Fund: Zenkel Family Foundation, Ian's Friends Foundation, or Precision Health at the University of Michigan. We are grateful to the reviewers for their helpful review and feedback.

References

Jacob Austin, Daniel D Johnson, Jonathan Ho, Daniel Tarlow, and Rianne van den Berg. 2021. Structured denoising diffusion models in discrete state-spaces. *Advances in Neural Information Processing Systems*, 34:17981–17993.

Tom Brown, Benjamin Mann, Nick Ryder, Melanie Subbiah, Jared D Kaplan, Prafulla Dhariwal, Arvind Neelakantan, Pranav Shyam, Girish Sastry, Amanda Askell, et al. 2020. Language models are few-shot learners. *Advances in neural information processing systems*, 33:1877–1901.

Asli Celikyilmaz, Li Deng, and Dilek Hakkani-Tür. 2018. Deep learning in spoken and text-based dialog systems. In *Deep Learning in Natural Language Processing*, pages 49–78. Springer.

Shansan Gong, Mukai Li, Jiangtao Feng, Zhiyong Wu, and LingPeng Kong. 2022. Diffuseq: Sequence to sequence text generation with diffusion models. *arXiv preprint arXiv:2210.08933*.

Kelvin Guu, Tatsunori B Hashimoto, Yonatan Oren, and Percy Liang. 2018. Generating sentences by editing prototypes. *Transactions of the Association for Computational Linguistics*, 6:437–450.

Tatsunori B Hashimoto, Kelvin Guu, Yonatan Oren, and Percy S Liang. 2018. A retrieve-and-edit framework for predicting structured outputs. In *Advances in Neural Information Processing Systems*, pages 10052–10062.

Junxian He, Xinyi Wang, Graham Neubig, and Taylor Berg-Kirkpatrick. 2020. A probabilistic formulation of unsupervised text style transfer. *arXiv preprint arXiv:2002.03912*.

Jonathan Ho, Ajay Jain, and Pieter Abbeel. 2020. Denoising diffusion probabilistic models. *Advances in Neural Information Processing Systems*, 33:6840–6851.

Emiel Hoogeboom, Didrik Nielsen, Priyank Jaini, Patrick Forré, and Max Welling. 2021. Argmax flows and multinomial diffusion: Learning categorical distributions. *Advances in Neural Information Processing Systems*, 34:12454–12465.

Eduard Hovy. 1987. Generating natural language under pragmatic constraints. *Journal of Pragmatics*, 11(6):689–719.

Elizabeth S Kim, Lauren D Berkovits, Emily P Bernier, Dan Leyzberg, Frederick Shic, Rhea Paul, and Brian Scassellati. 2013. Social robots as embedded reinforcers of social behavior in children with autism. *Journal of autism and developmental disorders*.

Yoon Kim. 2021. Sequence-to-sequence learning with latent neural grammars. *Advances in Neural Information Processing Systems*, 34:26302–26317.

Guillaume Lample, Sandeep Subramanian, Eric Smith, Ludovic Denoyer, Marc'Aurelio Ranzato, and Y-Lan Boureau. 2019. Multiple-attribute text rewriting. In *International Conference on Learning Representations*.

Juncen Li, Robin Jia, He He, and Percy Liang. 2018. Delete, retrieve, generate: a simple approach to sentiment and style transfer. In *Proceedings of the 2018 Conference of the North American Chapter of the Association for Computational Linguistics: Human Language Technologies, Volume 1 (Long Papers)*, pages 1865–1874. Association for Computational Linguistics.

Xiang Lisa Li, John Thickstun, Ishaan Gulrajani, Percy Liang, and Tatsunori B Hashimoto. 2022. Diffusion-lm improves controllable text generation. *arXiv preprint arXiv:2205.14217*.

Paul Pu Liang, Jeffrey Chen, Ruslan Salakhutdinov, Louis-Philippe Morency, and Satwik Kottur. 2020. On emergent communication in competitive multi-agent teams. In *AAMAS*.

Yiwei Lyu, Paul Pu Liang, Hai Pham, Eduard Hovy, Barnabás Póczos, Ruslan Salakhutdinov, and Louis-Philippe Morency. 2021. Styleptb: A compositional benchmark for fine-grained controllable text style transfer. *arXiv preprint arXiv:2104.05196*.

Aman Madaan, Amrith Setlur, Tanmay Parekh, Barnabas Poczos, Graham Neubig, Yiming Yang, Ruslan Salakhutdinov, Alan W Black, and Shrimai Prabhumoye. 2020. Politeness transfer: A tag and generate approach. *arXiv preprint arXiv:2004.14257*.

Mitchell P. Marcus, Beatrice Santorini, and Mary Ann Marcinkiewicz. 1993. Building a large annotated corpus of English: The Penn Treebank. *Computational Linguistics*, 19(2):313–330.

Johannes Pittermann, Angela Pittermann, and Wolfgang Minker. 2010. Emotion recognition and adaptation in spoken dialogue systems. *International Journal of Speech Technology*.

Shrimai Prabhumoye, Yulia Tsvetkov, Ruslan Salakhutdinov, and Alan W Black. 2018. Style transfer through back-translation. In *Proceedings of the 56th Annual Meeting of the Association for Computational Linguistics (Volume 1: Long Papers)*, pages 866–876. Association for Computational Linguistics.

Alec Radford, Jeff Wu, Rewon Child, David Luan, Dario Amodei, and Ilya Sutskever. 2019. Language models are unsupervised multitask learners.

Sudha Rao and Joel Tetreault. 2018. Dear sir or madam, may i introduce the gyafc dataset: Corpus, benchmarks and metrics for formality style transfer. *arXiv preprint arXiv:1803.06535*.

Robin Rombach, Andreas Blattmann, Dominik Lorenz, Patrick Esser, and Björn Ommer. 2022. High-resolution image synthesis with latent diffusion models. In *Proceedings of the IEEE/CVF Conference on Computer Vision and Pattern Recognition*, pages 10684–10695.

Alexis Ross, Tongshuang Wu, Hao Peng, Matthew E Peters, and Matt Gardner. 2021. Tailor: Generating and perturbing text with semantic controls. *arXiv preprint arXiv:2107.07150*.

Shikhar Sharma, Layla El Asri, Hannes Schulz, and Jeremie Zumer. 2017. Relevance of unsupervised metrics in task-oriented dialogue for evaluating natural language generation. *CoRR*, abs/1706.09799.

Tianxiao Shen, Tao Lei, Regina Barzilay, and Tommi Jaakkola. 2017. Style transfer from non-parallel text by cross-alignment. In *Advances in Neural Information Processing Systems*, pages 6833–6844.

Nishant Subramani, Nivedita Suresh, and Matthew E Peters. 2022. Extracting latent steering vectors from pretrained language models. *arXiv preprint arXiv:2205.05124*.

Akhilesh Sudhakar, Bhargav Upadhyay, and Arjun Maheswaran. 2019. Transforming delete, retrieve, generate approach for controlled text style transfer. *arXiv preprint arXiv:1908.09368*.

Ilya Sutskever, Oriol Vinyals, and Quoc V Le. 2014. Sequence to sequence learning with neural networks. In *Advances in neural information processing systems*, pages 3104–3112.

Wei Xu, Alan Ritter, Bill Dolan, Ralph Grishman, and Colin Cherry. 2012. Paraphrasing for style. In *Proceedings of COLING 2012*, pages 2899–2914.

Enhancing text comprehension for Question Answering with Contrastive Learning

Seungyeon Lee[1], **Minho Lee**[1,2,3,*]
[1]Department of Artificial Intelligence, Kyungpook National University
[2]School of Electronics Engineering, Kyungpook National University
[3]ALI Co., Ltd.
statai3237@knu.ac.kr, mholee@knu.ac.kr

Abstract

Although Question Answering (QA) have advanced to the human-level language skills in NLP tasks, there is still a problem: the QA model gets confused when there are similar sentences or paragraphs. Existing studies focus on enhancing the text understanding of the candidate answers to improve the overall performance of the QA models. However, since these methods focus on re-ranking queries or candidate answers, they fail to resolve the confusion when many generated answers are similar to the expected answer. To address these issues, we propose a novel contrastive learning framework called ContrastiveQA that alleviates the confusion problem in answer extraction. We propose a supervised method where we generate positive and negative samples from the candidate answers and the given answer, respectively. We thus introduce ContrastiveQA, which uses contrastive learning with sampling data to reduce incorrect answers. Experimental results on four QA benchmarks show the effectiveness of the proposed method.

(Title : Hunter Davies)
Edward Hunter Davies, OBE (born 7 January 1936) is a British author, journalist and broadcaster. He is the author of a number of books, including the only authorized biograph of the Beatles.

(Title : Here We Go Round the Mulberry Bush (film))
Here We Go Round the Mulberry Bush is a 1967 British film made based on the novel of the same name by Hunter Davies.
It was listed to compete at the 1968 Cannes Film Festival, but the festival was cancelled due to the events of May 1968 in France.

(Title : Clive Donner)
Clive Stanley Donner (21 January 1926 – 6 September 2010) was a British film director who was a defining part of the British New Wave, director films such as "The Caretaker", "Nothing But the Best", "Here We Go Round the Mulberry Bush" and "What's New Pussy cat?". He also directed television movies and commercials through the mid-1990s.

(Title : Christopher Mitchell (actor))
Christopher Mitchell (21 May 1947 – 22 February 2001) was a British actor most notable for his role in the BBC sitcom "It Ain't Half Hot Mum" as Gunner Nigel 'Parky' Parkin. His film credits include "Here We Go Round the Mulberry Bush" (1967), "This, That and the Other" (1969), "The Sex Theif " (1973) and "What's Up Superdoc !" (1978).

Question : When was the British author who wrote the novel on which "Here We Go Round the Mulberry Bush" was based born?
Answer : 7 January 1936

Figure 1: An example of HotpotQA dataset that consists of several paragraphs in one context. HotpotQA consists of two supporting paragraphs and eight distractor settings. A distractor paragraph appears to be related to the question but is used to induce confusion.

1 Introduction

Large language model (LLM) is developing rapidly, and ChatGPT (Ouyang et al., 2022), which can perform almost all natural language processing tasks, is receiving tremendous attention. ChatGPT can be easily used by anyone through a conversation interface, and ChatGPT responds appropriately to the user's query. It is clear that ChatGPT has led to tremendous development and success, but it has a fatal problem called hallucination (Alkaissi and McFarlane, 2023; Bang et al., 2023). A generative model such as ChatGPT can have serious consequences if poor decisions are made when it is used in specific domains such as finance, law, and medicine (Shahriar and Hayawi, 2023). To avoid this hallucination problem in specific domains, finding the correct answer within a given document is more reliable. In this paper, we focus on extractive question answering (QA), which extracts the correct answer to a given question in a context. In the field of natural language processing, there are several attempts to solve extractive QA problems that can increase the ability to answer and reason like humans, such as HotpotQA dataset (Yang et al., 2018; Gao et al., 2021; Saxena et al., 2020). However, it is still challenging for the extractive QA model to have a human-level understanding or comprehension skills. In general, humans can easily find and select the correct answer among many similar answers related to the given question. On the contrary, the current QA model is somewhat less capable of selecting the correct answer if the correct answer is confused within the context (Gupta et al., 2018; Kratzwald et al.,

*Corresponding author

Proceedings of the 8th Workshop on Representation Learning for NLP (RepL4NLP 2023), pages 75–86
July 13, 2023

2019; Mao et al., 2021; Glass et al., 2022). To deal with these issues, the conventional methods for improving QA performance use answer re-ranking methods to find the correct answers (Iyer et al., 2021; Majumder et al., 2021). In (Iyer et al., 2021), they use a cross-attention method to build an answer re-ranking model. The (Majumder et al., 2021) seeks to improve the performance of the QA model by explicitly assigning scores to candidate sentences according to the overlap of named entities in the question and sentence. Although the answer re-ranking methods are simple and intuitive, they employ methods of re-ranking answers over a smaller set of candidates rather than considering confusing cases of answer selection. As shown in Fig. 1, a typical QA model explores each sentence to extract an answer to a question. For complex cases like Fig. 1, the QA model may confuse selecting a correct answer during answer extraction and extracting other similar answers. These cases are mainly because the distractor words confuse finding the correct answer.

With this motivation, we propose a novel QA model called ContrastiveQA that uses contrastive learning to pull semantically similar sentences closer and push different sentences further. In addition, the proposed model introduces a method of positive and negative sampling with candidate answers. ContrastiveQA performs the contrastive learning by generating positive and negative samples with the given answer and candidate answers obtained from a pre-finetuned QA model. The proposed model extracts an answer close to the correct answer because the QA model uses a contrastive objective to alleviate the confusing problem of selecting the correct answer.

We demonstrate the effectiveness of our approach on four extractive QA datasets: HotpotQA (Yang et al., 2018), SQuAD (Rajpurkar et al., 2016), TriviaQA (Joshi et al., 2017) and NewsQA (Trischler et al., 2017). We obtain notable performance for the proposed ContrastiveQA, a method learned by contrastive learning, on extractive QA datasets. In particular, the experimental results demonstrate that the proposed method performs significantly better than the previous approaches due to the positive and negative sampling.

Contributions. The main contributions of the proposed ContrastiveQA are as follows :

- We propose a novel method called, ContrastiveQA that effectively solves the problem of ambiguous answer selection and confusion.
- We introduce positive and negative sampling to perform contrastive learning better using QA datasets.
- Experimental results show that the proposed models outperform the baseline models on the extractive QA datasets.

2 Related Works

Contrastive learning for Question Answering. Contrastive learning has achieved remarkable performance in supervised/unsupervised learning and is actively used in image processing (Liang et al., 2020; Wang et al., 2021, 2022). The main goal of contrastive learning is to learn representations that keep similar samples close together and dissimilar samples far apart. In the field of natural language processing, contrastive learning is used to train text representation. Contrastive Domain Adaptive For Question Answering (CAQA) (Yue et al., 2021) proposes a framework for answering out-of-domain questions combining question generation and contrastive domain adaptation to learn domain invariants. This setup can transfer knowledge to the target domain without additional training that can effectively answer the out-of-domain questions. Cross Momentum Contrastive Learning (xMoCo) (Yang et al., 2021) used fast and slow encoders to learn and optimize phrase-question and question-phrase matching. They demonstrated its effectiveness in open-domain QA similar to MoCo (He et al., 2020). It effectively retained large speech samples requiring different question and phrase encoders. (Hu et al., 2022) proposed Momentum Contrastive Pre-Training for Question AnSwering (MCROSS) that employed contrastive learning to align knowledge learned from cloze-type samples to answer natural language questions. This momentum contrastive learning method improved the performance of pre-trained models when answering questions by maximizing the consistency of the distribution of predicted answers. It showed remarkable performance in QA tasks for supervised and zero-shot settings. (Caciularu et al., 2022) applied contrastive learning to reinforce the similarity between the question and evidence sentences. They introduced information encoding to relate the questions to the sentences in order to optimize questions.

They also used similarity mechanisms in specific subspaces by linear projections of raw representations. This method showed consistent improvement in benchmarks with long document context (Yang et al., 2018; Dasigi et al., 2021).

Unlike previous studies, our proposed approach aims to avoid ambiguous answer extraction by processing candidates similar to the correct answer in a set of candidates using contrastive learning.

3 Proposed model

In this work, we propose a novel question-answering (QA) model, called ContrastiveQA. The proposed model allows accurate answers to be extracted by adding a contrastive loss term, which alleviates the confusion and errors that may occur when using the existing QA model.

To achieve this purpose, we divide the training phase into three main steps: candidate answer extraction, positive and negative sampling, and ContrastiveQA to perform contrastive learning. In particular, we introduce a method for creating data to perform ContrastiveQA, where the correct answer is known, in the positive and negative sampling step.

The overall flow of the proposed ContrastiveQA model is shown in Fig. 2.

3.1 Candidate answer extraction

We use the pre-finetuned QA model to perform candidate answer extraction [1]. Like the existing QA models, inputs are questions and contexts, and outputs are answers. When extracting answers, we do not extract only one answer but multiple answers in the order of high confidence score. The QA model gives a confidence score for each of the output answers. And, from among the multiple answers obtained, the most optimal number of candidate answers required for learning are heuristically obtained through experiments (see as subsection 5.2).

Such an extracted candidate answer has a start position and an end position that indicates the answer location within a given context. We represent the candidate answer set by $\mathbb{A}$ that has $\mathbb{A}^{start}$ and $\mathbb{A}^{end}$ in Eq. (1) :

$$\mathbb{A}_{ik}(\mathbb{A}_{ik}^{start}, \mathbb{A}_{ik}^{end}) = QA(q_i, c_i) \tag{1}$$

In $\mathbb{A}_{ik}$, i is the number of contexts and k is the number of candidate answer sets.

3.2 Positive and Negative Sampling

In this subsection, we describe the process of obtaining positive and negative samples to perform contrastive learning. In general, dropout, masking, random change, and back-translation are used to obtain positive and negative samples for contrastive learning in NLP tasks. These methods can be easily applied to obtain samples, but it is challenging to apply to QA tasks because finding correct answers to questions is crucial. We thus utilize the answer's span (start, end) position information to reconstruct the data.

We refer to positive and negative samples as the set of extracted candidates to mitigate the confusing problem of QA models in subsection 3.1. We distinguish between positive and negative samples by comparing the given answers in the training data with the candidate answers.

We consider a candidate answer with the same token as a correct answer token and the same span position (start, end) as a positive sample. We consider a positive sample when the candidate answer and the actual correct answer have the same token positions. Conversely, if the candidate answer and the actual correct answer do not have the same token position, it is considered a negative sample.

Algorithm 1 Procedure of positive and negative sampling for Supervised ContrastiveQA

Input: Candidate answer ($\mathbb{A}_{ik}$), Given answer (A_i)
Output: Positive, Negative samples

Compare the span positions of the candidate answer and the given answer.
Given answer (start, end) position : (A_i^s, A_i^e)
Candidate answer (start, end) position : $(\mathbb{A}_{ik}^s, \mathbb{A}_{ik}^e)$
if $(A_i^s, A_i^e) = (\mathbb{A}_{ik}^s, \mathbb{A}_{ik}^e)$ **then**
    Positive sample
else if $A_i = \mathbb{A}_{ik}$ **and** $(A_i^s, A_i^e) \neq (\mathbb{A}_{ik}^s, \mathbb{A}_{ik}^e)$ **then**
    Negative sample
end if
return Positive, Negative samples for each context

[1]The QA model used to extract the candidate answer is Longformer (Beltagy et al., 2020), which is the backbone model in the experiments. To train the pre-finetuned QA model, we use the data except for the unanswerable of SQuAD v2.0 (Rajpurkar et al., 2018) for training to avoid overlapping data contents. Here, we use the answerable context-question-answer pair of SQuAD v2.0.

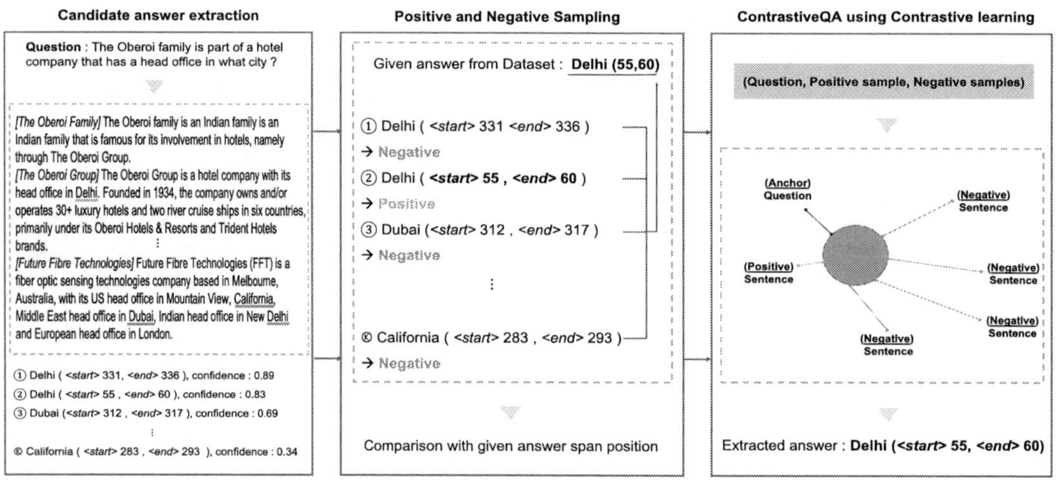

Figure 2: The overall flow of our ContrastiveQA model using the example of HotpotQA. (Left): The process of extracting candidate answers through a pre-finetuned QA model. (Center): In the positive and negative sampling step, positive and negative samples are designated using the given answer information. (Right): Contrastive learning is performed using positive and negative sampling data.

To utilize the positive and negative samples created in long sequences, the sentences with each sample are also designated as candidate sentences corresponding to the candidate answers. We define a candidate sentence set as Eq. (2) :

$$\mathbb{S}_{ik} = \{s_{ij} | \mathbb{A}_{ik} \subset s_{ij}, 1 \leq j \leq M\} \quad (2)$$

where the i-th context has M sentences, and $\mathbb{S}_{ik}$ indicates the sentence to which $\mathbb{A}_{ik}$ belongs. In Algorithm 1, we explain the overall flow for the positive and negative sampling phase.

3.3 ContrastiveQA using contrastive learning

We attempt to address QA problems that can be misleading for distractor words or similar answers using positive and negative samples. First, we use Longformer (Beltagy et al., 2020) as a backbone model to extract an answer with a question and context. We use the context consisting of 15 candidate sentences rather than using the given context. We detail the experiments and analysis of context construction in subsection 5.2. As in previous studies (Beltagy et al., 2020; Zaheer et al., 2020; Caciularu et al., 2021, 2022), we use the special tokens <q> and </s> to indicate question and sentence boundaries to represent sentences in a long context or document as one long sequence. We configure the ContrastiveQA model's input as $[CLS]$ <q> $q_1, q_2, q_3, \cdots$ </s> $s_{11}, s_{12}, \cdots$ </s> $s_{21}, s_{22}, \cdots$ </s> $s_{n1}, s_{n2}, \cdots$ by adding a special token like the input format introduced in Longformer (Beltagy et al., 2020). In the input format, q_i represents a question token, and s_{jk} represents the kth token of the jth sentence. The special tokens are added to the vocabulary and initialized before fine-tuning the model. We define L_{CE} using the cross-entropy loss and L_{QC} using the InfoNCE loss (Oord et al., 2018) to perform contrastive objectives. Then, we define the final loss, L_{CL}, by adjusting L_{CE} and L_{QC} with λ. In the final loss (L_{CL}), λ is weight hyperparameter. We heuristically adjust the λ value to 0.6.

$$\mathcal{L}_{CL} = \lambda \mathcal{L}_{CE} + (1 - \lambda)\mathcal{L}_{QC} \quad (3)$$

L_{CE} calculates the difference between the probability distribution of y and $\hat{y}$, and during training, it learns to reduce this difference. We define it as Eq. (4) :

$$\mathcal{L}_{CE} = -\frac{1}{N}\sum_{i=1}^{N} y_i \log(\hat{y}_i) + (1 - y_i)\log(1 - \hat{y}_i) \quad (4)$$

In L_{QC}, positive sentences (s^+) and question (q) representations are pulled to be close to each other, while negative samples (s^-) are pushed to be far apart from each other. We define it as Eq. (5) :

$$\mathcal{L}_{QC_i} = -log\frac{e^{sim(q_i,s^+)/\tau}}{e^{sim(q_i,s^+)/\tau} + \sum_j^{k-1} e^{sim(q_i,s_j^-)/\tau}} \quad (5)$$

Dataset	Task	QA type	Source	Train set
HotpotQA	Multi-hop question answering	Extractive	Wikipedia	90.4k
SQuAD	Question answering	Extractive	Wikipedia	87.5k
TriviaQA	Reading Comprehension	Extractive	Wikipedia, Web	110k
NewsQA	Reading Comprehension	Extractive	CNN news article	92.5k

Table 1: HotpotQA, SQuAD, TriviaQA, and NewsQA datasets used for experiments.

where sim(·,·) represents similarity between two elements and τ is a configurable temperature parameter. We use Sentence-BERT (SBERT)[2] to calculate the similarity between two sentences. In detail, we experiment with the similarity function in subsection 5.4 and discuss it. Formally, we define the contrastive loss as the sum of the negative log-likelihood losses over all input examples, as introduced in (Caciularu et al., 2022). Here, each loss term distinguishes between positive and negative samples. L_{QC_i} serves one example each, and the final loss (L_{QC}) is obtained as the average loss value over all the examples.

4 Experiment Setup

In this section, we provide experimental datasets and detail about the experiments. We summarize the number of train datasets and the source of the dataset in Table 1.

4.1 Datasets

We use HotpotQA (Yang et al., 2018), SQuAD (Rajpurkar et al., 2016), TriviaQA (Joshi et al., 2017), and NewsQA (Trischler et al., 2017) validation datasets for evaluation.

HotpotQA (Yang et al., 2018) is an multi-hop QA dataset that requires reasoning. In this experiment, we use the HotpotQA-distractor setting. HotpotQA includes yes and no as the answer type, so we add 'yes no' character at the beginning of the context.

SQuAD (Rajpurkar et al., 2016) is a set of QA pairs derived from Wikipedia articles. In SQuAD, the correct answer can be found as a sequence of tokens within the given context. This dataset consists of over 100,000 question-answer pairs.

TriviaQA (Joshi et al., 2017) is a realistic text-based QA dataset obtained from Wikipedia and the Web. TriviaQA has relatively complex and structured questions, with considerable syntactic and lexical variability.

NewsQA (Trischler et al., 2017) is a reading comprehension dataset for CNN news articles. Some answers to questions in the NewsQA dataset may sometimes require reasoning.

4.2 Training details

In the experiment, we evaluate the ContrastiveQA to alleviate the problem of confusion in answer extraction. We use the Longformer-base model of the Huggingface Transformer as the backbone model[3] (Wolf et al., 2020). We use four RTX 8000 GPUs in our experiments. We experiment with a batch size of 8 for the Longformer-based model and 32 for the BERT-based model. We conduct experiments in different optimal experimental settings for each dataset. The learning rate for the datasets HotpotQA and TriviaQA is set to $3e^{-5}$, and the model is trained for five epochs. For other two datasets, SQuAD and NewsQA, the learning rates are set to $5e^{-5}$ and $1e^{-4}$, respectively, and the model is trained for three epochs and five epochs, respectively.

4.3 Baselines

We compare the ContrastiveQA model with eight baselines below :

- **Long-context QA Models**
  - Longformer (Beltagy et al., 2020) encodes long inputs using both sliding-window local attention and global attention.
  - CDLM (Caciularu et al., 2021) is a cross-document language model that learns relationships between documents by pre-training a set of related documents.
  - BigBird (Zaheer et al., 2020) uses up to 4,096 tokens by applying block sparse attention to efficiently look at the tokens.
- **Extractive QA Models**

[2]SBERT(Reimers and Gurevych, 2019) is modified BERT that uses siamese and triplet network structure to derive semantically meaningful sentence embeddings. The code is available at `https://www.sbert.net/`.

[3]`https://huggingface.co/`

Model	Supervised Setting		
	Ans	Sup	Joint
Longformer	76.4	82.2	69.3
CDLM	77.2	85.4	71.7
BigBird	76.8	83.1	70.2
BERT	69.7	74.3	62.1
RoBERTa	73.1	79.2	65.0
SpanBERT	71.5	78.6	63.4
SLED	75.8	80.4	67.9
HGN	81.3	86.2	72.5
ContrastiveQA (ours)	**83.9**	**89.4**	**75.6**

Table 2: Experimental results on the HotpotQA dataset. The best performance is indicated in bold. In this table, **Ans** refers to the answer span, and **Sup** refers to the results of supporting facts. **Joint** is the harmonic mean value obtained by multiplying the recall and precision of **Ans** and **Sup**. The metric for evaluation is the F1 score.

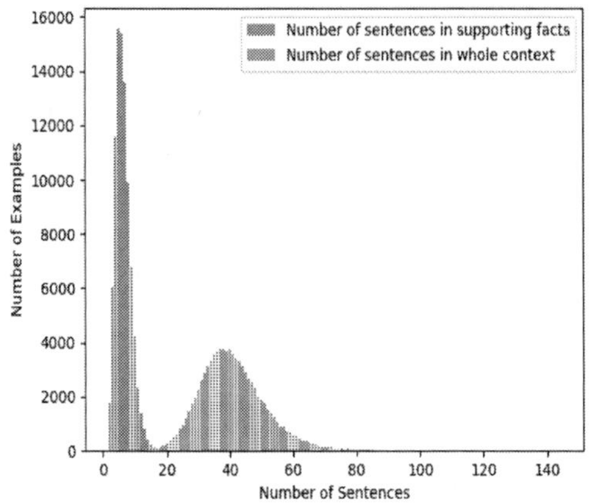

Figure 3: Distribution of the number of sentences in a given context and the number of sentences in supporting facts on the HotpotQA dataset.

- BERT (Devlin et al., 2019) is a pre-trained language model that can understand the context by pre-training MLM (masked language model) and NSP (next sentence prediction).

- RoBERTa (Liu et al., 2019) is a Robustly Optimized BERT Pretraining Approach, and it shows better performance than the existing BERT by adjusting the hyperparameters and training data size of BERT.

- SpanBERT (Joshi et al., 2020) is a model that masks random spans unlike BERT, which masks random tokens and learns a span boundary representation to represent and predict text spans well.

• **Previous Multi-hop QA Models**

- HGN[4] (Fang et al., 2020) is a hierarchical graph network that reinforces answer/evidence prediction through graphs subdivided step by step in a hierarchical framework.

- SLED[5] (Ivgi et al., 2023) is a method of processing long texts using a fusion-in-decoder-based encoder-decoder language model.

5 Model Analysis

5.1 Extractive QA Results

We compare previously superior baseline models for extractive QA with ContrastiveQA.

Supervised ContrastiveQA. We evaluate the performance of models using the F1-score for four benchmarks. Table 2 shows the results of HotpotQA trained by the supervised learning method. Our proposed model results demonstrate improved performance compared to the baseline. In particular, HopotQA, which we used in this experiment, is based on a distractor setting. HotpotQA contains distractor words within the context, causing more confusion in QA tasks. The proposed ContrastiveQA model improves performance by avoiding confusion. In addition, we show excellent performance compared to the existing baseline model based on F1-score for the SQuAD, TriviaQA, and NewsQA datasets in Table 3. Those results demonstrate the effectiveness of positive and negative sampling and contrastive objectives to create positive and negative samples to avoid confusion in a supervised setting.

5.2 Effect of Selecting Candidate sets

We conduct an ablation study with experimental data to prove the effectiveness of the components of the proposed model, ContrastiveQA. We perform an ablation experiment to find the optimal number of candidates in candidate answer extraction introduced in section 3.1. As shown in Fig. 3, the HotpotQA data of the distractor setting has two gold paragraphs and eight distractor paragraphs, so the number of total sentences is very large. However, in practice, the number of sentences required to infer the correct answer is significantly less than

[4]https://github.com/yuwfan/HGN

[5]https://github.com/Mivg/SLED

Model	Supervised Setting		
	SQuAD	TriviaQA	NewsQA
Longformer	91.3	75.8	72.4
CDLM	91.7	76.9	71.8
BigBird	92.0	77.4	73.7
BERT	87.6	70.9	66.1
RoBERTa	89.0	72.2	68.6
SpanBERT	90.2	73.5	71.2
ContrastiveQA (ours)	**93.8**	**81.7**	**77.8**

Table 3: Experimental results on the SQUAD, TriviaQA, and NewsQA dataset. The best performances are indicated in bold. The metric for evaluation is the F1 score.

Model	k	F1-score
	5	69.8
	10	72.3
Longformer	**15**	**76.4**
	20	75.6
	All	73.9
	5	70.4
	10	74.2
CDLM	**15**	**77.2**
	20	76.5
	All	76.0
	5	79.5
	10	82.6
ContrastiveQA (ours)	**15**	**83.9**
	20	82.3
	All	81.8

Table 4: Selection of the optimal number of candidate sets (k) on the HotpotQA validation set. Comparison of performance among Longformer, CDLM, and ContrastiveQA, where k is set to 5, 10, 15, 20, and all data. The best performance is in bold.

the total number of sentences. For this reason, we adopt a method of extracting and using sentences related to the correct answer rather than considering the entire sentence. We experiment using the HotpotQA validation set that has the longest sequence with ten paragraphs as a representative example. We experiment by setting k, the number of candidate sets, to 5, 10, 15, 20, and all data. One becomes a positive sample from the total number of candidates, and the rest becomes negative samples. As shown in Table 4, we get the best performance when the number of candidates is 15 in all three models. Since HotpotQA data are complex and require reasoning, the performance may be reduced if the candidate set is too small. Moreover, if the entire dataset is used up, performance may be deteriorated because the sequence length exceeds the capacity (e.g., 512, 1024, 4096) the model can accommodate. We obtain the optimal k of 15 in the ablation experiment. This means we set one positive sample and the rest as negative samples, 15 samples in the experiment.

λ	HotpotQA (F1)
0.4	79.1
0.5 (Standard)	81.6
0.6 (Optimal)	83.9
0.7	80.7
1.0 (Cross-Entropy loss)	76.4

Table 5: Experimental results on the effect of contrastive loss. When λ is 1.0, it is the same case as using only the cross-entropy loss.

5.3 Effect of Contrastive Loss

In this subsection, we analyze the effect of contrastive loss, a key component of our proposed model. Through experiments, we derive the most optimal result when λ is 0.6. First, we set the weight as 0.5 between the cross-entropy and contrastive loss to find the optimal λ value. Then, we experiment with 0.4 and 0.6 and confirm that the performance is lower when the weight is 0.4 than when the weight is 0.5, but the performance is better when the weight is 0.6. As shown in Table 5, when λ is 1, this is the result of using only the cross-entropy loss, and we demonstrate that the QA result is improved by using the contrastive loss through this ablation experiment. In Table 6, we show an example of both when the contrastive loss is applied and when it is not to demonstrate the effect of contrastive loss more intuitively.

Data fields	Example
Question	Where is the stadium at which 1964 Georgia Tech Yellow Jacket football team played their home game located?
Context	The 1964 Georgia Tech Yellow Jackets football team represented the Georgia Institute of Technology during the 1964 college football season. The Yellow Jackets were led by 20th-year head coach Bobby Dodd, and played their home games at Grant Field in Atlanta, Georgia. They competed as independents for the first time since 1920, after dropping from the Southeastern Conference in 1963. Bobby Dodd Stadium at Historic Grant Field is the football stadium located at the corner of North Avenue at Techwood Drive on the campus of the Georgia Institute of Technology in Atlanta. It has been home to the Georgia Tech Yellow Jackets football team, often referred to as the "RamblinẂreck", in rudimentary form since 1905 and as a complete stadium since 1913. · · · .
Expected Answer (Label)	North Avenue at Techwood Drive
Answer (Longformer)	Grant Field (confidence score : 0.4751)
Answer (ContrastiveQA)	North Avenue at Techwood Drive (confidence score: 0.6833)

Table 6: Example results of Longformer and ContrastiveQA for the HotpotQA validation set. QA results for Longformer and ContrastiveQA are indicated in pink and cyan, respectively.

Similarity	HotpotQA		
	Ans	Sup	Joint
Cosine-similarity	83.5	89.1	74.3
SBERT	83.9	89.4	75.6

Table 7: Experimental results for the similarity function of the contrastive loss. HotpotQA validation set results (F1) for cosine-similarity and SentenceBERT (SBERT).

5.4 Effect of Similarity Function

As briefly described in subsection 3.3, we perform experiments on the similarity function of the contrastive loss term. We experiment using SBERT (Reimers and Gurevych, 2019), which applies not only cosine-similarity, commonly used to calculate the similarity of two sentences (question, sentence), but also sentence-level embedding. In Table 7, we show the results obtained using cosine-similarity and SBERT on the HotpotQA validation set. As a result of HotpotQA, we demonstrate that SBERT performs better than cosine similarity in all three items: answer span, supporting facts, and joint F1.

6 Conclusion

In this work, we proposed a novel ContrastiveQA to alleviate the problem of confusion in answer extraction using contrastive learning. The proposed model ContrastiveQA consists of three tasks: 1) candidate answer extraction, 2) positive and negative sampling, 3) ContrastiveQA using contrastive learning. We demonstrated the effectiveness of the proposed model by outperforming the performance of the baseline models on four benchmark datasets. In the future, we would like to adopt a method to specify the number of samples required in contrastive learning dynamically. This approach created an adaptive mechanism to use the number of samples for each input. This method could improve the overall performance of the model.

7 Limitations

We obtain notable QA performance through experiments. However, we conduct many experiments to find the optimal candidate for ContrastiveQA. Many of these experiments inevitably consume a lot of time and energy, and we have to heuristically determine the number of candidate sets through experiments in a limited environment. We intend to alleviate the current problems by adding a module that can solve these problems in our future research. For example, the Longformer model takes almost a day to process long text for each epoch to train. Therefore, we use smaller batch sizes with a limited number of GPUs to train the LongFormer model. However, due to the lack of GPU resources, the optimal weight of the proposed framework cannot be learned. Thus, it is necessary for further research on model weight reduction to mitigate computational resource problems.

Acknowledgements

This work was partly supported by Institute of Information & communications Technology Planning & Evaluation (IITP) grant funded by the Korea government(MSIT) (No. 2021-0-02068, Artificial Intelligence Innovation Hub), and Center for Applied Research in Artificial Intelligence (CARAI) grant funded by DAPA and ADD (UD230017TD).

References

Hussam Alkaissi and Samy I McFarlane. 2023. Artificial hallucinations in chatgpt: implications in scientific writing. *Cureus*, 15(2).

Yejin Bang, Samuel Cahyawijaya, Nayeon Lee, Wenliang Dai, Dan Su, Bryan Wilie, Holy Lovenia, Ziwei Ji, Tiezheng Yu, Willy Chung, et al. 2023. A multitask, multilingual, multimodal evaluation of chatgpt on reasoning, hallucination, and interactivity. *arXiv preprint arXiv:2302.04023*.

Iz Beltagy, Matthew E. Peters, and Arman Cohan. 2020. Longformer: The long-document transformer. *arXiv:2004.05150*.

Avi Caciularu, Arman Cohan, Iz Beltagy, Matthew Peters, Arie Cattan, and Ido Dagan. 2021. CDLM: Cross-document language modeling. In *Findings of the Association for Computational Linguistics: EMNLP 2021*, pages 2648–2662, Punta Cana, Dominican Republic. Association for Computational Linguistics.

Avi Caciularu, Ido Dagan, Jacob Goldberger, and Arman Cohan. 2022. Long context question answering via supervised contrastive learning. In *Proceedings of the 2022 Conference of the North American Chapter of the Association for Computational Linguistics: Human Language Technologies*, pages 2872–2879, Seattle, United States. Association for Computational Linguistics.

Pradeep Dasigi, Kyle Lo, Iz Beltagy, Arman Cohan, Noah A. Smith, and Matt Gardner. 2021. A dataset of information-seeking questions and answers anchored in research papers. In *Proceedings of the 2021 Conference of the North American Chapter of the Association for Computational Linguistics: Human Language Technologies*, pages 4599–4610, Online. Association for Computational Linguistics.

Jacob Devlin, Ming-Wei Chang, Kenton Lee, and Kristina Toutanova. 2019. BERT: Pre-training of deep bidirectional transformers for language understanding. In *Proceedings of the 2019 Conference of the North American Chapter of the Association for Computational Linguistics: Human Language Technologies, Volume 1 (Long and Short Papers)*, pages 4171–4186, Minneapolis, Minnesota. Association for Computational Linguistics.

Yuwei Fang, Siqi Sun, Zhe Gan, Rohit Pillai, Shuohang Wang, and Jingjing Liu. 2020. Hierarchical graph network for multi-hop question answering. In *Proceedings of the 2020 Conference on Empirical Methods in Natural Language Processing (EMNLP)*, pages 8823–8838, Online. Association for Computational Linguistics.

Yifan Gao, Henghui Zhu, Patrick Ng, Cicero Nogueira dos Santos, Zhiguo Wang, Feng Nan, Dejiao Zhang, Ramesh Nallapati, Andrew O. Arnold, and Bing Xiang. 2021. Answering ambiguous questions through generative evidence fusion and round-trip prediction. In *Proceedings of the 59th Annual Meeting of the Association for Computational Linguistics and the 11th International Joint Conference on Natural Language Processing (Volume 1: Long Papers)*, pages 3263–3276, Online. Association for Computational Linguistics.

Michael Glass, Gaetano Rossiello, Md Faisal Mahbub Chowdhury, Ankita Naik, Pengshan Cai, and Alfio Gliozzo. 2022. Re2G: Retrieve, rerank, generate. In *Proceedings of the 2022 Conference of the North American Chapter of the Association for Computational Linguistics: Human Language Technologies*, pages 2701–2715, Seattle, United States. Association for Computational Linguistics.

Vishal Gupta, Manoj Chinnakotla, and Manish Shrivastava. 2018. Retrieve and re-rank: A simple and effective IR approach to simple question answering over knowledge graphs. In *Proceedings of the First Workshop on Fact Extraction and VERification (FEVER)*, pages 22–27, Brussels, Belgium. Association for Computational Linguistics.

Kaiming He, Haoqi Fan, Yuxin Wu, Saining Xie, and Ross Girshick. 2020. Momentum contrast for unsupervised visual representation learning. In *Proceedings of the IEEE/CVF conference on computer vision and pattern recognition*, pages 9729–9738.

Minda Hu, Muzhi Li, Yasheng Wang, and Irwin King. 2022. Momentum contrastive pre-training for question answering. *arXiv preprint arXiv:2212.05762*.

Maor Ivgi, Uri Shaham, and Jonathan Berant. 2023. Efficient long-text understanding with short-text models. *Transactions of the Association for Computational Linguistics*, 11:284–299.

Srinivasan Iyer, Sewon Min, Yashar Mehdad, and Wen-tau Yih. 2021. RECONSIDER: Improved re-ranking using span-focused cross-attention for open domain question answering. In *Proceedings of the 2021 Conference of the North American Chapter of the Association for Computational Linguistics: Human Language Technologies*, pages 1280–1287, Online. Association for Computational Linguistics.

Mandar Joshi, Danqi Chen, Yinhan Liu, Daniel S. Weld, Luke Zettlemoyer, and Omer Levy. 2020. SpanBERT: Improving pre-training by representing and predicting spans. *Transactions of the Association for Computational Linguistics*, 8:64–77.

Mandar Joshi, Eunsol Choi, Daniel Weld, and Luke Zettlemoyer. 2017. TriviaQA: A large scale distantly supervised challenge dataset for reading comprehension. In *Proceedings of the 55th Annual Meeting of the Association for Computational Linguistics (Volume 1: Long Papers)*, pages 1601–1611, Vancouver, Canada. Association for Computational Linguistics.

Bernhard Kratzwald, Anna Eigenmann, and Stefan Feuerriegel. 2019. Rankqa: Neural question answering with answer re-ranking. In *Annual Meeting of the Association for Computational Linguistics (ACL)*.

Zujie Liang, Weitao Jiang, Haifeng Hu, and Jiaying Zhu. 2020. Learning to contrast the counterfactual samples for robust visual question answering. In *Proceedings of the 2020 Conference on Empirical Methods in Natural Language Processing (EMNLP)*, pages 3285–3292, Online. Association for Computational Linguistics.

Yinhan Liu, Myle Ott, Naman Goyal, Jingfei Du, Mandar Joshi, Danqi Chen, Omer Levy, Mike Lewis, Luke Zettlemoyer, and Veselin Stoyanov. 2019. Roberta: A robustly optimized bert pretraining approach. *arXiv preprint arXiv:1907.11692*.

Sagnik Majumder, Chinmoy Samant, and Greg Durrett. 2021. Model agnostic answer reranking system for adversarial question answering. In *Proceedings of the 16th Conference of the European Chapter of the Association for Computational Linguistics: Student Research Workshop*, pages 50–57, Online. Association for Computational Linguistics.

Yuning Mao, Pengcheng He, Xiaodong Liu, Yelong Shen, Jianfeng Gao, Jiawei Han, and Weizhu Chen. 2021. Reader-guided passage reranking for open-domain question answering. In *Findings of the Association for Computational Linguistics: ACL-IJCNLP 2021*, pages 344–350, Online. Association for Computational Linguistics.

Aaron van den Oord, Yazhe Li, and Oriol Vinyals. 2018. Representation learning with contrastive predictive coding. *arXiv preprint arXiv:1807.03748*.

Long Ouyang, Jeffrey Wu, Xu Jiang, Diogo Almeida, Carroll Wainwright, Pamela Mishkin, Chong Zhang, Sandhini Agarwal, Katarina Slama, Alex Ray, et al. 2022. Training language models to follow instructions with human feedback. *Advances in Neural Information Processing Systems*, 35:27730–27744.

Pranav Rajpurkar, Robin Jia, and Percy Liang. 2018. Know what you don't know: Unanswerable questions for SQuAD. In *Proceedings of the 56th Annual Meeting of the Association for Computational Linguistics (Volume 2: Short Papers)*, pages 784–789, Melbourne, Australia. Association for Computational Linguistics.

Pranav Rajpurkar, Jian Zhang, Konstantin Lopyrev, and Percy Liang. 2016. SQuAD: 100,000+ questions for machine comprehension of text. In *Proceedings of the 2016 Conference on Empirical Methods in Natural Language Processing*, pages 2383–2392, Austin, Texas. Association for Computational Linguistics.

Nils Reimers and Iryna Gurevych. 2019. Sentence-bert: Sentence embeddings using siamese bert-networks. In *Proceedings of the 2019 Conference on Empirical Methods in Natural Language Processing*. Association for Computational Linguistics.

Apoorv Saxena, Aditay Tripathi, and Partha Talukdar. 2020. Improving multi-hop question answering over knowledge graphs using knowledge base embeddings. In *Proceedings of the 58th Annual Meeting of the Association for Computational Linguistics*, pages 4498–4507, Online. Association for Computational Linguistics.

Sakib Shahriar and Kadhim Hayawi. 2023. Let's have a chat! a conversation with chatgpt: Technology, applications, and limitations. *arXiv preprint arXiv:2302.13817*.

Adam Trischler, Tong Wang, Xingdi Yuan, Justin Harris, Alessandro Sordoni, Philip Bachman, and Kaheer Suleman. 2017. NewsQA: A machine comprehension dataset. In *Proceedings of the 2nd Workshop on Representation Learning for NLP*, pages 191–200, Vancouver, Canada. Association for Computational Linguistics.

Xinlong Wang, Rufeng Zhang, Chunhua Shen, Tao Kong, and Lei Li. 2021. Dense contrastive learning for self-supervised visual pre-training. In *Proc. IEEE Conf. Computer Vision and Pattern Recognition (CVPR)*.

Zhaoqing Wang, Yu Lu, Qiang Li, Xunqiang Tao, Yandong Guo, Mingming Gong, and Tongliang Liu. 2022. Cris: Clip-driven referring image segmentation. In *Proceedings of the IEEE/CVF conference on computer vision and pattern recognition*.

Thomas Wolf, Lysandre Debut, Victor Sanh, Julien Chaumond, Clement Delangue, Anthony Moi, Pierric Cistac, Tim Rault, Remi Louf, Morgan Funtowicz, Joe Davison, Sam Shleifer, Patrick von Platen, Clara Ma, Yacine Jernite, Julien Plu, Canwen Xu, Teven Le Scao, Sylvain Gugger, Mariama Drame, Quentin Lhoest, and Alexander Rush. 2020. Transformers: State-of-the-art natural language processing. In *Proceedings of the 2020 Conference on Empirical Methods in Natural Language Processing: System Demonstrations*, pages 38–45, Online. Association for Computational Linguistics.

Nan Yang, Furu Wei, Binxing Jiao, Daxing Jiang, and Linjun Yang. 2021. xMoCo: Cross momentum contrastive learning for open-domain question answering. In *Proceedings of the 59th Annual Meeting of the Association for Computational Linguistics and the 11th International Joint Conference on Natural Language Processing (Volume 1: Long Papers)*, pages 6120–6129, Online. Association for Computational Linguistics.

Zhilin Yang, Peng Qi, Saizheng Zhang, Yoshua Bengio, William Cohen, Ruslan Salakhutdinov, and Christopher D. Manning. 2018. HotpotQA: A dataset for diverse, explainable multi-hop question answering. In *Proceedings of the 2018 Conference on Empirical Methods in Natural Language Processing*, pages 2369–2380, Brussels, Belgium. Association for Computational Linguistics.

Zhenrui Yue, Bernhard Kratzwald, and Stefan Feuerriegel. 2021. Contrastive domain adaptation for question answering using limited text corpora. In *Proceedings of the 2021 Conference on Empirical Methods in Natural Language Processing*, pages 9575–9593, Online and Punta Cana, Dominican Republic. Association for Computational Linguistics.

Manzil Zaheer, Guru Guruganesh, Kumar Avinava Dubey, Joshua Ainslie, Chris Alberti, Santiago Ontanon, Philip Pham, Anirudh Ravula, Qifan Wang, Li Yang, and Amr Ahmed. 2020. Big bird: Transformers for longer sequences. In *Advances in Neural Information Processing Systems*, volume 33, pages 17283–17297. Curran Associates, Inc.

Appendix

A Experimental result examples

A.1 Supervised ContrastiveQA examples

Data fields	Example
Answer	Mark Masons' Hall
Our proposed model answer prediction	Mark Masons' Hall
Baseline model answer prediction	86 St James's Street
Context	Mark Masons' Hall in London is the headquarters of The Grand Lodge of Mark Master Masons of England and Wales, which also controls the Royal Ark Mariner degree. It is located in **86 St James's Street** in the central London district of St James's, opposite St James's Palace. While Freemasons' Hall is the headquarters of the United Grand Lodge of England and the Supreme Grand Chapter of Royal Arch Masons of England, **Mark Masons' Hall** is the home of several other important appendant orders of Freemasonry in England and Wales. St James's Palace is the most senior royal palace in the United Kingdom. Located in the City of Westminster, although no longer the principal residence of the monarch, it is the ceremonial meeting place of the Accession Council and the London residence of several members of the royal family.
Question	What building is opposite the ceremonial meeting place of the Accession Council in the United Kingdom?
Answer	Adelaide
Our proposed model answer prediction	Adelaide
Baseline model answer prediction	Adelaide, about 4 km east of the Adelaide city centre. The suburb is in the City of Norwood
Context	Frewville is a small suburb in the South Australian city of Adelaide. It is three xa0kilometres south-east of Adelaide's central business district (CBD). Norwood is a suburb of **Adelaide, about 4 km east of the Adelaide city centre. The suburb is in the City of Norwood** Payneham & St Peters, the oldest South Australian local government municipality, with a city population over 34,000. Walter Frank Giffen (20 September 1861 in Norwood – 28 June 1949 in Adelaide) was an Australian cricketer who played in 3 Tests between 1887 and 1892. He was the brother of the great all-rounder George Giffen. Glenunga is a small southern suburb of 2,539 people in the South Australian city of Adelaide. It is located five kilometres southeast of the Adelaide city centre. Glenunga is a small southern suburb of 2,539 people in the South Australian city of Adelaide. It is located five kilometres southeast of the Adelaide city centre.
Question	Walter Giffen is from a suburb of which South Australian city?
Answer	2013
Our proposed model answer prediction	2013
Baseline model answer prediction	2015
Context	Frozen Fever is a **2015** American computer-animated musical fantasy short film produced by Walt Disney Animation Studios and released by Walt Disney Pictures. It is a sequel to the **2013** feature film "Frozen", and tells the story of Anna's birthday party given by Elsa with the help of Kristoff, Sven, and Olaf. Chris Buck and Jennifer Lee again served as the directors with Kristen Bell, Idina Menzel, Jonathan Groff, and Josh Gad providing the lead voices. "Making Today a Perfect Day" is a song from the 2015 Walt Disney Animation Studios computer-animated short film "Frozen Fever", with music and lyrics by Kristen Anderson-Lopez and Robert Lopez and performed throughout most of the short. It was released as a single in the United States on March 12, 2015.
Question	What is the year of the event that occured first, Making Today a Perfect Day was produced, or Frozen was produced?

Table A1: Example of answer extraction of Baseline and ContrastiveQA.

In Table A.1, we classify into positive and negative samples using the information of the given correct answer and train them with contrastive loss to derive a result that is closer to the original correct answer when compared with the baseline.

Towards Flow Graph Prediction of Open-Domain Procedural Texts

Keisuke Shirai[1] **Hirotaka Kameko**[2] **Shinsuke Mori**[2]
[1]Graduate School of Informatics, Kyoto University
[2]Academic Center for Computing and Media Studies, Kyoto University
shirai.keisuke.64x@st.kyoto-u.ac.jp {kameko,forest}@i.kyoto-u.ac.jp

Abstract

Machine comprehension of procedural texts is essential for reasoning about the steps and automating the procedures. However, this requires identifying entities within a text and resolving the relationships between the entities. Previous work focused on the cooking domain and proposed a framework to convert a recipe text into a flow graph (FG) representation. In this work, we propose a framework based on the recipe FG for flow graph prediction of open-domain procedural texts. To investigate flow graph prediction performance in non-cooking domains, we introduce the wikiHow-FG corpus from articles on wikiHow, a website of how-to instruction articles. In experiments, we consider using the existing recipe corpus and performing domain adaptation from the cooking to the target domain. Experimental results show that the domain adaptation models achieve higher performance than those trained only on the cooking or target domain data.

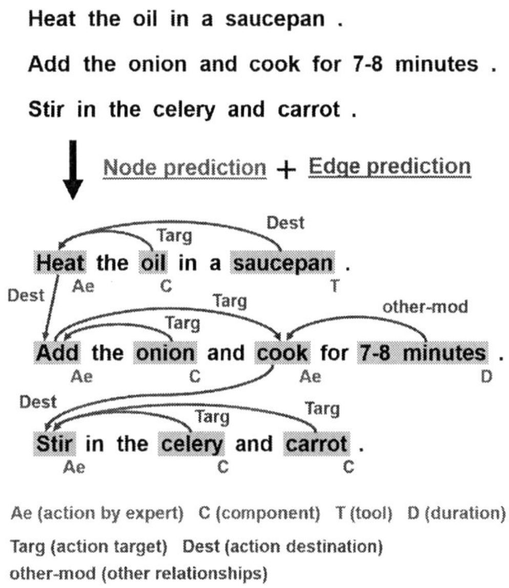

Figure 1: Example of flow graph prediction with our framework. The prediction is in two stages: node prediction (colored in blue) and edge prediction (colored in red). In this work, we use this framework to predict flow graphs of open-domain procedural texts.

1 Introduction

A procedural text guides a human to complete daily activities like cooking and furniture assembly. Machine comprehension of these texts is essential for reasoning about the steps (Zhang et al., 2020b) and automating the procedures (Bollini et al., 2013). However, it needs to identify entities within a text and resolve relationships between the entities. Converting the text into an actionable representation (e.g., flow graph (Momouchi, 1980)) is an approach for solving these problems.

There are several works on converting a procedural text into an action graph (Mori et al., 2014; Kulkarni et al., 2018; Kuniyoshi et al., 2020). In the cooking domain, various approaches (Mori et al., 2014; Kiddon et al., 2015; Pan et al., 2020; Papadopoulos et al., 2022) have been taken because there are a rich amount of available resources on the web. Among them, recipe flow graph (FG) (Mori et al., 2014) has the advantage of capturing fine-grained relationships at entity-level. While the original work (Mori et al., 2014) introduced a framework and corpus in Japanese, the recent work (Yamakata et al., 2020) proposed those in English. The current FG framework has two issues. Since FG is designed to represent the flow of actions in a procedural text, it should be applicable to other procedural domains such as crafting. One is that the framework has only been applied to the cooking domain. The other is that preparing a large number of annotations (e.g., thousands of articles) is unrealistic due to its complex annotation procedures.

In this work, we propose a framework based on the English recipe flow graph (English-FG) (Yamakata et al., 2020) for FG prediction of open-

Proceedings of the 8th Workshop on Representation Learning for NLP (RepL4NLP 2023), pages 87–96
July 13, 2023 ©2023 Association for Computational Linguistics

Tag	Meaning
C (F)	Component (Food)
T	Tool
D	Duration
Q	Quantity
Ae (Ac)	Action by expert (chef)
Ae2 (Ac2)	Discontinuous Ae (Ac)
Ac (Af)	Action by component (food)
At	Action by tool
Sc (Sf)	State of component (food)
St	State of tool

Table 1: Tags and their meanings. The inside of the parenthesis represents a tag and its meaning in English-FG.

Label	Meaning
Agent	Action agent
Targ	Action target
Dest	Action destination
T-comp	Tool complement
C-comp (F-comp)	Component (Food) complement
C-eq (F-eq)	Component (Food) equality
C-part-of (F-part-of)	Component (Food) part-of
C-set (F-set)	Component (Food) set
T-eq	Tool equality
T-part-of	Tool part-of
A-eq	Action equality
V-tm	Head of clause for timing
other-mod	Other relationships

Table 2: Labels and their meanings. The inside of the parenthesis represents a label and its meaning in English-FG.

domain procedural texts. We show the overview of our framework in Figure 1. Our motivation is to expand the scope of the recipe FG to non-cooking domains by treating food ingredients as final product components. Our framework predicts an FG in two stages: node prediction and edge prediction, following Maeta et al. (2015). Our framework is compatible with the English-FG, and we can jointly learn representations from data in the cooking and non-cooking domains. To investigate FG prediction performance in non-cooking domains, we introduce the wikiHow-FG corpus from wikiHow articles. The corpus was constructed by selecting four domains from the wikiHow categories and annotating 30 articles for each domain.

In experiments, we assume a low-resource scenario in which we can access only a few training examples in the target domain. This is a realistic scenario considering the huge annotation cost for FG. To tackle this issue, we consider domain adaptation from the existing cooking domain to the target domain. Experimental results show that domain adaptation models obtain higher performance than those trained only on the cooking or target domain data. We also considered two data augmentation techniques to boost performance. From the results, we found that they improve performance in particular domains.

Our contributions are three-fold:

- We propose a framework based on the English-FG for flow graph prediction of open-domain procedural texts.
- We introduce the wikiHow-FG corpus, a new corpus from wikiHow articles. This corpus is based on four wikiHow domains and has 30 annotated articles for each domain.
- We assume a low-resource scenario in the target domain and consider domain adaptation from the cooking to the target domain. Experimental results show that domain adaptation models outperform those trained only on the cooking or target domain data.

2 Recipe flow graph

In this section, we provide a brief description of the recipe flow graph (FG) (Mori et al., 2014). A recipe FG is a directed acyclic graph $G(V, E)$, where V represents entities as nodes, while E represents the relationships between the nodes as labeled edges. Currently, FG annotations are available in Japanese (Mori et al., 2014) and English (Yamakata et al., 2020), and these corpora provide annotations of hundreds of recipes. Note that Japanese and English frameworks for FG are not compatible since the English FG uses additional tags to handle English-specific expressions. As we focus on texts in English, we consider the English-FG framework (Yamakata et al., 2020) in the following sections.

2.1 Flow graph representation

A recipe FG representation is divided into two types of annotations; node and edge annotations. Nodes represent entities with tags in the IOB-format (Ramshaw and Marcus, 1995). As listed in Table 1, 10 types of tags are used in the English-FG. Labeled edges represent the relationships between the nodes. As listed in Table 2, 13 types of labels are used in the English-FG.

2.2 Flow graph prediction

For the automatic prediction of the FG, previous work (Maeta et al., 2015) proposed to divide the problem into two subtasks: node prediction and edge prediction. In both subtasks, models are trained in a supervised fashion.

Node prediction identifies nodes in an article with the tags. Maeta et al. (2015); Yamakata et al. (2020) formulated this problem as a sequence labeling problem and used NER model (Lample et al., 2016). While predicting tags at sentence-level is common in NER (Lample et al., 2016), previous work (Yamakata et al., 2020) used an entire recipe text as input.[1]

Edge prediction constructs a directed acyclic graph by predicting labeled edges between the nodes. This is formulated as a problem of finding the maximum spanning tree as:

$$\hat{G} = \underset{G \in \mathcal{G}}{\operatorname{argmax}} \sum_{(u,v,l)} s(u, v, l), \tag{1}$$

where $s(u, v, l)$ represents the score of a labeled edge from u to v with label l. We can solve this problem by using the Chu-Liu-Edmonds algorithm. The scores are calculated using a graph-based dependency parser (McDonald et al., 2005).

3 Flow graph prediction of open-domain procedural texts

Our framework is based on the English-FG and applies to non-cooking domains by treating foods in recipe texts as final product components. Examples of the components include tomato and beef for cooking, cardboard and glue for crafting, and gear and tire for vehicle maintenance. The framework uses tags and labels defined in Table 1 and Table 2, respectively. These tags and labels are slightly modified from the definitions in the English-FG to avoid confusion, and we did not add or delete any tags and labels. Therefore, our framework is compatible with the English-FG, and we can learn representations jointly from the cooking and non-cooking domains.

[1]In our preliminary experiments, we found that predicting the tags at document-level improves accuracy by 10% compared to the prediction at sentence-level.

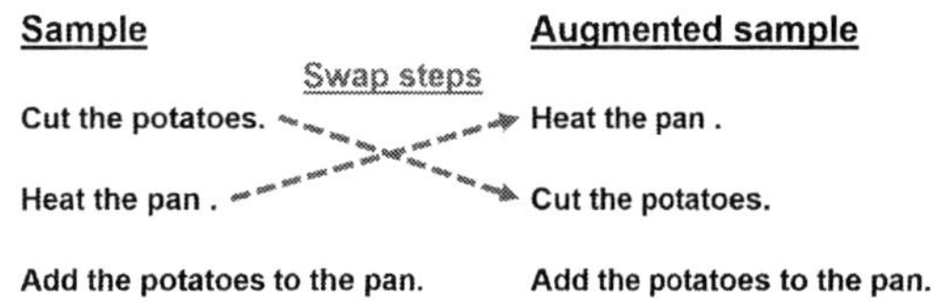

Figure 2: Example of swapping steps. The first and second steps are swappable without violating causality.

With this framework, we consider predicting flow graphs of open-domain procedural texts. The prediction is performed in two stages: node prediction and edge prediction as in Section 2. Models are trained in a supervised way as the previous approach (Maeta et al., 2015). However, preparing a large number of examples in a new domain is unrealistic, considering the huge FG annotation cost. Thus, we assume that only a few training examples are available in the target domain. To tackle this issue, we consider domain adaptation from the existing cooking domain data to the target domain data. In the rest of this section, we formulate the task in Section 3.1, then consider data augmentation techniques that fit our setting in Section 3.2.

3.1 Task definition

We are given N examples in the cooking domain $(V_1^C, E_1^C), \cdots, (V_N^C, E_N^C)$ and M examples in the target domain $(V_1^T, E_1^T), \cdots, (V_M^T, E_M^T)$, where V^C and E^C are a set of vertices and edges in the cooking domain, while V^T and E^T are those in the target domain. Our goal is to maximize the performance of node and edge prediction models in the target domain. In this work, we use the English-FG corpus (300 articles) as the cooking domain examples and the wikiHow-FG corpus (Section 4) as the target domain examples. Note that M is a minimal number (namely, $M = 5$) in our setting, and the task has an aspect of low-resource domain adaptation (Xu et al., 2021). Note also that training with only the cooking or target-domain examples becomes zero-shot or few-shot learning scenarios, respectively.

3.2 Data augmentation

For improving performance in a low-resource setting, data augmentation is one of possible solutions (Fadaee et al., 2017; Ding et al., 2020). In this work, we consider the following two data augmentation techniques: step swapping and word replacement.

Domain	Task examples
Food and Entertaining	*Cooking acorn squash, Making lavender tea, Baking a cherry pie*
Hobbies and Crafts	*Making a bar soap, Making a duct tape bow, Making a paper box*
Home and Garden	*Cleaning a mattress pad, Installing a microwave, Making a scented candle*
Cars & Other Vehicles	*Fixing a slipped bike chain, Cleaning car window, Cleaning tail lights*

Table 3: Examples of article titles for each domain.

Domain	# Characters	# Words	# Steps	# Tags	# Labels
Food and Entertaining	10,167	2,761	224	1,132	1,124
Hobbies and Crafts	9,407	2,556	247	1,062	1,076
Home and Garden	7,700	2,010	205	894	886
Cars & Other Vehicles	6,432	1,622	173	625	622

Table 4: Statistics of the wikiHow-FG corpus.

Step swapping augments an example by replacing two arbitrary steps in an article as illustrated in Figure 2. However, randomly choosing and swapping two steps might break their causal relationship. For example, we cannot swap two steps "Cut the potatoes." and "Add the potatoes to the pan." in Figure 2. In this work, we augment examples keeping this constraint by using flow graph annotations.

Word replacement augments an example by replacing a word with an arbitrary one. For each word in a step, we replace a word with one of its synonyms from WordNet (Dai and Adel, 2020) with a probability p.

4 wikiHow-FG corpus

The wikiHow-FG corpus is a new flow graph corpus from articles on wikiHow[2], a website with more than 110K how-to articles. wikiHow articles have been used as a language resource for procedural texts (Zhou et al., 2019; Zellers et al., 2019; Zhang et al., 2020b,a; Zhou et al., 2022). In the following, we describe the data collection, annotation procedure, and statistics of the annotation results.

4.1 Data collection

For the target domains, we selected four categories from wikiHow: (i) *Food and Entertaining*, (ii) *Hobbies and Crafts*, (iii) *Home and Garden*, and (iv) *Cars & Other Vehicles*. We decided on those domains because many articles target and interact with substantial objects. We show examples of article titles in Table 3. *Food and Entertaining* is a domain close to the cooking domain as with the English-FG. *Hobbies and Crafts* is far from the cooking domain in the sense that they assemble non-edible materials (e.g., *making a bar soap*). The remaining two domains are further from these domains because they contain non-assembly tasks (e.g., *cleaning a table* and *fixing a broken chain*).

We collected 30 articles for each domain from the wikiHow corpus (Zhang et al., 2020b). To exclude low-quality articles, we collected articles with 25 or more words and more than 50% user ratings. We then manually excluded articles with too abstract goals or not targeting substantial objects. We used article headlines as steps for annotation and experiments. Note that each article has a title and visual information (e.g., images or videos) describing the procedures. Exploiting them is interesting, but we leave that direction for future work.

4.2 Annotation procedure

Due to the dense, complex nature of the flow graph, constructing a high-quality corpus is a challenging problem. In order to guarantee the annotation quality, we first trained an annotator with 10 recipes sampled from the English-FG corpus (Yamakata et al., 2020). The training continued until the inter-annotator agreements with the ground-truth annotations reached over 80%. We then asked the annotator to annotate wikiHow articles. For both the node and edge annotations, we used the flow graph annotation tool (Shirai et al., 2022).[3] The whole annotation took 40 hours.

4.3 Statistics

We show statistics of the wikiHow corpus in Table 4. The articles comprise 280.9 characters,

[2] https://www.wikihow.com

[3] Before the annotation, we tokenized steps into words with the stanza toolkit (Qi et al., 2020).

Annotation type	Agreement
Node annotation	90.17%
Edge annotation	57.43%

Table 5: Inter-annotator agreements.

74.6 words, and 7.08 steps on average. The average number of tags and labels per article is 37.73 (±16.48) and 37.47 (±17.21) on *Food and Entertaining*, 35.40 (±9.08) and 35.87 (±9.44) on *Hobbies and Crafts*, 29.80 (±7.83) and 29.53 (±8.29) on *Home and Garden*, and 20.83 (±6.40) and 20.73 (±7.14) on *Cars & Other Vehicles*. Since articles on *Home and Garden* and *Cars & Other Vehicles* have fewer words than the other two domains, the number of tags and labels also becomes smaller.

4.4 Inter-annotator agreements

To assess the consistency of the annotations, we asked another annotator to re-annotate 10% of articles for each domain. We then measured F1 scores between the two sets of annotations using the original annotations as the ground-truth ones. Table 5 shows the results. The agreement for the node annotation (90.14%) was high, considering entities corresponding to the tags greatly change depending on the domain. For the edge annotation, the agreement (57.43%) drops from the one for node annotation. However, this agreement is also high considering errors from the node annotation influence this step and that a large number of candidate edges for the annotation.

5 Node prediction

5.1 Experimental settings

Model. We adopted a BiLSTM-CRF model (Lample et al., 2016) for node prediction by replacing a BiLSTM encoder with a pre-trained language model (LM) (Devlin et al., 2019; Liu et al., 2019; He et al., 2021). While previous work (Yamakata et al., 2020) used a pre-trained BERT (Devlin et al., 2019) as the encoder, we used a pre-trained DeBERTa (He et al., 2021).[4] This model has 140M parameters in total.

Training. We trained a domain adaptation model by first training on the cooking domain data (English-FG) and then training again on the target domain data (wikiHow-FG). Note that we use only target domain examples of the wikiHow-FG corpus (e.g., when targeting *Hobbies and Crafts*, we do not use examples in the other three domains.). We also train models only on the cooking or target domain data and report the results to compare with the domain adaptation results.

For an optimization method, we used AdamW (Loshchilov and Hutter, 2019) with an initial learning rate of 5.0×10^{-5} and a weight decay of 1.0×10^{-5}. We tuned a learning rate with a cosine-annealing (Loshchilov and Hutter, 2019) (S_{d} steps) with a linear warm-up (S_{w} steps) at every iteration. We created a mini-batch from B articles. We set $(B, S_{\mathrm{w}}, S_{\mathrm{d}}) = (5, 500, 4500)$ and $(B, S_{\mathrm{w}}, S_{\mathrm{d}}) = (3, 100, 900)$ for training on the English-FG corpus and the wikiHow-FG corpus, respectively. We tuned these hyper-parameters on the development set. We used the data augmentation techniques only for the target domain data. For the step swapping, we created 5 augmented examples at maximum from one example. For the word replacement, we set 0.5 to p and created 10 examples from one example.

Evaluation. We split the English-FG corpus into 80% for training, 10% for validation, and the rest of 10% for testing. For the wikiHow-FG corpus, we split 30 articles of each domain into 6 folds. For more reliable results, we performed 6-fold cross-validation by using 1 fold for training, 1 fold for validation, and the remaining 4 folds for testing. We used precision, recall, and F1 for evaluation metrics, following Yamakata et al. (2020). On the evaluation, we report the average scores of the models on the test set.

Model configurations. We refer to the domain adaptation models as **domain-adaptation** models. We also refer to the models trained only on the English-FG or the wikiHow-FG corpus as **cooking-only** and **target-only** models, respectively.

5.2 Results

The results are shown in Table 6. We see that the **target-only** models achieve an F1 score of 66.9% or more in all the target domains. This implies that the node prediction model can predict nodes to an extent with a few annotated articles. We also see that the **cooking-only** models achieve competitive performance with the **target-only** ones and outperform them in the two domains of *Food and*

[4] In our preliminary experiments, we confirmed that DeBERTa improves the accuracy of BERT by 0.47% on the English-FG corpus.

Domain	Model	Augmentation		Prec.	Recall	F1
		Step-swap	Word-replace			
Food and Entertaining	Target-only			0.770	0.784	0.777
	Cooking-only			0.884	0.877	0.880
	Domain-adaptation			0.890	0.892	0.891
	Domain-adaptation	✓		**0.894**	**0.895**	**0.895**
	Domain-adaptation		✓	0.885	0.891	0.888
Hobbies and Crafts	Target-only			0.698	0.707	0.702
	Cooking-only			0.703	0.684	0.693
	Domain-adaptation			**0.794**	**0.805**	**0.799**
	Domain-adaptation	✓		0.784	0.795	0.789
	Domain-adaptation		✓	0.781	0.790	0.785
Home and Garden	Target-only			0.663	0.676	0.669
	Cooking-only			0.734	0.742	0.738
	Domain-adaptation			0.780	0.786	0.783
	Domain-adaptation	✓		**0.787**	**0.791**	**0.786**
	Domain-adaptation		✓	0.765	0.773	0.769
Cars & Other Vehicles	Target-only			0.650	0.690	0.669
	Cooking-only			0.646	0.695	0.670
	Domain-adaptation			**0.748**	**0.784**	**0.765**
	Domain-adaptation	✓		0.734	**0.784**	0.761
	Domain-adaptation		✓	0.729	0.772	0.750

Table 6: Results of the node prediction experiments. The check mark symbol (✓) indicates the used training data (in cooking and target domains) and augmentation techniques (step-swap and word-replace).

Domain	Ae			C			T		
	Duplicates	F1		Duplicates	F1		Duplicates	F1	
		Src	Adpt		Src	Adpt		Src	Adpt
Food and Entertaining	92.06%	0.941	0.952	72.11%	0.932	0.933	77.94%	0.896	0.882
Hobbies and Crafts	69.03%	0.943	0.951	10.33%	0.717	0.833	51.79%	0.398	0.588
Home and Garden	65.19%	0.954	0.961	18.40%	0.716	0.795	43.55%	0.567	0.678
Cars & Other Vehicles	46.04%	0.905	0.919	6.88%	0.666	0.805	27.47%	0.459	0.557

Table 7: F1 scores of Ae, C, and T tags with the percentage of entities that appeared in the English-FG corpus and also in the wikiHow-FG corpus. Src and Adpt denote **cooking-only** and **domain-adaptation** models, respectively.

Entertaining and *Home and Garden*. Particularly in *Food and Entertaining*, the **cooking-only** model surpasses the **target-only** one by 10.3% in F1. We consider that this domain is close to the cooking domain of the English-FG; thus, the **cooking-only** model is more advantageous as it can access more examples.

Next, the **domain-adaptation** models achieve the best performance in all the domains compared with the **cooking-only** and **target-only** models (76.5% or more F1). The most significant improvements are obtained in the two domains of *Hobbies and Crafts* and *Cars & Other Vehicles* (9.5% and 10.5% improvements in F1). These results indicate that domain adaptation from the cooking to the target domain is effective for training the node prediction model.

Third, we see that using the augmented data by the step swapping slightly improves performance from the **domain-adaptation** models in *Food and Entertaining* and *Home and Garden*. On the other hand, the word replacement does not contribute to any improvement. One possible reason is that a replaced word does not necessarily match the corresponding tag, and this disrupts the improvement.

5.3 Tag-level prediction performance

Entities for each tag can greatly change depending on the domain. In that case, the degree of improvement from the **cooking-only** to the **domain-adaptation** model is expected to increase as the duplicate entities between the domains decrease.

Domain	Model	Augmentation		Prec.	Recall	F1
		Step-Swap	Word-Replace			
Food and Entertaining	Target-only			0.335	0.338	0.337
	Cooking-only			0.725	0.731	0.728
	Domain-adaptation			0.750	**0.756**	**0.753**
	Domain-adaptation	✓		0.747	0.752	0.750
	Domain-adaptation		✓	**0.761**	0.752	0.749
Hobbies and Crafts	Target-only			0.285	0.281	0.283
	Cooking-only			0.613	0.605	0.609
	Domain-adaptation			0.649	0.640	0.644
	Domain-adaptation	✓		0.646	0.638	0.642
	Domain-adaptation		✓	**0.653**	**0.644**	**0.648**
Home and Garden	Target-only			0.229	0.232	0.231
	Cooking-only			0.644	0.649	0.646
	Domain-adaptation			0.659	0.665	0.662
	Domain-adaptation	✓		0.656	0.662	0.659
	Domain-adaptation		✓	**0.674**	**0.680**	**0.677**
Cars & Other Vehicles	Target-only			0.154	0.155	0.154
	Cooking-only			0.587	0.590	0.587
	Domain-adaptation			0.607	0.610	0.609
	Domain-adaptation	✓		0.607	0.610	0.608
	Domain-adaptation		✓	**0.617**	**0.620**	**0.618**

Table 8: Results of the edge prediction experiments. The check mark symbol (✓) indicates the used training data (in cooking and target domains) and augmentation techniques (step-swap and word-replace).

To investigate this assumption, we measured tag-level prediction performance in F1 with the duplicate ratio of entities of the wikiHow-FG in the English-FG. We targeted the three tags of Ae, C, and T because these tags frequently appear in all the domains.

The results are shown in Table 7. For Ae, the degree of improvement from the **cooking-only** to the **domain-adaptation** model is small regardless of the duplicate ratios, which is contrary to our assumption. These results imply that recognizing entities for Ae is easy irrespective of the domain. For C and T, the **domain-adaptation** models significantly outperform the **cooking-only** ones in the three domains other than *Food and Entertaining*. These results imply that the domain adaptation is effective for recognizing C and T tags when the domain is further from the cooking domain.

6 Edge prediction

6.1 Experimental settings

Model. We adopted a biaffine dependency parser (Dozat and Manning, 2018) for edge prediction.[5] This model uses separate modules for edge prediction and label prediction. The resulting loss l is defined as a weighted sum of losses from the two modules:

$$l = \lambda l^{(\text{edge})} + (1 - \lambda) l^{(\text{label})}, \quad (2)$$

where λ controls the strength of the two losses. We empirically set 0.5 to λ. We used a pre-trained DeBERTa (He et al., 2021) to obtain contextualized word representations. This model has 149M parameters in total.

Training. Similarly to Section 5.1, we trained a domain adaptation model for edge prediction first on the English-FG corpus and then on the wikiHow-FG corpus. For an optimization method, we used AdamW (Loshchilov and Hutter, 2019) with a combination of a cosine-annealing and linear warm-up learning rate scheduling method. We used the same hyperparameters in Section 5.1.

Evaluation. We used the same splits of the English-FG and wikiHow-FG corpora as in Section 5 and performed 6-fold cross-validation for

[5] Previous work (Maeta et al., 2015) used a linear model, but we confirmed that our model achieves higher performance on the English-FG corpus.

Domain	F1
Food and Entertaining	0.679 (-9.8%)
Hobbies and Crafts	0.501 (-22.2%)
Home and Garden	0.494 (-25.4%)
Cars & Other Vehicles	0.449 (-26.3%)

Table 9: Results of the pipeline experiments. The inside of the parenthesis represents the performance drop from the **domain-adaptation** model with ground-truth tags.

more reliable results. We report the average scores of the models on the test set. For evaluation metrics, we used precision, recall, and F1 between predicted and ground-truth labeled edges of (u, v, l).

Model configurations. We used the same model notations of **cooking-only**, **target-only**, and **domain-adaptation** models as in Section 5.

6.2 Results

The results are shown in Table 8. We used ground-truth tags to identify nodes. Contrary to the node prediction results, the **target-only** models achieve poor performance in all the domains (33.8% or less in all the metrics). On the other hand, the scores of the **cooking-only** models are more than twice those of the **target-only** models. These results show that the edge prediction model requires more training examples than the node prediction one. These also show that with the English-FG corpus, predicting edges with 58.7% or more F1 is possible in non-cooking domains.

Next, the **domain-adaptation** models outperform the **target-only** and **cooking-only** ones in all the domains. This is consistent with the results in the node prediction task. These results mean that the domain adaptation from the cooking to the target domain is also effective for the edge prediction model. For the results with the data augmentation techniques, the step swapping does not contribute to any improvement, contrary to Section 5.2. The word replacement improves the performance of the **domain-adaptation** models in the three domains other than *Food and Entertaining*.

6.3 Pipeline experiments

So far, the model has used ground-truth tags to identify nodes. However, in a realistic scenario, the model must predict labeled edges with the predicted nodes. In this scenario, errors in the node prediction step would affect performance in the edge prediction step. To investigate edge prediction performance in this setting, we conducted experiments of edge prediction with the predicted nodes. We predicted nodes using the models in Section 5.2. In order to evaluate the model with tag information, we measured F1 of tuples of (u, v, l, n_u, n_v) between ground-truth and predicted ones, where n_u and n_v are the tags of the starting and ending nodes, respectively.

Table 9 shows the results with performance drops from those in Table 8. We see that 9.8% drops in *Food and Entertaining*, and more significant drops occur in the other three domains (about 24.6%). In these three domains, F1 scores of the node prediction are about 10% smaller than that of *Food and Entertaining*, and this gap would cause such large performance drops. We consider that improving node prediction performance would alleviate these drops.

7 Related work

Mori et al. (2014) designed a flow graph (FG) representation in the cooking domain and introduced a corpus of recipe texts. Subsequent works introduced a corpus in English (Yamakata et al., 2020) and corpora with visual annotations (Nishimura et al., 2020; Shirai et al., 2022). Maeta et al. (2015) proposed a method for an automatic FG prediction. Our work stems from this line of research and is the first attempt to apply the framework to non-cooking domains. Ours is also the first work to use a neural network-based method for the edge prediction.

Other than the recipe FG, there are several works that focus on obtaining an actionable representation from a procedural text. In cooking, Kiddon et al. (2015) proposed an unsupervised EM algorithm, while Pan et al. (2020); Papadopoulos et al. (2022) proposed supervised approaches. In biochemistry, Kulkarni et al. (2018); Tamari et al. (2021) introduced datasets for mapping wet lab protocols to an action graph. In material science, Kuniyoshi et al. (2020) represented the synthesis process with flow graphs. The works (Pan et al., 2020; Papadopoulos et al., 2022; Tamari et al., 2021; Kuniyoshi et al., 2020) are especially close to ours in the sense that they aim to obtain a document-level action graph in a supervised way.

8 Conclusion

We proposed a framework based on the English-FG and investigated flow graph prediction performance in non-cooking domains. We presented the wikiHow-FG corpus from wikiHow articles. We considered domain adaptation from the cooking to the target domain. Experimental results show that domain adaptation models outperform those trained only on the cooking or target domain data. In future work, we consider applying this framework to other domains, such as material science and biochemistry. One can also try improving performance using more sophisticated data augmentation techniques. We hope that our work will provide new insights into procedural text understanding.

Acknowledgments

We would like to thank anonymous reviewers for their insightful comments. This work was supported by JSPS KAKENHI Grant Number 20H04210 and 21H04910.

References

Mario Bollini, Stefanie Tellex, Tyler Thompson, Nicholas Roy, and Daniela Rus. 2013. Interpreting and executing recipes with a cooking robot. In *Experimental Robotics*, pages 481–495. Springer.

Xiang Dai and Heike Adel. 2020. An analysis of simple data augmentation for named entity recognition. In *Proceedings of the 28th International Conference on Computational Linguistics*, pages 3861–3867. International Committee on Computational Linguistics.

Jacob Devlin, Ming-Wei Chang, Kenton Lee, and Kristina Toutanova. 2019. BERT: Pre-training of deep bidirectional transformers for language understanding. In *Proceedings of the 2019 Conference of the North American Chapter of the Association for Computational Linguistics: Human Language Technologies (Volume 1: Long and Short Papers)*, pages 4171–4186. Association for Computational Linguistics.

Bosheng Ding, Linlin Liu, Lidong Bing, Canasai Kruengkrai, Thien Hai Nguyen, Shafiq Joty, Luo Si, and Chunyan Miao. 2020. DAGA: Data augmentation with a generation approach for low-resource tagging tasks. In *Proceedings of the 2020 Conference on Empirical Methods in Natural Language Processing (EMNLP)*, pages 6045–6057. Association for Computational Linguistics.

Timothy Dozat and Christopher D. Manning. 2018. Simpler but more accurate semantic dependency parsing. In *Proceedings of the 56th Annual Meeting of the Association for Computational Linguistics (Volume 2: Short Papers)*, pages 484–490. Association for Computational Linguistics.

Marzieh Fadaee, Arianna Bisazza, and Christof Monz. 2017. Data augmentation for low-resource neural machine translation. In *Proceedings of the 55th Annual Meeting of the Association for Computational Linguistics (Volume 2: Short Papers)*, pages 567–573. Association for Computational Linguistics.

Pengcheng He, Xiaodong Liu, Jianfeng Gao, and Weizhu Chen. 2021. Deberta: decoding-enhanced bert with disentangled attention. In *9th International Conference on Learning Representations*.

Chloé Kiddon, Ganesa Thandavam Ponnuraj, Luke Zettlemoyer, and Yejin Choi. 2015. Mise en place: Unsupervised interpretation of instructional recipes. In *Proceedings of the 2015 Conference on Empirical Methods in Natural Language Processing*, pages 982–992. Association for Computational Linguistics.

Chaitanya Kulkarni, Wei Xu, Alan Ritter, and Raghu Machiraju. 2018. An annotated corpus for machine reading of instructions in wet lab protocols. In *Proceedings of the 2018 Conference of the North American Chapter of the Association for Computational Linguistics: Human Language Technologies, Volume 2 (Short Papers)*, pages 97–106. Association for Computational Linguistics.

Fusataka Kuniyoshi, Kohei Makino, Jun Ozawa, and Makoto Miwa. 2020. Annotating and extracting synthesis process of all-solid-state batteries from scientific literature. In *Proceedings of the Twelfth Language Resources and Evaluation Conference*, pages 1941–1950. European Language Resources Association.

Guillaume Lample, Miguel Ballesteros, Sandeep Subramanian, Kazuya Kawakami, and Chris Dyer. 2016. Neural architectures for named entity recognition. In *Proceedings of the 2016 Conference of the North American Chapter of the Association for Computational Linguistics: Human Language Technologies*, pages 260–270. Association for Computational Linguistics.

Yinhan Liu, Myle Ott, Naman Goyal, Jingfei Du, Mandar Joshi, Danqi Chen, Omer Levy, Mike Lewis, Luke Zettlemoyer, and Veselin Stoyanov. 2019. Roberta: A robustly optimized bert pretraining approach. *arXiv preprint arXiv:1907.11692*.

Ilya Loshchilov and Frank Hutter. 2019. Decoupled weight decay regularization. In *Proceedings of the 7th International Conference on Learning Representations*.

Hirokuni Maeta, Tetsuro Sasada, and Shinsuke Mori. 2015. A framework for procedural text understanding. In *Proceedings of the 14th International Conference on Parsing Technologies*, pages 50–60. Association for Computational Linguistics.

Ryan McDonald, Fernando Pereira, Kiril Ribarov, and Jan Hajič. 2005. Non-projective dependency parsing using spanning tree algorithms. In *Proceedings of Human Language Technology Conference and Conference on Empirical Methods in Natural Language*

Processing, pages 523–530. Association for Computational Linguistics.

Yoshio Momouchi. 1980. Control structures for actions in procedural texts and PT-chart. In *COLING 1980 Volume 1: The 8th International Conference on Computational Linguistics*.

Shinsuke Mori, Hirokuni Maeta, Yoko Yamakata, and Tetsuro Sasada. 2014. Flow graph corpus from recipe texts. In *Proceedings of the Ninth International Conference on Language Resources and Evaluation*, pages 2370–2377.

Taichi Nishimura, Suzushi Tomori, Hayato Hashimoto, Atsushi Hashimoto, Yoko Yamakata, Jun Harashima, Yoshitaka Ushiku, and Shinsuke Mori. 2020. Visual grounding annotation of recipe flow graph. In *Proceedings of the 12th Language Resources and Evaluation Conference*, pages 4275–4284. European Language Resources Association.

Liang-Ming Pan, Jingjing Chen, Jianlong Wu, Shaoteng Liu, Chong-Wah Ngo, Min-Yen Kan, Yugang Jiang, and Tat-Seng Chua. 2020. Multi-modal cooking workflow construction for food recipes. In *Proceedings of the 28th ACM International Conference on Multimedia*, page 1132–1141. Association for Computing Machinery.

Dim P. Papadopoulos, Enrique Mora, Nadiia Chepurko, Kuan Wei Huang, Ferda Ofli, and Antonio Torralba. 2022. Learning program representations for food images and cooking recipes. In *Proceedings of the IEEE/CVF Conference on Computer Vision and Pattern Recognition (CVPR)*, pages 16559–16569.

Peng Qi, Yuhao Zhang, Yuhui Zhang, Jason Bolton, and Christopher D. Manning. 2020. Stanza: A python natural language processing toolkit for many human languages. In *Proceedings of the 58th Annual Meeting of the Association for Computational Linguistics: System Demonstrations*, pages 101–108. Association for Computational Linguistics.

Lance Ramshaw and Mitch Marcus. 1995. Text chunking using transformation-based learning. In *Third Workshop on Very Large Corpora*.

Keisuke Shirai, Atsushi Hashimoto, Taichi Nishimura, Hirotaka Kameko, Shuhei Kurita, Yoshitaka Ushiku, and Shinsuke Mori. 2022. Visual recipe flow: A dataset for learning visual state changes of objects with recipe flows. In *Proceedings of the 29th International Conference on Computational Linguistics*, pages 3570–3577. International Committee on Computational Linguistics.

Ronen Tamari, Fan Bai, Alan Ritter, and Gabriel Stanovsky. 2021. Process-level representation of scientific protocols with interactive annotation. In *Proceedings of the 16th Conference of the European Chapter of the Association for Computational Linguistics: Main Volume*, pages 2190–2202. Association for Computational Linguistics.

Haoran Xu, Seth Ebner, Mahsa Yarmohammadi, Aaron Steven White, Benjamin Van Durme, and Kenton Murray. 2021. Gradual fine-tuning for low-resource domain adaptation. In *Proceedings of the Second Workshop on Domain Adaptation for NLP*, pages 214–221. Association for Computational Linguistics.

Yoko Yamakata, Shinsuke Mori, and John A Carroll. 2020. English recipe flow graph corpus. In *Proceedings of the 12th Language Resources and Evaluation Conference*, pages 5187–5194. European Language Resources Association.

Rowan Zellers, Ari Holtzman, Yonatan Bisk, Ali Farhadi, and Yejin Choi. 2019. HellaSwag: Can a machine really finish your sentence? In *Proceedings of the 57th Annual Meeting of the Association for Computational Linguistics*, pages 4791–4800. Association for Computational Linguistics.

Li Zhang, Qing Lyu, and Chris Callison-Burch. 2020a. Intent detection with WikiHow. In *Proceedings of the 1st Conference of the Asia-Pacific Chapter of the Association for Computational Linguistics and the 10th International Joint Conference on Natural Language Processing*, pages 328–333. Association for Computational Linguistics.

Li Zhang, Qing Lyu, and Chris Callison-Burch. 2020b. Reasoning about goals, steps, and temporal ordering with WikiHow. In *Proceedings of the 2020 Conference on Empirical Methods in Natural Language Processing*, pages 4630–4639. Association for Computational Linguistics.

Shuyan Zhou, Li Zhang, Yue Yang, Qing Lyu, Pengcheng Yin, Chris Callison-Burch, and Graham Neubig. 2022. Show me more details: Discovering hierarchies of procedures from semi-structured web data. In *Proceedings of the 60th Annual Meeting of the Association for Computational Linguistics (Volume 1: Long Papers)*, pages 2998–3012. Association for Computational Linguistics.

Yilun Zhou, Julie Shah, and Steven Schockaert. 2019. Learning household task knowledge from WikiHow descriptions. In *Proceedings of the 5th Workshop on Semantic Deep Learning (SemDeep-5)*, pages 50–56. Association for Computational Linguistics.

One does *not* fit all!
On the Complementarity of Vision Encoders for Vision and Language Tasks

Gregor Geigle[*], **Chen Cecilia Liu**, **Jonas Pfeiffer**[†], **Iryna Gurevych**
Ubiquitous Knowledge Processing Lab (UKP Lab)
Department of Computer Science and Hessian Center for AI (hessian.AI)
Technical University of Darmstadt
www.ukp.tu-darmstadt.de

Abstract

Current multimodal models, aimed at solving Vision and Language (V+L) tasks, predominantly repurpose Vision Encoders (VE) as feature extractors. While many VEs—of different architectures, trained on different data and objectives—are publicly available, they are not designed for the downstream V+L tasks. Nonetheless, most current work assumes that a *single* pre-trained VE can serve as a general-purpose encoder. In this work, we focus on analysis and aim to understand whether the information stored within different VEs is complementary, i.e. if providing the model with features from multiple VEs can improve the performance on a target task, and how they are combined. We exhaustively experiment with three popular VEs on six downstream V+L tasks and analyze the attention and VE-dropout patterns. Our analyses suggest that diverse VEs complement each other, resulting in improved downstream V+L task performance, where the improvements are not due to simple ensemble effects (i.e. the performance does not always improve when increasing the number of encoders). We demonstrate that future VEs, which are not *repurposed*, but explicitly *designed* for V+L tasks, have the potential of improving performance on the target V+L tasks.

1 Introduction

The dominant strategy for solving Vision+Language (V+L) tasks involves using Transformer models (Vaswani et al., 2017) that jointly attend over the representations of the respective modalities (Lu et al., 2019; Su et al., 2020; Li et al., 2020b; Chen et al., 2020; Huang et al., 2020, *inter alia*). While representation-learning of the text modality is comparatively straightforward using token embeddings,[1] image representations are more difficult to learn. Given an image, a common approach is to use pre-trained Vision Encoders (VE), where the VE's output features are passed as inputs, together with the text embeddings, into a Transformer model. The attention mechanism then learns a cross-modal representation space over the text and image features to solve the target V+L task.

Consequently, the success of a multimodal model builds heavily on the features extracted from a VE and is thus highly dependent on the VE's architecture, training objectives (e.g. image classification, image encoding, object detection, etc.), and pre-training data. This dependency is further exacerbated for multimodal models that utilize VEs as static feature extractors (i.e. the weights of the VE are frozen), but also for models that are trained end-to-end, as the biases introduced by the architecture, objectives, and data of the VE remain.

Since many computer vision models can be *repurposed* as VEs for V+L tasks, a few prior works have focused on identifying *individual* VEs that perform the best on downstream tasks (Jiang et al., 2020; Shen et al., 2022; Eichenberg et al., 2022; Zhang et al., 2021). A common assumption is that a *single* pre-trained VE can perform the best for a target task or even serve as a general-purpose encoder for a wide range of V+L tasks. However, a natural question arises: to what extent is this assumption correct? Given that all VEs differ in architecture, objectives, and pre-training data, we hypothesize that the extracted features of multiple different VEs encode *complementary* information.

In this work, we focus on answering: 1) Do different VEs encode complementary features? 2) *How* are features from different VEs utilized by Transformers? We provide comprehensive analyses for multi-VE models and test whether combining VEs is beneficial over a single-VE setup under the viewpoint of feature complementarity. Similar to prior work that analyzed other components of V+L

[*] Gregor is now affiliated with WüNLP & Computer Vision Lab, CAIDAS, University of Würzburg.

[†] Jonas is now affiliated with Google DeepMind.

[1] But still far from solved especially in multilingual settings (Rust et al., 2021; Clark et al., 2022; Xue et al., 2022)

Proceedings of the 8th Workshop on Representation Learning for NLP (RepL4NLP 2023), pages 97–117
July 13, 2023 ©2023 Association for Computational Linguistics

Transformers (Bugliarello et al., 2021; Hendricks et al., 2021), we will not focus on improving the performance through ensembling like Yan et al. (2021b). Rather, we utilize combinations of VEs as the setting for answering our research questions.

We cover three popular classes of VEs in our experiments: 1) object detection models providing a feature representation of salient image parts containing objects (*Region*) (Anderson et al., 2018), 2) CNN models computing a feature map of the image for grid features (*Grid*), and 3) Vision Transformers (ViT) (Dosovitskiy et al., 2021) computing contextualized patch features of the image (*Patch*). As the downstream domain and task type can be heavily impacted by the different VEs, we probe all combinations of the **three** VEs on **six** different V+L tasks, covering retrieval, Q&A, and reasoning.

To investigate the VE complementarity and feature utilization, we analyze 1) the attention patterns across modalities and VEs, and 2) the dependency of specific VEs when performing VE-dropout during training and inference. While multi-VE seems to perform better than single-VE (which could partially attribute to the increased parameter count), we consistently observe performance gaps between different multi-VE configurations (e.g. a gap as large as 8.9 points for the same task) and no single winning combination for all task types. Our attention patterns analysis across the different VEs reveals that the distinctive information encoded in the VEs is important for different tasks, and the model composes the representations by enriching a dominant VE with complementary information of the other VEs.

To sum up, our results and analysis suggest that VEs trained on different objectives, architectures, and data can have a high impact on the model's V+L task performance. We cannot rely on simple ensemble effects to improve performance; selecting and repurposing off-the-shelf VEs is non-trivial, which emphasizes the necessity to design VEs explicitly for V+L tasks in the future.

2 Related Work

Multimodal Transformer Architectures. Multimodal Transformer architectures can be divided into single-stream and dual-stream models (Bugliarello et al., 2021). The single-stream Transformer takes the concatenated visual and text tokens as input and processes them modality-agnostic, i.e. the self-attention jointly attends over the tokens of both modalities. Dual-stream models use separate Transformers for each modality that are connected through a co-attention mechanism (Tan and Bansal, 2019; Lu et al., 2019), concatenated in a single-stream model on top (Singh et al., 2022; Kamath et al., 2021), or the image model output is used asymmetrically for cross-attention in the text model (Li et al., 2021, 2022).

The Faster R-CNN (Ren et al., 2015) object detector has been the dominant choice for multimodal models as a *Region* VE, where most methods propose to use it as a static feature extractor (Tan and Bansal, 2019; Lu et al., 2019; Su et al., 2020; Chen et al., 2020; Gan et al., 2020; Li et al., 2020b; Zhang et al., 2021; Cho et al., 2021), with the notable exception being Su et al. (2020) who backpropagate through the Faster R-CNN model. Less popular VEs are *Grid* (Huang et al., 2020; Kamath et al., 2021; Yan et al., 2021a; Shen et al., 2022; Eichenberg et al., 2022), and *Patch* (Kim et al., 2021; Wang et al., 2022; Eichenberg et al., 2022). In contrast to *Region* VEs, *Grid* and *Patch* VEs are commonly fine-tuned on the target V+L task, with the notable exception being Yan et al. (2021a). Following Bugliarello et al. (2021); Hendricks et al. (2021) we focus on single-stream models as they have been shown to perform on par with dual-stream models while being easier to extend to multi-VE setups.

Comparing and Combining VEs. Recently, several works aim to compare different VEs for V+L tasks. Jiang et al. (2020) compare *Region* and *Grid* for visual QA tasks, showing that training data, objectives and other factors all affect the downstream task performance. Shen et al. (2022); Eichenberg et al. (2022) compare different pre-trained *Grid* and *Patch* VEs building on CLIP (Radford et al., 2021). Zhang et al. (2021) compare different design choices for *Region* VEs with *Grid* VEs trained on the same data. Dai et al. (2023) compares different VEs in influence object hallucinations in caption generation. Closest to our work is the work by Yan et al. (2021b). While they also experiment with combining representations of *Grid-*, *Patch-*, and *Region* VEs, they only focus on the Visual Question Answering (VQA; Goyal et al., 2017) dataset and only use the combination of all three VEs. Our work provides a more in-depth evaluation of different multi-VE setups while experimenting with six diverse tasks, and shows that different combinations work best for each task.

Analysis of Multimodal Transformers. Our analysis methods draw inspiration from recent works that probe and analyze pre-trained multimodal Transformers for a better understanding of their different components (Bugliarello et al., 2021; Cao et al., 2020; Li et al., 2020a; Frank et al., 2021; Hendricks et al., 2021). Cao et al. (2020) propose a range of different probing tasks to understand the inner workings of multimodal models. Li et al. (2020a) analyze how accurate the attention heads of pre-trained models can perform visual grounding. Frank et al. (2021) mask parts of the text and image input and measure how the prediction performance changes for the respective other modality to test how symmetric the learned cross-modal connection is. Bugliarello et al. (2021); Hendricks et al. (2021) evaluate and disentangle which components of multimodal pre-training proposed in different works are important for their success. While previous work has only focused on models with a *Region* VE, we also experiment with *Grid* and *Patch* VEs.

In summary, our work is the first in-depth study of multimodal Transformers that use multiple VEs.

3 Multimodal Multi-VE Transformers

Recently, cross-modal attention is the dominant strategy to learn multimodal representations with V+L Transformers. In this work, we follow Bugliarello et al. (2021) and focus on the single-stream architecture, which shares the attention components across all modalities, i.e. the concatenated visual and text tokens are processed modality-agnostic. This architecture achieves state-of-the-art results (Bugliarello et al., 2021) while being easily extendable to multiple VEs, by concatenating all vision tokens.[2] Figure 1 illustrates our architecture.

Multimodal input representations. The raw data for a V+L task consists of either discrete tokens/characters (text-modality) or high-resolution pixel values (image-modality). To extract dense representations of the respective modalities we follow the standard pre-processing strategies: The *text* modality is tokenized using word-piece tokenization (Devlin et al., 2019) and mapped to their corresponding dense embedding representations. At the input to the first Transformer layer, positional embeddings are added to the respective token embeddings. For the *vision* modality, pre-trained VEs

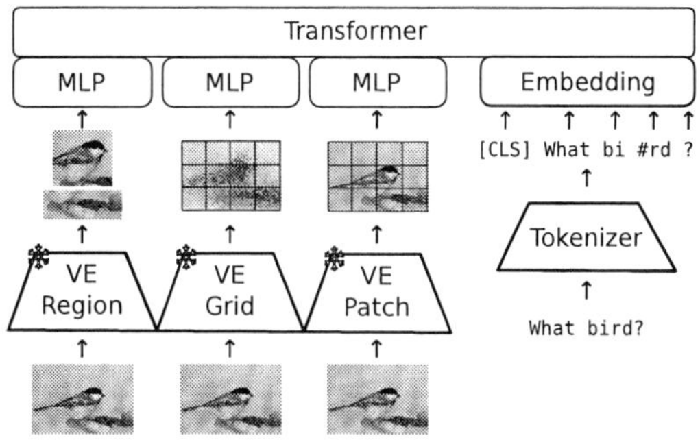

Figure 1: Our Multi-VE Architecture: Each VE produces a list of visual tokens, which are passed through MLPs and concatenated with the text embeddings. The Transformer is modality-agnostic and attends over all tokens. We freeze the VEs during training and only optimize the MLPs, embeddings, and the Transformer.

are utilized which encode the raw pixel values of the respective image into dense high-dimensional feature vectors. These VEs can either encode designated sections (e.g. *Region*), or an entire image (e.g. *Grid* and *Patch*). The extracted feature vectors are then passed through a multi-layer perceptron (MLP), and subsequently into the Transformer. This procedure can be repeated for any number of VEs of interest. In other words, the image features (from multiple VEs) and the text embeddings are concatenated and jointly passed through a shared Transformer model which learns to attend over the multimodal representations.

V+L task training. We place a classification head on the output of the [CLS] token (following Devlin et al. (2019)) and fine-tune the model with cross-entropy loss on the training data of the target task.

4 Experiments

We evaluate the impact of three different VEs on six downstream V+L tasks to assess the complementarity of different image representations. Here, we experiment with all possible combinations of the three VEs (i.e. *single VE*, *2-VE*, and *3-VE* setups).[3] To fairly compare the information stored in the respective VEs, we only fine-tune the multimodal models on the target V+L task in order to circumvent potentially beneficial information leaking into the multimodal model from auxiliary tasks. We therefore initialize all models with *BERT weights*

[2]We concatenate all VE for analysis in §5. In practice, concatenation increases the sequence length and incurs a high computational cost. More efficient methods like resampling (Alayrac et al., 2022) can be explored in future work.

[3]While we report the results of a single VE, we do not aim to show that one VE outperforms others, as this would require a more controlled experimental setup, e.g. training dataset and training objectives amongst other factors (Jiang et al., 2020; Zhang et al., 2021), which is outside the scope of this work.

VE	Model	# Train	Tasks	# V. Tok.	Dim.
Region	VinVL (Zhang et al., 2021)	2.5M[1]	bounding box prediction, object & attribute classification	36	2054
Grid	CLIP RN50x4 (Radford et al., 2021)	400M[2]	image-text contrastive loss	36	2560
Patch	CLIP ViT/B-32 (Radford et al., 2021)	400M[2]	image-text contrastive loss	49	768

Table 1: The three VE models used in our experiments with the number of pre-training images, training objectives, the number of visual tokens (V.Tok.), and the output feature dimension. **Train Datasets**: **1**: Combination of multiple object detection datasets (see (Zhang et al., 2021)). **2**: Web-crawled & cleaned image-caption pairs (proprietary).

(Devlin et al., 2019) (base-size). We note, however, that gains can be achieved when pre-training the multimodal model on auxiliary data prior to fine-tuning on the target V+L task (Tan and Bansal, 2019; Lu et al., 2019; Chen et al., 2020, *inter alia*).

4.1 Vision Encoders

We follow the standard approach and repurpose three pre-trained vision models as VEs. In a best-effort attempt for a fair setup, we use the current best publicly available models of similar sizes. Each VE has a designated, randomly initialized 2-layer perceptron (MLP) that maps the representations to the input of the Transformer and is trained on the target V+L task along with the multimodal Transformer weights. We keep the VE weights *frozen* during training. For a full summary of the VEs including pre-training data, the number of extracted tokens as well as dimensions, see Table 1.

***Region* VE.** We utilize Faster R-CNN (Ren et al., 2015), an object detection model that outputs a list of bounding boxes and feature vectors for Regions of Interest—salient parts of the image that likely contain an object. Here we select the pre-trained VinVL object detector (Zhang et al., 2021),[4] which outperforms previous object detectors on V+L tasks. We follow Li et al. (2020b); Zhang et al. (2021) and concatenate each extracted feature vector with the corresponding normalized box coordinates and width / height. We extract the top-36 regions from the VinVL object detector.

***Grid* VE.** *Grid* VEs linearize the grid feature map of a CNN (before final pooling or classification layers) to a list of visual tokens. Each visual token corresponds to a specific part of the image with image features on different scales (through different pooling operations and convolution sizes throughout the CNN) encoded in it. We use adaptive max pooling[5] on the feature map to reduce the number of tokens to 36 per image. We use the CLIP CNN (RN50x4) (Radford et al., 2021) as initialization, given it's recent success on V+L tasks (Shen et al., 2022; Eichenberg et al., 2022; Alayrac et al., 2022).

***Patch* VE.** *Patch* VEs use the contextualized output representations of a Vision Transformer (ViT) (Dosovitskiy et al., 2021) as visual tokens. The ViT splits an image into uniform patches, which are used as input tokens. Different from a CNN, the ViT tokens are fixed in size throughout the model but they have a global receptive field through the ViT's attention mechanism. We exclude the ViT's special classification token from the Transformer input. We also utilize the CLIP-based ViT models (ViT/B-32) (Radford et al., 2021) for our *Patch*-VE. We extract all 49 tokens for the CLIP ViT due to their smaller feature dimension size.

4.2 Tasks

We experiment with a set of six V+L tasks: *Image-text retrieval* (**Flickr30k** (Young et al., 2014) and **MSCOCO** (Lin et al., 2014)), *visual question answering* (**GQA** (Hudson and Manning, 2019) and **VQA2.0** (Goyal et al., 2017)), *visual entailment* (**SNLI-VE** (Xie et al., 2019)) and *memes classification* (**Hateful Memes** (Kiela et al., 2020)). For all experiments we report the mean and standard deviations over three random seeds and present training details and hyperparameters in Appendix A. We train all models with a single Nvidia V100 GPU, training a single model (all tasks, three seeds) takes approximately 10 GPU days.

4.3 Results & Discussion

We report the results on the six tasks with all possible combinations of VEs in Table 2.

No "one encoder to rule them all". When comparing the results of the single-VE models, there is no clear single winning VE that outperforms all other VEs across all tasks. While for QA tasks *Region* VE models perform best, for the other tasks *Grid* VE outperforms the others. We hypothesize

[4]Not to be confused with their Transformer.

[5]torch.nn.AdaptiveMaxPool2d

Vision Encoders	Retrieval Flickr30k R@1	Retrieval MSCOCO R@1	Question Answering GQA Acc.	Question Answering VQA Acc.	Reasoning SNLI-VE Acc.	Reasoning Hateful M. AUROC
Region	57.46 ±2.74	50.79 ±3.28	**55.32** ±0.33	**65.73** ±0.54	76.57 ±0.10	74.83 ±0.73
Grid	**66.93** ±3.59	**58.30** ±3.56	51.51 ±0.17	62.99 ±1.25	**77.32** ±0.11	**79.03** ±0.27
Patch	54.99 ±6.00	46.30 ±2.07	51.56 ±0.44	62.96 ±0.71	76.32 ±0.09	75.78 ±1.57
Region+Grid	63.43 ±5.85	54.87 ±6.88	55.08 ±0.44	66.30 ±1.52	77.66 ±0.11	78.68 ±1.82
Region+Patch	58.60 ±4.44	<u>**58.73**</u> ±4.02	<u>**55.58**</u> ±0.09	<u>**67.05**</u> ±0.42	76.60 ±0.19	75.87 ±0.63
Grid+Patch	<u>**67.53**</u> ±2.07	56.44 ±3.80	51.55 ±0.16	62.64 ±0.30	77.39 ±0.35	<u>**79.88**</u> ±0.95
Region+Grid+Patch	62.30 ±2.04	58.33 ±2.51	54.39 ±0.59	66.82 ±1.57	<u>**77.87**</u> ±0.24	78.81 ±0.38
With VE-Dropout Training §5.5						
Region+Grid	55.11 ±13.44	54.28 ±4.97	**54.91** ±0.26	64.72 ±3.93	77.07 ±0.21	75.75 ±0.93
Region+Patch	51.53 ±7.75	52.07 ±4.44	54.46 ±0.70	**65.07** ±0.63	76.42 ±0.15	73.57 ±0.69
Grid+Patch	**63.13** ±4.16	**55.56** ±3.92	51.80 ±0.25	60.62 ±1.38	**77.41** ±0.16	**77.30** ±0.43

Table 2: Mean and standard deviation over three seeds. Metrics: for retrieval the average recall at 1 between image-text and text-image retrieval, for Hateful Memes AUROC, and accuracy otherwise. Best single- and multi-VE setup is **bolded** and overall best score is <u>underlined</u>. We also report the results for VE-Dropout Training (see §5.5).

that the object-centric regions are useful for QA tasks, which focus on specific elements, while the uniform grid encoding might be useful for retrieval and other tasks that look at the entire image. Isolating *why* certain VEs are useful for specific tasks, and the role of training objectives, data, and architecture, requires a controlled setup of training VEs from scratch (Jiang et al., 2020), which we leave to future work. Interestingly, the *Patch* VE never achieves the best performance, which aligns with previous findings by Shen et al. (2022); Eichenberg et al. (2022). These single-VE results demonstrate that each VE encodes different types of information that impacts the downstream performance.

VEs can complement each other. When combining the representations from different VEs, we witness improvements across all V+L tasks. Interestingly, MSCOCO benefits greatly from combining the two weakest VEs (i.e. *Region* and *Patch*), surpassing their corresponding single VE results by 7.94 and 12.43 points respectively, achieving the best performance on this task. Although the *Patch* VE never achieves the best performance in single-VE setups, it provides complementary information in combination with the best performing VE, achieving the best overall performance for many tasks.[6] However, we see that simply using more encoders does *not* guarantee improvements as is evident by the 3-encoder model. While the 3-encoder model consistently achieves near-best results, it is rarely the best model (only on 1 out of 6 tasks). This result shows that simply using more encoders does ***not*** guarantee improvement (i.e. model performance is not monotonically improving with more VEs.). Hence, it is unlikely that the improvements are due to an ensemble effect.

One does not fit all. In summary, we see that neither one VE alone nor a fixed combination of VEs gives the best results for the entire breadth of V+L tasks. This shows the current limitations of repurposed vision encoders and highlights the need for encoders designed specifically for V+L tasks.

5 Analysis

To better understand how the representations are combined in different multi-VE setups, we analyze the *flow of attention*, *phrase-to-image grounding*, and the robustness to *dropping VEs* at test time. We overload 'cross-modality' to include both VE-text but also VE-VE interactions for simplicity. We present the analysis for the best performing model combinations in what follows but provide a full list of results in Appendix B.

5.1 CLS Attention Flow

The CLS token can be seen as the fused representation of the modalities that are used for the final classification (Cao et al., 2020). We can thus estimate which VEs are important for classification by considering which VEs the CLS token attends to.[7]

[6] Grid+Patch performs better than Grid for Flickr30k, Region+Patch performs better than Region for GQA, etc.

[7] This is only an estimation because the modalities combine information through attention, too.

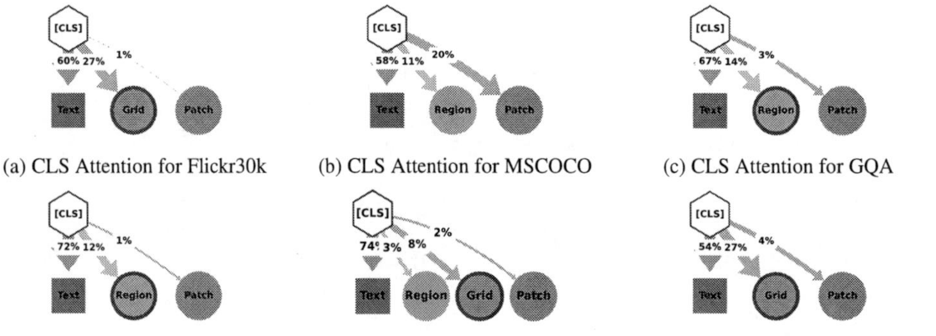

(a) CLS Attention for Flickr30k (b) CLS Attention for MSCOCO (c) CLS Attention for GQA

(d) CLS Attention for VQA (e) CLS Attention for SNLI-VE (f) CLS Attention for Hateful Memes

Figure 2: CLS attention (in %) to each modality/ VE averaged over all heads. We add an **outline** to the VE with the best single-VE results. Numbers do not add to 100% because of CLS self-attention. We present the best multi-VE results here and all other results in Figure 8 in the Appendix.

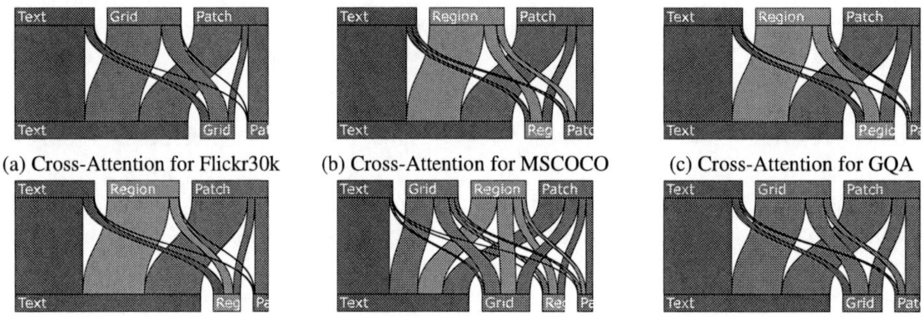

(a) Cross-Attention for Flickr30k (b) Cross-Attention for MSCOCO (c) Cross-Attention for GQA

(d) Cross-Attention for VQA (e) Cross-Attention for SNLI-VE (f) Cross-Attention for Hateful Memes

Figure 3: Cross-modal attention flow (in %) from each modality/ VEs (top) to all modalities/ VEs (bottom). Flow is the sum of all attention weights between two modalities, averaged over all modality tokens and attention heads. We present the best multi-VE results here and all other results in Figure 9 in the Appendix.

Following Cao et al. (2020), we compute the sum of attention from the CLS token to each modality and then average those scores over all heads.

We present the CLS attention for the best multi-VE setups in Figure 2. We see that for most tasks, the VE which performed best in the single-VE setup receives the majority of VE-attention. This suggests that one VE dominates in multi-VE setups while the others are complementary.

5.2 Cross-Modal Attention Flow

The attention flow between the different modalities can indicate which VEs are used by the model to reason over the input. We assume that more attention to a modality suggests that it contains useful information for others. We compute the average attention flow between two modalities M and N for an attention head as $\frac{1}{|M|}\sum_{m\in M, n\in N} a_{m\to n}$ with $a_{m\to n}$ as the attention weight from token m to n (excluding CLS). We average over all heads.

We present the attention flow for the best multi-VE setups in Figure 3. Similar to §5.1, the majority of attention is paid to the VE that achieved better results in the single-VE experiment for that task.

5.3 Overlapping Token Surplus Attention

The attention flow between different VEs' visual tokens that *overlap*—i.e. encode the same part of the image—can tell us if the model combines the VEs to complement the image representation. For each attention head we therefore compute the average per-token attention from a token t of *one* VE to overlapping tokens $I_{|t}$ of *another* VE, and compare this—i.e. compute the surplus—to the non-overlapping tokens of that VE $I\backslash t$ as $(\frac{1}{|I_{|t}|}\sum_{i\in I_{|t}} a_{t\to i}) - (\frac{1}{|I\backslash t|}\sum_{i\in I\backslash t} a_{t\to i})$ with $a_{t\to i}$ being the attention weight between the tokens. We average over all tokens to get the surplus attention of an attention head for a VE pair.

We present the results for the best performing setups in Figure 4. For most VEs we can identify heads—indicated by larger dot sizes—which

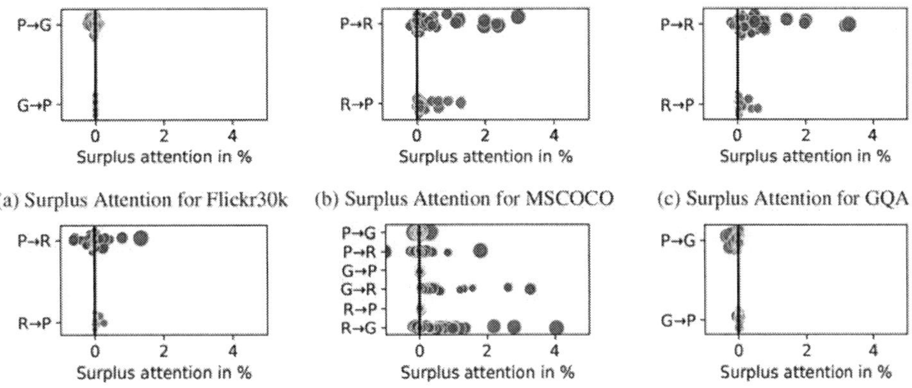

(a) Surplus Attention for Flickr30k (b) Surplus Attention for MSCOCO (c) Surplus Attention for GQA

(d) Surplus Attention for VQA (e) Surplus Attention for SNLI-VE (f) Surplus Attention for Hateful M.

Figure 4: Surplus attention of attention heads from one VE's tokens to another target VE's overlapping tokens compared to the other non-overlapping tokens of the target VE. **Dot size** represents the average total attention paid to the target VE by the respective head. Positive values indicate that the respective head attributes *more* attention, negative values that *less* attention is attributed to overlapping tokens. We present the best multi-VE results here and all other results in Figure 10 in the Appendix. (Abbreviations: **R**egion, **G**rid, **P**atch).

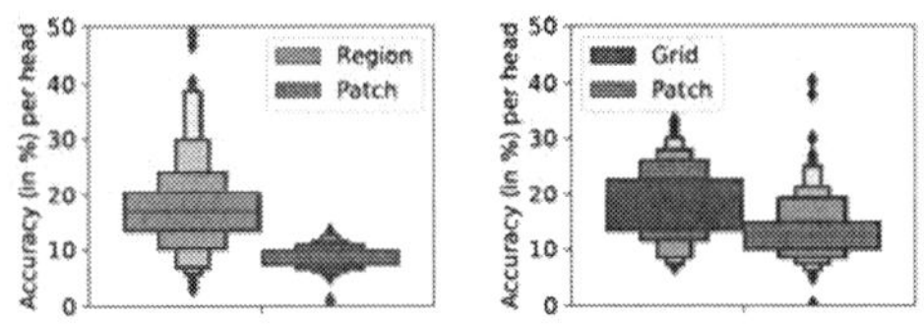

(a) Visual Grounding GQA (b) Visual Ground. Flickr30k

Figure 5: Visual Entity Grounding accuracy of all attention heads. An entity is grounded correctly to a VE if the attention weight from the phrase to the matching visual tokens is the highest over all the VE's tokens. Other results can be found in Figure 11 in the Appendix.

attend particularly to *another* VE's tokens. For most settings, these heads are also those which attend to the overlapping tokens of the respective other VE. While we witness a large surplus in attention for overlapping tokens between *Region* and *Grid*/*Patch*, this is not the case for *Grid-Patch*. This indicates that the complementarity of *Region* features is higher for the respective other VEs, which provides more evidence that training the VE on different data and objectives is important.

5.4 Visual Entity Grounding

Visual grounding is the task of matching text phrases to their corresponding parts in the image. To analyze whether or not there are dominant VEs which learn to ground, we follow Li et al. (2020a) and count how often the highest attention weight from a text phrase is assigned to the corresponding visual token. We use the gold phrase-to-bounding box annotations available for Flickr30k (Plummer et al., 2015) and GQA. Formally, a head correctly grounds a phrase to the gold box g if the *maximum attention* from the last phrase token t to any of a VE's tokens I goes to any token $I_{|g}$ overlapping with the gold box,[8] i.e. if $\arg\max_{i \in I} a_{t \to i} \in I_{|g}$. We calculate the accuracy by counting the number of correct groundings where $I_{|g}$ is not empty.

We report the results for all heads of the best GQA and Flickr30k models in Figure 5. We can see that the accuracy of the dominant VE (*Grid* and *Region*, respectively) is generally higher than for *Patch*. While there is a clear pattern of the dominant VE achieving significantly higher accuracy, the complementary VE also achieves accuracies beyond 10%, indicating that the model learns to reason over, and utilize *both* VE's representations.

5.5 VE-Dropout

Our analyses in the previous sections suggest that there are dominant and complementary encoders, the former contributing the most to the model's performance on the target task. To further evaluate the importance of the respective VEs we experiment with dropping all VE-specific features during test time. The results in Figure 6 show that drop-

[8] We consider all visual tokens with Intersection over Union between the token box and the gold box over 0.5 for region tokens (based on Li et al. (2020a)) and over 0.1 for grid and patch tokens (because a single object can be distributed over many tokens due to the uniform grid).

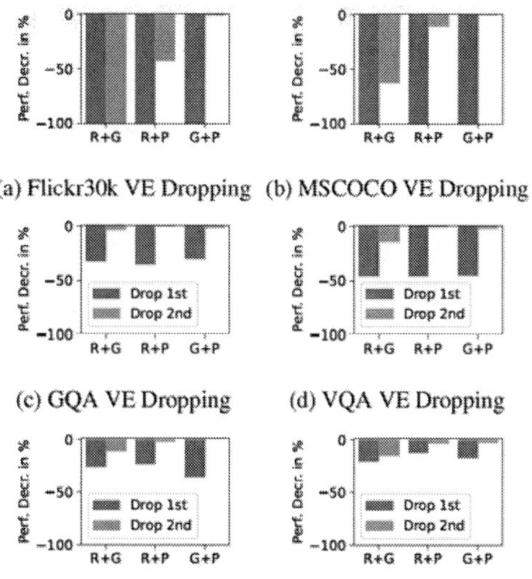

(a) Flickr30k VE Dropping (b) MSCOCO VE Dropping

(c) GQA VE Dropping (d) VQA VE Dropping

(e) SNLI-VE VE Dropping (f) Hateful M. VE Dropping

Figure 6: Relative performance decrease of 2-encoder models after dropping the entire first or second VE from the input compared to evaluation with both encoders in use. (Abbreviations: **R**egion, **G**rid, **P**atch).

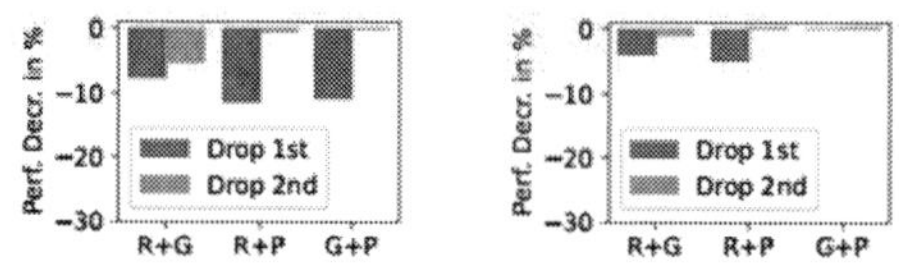

(a) MSCOCO VE Dropping (b) GQA VE Dropping

Figure 7: Relative performance decrease of 2-encoder models as in Figure 6 **after** VE-Dropout Training. Other tasks in Figure 12 in the Appendix.

ping the dominant encoder results in a catastrophic performance decrease, especially for the retrieval tasks. While QA and reasoning tasks have a 20% to 40% decrease in performance, for retrieval tasks R@1 decreases by almost 100%.

However, the detrimental performance of dropping out of the VE features at test time might be a result of the multi-VE models never being trained for this setting. Consequently, we train the 2-encoder models with VE-wise dropout per batch.[9] We hypothesize that this would force the model to take the complementary VE into account while being more robust during inference. As reported in Figure 7, the robustness in terms of dropping VEs improves, however, we see a slight drop in the final task performance, as reported in Table 2.[10]

6 Discussion and Future Directions

Our analyses demonstrate that, while combining multiple VEs consistently outperforms single VE setups, there is not a single VE or a fixed strategy on combining VEs that works best for all tasks. In particular, simply ensembling all VEs is rarely the optimal choice; consequently, best-performing combinations of VEs need to be identified for each individual task (§ 4.3). By further analyzing the attention patterns, we find a clear dominating VE (§ 5.5, Figures 6 & 7) that both the [CLS] (§ 5.1, Figure 2) and the multimodal tokens (§ 5.2, Figure 3) predominantly attend to, whereas the secondary VEs provide complementary information, supporting the model's overall performance. The complementarity of VEs is highlighted by analyzing the cross-modal attention patterns for overlapping parts of the image (§ 5.3, Figure 4). VEs trained on different data and objectives (e.g. *Grid* and *Region*) cross-attend to the tokens of the respective *other* VE that encode the same parts of the image, aggregating their information. Further, the model learns to visually ground the text representations to all VEs, as demonstrated by their attention patterns (§ 5.4, Figure 5), and the text modality aggregates information from different VEs.

In summary, our results indicate that VEs, trained on different data and objectives, encode complementary information, resulting in improvements over approaches which only utilize a single VE. This indicates that VEs, explicitly designed for V+L tasks—e.g. by incorporating more diverse training data and objectives during pre-training—have the potential to significantly impact the performance on the target V+L tasks.

7 Conclusion

In this work, we investigated whether different VEs—based on repurposed pre-trained vision models—encode complementary information, which improves the performance on downstream V+L tasks. We experimented with three popular VE classes *Region*, *Grid*, and *Patch*, and trained models with all possible combinations on six different V+L tasks. While combining VEs improve over single-VE setups, our further analysis of attention patterns reveals that diverse VEs encode complementary information, which motivates future work on designing VEs explicitly for V+L tasks—e.g. by

[9] Uniformly dropping the *first*, *second*, or *no* VE.

[10] We notice no significant changes in the attention patterns after VE-Dropout training (see Appendix C).

incorporating more diverse datasets, and training objectives.

Limitations

The main limitation of our concatenation-based multi-VE models is efficiency: The models are significantly slower than single-VE models because of the additional visual tokens in the input; the 3-VE model requires almost twice the time to train (in real time, not training steps) compared to the single-VE models. Also, in cases where images are not pre-encoded, multi-VE setups are significantly slower at inference time. However, as mentioned before, we concatenate the tokens for analysis purposes only (§5) and leave more efficient alternatives like resampling (Alayrac et al., 2022) to the future.

Several limitations could be investigated in the future, assuming access to a larger computational budget:

1. We focused on single-stream Transformers and did not take into account dual-stream or other multimodal Transformer architectures.
2. We only experimented with three popular VEs (one version per VE class). There are many other VEs we could investigate in the future.
3. We do not pre-train our multimodal models on intermediate, auxiliary multimodal tasks (Tan and Bansal, 2019; Lu et al., 2019; Chen et al., 2020, *inter alia*) as achieving state-of-the-art is not our goal.

Acknowledgements

This work has been funded by the German Federal Ministry of Education and Research (BMBF) under the promotional reference 13N15897 (MISRIK) and by the LOEWE initiative (Hesse, Germany) within the emergenCITY center.

We thank Mert Tiftikci, Pooneh Mousavi, and Neha Warikoo for insightful feedback and suggestions on a draft of this paper.

References

Jean-Baptiste Alayrac, Jeff Donahue, Pauline Luc, Antoine Miech, Iain Barr, Yana Hasson, Karel Lenc, Arthur Mensch, Katherine Millican, Malcolm Reynolds, Roman Ring, Eliza Rutherford, Serkan Cabi, Tengda Han, Zhitao Gong, Sina Samangooei, Marianne Monteiro, Jacob Menick, Sebastian Borgeaud, Andrew Brock, Aida Nematzadeh, Sahand Sharifzadeh, Mikolaj Binkowski, Ricardo Barreira, Oriol Vinyals, Andrew Zisserman, and Karen Simonyan. 2022. Flamingo: a visual language model for few-shot learning. In *Advances in Neural Information Processing Systems 35: Annual Conference on Neural Information Processing Systems 2022, NeurIPS 2022*.

P. Anderson, X. He, C. Buehler, D. Teney, M. Johnson, S. Gould, and L. Zhang. 2018. Bottom-Up and Top-Down Attention for Image Captioning and Visual Question Answering. In *2018 IEEE/CVF Conference on Computer Vision and Pattern Recognition*, pages 6077–6086.

Emanuele Bugliarello, Ryan Cotterell, Naoaki Okazaki, and Desmond Elliott. 2021. Multimodal Pretraining Unmasked: A Meta-Analysis and a Unified Framework of Vision-and-Language BERTs. *Transactions of the Association for Computational Linguistics*, 9:978–994.

Jize Cao, Zhe Gan, Yu Cheng, Licheng Yu, Yen-Chun Chen, and Jingjing Liu. 2020. Behind the Scene: Revealing the Secrets of Pre-trained Vision-and-Language Models. In *Computer Vision - ECCV 2020 - 16th European Conference, Glasgow, UK, August 23-28, 2020, Proceedings, Part VI*, volume 12351 of *Lecture Notes in Computer Science*, pages 565–580. Springer.

Yen-Chun Chen, Linjie Li, Licheng Yu, Ahmed El Kholy, Faisal Ahmed, Zhe Gan, Yu Cheng, and Jingjing Liu. 2020. UNITER: UNiversal Image-TExt Representation Learning. In *Computer Vision - ECCV 2020 - 16th European Conference, Glasgow, UK, August 23-28, 2020, Proceedings*, volume 12375 of *Lecture Notes in Computer Science*, pages 104–120. Springer.

Jaemin Cho, Jie Lei, Hao Tan, and Mohit Bansal. 2021. Unifying vision-and-language tasks via text generation. In *Proceedings of the 38th International Conference on Machine Learning, ICML 2021, 18-24 July 2021, Virtual Event*, volume 139 of *Proceedings of Machine Learning Research*, pages 1931–1942. PMLR.

Jonathan H. Clark, Dan Garrette, Iulia Turc, and John Wieting. 2022. Canine: Pre-training an Efficient Tokenization-Free Encoder for Language Representation. *Transactions of the Association for Computational Linguistics*, 10:73–91.

Wenliang Dai, Zihan Liu, Ziwei Ji, Dan Su, and Pascale Fung. 2023. Plausible may not be faithful: Probing object hallucination in vision-language pre-training. In *Proceedings of the 17th Conference of the European Chapter of the Association for Computational Linguistics*, pages 2136–2148, Dubrovnik, Croatia. Association for Computational Linguistics.

Jacob Devlin, Ming-Wei Chang, Kenton Lee, and Kristina Toutanova. 2019. BERT: Pre-training of

Deep Bidirectional Transformers for Language Understanding. In *Proceedings of the 2019 Conference of the North American Chapter of the Association for Computational Linguistics: Human Language Technologies, NAACL-HLT 2019, Minneapolis, MN, USA, June 2-7, 2019, Volume 1 (Long and Short Papers)*, pages 4171–4186. Association for Computational Linguistics.

Alexey Dosovitskiy, Lucas Beyer, Alexander Kolesnikov, Dirk Weissenborn, Xiaohua Zhai, Thomas Unterthiner, Mostafa Dehghani, Matthias Minderer, Georg Heigold, Sylvain Gelly, Jakob Uszkoreit, and Neil Houlsby. 2021. An image is worth 16x16 words: Transformers for image recognition at scale. In *9th International Conference on Learning Representations, ICLR 2021, Virtual Event, Austria, May 3-7, 2021*. OpenReview.net.

Constantin Eichenberg, Sidney Black, Samuel Weinbach, Letitia Parcalabescu, and Anette Frank. 2022. MAGMA – multimodal augmentation of generative models through adapter-based finetuning. In *Findings of the Association for Computational Linguistics: EMNLP 2022*, pages 2416–2428, Abu Dhabi, United Arab Emirates. Association for Computational Linguistics.

Stella Frank, Emanuele Bugliarello, and Desmond Elliott. 2021. Vision-and-Language or Vision-for-Language? On Cross-Modal Influence in Multimodal Transformers. In *Proceedings of the 2021 Conference on Empirical Methods in Natural Language Processing, EMNLP 2021, Virtual Event / Punta Cana, Dominican Republic, 7-11 November, 2021*, pages 9847–9857. Association for Computational Linguistics.

Zhe Gan, Yen-Chun Chen, Linjie Li, Chen Zhu, Yu Cheng, and Jingjing Liu. 2020. Large-Scale Adversarial Training for Vision-and-Language Representation Learning. In *Advances in Neural Information Processing Systems 33: Annual Conference on Neural Information Processing Systems 2020, NeurIPS 2020, December 6-12, 2020, virtual.*

Y. Goyal, T. Khot, D. Summers-Stay, D. Batra, and D. Parikh. 2017. Making the V in VQA Matter: Elevating the Role of Image Understanding in Visual Question Answering. In *2017 IEEE Conference on Computer Vision and Pattern Recognition (CVPR)*, pages 6325–6334.

Lisa Anne Hendricks, John Mellor, Rosalia Schneider, Jean-Baptiste Alayrac, and Aida Nematzadeh. 2021. Decoupling the role of data, attention, and losses in multimodal transformers. *Transactions of the Association for Computational Linguistics*, 9:570–585.

Zhicheng Huang, Zhaoyang Zeng, Bei Liu, Dongmei Fu, and Jianlong Fu. 2020. Pixel-BERT: Aligning Image Pixels with Text by Deep Multi-Modal Transformers. *arXiv preprint*.

Drew A. Hudson and Christopher D. Manning. 2019. GQA: A New Dataset for Real-World Visual Reasoning and Compositional Question Answering. In *IEEE Conference on Computer Vision and Pattern Recognition, CVPR 2019, Long Beach, CA, USA, June 16-20, 2019*, pages 6700–6709. Computer Vision Foundation / IEEE.

Huaizu Jiang, Ishan Misra, Marcus Rohrbach, Erik G. Learned-Miller, and Xinlei Chen. 2020. In Defense of Grid Features for Visual Question Answering. In *2020 IEEE/CVF Conference on Computer Vision and Pattern Recognition, CVPR 2020, Seattle, WA, USA, June 13-19, 2020*, pages 10264–10273. Computer Vision Foundation / IEEE.

Aishwarya Kamath, Mannat Singh, Yann LeCun, Gabriel Synnaeve, Ishan Misra, and Nicolas Carion. 2021. MDETR - modulated detection for end-to-end multi-modal understanding. In *2021 IEEE/CVF International Conference on Computer Vision, ICCV 2021, Montreal, QC, Canada, October 10-17, 2021*, pages 1760–1770. IEEE.

Douwe Kiela, Hamed Firooz, Aravind Mohan, Vedanuj Goswami, Amanpreet Singh, Pratik Ringshia, and Davide Testuggine. 2020. The Hateful Memes Challenge: Detecting Hate Speech in Multimodal Memes. In *Advances in Neural Information Processing Systems 33: Annual Conference on Neural Information Processing Systems 2020, NeurIPS 2020, December 6-12, 2020, virtual.*

Wonjae Kim, Bokyung Son, and Ildoo Kim. 2021. Vilt: Vision-and-language transformer without convolution or region supervision. In *Proceedings of the 38th International Conference on Machine Learning, ICML 2021, 18-24 July 2021, Virtual Event*, volume 139 of *Proceedings of Machine Learning Research*, pages 5583–5594. PMLR.

Junnan Li, Dongxu Li, Caiming Xiong, and Steven C. H. Hoi. 2022. BLIP: bootstrapping language-image pretraining for unified vision-language understanding and generation. In *International Conference on Machine Learning, ICML 2022, 17-23 July 2022, Baltimore, Maryland, USA*, volume 162 of *Proceedings of Machine Learning Research*, pages 12888–12900. PMLR.

Junnan Li, Ramprasaath R. Selvaraju, Akhilesh Gotmare, Shafiq R. Joty, Caiming Xiong, and Steven Chu-Hong Hoi. 2021. Align before fuse: Vision and language representation learning with momentum distillation. In *Advances in Neural Information Processing Systems 34: Annual Conference on Neural Information Processing Systems 2021, NeurIPS 2021, December 6-14, 2021, virtual*, pages 9694–9705.

Liunian Harold Li, Mark Yatskar, Da Yin, Cho-Jui Hsieh, and Kai-Wei Chang. 2020a. What Does BERT with Vision Look At? In *Proceedings of the 58th Annual Meeting of the Association for Computational Linguistics, ACL 2020, Online, July 5-10,*

2020, pages 5265–5275. Association for Computational Linguistics.

Xiujun Li, Xi Yin, Chunyuan Li, Pengchuan Zhang, Xiaowei Hu, Lei Zhang, Lijuan Wang, Houdong Hu, Li Dong, Furu Wei, Yejin Choi, and Jianfeng Gao. 2020b. Oscar: Object-Semantics Aligned Pre-training for Vision-Language Tasks. In *Computer Vision - ECCV 2020 - 16th European Conference, Glasgow, UK, August 23-28, 2020, Proceedings, Part XXX*, volume 12375 of *Lecture Notes in Computer Science*, pages 121–137. Springer.

Tsung-Yi Lin, Michael Maire, Serge J. Belongie, James Hays, Pietro Perona, Deva Ramanan, Piotr Dollár, and C. Lawrence Zitnick. 2014. Microsoft COCO: Common Objects in Context. In *Computer Vision - ECCV 2014 - 13th European Conference, Zurich, Switzerland, September 6-12, 2014, Proceedings, Part V*, volume 8693 of *Lecture Notes in Computer Science*, pages 740–755. Springer.

Ilya Loshchilov and Frank Hutter. 2019. Decoupled Weight Decay Regularization. In *7th International Conference on Learning Representations, ICLR 2019, New Orleans, LA, USA, May 6-9, 2019*. OpenReview.net.

Jiasen Lu, Dhruv Batra, Devi Parikh, and Stefan Lee. 2019. ViLBERT: Pretraining Task-Agnostic Visiolinguistic Representations for Vision-and-Language Tasks. In *Advances in Neural Information Processing Systems 32: Annual Conference on Neural Information Processing Systems 2019, NeurIPS 2019, December 8-14, 2019, Vancouver, BC, Canada*, pages 13–23.

Bryan A. Plummer, Liwei Wang, Chris M. Cervantes, Juan C. Caicedo, Julia Hockenmaier, and Svetlana Lazebnik. 2015. Flickr30k Entities: Collecting Region-to-Phrase Correspondences for Richer Image-to-Sentence Models. In *2015 IEEE International Conference on Computer Vision, ICCV 2015, Santiago, Chile, December 7-13, 2015*, pages 2641–2649.

Alec Radford, Jong Wook Kim, Chris Hallacy, Aditya Ramesh, Gabriel Goh, Sandhini Agarwal, Girish Sastry, Amanda Askell, Pamela Mishkin, Jack Clark, Gretchen Krueger, and Ilya Sutskever. 2021. Learning transferable visual models from natural language supervision. In *Proceedings of the 38th International Conference on Machine Learning, ICML 2021, 18-24 July 2021, Virtual Event*, volume 139 of *Proceedings of Machine Learning Research*, pages 8748–8763. PMLR.

Shaoqing Ren, Kaiming He, Ross B. Girshick, and Jian Sun. 2015. Faster R-CNN: Towards Real-Time Object Detection with Region Proposal Networks. In *Advances in Neural Information Processing Systems 28: Annual Conference on Neural Information Processing Systems 2015, December 7-12, 2015, Montreal, Quebec, Canada*, pages 91–99.

Phillip Rust, Jonas Pfeiffer, Ivan Vulic, Sebastian Ruder, and Iryna Gurevych. 2021. How good is your tokenizer? on the monolingual performance of multilingual language models. In *Proceedings of the 59th Annual Meeting of the Association for Computational Linguistics and the 11th International Joint Conference on Natural Language Processing, ACL/IJCNLP 2021, (Volume 1: Long Papers), Virtual Event, August 1-6, 2021*, pages 3118–3135. Association for Computational Linguistics.

Sheng Shen, Liunian Harold Li, Hao Tan, Mohit Bansal, Anna Rohrbach, Kai-Wei Chang, Zhewei Yao, and Kurt Keutzer. 2022. How much can CLIP benefit vision-and-language tasks? In *The Tenth International Conference on Learning Representations, ICLR 2022, Virtual Event, April 25-29, 2022*. OpenReview.net.

Amanpreet Singh, Ronghang Hu, Vedanuj Goswami, Guillaume Couairon, Wojciech Galuba, Marcus Rohrbach, and Douwe Kiela. 2022. FLAVA: A foundational language and vision alignment model. In *IEEE/CVF Conference on Computer Vision and Pattern Recognition, CVPR 2022, New Orleans, LA, USA, June 18-24, 2022*, pages 15617–15629. IEEE.

Weijie Su, Xizhou Zhu, Yue Cao, Bin Li, Lewei Lu, Furu Wei, and Jifeng Dai. 2020. VL-BERT: Pre-training of Generic Visual-Linguistic Representations. In *8th International Conference on Learning Representations, ICLR 2020, Addis Ababa, Ethiopia, April 26-30, 2020*. OpenReview.net.

Hao Tan and Mohit Bansal. 2019. LXMERT: Learning Cross-Modality Encoder Representations from Transformers. In *Proceedings of the 2019 Conference on Empirical Methods in Natural Language Processing and the 9th International Joint Conference on Natural Language Processing, EMNLP-IJCNLP 2019, Hong Kong, China, November 3-7, 2019*, pages 5099–5110. Association for Computational Linguistics.

Ashish Vaswani, Noam Shazeer, Niki Parmar, Jakob Uszkoreit, Llion Jones, Aidan N. Gomez, Lukasz Kaiser, and Illia Polosukhin. 2017. Attention is All you Need. In *Advances in Neural Information Processing Systems 30: Annual Conference on Neural Information Processing Systems 2017, December 4-9, 2017, Long Beach, CA, USA*, pages 5998–6008.

Zirui Wang, Jiahui Yu, Adams Wei Yu, Zihang Dai, Yulia Tsvetkov, and Yuan Cao. 2022. SimVLM: Simple visual language model pretraining with weak supervision. In *11th International Conference on Learning Representations, ICLR 2022,*.

Ning Xie, Farley Lai, Derek Doran, and Asim Kadav. 2019. Visual Entailment: A Novel Task for Fine-Grained Image Understanding. *arXiv preprint*.

Linting Xue, Aditya Barua, Noah Constant, Rami Al-Rfou, Sharan Narang, Mihir Kale, Adam Roberts, and Colin Raffel. 2022. Byt5: Towards a token-free future with pre-trained byte-to-byte models. *Transactions of the Association for Computational Linguistics*, 10(0):291–306.

Ming Yan, Haiyang Xu, Chenliang Li, Bin Bi, Junfeng Tian, Min Gui, and Wei Wang. 2021a. Grid-VLP: Revisiting Grid Features for Vision-Language Pre-training. *arXiv preprint*.

Ming Yan, Haiyang Xu, Chenliang Li, Junfeng Tian, Bin Bi, Wei Wang, Weihua Chen, Xianzhe Xu, Fan Wang, Zheng Cao, Zhicheng Zhang, Qiyu Zhang, Ji Zhang, Songfang Huang, Fei Huang, Luo Si, and Rong Jin. 2021b. Achieving Human Parity on Visual Question Answering. *arXiv preprint*.

Peter Young, Alice Lai, Micah Hodosh, and Julia Hockenmaier. 2014. From image descriptions to visual denotations: New similarity metrics for semantic inference over event descriptions. *Transactions of the Association for Computational Linguistics*, 2:67–78.

Pengchuan Zhang, Xiujun Li, Xiaowei Hu, Jianwei Yang, Lei Zhang, Lijuan Wang, Yejin Choi, and Jianfeng Gao. 2021. VinVL: Revisiting Visual Representations in Vision-Language Models. In *Proceedings of the IEEE/CVF Conference on Computer Vision and Pattern Recognition (CVPR)*, pages 5579–5588.

A Training and Hyperparameters

We report the hyperparameters along with the task-specific training details.

A.1 Hyperparameters

We report our hyperparameters in Table 3,4. For each task, we select the learning rate in $\{2e-5, 3e-5, 5e-5\}$ with the best validation performance for the model trained with all three VEs. We train all VE combinations for one task with the same hyperparameters. We use the training checkpoint with the best validation performance (computed each epoch) for testing.

Name	Value
Optimizer	AdamW (Loshchilov and Hutter, 2019)
Schedule	linear
Warmup steps	5%
Weight decay	0.05
Batch size	64
Max. text sequence	96

Table 3: Shared hyperparameters used during training for the different tasks.

Task	Learning Rate	Epochs
Flickr30k	2e-5	10
MSCOCO	2e-5	3
GQA	5e-5	6
VQA	5e-5	10
SNLI-VE	5e-5	10
Hateful Memes	3e-5	50

Table 4: The per-task hyperparameters used during training.

A.2 Task Details

We describe the training details for each task. Unless noted otherwise, we use the standard splits of all tasks as described in Li et al. (2020b); Zhang et al. (2021).

Flickr30k, MSCOCO: We use a cross-encoder following Li et al. (2020b); Zhang et al. (2021). The model either receives the caption and the paired image or a random image (each with 50% chance). The task is to predict if the caption and image match. We use cross entropy as loss as the training objective.

During evaluation, we compute the logits for all possible image-caption pairs and use these scores as ranking to compute the recall at k. We evaluate MSCOCO on the 1k image test set.

GQA, VQA, SNLI-VE, Hateful Memes: We train all three tasks as standard classification task with cross entropy loss. For GQA, each class corresponds to a label appearing in the train, test, or validation set. We also use the *balanced* training data for GQA as it produces similar results to the much larger *unbalanced* training set with a fraction of the training time. For VQA, we follow Li et al. (2020b) and use the top-3000 labels for classification and we train the model with a multilabel objective using the relevance scores as soft probabilities. For testing, we use the maximum logit as the single predicted class.

B Full Analysis Results

We present the full results for all VE combinations from the analysis of §5. Figure 8 shows the CLS attention, Figure 9 the attention flow, Figure 10 the surplus attention for overlapping tokens, and Figure 11 the visual grounding.

C Analysis Results after VE-Dropout Training

We present the full results for all VE combinations from the analysis of §5 **after** VE-Dropout training. Figure 12 show the results for VE-Dropout at test time, Figure 14 the CLS attention, Figure 15 the attention flow, Figure 16 the surplus attention for overlapping tokens, and Figure 13 the visual grounding.

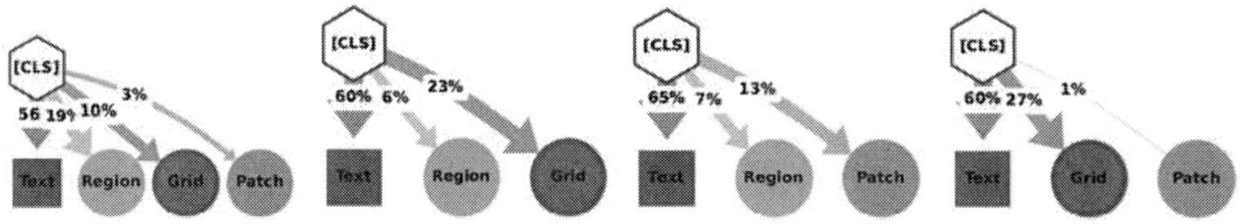

(a) CLS Attention Flickr30k

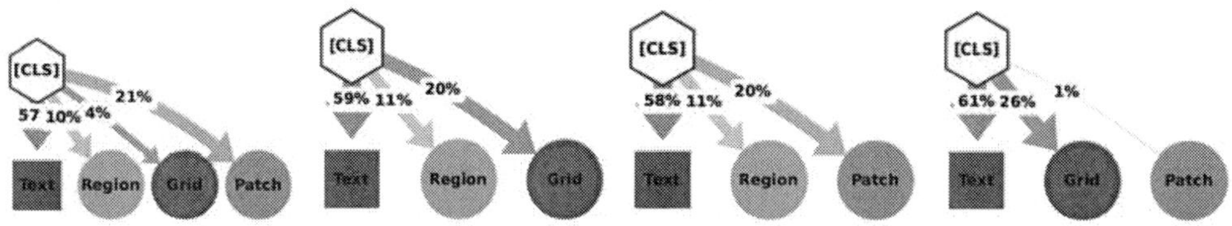

(b) CLS Attention MSCOCO

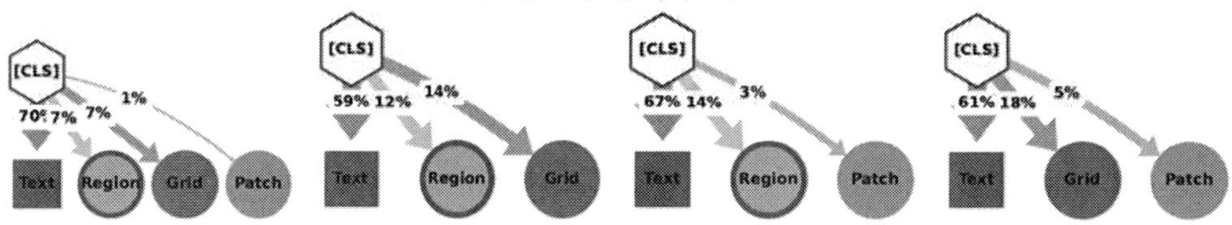

(c) CLS Attention GQA

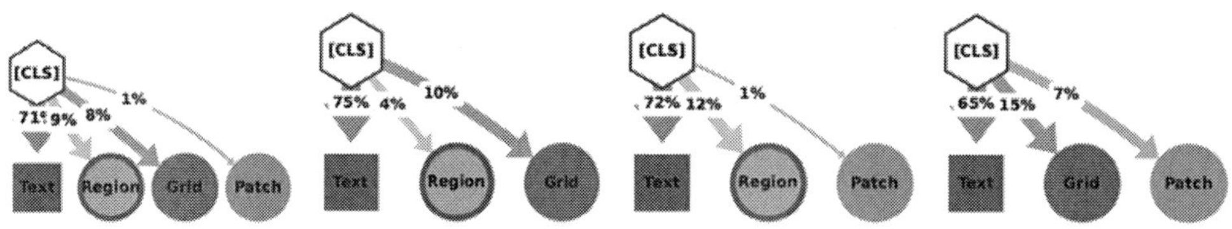

(d) CLS Attention VQA

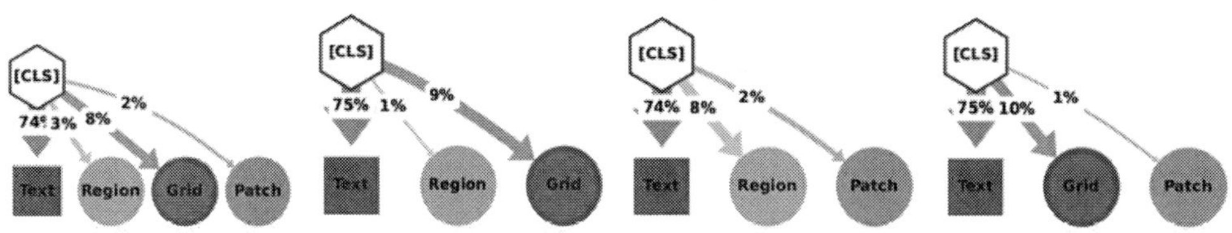

(e) CLS Attention SNLI-VE

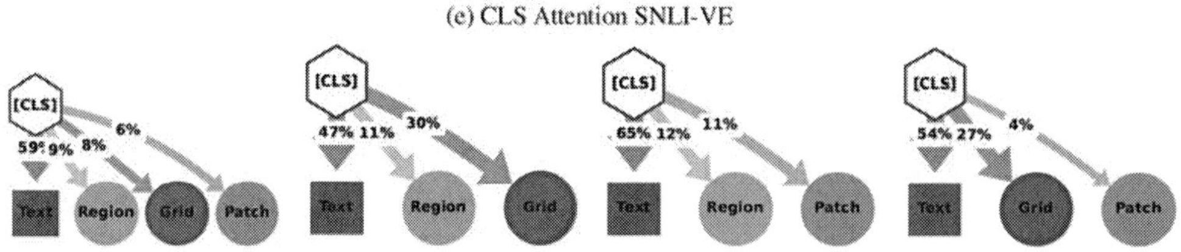

(f) CLS Attention Hateful Memes

Figure 8: CLS attention weights (in %) averaged over all heads to the modalities. Numbers do not add to 100% because of CLS self-attention.

(a) Cross-Attention for Flickr30k

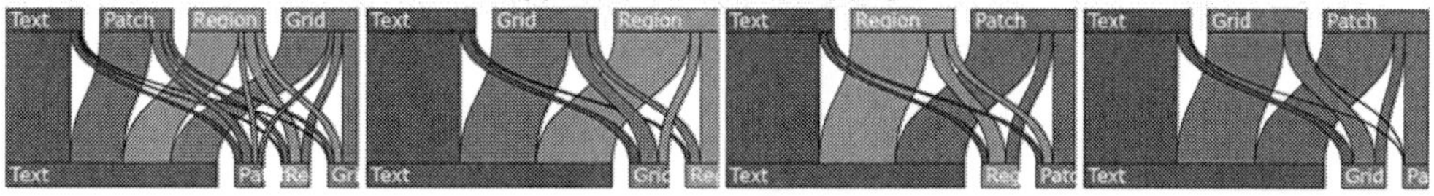

(b) Cross-Attention for MSCOCO

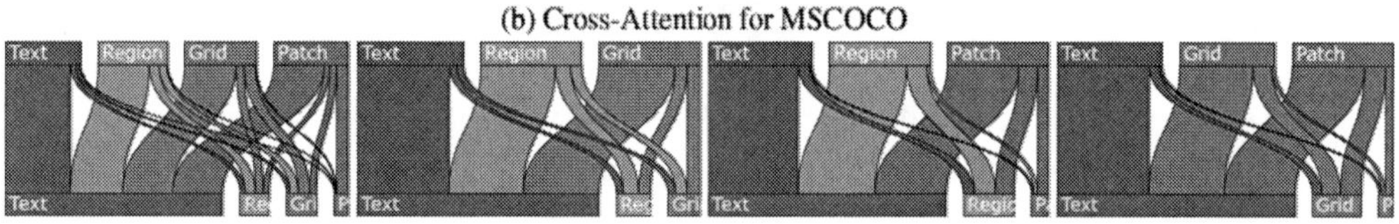

(c) Cross-Attention for GQA

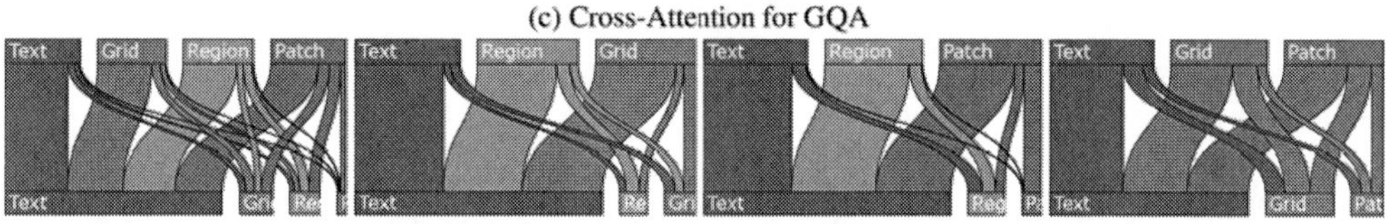

(d) Cross-Attention for VQA

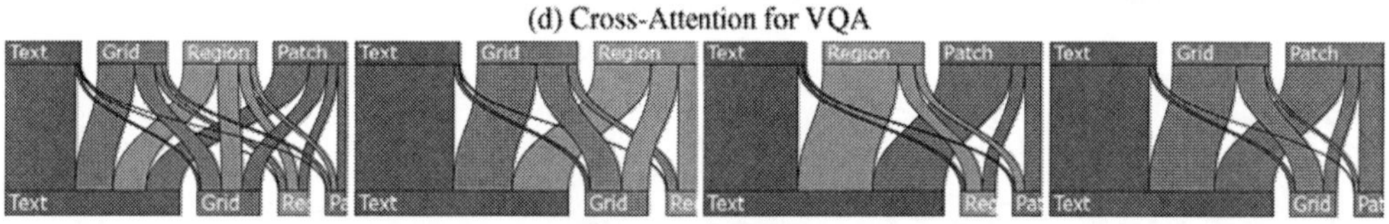

(e) Cross-Attention for SNLI-VE

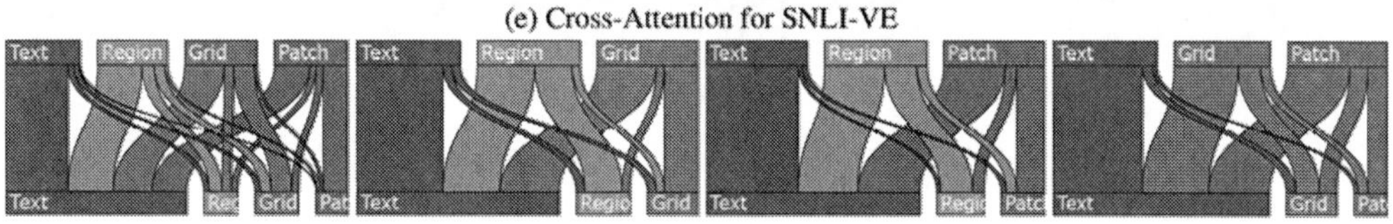

(f) Cross-Attention for Hateful Memes

Figure 9: Attention flow (in %) from each modality (top) to all modalities (bottom). Flow is the sum of all attention weights between the modalities, averaged over all modality tokens and all attention heads.

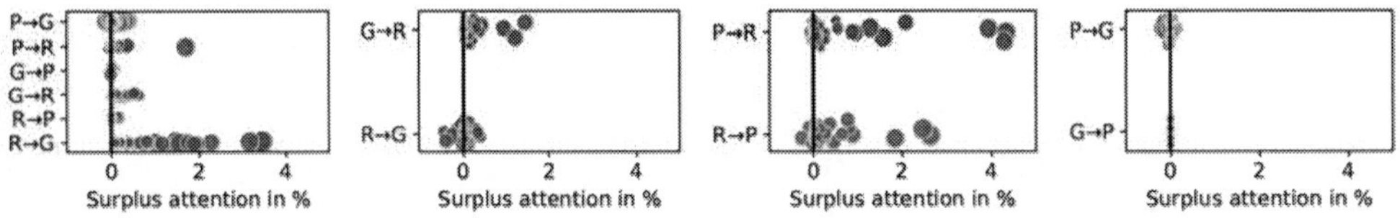

(a) Surplus Attention Flickr30k

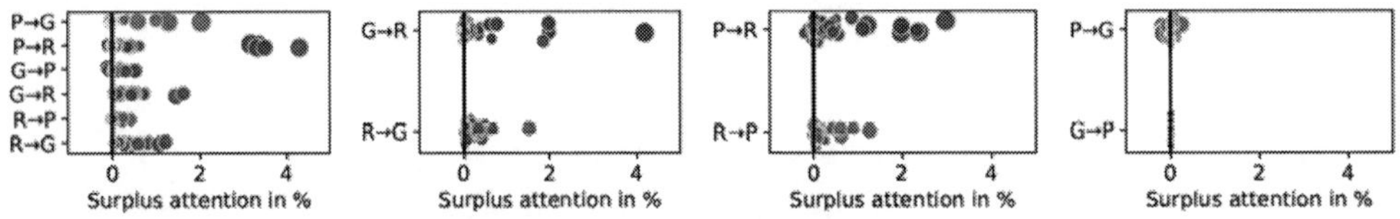

(b) Surplus Attention MSCOCO

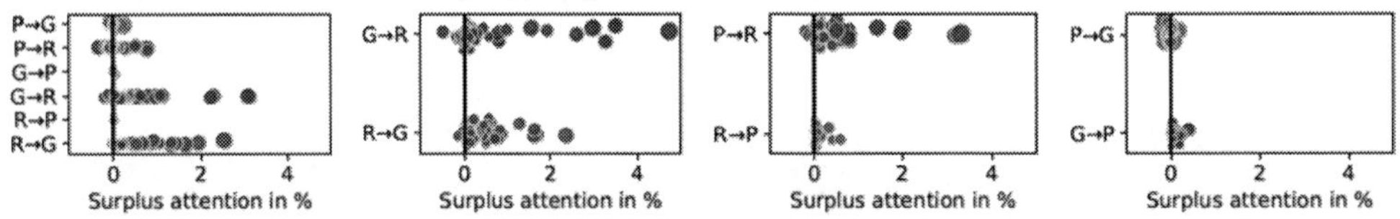

(c) Surplus Attention GQA

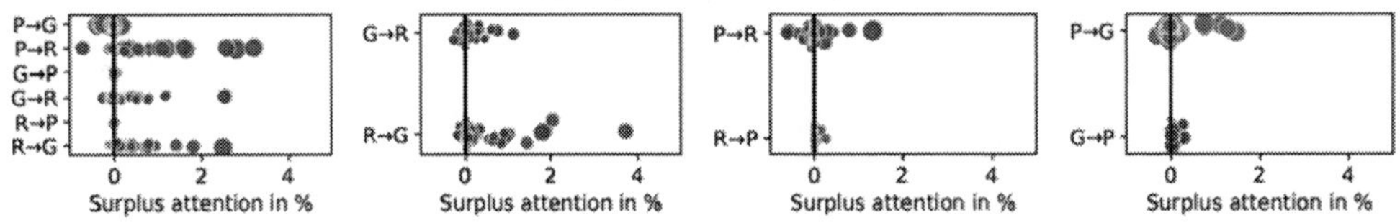

(d) Surplus Attention VQA

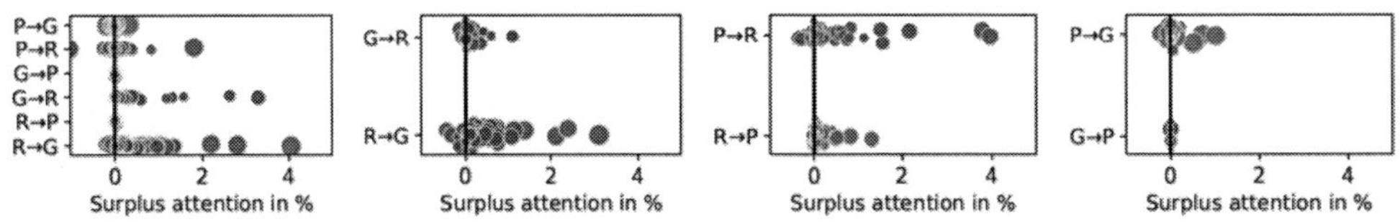

(e) Surplus Attention SNLI-VE

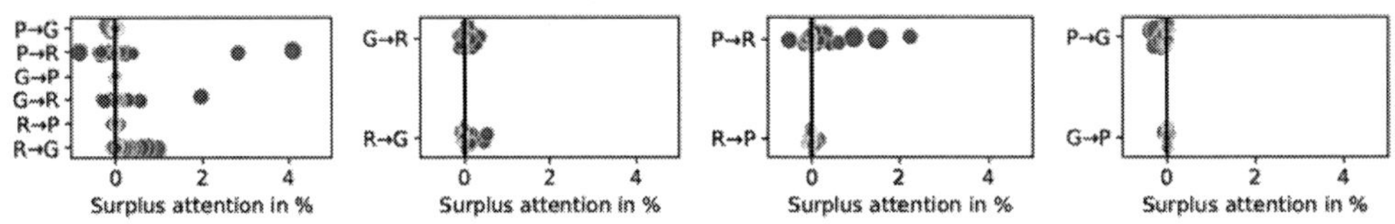

(f) Surplus Attention Hateful Memes

Figure 10: Surplus attention of attention heads from one VE's tokens to another target VE's overlapping tokens compared to the other non-overlapping tokens of the target VE. **Dot size** represents the average total attention paid to the target VE by each head. (Abbreviations: **R**egion, **G**rid, **P**atch).

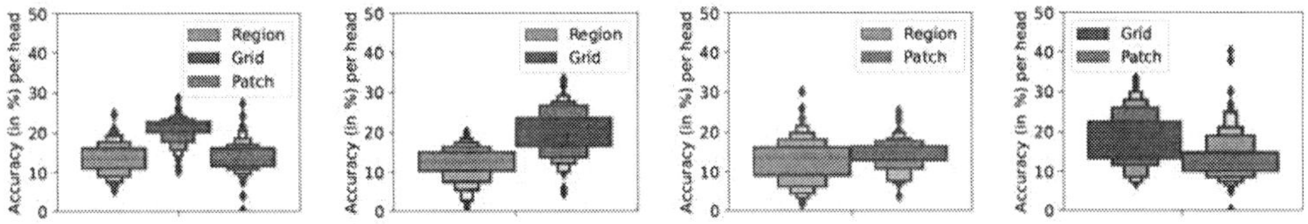

(a) Visual Grounding of attention heads on Flickr30k

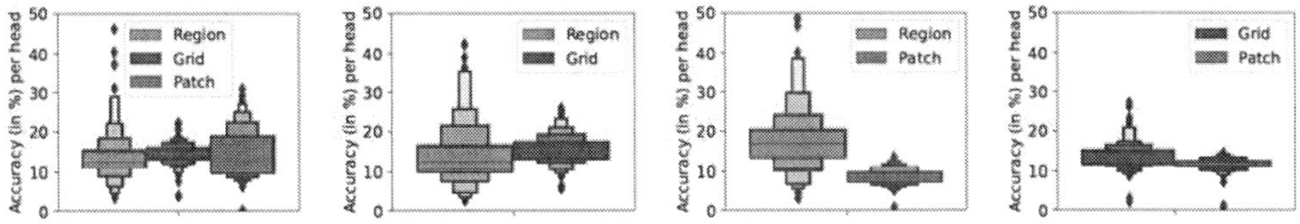

(b) Visual Grounding of attention heads on GQA

Figure 11: Visual Entity Grounding accuracy of all attention heads. An entity is grounded correctly to a VE if the attention weight from the phrase to the matching visual tokens is the highest over all the VE's tokens.

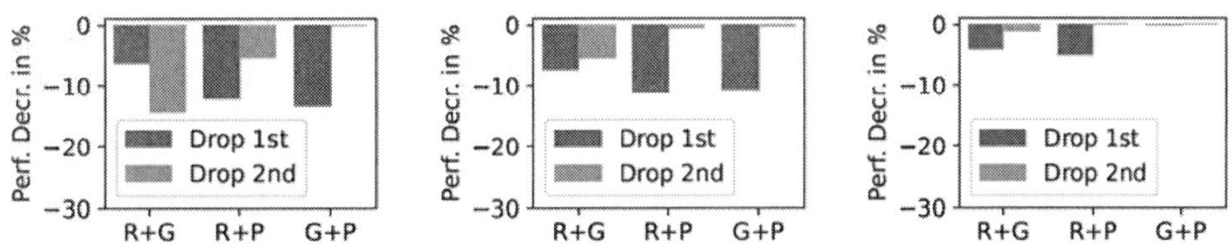

(a) Flickr30k Pruning (b) MSCOCO Pruning (c) GQA Pruning

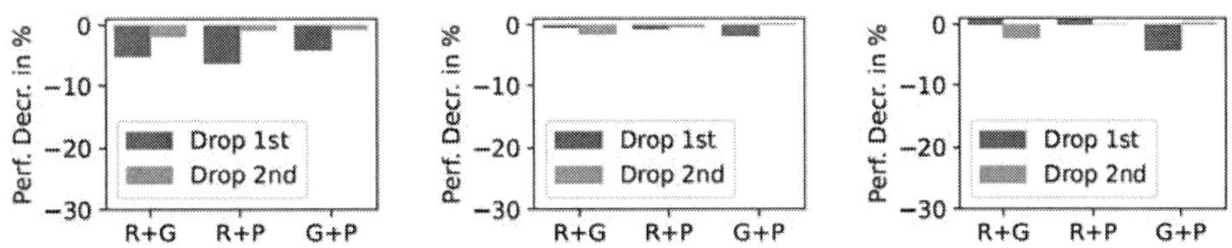

(d) VQA Pruning (e) SNLI-VE Pruning (f) Hateful Memes Pruning

Figure 12: (After VE-Dropout Training) Relative performance decrease of 2-encoder models after dropping the entire first or second VE from the input compared to evaluation with both encoders in use. (Abbreviations: **R**egion, **G**rid, **P**atch).

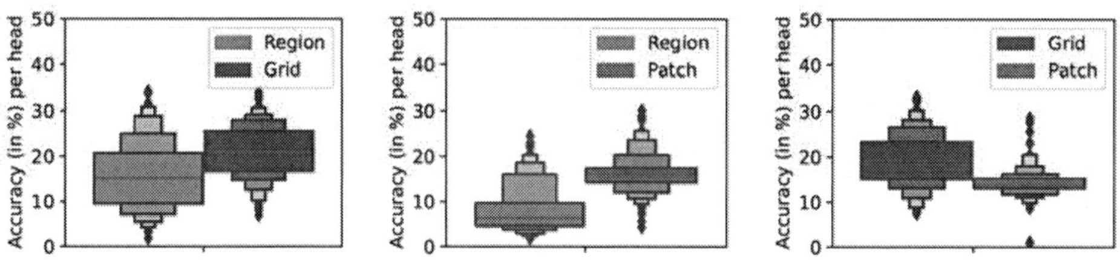

(a) Visual Grounding of attention heads on Flickr30k

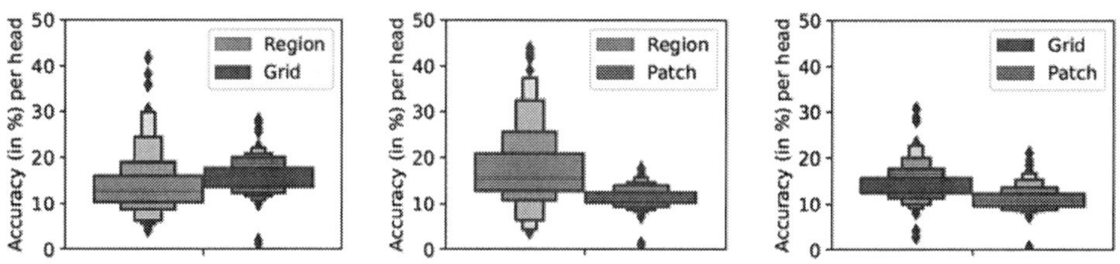

(b) Visual Grounding of attention heads on GQA

Figure 13: (After VE-Dropout Training) Visual Entity Grounding accuracy of all attention heads. An entity is grounded correctly to a VE if the attention weight from the phrase to the matching visual tokens is the highest over all the VE's tokens.

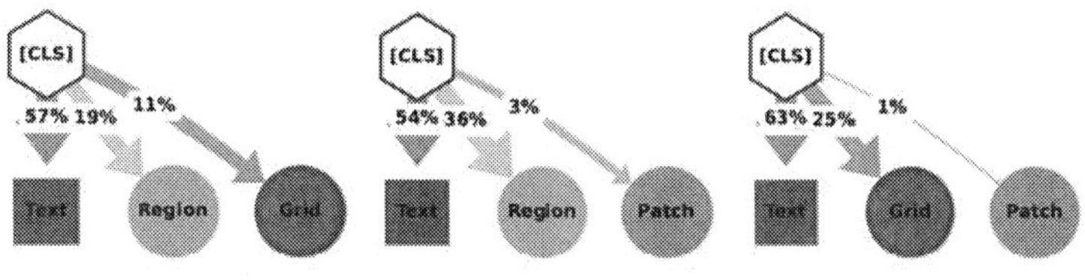

(a) CLS Attention Flickr30k

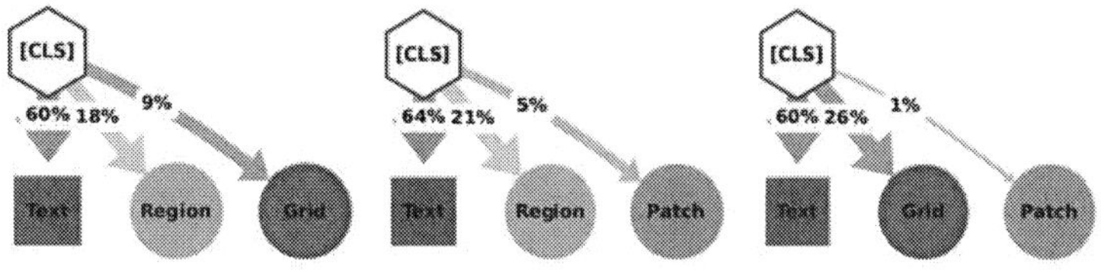

(b) CLS Attention MSCOCO

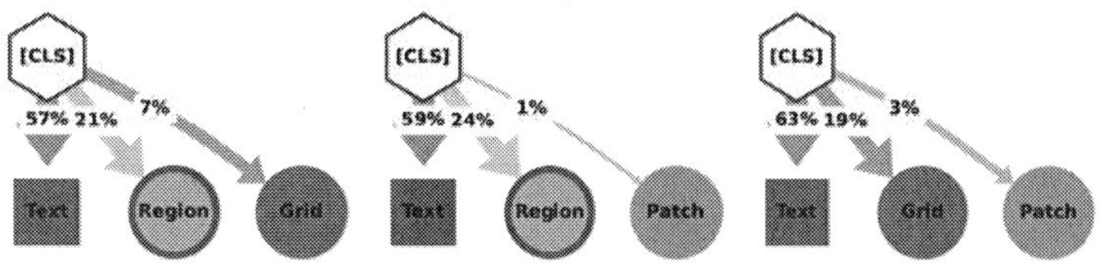

(c) CLS Attention GQA

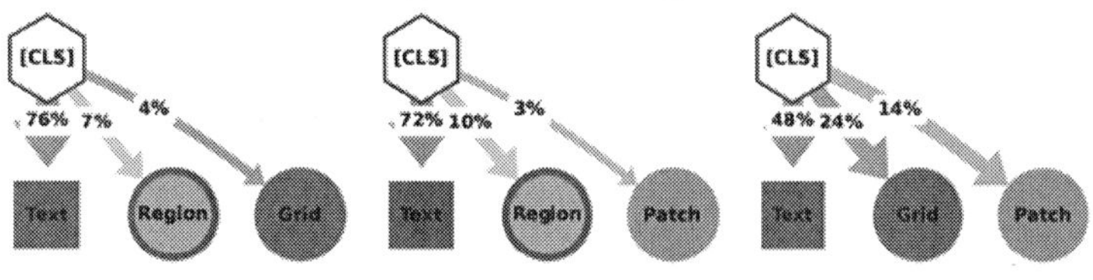

(d) CLS Attention VQA

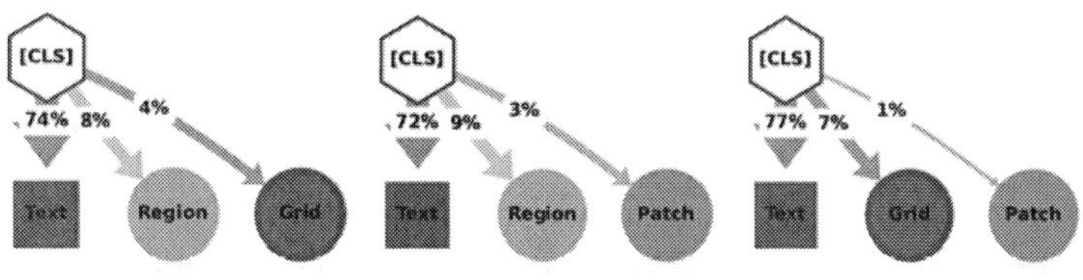

(e) CLS Attention SNLI-VE

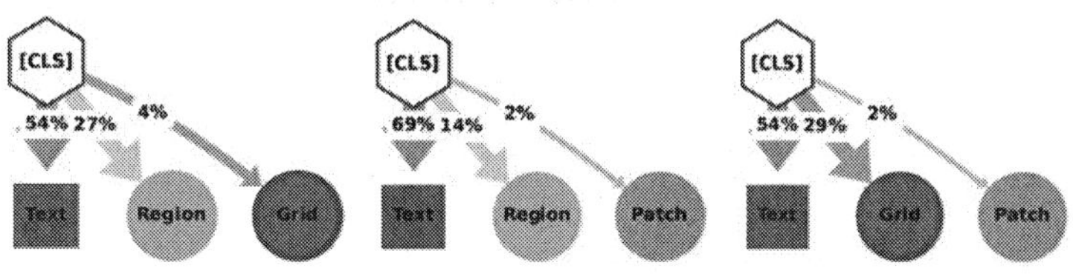

(f) CLS Attention Hateful Memes

Figure 14: (After VE-Dropout Training) CLS attention weights (in %) averaged over all heads to the modalities. Numbers do not add to 100% because of CLS self-attention.

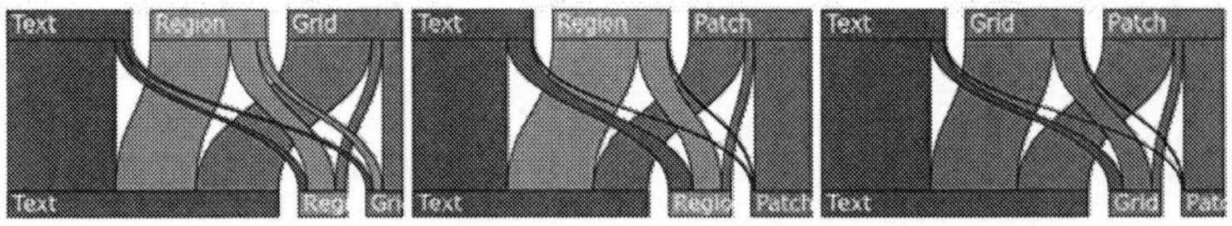

(a) Cross-Attention for Flickr30k

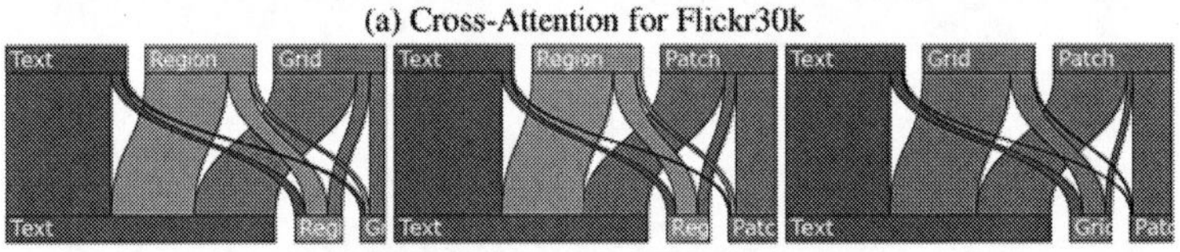

(b) Cross-Attention for MSCOCO

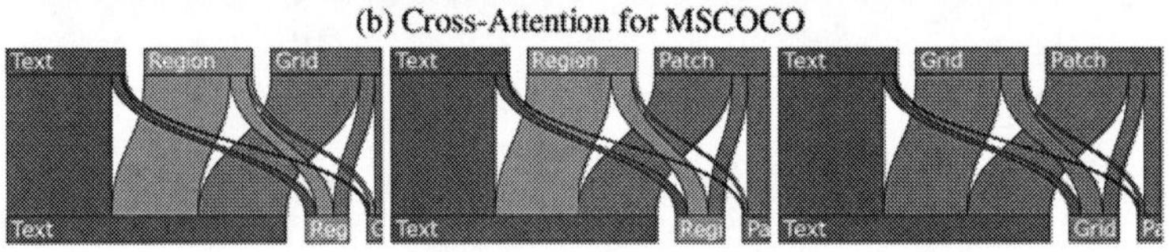

(c) Cross-Attention for GQA

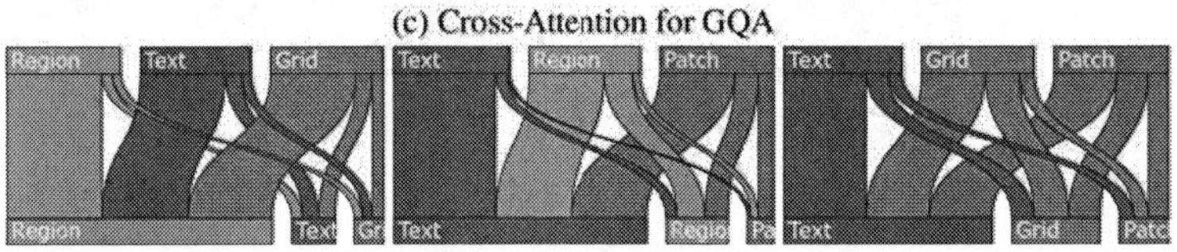

(d) Cross-Attention for VQA

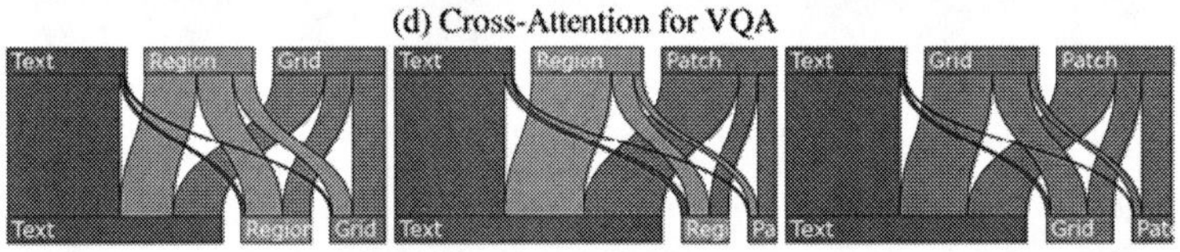

(e) Cross-Attention for SNLI-VE

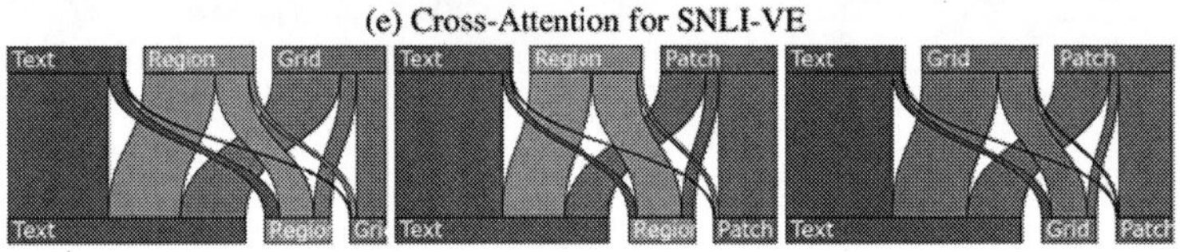

(f) Cross-Attention for Hateful Memes

Figure 15: (After VE-Dropout Training) Attention flow (in %) from each modality (top) to all modalities (bottom). Flow is the sum of all attention weights between the modalities, averaged over all modality tokens and all attention heads.

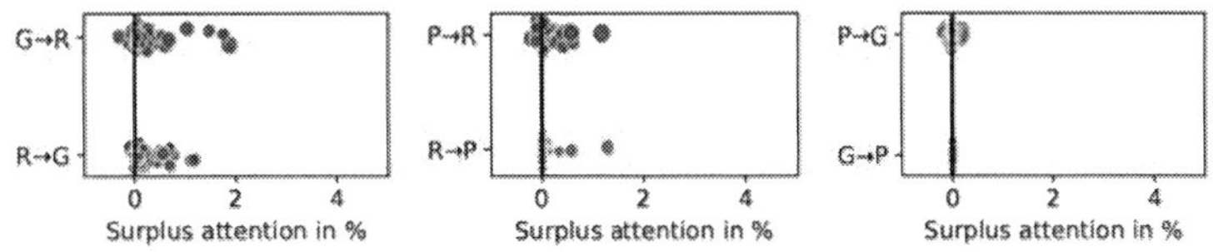

(a) Surplus Attention Flickr30k

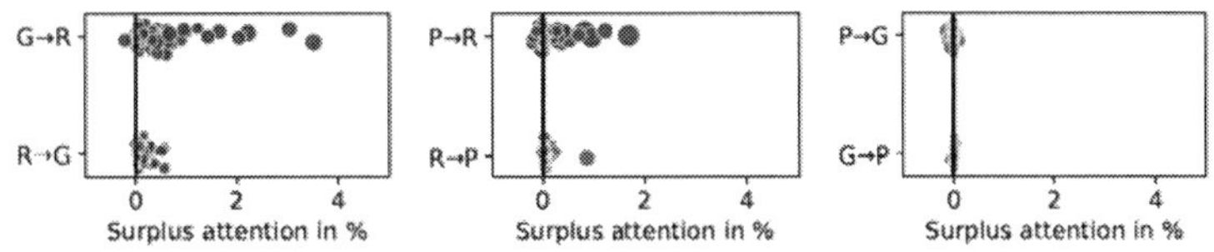

(b) Surplus Attention MSCOCO

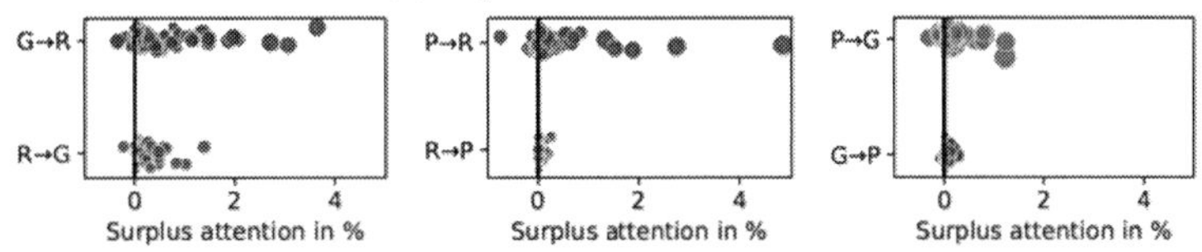

(c) Surplus Attention GQA

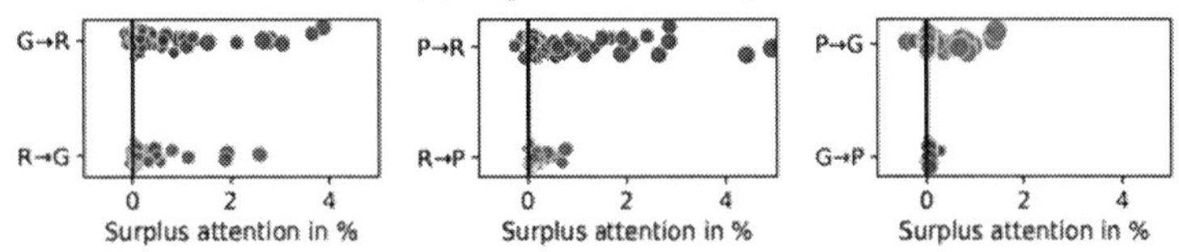

(d) Surplus Attention VQA

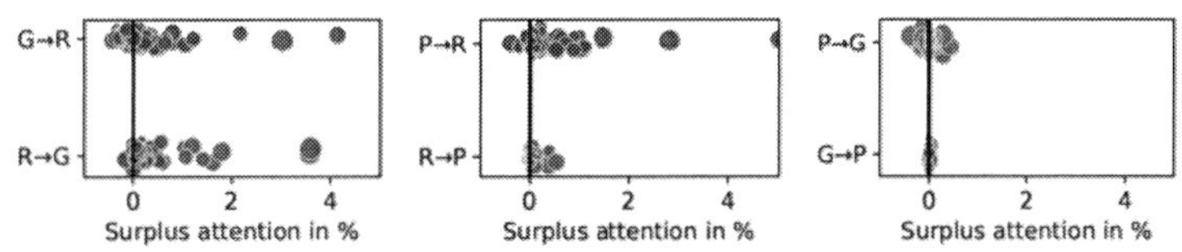

(e) Surplus Attention SNLI-VE

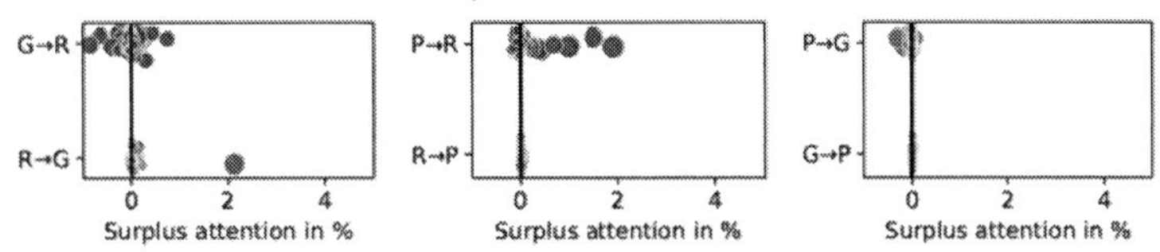

(f) Surplus Attention Hateful Memes

Figure 16: (After VE-Dropout Training) Surplus attention of attention heads from one VE's tokens to another target VE's overlapping tokens compared to the other non-overlapping tokens of the target VE. **Dot size** represents the average total attention paid to the target VE by each head. (Abbreviations: **R**egion, **G**rid, **P**atch).

SPC: Soft Prompt Construction for Cross Domain Generalization

Wenbo Zhao[1], **Arpit Gupta**[1], **Tagyoung Chung**[1] and **Jing Huang**[2]
Alexa AI, Amazon, USA
[1]{wenbzhao,guparpit,tagyoung}@amazon.com
[2]jinghuang.zhu@gmail.com

Abstract

Recent advances in prompt tuning have proven effective as a new language modeling paradigm for various natural language understanding tasks. However, it is challenging to adapt the soft prompt embeddings to different domains or generalize to low-data settings when learning soft prompts itself is unstable, task-specific, and bias-prone. This paper proposes a principled learning framework—soft prompt construction (SPC)—to facilitate learning domain-adaptable soft prompts. Derived from the SPC framework is a simple loss that can plug into various models and tuning approaches to improve their cross-domain performance. We show SPC can improve upon SOTA for contextual query rewriting, summarization, and paraphrase detection by up to 5%, 19%, and 16%, respectively.

1 Introduction

Prompting has emerged as a new paradigm for tuning language models (LMs), drawing increasing research attention. It shows impressive utility in stimulating an LM' hidden knowledge without fine-tuning it (Petroni et al., 2019). Simply adding some descriptive words to the input can steer a general-purpose LM to a specific task in a zero-shot fashion. Table 1 shows some examples of prompting. The prompt "in other words" is added after the conversation as additional input, turning the LM into a contextual query rewriter. Any natural language understanding task can be reformulated into a generation task with proper prompting (Liu et al., 2021b; Raffel et al., 2020). As shown in Table 1, the dialogue state tracking task is converted to generating the slot value given the prompted input. As a result, a natural language understanding task turns into a prompt design task. More sophisticated prompting techniques are derived to better adapt the LM, such as in-context learning (Xie et al., 2021), chain-of-thought (Wei et al., 2022). Researchers hypothesize that these prompting techniques make the LM understand the task instructions and do implicit task adaptation (Xie et al., 2021; Wang et al., 2022a).

Albeit the impressive utility of these prompting techniques, they have some limitations that encourage further research. One major drawback is that the prompt templates significantly impact model performance but require handcrafting, which is why there is increasing prompt engineering and sharing of "good" templates (Zhou et al., 2022). Chosen unwisely, a prompt template would not work or even hurt the model inference (Liu and Chilton, 2022; Wang et al., 2022b). Further, one has to design prompts for each task, making it inefficient and less robust to transfer across models or tasks (Sanh et al., 2022). The other drawback of prompting is that it works best for large models (Reynolds and McDonell, 2021). However, training and serving large LMs are known to be costly.

These limitations drive us to study new prompting methods that require little manual effort and work for large and small models. Soft prompting is one of these approaches. Unlike prompting that adds words to the input, soft prompting adds embeddings to the model, such as injecting embeddings to the token embedding layer or other model layers (Asai et al., 2022). Such embeddings, or *soft prompts*, can be automatically learned. Many studies have shown that soft prompting works well for smaller-sized models and can be as effective as fine-tuning large LMs with orders of magnitude fewer trainable parameters (Lester et al., 2021; Li and Liang, 2021; Liu et al., 2021c; Su et al., 2022).

Soft prompting is a promising approach to further improve cross-domain generalization and task adaptation for all-sized models. However, some barriers need to be removed. First, learning soft prompts lacks guidance, and traditional learning objectives (such as cross-entropy) often lead to unstable training, sub-optimality, and unstable performance. Further, the unstable performance is am-

Proceedings of the 8th Workshop on Representation Learning for NLP (RepL4NLP 2023), pages 118–130

Task	Input	Prompted Input	Output
Contextual Query Rewrite	User: Show me the latest movie by Tom Hanks. Agent: Here is Finch by Tom Hanks. User: Who directed it?	[Input] In other words,	Who directed Finch?
Summarization	Las Vegas police ...	[Input] TL;DR:	The victim ...
Dialogue State Tracking	I am looking for a gastropub.	[Input] What is ${restaurant.food}?	gastropub
Paraphrase Detection	Useless math. Algebraic topology.	Sentence 1 [S1] and sentence 2 [S2] are	equivalent

Table 1: Prompting examples.

plified in cross-domain settings. Soft prompts are often biased by a specific domain and hence less effective for other domains. In low-data settings, it is particularly difficult to learn soft prompts with consistent cross-domain performance (Su et al., 2022; Lester et al., 2021; Liu et al., 2021b; Chen et al., 2022a).

Our objective is to derive a principled paradigm for learning domain-adaptable soft prompts, for which we propose the soft prompt construction (SPC) framework. Using this SPC framework, we further derive a simple loss: the SPC loss. The loss supervises the optimization of soft prompts without re-tuning the entire model. The learned soft prompts demonstrate superior cross-domain generalization than other fine-tuning and prompt tuning approaches. Our contributions are the following:

(1) We propose an SPC framework that learns soft prompts in a zero/few-shot manner and demonstrates superior cross-domain generalization in extensive experiments on diverse tasks.

(2) We propose an SPC loss that can simply plug into various language models and boost their in/cross-domain performance.

(3) Our SPC framework builds upon the simplest soft prompt tuning approach, requiring orders of magnitude fewer trainable parameters than finetuning or other soft prompt tuning approaches.

2 Related Work

Prompting adds token-level templates to the model input, often designed manually (Petroni et al., 2019; Liu et al., 2021b). AutoPrompt automates prompt design via gradient-based search (Shin et al., 2020). Other approaches like (Gao et al., 2021; Sun et al., 2021) may use LMs to generate the prompts. Two prompting techniques are particularly useful for large LMs (LLMs): in-context learning (ICL) and chain-of-thought (CoT). ICL uses a few examples to demonstrate the task, and the LLM can perform the task in a few-shot manner (Xie et al., 2021). CoT instructs an LLM to reason step-by-step to perform a task (Wei et al., 2022). CoT can be seen as a special case of ICL as it often provides examples to demonstrate step-by-step reasoning, such as ReAct (Yao et al., 2022), self-consistency (Wang et al., 2022a). Token-based prompts' performance is highly dependent on prompt selection and constraint on natural language words.

On the other hand, soft prompt tuning uses embedding-level prompts and is optimized by gradients. The prompt embeddings do not necessarily represent natural language words and can generalize to different domains. DART (Zhang et al., 2021) treats input token embeddings as prompt templates. Qin and Eisner (2021) optimize soft prompts via perturbing a prompt mixture. PrefixTuning (Li and Liang, 2021) prepends prompt embeddings to the model layers and uses additional networks to re-parameterize them. P-Tuning v2 (Liu et al., 2021c) extends PrefixTuning and achieves performance comparable to fine-tuning. Such works often use deep prompts (adding prompt embeddings to all model layers) or reparameterization, introducing a large number of new parameters (Li and Liang, 2021; Jiang and Wang, 2022). Lester et al. (2021) add task-specific soft prompts to the model input and obtain performance comparable to fine-tuning large LMs, especially on low-resource domain adaptation tasks.

However, soft prompts' performance is unstable and sensitive to initialization (Qin and Eisner, 2021). Learning soft prompts across tasks is challenging, especially in low-data scenarios (Gu et al., 2022). To this end, Chen et al. (2021) construct soft prompts via knowledge injection and implicit relation constraint. Gu et al. (2022) pretrain soft prompts on varied tasks to improve generalization but require prompts to be added during pre-training. Qin et al. (2021) study the generalization of soft prompts via (nonlinear) subspace decomposition. However, Su et al. (2022) find that the prompt dis-

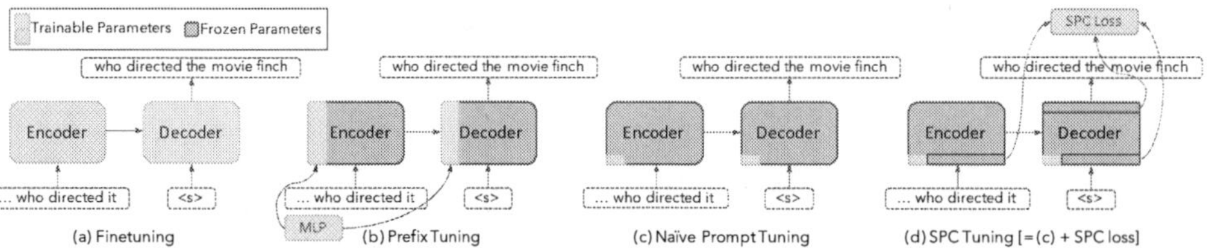

Figure 1: Model diagrams for (a) fine-tuning, (b) PrefixTuning, (c) naive prompt tuning, and (d) SPC + prompt tuning. SPC loss can plug into *any* tuning methods and language models. SPC prompt embeddings are shown as prefixes, but they can be placed *anywhere*.

tance cannot be appropriately quantified by Euclidean or cosine distances, implying a nonlinear and (potentially) non-metrizable prompt embedding space. Hence, constructing the prompt embedding space via decomposition is challenging.

3 Soft Prompt Construction

Using the examples in Table 1, prompting requires us to design different templates for different tasks, such as "in other words" for contextual query rewriting and "TL;DR" for summarization. Such handcrafting process is inefficient, does not generalize, and the performance is unstable. We aim to replace these prompt tokens with soft prompt embeddings and automatically learn domain-adaptable soft prompts. Instead of designing prompt templates, we devise a method to learn prompt embeddings that are universal to all tasks. Such prompt embeddings aim to align the model s.t. `[Input] + [Prompt] yields [Output]`; e.g., `[Input] In other words -> [Output]` $\Rightarrow$ `[input token embeddings][prompt embeddings] -> [output embeddings]`. We present a soft prompt construction (SPC) framework for learning cross-domain generalizable soft prompts.

Consider the data on cross-domain tasks $\mathbb{D} = \mathbb{X} \times \mathbb{Y}$ consisting of the input set $\mathbb{X}$ and output set $\mathbb{Y}$. For text generation tasks, for example, each element in $\mathbb{X}$ or $\mathbb{Y}$ represents a sequence of tokens. Given the generality of the tasks and data structures, we omit the dimensionality in the notations when there is no confusion. The objective of a language model is to maximize the expected log-likelihood

$$\max \mathbb{E}_{F_{\mathrm{y}}} \left[\log f_\theta(\mathrm{y} \mid x)\right] \tag{1}$$

where $x \in \mathbb{X}$, F_{y} is the probability measure w.r.t. random variable y (note we use different fonts for a random variable y and a sample y), and f_θ is the likelihood function with model parameter θ and the conditional density $f(\mathrm{y} \mid x)$. To help this objective, prompting is introduced and prompts p are added to the input $[p, x]$

$$\max \mathbb{E}_{F_{\mathrm{y}}} \left[\log \int_p f_\theta(\mathrm{y} \mid p, x) d\nu_{\mathrm{p}}\right] \tag{2}$$

where ν_{p} is the probability measure of the prompt, and we will omit this for notional simplicity when there is no confusion. Let $L = \log \int_p f_\theta(\mathrm{y} \mid p, x)$. We have

$$L = \log \int_p f_\theta(\mathrm{y} \mid p) f_\theta(p \mid x) \tag{3}$$

$$\geq \int_p \left[\log f_\theta(\mathrm{y} \mid p) + \log f_\theta(p \mid x)\right] \tag{4}$$

where from (3) to (4) we apply Jensen's inequality. To maximize (2), we need to find a maximizer of the lower-bound (4). Taking the partial derivative of (4) w.r.t. p and setting it to zero, one of the feasible maximizers p^* is obtained by (5)

$$p^* = x \oplus y \tag{5}$$

where $\oplus$ means direct sum. Indeed, if we plug (5) into (4), it achieves the maximal (3). When using soft prompts $[p, x] \overset{f_\theta}{\mapsto} y \Rightarrow [e_p, e_x] \overset{f_\theta}{\mapsto} e_y$ where e_x, e_y, e_p are embeddings of x, y, and p, relation (5) naturally extends to the embedding representations

$$e_p^* = e_x \oplus e_y \tag{6}$$

We propose to enforce such a relation using an SPC loss

$$l_{\text{spc}} = \|W[W_x e_x; W_y e_y] - W_p e_p\|_2 \tag{7}$$

where $[\cdot;\cdot]$ is embedding concatenation, Ws are linear transformations that will be learned during model training. The SPC loss is directly added to the original loss (e.g., cross-entropy) to supervise the training.

For those interested, we also provide an algebraic view for our methodology in Appendix B.

Implementation details A backbone language model is used and its parameters are *frozen*. The prompt embeddings e_p have fixed length and are concatenated to the input token embeddings e_x, effectively increasing the input length. Prompt length and concatenation are explained in Section 4. Output embeddings e_y are taken from the last output layer. During training, the SPC loss (7) is directly added to the original loss (e.g., cross-entropy loss). The prompt embeddings and the linear weights of the SPC loss are learned. At inference time, the linear weights are discarded, and only the learned prompt embeddings are concatenated to the input token embeddings. *Only one soft prompt is learned, and it is universal for all domains and tasks.* An illustration is shown in Figure 1. Code 1 shows the code for computing the SPC loss.

4 Experiments

We design experiments to validate the main claims of our SPC framework: (1) SPC loss can be plugged into any model or tuning method, and (2) improve the zero/few-shot in/cross-domain generalization. We will explain our selected tasks, data, model, implementation, and results.

4.1 Task description

We select standard text generation and classification tasks: (1) contextual query rewriting (CQR), (2) abstractive summarization, and (3) paraphrase detection.

CQR refers to rewriting a contextual query in dialogue into a non-contextual query such that any missing information from the context is completed. CQR plays a crucial role in conversation systems, and the rewritten query can be used for downstream tasks such as question answering, information retrieval, and reading comprehension. CQR can be addressed by rule-based approaches, retrieval-based approaches (Fan et al., 2021), pointer-based models (Rastogi et al., 2019; Elgohary et al., 2019; Quan et al., 2019), generation-based models (Anantha et al., 2021; Yu et al., 2020; Liu et al., 2021a; Regan et al., 2019). We combine the end-to-end generation-based approach with prompt tuning to exploit both. Yilmaz and Toraman (2021) have attempted a soft prompt tuning approach for query rewriting. **Abstractive summarization** refers to generating a summary of a given text. Unlike extractive summarization, which extracts phrases from the original text, abstractive summarization may generate new phrases (Lin and Ng, 2019). The difficulty is to balance the semantic cohesion between the text and the new generation. Such problem is addressed by attention methods (Narayan et al., 2018; Gehrmann et al., 2018), extraction-abstraction-based methods (Chen and Bansal, 2018), pointer-generator-based models (See et al., 2017), generation-based methods (Zhang et al., 2020). Only a few use a prompt tuning approach (Li and Liang, 2021; Liu et al., 2022). **Paraphrase detection** refers to telling if two sentences mean the same (Yin and Schütze, 2015). Prompt tuning approaches have proven effective for this task (Lester et al., 2021; Gu et al., 2022).

Zero/few-shot cross-domain settings We train with all training data for in-domain tasks and evaluate on the test data. For cross-domain experiments, we adopt a few-shot one-to-one domain-transfer setting: first train with the source domain training data and then train with a single batch (16 samples in our settings) from the target domain training data. No target domain validation data is used. For the summarization task, we select five domains: sport, business, politics, entertainment, and technology. For the paraphrase detection task, we evaluate the few-shot cross-domain transfer between QQP and MRPC in both directions.

Zero/few-shot cross-task settings We conduct zero/few-shot cross-task transfer evaluation between CQR and summarization: take the trained model from the CQR task, evaluate on the summarization task, and vice-versa.

4.2 Data and metrics

The QReCC dataset for the CQR task consists of 14K open-domain dialogues with 80K (query, rewrite, answer) triples (Anantha et al., 2021). The XSum dataset for the abstractive summarization task consists of 227K (document, summary) pairs. The documents are collected from BBC news articles covering topics like sport, business, politics, entertainment, and technology. The summaries are of one-sentence length (Narayan et al., 2018). For both tasks, the original data split is used. Rouge score (Lin, 2004) is used as a standard evaluation metric.

Following Lester et al. (2021), we use the QQP (Shankar et al., 2017) and MRPC (Dolan and Brockett, 2005) dataset from the GLUE (Wang et al., 2019) benchmark for the paraphrase detection task. QQP consists of 795K question pairs from Quora. Since there is no label for QQP's test set, we use the validation set for testing and use 10% of the training set for validation. MRPC consists of 5.8K sentence pairs from online news articles. The original data split is used. Following Lester et al. (2021) and Raffel et al. (2020), we format the QQP question pairs as [question 1: <question 1 text> question 2: <question 2 text>]. For MRPC, we format the sentence pairs as [sentence 1: <sentence 1 text> sentence 2: <sentence 2 text>]. We convert the binary class labels (1, 0) to "same" and "different" to better situate the task in a generative setting. Only exact matches with the label word are considered correct. [1] F1 score is used as a standard metric.

4.3 Model and baselines

We test the utility of the SPC loss by plugging it into fine-tuning and prompt tuning approaches and comparing the before/after performance. Admittedly, many prompt tuning work surfaces at the time of this manuscript (Liu et al., 2021c; Chen et al., 2022b; Gu et al., 2022). However, it is not our intention to build a better mousetrap but to present a new problem—that of learning domain-adaptable soft prompts—that naturally leads to a new learning paradigm. With this consideration, we select fine-tuning, PrefixTuning (Li and Liang, 2021), and (naive) prompt tuning (Lester et al., 2021) as our baselines because they are SOTA for respective tasks, most widely compared, and do not involve any additional components/tricks. Comparing these clean baselines present a clearer picture of SPC's benefits. The baselines are:

(1) **Fine-tuning** the BART model (Lewis et al., 2020).

(2) **PrefixTuning** (Li and Liang, 2021), a strong baseline commonly compared by other work. It uses the pretrained BART model as the backbone and prepends prompt embeddings to the encoder and decoder layers. The prefix embeddings are reparameterized by feedforward neural networks (see Figure 1). We also implement a variant of PrefixTuning—only prepending prompt embeddings at the decoder layers.

(3) **(Naive) prompt tuning** (Lester et al., 2021), the simplest soft prompt tuning. It prepends prompt embeddings to the input layer (not all layers, see Figure 1). We use the same BART backbone model for CQR and summarization tasks and add prompt embeddings to decoder input. For the paraphrase detection task, we use the same pretrained and LM-adapted T5 models (Lester et al., 2021; Raffel et al., 2020) and add prompt embeddings to encoder input.

4.4 Training and implementation

CQR, summarization We use the pretrained BART-large model (Lewis et al., 2019) for fine-tuning. For PrefixTuning and SPC, we freeze the BART model and only tune the prompt-related parameters. PrefixTuning requires training prefix embeddings and the reparameterization networks. SPC requires training prefix embeddings and the weights in the loss equation (7).

Paraphrase detection The pretrained and LM-adapted T5 models are used (Lester et al., 2021; Raffel et al., 2020). The T5-small model has 77M parameters, and the T5-XL model has 3B parameters.

All training and evaluation use comparable configurations and hyperparameters (e.g., batch size, learning rate, training epochs, prompt length, generation length, beam size). We find the optimal set of hyperparameters through searching, as shown in Table 8. The implementation is based on the HuggingFace's Transformers library (Wolf et al., 2020). We also re-implement the PrefixTuning model (Li and Liang, 2021). We use the metrics code that comes with the HuggingFace datasets. Training is done on the AWS cluster with eight NVIDIA V100 or A100 GPUs. More details on hyper-parameters and computation costs are shown in Appendix A.

4.5 In-domain results

CQR Table 2 shows the results on the CQR task using fine-tuning, PrefixTuning, and prompt tuning with/without SPC loss. For each prompt tuning approach, we compare random prompt initialization (*rand*) and BART word embedding initialization (*bart*). Results show that the SPC loss plugin (*row 8–12*) uniformly increases performance over fine-tuning, PrefixTuning, and prompt tuning (*row 1–7*),

[1]During inference, the generation length is 2 (including a start token). We observe that the T5 model can generate the exact "same/different" tokens with rare exceptions, so no words in vocabulary are masked off.

#	Approach	Rouge-2	Rouge-L	Gain/Loss (+/-%)
1	Finetune	74.93	**83.29**	
2	$\text{Prefix}_{\text{both,rand}}$	37.14	53.57	
3	$\text{Prefix}_{\text{both,bart}}$	55.10	68.94	
4	$\text{Prefix}_{\text{dec,rand}}$	69.68	79.13	
5	$\text{Prefix}_{\text{dec,bart}}$	72.08	81.13	
6	$\text{Prompt}_{\text{rand}}$	68.39	78.16	
7	$\text{Prompt}_{\text{bart}}$	67.13	77.34	
8	SPC+Finetune	**75.40**	83.24	+0.6/-0.06
9	SPC+$\text{Prefix}_{\text{dec,rand}}$	**72.77**	**81.60**	+4.5/+3.1
10	SPC+$\text{Prefix}_{\text{dec,bart}}$	**73.33**	**81.97**	+1.7/+1.0
11	SPC+$\text{Prompt}_{\text{rand}}$	**70.86**	**80.33**	+3.6/+2.8
12	SPC+$\text{Prompt}_{\text{bart}}$	**72.84**	**81.67**	+8.5/+5.6

Table 2: Before/after SPC results on contextual query rewriting task with fine-tuning (Finetune), PrefixTuing (Prefix), and prompt tuning (Prompt).

Approach	Rouge-2	Rouge-L	Gain/Loss (+/-%)
Finetune	20.66	35.48	
$\text{Prefix}_{\text{both,rand}}$	10.49	24.57	
$\text{Prefix}_{\text{both,bart}}$	12.47	26.63	
$\text{Prefix}_{\text{dec,rand}}$	**19.39**	**34.30**	
$\text{Prefix}_{\text{dec,bart}}$	18.81	**33.79**	
$\text{Prompt}_{\text{rand}}$	16.33	31.08	
$\text{Prompt}_{\text{bart}}$	16.66	31.63	
SPC+Finetune	**20.82**	**35.55**	+0.8/+0.2
SPC+$\text{Prefix}_{\text{dec,rand}}$	18.66	33.62	-3.8/-2.0
SPC+$\text{Prefix}_{\text{dec,bart}}$	**18.88**	33.76	+0.4/-0.09
SPC+$\text{Prompt}_{\text{rand}}$	**17.02**	**32.15**	+4.2/+3.4
SPC+$\text{Prompt}_{\text{bart}}$	**17.91**	**32.91**	+7.5/+4.0

Table 3: Before/after SPC results on abstractive summarization task with fine-tuning (Finetune), PrefixTuing (Prefix), and prompt tuning (Prompt).

with the gain ranging from 0.6%–8.5%. For PrefixTuning (*row 2–5*), prompting only at the decoder layers (*row 5*) is the best among its variations. SPC loss also significantly reduces sensitivity to prompt initialization.

Summarization Table 3 shows the results on the summarization task. We observe similar trends to CQR. [2] The SPC loss increases performance over fine-tuning, PrefixTuning, and prompt tuning, with the gain ranging from 0.2%–7.5%. SPC loss also significantly reduces sensitivity to prompt initialization.

4.6 Cross-domain results

Given the performance boost of SPC on top of other tuning approaches demonstrated in the last section, we choose to use the **simplest and most parameter-efficient** SPC loss + prompt tuning (*SPC+Prompt*) to demonstrate SPC's utility in cross-domain settings.

Summarization Table 4 presents the results for both in-domain and few-shot (16) cross-domain summarization tasks obtained with fine-tuning, PrefixTuning at the decoder with BART initialization, and SPC+Prompt with BART initialization. For in-domain, fine-tuning outperforms the prompt tuning methods. This aligns with our expectations, given that fine-tuning tunes the entire model, thereby utilizing a significantly larger number of trainable parameters compared to prompt tuning approaches. Remarkably, despite having far fewer trainable parameters, SPC+Prompt manages to achieve performance that is either comparable to or better than that of PrefixTuning. In some domains, it even matches the performance of fine-tuning. Furthermore, when plugged into fine-tuning, SPC has the potential to enhance its performance even further (as shown in Table 3). Most impressively, despite less sufficient in-domain training, SPC+Prompt surpasses other state-of-the-art methods in cross-domain performance. This greatly improves cross-domain adaptation.

Paraphrase detection Table 5 shows the results on the paraphrase detection task for both in-domain and few(16)-shot cross-domain between QQP and MRPC. SPC+Prompt initializes prompt embeddings with the first prompt-length token embeddings of the T5 model. SPC+Prompt outperforms prompt tuning with large margins, validating the cross-domain generalization of the soft prompts learned by SPC.

Cross-task Table 6 shows the results for zero/few-shot cross-task experiments between CQR and summarization. SPC+Prompt is at par or better in all settings. Prompt tuning approaches perform better than fine-tuning in low-resource settings, consistent with the findings by Chen et al. (2022a).

4.7 Analysis and discussion

Number of parameters PrefixTuning has around 7% trainable parameters (including prefix embeddings and reparameterization networks) compared to fine-tuning. Our SPC method drastically reduces the number of trainable parameters by using 0.07% parameters (including prompt embeddings and SPC loss parameters) as shown in Table 7. This ratio

[2]Our implementation does not achieve the performance reported in (Li and Liang, 2021). This may arise from different experiment configurations: compared to (Li and Liang, 2021), we do not use BPE tokens and length normalization, and we use smaller batch sizes and only 10% validation data.

Domain	Approach	Sport	Business	Politics	Entertainment	Technology
Sport	Finetune	23.89, 37.83	9.79, 23.75	11.34, 24.35	15.02, 29.16	7.69, 22.13
	Prefixtune	18.83, 33.10	13.16, 26.71	14.49, 28.14	19.02, 32.58	**12.73, 28.03**
	SPC+Prompt	18.38, 33.00	**14.04, 28.25**	**15.03, 28.68**	**20.53, 34.73**	11.38, 27.06
Business	Finetune	14.99, 29.06	15.79, 30.65	14.07, 27.44	18.28, 32.71	11.08, 25.96
	Prefixtune	15.03, 29.98	14.52, 28.80	15.12, 28.30	19.64, 32.63	12.00, 26.27
	SPC+Prompt	**16.51, 30.92**	14.70, 29.31	**15.52, 28.84**	**20.61, 34.17**	**12.25, 27.54**
Politics	Finetune	11.65, 24.98	10.49, 24.24	16.35, 29.20	16.03, 29.38	8.12, 21.93
	Prefixtune	16.04, 30.10	13.42, 27.61	15.57, 28.84	19.98, 33.63	11.52, 26.42
	SPC+Prompt	**16.50, 30.97**	**13.92, 28.15**	15.78, 29.36	**20.60, 34.80**	**12.62, 28.04**
Entertainment	Finetune	14.60, 28.67	13.01, 27.31	**15.62, 28.82**	23.62, 37.76	10.31, 25.28
	Prefixtune	16.59, 31.02	**14.07**, 28.42	15.23, 28.31	21.09, 35.26	11.56, 26.33
	SPC+Prompt	**16.60, 31.11**	**14.07, 28.50**	15.17, 28.05	20.88, 35.24	**12.15, 27.56**
Technology	Finetune	15.08, 28.81	12.90, 27.17	14.41, 27.82	18.95, 32.50	11.30, 26.15
	Prefixtune	**16.28, 30.66**	**14.16, 28.55**	**15.09, 28.52**	**32.56, 42.25**	12.00, 26.90
	SPC+Prompt	15.49, 29.74	13.22, 27.13	13.65, 26.55	19.38, 33.06	11.56, 26.31

Table 4: Few-shot cross-domain results on summarization task with fine-tuning (Finetune), PrefixTuing (Prefix), and SPC+prompt tuning (SPC+Prompt). SPC+Prompt uses significantly fewer trainable parameters. Reported as (Rouge-2, Rouge-L) pairs. **Bold numbers** represent the best of the three approaches for each domain–domain pair. Underlined numbers represent *in-domain* full-data results.

Source Domain	Target Domain	Approach	T5-small (F1)	T5-xl (F1)
QQP	QQP	Prompttune	69.93	81.26
		SPC+Prompt	**73.68**	**81.42**
	MRPC	Prompttune	68.49	70.45
		SPC+Prompt	**79.32**	**77.78**
MRPC	MRPC	Prompttune	79.89	79.87
		SPC+Prompt	**81.22**	**81.29**
	QQP	Prompttune	53.13	54.02
		SPC+Prompt	**63.64**	**60.87**

Table 5: In-domain & 16-shot cross-domain results on paraphrase detection task with prompt tuning (Prompttune) and SPC+prompt tuning (SPC+Prompt).

Source Task	Target Task	Approach	Zero-Shot	Few-Shot
QReCC	XSum	Finetune	**2.29, 11.79**	6.15, 18.56
		Prefixtune	2.01, 11.05	10.26, 24.08
		SPC+Prompt	2.14, 11.13	**13.98, 28.39**
XSum	QReCC	Finetune	9.33, 19.66	42.29, 54.22
		Prefixtune	10.61, 19.77	33.20, 45.72
		SPC+Prompt	**19.33, 31.69**	**43.26, 54.96**

Table 6: Zero/Few-shot cross-task results with fine-tuning (Finetune), PrefixTuing (Prefix), and SPC+prompt tuning (SPC+Prompt). Reported as (Rouge-2, Rouge-L) pairs.

becomes negligible as the LM goes larger (e.g., T5-XL, GPT-3). We do not show SPC results with reparameterization as its effect is inconsistent across tasks (Liu et al., 2021c).

Ablation study Table 2, 3, and Figure 2 show the effectiveness of our SPC framework in comparison with baselines. The SPC loss significantly improves the performance of fine-tuning, Prefix-

Approach	Total Parameters	Trainable Parameters (#/%)
Finetuning	406,291,456	406,291,456 / 100%
PrefixTuning	447,507,008	41,215,552 / 9.21%
PrefixTuning$_{\text{dec}}$	426,899,232	20,607,776 / 4.83%
Prompt Tuning	406,393,856	102,400 / 0.025%
SPC+Prompt	406,589,225	297,769 / 0.073%

Table 7: Trainable parameter count w.r.t. BART model and fixed prompt length 100.

Tuning, and prompt tuning.

Prompt length Prompt length significantly affects the performance of prompt tuning approaches (Li and Liang, 2021; Liu et al., 2021c), as shown in Figure 3. Their relationship is non-linear. A longer prompt (hence more parameters) does not translate to better performance, suggesting prompt tuning's high variance that cannot be stabilized by using more parameters or larger models (Chen et al., 2022a). Generally, simpler tasks require a shorter prompt (Liu et al., 2021c).

Prompt initialization Prompt tuning methods generally benefit from "meaningful" prompt initialization, such as initializing from model word embeddings as shown in Table 2 and 3. Our SPC approach is less sensitive to the initialization method than PrefixTuning (Chen et al., 2022a), and the SPC loss helps stabilize performance.

Prompt position Our experiments suggest that generation tasks favor prompting after the original input, i.e., at the decoder. For the text classification

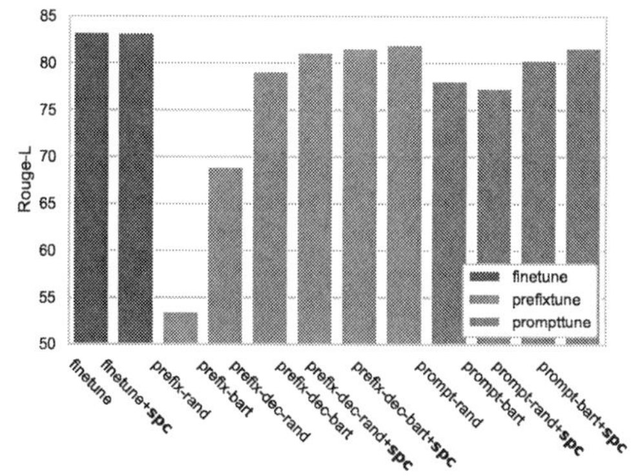

Figure 2: Ablation study on CQR task. Y-axis is the Rouge-L score and X-axis represents model variants.

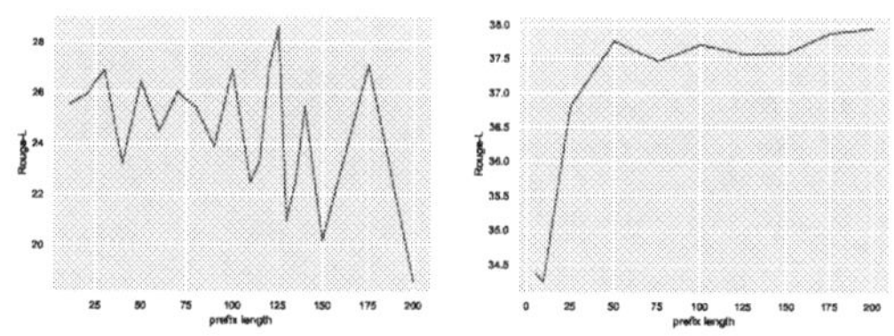

(a) QReCC (b) XSum

Figure 3: Prompt length *v.s.* SPC performance on (a) QReCC and (b) XSum. Results obtained with (a) 10% validation and 25% training data; (b) 10% validation and 20% training data.

task (paraphrase detection), we prompt before the original input as suggested by Liu et al. (2021c); Lester et al. (2021). However, in our experience prompting after the original input still performs better for most tasks.

Interpretability There is an ongoing debate on whether soft prompts are interpretable. Webson and Pavlick (2021) find little evidence supporting language models understanding the prompts' meaning. Other works suggest that soft prompts form semantically close clusters (Lester et al., 2021; Zhang et al., 2021) and task-specific clusters (Su et al., 2022). However, the prompted embedding space may be highly nonlinear and potentially non-metrizable; hence, the clusters induced by Euclidean or cosine distance may not imply semantic similarity (Su et al., 2022). Instead, the clusters may be illusions arising from certain initialization strategies or the clustering tendency in high dimensions—namely, the probability for high-dimensional vectors to be uniformly distributed across dimensions is low. Our experiments find that the learned soft prompts do not convert to meaningful phrases. However, carefully controlled experiments are required to exclude confounding factors, and we leave this exploration to future work.

5 Conclusions

This paper proposes a soft prompt construction (SPC) framework to learn domain-adaptable soft prompts. The derived SPC loss is model/task-agnostic and can plug into other models and tuning methods to improve their cross-domain performance. Experiments on three tasks (contextual query rewriting, abstractive summarization, paraphrase detection) demonstrate that SPC improves significantly over strong SOTA: PrefixTuning (Li and Liang, 2021), prompt tuning (Lester et al., 2021), and fine-tuning in zero/few-shot cross-domain/task settings across different LMs (BART, T5 family). Various properties of SPC are also analyzed. This study paves the way for loss-guided domain-adaptable prompt learning.

Limitations

The proposed SPC framework is model and task agnostic and can scale to different models and tasks. It is adaptable to domain/task shifts and generalizes well with low data. However, the prompt length has to be tuned for each task, and there is no principled way of determining the optimal prompt length. This work does not explore the interpretation of soft prompts or prompt ensemble. Future work can investigate other loss forms derived from our SPC framework, explore the combination of fine-tuning's strong in-domain performance and SPC's cross-domain performance, and apply SPC and other parameter-efficient tuning approaches to large LMs.

Ethical Statement

We hereby state that our study adheres to the ACL Code of Ethics and Professional Conduct. We do not see an immediate negative impact or potential misuse of the proposed SPC method. Should our method fail in real-world applications, it will not cause potential harm to vulnerable populations. We examine the dataset and trained models and do not see bias incurred by our method. Our study does not use demographic or identity characteristics from users. No data is or will be collected from users. Our method does not increase energy and carbon costs but will potentially reduce them due to its data- and parameter-efficient training.

References

Raviteja Anantha, Svitlana Vakulenko, Zhucheng Tu, Shayne Longpre, Stephen Pulman, and Srinivas Chappidi. 2021. Open-domain question answering goes conversational via question rewriting. In *Proceedings of the 2021 Conference of the North American Chapter of the Association for Computational Linguistics: Human Language Technologies*, pages 520–534.

Akari Asai, Mohammadreza Salehi, Matthew E Peters, and Hannaneh Hajishirzi. 2022. Attempt: Parameter-efficient multi-task tuning via attentional mixtures of soft prompts. In *Proceedings of the 2022 Conference on Empirical Methods in Natural Language Processing*, pages 6655–6672.

Michael Barr and Charles Wells. 1990. *Category theory for computing science*, volume 1. Prentice Hall New York.

Guanzheng Chen, Fangyu Liu, Zaiqiao Meng, and Shangsong Liang. 2022a. Revisiting parameter-efficient tuning: Are we really there yet? *arXiv preprint arXiv:2202.07962*.

Xiang Chen, Ningyu Zhang, Xin Xie, Shumin Deng, Yunzhi Yao, Chuanqi Tan, Fei Huang, Luo Si, and Huajun Chen. 2021. Knowprompt: Knowledge-aware prompt-tuning with synergistic optimization for relation extraction. *arXiv preprint arXiv:2104.07650*.

Xiang Chen, Ningyu Zhang, Xin Xie, Shumin Deng, Yunzhi Yao, Chuanqi Tan, Fei Huang, Luo Si, and Huajun Chen. 2022b. Knowprompt: Knowledge-aware prompt-tuning with synergistic optimization for relation extraction. In *Proceedings of the ACM Web Conference 2022*, pages 2778–2788.

Yen-Chun Chen and Mohit Bansal. 2018. Fast abstractive summarization with reinforce-selected sentence rewriting. In *Proceedings of the 56th Annual Meeting of the Association for Computational Linguistics (Volume 1: Long Papers)*, pages 675–686.

Bill Dolan and Chris Brockett. 2005. Automatically constructing a corpus of sentential paraphrases. In *Third International Workshop on Paraphrasing (IWP2005)*.

Ahmed Elgohary, Denis Peskov, and Jordan Boyd-Graber. 2019. Can you unpack that? learning to rewrite questions-in-context. In *Proceedings of the 2019 Conference on Empirical Methods in Natural Language Processing and the 9th International Joint Conference on Natural Language Processing (EMNLP-IJCNLP)*, pages 5918–5924.

Xing Fan, Eunah Cho, Xiaojiang Huang, and Chenlei Guo. 2021. Search based self-learning query rewrite system in conversational ai. In *2nd International Workshop on Data-Efficient Machine Learning (DeMaL)*.

Tianyu Gao, Adam Fisch, and Danqi Chen. 2021. Making pre-trained language models better few-shot learners. In *Proceedings of the 59th Annual Meeting of the Association for Computational Linguistics and the 11th International Joint Conference on Natural Language Processing (Volume 1: Long Papers)*, pages 3816–3830.

Sebastian Gehrmann, Yuntian Deng, and Alexander M Rush. 2018. Bottom-up abstractive summarization. In *Proceedings of the 2018 Conference on Empirical Methods in Natural Language Processing*, pages 4098–4109.

Yuxian Gu, Xu Han, Zhiyuan Liu, and Minlie Huang. 2022. Ppt: Pre-trained prompt tuning for few-shot learning. In *Proceedings of the 60th Annual Meeting of the Association for Computational Linguistics (Volume 1: Long Papers)*, pages 8410–8423.

Yuxin Jiang and Wei Wang. 2022. Deep continuous prompt for contrastive learning of sentence embeddings. *arXiv preprint arXiv:2203.06875*.

Serge Lang, FW Gehring, and KA Ribet. 2002. *Introduction to differentiable manifolds*, volume 32. Springer.

Brian Lester, Rami Al-Rfou, and Noah Constant. 2021. The power of scale for parameter-efficient prompt tuning. In *Proceedings of the 2021 Conference on Empirical Methods in Natural Language Processing*, pages 3045–3059.

Mike Lewis, Yinhan Liu, Naman Goyal, Marjan Ghazvininejad, Abdelrahman Mohamed, Omer Levy, Veselin Stoyanov, and Luke Zettlemoyer. 2019. BART: denoising sequence-to-sequence pre-training for natural language generation, translation, and comprehension. *CoRR*, abs/1910.13461.

Mike Lewis, Yinhan Liu, Naman Goyal, Marjan Ghazvininejad, Abdelrahman Mohamed, Omer Levy, Veselin Stoyanov, and Luke Zettlemoyer. 2020. Bart: Denoising sequence-to-sequence pre-training for natural language generation, translation, and comprehension. In *Proceedings of the 58th Annual Meeting of the Association for Computational Linguistics*, pages 7871–7880.

Xiang Lisa Li and Percy Liang. 2021. Prefix-tuning: Optimizing continuous prompts for generation. In *Proceedings of the 59th Annual Meeting of the Association for Computational Linguistics and the 11th International Joint Conference on Natural Language Processing (Volume 1: Long Papers)*, pages 4582–4597.

Chin-Yew Lin. 2004. Rouge: A package for automatic evaluation of summaries. In *Text summarization branches out*, pages 74–81.

Hui Lin and Vincent Ng. 2019. Abstractive summarization: A survey of the state of the art. In *Proceedings of the AAAI Conference on Artificial Intelligence*, volume 33, pages 9815–9822.

Hang Liu, Meng Chen, Youzheng Wu, Xiaodong He, and Bowen Zhou. 2021a. Conversational query rewriting with self-supervised learning. In *ICASSP 2021-2021 IEEE International Conference on Acoustics, Speech and Signal Processing (ICASSP)*, pages 7628–7632. IEEE.

Pengfei Liu, Weizhe Yuan, Jinlan Fu, Zhengbao Jiang, Hiroaki Hayashi, and Graham Neubig. 2021b. Pre-train, prompt, and predict: A systematic survey of prompting methods in natural language processing. *arXiv preprint arXiv:2107.13586*.

Vivian Liu and Lydia B Chilton. 2022. Design guidelines for prompt engineering text-to-image generative models. In *Proceedings of the 2022 CHI Conference on Human Factors in Computing Systems*, pages 1–23.

Xiao Liu, Kaixuan Ji, Yicheng Fu, Zhengxiao Du, Zhilin Yang, and Jie Tang. 2021c. P-tuning v2: Prompt tuning can be comparable to fine-tuning universally across scales and tasks. *arXiv preprint arXiv:2110.07602*.

Xiaochen Liu, Yu Bai, Jiawei Li, Yinan Hu, and Yang Gao. 2022. Psp: Pre-trained soft prompts for few-shot abstractive summarization. *arXiv preprint arXiv:2204.04413*.

William S Massey. 2019. *A basic course in algebraic topology*, volume 127. Springer.

Shashi Narayan, Shay B. Cohen, and Mirella Lapata. 2018. Don't give me the details, just the summary! Topic-aware convolutional neural networks for extreme summarization. In *Proceedings of the 2018 Conference on Empirical Methods in Natural Language Processing*, Brussels, Belgium.

Fabio Petroni, Tim Rocktäschel, Sebastian Riedel, Patrick Lewis, Anton Bakhtin, Yuxiang Wu, and Alexander Miller. 2019. Language models as knowledge bases? In *Proceedings of the 2019 Conference on Empirical Methods in Natural Language Processing and the 9th International Joint Conference on Natural Language Processing (EMNLP-IJCNLP)*, pages 2463–2473.

Guanghui Qin and Jason Eisner. 2021. Learning how to ask: Querying lms with mixtures of soft prompts. In *Proceedings of the 2021 Conference of the North American Chapter of the Association for Computational Linguistics: Human Language Technologies*, pages 5203–5212.

Yujia Qin, Xiaozhi Wang, Yusheng Su, Yankai Lin, Ning Ding, Zhiyuan Liu, Juanzi Li, Lei Hou, Peng Li, Maosong Sun, et al. 2021. Exploring low-dimensional intrinsic task subspace via prompt tuning. *arXiv preprint arXiv:2110.07867*.

Jun Quan, Deyi Xiong, Bonnie Webber, and Changjian Hu. 2019. Gecor: An end-to-end generative ellipsis and co-reference resolution model for task-oriented dialogue. In *Proceedings of the 2019 Conference on Empirical Methods in Natural Language Processing and the 9th International Joint Conference on Natural Language Processing (EMNLP-IJCNLP)*, pages 4547–4557.

Colin Raffel, Noam Shazeer, Adam Roberts, Katherine Lee, Sharan Narang, Michael Matena, Yanqi Zhou, Wei Li, and Peter J Liu. 2020. Exploring the limits of transfer learning with a unified text-to-text transformer. *Journal of Machine Learning Research*, 21:1–67.

Pushpendre Rastogi, AI Alexa, Arpit Gupta, and Tongfei Chen. 2019. Scaling multi-domain dialogue state tracking via query reformulation. *NAACL HLT 2019*, pages 97–105.

Michael Regan, Pushpendre Rastogi, Arpit Gupta, and Lambert Mathias. 2019. A dataset for resolving referring expressions in spoken dialogue via contextual query rewrites (cqr). *arXiv preprint arXiv:1903.11783*.

Laria Reynolds and Kyle McDonell. 2021. Prompt programming for large language models: Beyond the few-shot paradigm. In *Extended Abstracts of the 2021 CHI Conference on Human Factors in Computing Systems*, pages 1–7.

Victor Sanh, Albert Webson, Colin Raffel, Stephen Bach, Lintang Sutawika, Zaid Alyafeai, Antoine Chaffin, Arnaud Stiegler, Teven Le Scao, Arun Raja, et al. 2022. Multitask prompted training enables zero-shot task generalization. In *The Tenth International Conference on Learning Representations*.

Abigail See, Peter J Liu, and Christopher D Manning. 2017. Get to the point: Summarization with pointer-generator networks. *arXiv preprint arXiv:1704.04368*.

Iyer Shankar, Dandekar Nikhil, and Csernai Kornel. 2017. First quora dataset release: question pairs (2017). *URL https://www. quora. com/q/quoradata/First-Quora-Dataset-Release-Question-Pairs*.

Taylor Shin, Yasaman Razeghi, Robert L Logan IV, Eric Wallace, and Sameer Singh. 2020. Autoprompt: Eliciting knowledge from language models with automatically generated prompts. In *Proceedings of the 2020 Conference on Empirical Methods in Natural Language Processing (EMNLP)*, pages 4222–4235.

Edwin H Spanier. 1989. *Algebraic topology*. Springer Science & Business Media.

Yusheng Su, Xiaozhi Wang, Yujia Qin, Chi-Min Chan, Yankai Lin, Huadong Wang, Kaiyue Wen, Zhiyuan Liu, Peng Li, Juanzi Li, et al. 2022. On transferability of prompt tuning for natural language processing. In *Proceedings of the 2022 Conference of the North American Chapter of the Association for Computational Linguistics: Human Language Technologies*, pages 3949–3969.

Yi Sun, Yu Zheng, Chao Hao, and Hangping Qiu. 2021. Nsp-bert: A prompt-based zero-shot learner through an original pre-training task–next sentence prediction. *arXiv preprint arXiv:2109.03564*.

Alex Wang, Amanpreet Singh, Julian Michael, Felix Hill, Omer Levy, and Samuel R Bowman. 2019. Glue: A multi-task benchmark and analysis platform for natural language understanding. In *7th International Conference on Learning Representations, ICLR 2019*.

Xuezhi Wang, Jason Wei, Dale Schuurmans, Quoc Le, Ed Chi, and Denny Zhou. 2022a. Self-consistency improves chain of thought reasoning in language models. *arXiv preprint arXiv:2203.11171*.

Yihan Wang, Si Si, Daliang Li, Michal Lukasik, Felix Yu, Cho-Jui Hsieh, Inderjit S Dhillon, and Sanjiv Kumar. 2022b. Preserving in-context learning ability in large language model fine-tuning. *arXiv preprint arXiv:2211.00635*.

Albert Webson and Ellie Pavlick. 2021. Do prompt-based models really understand the meaning of their prompts? *arXiv preprint arXiv:2109.01247*.

Jason Wei, Xuezhi Wang, Dale Schuurmans, Maarten Bosma, Ed Chi, Quoc Le, and Denny Zhou. 2022. Chain of thought prompting elicits reasoning in large language models. *arXiv preprint arXiv:2201.11903*.

Charles A Weibel. 1995. *An introduction to homological algebra*. 38. Cambridge university press.

Thomas Wolf, Lysandre Debut, Victor Sanh, Julien Chaumond, Clement Delangue, Anthony Moi, Pierric Cistac, Tim Rault, Rémi Louf, Morgan Funtowicz, et al. 2020. Transformers: State-of-the-art natural language processing. In *Proceedings of the 2020 conference on empirical methods in natural language processing: system demonstrations*, pages 38–45.

Sang Michael Xie, Aditi Raghunathan, Percy Liang, and Tengyu Ma. 2021. An explanation of in-context learning as implicit bayesian inference. *arXiv preprint arXiv:2111.02080*.

Shunyu Yao, Jeffrey Zhao, Dian Yu, Nan Du, Izhak Shafran, Karthik Narasimhan, and Yuan Cao. 2022. React: Synergizing reasoning and acting in language models. *arXiv preprint arXiv:2210.03629*.

Eyup Halit Yilmaz and Cagri Toraman. 2021. Conqx: Semantic expansion of spoken queries for intent detection based on conditioned text generation. *arXiv preprint arXiv:2109.00729*.

Wenpeng Yin and Hinrich Schütze. 2015. Convolutional neural network for paraphrase identification. In *Proceedings of the 2015 Conference of the North American Chapter of the Association for Computational Linguistics: Human Language Technologies*, pages 901–911.

Shi Yu, Jiahua Liu, Jingqin Yang, Chenyan Xiong, Paul Bennett, Jianfeng Gao, and Zhiyuan Liu. 2020. Few-shot generative conversational query rewriting. In *Proceedings of the 43rd International ACM SIGIR conference on research and development in Information Retrieval*, pages 1933–1936.

Jingqing Zhang, Yao Zhao, Mohammad Saleh, and Peter Liu. 2020. Pegasus: Pre-training with extracted gap-sentences for abstractive summarization. In *International Conference on Machine Learning*, pages 11328–11339. PMLR.

Ningyu Zhang, Luoqiu Li, Xiang Chen, Shumin Deng, Zhen Bi, Chuanqi Tan, Fei Huang, and Huajun Chen. 2021. Differentiable prompt makes pre-trained language models better few-shot learners. *arXiv preprint arXiv:2108.13161*.

Yongchao Zhou, Andrei Ioan Muresanu, Ziwen Han, Keiran Paster, Silviu Pitis, Harris Chan, and Jimmy Ba. 2022. Large language models are human-level prompt engineers. *arXiv preprint arXiv:2211.01910*.

A Additional Experiment Details

```
# Using PyTorch as demonstration
freeze_params(model)
model.train()

# Initialize prompt embedding
prompt_embedder = torch.nn.Embedding(
    prompt_length, embedding_dim)
prompt_embedder.weight = torch.nn.
    Parameter(model.shared.weight[:
    prompt_length, :].clone().detach())
prompt_embedding = prompt_embedder(range
    (prompt_length))

# Add prompt embedding to model input
    and run forward pass
inputs_embeds = torch.cat((
    prompt_embedding.clone(),
    input_embeds), dim=1)
outputs = model.forward(input_embeds)

# Get embeddings
E_x = outputs.encoder_hidden_states[0]
    # shape (batch_size, sequence_length
    , embedding_dim)
E_y = outputs.decoder_hidden_states[-1]
E_p = outputs.decoder_hidden_states[0]
    or outputs.encoder_hidden_states
    [0][:, <prompt indices>, :]

# Transform embeddings
E_x = W_x(E_x).squeeze(-1)
E_y = W_y(E_y).squeeze(-1)
E_xy = torch.cat((E_x, E_y), dim=1)
E_xy = W(E_xy)
E_p = W_p(E_p).squeeze(-1)

# Compute loss
spc_loss = (E_xy - E_p).pow(2).sum(dim
    =1).sqrt().mean()
loss = outputs.loss + spc_loss
loss.backward()
```

Code 1: Pseudo-code for SPC loss.

Table 8 shows the hyperparameter search space. The prompt lengths we used for CQR, summarization, and paraphrase detection are 200, 200, and 120. To conduct a fair comparison, we use the same batch size and number of epochs for all model variants on the same task, regardless of tuning approaches. The (batch size, training epochs) for CQR, summarization, and paraphrase detection tasks are: (16, 50), (16, 50), (16, 200).

Fine-tuning tends to converge faster than parameter-efficient approaches. For example, fine-tuning (with/without SPC) reaches high validation performance with fewer epochs and slowly improves after that. Parameter-efficient approaches (PrefixTuning, prompt tuning, with/without SPC) take more epochs to reach the same performance. However, we do not use early stopping and use the best checkpoint for evaluation after finishing all epochs.

Hyperparameter	Search Space
prompt position	{encoder, decoder, both}
prompt length	{1, 5, 10, 20, 30, ..., 200}
prompt initialization	{random, model token embedding}
max/min generation length	(vary with tasks)
beam size	{1, 2, 3, 4, 5, 6}
length penalty	{1}
batch size	{8, 16}
learning rate	{5e-5, 1e-5, 1e-4, 1e-3, 1e-2}
learning rate scheduler	{none, linear}
warmup steps	{none, 10%}
epochs	full-data: $\leq$ 200; few-shot: $\leq$ 1000

Table 8: Hyperparameter search space.

The exact number of epochs for stabilizing performance varies with each setting and task. However, we can compare their *effective FLOP* (= number of trainable parameters $\times$ number of epochs to stabilization). For example, for the CQR task, the effective FLOP for fine-tuning, PrefixTuning, and SPC+Prompt are: 406M params $\times$ 20 epochs = 8120M FLOP, 41M params $\times$ 40 epochs = 1640M FLOP, 0.3M params $\times$ 45 epochs = 13.5M FLOP. Hence, even with more epochs, SPC+Prompt has a drastically smaller effective FLOP.

B Methodology: Algebraic Perspective

The soft prompt tuning problem aims to generate the target conditioned on the prompted input, which is achieved by simply tuning the prompt embeddings rather than designing the prompt tokens. We aim to improve soft prompts' cross-domain generalizability by proposing a domain-adaptable learning paradigm.

We examine the three spaces that play a crucial role here: general task (or input) space, prompted space, and specific task (or output) space. Denote the tuple (input space, prompted space, output space) as the *three-spaces*. The input space is the general task space because it contains the task information without referring to a specific task or target. For example, an LM cannot tell if text input is for rewriting or summarization without fine-tuning on the specific task (see Table 1). However, prompts in the prompted space provide the context to specify the task and steer the LM to predict targets in the specific task space (Reynolds and McDonell, 2021). For instance, Table 1 shows how a prompted input, which combines input and prompt, contains both the original text and task-specific information. Nonetheless, the hand-designed prompts are not scalable to other tasks as they require manual labor, and traditional soft prompt tuning approaches do not generalize to new domains.

So how do we learn domain-generalizable soft prompts? We take an algebraic approach and resort to the category theory. Category theory is fundamental to other (modern) math streams and applied to other fields, such as computer science. It studies the universal properties of mathematical objects, their structures, and the relations between them (Barr and Wells, 1990). Using category theory, we can derive the universal properties of the three-spaces and their relations, and such properties will be natural to domains, i.e., they will be domain-invariant.

First, let us formalize the three-spaces into categories. The input space, prompted space, and output space carry the canonical structure of sets, so they are categories of sets (Barr and Wells, 1990): $\mathbf{Set}_i$, $\mathbf{Set}_p$, $\mathbf{Set}_o$. Within the category, the objects are sets of tokens (i.e., tokens of inputs, prompts, and outputs), and the morphisms are functions between sets. We introduce the functor: structure-preserving map between categories $F : \mathbf{Set}_i \to \mathbf{Set}_o$, such that for any object $x \in \mathbf{Set}_i$, $F(x) \in \mathbf{Set}_o$, and for any morphism $f : x \to y \in \mathbf{Set}_i$, $F(f) : F(x) \to F(y) \in \mathbf{Set}_o$. Similarly, we introduce functors $G : \mathbf{Set}_p \to \mathbf{Set}_o$ and $H : \mathbf{Set}_i \to \mathbf{Set}_p$. A commutative diagram 4 shows such relations.

Next, we push the category of sets to the category of vector spaces—that is, we move to the corresponding embedding spaces of the three-spaces. Embedding spaces naturally carry the structure of vector spaces, so they are categories of vector spaces: $\mathbf{Vect}_i$, $\mathbf{Vect}_p$, $\mathbf{Vect}_o$ (they are actually categories of topological vector spaces as the embeddings carry manifold structure, but we omit this structure for simplicity) (Lang et al., 2002). For notional convenience, we omit the underlying field of real numbers for the vector space. The objects in the $\mathbf{Vect}$ category are vector spaces, and the morphisms are linear maps between vector spaces. Similarly, we have functors $\bar{F} : \mathbf{Vect}_i \to \mathbf{Vect}_o$, $\bar{G} : \mathbf{Vect}_p \to \mathbf{Vect}_o$, $\bar{H} : \mathbf{Vect}_i \to \mathbf{Vect}_p$. The map from the category of sets to the category of vector spaces is also a functor: the "embedding" functor.

To make $\mathbf{Vect}_p$ domain-invariant, we must find invariance between functorial maps. We resort to homology: algebraic objects that are topolog-

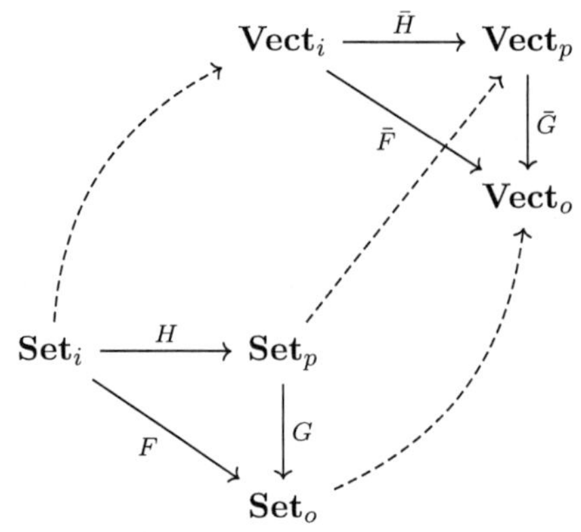

Figure 4: Commutative diagram between categories.

ically invariant (Weibel, 1995). Denote the category of chain complexes over $\mathbf{Vect}$ as $\partial\mathbf{Vect}$ whose objects are chain complexes in $\mathbf{Vect}$ and morphisms are chain maps. There is a homology functor (Spanier, 1989): $\mathring{H} : \partial\mathbf{Vect} \to \mathbf{Vect}$ that maps from chain complexes to their homology (modules). However, computing the homology is non-trivial. To simplify the problem, we introduce a short exact sequence—simplest form of chain complexes and can be used to construct longer chain complexes (Massey, 2019; Weibel, 1995)—in $\mathbf{Vect}$: $\mathcal{K} \equiv \mathbf{0} \to \boldsymbol{E}_i \xrightarrow{h} \boldsymbol{E}_p \xrightarrow{g} \boldsymbol{E}_o \to \mathbf{0}$ where $\boldsymbol{E}_i$, $\boldsymbol{E}_p$, $\boldsymbol{E}_o$ are the input, prompted, output embedding spaces, and $\mathbf{0}$ is the zero object (exercise for readers to check such exact sequence exists). This indicates $\mathcal{K}$'s homology $\mathring{H}(\mathcal{K}) \equiv \frac{\ker(g)}{\mathrm{im}(h)} = \mathbf{0}_{\mathrm{id}}$ is trivial and $\boldsymbol{E}_p$ is acyclic and invariant. Further, there exists a morphism $h^{-1} : \boldsymbol{E}_p \to \boldsymbol{E}_i$ such that $h^{-1} \circ h = \mathrm{id}_{\boldsymbol{E}_i}$. By the splitting lemma (Weibel, 1995), we have $\boldsymbol{E}_p \cong \boldsymbol{E}_i \oplus \boldsymbol{E}_o$. Hence, we can construct the prompted embedding space $\boldsymbol{E}_p$ from the direct sum of input embedding space $\boldsymbol{E}_i$ and output embedding space $\boldsymbol{E}_o$, hence the name "soft prompt construction" (SPC). There are more than one approaches to enforce such a domain-invariant property. We choose the most straightforward one: the SPC loss (7).

Friendly Neighbors: Contextualized Sequence-to-Sequence Link Prediction

Adrian Kochsiek
University of Mannheim
Germany
akochsiek
@uni-mannheim.de

Apoorv Saxena
Adobe Research
India
apoorvs
@adobe.com

Inderjeet Nair
Adobe Research
India
inderjeetnair1
@gmail.com

Rainer Gemulla
University of Mannheim
Germany
rgemulla
@uni-mannheim.de

Abstract

We propose *KGT5-context*, a simple sequence-to-sequence model for link prediction (LP) in knowledge graphs (KG). Our work expands on KGT5, a recent LP model that exploits textual features of the KG, has small model size, and is scalable. To reach good predictive performance, however, KGT5 relies on an ensemble with a knowledge graph embedding model, which itself is excessively large and costly to use. In this short paper, we show empirically that adding contextual information—i.e., information about the direct neighborhood of the query entity—alleviates the need for a separate KGE model to obtain good performance. The resulting KGT5-context model is simple, reduces model size significantly, and obtains state-of-the-art performance in our experimental study.

1 Introduction

A knowledge graph (KG) is a collection of facts describing relations between real-world entities. Facts are represented in the form of subject-relation-object ((s, r, o)) triples such as *(Brendan Fraser, hasWonPrize, Oscar)*. In this paper, we study the link prediction (LP) problem, which is to infer missing links in the KG. We focus on KGs in which the entities and relations have textual features, such as mention names or descriptions.

Saxena et al. (2022) made a case for large language models (LM) for this task. They proposed the KGT5 model, which posed the link prediction problem as a sequence-to-sequence (seq2seq) task. The main advantages of this approach are that

(i) it allows for small model sizes, and

(ii) it decouples inference cost from the graph size (and, in particular, the number of entities).

They found that KGT5's performance was particularly strong when predicting the object of new relations for a query entity (e.g., the birthplace of a person), but fell short of alternative approaches when predicting additional objects for a known relation (e.g., additional awards won by someone).

To avoid this problem, Saxena et al. (2022) used an ensemble of KGT5 with a large knowledge graph embedding (KGE) model (ComplEx (Trouillon et al., 2016)). This ensemble did reach good performance but destroyed both advantages (i) and (ii) of using a LM. In fact, KGE models learn a low-dimensional representation of each entity and each relation in the graph (Bordes et al., 2013; Sun et al., 2019; Trouillon et al., 2016). Consequently, model size and LP cost are linear in the number of entities in the graph, which can be expensive to use for large-scale KGs. For example, the currently best-performing model (Cattaneo et al., 2022) for the large-scale WikiKG90Mv2 benchmark (Hu et al., 2021) consists of an ensemble of 85 KGE models; each taking up more than 86 GB of space for parameters. Though KGE model sizes can be reduced by using compositional embeddings based on text mentions (Wang et al., 2021; Clouatre et al., 2021; Wang et al., 2022; Jiang et al., 2023), inference cost remains high for large graphs.

We propose and study KGT5-context, which expands on KGT5 by providing contextual information about the query entity—i.e., information about the direct neighborhood of the query entity—to facilitate link prediction. Our work is motivated by the KGE model HittER (Chen et al., 2021), which follows a similar approach; we use the seq2seq model KGT5 instead of a Transformer-based KGE model. KGT5-context is very simple: The only change to KGT5 is that we add a verbalization of the neighborhood of the query entity to the description of a given LP task; see Fig. 1 for an example. KGT5-context retains advantages (i) and (ii) of KGT5.

We performed an experimental study using the Wikidata5M (Wang et al., 2021) and

Proceedings of the 8th Workshop on Representation Learning for NLP (RepL4NLP 2023), pages 131–138
July 13, 2023

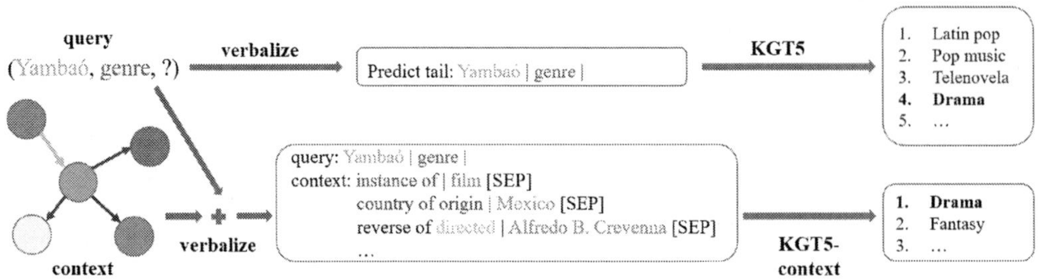

Figure 1: Overview of KGT5-context (at bottom) and comparison to KGT5 (on top); real example from Wikidata5M, best viewed in color. KGT5-context differs from KGT5 in that it appends the neighboring relations and entities of *Yambaó* (a drama movie) to the verbalized query. Both models then apply T5, sample predictions from the decoder, map the samples to entities, and rank by sample logit scores.

WikiKG90Mv2 (Hu et al., 2021) benchmarks. We found that—without further hyperparameter tuning—KGT5-context reached or exceeded state-of-the-art performance on both benchmarks using a significantly smaller model size than alternative approaches. The simple KGT5-context model thus provides a suitable baseline for further research.

2 Expanding KGT5 with Context

Given a *query* $(s, r, ?)$ and a KG, LP is the task to predict new answer entities, i.e., the ? slot of the query. An example is given in Fig. 1.

KGT5 (Saxena et al., 2022) treats link prediction as a seq2seq task. It exploits available textual information for entities and relations, such as mention names (for both entities and relations) or descriptions. KGT5's architecture is based on the encoder-decoder Transformer model T5 (Raffel et al., 2020). It uses canonical mentions to verbalize the LP query to a text sequence of form "`predict tail: <subject mention> | <relation mention> |` ". To predict answers, KGT5 samples (exact) candidate mentions from the decoder; the cost of sampling is independent of the number of entities in the KG. To train KGT5, Saxena et al. (2022) use standard training techniques for LLMs: KGT5 is trained on facts in the KG and asked to generate the true answer using teacher forcing and a cross-entropy loss.

KGT5-context (ours) proceeds in the same way as KGT5 but extends the verbalization of the query. In particular, we append a textual sequence of the one-hop neighborhood of the query entity s to the verbalized query of KGT5. As a result, the query entity is contextualized, an approach that has been applied successfully to KGE models before (Chen et al., 2021). KGT5-context simplifies the prediction problem because additional information that is readily available in the KG is provided along with the query. In the example of Fig. 1, the contextual information states that *Yambaó* is a Mexican movie. This information is helpful; e.g., it already rules out the top two predictions of KGT5, which incorrectly suggest that *Yambaó* is a piece of music. For a more detailed analysis, see Sec. 3.3.

Verbalization details. To summarize, we obtain mentions of the entities and relations in the query as well as in the one-hop neighborhood of the query entity. We use these mentions to verbalize the query together with the neighborhood as "`query: <query entity mention> | <query relation mention> | context: <context relation 1 mention> | <context entity 1 mention> <SEP> ...`".[1] To keep direction of relations, we prepend the relation mention with "`reverse of`" if the query entity acts as an object, i.e., the relation "points towards" the query entity. A real-world example is given in Fig. 1. Inspired by neighborhood sampling in GNNs (Hamilton et al., 2017), we sample up to k (default: $k = 100$) relation-neighbor pairs uniformly, at random, and without replacement.

3 Experimental Study

We conducted an experimental study to investigate (i) to what extent integrating context in terms of the entity neighborhood into KGT5 improves link prediction performance, (ii) whether the use of context can mitigate the necessity for an ensemble of the text-based KGT5 model with a KGE model, and

[1]When entity descriptions are available, we include "`description: <description of query entity>`" right before the query context.

Dataset	Entities	Relations	Edges
Wikidata5M	4.8M	828	21M
WikiKG90Mv2	91M	1,387	601M

Table 1: Dataset statistics.

(iii) for what kind of queries context is helpful. We found that:

1. KGT5-context improved the state-of-the-art performance on Wikidata5M using a smaller model (Tab. 2).
2. KGT5-context was orders of magnitudes smaller than the leading models on WikiKG90Mv2 and reached competitive performance (Tab. 3).
3. KGT5-context did not benefit further from ensembling with a KGE model (Tab. 4).

3.1 Experimental Setup

Source code and configuration are available at `https://github.com/uma-pi1/kgt5-context`.

Datasets. We evaluate KGT5-context on two commonly used large-scale link prediction benchmarks. Wikidata5M (Wang et al., 2021) is the induced graph of the 5M most-frequent entities of the Wikidata KG. WikiKG90Mv2 (Hu et al., 2021) contains more than 90M entities and over 600M facts. In contrast to Wikidata5M, it is only evaluated on tail prediction, i.e., $(s, r, ?)$ queries. Dataset statistics are summarized in Tab. 1. For Wikidata5M and WikiKG90Mv2[2], we used the entity mentions provided on the KGT5 webpage. For Wikidata5M, we also consider the usefulness of entity descriptions, which are provided with the dataset and have been used in some prior studies (Wang et al., 2022; Jiang et al., 2023). Note that we do not use these descriptions by default, and clearly mark throughout when they have been used.

Metrics. We follow the standard procedure to evaluate model quality for the link prediction task. In particular, for each test triple (s, r, o), we rank all triples of the form $(s, r, ?)$ (and $(?, r, o)$ on Wikidata5M) by their predicted scores. For KGT5 and KGT5-context, we instead sample from the decoder and ignore outputs that do not correspond to an existing entity mention. For all models, we filter out all true answers other than the test triple that occur either in the train, valid or test data. Finally, we determine the mean reciprocal rank (MRR) and Hits@K over all test triples. In case of ties, we use the mean rank to avoid misleading results (Sun et al., 2020).

Settings. We mainly follow the setting of KGT5. For all experiments, we used the same T5 architecture (T5-small for Wikidata5M, T5-base for WikiKG90Mv2) without any pretrained weights. Training from scratch ensures test data is unseen during (pre-)training and avoids leakage. We used the SentencePiece tokenizer pretrained by (Raffel et al., 2020). We trained on 8 A100-GPUs with a batch size of 32 (effective batch size of 256) using the AdaFactor optimizer. No dataset-specific hyperparameter optimization was performed. For KGT5-context, we sampled up to 100 neighbors per query entity or up to an input sequence length of 512 tokens. For inference, we obtained 500 samples from the decoder.

Models. On Wikidata5M, we compare KGT5-context to the KGE models ComplEx (Trouillon et al., 2016) and SimplE (Kazemi and Poole, 2018) (only graph structure used), the compositional KGE model SimKGC (Wang et al., 2022), its extension utilizing hard negatives (Jiang et al., 2023), and the seq2seq model KGT5 (Saxena et al., 2022). The model of Jiang et al. (2023) is an ensemble of multiple SimKGC models, each trained with a different strategy for selecting negatives. Note that in contrast to KGT5 and KGT5-context, SimKGC is based on pretrained models (BERT transformers). During prediction, all text-based models require access to entity and relation mentions and, when used, the description of the query entity. SimKGC additionally requires access to precomputed entity embeddings, KGT5-context to the 1-hop neighborhood of the query entity in the KG.

On WikiKG90M, we compare to the models presented on the official leaderboard.[2] Here, the best-performing approaches are large ensembles of multiple KGE models.

3.2 Link Prediction Performance

Link prediction performance on Wikidata5M is shown in Tab. 2; additional baselines are given in Tab. 5 (appendix). Generally, we found that textual

[2]We directly used mentions of entities and relations for WikiKG90Mv2, instead of the textual embeddings used by other models. For this reason, the benchmark authors (Hu et al., 2021) did not provide us with scores on the hidden test set. The mentions used to be provided with the dataset but have been removed by now; we obtained them from `https://github.com/apoorvumang/kgt5`.

Model	MRR	Hits@1	Hits@3	Hits@10	Params	Add. requirements for inference	Pre-trained
SimplE †	0.296	0.252	0.317	0.377	2,400M	-	no
ComplEx ††	0.308	0.255	-	0.398	614M	-	no
SimKGC	0.212	0.182	0.223	0.266	220M	entity embeddings	yes
KGT5 ‡	0.300	0.267	0.318	0.365	60M	-	no
+ ComplEx ‡	0.336	0.286	0.362	0.426	674M	-	no
KGT5-context (ours)	0.378	0.350	0.396	0.427	60M	1-hop neighborhood	no
SimKGC + Desc. ‡‡	0.358	0.313	0.376	0.441	220M	entity embeddings	yes
+ Hard Negative Ensemble $	0.420	0.381	0.435	**0.490**	1,100M	entity embeddings	yes
KGT5 + Desc.	0.381	0.357	0.397	0.422	60M	-	no
KGT5-context + Desc. (ours)	**0.426**	**0.406**	**0.440**	0.460	60M	1-hop neighborhood	no

Table 2: Link prediction results on Wikidata5M, test split. The first group does not make use of textual information, the second group uses mention names, the third group additionally entity descriptions. Best per group underlined, best overall bold. Marked results are from † Zhu et al. (2019), †† Kochsiek and Gemulla (2021), ‡ Saxena et al. (2022), ‡‡ Wang et al. (2022), $ Jiang et al. (2023). Additional results in Tab. 5 (appendix).

information was highly beneficial. KGT5-context was the only model that improved upon KGE models (which do not use textual information) when only mention information was available. Moreover, KGT5-context obtained better predictive performance than the ensemble of KGT5 with the ComplEx KGE model. Entity descriptions provided further improvements; they hold valuable information for this benchmark. With these descriptions, KGT5-context outperformed traditional KGE models by up to 12pp in terms of MRR, with a model size reduction of 90-98%. Likewise, KGT5-context improved on KGT5 by 12pp, on the KGT5+Complex ensemble by almost 9pp, and performed roughly on-par with the current state-of-the-art SimKGC ensemble model, which is significantly larger.

The results on the much larger WikiKG90Mv2 are shown in Tab. 3.[2] Here, KGT5-context is multiple orders of magnitude smaller than the currently best-performing models,[3] and improves validation MRR by almost 1pp.

Model	Test MRR	Valid MRR	Params
ComplEx	0.141	0.182	18.2B
TransE	0.082	0.110	18.2B
ComplEx-Concat	0.176	0.205	18.2B
TransE-Concat	0.176	0.206	18.2B
PIE-RM	0.212	0.254	18.2B[3]
DGLKE + Rule Mining	0.249	0.292	18.2B[3]
BESS	**0.254**	0.292	23.3B[3]
KGT5, T5 small[2]	-	0.221	60M
KGT5-context, T5 base (ours)[2]	-	**0.301**	220M

Table 3: Link prediction results on WikiKG90Mv2. Baseline numbers are from the official leaderboard of OGB-LSC (Hu et al., 2021).

Model	0	1-10	>10	All
ComplEx	0.534	0.351	**0.045**	0.296
KGT5	0.624	0.215	0.015	0.300
KGT5-context (ours)	**0.738**	**0.415**	0.014	0.378
KGT5 + ComplEx	0.624	0.351	0.045	0.336
KGT5-context + ComplEx	**0.738**	0.351	**0.045**	**0.379**

Table 4: Test MRR on Wikidata5M grouped by query frequency during training.

3.3 Analysis

To investigate in which cases context information was beneficial, we empirically analyzed LP performance w.r.t. (i) query frequency and (ii) the degree of the query entity. We also sampled predictions and summarize our general observations.

Query frequency. The *frequency* of a test query $(s, r, ?)$ is the number of answers to the query already available in the training data. For example, queries for N:1 relations have frequency 0, whereas queries for 1:N relations can have large frequency for high-degree query entities. We bucketized the test queries of Wikidata5M into low, medium, and high frequency queries and report average MRR for various models in Tab. 4. Generally, high-frequency queries appear harder to answer. These queries have many known true answers already (tying up model capacity); there may be many additional, potentially unrelated answers and incom-

[3]The parameter count in Tab. 3 corresponds to the size of the largest model in an ensemble, not the overall model size. For example, BESS (Cattaneo et al., 2022) consists of 85 models and the complete ensemble has 2.6T parameters; the KGT5-context model is 5 orders of magnitude smaller.

pleteness of the KG may be a concern during evaluation. In contrast, a low-frequency query such as *(Brendan Fraser, instance Of, ?)* has few or no known answer and might be easier to infer, even when the combination of this particular subject and relation was not yet seen during training.

Ensemble with KGE models. In general, the prior KGT5 model performed reasonably well on queries that did not occur in the training data, but was outperformed by a large amount by ComplEx on queries seen multiple times. Hence, both models complemented each other in an ensemble. KGT5-context strongly improved performance over ComplEx, KGT5, and the KGT5+Complex ensemble for low- and medium-frequency queries. For this reason, an ensemble between KGT5-context and ComplEx only brought negligible benefits, but has substantial drawbacks. Consequently, an ensemble of KGT5-context with a KGE model is not needed and should not be used.

Entity degree. We also investigated the benefit of contextual information w.r.t. to the degree of the query entity (see Fig. 2 in the appendix). We found that KGT5-context was beneficial and performed well on query entities with a degree of up to 100. For entities with very large degrees (i.e., nodes with more than 100 or even 1000s of neighbors), ComplEx showed benefits. As before, we feel that these performance benefits are negligible considering the increase in model size and decrease in scalability.

Anecdotal results. We manually probed some predictions of KGT5-context and found the context is especially beneficial when (i) the entity mention only provides limited information about the entity, and/or when (ii) the answer to the query is contained in the one-hop neighborhood.

A case of (i) is shown in Fig. 1, a real example. Here, KGT5 was able to capture the geographic region of the real-world entity only based on its mention. Based on this geographic notion, it proposed the music genre *Latin pop* but was unaware that the entity is a movie. This useful information can be obtained directly from the one-hop neighborhood and, indeed, was exploited by KGT5-context.

For Wikidata5M, the correct answer entity appears in the one-hop neighborhood of the query entity for about 7% of the validation triples. But even when the answer does not directly appear in the context, it may contain entities strongly hinting at the correct answer. For example, it is easier to predict that an entity has occupation *biochemist*, when the context already contains the information that the entity is a *chemist*.

4 Conclusion

We proposed and studied KGT5-context, a sequence-to-sequence model for link prediction in knowledge graphs. KGT5-context extends the KGT5 model of Saxena et al. (2022) by using contextual information of the query entity for prediction. KGT5-context is simple, small, and scalable, and it obtained or exceeded state-of-the-art performance in our experimental study. It thus provides a suitable baseline for further research in this area. A natural direction, for example, is to explore approaches that integrate contextual information in a less naive way than KGT5-context does.

Limitations

KGT5-context relies on the textual mentions of entities and relations (and, optionally, entity descriptions). Therefore, it is only applicable to KGs that provide such information. KGT5-context may be able to handle some entities without textual features when well-described by their neighborhood; we did not investigate this though.

To use KGT5-context for prediction, the KG has to be queried to obtain context information, i.e., the one-hop neighborhood of the query entity. KGT5-context thus cannot be used without the underlying KG.

The verbalized neighborhood of the query entity leads to long input sequences, which in turn may induce higher memory consumption and higher computational cost during training. Overall, training KGT5-context is typically more expensive than training traditional KGE models, which can be tuned (Kochsiek et al., 2022) and trained efficiently (Lerer et al., 2019; Kochsiek and Gemulla, 2021; Zheng et al., 2020).

For inference, KGT5-context first samples relation-neighbor pairs for contextualization, and then samples possible answers from the decoder. These sampling steps can lead to variance in predictive performance. We found this effect to be negligible on Wikidata5M, but it may be larger on other datasets.

Ethics Statement

This research uses publicly available data and benchmarks for evaluation. We believe that this research was conducted in an ethical manner and in compliance with all relevant laws and regulations.

References

Antoine Bordes, Nicolas Usunier, Alberto Garcia-Duran, Jason Weston, and Oksana Yakhnenko. 2013. Translating embeddings for modeling multi-relational data. In *Neural Information Processing Systems (NIPS)*, pages 1–9.

Alberto Cattaneo, Daniel Justus, Harry Mellor, Douglas Orr, Jerome Maloberti, Zhenying Liu, Thorin Farnsworth, Andrew Fitzgibbon, Blazej Banaszewski, and Carlo Luschi. 2022. Bess: Balanced entity sampling and sharing for large-scale knowledge graph completion. *arXiv preprint arXiv:2211.12281*.

Sanxing Chen, Xiaodong Liu, Jianfeng Gao, Jian Jiao, Ruofei Zhang, and Yangfeng Ji. 2021. Hitter: Hierarchical transformers for knowledge graph embeddings. In *Proceedings of the 2021 Conference on Empirical Methods in Natural Language Processing*, pages 10395–10407.

Louis Clouatre, Philippe Trempe, Amal Zouaq, and Sarath Chandar. 2021. Mlmlm: Link prediction with mean likelihood masked language model. In *Findings of the Association for Computational Linguistics: ACL-IJCNLP 2021*, pages 4321–4331.

William L. Hamilton, Rex Ying, and Jure Leskovec. 2017. Inductive representation learning on large graphs. In *Proceedings of the 31st International Conference on Neural Information Processing Systems*, NIPS'17, pages 1025–1035, Red Hook, NY, USA. Curran Associates Inc.

Weihua Hu, Matthias Fey, Hongyu Ren, Maho Nakata, Yuxiao Dong, and Jure Leskovec. 2021. Ogb-lsc: A large-scale challenge for machine learning on graphs. *Advances in Neural Information Processing Systems*, 35.

Fan Jiang, Tom Drummond, and Trevor Cohn. 2023. Don't mess with mister-in-between: Improved negative search for knowledge graph completion. In *Proceedings of the 17th Conference of the European Chapter of the Association for Computational Linguistics*, pages 1810–1824.

Seyed Mehran Kazemi and David Poole. 2018. Simple embedding for link prediction in knowledge graphs. In *Advances in Neural Information Processing Systems*.

Adrian Kochsiek and Rainer Gemulla. 2021. Parallel training of knowledge graph embedding models: a comparison of techniques. *Proceedings of the VLDB Endowment*, 15(3):633–645.

Adrian Kochsiek, Fritz Niesel, and Rainer Gemulla. 2022. Start small, think big: On hyperparameter optimization for large-scale knowledge graph embeddings. In *Machine Learning and Knowledge Discovery in Databases: European Conference, ECML PKDD 2022, Grenoble, France, September 19–23, 2022, Proceedings, Part II*, pages 138–154. Springer.

Adam Lerer, Ledell Wu, Jiajun Shen, Timothee Lacroix, Luca Wehrstedt, Abhijit Bose, and Alex Peysakhovich. 2019. Pytorch-biggraph: A large scale graph embedding system. *Proceedings of Machine Learning and Systems*, 1:120–131.

Colin Raffel, Noam Shazeer, Adam Roberts, Katherine Lee, Sharan Narang, Michael Matena, Yanqi Zhou, Wei Li, and Peter J. Liu. 2020. Exploring the limits of transfer learning with a unified text-to-text transformer. *Journal of Machine Learning Research*, 21(140):1–67.

Apoorv Saxena, Adrian Kochsiek, and Rainer Gemulla. 2022. Sequence-to-sequence knowledge graph completion and question answering. In *Proceedings of the 60th Annual Meeting of the Association for Computational Linguistics (Volume 1: Long Papers)*, pages 2814–2828.

Zhiqing Sun, Zhi-Hong Deng, Jian-Yun Nie, and Jian Tang. 2019. Rotate: Knowledge graph embedding by relational rotation in complex space. In *International Conference on Learning Representations*.

Zhiqing Sun, Shikhar Vashishth, Soumya Sanyal, Partha Talukdar, and Yiming Yang. 2020. A re-evaluation of knowledge graph completion methods. In *Proceedings of the 58th Annual Meeting of the Association for Computational Linguistics*, pages 5516–5522.

Théo Trouillon, Johannes Welbl, Sebastian Riedel, Éric Gaussier, and Guillaume Bouchard. 2016. Complex embeddings for simple link prediction. In *International conference on machine learning*, pages 2071–2080. PMLR.

Liang Wang, Wei Zhao, Zhuoyu Wei, and Jingming Liu. 2022. Simkgc: Simple contrastive knowledge graph completion with pre-trained language models. In *Proceedings of the 60th Annual Meeting of the Association for Computational Linguistics (Volume 1: Long Papers)*, pages 4281–4294.

Xiaozhi Wang, Tianyu Gao, Zhaocheng Zhu, Zhengyan Zhang, Zhiyuan Liu, Juanzi Li, and Jian Tang. 2021. Kepler: A unified model for knowledge embedding and pre-trained language representation. *Transactions of the Association for Computational Linguistics*, 9:176–194.

Ruobing Xie, Zhiyuan Liu, Jia Jia, Huanbo Luan, and Maosong Sun. 2016. Representation learning of knowledge graphs with entity descriptions. *Proceedings of the AAAI Conference on Artificial Intelligence*, 30(1).

Bishan Yang, Scott Wen-tau Yih, Xiaodong He, Jianfeng Gao, and Li Deng. 2015. Embedding entities and relations for learning and inference in knowledge bases. In *Proceedings of the International Conference on Learning Representations (ICLR) 2015*.

Da Zheng, Xiang Song, Chao Ma, Zeyuan Tan, Zihao Ye, Jin Dong, Hao Xiong, Zheng Zhang, and George Karypis. 2020. Dgl-ke: Training knowledge graph embeddings at scale. In *Proceedings of the 43rd International ACM SIGIR Conference on Research and Development in Information Retrieval*, pages 739–748.

Zhaocheng Zhu, Shizhen Xu, Meng Qu, and Jian Tang. 2019. Graphvite: A high-performance cpu-gpu hybrid system for node embedding. In *The World Wide Web Conference*, pages 2494–2504. ACM.

Appendix

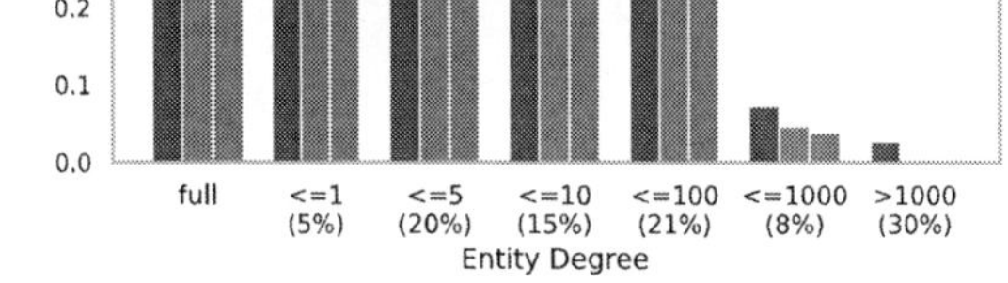

Figure 2: MRR grouped by entity degree on Wikidata5M. Group weight is given in brackets.

Model	MRR	Hits@1	Hits@3	Hits@10	Params
TransE (Bordes et al., 2013) †	0.253	0.170	0.311	0.392	2,400M
DistMult (Yang et al., 2015) †	0.253	0.209	0.278	0.334	2,400M
RotatE (Sun et al., 2019) †	0.290	0.234	0.322	0.390	2,400M
DKRL (Xie et al., 2016) $	0.160	0.120	0.181	0.229	20M
KEPLER (Wang et al., 2021) $	0.210	0.173	0.224	0.277	125M
MLMLM (Clouatre et al., 2021) ††	0.223	0.201	0.232	0.264	355M

Table 5: Additional link prediction results on Wikidata5M from prior work. Results are from † Zhu et al. (2019). $ Wang et al. (2021). †† Clouatre et al. (2021).

Extracting Multi-valued Relations from Language Models

Sneha Singhania, Simon Razniewski, Gerhard Weikum
Max Planck Institute for Informatics
{ssinghan, srazniew, weikum}@mpi-inf.mpg.de

Abstract

The widespread usage of latent language representations via pre-trained language models (LMs) suggests that they are a promising source of structured knowledge. However, existing methods focus only on a single object per subject-relation pair, even though often multiple objects are correct. To overcome this limitation, we analyze these representations for their potential to yield materialized multi-object relational knowledge. We formulate the problem as a *rank-then-select* task. For *ranking* candidate objects, we evaluate existing prompting techniques and propose new ones incorporating domain knowledge. Among the *selection* methods, we find that choosing objects with a likelihood above a learned relation-specific threshold gives a 49.5% F1 score. Our results highlight the difficulty of employing LMs for the multi-valued slot-filling task, and pave the way for further research on extracting relational knowledge from latent language representations.

1 Introduction

Petroni et al. (2019) showcased the potential of relation-specific probes for extracting implicit knowledge from latent language representations. But the viability of materializing factual knowledge directly from LMs remain open problems (Razniewski et al., 2021; AlKhamissi et al., 2022).

Building upon the LAMA framework, where an LM predicts an object in the slot for given a cloze-style prompt such as "Dante was born in [MASK]", several methods (Jiang et al., 2020b; Shin et al., 2020; Zhong et al., 2021; Qin and Eisner, 2021) design effective prompts for factual information extraction. Importantly, however, all these methods implicitly assume the existence of a single correct object per (subject, relation)-pair and evaluate on precision at rank 1. In reality, many relations have multiple correct values as illustrated in Figure 1.

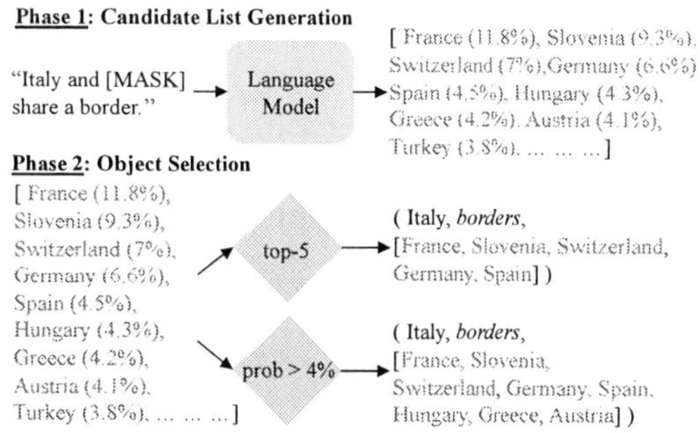

Figure 1: Probing LMs to extract objects for multi-valued relations.

In this paper, we focus on probing LMs directly for multi-valued slot-filling task. In a zero-shot setting, an LM is probed using prompts that include *a subject and a multi-valued relation* to generate a list of candidate objects. However, prior knowledge of the no. of correct objects is generally unknown. Since the LM's probabilities alone do not provide a clear indication of the objects' factual accuracy (Jiang et al., 2021; Holtzman et al., 2021), we apply various selection mechanisms on the generated list to choose the correct objects.

We probe LMs using existing prompting techniques and introduce new relation-specific prompts. The generated object lists are evaluated by their order, and our manual prompts result in higher-quality lists than the state-of-the-art automated methods. Our prompts outperform the best baseline, SoftPrompts, by ca. 5% points on the three most challenging relations (parts of chemical compounds, official languages of countries, instruments of musicians), while being competitive on the other four relations. While evaluating the output of selection mechanisms, our best approach achieves 54.1% precision, 50.8% recall, and 49.5% F1 score. These trends in scores demonstrate the difficulty of extracting complete knowledge from internal LMs representations.

Proceedings of the 8th Workshop on Representation Learning for NLP (RepL4NLP 2023), pages 139–154

2 Background

The idea of knowledge extraction using LMs representations was put forward by Radford et al. (2019); Petroni et al. (2019), and has since received much attention. Several approaches (Bouraoui et al., 2019; Goswami et al., 2020; Chen et al., 2022) use relational metadata and textual corpora to tune the LM using knowledge-enriched representations and efficiently extract knowledge. Jiang et al. (2020a); Kassner et al. (2021) focus on multilingual knowledge extraction, while Dhingra et al. (2022) looks at extracting temporal knowledge from LMs. Current methods usually sample from correct objects for a given subject-relation pair by employing the hits@k metric and do not enforce deliberate accept/reject decisions on the outputs.

3 Methodology

Candidate List Generation When probing an LM using a cloze-style prompt, the LM generates a probability distribution over the vocabulary tokens to fill in the masked position. For our task, we use prompts mentioning a subject-relation ⟨s, r⟩ pair and consider the resulting ranked list of tokens (w/ their corresponding probability scores) as candidates. In a zero-shot setting, the LM is probed using two types of prompts: (i) *discrete prompts* such as LPAQA (Jiang et al., 2020b) and AUTOPROMPT (Shin et al., 2020), and (ii) *continuous prompts* such as OPTIPROMPT (Zhong et al., 2021) and SoftPrompts (Qin and Eisner, 2021).

In addition, we propose a collection of carefully designed manual prompts to evaluate and compare the generated objects for multi-valued relations. We create 50 diverse relation-specific prompts by incorporating domain knowledge, relation type, and variations in sentence structure and grammar. Our prompts differ in verb form, tense, placement of the masked token (whether it is predicted in a prefix, suffix, or cloze-style), and whether or not there is a period and object type in the context.

Selection Mechanisms We experiment with the following parameterized mechanisms on the generated object lists to get a valid subset of triples.
Top-k: The most probable k objects are selected.
Prob-x: Objects with a probability greater than or equal to x are chosen.
Cumul-x: Retain all objects, in order of probability, whose summed probability is no larger than x. In difference with Prob-x, it would enable retaining candidates of similarly moderate probability.
Count Probe: We probe the LM again to get an object count prediction for a ⟨s, r⟩. A count probe could be as follows, *"Italy borders a total of* [MASK] *countries"*. From the list of generated tokens, the highest-ranked integer type token (either in alphabetical or numerical form) is used to subset the original object list.
Verification Probe: We probe the same LM again on each candidate object to factually verify the generated subject-relation-object ⟨s, r, o⟩ triple. A verification probe could be as follows, *"Italy and France share a border? Answer:* [MASK]*"*. We compare the relative probabilities of the _yes versus _no tokens in the masked position, using ($p_{\_yes} - p_{\_no} > \alpha$), with α is a hyper-parameter, to determine the correctness of the original candidate object, France. All the original candidate objects satisfying the comparison condition are selected.

4 Experiment

Dataset The seven diverse multi-valued relations appearing in LAMA benchmark (Petroni et al., 2019) are chosen. For each relation, approx. 200 subjects and a complete list of objects from the popular Wikidata KB (Vrandečić and Krötzsch, 2014) are sampled. The subjects were picked based on popularity, measured using Wikidata ID and count of Twitter followers for person-type subjects[1].

Evaluation In the *ranking* phase, the quality of a candidate list is assessed using the maximally possible F1 score, defined as the highest possible F1 score achieved by applying the top-k selection mechanism with the optimal k value. The optimal k is found by iterating over all possible choices of k and calculating the respective F1 score on the subset of candidate objects and ground-truth objects. In the *selection* phase, the output triples obtained after applying a selection mechanism are evaluated using precision, recall, and F1 score.

Setup We reuse the best prompts reported by each prompting baseline, which are tuned on much larger data. We probe BERT (Devlin et al., 2019) on each ⟨s, r⟩ and generate the 500 most probable candidate objects. The generated list is post-processed to remove stopwords and other type-irrelevant objects depending on the relation type, only to retain sensible candidate objects. Our dataset is split into train, dev, and test, with

[1]https://anonymous.4open.science/r/acl_dataset-00B6/

⟨subject, relation⟩	Ours	Mined	Para	AUTO	OPTI	Soft
compound, *has-parts*	**78.5**	38.1	29.5	51.4	68.1	71.6
country, *borders*	72.8	66.4	64.9	71.6	73.2	**75.6**
country, *official-lang*	**83.6**	81.9	75.2	71.8	75.9	79.9
person, *instrument*	62.5	**63.4**	61.3	61.7	52.7	57.0
person, *speaks-lang*	**72.8**	69.1	41.1	52.8	71.5	69.0
person, *occupation*	33.2	40.2	**44.9**	37.5	36.6	36.9
state, *borders*	25.7	23.8	24.3	24.4	25.9	**25.9**
Overall (avg.)	**61.3**	54.7	48.7	53.0	57.7	59.4

Table 1: Comparing generated object lists by probing BERT-large using macro-averaged max-F1(%) scores. Mined is LPAQA's mining-based prompts and Para is LPAQA's paraphrasing-based prompts. AUTO uses the open-sourced AUTOPROMPT templates. OPTI and Soft are OPTIPROMPT and SoftPrompts obtained by training the LM using author-released data and code.

100/∼50/50 subjects per relation, for tuning and estimating parameters in the selection mechanisms.

5 Results

Candidate List Generation We compare the candidate list generated by each prompting method in Table 1. Our prompts generate the best object lists in terms of macro-averaged max-F1 score. Unlike our prompts, discrete prompts have a lower performance, while continuous counterparts have a similar performance. Surprisingly, OPTIPROMPT obtained by initializing its continuous vectors using our prompts has a lower score.

To validate the effectiveness of our prompts and inspect if optimizing prompts on precision@1 is sufficient for extraction on multi-valued relations, we compare the best prompts in terms of precision@1 and max-F1 score. In Table 2, we see that prompts performing well on precision@1 are not necessarily the best on max-F1. Overall, prompts suitable for multi-valued extraction are more often of the prefix type, while prompts in the single-object case show more variance. In Appendix, Table 4 shows examples of generated lists, and Tables 9-15 lists all the prompt templates. The large gap between precision@1 and max-F1 indicates the difficulty in designing task-specific prompts and raises the need for developing more robust prompts.

Object Selection The candidate objects retained after applying a selection mechanism are compared against the ground-truth objects, and the results are shown in Table 3. The top-k method achieves the best overall F1 score, which is the macro-average of individual ⟨s, r⟩ tuple-specific F1 scores. The individual F1 scores and max-F1 (upper bound) have a large gap since the probabilities of predicted tokens are not calibrated enough to match the actual factuality of the ⟨s, r, o⟩ triple. Table 5 in Appendix gives the prompt templates and learned parameters of each selection mechanism.

6 Discussion

Although BERT was probed for 500 objects when generating object lists, only 119.7 objects were retained after post-processing. Objects with invalid types occur due to the zero-shot setting. Also, other eminent masked LMs, including BERT-base, RoBERTa-base, and RoBERTa-large, achieve 60.61%, 54.82%, and 58.90% max-F1 scores.

The max-F1 scores in Table 1 & 2 are far from 100%, i.e., LMs do not generate candidate lists that correctly rank all true objects above the false ones. In particular, max-F1 will not reach 100% when correct objects are ranked too low or absent. We found that 26.90% of valid objects in a candidate list were ranked below the optimal threshold and 27.75% of valid objects were not generated at all.

In Table 3, the top-k and prob-x achieve balanced precision and recall scores. The count-probe achieves a high recall since almost always a count greater than 10 is predicted, and in our dataset, the average count of ground-truth objects across all ⟨s, r⟩ is in [1,10] range. In the verification probe, the parameter α is near zero for most relations, and the probability of _yes is greater than _no, leading to a selection of all the candidate objects. Although Schick and Schütze (2021) and others show the effect of verbalizing labels to _yes and _no tokens in the few-shot setting on classification and inference tasks, optimally using them for factual knowledge extraction remains an open challenge.

Effect of Prompt Template In Table 3, each mechanism is evaluated on the candidate list generated using prompt templates shown in max-F1 column in Table 2. However, by choosing a different set of prompts, a higher overall F1 score of 51.3% with a lower 59.9% max-F1 can be achieved by using the prob-x method. Table 6 in Appendix gives more details. This change in F1 scores shows the hardness of designing robust prompts.

Effect of Relation Type The candidate lists generated for popular subjects tend to have higher precision and recall. For instance, F1 score for (state, *borders*) with top-k is the lowest due to the pres-

⟨subject, relation⟩	Our Prompts with best precision@1	hits@1	Our Prompts with best max-F1	max-F1
compound, *has-parts*	[X] contains [MASK] atom	78.50	[X] has [MASK], which is an atom.	78.52
country, *borders*	[X] and [MASK] share a border	84.86	[X] and [MASK] share a border.	72.82
country, *official-lang*	People of [X] mostly speak in [MASK].	93.37	[MASK] is the main language of [X].	83.57
person, *instrument*	Musician [X] plays [MASK].	67.50	[X] plays [MASK], which is an instrument	62.45
person, *speaks-lang*	In which language can [X] talk? Answer: [MASK].	92.50	[X] speaks in [MASK].	72.78
person, *occupation*	[X] is a well-known [MASK].	59.00	[X] is a well-known [MASK]	33.21
state, *borders*	[MASK], which is a [Y], borders [X].	37.50	[X] and [MASK] share a border	25.71

Table 2: Our best prompts among the 50 relation-specific prompts on precision@1 (%) and max-F1 (%). The [Y] slot takes the object-type information, e.g., in ⟨state, *borders*⟩, [Y] could be "state", "governate", "prefecture", etc.

⟨subject, relation⟩	top-k			prob-x			cumul-x			count-probe			verify-probe			max-F1
	p	r	f1	p	r	f1	p	r	f1	p	r	f1	p	r	f1	
compound, *has-parts*	62.5	78.1	68.0	60.3	76.4	65.4	37.8	74.7	37.8	54.2	78.7	61.8	16.1	70.7	22.9	78.5
country, *borders*	64.0	55.4	54.2	63.4	58.7	55.4	56.0	58.4	46.5	21.9	71.7	30.5	1.9	68.2	3.6	72.8
country, *official-lang*	96.0	74.1	80.1	94.0	75.8	80.5	52.8	71.3	43.2	28.9	82.3	40.5	27.0	32.4	4.9	83.6
person, *instrument*	46.0	42.3	38.8	51.7	40.8	39.1	51.8	41.4	33.8	18.2	60.9	25.5	7.1	24.4	4.8	62.5
person, *speaks-lang*	52.5	59.8	55.1	69.6	56.7	60.0	56.2	57.3	46.8	37.4	69.0	47.3	3.5	53.0	6.4	72.8
person, *occupation*	33.3	23.5	27.3	3.2	85.1	6.1	30.1	36.2	18.6	23.1	30.0	25.9	5.5	41.7	9.0	33.2
state, *borders*	24.4	22.6	22.9	63.1	21.1	24.9	21.9	18.3	13.7	10.0	24.3	13.9	2.4	26.2	4.3	25.7
Overall (averaged)	54.1	50.8	**49.5**	**57.9**	59.2	47.4	43.8	51.1	34.4	27.7	**59.5**	35.1	9.1	45.3	8.0	61.3

Table 3: Results on comparing triples using precision, recall, and F1 score when probing BERT-large and applying a selection mechanism. The bold-faced numbers are the highest achieved precision, recall, and F1 scores.

ence of long-tail subjects. Also for a large possible set of valid objects, e.g., in *occupation*, LM only generates common professions with a high probability and negatively impacts the F1 scores. This behavior, however, helps in *language* type relations. A similar difference in performance can be observed in Shin et al. (2020); Zhong et al. (2021).

Calibrate using Web Signals We used the query hit rate from Bing to calibrate and select objects from the candidate list. Bing receives each ⟨s, r, o⟩ triple in the form of a natural language query. The hit rate is used in two ways: (i) subset, objects with non-zero hit rate, (ii) rerank, objects with non-zero hit rate are calibrated to the highest probability. In contrast to prob-x F1 scores, we observe a high increase in precision and decrease in recall applying (I) with a lower overall F1 score of 34.7%, while the (II) method achieves higher recall and lower precision with a similar overall F1 score of 45.7%. Table 7 in Appendix shows all the scores.

Effect of LM Size We probed larger LMs like T5 (Raffel et al., 2020) and BART (Lewis et al., 2020), which can generate a list of tokens with likelihoods using Beam search decoding algorithm, similar to masked LMs. With top-k method, T5-large achieves 43.6% precision, 41.7% recall, and 40.3% F1 score. BART-large achieves an even lower 32.0% precision, 34.3% recall, and 30.8% F1 score. Table 8 in Appendix gives all the scores. These models tend to generate common objects and exhibit repetitive behavior. Also, the current trend is towards using autoregressive models like (chat-)GPT, like Alivanistos et al. (2022); Cohen et al. (2023) used to extract multi-valued relations. However, unlike in our method, with no control over the selection mechanism, the LM directly outputs one final list in both works. While internally autoregressive models also use token probabilities that could be used for our approach, once one generates a full list, previously generated list items conflate the probabilities of items.

7 Conclusion

In this work, we evaluate using LM's internal representation for materializing factual knowledge on multi-valued relations. We utilize existing prompt engineering techniques and propose new prompts tailored for multi-valued relations. The suggested selection mechanism approaches help to filter out valid triples. Our detailed analysis of the model's performance highlights the limitations of using zero-shot probing for the multi-valued slot-filling task. Future work could aim to improve overall precision and recall and measure the impact of using LMs to fill gaps in KBs.

References

Dimitrios Alivanistos, Selene Báez Santamaría, Michael Cochez, Jan-Christoph Kalo, Emile van Krieken, and Thiviyan Thanapalasingam. 2022. Prompting as probing: Using language models for knowledge base construction. In *LM-KBC*.

Badr AlKhamissi, Millicent Li, Asli Celikyilmaz, Mona Diab, and Marjan Ghazvininejad. 2022. A review on language models as knowledge bases. arXiv:2204.06031.

Zied Bouraoui, José Camacho-Collados, and Steven Schockaert. 2019. Inducing relational knowledge from bert. In *AAAI Conference on Artificial Intelligence*.

Xiang Chen, Ningyu Zhang, Xin Xie, Shumin Deng, Yunzhi Yao, Chuanqi Tan, Fei Huang, Luo Si, and Huajun Chen. 2022. Knowprompt: Knowledge-aware prompt-tuning with synergistic optimization for relation extraction. In *Proceedings of the ACM Web Conference 2022*, page 2778–2788, New York, NY, USA. Association for Computing Machinery.

Roi Cohen, Mor Geva, Jonathan Berant, and Amir Globerson. 2023. Crawling the internal knowledge-base of language models. *Findings of EACL*.

Jacob Devlin, Ming-Wei Chang, Kenton Lee, and Kristina Toutanova. 2019. BERT: Pre-training of deep bidirectional transformers for language understanding. In *Proceedings of the 2019 Conference of the North American Chapter of the Association for Computational Linguistics: Human Language Technologies, Volume 1 (Long and Short Papers)*, pages 4171–4186, Minneapolis, Minnesota. Association for Computational Linguistics.

Bhuwan Dhingra, Jeremy R. Cole, Julian Martin Eisenschlos, Daniel Gillick, Jacob Eisenstein, and William W. Cohen. 2022. Time-aware language models as temporal knowledge bases. *Transactions of the Association for Computational Linguistics*, 10:257–273.

Ankur Goswami, Akshata Bhat, Hadar Ohana, and Theodoros Rekatsinas. 2020. Unsupervised relation extraction from language models using constrained cloze completion. In *Findings of the Association for Computational Linguistics: EMNLP 2020*, pages 1263–1276, Online. Association for Computational Linguistics.

Ari Holtzman, Peter West, Vered Shwartz, Yejin Choi, and Luke Zettlemoyer. 2021. Surface form competition: Why the highest probability answer isn't always right. In *Proceedings of the 2021 Conference on Empirical Methods in Natural Language Processing*, pages 7038–7051, Online and Punta Cana, Dominican Republic. Association for Computational Linguistics.

Zhengbao Jiang, Antonios Anastasopoulos, Jun Araki, Haibo Ding, and Graham Neubig. 2020a. X-FACTR: Multilingual factual knowledge retrieval from pretrained language models. In *Proceedings of the 2020 Conference on Empirical Methods in Natural Language Processing (EMNLP)*, pages 5943–5959, Online. Association for Computational Linguistics.

Zhengbao Jiang, Jun Araki, Haibo Ding, and Graham Neubig. 2021. How can we know when language models know? on the calibration of language models for question answering. *Transactions of the Association for Computational Linguistics*, 9:962–977.

Zhengbao Jiang, Frank F. Xu, Jun Araki, and Graham Neubig. 2020b. How can we know what language models know? *Transactions of the Association for Computational Linguistics*, 8:423–438.

Nora Kassner, Philipp Dufter, and Hinrich Schütze. 2021. Multilingual LAMA: Investigating knowledge in multilingual pretrained language models. In *Proceedings of the 16th Conference of the European Chapter of the Association for Computational Linguistics: Main Volume*, pages 3250–3258, Online. Association for Computational Linguistics.

Mike Lewis, Yinhan Liu, Naman Goyal, Marjan Ghazvininejad, Abdelrahman Mohamed, Omer Levy, Veselin Stoyanov, and Luke Zettlemoyer. 2020. BART: Denoising sequence-to-sequence pre-training for natural language generation, translation, and comprehension. In *Proceedings of the 58th Annual Meeting of the Association for Computational Linguistics*, pages 7871–7880, Online. Association for Computational Linguistics.

Fabio Petroni, Tim Rocktäschel, Sebastian Riedel, Patrick Lewis, Anton Bakhtin, Yuxiang Wu, and Alexander Miller. 2019. Language models as knowledge bases? In *Proceedings of the 2019 Conference on Empirical Methods in Natural Language Processing and the 9th International Joint Conference on Natural Language Processing (EMNLP-IJCNLP)*, pages 2463–2473, Hong Kong, China. Association for Computational Linguistics.

Guanghui Qin and Jason Eisner. 2021. Learning how to ask: Querying LMs with mixtures of soft prompts. In *Proceedings of the 2021 Conference of the North American Chapter of the Association for Computational Linguistics: Human Language Technologies*, pages 5203–5212, Online. Association for Computational Linguistics.

Alec Radford, Jeff Wu, Rewon Child, David Luan, Dario Amodei, and Ilya Sutskever. 2019. Language models are unsupervised multitask learners.

Colin Raffel, Noam Shazeer, Adam Roberts, Katherine Lee, Sharan Narang, Michael Matena, Yanqi Zhou, Wei Li, and Peter J. Liu. 2020. Exploring the limits of transfer learning with a unified text-to-text transformer. *Journal of Machine Learning Research*, 21(140):1–67.

Simon Razniewski, Andrew Yates, Nora Kassner, and Gerhard Weikum. 2021. Language models as or for knowledge bases. In *Proceedings of the Workshop on Deep Learning for Knowledge Graphs (DL4KG 2021)*. CEUR Workshop Proceedings.

Timo Schick and Hinrich Schütze. 2021. Exploiting cloze-questions for few-shot text classification and natural language inference. In *Proceedings of the 16th Conference of the European Chapter of the Association for Computational Linguistics: Main Volume*, pages 255–269, Online. Association for Computational Linguistics.

Taylor Shin, Yasaman Razeghi, Robert L. Logan IV, Eric Wallace, and Sameer Singh. 2020. AutoPrompt: Eliciting Knowledge from Language Models with Automatically Generated Prompts. In *Proceedings of the 2020 Conference on Empirical Methods in Natural Language Processing (EMNLP)*, pages 4222–4235, Online. Association for Computational Linguistics.

Denny Vrandečić and Markus Krötzsch. 2014. Wikidata: a free collaborative knowledgebase. *Communications of ACM*, 57:78–85.

Zexuan Zhong, Dan Friedman, and Danqi Chen. 2021. Factual probing is [MASK]: Learning vs. learning to recall. In *Proceedings of the 2021 Conference of the North American Chapter of the Association for Computational Linguistics: Human Language Technologies*, pages 5017–5033, Online. Association for Computational Linguistics.

A Appendix

⟨subject, relation⟩	Generated Object List	|GT|
(compound, *has-parts*)		
Calcium Carbonate	carbon (0.47), hydrogen (0.03), oxygen (0.02), calcium (0.01), silicon (0.01), nitrogen (0.002), sulfur (0.002)	3
Dopamine	hydrogen (0.09), nitrogen (0.05), carbon (0.05), oxygen (0.05), calcium (0.02), sodium (0.011), sulfur (0.009)	4
Sodium Chloride	carbon (0.15), hydrogen (0.09), oxygen (0.03), silicon (0.01), nitrogen (0.01), sulfur (0.006), sodium (0.006)	2
Thiocyanic Acid	hydrogen (0.1), carbon (0.1), oxygen (0.03), nitrogen (0.02), sulfur (0.01), silicon (0.003), sodium (0.002)	4
Water	oxygen (0.17), hydrogen (0.17), carbon (0.05), nitrogen (0.02), sodium (0.01), mercury (0.004), sulfur (0.003)	2
(country, *borders*)		
Germany	poland (0.14), austria (0.12), france (0.09), italy (0.06), belgium (0.05), russia (0.04), switzerland (0.04)	9
India	pakistan (0.34), bangladesh (0.19), myanmar (0.1), nepal (0.1), china (0.05), iran (0.02), bhutan (0.02)	8
Palau	japan (0.06), indonesia (0.05), taiwan (0.04), fiji (0.03), china (0.02), australia (0.02), philippines (0.01)	3
Malta	gibraltar (0.12), italy (0.11), cyprus (0.07), ireland (0.06), greece (0.05), tunisia (0.04), serbia (0.04)	1
Singapore	malaysia (0.7), thailand (0.1), indonesia (0.1), vietnam (0.02), myanmar (0.02), china (0.01), taiwan (0.01)	2
(country, *official-lang*)		
Algeria	french (0.47), arabic (0.4), spanish (0.04), english (0.03), algerian (0.007), italian (0.005), latin (0.003)	2
Bolivia	spanish (0.9), english (0.07), portuguese (0.01), french (0.006), arabic (0.003), italian (0.002), latin (0.001)	4
Ethiopia	somali (0.52), arabic (0.08), english (0.05), ethiopian (0.04), italian (0.02), spanish (0.01), french (0.01)	1
Singapore	english (0.7), malay (0.18), chinese (0.03), tamil (0.03), mandarin (0.02), indonesian (0.005), arabic (0.003)	4
South Africa	english (0.9), dutch (0.03), french (0.03), portuguese (0.02), spanish (0.01), german (0.006), arabic (0.004)	11
(person, *instrument*)		
A. R. Rahman	guitar (0.29), flute (0.18), piano (0.16), violin (0.08), saxophone (0.05), harmonica (0.04), clarinet (0.03)	16
Andy Hurley	guitar (0.36), piano (0.11), bass (0.06), violin (0.05), cello (0.04), accordion (0.03), drums (0.03)	1
Bruce Springsteen	guitar (0.54), piano (0.08), bass (0.05), drums (0.04), mandolin (0.03), harmonica (0.03), trumpet (0.03)	3
Owen Pallett	guitar (0.34), piano (0.15), violin (0.06), bass (0.05), cello (0.05), trumpet (0.03), drums (0.03)	4
Rino Sashihara	guitar (0.2815), flute (0.12), piano (0.12), violin (0.07), cello (0.04), accordion (0.04), clarinet (0.03)	1
(person, *speaks-lang*)		
Alessandra Ambrosio	italian (0.9), english (0.1), spanish (0.02), french (0.02), german (0.01), portuguese (0.01), latin (0.01)	3
Amy Jackson	english (0.6), spanish (0.1), french (0.1), japanese (0.03), german (0.03), russian (0.02), italian (0.02)	4
Gustavo Petro	spanish (0.7), english (0.2), italian (0.03), portuguese (0.03), french (0.02), german (0.01), catalan (0.006)	4
Gad Elmaleh	english (0.4), arabic (0.4), french (0.13), hebrew (0.03), spanish (0.01), persian (0.007), russian (0.007)	4
Petro Poroshenko	russian (0.4), ukrainian (0.3), english (0.13), polish (0.05), belarusian (0.03), bulgarian (0.006), german (0.006)	6
(person, *occupation*)		
Donald Trump	politician (0.0005), american (0.0005), speaker (0.0004), name (0.0003), personality (0.0003), person (0.0003)	17
Neil Gaiman	author (0.001), writer (0.001), novelist (0.0003), artist (0.0003), contributor (0.0002), character (0.0002)	11
Richard Dawkins	author (0.0024), biologist (0.0019), writer (0.0018), psychologist (0.001), philosopher (0.001), scientist (0.0008)	15
George R. R. Martin	author (0.0032), historian (0.0025), writer (0.0013), scholar (0.0012), biologist (0.0005), novelist (0.0004)	10
Yoko Ono	artist (0.001), singer (0.001), musician (0.0004), actress (0.0003), author (0.0002), writer (0.0002), painter (0.0002)	10
(river, *basins*)		
Aras River	russia (0.18), uzbekistan (0.08), azerbaijan (0.07), armenia (0.06), kazakhstan (0.04), iran (0.04), ukraine (0.03)	4
Draa River	somalia (0.07), ethiopia (0.07), afghanistan (0.02), turkey (0.02), egypt (0.02), algeria (0.02), morocco (0.02)	1
Mekong River	vietnam (0.2001), cambodia (0.19), thailand (0.05), laos (0.03), china (0.01), myanmar (0.003), cameroon (0.003)	6
Limpopo River	botswana (0.25), zambia (0.16), namibia (0.13), zimbabwe (0.08), mozambique (0.07), angola (0.02), africa (0.02)	4
Jordan River	jordan (0.33), israel (0.06), syria (0.05), iraq (0.02), iran (0.02), egypt (0.02), palestine (0.02), lebanon (0.01)	6
(state, *borders*)		
Alabama	mississippi (0.4), georgia (0.3), tennessee (0.1), louisiana (0.05), florida (0.04), arkansas (0.02), texas (0.02)	4
Castile and León	navarre (0.26), galicia (0.22), catalonia (0.14), aragon (0.04), castile (0.02), valencia (0.01), mexico (0.003)	10
La Rioja Province	mendoza (0.05), navarre (0.05), galicia (0.02), madrid (0.01), catalonia (0.007), piedmont (0.006)	5
Gelderland	utrecht (0.40), holland (0.06), hesse (0.02), hamburg (0.01), jersey (0.003), bremen (0.002), berlin (0.001)	7
Fukushima Prefecture	tokyo (0.23), hiroshima (0.14), okinawa (0.13), kyoto (0.1), osaka (0.03), nagoya (0.03), saga (0.01)	6

Table 4: Samples of generated object list for five unique subjects on multi-valued relations. The green highlighted valid objects, while the red ones are wrong. The |GT| column gives the total no. of ground-truth objects for the corresponding subject.

⟨subject, relation⟩	Metric	avg-cutoff	Our Prompts
	top-k	4	
	prob-x	0.02	[X] has [MASK], which is an atom
compound, *has-parts*	cumul-x	0.53	
	count-alpha	2.26	[X] consists of [MASK] elements.
	count-num	4.64	[X] consists of [MASK] elements
	verify-probe	$\alpha = 0.06$	[X] consists of [Y] atom. Is this correct? Answer: [MASK].
	top-k	3	
	prob-x	0.05	[X] and [MASK] share a border.
country, *borders*	cumul-x	0.79	
	count-alpha	2.54	[X] shares border with [MASK] countries.
	count-num	13.36	[X] shares border with [MASK] countries
	verify-probe	$\alpha = 0$	[X] and [Y] share a border. Is this correct? Answer: [MASK].
	top-k	1	
	prob-x	0.22	[MASK] is the main language of [X].
country, *official-lang*	cumul-x	0.91	
	count-alpha	3.42	[X] has [MASK] official languages.
	count-num	2.18	[X] has [MASK] official languages
	verify-probe	$\alpha = 0.11$	[Y] is the official language of [X]. Is this correct? Answer: [MASK].
	top-k	2	
	prob-x	0.12	[X] plays [MASK], which is an instrument
person, *instrument*	cumul-x	0.54	
	count-alpha	2.98	[X] plays [MASK] instruments.
	count-num	6.88	[X] plays [MASK] instruments
	verify-probe	$\alpha = 0.28$	[X] plays [Y]. Is this correct? Answer: [MASK].
	top-k	4	
	prob-x	0.05	[X] speaks in [MASK].
person, *speaks-lang*	cumul-x	0.87	
	count-alpha	4.16	[X] speaks in [MASK] languages.
	count-num	6	
	verify-probe	$\alpha = 0.24$	[X] can speak in [Y]. Is this correct? Answer: [MASK].
	top-k	8	
	prob-x	0	[X] is a well-known [MASK]
person, *occupation*	cumul-x	0.01	
	count-alpha	4.74	[X] had a total of [MASK] different professions.
	count-num	13.64	
	verify-probe	$\alpha = 0$	[X] is a well-known [Y]. Is this correct? Answer: [MASK].
	top-k	5	
	prob-x	0.04	[X] and [MASK] share a border
state, *borders*	cumul-x	0.75	
	count-alpha	3.16	[X] shares border with [MASK] states
	count-num	13.04	[X] shares border with a total of [MASK] states.
	verify-probe	$\alpha = 0$	[X] and [Y] share a border. Is this correct? Answer: [MASK].

Table 5: The prompt templates used for generating the object list. The avg-cutoff shows the learned parameters of each selection mechanism averaged across all subjects.

⟨subject, relation⟩	Our Prompts	avg-cutoff	Precision	Recall	F1 score	Max-F_1
compound, *has-parts*	[X] has [MASK], which is an atom.	0.02	60.33	76.40	65.41	78.52
country, *borders*	[X] has borders with [MASK].	0.07	74.73	55.41	58.45	71.41
country, *official-lang*	The official language of [X] is [MASK].	0.15	94.33	79.97	83.38	83.54
person, *instrument*	[X] likes to play the [MASK].	0.12	51.33	46.52	41.48	58.19
person, *speaks-lang*	[X] speaks in [MASK].	0.05	69.60	56.72	59.99	72.78
person, *occupation*	[X] is a [MASK].	0.01	22.79	31.26	25.42	29.30
state, *borders*	[X] and [MASK] share a border	0.04	63.10	21.12	24.91	25.71
Overall			62.32	52.49	51.29	59.9

Table 6: Higher F1 score achieved by using a different set of our proposed prompts and prob-x mechanism.

⟨subject, relation⟩	Our Prompts	Prob-x			Nonzero Hit-rate			ReRank		
		p	r	f1	p	r	f1	p	r	f1
compound, *has-parts*	[X] has [MASK], which is an atom.	60.3	76.4	**65.4**	84.2	17.7	17.0	57.0	80.9	64.1
country, *borders*	[X] has borders with [MASK].	74.7	55.4	58.5	82.3	53.5	56.0	58.9	69.4	**58.8**
country, *official-lang*	The official language of [X] is [MASK].	94.3	80.0	**83.4**	91.7	68.3	71.1	69.3	81.6	69.3
person, *instrument*	[X] likes to play the [MASK].	51.3	46.5	**41.5**	83.0	30.1	33.8	27.7	53.2	32.4
person, *speaks-lang*	[X] speaks in [MASK].	69.6	56.7	**60.0**	83.0	19.7	22.1	48.5	66.3	51.2
person, *occupation*	[X] is a [MASK].	23.0	31.3	**25.4**	19.7	23.7	20.3	19.8	24.1	20.5
state, *borders*	[X] and [MASK] share a border	63.1	21.1	**24.9**	93.0	18.3	22.3	69.0	21.9	23.4
Overall		57.9	59.2	**47.4**	76.7	33.1	34.7	50.1	56.8	45.7

Table 7: Results on calibrating object probabilities with Bing hit rates

⟨subject, relation⟩	Our Prompts	T5-large			BART-large		
		p	r	f1	p	r	f1
compound, *has-parts*	[X] has [MASK], which is an atom.	67.3	64.9	61.5	58.7	56.2	56.2
country, *borders*	[X] and [MASK] share a border.	43.8	53.1	45.0	44.8	60.4	47.3
country, *official-lang*	[MASK] is the main language of [X].	82.0	61.1	66.8	0	0	0
person, *instrument*	[X] plays [MASK], which is an instrument	13.3	14.8	12.6	40.0	36.1	33.5
person, *speaks-lang*	[X] speaks in [MASK].	47.0	40.4	43.0	22.1	28.7	24.5
person, *occupation*	[X] is a well-known [MASK]	27.2	36.4	30.8	36.5	37.1	34.4
state, *borders*	[X] and [MASK] share a border	24.6	21.5	22.3	21.5	21.4	19.8
Overall		43.6	41.7	40.3	32.0	34.3	30.8

Table 8: Results on probing T5 and BART model with top-k selection mechanism

Prompt Template	optimal k	precision	recall	max-F1	p@1
[X] consists of [MASK].	81.08	42.68	68.58	45.14	31.66
[X] consists of [MASK]	251.54	22.73	26.18	20.08	11.05
[X] consists of [MASK] element.	48.12	49.8	66.64	49.28	37.56
[X] consists of [MASK] element	142.47	33.57	54.88	36.63	13.13
[X] consists of [MASK], which is an element.	33.44	67.84	72.2	64.11	68.00
[X] consists of [MASK], which is an element	39.69	60.18	70.56	57.03	54.27
The chemical compound [X] consists of [MASK].	23.11	50.65	73.09	52.23	42.00
The chemical compound [X] consists of [MASK]	196.56	26.73	27.74	23.52	13.00
The chemical compound [X] consists of [MASK] element.	26.91	47.05	64.6	43.38	33.00
The chemical compound [X] consists of [MASK] element	51.63	36.05	66.4	39.33	15.00
The chemical compound [X] consists of [MASK], which is an element.	21.43	63.34	69.99	59.83	56.50
The chemical compound [X] consists of [MASK], which is an element	28.12	56.23	69.19	51.97	48.50
[X] contains [MASK].	42.52	46.27	75.88	52.78	36.50
[X] contains [MASK] atom	20.13	72.82	78.49	72.45	78.50
[X] is composed of [MASK], which is an element.	23.99	66.23	74.15	64.01	65.50
[X] is composed of [MASK], which is an element	30.2	56.93	71.69	55.02	52.00
[X] is composed of [MASK] atom.	20.82	68.12	79.93	69.18	62.50
[X] is composed of [MASK] atom	21.11	70.26	75.46	67.22	71.00
[X] is composed of [MASK].	58.15	47.92	72.85	50.77	36.00
[X] is composed of [MASK]	172.04	28.28	35.87	26.18	14.75
[MASK] atom is present in [X].	32.04	35.01	79.21	45.23	4.50
[MASK] atom is present in [X]	35.25	33.03	76.98	42.03	5.50
[MASK] element is present in [X].	377.61	8.5	10.58	8.27	1.00
[MASK] element is present in [X]	312.44	12.47	15.98	12.47	2.51
[MASK] is present in [X].	79.54	27.81	66.19	35.53	7.54
[MASK] is present in [X]	111.5	27.42	61.21	33.08	8.25
[X] has [MASK], which is an element.	27.92	69.34	77.11	69.02	68.00
[X] has [MASK], which is an element	32.81	70.32	73.68	67.91	68.84
[X] has [MASK], which is an atom.	20.07	78.75	82.76	78.52	76.00
[X] has [MASK], which is an atom	20.02	74.81	81.77	75.95	74.50
[X] molecule is composed of [MASK], which is an element.	20.5	73.41	78.48	72.04	76.00
[X] molecule is composed of [MASK], which is an element	23.7	65.93	74.53	63.84	62.50
[X] molecule is composed of [MASK] atom.	20.62	70.35	80.6	71.32	69.00
[X] molecule is composed of [MASK] atom	20.77	71.7	77.44	69.94	73.00
[X] molecule is composed of [MASK].	21.23	63.81	80.4	67.24	53.00
[X] molecule is composed of [MASK]	149.31	37.28	34.97	30.58	24.00
[MASK] atom is present in [X] molecule.	23.69	41.1	79.8	50.42	10.50
[MASK] atom is present in [X] molecule	24.7	36.06	78.64	45.96	7.00
[MASK] element is present in [X] molecule.	144.71	19.53	47.54	25.17	1.50
[MASK] element is present in [X] molecule	190.69	20.99	38.21	22.93	4.50
[MASK] is present in [X] molecule.	71.54	31.73	68.47	37.97	10.00
[MASK] is present in [X] molecule	69.52	29.54	72.49	38.01	6.00
The [X] molecule consists of [MASK].	20.48	72.41	81.54	73.33	59.50
The [X] molecule consists of [MASK]	297.46	27.53	19.48	20.14	17.00
The [X] molecule consists of [MASK] element.	31.69	56.43	73.09	57.56	51.50
The [X] molecule consists of [MASK] element	54.96	39.27	64.37	43.4	11.50
The [X] molecule consists of [MASK], which is an element.	20.32	75.89	78.82	73.64	76.00
The [X] molecule consists of [MASK], which is an element	23.21	70.36	76.15	67.98	66.50
[X] molecule has [MASK], which is an element.	20.05	75.17	82.05	75.9	75.50
[X] molecule has [MASK], which is an element	20.1	75.67	81.32	75.68	77.00

Table 9: Our proposed prompts for (chemical compound, has parts) relation.

Prompt Template	optimal k	precision	recall	max-F1	p@1
[X] shares border with [MASK].	9.3	76.73	77.11	71.29	83.24
[X] shares border with [MASK]	10.92	65.44	70.6	62.02	70.81
[X] shares a border with [MASK].	9.49	78.63	76.59	72.1	83.78
[X] shares a border with [MASK]	11.62	61.24	69.24	58.22	65.95
[X] borders [MASK].	10.37	72.79	74.9	67.98	80.00
[X] borders [MASK]	25.04	25.82	60.28	28.67	12.97
[X] has borders with [MASK].	9.54	79.26	75.14	71.41	82.70
[X] has borders with [MASK]	19.76	49.49	62.74	43.75	48.65
[X] shares border with [MASK], which is a country.	10.01	77.89	77.04	71.49	82.16
[X] shares border with [MASK], which is a country	10.08	78.13	76.62	71.38	81.62
The neighbouring country of [X] is [MASK].	11.07	76.04	74.02	69.13	80.00
The neighbouring country of [X] is [MASK]	74.58	21.43	56.52	28.12	4.32
The neighbouring countries of [X] are [MASK].	46.29	35.97	61.2	39.71	21.08
The neighbouring countries of [X] are [MASK]	149.41	23.07	43.63	24.41	8.65
[X] shares a border with [MASK], which is a country.	10.46	77.38	77.05	71.45	82.16
[X] shares a border with [MASK], which is a country	10.27	78.38	76.07	71.32	83.78
[X] borders [MASK], which is a country.	10.08	78.15	75.92	71.54	82.16
[X] borders [MASK], which is a country	10.03	76.53	76.39	71.04	81.62
[MASK] is a neighbouring country of [X].	10.14	76.35	75.51	70.02	83.24
[MASK] is a neighbouring country of [X]	10.51	73.66	74.97	68.1	80.00
Which country shares border with [X]? Answer: [MASK].	8.74	58.42	71.62	57.49	53.51
Which country shares border with [X]? Answer: [MASK]	119.09	19.56	45.47	22.45	5.41
Which country is near [X]? Answer: [MASK].	8.12	55.89	70.71	56.9	45.95
Which country is near [X]? Answer: [MASK]	89.11	19.21	45.86	22.92	5.95
[MASK], which is a country, is near [X].	9.75	76.37	76.25	70.35	82.16
[MASK], which is a country, is near [X]	9.63	69.4	72.55	64.93	71.89
The country, [MASK], shares border with [X].	9.42	71.85	71.59	64.32	74.59
The country, [MASK], shares border with [X]	11.21	62.09	67.23	56.32	64.32
[MASK] is the bordering country of [X].	10.91	75.9	75.07	69.37	81.62
[MASK] is the bordering country of [X]	12.69	65.9	71.83	61.78	70.27
The country, [MASK], shares border with [X], which is a country.	8.52	71.85	74.25	66.52	75.68
The country, [MASK], shares border with [X], which is a country	8.69	71.83	73.57	66.28	76.76
[MASK], which is a country, shares a border with [X].	11.26	75.08	74.45	68.71	80.00
[MASK], which is a country, shares a border with [X]	11.98	68.41	72.85	64.18	74.05
[MASK], which is a country, borders [X].	11.23	75.63	75.7	69.52	80.54
[MASK], which is a country, borders [X]	11.9	72.8	74.06	67.23	75.68
[MASK], which is a country, has borders with [X].	13.42	72.52	74.88	67.53	77.84
[MASK], which is a country, has borders with [X]	12.77	67.38	71.64	62.24	71.89
The neighbouring country of [X] is [MASK], which is a country.	9.43	78.01	75.52	71.19	83.24
The neighbouring country of [X] is [MASK], which is a country	8.99	76.85	75.96	70.78	83.24
Which country shares border with [X]? The answer is [MASK].	234.62	27.4	28.8	24.76	21.62
Which country shares border with [X]? The answer is [MASK]	477.46	2.52	1.52	1.82	1.08
Which country shares border with [X]? Answer: [MASK], which is a country.	7.36	67.73	73.18	64.68	67.57
Which country shares border with [X]? Answer: [MASK], which is a country	7.92	61.61	73.56	61.44	61.62
[X] and [MASK] share a border.	9.19	80.08	76.7	72.82	83.78
[X] and [MASK] share a border	9.18	78.29	77.21	71.96	84.86
[X] and [MASK] are neighbouring countries.	10.86	73.27	73.9	67.27	77.30
[X] and [MASK] are neighbouring countries	11.32	72.26	73.86	66.7	77.30
[X] and [MASK] are neighbours.	11.08	77.04	75.67	70.76	83.24
[X] and [MASK] are neighbours	8.22	75.98	75.1	70.06	82.70

Table 10: Our proposed prompts for (country, shares borders) relation.

Prompt Template	optimal k	precision	recall	max-F1	p@1
The official language of [X] is [MASK].	18.18	92.58	80.43	83.54	91.84
The official language of [X] is [MASK]	18.22	90.73	79.66	81.66	88.27
[MASK] is the official language of [X].	18.16	93.09	80.04	83.4	92.35
[MASK] is the official language of [X]	18.2	92.15	80.17	83.1	91.33
[X] has [MASK] as its official language.	18.3	87.26	79.62	79.51	83.16
[X] has [MASK] as its official language	18.43	83.35	79.92	77.36	75.00
The official languages of [X] are [MASK].	18.19	92.08	80.3	83.02	90.31
The official languages of [X] are [MASK]	25.24	29.18	77.04	33.08	16.84
The main language spoken in [X] is [MASK].	18.22	92.43	79.69	83.41	92.35
The main language spoken in [X] is [MASK]	18.42	86.31	79.28	79.09	82.14
People of [X] mostly speak in [MASK], which is a language.	18.2	92.17	80.03	83.26	91.84
People of [X] mostly speak in [MASK], which is a language	18.18	92.31	79.86	83.26	92.86
People of [X] mostly speak in [MASK].	18.13	93.37	79.66	83.41	93.37
People of [X] mostly speak in [MASK]	18.26	88.45	79.75	80.4	84.69
[MASK] is the main spoken language of [X].	18.14	93.22	79.66	83.43	92.35
[MASK] is the main spoken language of [X]	18.16	92.49	79.66	83.05	91.84
[MASK] is spoken in [X].	26.31	66.55	78.05	63.59	60.20
[MASK] is spoken in [X]	26.92	59.87	77.15	58.95	50.51
Language spoken in [X] is [MASK].	18.27	91.67	79.95	82.86	91.33
Language spoken in [X] is [MASK]	19.35	75.56	78.09	70.91	67.86
Languages spoken in [X] are [MASK].	18.95	75.13	78.81	71.35	66.33
Languages spoken in [X] are [MASK]	49.03	12.19	75.08	18.92	0.00
What are the main languages spoken in [X]? Answer: [MASK].	18.44	81.97	80.09	76.73	71.94
What are the main languages spoken in [X]? Answer: [MASK]	119	13.16	61.35	18.35	2.55
What are the official languages of [X]? Answer: [MASK].	18.4	83.09	80.47	77.59	72.45
What are the official languages of [X]? Answer: [MASK]	61.16	14.15	69.61	20.96	1.02
What is the official language of [X]? Answer: [MASK].	18.35	84.53	80.17	78.37	73.98
What is the official language of [X]? Answer: [MASK]	68.94	15.07	69.35	21.67	3.06
Which language is officially spoken in [X]? Answer: [MASK].	18.44	82.86	80.47	77.3	74.49
Which language is officially spoken in [X]? Answer: [MASK]	80.3	14.68	66.10	19.17	4.08
[MASK] is the main language of [X].	18.15	93.22	80.04	83.57	92.35
[MASK] is the main language of [X]	18.16	92.71	79.92	83.32	91.84
In [X], people speak in [MASK].	18.26	91.93	79.86	82.93	92.35
In [X], people speak in [MASK]	19.64	78.75	78.74	72.13	71.94
In [X], people speak in [MASK], which is an official language.	18.22	92.36	79.78	83.18	92.86
In [X], people speak in [MASK], which is an official language	18.23	92.39	79.69	83.18	92.35
In [X], people speak in [MASK], which is a language.	18.21	91.8	79.78	82.9	91.84
In [X], people speak in [MASK], which is a language	18.19	91.89	79.35	82.78	90.82
In [X], people mainly speak in [MASK].	18.14	92.73	79.66	83.15	92.35
In [X], people mainly speak in [MASK]	18.49	87.07	79.16	78.43	83.67
In [X], people mainly speak in [MASK], which is an official language.	18.17	92.46	79.92	82.96	93.37
In [X], people mainly speak in [MASK], which is an official language	18.21	92.35	79.52	83.05	92.35
In [X], people mainly speak in [MASK], which is a language.	18.21	91.78	79.78	82.91	90.82
In [X], people mainly speak in [MASK], which is a language	18.17	92.19	79.35	82.98	91.33
The national language of [X] is [MASK].	18.18	92.62	80.17	83.38	91.33
The national language of [X] is [MASK]	18.37	89.85	78.85	80.39	86.73
[X] is a country and [MASK] is the official language.	18.23	90.15	80.00	81.59	87.76
[X] is a country and [MASK] is the official language	18.28	88.03	80.17	80.49	83.67
[MASK] is the national language of [X].	18.2	92.24	80.43	83.23	91.84
[MASK] is the national language of [X]	18.2	92.24	80.17	83.2	91.84

Table 11: Our proposed prompts for (country, has official language) relation.

Prompt Template	optimal k	precision	recall	max-F1	p@1
[X] plays [MASK].	83.77	52.59	60.22	49.03	49.00
[X] plays [MASK]	56.31	31.27	66.57	32.52	20.50
[X] plays [MASK] instrument.	17.48	36.88	76.01	42.07	24.00
[X] plays [MASK] instrument	19.72	35.9	73.79	39.48	20.00
[X] plays [MASK] musical instrument.	59.91	16.09	62.72	19.48	5.00
[X] plays [MASK] musical instrument	71.2	11.67	61.89	15.84	2.50
[X] plays [MASK], which is an instrument.	14.12	65.16	74.57	61.24	61.50
[X] plays [MASK], which is an instrument	14.1	67.33	74.74	62.45	66.00
Musician [X] plays [MASK].	15.1	67.36	74.24	61.23	67.50
Musician [X] plays [MASK]	54.72	21.35	66.87	26.93	8.00
Musician [X] plays [MASK] instrument.	30.13	17.17	72.3	23.44	2.50
Musician [X] plays [MASK] instrument	35.04	17.36	68.15	22.46	2.50
Musician [X] plays [MASK], which is an instrument.	14.12	66.99	73.75	61.72	65.50
Musician [X] plays [MASK], which is an instrument	13.81	68.78	72.2	61.11	65.00
[X] played the [MASK].	14.77	63.76	74.19	59.37	63.00
[X] played the [MASK]	18.53	48.28	72.43	48.46	44.50
[X] played the [MASK], which is an instrument.	14.39	59.86	73.18	57.25	58.00
[X] played the [MASK], which is an instrument	14.21	63.68	70.63	56.69	57.50
[MASK], which is an instrument, was played by [X].	15.02	58.45	74.3	55.99	49.50
[MASK], which is an instrument, was played by [X]	14.68	61.6	73.21	56.85	52.00
[X] likes to play the [MASK].	14.29	66.32	70.17	58.19	62.50
[X] likes to play the [MASK]	24.56	42.42	65.56	41.5	26.00
[X] performed on (her|his) [MASK], which is an instrument.	14.08	63.14	72.04	57.15	64.00
[X] performed on (her|his) [MASK], which is an instrument	14.06	65.43	71.42	58.36	67.00
[X] likes to play the [MASK], which is an instrument.	13.83	66.84	69.79	58.34	61.00
[X] likes to play the [MASK], which is an instrument	13.68	68.08	69.25	58.29	63.50
[X] knows to play the [MASK].	13.97	65.89	69.83	58.75	62.00
[X] knows to play [MASK]	486.81	0.40	1.20	0.32	0.00
[X] knows to play the [MASK] instrument.	20.21	26.09	72.71	32.17	10.50
[X] knows to play [MASK] instrument	17.64	47.08	72.52	47.46	35.50
[X] knows to play the [MASK], which is an instrument.	13.96	64.67	70.09	57.21	58.00
[X] knows to play the [MASK], which is an instrument	13.93	64.96	69	56.24	57.50
[X] can play [MASK].	15.03	59.04	74.3	56.56	57.00
[X] can play [MASK]	292.6	9.42	26.31	11.35	2.00
[X] can play [MASK], which is an instrument.	14.16	67.2	73.89	61.7	66.00
[X] can play [MASK] instrument.	19.54	34.77	72.25	37.44	23.00
[X] is noted for playing [MASK] instrument.	32.89	14.19	70.87	19.81	3.00
[X] is noted for playing [MASK] instrument	35.96	16.07	71.73	21.05	1.50
[X] is noted for playing [MASK], which is an instrument.	14.14	66.44	74.48	61.75	64.50
[X] is noted for playing [MASK], which is an instrument	14.18	65.82	73.17	60.11	65.50
[X] is noted for playing [MASK].	17.33	63.09	73.6	58.68	64.50
[X] is noted for playing [MASK]	38.19	18.92	69.68	23.92	5.50
[X] is noted for playing [MASK], which is an instrument.	14.14	66.44	74.48	61.75	64.50
[X] is noted for playing [MASK], which is an instrument	14.18	65.82	73.17	60.11	65.50
[X] practised [MASK], which is an instrument.	14.31	66.18	70.75	58.3	61.50
[X] practised [MASK], which is an instrument	14.38	66.34	71.79	58.92	64.50
[X] taught [MASK], which is an instrument.	14.27	67.04	72.28	60.67	65.00
[X] taught [MASK], which is an instrument	14.1	67.6	72.64	61.16	66.50
[X] performed on (his|her) [MASK], which is an instrument.	14.44	51.89	73.1	51.84	40.50
[X] performed on (his|her) [MASK], which is an instrument	14.01	63.91	71.72	57.67	67.00

Table 12: Our proposed prompts for (person, plays an instrument) relation.

Prompt Template	optimal k	precision	recall	max-F1	p@1
[X] speaks in [MASK].	2.61	82.13	72.35	72.78	83.50
[X] speaks in [MASK]	5.73	54.6	61.08	48.62	47.50
[X] can speak in [MASK].	2.56	81.63	69.37	70.76	82.50
[X] can speak in [MASK]	7.26	63.35	66.07	57.14	60.50
[X] communicates in [MASK].	2.94	77.04	71.28	69.93	74.50
[X] communicates in [MASK]	6.71	48.41	64.69	47.07	36.50
[X] spoke in [MASK].	2.59	82.62	70.24	71.32	86.00
[X] spoke in [MASK]	7.28	38.36	59.67	39.74	20.00
[X] communicated in [MASK].	3.09	77.38	71.76	69.41	79.50
[X] communicated in [MASK]	13.03	32.09	58.54	35.86	11.00
[X] knows the [MASK] language.	3.18	76.9	68.85	67.49	78.50
[X] knows the [MASK] language	4.04	70.16	70.24	63.91	75.50
[X] learnt [MASK], which is a language.	2.68	79.65	70.03	70.23	81.00
[X] learnt [MASK], which is a language	3.18	74.11	72.93	68.82	79.00
[X] knows [MASK], which is a language.	2.58	82.19	68.29	69.92	88.50
[X] knows [MASK], which is a language	2.54	81.04	68.78	70.12	87.00
Languages spoken by [X] are [MASK].	2.64	78.99	68.52	68.6	86.50
Languages spoken by [X] are [MASK]	19.64	24.57	57.63	29.39	5.50
In which language can [X] speak? Answer: [MASK].	2.45	82.8	65.31	68.18	91.50
In which language can [X] speak? Answer: [MASK]	110.26	19.29	39.12	23.86	1.00
In which language can [X] talk? Answer: [MASK].	2.53	82.43	64.67	67.2	92.50
In which language can [X] talk? Answer: [MASK]	157.13	18.64	37.15	22.08	3.00
In which language can [X] communicates? Answer: [MASK]	142.3	19.28	36.47	22.15	3.00
In which language can [X] communicates? Answer: [MASK]	142.3	19.28	36.47	22.15	3.00
[X] knows to speak in [MASK].	2.6	82.13	69.34	70.88	86.50
[X] knows to speak in [MASK]	18.97	50.01	61.15	45.91	42.50
[X] speaks in [MASK], which is a language.	2.85	78.28	70.92	70.02	82.00
[X] speaks in [MASK], which is a language	3.06	74.5	70.92	68.25	78.00
[X] can speak in [MASK], which is a language.	2.61	81.86	70.11	71.22	85.50
[X] can speak in [MASK], which is a language	2.88	77.43	71.18	69.82	84.50
In [MASK], [X] spoke.	3.12	72.21	62.23	61.27	74.50
In [MASK], [X] spoke	9.81	39.6	57.87	40.93	26.50
In [MASK], which is a language, [X] spoke.	2.83	77.59	69.16	68.24	80.50
In [MASK], which is a language, [X] spoke	2.91	77.5	69.2	68.11	78.50
[X] learned to speak [MASK] fluently.	2.89	78.81	71.55	70.46	80.00
[X] learned to speak [MASK] fluently	2.91	80.46	72.49	71.38	83.50
[X] learned to speak [MASK], which is a language.	2.73	80.59	70.28	70.4	82.50
[X] learned to speak [MASK], which is a language	3.26	75.33	71.25	68.07	80.00
[X] communicates in [MASK], which is a language.	2.44	83.7	67.28	69.82	85.50
[X] communicates in [MASK], which is a language	2.47	82.43	68.62	70.25	80.50
[X] spoke in [MASK], which is a language.	3.17	74.57	69.58	66.67	79.00
[X] spoke in [MASK], which is a language	3.92	67.89	71.21	63.95	73.00
[X] knows to speak in [MASK], which is a language.	2.48	81.9	68.69	70.36	85.00
[X] knows to speak in [MASK], which is a language	2.97	77.49	70.76	69.88	81.00
[X] learned to speak [MASK].	2.99	76.54	70.91	68.95	80.00
[X] learned to speak [MASK]	76.98	18.98	42.24	22.06	3.50
[X] learnt [MASK] language.	4.46	60.35	66.61	56.26	55.00
[X] learnt [MASK] language	4.62	62.27	68.51	58.51	63.00
[X] addressed in [MASK], which is a language.	2.52	81.3	68.71	70.15	82.00
[X] addressed in [MASK], which is a language	2.69	79.85	70.65	70.75	82.00

Table 13: Our proposed prompts for (person, speaks a language) relation.

Prompt Template	optimal k	precision	recall	max-F1	p@1
[X] is a [MASK] by profession.	30.87	18.52	35.37	20.78	8.00
[X] is a [MASK] by profession	28.39	20.08	34.17	21.23	13.00
[X] is a [MASK].	19.23	35.01	35.98	29.3	40.50
[X] is a [MASK]	20.02	34.14	33.8	26.34	41.50
[X] is a [MASK], which is a profession.	23.15	30.17	36.72	26.81	31.00
[X] is a [MASK], which is a profession	17.87	35.11	31.63	26.43	40.00
[X]'s profession is [MASK].	61.53	13.22	44.71	17.2	3.00
[X]'s profession is [MASK]	111.9	6.14	22.31	6.72	1.50
[X] worked as a [MASK].	25.75	21.29	33.97	22.68	20.50
[X] worked as a [MASK]	16.41	30.66	27.78	24.41	25.50
[X] was a [MASK] for a living.	20.94	37.44	27.59	23.97	48.00
[X] is a [MASK] for a living.	15.66	38.35	30.19	27.14	53.00
[X] is a well-known [MASK].	14.58	39.76	33.36	30.8	59.00
[X] is a well-known [MASK]	11.64	45.35	32.37	33.21	54.50
[X] worked as a [MASK], which is a profession.	23.93	25.12	35.08	24.33	22.50
[X] worked as a [MASK], which is a profession	22.28	25.84	34.95	24.62	25.00
[X] worked as a [MASK] for a living.	29.44	25.35	32.45	21.22	27.00
[X] worked as a [MASK] for a living	27.66	23.66	32.75	21.08	26.00
[X] works as a [MASK].	32.09	17.79	38.41	21.05	19.00
[X] works as a [MASK]	21.62	25.43	31.52	23.02	20.50
What is the profession of [X]? Answer: [MASK].	158.97	2.68	20.45	4.11	0.00
What is the profession of [X]? Answer: [MASK]	216.16	5.51	6.41	3.68	1.50
What did [X] do for a living? Answer: [MASK].	225.71	1.8	8.83	2.33	0.00
What did [X] do for a living? Answer: [MASK]	326.04	3.28	3.27	2.23	1.00
[X] worked as a professional [MASK].	20.84	26.52	36.39	26.9	24.00
[X] worked as a professional [MASK]	39.51	14.9	27.85	15.78	1.00
[X] works as a professional [MASK].	22.99	25.73	38.29	26.45	23.00
[X] works as a professional [MASK]	35.24	16.39	30.64	17.54	2.00
[X] is a professional [MASK].	33.5	19.12	42.3	23.4	2.50
[X] is a professional [MASK]	30.51	15.1	31.41	18	3.50
[X] was a [MASK].	35.97	24.36	28.63	20.46	13.00
[X] was a [MASK]	29.84	31.56	26.78	21.66	33.00
[X] served as a [MASK].	34.84	19.08	28.5	17.56	3.00
[X] served as a [MASK]	30.13	20.31	25.71	17.14	9.00
[X] served as a [MASK], which is a profession.	26.62	25.43	29.37	21.94	13.00
[X] served as a [MASK], which is a profession	35.59	16.22	24.68	16.07	0.00
[X] became a [MASK].	24.79	22.97	30.52	21.71	20.00
[X] became a [MASK]	21.07	28.28	24.12	19.7	26.00
[X] became a [MASK], which is a profession.	24.82	23.87	35.55	24.4	24.50
[X] became a [MASK], which is a profession	23.56	23.95	30.41	21.78	19.00
[X] is an [MASK].	6.75	63.21	14.61	19.86	54.50
[X] is an [MASK]	14.35	26.24	13.94	15.54	11.00
[X] was an [MASK].	6.71	61.71	13.59	18.83	50.00
[X] was an [MASK]	20.49	31.84	13.04	14.65	18.00
[X] was a professional [MASK].	30.19	17.73	36.75	21.38	4.50
[X] was a professional [MASK]	51.69	12.68	29.00	14.65	0.50
[X] joined as a [MASK], which is a profession.	20.01	33.47	31.79	26.26	36.50
[X] joined as a [MASK], which is a profession	17.54	27.09	29.91	25.06	9.50
[X] joined as a [MASK].	21.72	23.88	31.06	24.16	8.00
[X] joined as a [MASK]	26.56	19.02	30.65	20.96	0.00

Table 14: Our proposed prompts for (person, has an occupation) relation.

Prompt Template	optimal k	precision	recall	max-F1	p@1
[X] shares border with [MASK].	285.62	35.78	21.85	25.18	32.50
[X] shares border with [MASK]	291.63	25.94	19.15	19.14	26.50
[X] shares a border with [MASK].	285.64	36.08	22.02	25.39	32.50
[X] shares a border with [MASK]	296.5	22.06	18.2	17.32	20.00
[X] borders [MASK].	285.81	35.48	21.51	24.63	34.00
[X] borders [MASK]	316.65	9.03	16.07	9.48	2.50
[X] has borders with [MASK].	286.25	32.6	21.67	24.1	30.00
[X] has borders with [MASK]	306.04	10.59	16.58	10.83	3.50
[X] shares border with [MASK], which is a [Y].	285.38	37.32	21.48	25.21	35.50
[X] shares border with [MASK], which is a [Y]	285.53	36.7	21.8	25.16	34.50
The neighbouring [Y] of [X] is [MASK].	290.67	32.64	20.87	23.52	32.50
The neighbouring [Y] of [X] is [MASK]	371.29	6.00	8.67	6.08	0.50
The [X] [Y] shares border with [MASK].	285.53	35.92	21.6	25.06	32.00
The [X] [Y] shares border with [MASK]	293.25	14.16	17.2	12.97	6.50
[X] shares a border with [MASK], which is a [Y].	285.4	37.27	21.6	25.3	35.00
[X] shares a border with [MASK], which is a [Y]	285.56	36.81	21.77	25.21	35.50
[X] borders [MASK], which is a [Y].	285.51	36.36	22.08	25.1	35.00
[X] borders [MASK], which is a [Y]	285.56	36.13	22.08	25.15	34.00
[MASK] is a neighbouring [Y] of [X].	285.45	35.96	21.79	25.04	34.50
[MASK] is a neighbouring [Y] of [X]	285.51	34.73	21.43	24.52	31.50
Which [Y] shares border with [X]? Answer: [MASK].	293.96	23.81	20.94	20.63	25.00
Which [Y] shares border with [X]? Answer: [MASK]	429.81	6.28	5.16	4.78	3.00
Which [Y] is near [X]? Answer: [MASK].	286.75	23.85	20.66	20.44	20.00
Which [Y] is near [X]? Answer: [MASK]	432.43	5.58	6.21	4.67	1.50
[MASK], which is a [Y], is near [X].	285.42	37.09	21.85	25.39	35.50
[MASK], which is a [Y], is near [X]	286.12	29.84	21.02	22.02	29.50
The [Y], [MASK], shares border with [X].	285.78	32.22	21.64	24.1	31.50
The [Y], [MASK], shares border with [X]	286.05	28.00	21.31	22.26	26.50
[MASK] is the bordering [Y] of [X].	285.41	37.06	21.94	25.43	35.50
[MASK] is the bordering [Y] of [X]	285.54	35.88	21.9	24.69	36.50
The [Y], [MASK], shares border with [X], which is a [Y].	285.61	34.00	21.25	24.23	34.00
The [Y], [MASK], shares border with [X], which is a [Y]	285.64	33.48	21.88	24.29	34.50
[MASK], which is a [Y], shares a border with [X].	285.37	37.96	21.86	25.49	37.00
[MASK], which is a [Y], shares a border with [X]	285.41	37.29	21.5	25.1	36.50
[MASK], which is a [Y], borders [X].	285.35	38.46	21.8	25.65	37.50
[MASK], which is a [Y], borders [X]	285.46	36.25	21.46	24.68	36.00
[MASK], which is a [Y], has borders with [X].	285.37	37.9	21.78	25.4	37.00
[MASK], which is a [Y], has borders with [X]	285.41	36.57	21.07	24.57	36.00
The neighbouring [Y] of [X] is [MASK], which is a [Y].	285.46	36.14	21.78	24.75	35.50
The neighbouring [Y] of [X] is [MASK], which is a [Y]	285.68	33.13	21.73	23.75	32.50
Which [Y] shares border with [X]? The answer is [MASK].	407.63	8.70	6.99	6.63	5.50
Which [Y] shares border with [X]? The answer is [MASK]	499.0	0.00	0.00	0.00	0.00
Which [Y] shares border with [X]? Answer: [MASK], which is a [Y].	285.71	32.77	21.72	23.74	30.50
Which [Y] shares border with [X]? Answer: [MASK], which is a [Y]	291.11	26.46	20.07	20.93	24.00
[X] and [MASK] share a border.	285.49	37.49	22.3	25.69	37.50
[X] and [MASK] share a border	285.49	37.54	22.3	25.71	37.00
The [X] [Y] shares border with [MASK], which is a [Y].	285.43	37.26	21.72	25.36	36.00
The [X] [Y] shares border with [MASK], which is a [Y]	285.51	37.11	21.55	25.22	35.50
[X] and [MASK] are neighbours.	288.2	33.55	21.78	23.96	33.00
[X] and [MASK] are neighbours	290.68	33.77	21.68	23.92	33.50

Table 15: Our proposed prompts for (state, shares border) relation.

Hierarchical Multi-Instance Multi-Label Learning for Detecting Propaganda Techniques

Anni Chen and **Bhuwan Dhingra**
Department of Computer Science
Duke University
Durham, NC, USA
anni.chen@alumni.duke.edu
bhuwan.dhingra@duke.edu

Abstract

Since the introduction of the SemEval 2020 Task 11 (Martino et al., 2020a), several approaches have been proposed in the literature for classifying propaganda based on the rhetorical techniques used to influence readers. These methods, however, classify one span at a time, ignoring dependencies from the labels of other spans within the same context. In this paper, we approach propaganda technique classification as a Multi-Instance Multi-Label (MIML) learning problem (Zhou et al., 2012) and propose a simple RoBERTa-based model (Zhuang et al., 2021) for classifying all spans in an article simultaneously. Further, we note that, due to the annotation process where annotators classified the spans by following a decision tree, there is an inherent hierarchical relationship among the different techniques, which existing approaches ignore. We incorporate these hierarchical label dependencies by adding an auxiliary classifier for each node in the decision tree to the training objective and ensembling the predictions from the original and auxiliary classifiers at test time. Overall, our model leads to an absolute improvement of 2.47% micro-F1 over the model from the shared task winning team in a cross-validation setup and is the best performing non-ensemble model on the shared task leaderboard.

1 Introduction

The development of the Web and social media has amplified the scale and effectiveness of propaganda (Barrón-Cedeno et al., 2019). Automatic propaganda detection through text analysis enables social science researchers to analyze its spread at scale (Glowacki et al., 2018; Martino et al., 2020b). Within text analysis, two broad approaches include the identification of rhetorical techniques used to influence readers and document-level propagandistic article classification. The former is more promising because propaganda techniques are easy to identify and are the very building blocks (Martino et al., 2020b). Hence, it is the focus of this paper.

Recent research on fine-grained propaganda detection has been spurred by the NLP4IF-2019 Shared Task (Da San Martino et al., 2019) and its follow-up SemEval 2020 Task 11 (Martino et al., 2020a). In this paper, we focus on its Technique Classification subtask where, given a news article text and spans identified as propagandistic, systems need to classify each of the spans into one or more of 14 different common propaganda techniques.

All top systems submitted to the task (Jurkiewicz et al., 2020; Chernyavskiy et al., 2020; Morio et al., 2020; Raj et al., 2020) employed a pretrained RoBERTa-based model (Zhuang et al., 2021) which was trained to classify one span at a time. However, labels of different spans within the same article clearly depend on each other. Thus, we approach the task within a Multi-Instance Multi-Label framework (Zhou et al., 2012), where we model each article as an object with multiple instances (spans), each with its own labels. This allows us to model the dependencies between different labels within the same article. We show that this $\text{MIML}_{\text{RoBERTa}}$ observes a 1.98% micro-F1 improvement over the replicated ApplicaAI system (referred to as baseline) (Jurkiewicz et al., 2020).

Besides, as a decision tree was used to guide annotations (Martino et al., 2020a), we explore incorporating this hierarchical relationship among the labels into classifiers. To do so, we add 7 more auxiliary classifiers on top of the span representations from RoBERTa, one for each intermediate node in the tree, and train these classifiers to predict the path to a leaf node and hence the corresponding label (see Figure 1). We show that incorporating the label hierarchy in this manner improves both the single-instance and the MIML versions of the RoBERTa model (referred to as hierarchical baseline and hierarchical $\text{MIML}_{\text{RoBERTa}}$ respectively).

Proceedings of the 8th Workshop on Representation Learning for NLP (RepL4NLP 2023), pages 155–163
July 13, 2023

2 Related Work

The MIML framework was first introduced by Zhou et al. (2012) aiming for better representing complicated objects composed of multiple instances, e.g., an image with several bounding boxes each with its own label. Since then, it has been applied to many tasks, such as relation extraction (Surdeanu et al., 2012) and aspect-category sentiment analysis (Li et al., 2020). The latter work uses a Bi-LSTM architecture which aggregates over the words in a sentence (instances) to classify the sentiments of different aspects (labels). MIML has also been applied to BERT-based models in the biomedical text analysis (Tian and Zhang, 2021). To our best knowledge, our work is the first one to apply it for propaganda technique classification.

Given the decision tree used for annotations (reproduced in Figure 4 in Appendix), this task can also be viewed as a hierarchical text classification problem, with mandatory leaf node prediction and a tree-structured hierarchy (Silla and Freitas, 2011). Exploiting hierarchical information has been useful in significantly enhancing the performance of the system for medical image annotations (Dimitrovski et al., 2011) and presents us with an opportunity to apply to the propaganda method detection. Similar to (Dumais and Chen, 2000; Weigend et al., 1999), we use the multiplicative rule to combine probabilities along the different paths in the hierarchy, leading to a distribution across the leaf nodes which can be combined with the distribution predicted by the non-hierarchical baseline. Different approaches to hierarchical classification across multiple domains can be found in Silla and Freitas (2011).

3 Methods[1]

Task Description. Given an article d with propagandistic spans $s_1, ..., s_m$ identified by their start and end indices, the task is to identify the sets of techniques $y_1, ..., y_m$ where $y_i \subseteq Y \; \forall i \in \{1, ..., m\}$ and Y represents the set of 14 techniques. Following the shared task, we assume that the number of labels $|y_i|$ for each span is known.

3.1 Single-Instance Baseline

The baseline system from the winning ApplicaAI team (Jurkiewicz et al., 2020) uses a RoBERTa-based classifier and applies to each span separately. The span is padded by special tokens <bop> and <eop> on either side. A total context of 256 tokens on both sides of the target span spanning multiple sentences are included in the input, unlike other systems (Chernyavskiy et al., 2020; Morio et al., 2020; Raj et al., 2020) on the leaderboard which limit to the target sentence. For classification, we use the <bop> representation output from RoBERTa and pass it through a linear layer followed by softmax. Jurkiewicz et al. (2020) further show marginal improvements by re-weighting the loss for under-represented classes, self-training over unlabeled data and a Span-CLS approach which adds a second transformer network on top of RoBERTa only over the tokens in the target span. In our experiments, we did not use any of the improvements.

3.2 MIML$_{\text{RoBERTa}}$

During the initial inspection of data, we observed high absolute pointwise mutual information between certain techniques. For example, in an article, if the *slogans* technique appears, the *flag-waving* technique usually follows. This observation motivates us to predict the labels of *all* spans in a text simultaneously.

During preprocessing, we pad the spans with pairs of <bop0>, <eop0>, <bop1>, <eop1>... to indicate the start and the end of a text fragment, even in cases where some spans are nested inside or overlapping with others. After padding, every article is split into windows of size 512 tokens with a stride of 256 tokens until there are no more labeled spans. Whenever there are spans that need to be truncated as we create a window, its corresponding <eop> is appended near the end of the window to ensure that the number of <bop>s and <eop>s match. In the case where there is a specific nesting structure between any two text fragments, its nesting structure is respected in appending the <eop> to represent the differences in text fragments even after truncation. Also, since only around 1.8% of the total annotations are spans with multiple labels (Martino et al., 2020a), for ease of implementation, we use the rarer label for every text span during preprocessing and the later training.

Let h_s denote the RoBERTa output at the <bop> for a span s, then we compute the logits for each of the labels as $p_{\text{flat}}(c) \propto \exp(h_s \cdot w_c)$, for $c = 0, \ldots, 13$. The model is trained using the cross-

[1]Code is available at `https://github.com/Dranoxgithub/propaganda-nlp-new`.

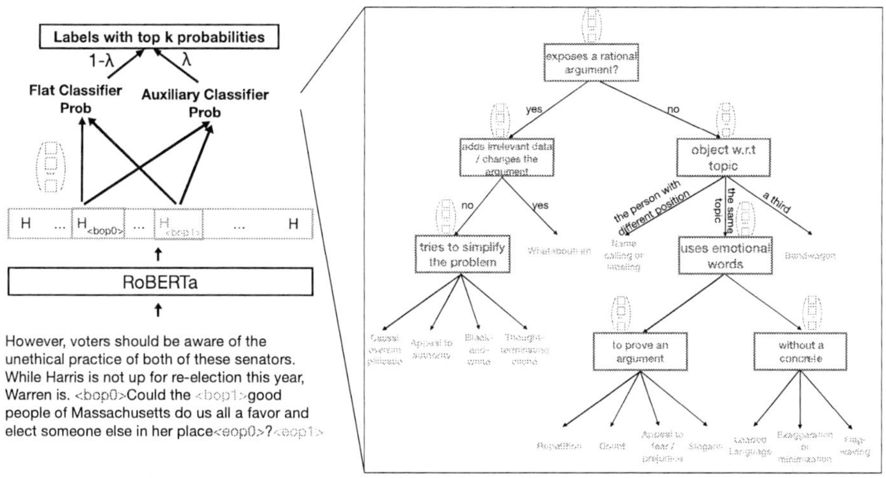

Figure 1: Overview of the hier $\text{MIML}_{\text{RoBERTa}}$. Multiple spans within the same text (instances) are classified together. We add an auxiliary classifier to the model at each intermediate node. Decision tree used for annotations (right).

entropy loss:

$$l_{\text{flat}} = \sum_{c=1}^{C} -\mathbb{1}_{y=c} \log p_{\text{flat}}(c), \tag{1}$$

where w_c is a weight vector and y is the ground truth label of the span. We compute l_{flat} simultaneously for all spans in the text and take an average.

During inference, we predict the number of labels requested for each span by selecting the classes with the highest in p_{flat}. Since some spans can appear in multiple windows, the set of predictions from the window where the span is least truncated and has the most surrounding context is chosen.

3.3 Hierarchical $\text{MIML}_{\text{RoBERTa}}$

Due to the complex and subjective nature of the task, span annotations by Martino et al. (2020a) were guided by a decision tree. For example, annotators first consider whether the argument is rational, followed by whether emotional words are used, and so on. This process induces a hierarchy among the labels, and to model such relationships, we use a simplified version of the decision tree whose leaf nodes are the 14 propaganda techniques (Figure 1, right). We add an auxiliary loss to the training objective based on hierarchical text classification which trains local classifiers at each intermediate node (Silla and Freitas, 2011).

Let K be the number of intermediate nodes and hence the number of auxiliary classifiers, and let $C_1, C_2, \ldots, C_K$ denote the number of outgoing edges or the number of labels for each classifier. Then, given the RoBERTa representation for a span h_s, we compute the probability of following an edge i from an intermediate node k as:

$$p_k(i) \propto \exp(h_s \cdot w_{k,i}), \quad \forall i = 0, \ldots, C_k \tag{2}$$

where $w_{k,i}$ is a weight vector and the probabilities are normalized across the C_k labels for each classifier. Given a leaf node label c, we denote the path of classifiers and edges from the root to it as $I_c = \{(k_1, i_1), (k_2, i_2), \ldots\}$, where each tuple in the set denotes a pair of classifier and its corresponding label along the path. Then we can compute the overall probability of selecting as:

$$p_{\text{aux}}(c) = \prod_{(k,i)\in I_c} p_k(i). \tag{3}$$

Note that p_{aux} forms a valid distribution over the leaf nodes since each probability along the path is normalized.

During training, we compute an auxiliary loss for each span which minimizes the negative log-likelihood of selecting the edges along the path to its correct label y:

$$l_{\text{aux}} = \frac{1}{|I_y|} \sum_{(k,i)\in I_y} \sum_{c=1}^{C_k} -\mathbb{1}_{i=c} \log p_k(i). \tag{4}$$

$\lambda_{\text{training}}$ and λ_{eval} are both hyperparameters. The overall training loss is a combination of the flat loss described in the previous section and the auxiliary loss above: $l_{\text{ovr}} = (1 - \lambda_{\text{training}}) \cdot l_{\text{flat}} + \lambda_{\text{training}} \cdot l_{\text{aux}}$.

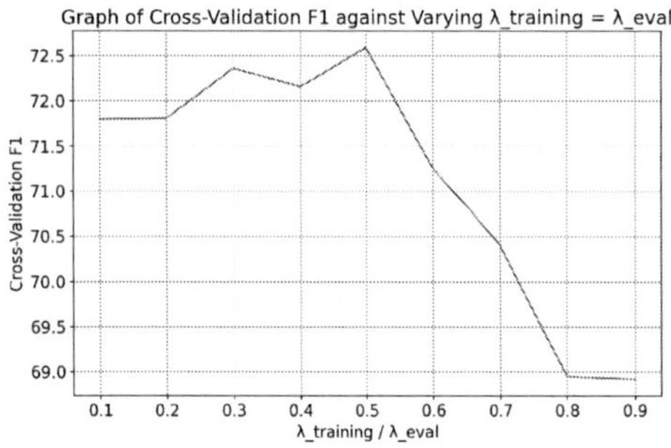

Figure 2: Cross-validation F1 against varying lambda values where $\lambda_{\text{training}} = \lambda_{\text{eval}}$. The performance is the best at $\lambda_{\text{training}} = \lambda_{\text{eval}} = 0.5$.

During inference, we combine the predicted probabilities over the labels from both the flat classifier and auxiliary classifiers: $p_{\text{ovr}}(c) = (1 - \lambda_{\text{eval}}) \cdot p_{\text{flat}}(c) + \lambda_{\text{eval}} \cdot p_{\text{aux}}(c)$.

4 Experiments

4.1 Dataset

The original training and development set respectively contains 357, 74 articles, and thus correspondingly 6128, 1063 data points. Following Jurkiewicz et al. (2020), we also evaluate using six-fold cross-validation where the folds are created by mixing the original training and development sets. As a result each fold roughly consists of 6000 training and 1200 evaluation data points. Below we report the average and standard deviation of the metrics across six folds. We also submit our best models, trained on the original training set, to the leaderboard for evaluation on the official test set.

4.2 Training & Evaluation

We tune both $\lambda_{\text{training}}$ between 0 and 1 with a step of 0.1. For every value of $\lambda_{\text{training}}$, we also tune λ_{eval} at 0, 1 and $\lambda_{\text{training}}$.The model's performance peaks at $\lambda_{\text{training}} = \lambda_{\text{eval}} = 0.5$ (Figure 2) and all the results reported use this set of values. Hyperparameter details are included in Appendix B.

The scorer script provided by the shared task organizers evaluates a micro-averaged F1 score, taking the best match between the predictions and ground truth labels when a span has multiple labels (Martino et al., 2020a). We use this script for evaluation in all our experiments. Additionally, we also use a *Tree-F1* score from the hierarchical text classification literature which measures the overlap between the paths from the root node to the ground truth and predicted nodes (Kosmopoulos et al., 2015) (details in Appendix C). In particular, we are interested in seeing if models with hierarchical information make mistakes closer to the ground truth in the tree.

5 Results and Discussion

Method		**Cross validation F1(%)**
Baseline	non-hier	70.12 ± 2.06
	hier	70.49 ± 2.01
MIML$_{\text{RoBERTa}}$	non-hier	72.10 ± 0.83
	random	69.54 ± 1.33
	hier	$\mathbf{72.59 \pm 1.02}$

Table 1: Mean and standard deviation of the F1 score across 6 folds for the single-instance baseline and MIML$_{\text{RoBERTa}}$, with and without hierarchical loss. *random* refers to an ablation where we randomly shuffle the nodes in the hierarchy.

Table 1 shows the micro-averaged F1 scores of the different models discussed in Section 3. We see a significant improvement when using the MIML framework: in cross validation, MIML$_{\text{RoBERTa}}$ has a micro-F1 of 72.10%, an absolute improvement of 1.98% compared to the baseline single-instance model (70.12%). This improvement holds whether we use the hierarchical loss or not – the hierarchical MIML$_{\text{RoBERTa}}$ has a 2.1% improvement over the hierarchical baseline (70.49%).

Method		**Tree-F1(%)**	
		(Incorrect)	**(All)**
Baseline	non-hier	51.19	85.44
	hier	51.71	85.78
MIML$_{\text{RoBERTa}}$	non-hier	51.33	86.53
	hier	51.64	86.76

Table 2: Tree-F1 scores for incorrect predictions and all predictions across different models. Incorporating loss$_{\text{aux}}$ improves the Tree-F1 score in both cases.

We also observe small but consistent improvements when training and predicting with hierarchical information in the form of auxiliary classifiers: the baseline model improves by 0.37%, while MIML$_{\text{RoBERTa}}$ improves by 0.49%. Table 2 shows the Tree-F1 scores over the full validation splits, as well as only for the incorrect predictions from the various models. Again, we observe a small improvement due to incorporating the hierarchical information – specifically, the incorrect predictions are now closer to the ground truth labels, as evidenced by the higher Tree-F1 over the mistakes.

To further confirm that these improvements are due to learning hierarchical information rather than any regularization effect from the additional auxiliary loss term, we also run the experiments with the labels on the decision tree randomly shuffled with the same lambda values. We obtain a micro-F1 of 69.54 with $\lambda_{\text{training}} = \lambda_{\text{eval}} = 0.5$, which is significantly lower. Particularly, when $\lambda_{\text{training}} = 0.5$ and $\lambda_{\text{eval}} = 1$, i.e. inference is done using only the auxiliary classifiers, the micro-F1 in cross validation is an extremely low 5.25%, in contrast to a 72.33% when not shuffled.

System		Test F1
Single	Singh et al. (2020)	58.436
	Dimov et al. (2020)	59.832
	non-Hier $\text{MIML}_{\text{RoBERTa}}$ (Ours)	62.179
	Hier $\text{MIML}_{\text{RoBERTa}}$ (Ours)	62.793
Ensemble	Morio et al. (2020)	63.129
	Chernyavskiy et al. (2020)	63.296
	Jurkiewicz et al. (2020)	63.743

Table 3: F1 score on the official test set of various systems on the leaderboard. See `https://propaganda.qcri.org/ptc/leaderboard.php`

The micro-F1 results on the official test set are in Table 3, where we see that the hierarchical $\text{MIML}_{\text{RoBERTa}}$ is the best performing single model. Other than improving accuracy, $\text{MIML}_{\text{RoBERTa}}$ also reduces the training and evaluation time, since it predicts multiple spans in a single forward pass through the RoBERTa model. One epoch of $\text{MIML}_{\text{RoBERTa}}$ (one evaluation every 25 steps) takes 5.04 minutes compared to 15.50 minutes by the single-instance baseline, a 68% reduction.

6 Conclusion

We propose two simple extensions to a RoBERTa-based model for propaganda technique classification, which lead to notable improvements. Our approach to incorporating hierarchical information about the labels into training could also be useful for other tasks where the annotation procedure involves making a series of decisions about instances. Future work can also explore other methods to incorporate the hierarchical information, e.g., via regularizing the label embeddings.

Limitations

The use of auxiliary classifiers at every node of the decision tree is not feasible when the hierarchical tree is huge, such as the large hierarchical terminologies for medical literature indexing (Gasco et al., 2021).

Besides, in Table 1, even though the integration of the hierarchical information shows a consistent improvement in both the baseline and $\text{MIML}_{\text{RoBERTa}}$ models, these improvements are still within one standard deviation of micro-F1.

Lastly, it is worth noting that we do not focus on large language models since our approach is to explore improvements on a published state-of-the-art model. While they might improve accuracy, a careful exploration of those on a new task is beyond the scope.

Ethics Statement

Propaganda detection is a sensitive topic and any practical application of the model needs to be carefully orchestrated. Both false positives and false negatives of the model can have harmful impacts. Moreover, there might be certain biases in the training data, and consequently this leads to systematic issues in the model, such as a higher tendency to mislabel certain kinds of text.

Furthermore, this paper follows the same definition as SemEval 2020 Task 11 (Martino et al., 2020a) whereas there might a broader debate on the definition of propaganda.

Lastly, we also acknowledge the concern that a perfect classifier for propaganda text can be used to train a language model that generates propaganda which in turn evades the classifier's detection.

References

Alberto Barrón-Cedeno, Giovanni Da San Martino, Israa Jaradat, and Preslav Nakov. 2019. Proppy: A system to unmask propaganda in online news. In *Proceedings of the AAAI Conference on Artificial Intelligence*, volume 33, pages 9847–9848.

Anton Chernyavskiy, Dmitry Ilvovsky, and Preslav Nakov. 2020. Aschern at semeval-2020 task 11: It takes three to tango: Roberta, crf, and transfer learning. *arXiv preprint arXiv:2008.02837*.

Giovanni Da San Martino, Alberto Barrón-Cedeño, and Preslav Nakov. 2019. Findings of the NLP4IF-2019 shared task on fine-grained propaganda detection. In *Proceedings of the Second Workshop on Natural Language Processing for Internet Freedom: Censorship,*

Disinformation, and Propaganda, pages 162–170, Hong Kong, China. Association for Computational Linguistics.

Ivica Dimitrovski, Dragi Kocev, Suzana Loskovska, and Saso Dzeroski. 2011. Hierarchical annotation of medical images. *Pattern Recognit.*, 44:2436–2449.

Ilya Dimov, Vladislav Korzun, and Ivan Smurov. 2020. NoPropaganda at SemEval-2020 task 11: A borrowed approach to sequence tagging and text classification. In *Proceedings of the Fourteenth Workshop on Semantic Evaluation*, pages 1488–1494, Barcelona (online). International Committee for Computational Linguistics.

Susan Dumais and Hao Chen. 2000. Hierarchical classification of web content. In *Proceedings of the 23rd Annual International ACM SIGIR Conference on Research and Development in Information Retrieval*, SIGIR '00, page 256–263, New York, NY, USA. Association for Computing Machinery.

Luis Gasco, Anastasios Nentidis, Anastasia Krithara, Darryl Estrada-Zavala, Renato Toshiyuki Murasaki, Elena Primo-Peña, Cristina Bojo Canales, Georgios Paliouras, Martin Krallinger, et al. 2021. Overview of bioasq 2021-mesinesp track. evaluation of advance hierarchical classification techniques for scientific literature, patents and clinical trials. CEUR Workshop Proceedings.

Monika Glowacki, Vidya Narayanan, Sam Maynard, Gustavo Hirsch, Bence Kollanyi, Lisa-Maria Neudert, Phil Howard, Thomas Lederer, and Vlad Barash. 2018. News and political information consumption in mexico: Mapping the 2018 mexican presidential election on twitter and facebook. *The Computational Propaganda Project*.

Dawid Jurkiewicz, Łukasz Borchmann, Izabela Kosmala, and Filip Graliński. 2020. Applicaai at semeval-2020 task 11: On roberta-crf, span cls and whether self-training helps them. *arXiv preprint arXiv:2005.07934*.

Aris Kosmopoulos, Ioannis Partalas, Eric Gaussier, Georgios Paliouras, and Ion Androutsopoulos. 2015. Evaluation measures for hierarchical classification: a unified view and novel approaches. *Data Mining and Knowledge Discovery*, 29(3):820–865.

Yuncong Li, Cunxiang Yin, Sheng-hua Zhong, and Xu Pan. 2020. Multi-instance multi-label learning networks for aspect-category sentiment analysis. In *Proceedings of the 2020 Conference on Empirical Methods in Natural Language Processing (EMNLP)*, pages 3550–3560, Online. Association for Computational Linguistics.

G Martino, Alberto Barrón-Cedeno, Henning Wachsmuth, Rostislav Petrov, and Preslav Nakov. 2020a. Semeval-2020 task 11: Detection of propaganda techniques in news articles. *arXiv preprint arXiv:2009.02696*.

Giovanni Da San Martino, Stefano Cresci, Alberto Barrón-Cedeño, Seunghak Yu, Roberto Di Pietro, and Preslav Nakov. 2020b. A survey on computational propaganda detection. *arXiv preprint arXiv:2007.08024*.

Gaku Morio, Terufumi Morishita, Hiroaki Ozaki, and Toshinori Miyoshi. 2020. Hitachi at SemEval-2020 task 11: An empirical study of pre-trained transformer family for propaganda detection. In *Proceedings of the Fourteenth Workshop on Semantic Evaluation*, pages 1739–1748, Barcelona (online). International Committee for Computational Linguistics.

Mayank Raj, Ajay Jaiswal, Rohit R.R, Ankita Gupta, Sudeep Kumar Sahoo, Vertika Srivastava, and Yeon Hyang Kim. 2020. Solomon at SemEval-2020 task 11: Ensemble architecture for fine-tuned propaganda detection in news articles. In *Proceedings of the Fourteenth Workshop on Semantic Evaluation*, pages 1802–1807, Barcelona (online). International Committee for Computational Linguistics.

Carlos N. Silla and Alex A. Freitas. 2011. A survey of hierarchical classification across different application domains. *Data Mining and Knowledge Discovery*, 22(1):31–72.

Paramansh Singh, Siraj Sandhu, Subham Kumar, and Ashutosh Modi. 2020. newsSweeper at SemEval-2020 task 11: Context-aware rich feature representations for propaganda classification. In *Proceedings of the Fourteenth Workshop on Semantic Evaluation*, pages 1764–1770, Barcelona (online). International Committee for Computational Linguistics.

Mihai Surdeanu, Julie Tibshirani, Ramesh Nallapati, and Christopher D Manning. 2012. Multi-instance multi-label learning for relation extraction. In *Proceedings of the 2012 joint conference on empirical methods in natural language processing and computational natural language learning*, pages 455–465.

Shubo Tian and Jinfeng Zhang. Team fsu2021 at biocreative vii litcovid track: Bert-based models using different strategies for topic annotation of covid-19 literature. In *Proceedings of the seventh BioCreative challenge evaluation workshop*.

Shubo Tian and Jinfeng Zhang. 2021. Multi-label topic classification for covid-19 literature annotation using an ensemble model based on pubmedbert. *bioRxiv*.

Andreas S. Weigend, Erik D. Wiener, and Jan O. Pedersen. 1999. Exploiting hierarchy in text categorization. *Information Retrieval*, 1(3):193–216.

Thomas Wolf, Lysandre Debut, Victor Sanh, Julien Chaumond, Clement Delangue, Anthony Moi, Pierric Cistac, Tim Rault, Rémi Louf, Morgan Funtowicz, et al. 2019. Huggingface's transformers: State-of-the-art natural language processing. *arXiv preprint arXiv:1910.03771*.

Zhi-Hua Zhou, Min-Ling Zhang, Sheng-Jun Huang, and Yu-Feng Li. 2012. Multi-instance multi-label learning. *Artificial Intelligence*, 176(1):2291–2320.

Liu Zhuang, Lin Wayne, Shi Ya, and Zhao Jun. 2021. A robustly optimized BERT pre-training approach with post-training. In *Proceedings of the 20th Chinese National Conference on Computational Linguistics*, pages 1218–1227, Huhhot, China. Chinese Information Processing Society of China.

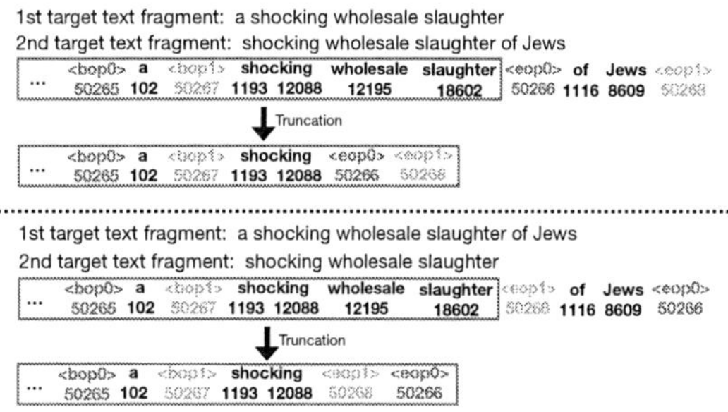

Figure 3: Illustration of how the truncation respects the nesting structure. The difference in text fragments (above and below the dotted line) is exemplified in different nesting structures before truncation. The difference is also preserved after truncation by the differences in the ordering of <eop0> and <eop1>.

A Techniques

The hierarchical diagram to guide the annotation of propaganda techniques can be found in Figure 4.

B Hyperparameters

We use HuggingFace's library (Wolf et al., 2019) and a single Nvidia RTX A6000 GPU. Both the baseline and the hierarchical baseline methods use a learning rate of $2e-5$, a dropout of 0 and a batch size of 16, while the $\text{MIML}_{\text{RoBERTa}}$ and its hierarchical version use a learning rate of $1e-5$, a dropout of 0.1 and a batch size of 8. All the models are trained for 20 epochs. More details can be found in Table 4.

C Tree-F1 Metric

Let Y be the ground truth label and Y' be the prediction, and let K be the lowest common ancestor between the two. Then the Tree-F1 is given by:

$$\text{Precision}_{\text{Tree}} = L_K / L_{Y'}$$

$$\text{Recall}_{\text{Tree}} = L_K / L_Y$$

$$\text{Tree-F1} = \frac{2 * \text{Precision}_{\text{Tree}} * \text{Recall}_{\text{Tree}}}{\text{Precision}_{\text{Tree}} + \text{Recall}_{\text{Tree}}}$$

where L_M refers to the number of nodes tracing from the root node down to node M.

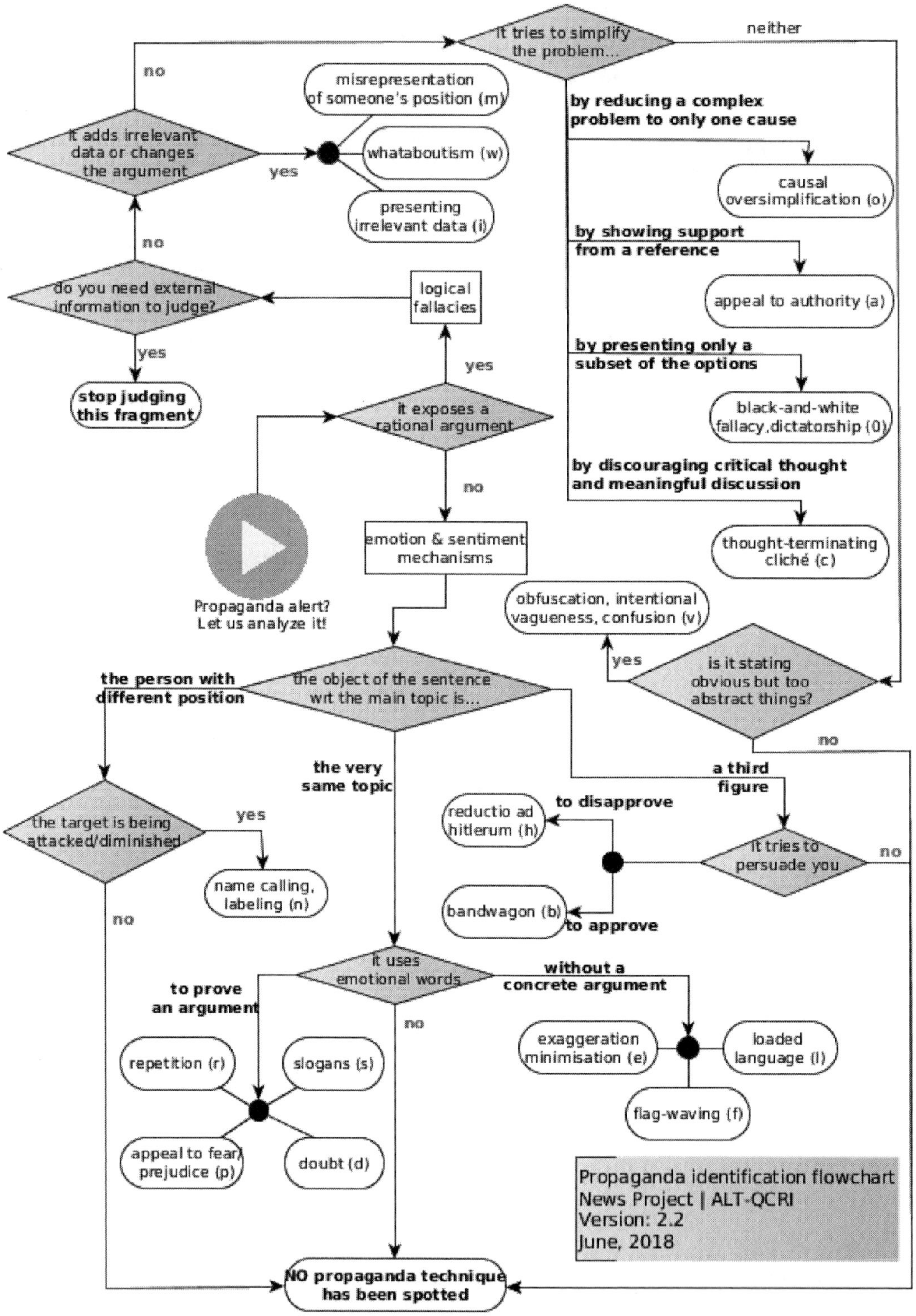

Figure 4: The hierarchical diagram to guide the annotation of propaganda techniques (Martino et al., 2020a).

Hyperparameter	Baseline	Hier Baseline	$MIML_{RoBERTa}$	Hier $MIML_{RoBERTa}$
Dropout	0	0	0.1	0.1
Learning Rate	2e-5	2e-5	1e-5	1e-5
Weight decay	0.01	0.01	0.1	0.1
Loss	BCE	BCE	CE	CE
Batch size	16	16	8	8
Context Size	512	512	512	512
Number of epochs	20	20	20	20
Optimizer	AdamW	AdamW	AdamW	AdamW

Table 4: Optimizers and hyperparameters for all different methods.

Technique	**Freq**
Loaded Language	2448
Name calling or labeling	1241
Repetition	766
Exaggeration or minimization	534
Doubt	559
Appeal to fear/prejudice	338
Flag-waving	316
Causal oversimplification	227
Slogans	169
Appeal to authority	158
Black-and-white fallacy, dictatorship	129
Thought-terminating cliché	93
Whataboutism, straw man, red herring	136
Bandwagon, reductio ad hilterum	77

Table 5: Summary of techniques and their frequency in the data. The definitions of the techniques are found in `https://propaganda.qcri.org/annotations/definitions.html`

Contrastive Loss is All You Need to Recover Analogies as Parallel Lines

Narutatsu Ri
Columbia University
wl2787@columbia.edu

Fei-Tzin Lee
Columbia University
feitzin@cs.columbia.edu

Nakul Verma
Columbia University
verma@cs.columbia.edu

Abstract

While static word embedding models are known to represent linguistic analogies as parallel lines in high-dimensional space, the underlying mechanism as to why they result in such geometric structures remains obscure. We find that an elementary contrastive-style optimization employed over distributional information performs competitively with popular word embedding models on analogy recovery tasks, while achieving dramatic speedups in training time. Further, we demonstrate that a contrastive loss is sufficient to create these parallel structures in word embeddings, and establish a precise relationship between the co-occurrence statistics and the geometric structure of the resulting word embeddings.

1 Introduction

Static word embeddings take inspiration from the distributional hypothesis (Firth, 1957) and assign vector representations to words based on co-occurrence statistics. Such embeddings are known to implicitly encode syntactic and semantic analogies as parallelogram-type structures (Mikolov et al., 2013a,b). This discovery inspired a series of theoretical investigations (Levy and Goldberg, 2014; Gittens et al., 2017; Allen and Hospedales, 2019; Ethayarajh et al., 2019).

Recent studies reconsider whether analogies are indeed represented as parallelograms in the embedding space (Schluter, 2018; Linzen, 2016; Fournier and Dunbar, 2021), and propose a weaker notion of viewing analogies as parallel *lines* (Arora et al., 2016) as a more appropriate model (cf. Figure 1). While this claim is shown to hold empirically for popular word embeddings (Fournier et al., 2020), few analyze the theoretical underpinnings of this phenomenon.

In this paper, we present a remarkable observation that a simple contrastive-style optimization (Chopra et al., 2005) performs just as well as highly-optimized versions of popular word embeddings while achieving 50× speedup in training time. Our work theoretically analyzes the precise conditions under which this optimization procedure can recover analogies as parallel lines. We further investigate the extent to which real-world data satisfies these conditions, and the contrastive loss recovers such parallel structures.

In Section 2, we review recent literature on the theory of word embeddings. Sections 3 and 4 present our contrastive learning objective and its analysis. Section 5 showcases the performance of our approach on analogy-based benchmarks.[1]

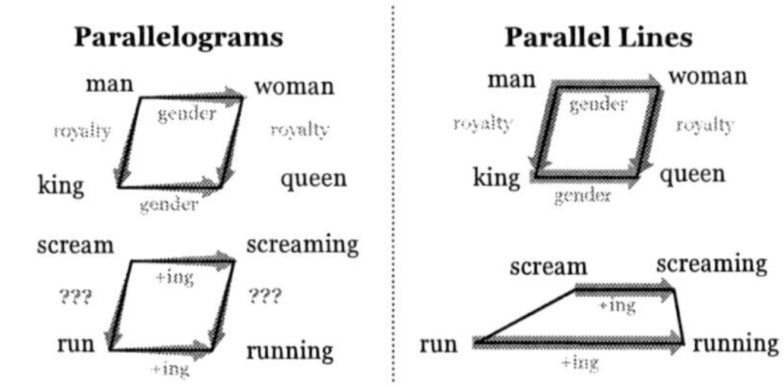

Figure 1: Visualization of analogies as parallelograms and as parallel lines. For the quadruple "`man, woman, king, queen`", two analogy relations coincide ("`man:woman = king:queen`" representing gender and "`man:king = woman:queen`" representing royalty). In contrast, the quadruple "`run, running, scream screaming`" contains only one analogy relation ("`run:running = scream:screaming`" representing present participle). Representing analogies as lines relaxes the geometric requirements on the analogy structure.

2 Related Work

Analogies as Parallelograms. Gittens et al. (2017) study the parallelogram phenomenon by analyzing analogies as a relation between paraphrases. Allen and Hospedales (2019) extend this line of work and show that analogies are captured as parallelo-

[1]Code can be found at `https://github.com/narutatsuri/cwm`.

Proceedings of the 8th Workshop on Representation Learning for NLP (RepL4NLP 2023), pages 164–173
July 13, 2023

grams when the vectors are linear projections of the *Pointwise Mutual Informaton* (PMI) matrix. Ethayarajh et al. (2019) further generalize Gittens' result by introducing the *co-occurrence shifted pointwise mutual information* (csPMI)[2] and analyze the conditions on the csPMI for which parallelograms emerge.

Analogies as Parallel Lines. To the best of our knowledge, the only theoretical work that explores analogies more generally as parallel lines is by Arora et al. (2019), who propose that analogies are encoded as such when the inner products between embeddings weakly recover the PMI of word co-occurrence statistics. We take an alternate approach and show that a contrastive-style optimization suffices to encode analogies as parallel lines.

3 The Contrastive Word Model (CWM)

Contrastive learning methods are based on an intuitive yet powerful idea that pulling similar items closer together while pushing dissimilar items away significantly improves model performance.

We can employ the same push-pull dynamics in word embeddings by placing the vector representations of words that co-occur closer together than those of words that do not. We call this the Contrastive Word Model (CWM), detailed below.

3.1 Notation & Formulation

Given a training corpus, we denote the vocabulary as W. We aim to learn a D-dimensional vector representation v_w for each word w in the vocabulary. The collection of all these vectors is denoted by $V = \{v_1, \ldots, v_{|W|}\}$. We refer to the length-normalized version of a vector v as $\hat{v}$.

Let $\#(i)$ be the occurrence count of word i and $\#(i, j)$ the co-occurrence count (for a context window of size Δ) of words i and j in the training corpus. We denote *window words* as words that co-occur with a reference *center word* (these are reminiscent of the target and context words in Mikolov et al., 2013b), and *negative window words* as words that do not co-occur with the center word. The center-, window-, and negative window words are denoted as c, w, w' respectively. Let $D_{c,w}$ be the set of negative window words for fixed c, w. We define the CWM objective as:

$$\sum_{c \in W} \sum_{w \in W} \#(c, w) \cdot \sum_{w' \in D_{c,w}} \Big[m - \underbrace{\hat{v}_c \cdot \hat{v}_w}_{\text{pull}} + \underbrace{\hat{v}_c \cdot \hat{v}_{w'}}_{\text{push}}\Big]_+ ,$$

where $[\cdot]_+$ is the hinge function and m is a tunable hyperparameter.

To better understand our proposed loss, consider its effect on a fixed center word c. The difference between the terms $\hat{v}_c \cdot \hat{v}_w$ and $\hat{v}_c \cdot \hat{v}_{w'}$ encourages the *angle* between vectors v_c and v_w to be smaller than that between v_c and $v_{w'}$ by at least a margin of m. The hinge function neutralizes the loss once the vectors satisfy the desired relationship. Such max-margin type losses among triples are well investigated in metric learning literature (Weinberger et al., 2005).

3.2 Relation to Popular Word Embeddings

Interestingly, popular word embedding models such as Skip-gram (Mikolov et al., 2013a) and GloVe (Pennington et al., 2014) can be viewed as implicitly employing a push-pull action similar to CWM. Consider Skip-gram's objective: for a fixed pair of co-occurring words c and w, the model updates the word vector v_c as:

$$v_c^{\text{new}} = v_c^{\text{old}} + \underbrace{\left(1 - \frac{e^{v_w^\intercal u_{c'}}}{\sum_{w' \in W} e^{v_w^\intercal u_{w'}}}\right) v_w}_{\text{pull}} \quad (1)$$
$$- \underbrace{\mathbb{E}_{w' \sim W}[v_{w'}]}_{\text{push}} + \text{additional terms.}$$

Here, the word c' (and its target vector $u_{c'}$) co-occurs with both c and w, encouraging all of them to be mapped together (pull), whereas the negative term pushes away randomly sampled words w' from c. See Appendix A.3 for a derivation.

The GloVe objective, on the other hand, performs a series of updates on c, w, and w' as:

$$\text{pull} \begin{cases} v_c^{\text{new}} &= v_c^{\text{old}} + g(c, c')u_{c'} \\ v_w^{\text{new}} &= v_w^{\text{old}} + g(w, c')u_{c'} \end{cases} \quad (2)$$
$$\text{push} \begin{cases} v_{w'}^{\text{new}} &= v_{w'}^{\text{old}} - g(w', c')u_{c'}, \end{cases}$$

where $g(\cdot, \cdot)$ always returns a positive value. Notice that the *positive* contribution of g in the first two updates encourages v_c and v_w to be closer together (pull), while the *negative* contribution to the $v_{w'}$ update encourages it to be pushed away. See Appendix A.4 for a derivation.

[2] $\text{csPMI}(a, b) = \text{PMI}(a, b) + \log p(a, b)$.

We believe that part of the success of these word embedding models is due to their implicit push-pull dynamics. Hence, a natural question to consider is what happens when one purely optimizes for the push-pull action alone.

4 Analysis

In this section, we provide a theoretical justification for the emergence of analogies as parallel lines when we optimize for the CWM objective.

Consider the expression for word vectors $v_c \in V$ that minimizes the global objective:

$$v_c = \rho_c \left(\sum_{w \in W} \left(\frac{\#(c,w)}{\#(c)} \hat{v}_w \right) - \mathop{\mathbb{E}}_{w' \sim U(W)} [\hat{v}_{w'}] \right), \quad (3)$$

where $\rho_c \in \mathbb{R}$ is a constant dependent on c. In essence, v_c is the difference between the weighted average of the window words and the mean of all word vectors. See Appendix A.1 for derivation.

Under Eq. (3), we consider the conditions that word co-occurrence statistics need to satisfy for a set of words a, b, c, d to form parallel geometric structures.

Theorem 1 *For any quadruple of words $a, b, c, d \in W$, if there exists a constant $\zeta \in \mathbb{R}$ where the co-occurrence statistics satisfy the condition:* $\forall w \in W$

$$\left(\frac{\#(a,w)}{\#(a)} - \frac{\#(b,w)}{\#(b)} \right) \Big/ \left(\frac{\#(c,w)}{\#(c)} - \frac{\#(d,w)}{\#(d)} \right) := \zeta, \quad (4)$$

then the corresponding word vectors satisfy the property:

$$\hat{v}_a - \hat{v}_b = \zeta \left(\hat{v}_c - \hat{v}_d \right).$$

Note that Theorem 1 establishes a direct relationship between word co-occurrence statistics—which are solely derived from the training corpus—and the geometric structure of the word embedding.

For a given quadruple $a, b, c, d \in W$ (regardless of whether they form an analogy), the existence of ζ induces parallel structures between $\hat{v}_a, \hat{v}_b, \hat{v}_c, \hat{v}_d$. If such a ζ exists and is equal to 1, then $\hat{v}_b - \hat{v}_a = \hat{v}_d - \hat{v}_c$ and the quadruple forms a parallelogram. When $\zeta \neq 1$, then the difference vectors $\hat{v}_b - \hat{v}_a$ and $\hat{v}_d - \hat{v}_c$ are mainly parallel, inducing a trapezoidal structure among $\hat{v}_a, \hat{v}_b, \hat{v}_c, \hat{v}_d$ (cf. Figure 1).

One would expect that the co-occurrence statistics of real data conform with the existence of such a ζ value for analogy quadruples, whereas ζ does not exist for random quadruples. This is empirically investigated in Section 5.3. The relationship between the value of ζ and the resulting parallelogram structure (parallelogram vs. trapezoid) is empirically verified in Section 5.4.

	Analogies		Training	
Model	**PCS**	**MSM**	**Time (hrs)**	**Speedup**
CWM	**0.677**	**0.469**	**0.59**	**49×**
SGNS	0.675	0.433	29.27	1×
GloVe	0.667	0.423	30.71	0.91×

Table 1: Performances for word embedding models. CWM refers to our contrastive word model. SGNS refers to Skip-gram with negative sampling. Best numbers are bolded.

5 Experiments

We first compare the performance of CWM to that of other popular word embedding methods on analogy recovery (Section 5.2). We then empirically verify the degree to which our assumptions regarding co-occurrences hold on real data (Section 5.3) as well as the relation between ζ and the parallelogram structure (Section 5.4).

5.1 Data and Training Procedure

We use the 03/2023 version of Wikimedia Downloads dump (Foundation, 2023) and train CWM for a single pass over the corpus using $\Delta = 5$ and $m = 0.2$ (chosen via cross validation from the range $0.1 \sim 1$). For comparison, we also train Skip-gram with Negative Sampling (SGNS) and GloVe over the same corpus with the default parameter settings provided by Mikolov et al. (2013b) and Pennington et al. (2014) respectively.

We utilize the BATS analogy dataset (Gladkova et al., 2016) for all analogy related tasks. For all word embeddings, we use dimension $D = 300$ and the vectors are length-normalized to follow practical conventions (Mikolov et al., 2013b). Training was done on 256 instances of AMD EPYC 7763 64-Core Processor machine.

5.2 Analogy Recovery

To assess the degree to which word embeddings encode analogies as lines consistently in the embedding space, we use two intuitive metrics proposed by Fournier et al. (2020): the *Pairing Consistency Score* (PCS) and *Mean Similarity Measure* (MSM). PCS assesses analogy alignment precision (the number of non-analogy offsets incorrectly aligned

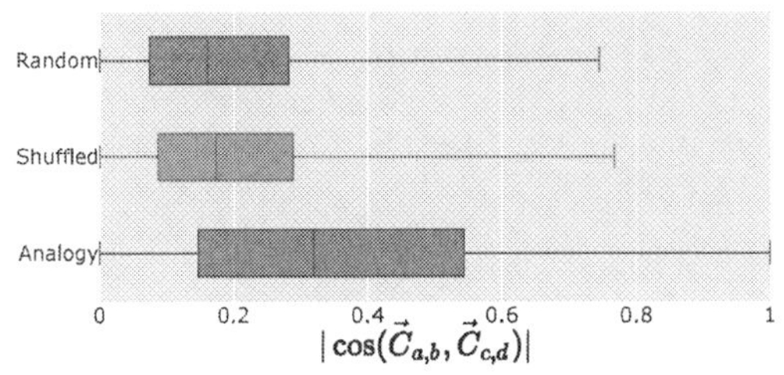

Figure 2: Cosine similarities between co-occurrence vectors $\vec{C}_{a,b}$ and $\vec{C}_{c,d}$ for words a, b, c, d from uniformly sampled word quadruples (Random), shuffled analogy pairs (Shuffled), and true analogy pairs (Analogy).

with true analogy offsets), while MSM measures absolute alignment.

Table 1 shows the relative performance of popular word embeddings. Notice that our method performs 7% better than popular word embeddings on the MSM metric, indicating that the word vectors learned by CWM exhibit higher alignment among analogy quadruples than Skip-gram and GloVe. CWM's performance on the PCS metric indicates that parallel lines are not erroneously encoded for non-analogy words. For completeness, see Appendix B.3 for parallelogram recovery performances (previous literature questions the validity of the standard evaluation method).

5.3 Existence of ζ and Analogies

Theorem 1 provides insight into the conditions required for CWM to induce parallel lines in the learned word vectors, but these conditions are not specific to analogy word pairs. Thus, the question remains: does ζ exist only when a quadruple forms an analogy?

Here, we study the level at which the co-occurrence statistics of analogy and non-analogy pairs satisfy the condition in Theorem 1. To assess the existence of ζ, consider the vectors $\vec{C}_{a,b}, \vec{C}_{c,d} \in \mathbb{R}^{|W|}$ (derived purely from co-occurrence counts):

$$\vec{C}_{a,b} = \left[\left(\frac{\#(a,w_1)}{\#(a)} - \frac{\#(b,w_1)}{\#(b)} \right), \ldots, \left(\frac{\#(a,w_{|W|})}{\#(a)} - \frac{\#(b,w_{|W|})}{\#(b)} \right) \right],$$

$$\vec{C}_{c,d} = \left[\left(\frac{\#(c,w_1)}{\#(c)} - \frac{\#(d,w_1)}{\#(d)} \right), \ldots, \left(\frac{\#(c,w_{|W|})}{\#(c)} - \frac{\#(d,w_{|W|})}{\#(d)} \right) \right].$$

Existence of a ζ where Eq. (4) holds for a, b, c, d, implies that all entries in $\vec{C}_{a,b}$ are equal to the corresponding entries in $\vec{C}_{c,d}$ scaled by a factor of ζ. This indicates that when ζ exists, $\vec{C}_{a,b}$ and $\vec{C}_{c,d}$ are collinear. Thus, we can approximate assessing the existence of ζ by evaluating whether the cosine similarity between $\vec{C}_{a,b}$ and $\vec{C}_{c,d}$ is sufficiently high.

Analogy Quadruple	Sim.
fall:rise = under:over	1.000
prevent:preventing = follow:following	0.9901
lancaster:lancashire = salford:manchester	0.9812
refer:referred = agree:agreed	0.9740
organized:arranged = dollars:bucks	0.0006
staircase:step = shilling:pence	0.0006
guitar:string = church:altar	0.0004
monkey:infant = fox:cub	0.0001

Table 2: Samples of analogy quadruples illustrating cosine similarity values between $\vec{C}_{a,b}$ and $\vec{C}_{c,d}$. "Sim." denotes the value of $|\cos(\vec{C}_{a,b}, \vec{C}_{c,d})|$.

We consider three settings from which the quadruples are obtained: randomly sampled word quadruples, false shuffled analogies, and true analogies using the BATS dataset. We compute the distribution of cosine similarities for all quadruples from these settings.

Results are shown in Figure 2. Observe that the cosine similarities of random and shuffled quadruples is significantly lower than that for analogy words. This indicates a positive association between ζ and analogy word quadruples in real world corpora.

Furthermore, it is worth noting the presence of "ambiguous" analogies within the BATS dataset. These include analogies with valid alternative replacements (e.g. `sun:orange = sea:blue` can also be `sun:red = sea:blue`), or analogies with unclear relationships (e.g. lexicographic analogies such as `father:dad = lady:madam`). We investigate whether the ambiguity of an analogy correlates with its cosine similarity between $\vec{C}_{a,b}$ and $\vec{C}_{c,d}$ by sampling from analogy quadruples with high and low values of $|\cos(\vec{C}_{a,b}, \vec{C}_{c,d})|$.

Results are shown in Table 2. Observe that analogy quadruples with high cosine similarity between $\vec{C}_{a,b}$ and $\vec{C}_{c,d}$ seems to demonstrate a clear relationships, whereas those with low cosine similarity exhibit weaker/ambiguous relationships.

5.4 ζ and Geometric Structure

We now examine the effect of ζ on the geometry of analogy word pairs. Recall that ζ exists for quadruples where $|\cos(\vec{C}_{a,b}, \vec{C}_{c,d})| = 1$. As this condition is unlikely to hold exactly on real data, we approximate ζ with the ratio $\hat{\zeta} := \|\vec{C}_{a,b}\| / \|\vec{C}_{c,d}\|$ for quadruples with high cosine similarity (which we define as $|\cos(\vec{C}_{a,b}, \vec{C}_{c,d})| \geq 0.9$). We expect the word vectors to form parallelograms when $\hat{\zeta} \approx 1$

	$k = 1$	$k = 5$
$\hat{\zeta} \not\approx 1$	0.800 (619/774)	0.862 (667/774)
$\hat{\zeta} \approx 1$	0.652 (137/210)	0.871 (183/210)

Table 3: Parallelogram/trapezoid recovery performances for different values of $\hat{\zeta}$. Parallelogram recovery for all analogy pairs is 0.27 (see Table 4 in Appendix), indicating dramatic performance increase for the analogy subset where $\hat{\zeta} \approx 1$.

$(0.95 \leq \hat{\zeta} \leq 1.05)$, and form trapezoids otherwise.

Specifically, for each such quadruple, we compute the word w that minimizes $\|\hat{v}_b - \hat{v}_a + \hat{v}_c - \hat{v}_w\|$ for parallelograms; ideally, w should equal d. For trapezoids, we retrieve the word w that maximizes the quantity $\cos(\hat{v}_b - \hat{v}_a, \hat{v}_w - \hat{v}_c)$. If the word d is among the top k words, we deem the quadruple to satisfy the corresponding geometric structure. For both cases, we consider $k = 1$ and 5.

Results are shown in Table 3. Observe that for $k = 5$, 87% of the quadruples form parallelograms when $\hat{\zeta} \approx 1$ (i.e., $0.95 \leq \hat{\zeta} \leq 1.05$), and 86% of quadruples form trapezoid-type structures when $\hat{\zeta} \not\approx 1$. This validates our expectation that parallelograms and trapezoids indeed form when $\hat{\zeta} \approx 1$ and $\hat{\zeta} \not\approx 1$ respectively.

6 Conclusion and Discussion

We demonstrate that optimizing a contrastive-style objective over word co-occurrences is indeed sufficient to encode analogies as parallel lines. Our analysis (Theorem 1) sheds light on the inner workings of word embeddings: parallel geometry is induced largely from word co-occurrence statistics for any push-pull model. Our work builds upon and generalizes previous literature that illuminates the underlying mechanisms governing the geometry of word embeddings.

Note that while our results demonstrate the sufficiency of the push-pull mechanism for recovering analogies as parallel lines, it remains unclear whether push-pull is a necessary condition for this phenomenon. Investigating alternative mechanisms and their ability to achieve similar results would provide further insight into the relationship between word co-occurrence statistics and the recovery of analogies.

References

Carl Allen and Timothy Hospedales. 2019. Analogies explained: Towards understanding word embeddings.

Sanjeev Arora, Yuanzhi Li, Yingyu Liang, Tengyu Ma, and Andrej Risteski. 2016. A latent variable model approach to PMI-based word embeddings. *Transactions of the Association for Computational Linguistics*, 4:385–399.

Sanjeev Arora, Yuanzhi Li, Yingyu Liang, Tengyu Ma, and Andrej Risteski. 2019. A latent variable model approach to pmi-based word embeddings.

Elia Bruni, Nam Khanh Tran, and Marco Baroni. 2014. Multimodal distributional semantics. *J. Artif. Intell. Res.*, 49:1–47.

S. Chopra, R. Hadsell, and Y. LeCun. 2005. Learning a similarity metric discriminatively, with application to face verification. In *2005 IEEE Computer Society Conference on Computer Vision and Pattern Recognition (CVPR'05)*, volume 1, pages 539–546 vol. 1.

Kawin Ethayarajh, David Duvenaud, and Graeme Hirst. 2019. Towards understanding linear word analogies. In *Proceedings of the 57th Annual Meeting of the Association for Computational Linguistics*, pages 3253–3262, Florence, Italy. Association for Computational Linguistics.

Lev Finkelstein, Evgeniy Gabrilovich, Y. Matias, Ehud Rivlin, Zach Solan, Gadi Wolfman, and Eytan Ruppin. 2002. Placing search in context: the concept revisited. *ACM Trans. Inf. Syst.*, 20:116–131.

J. Firth. 1957. A synopsis of linguistic theory 1930-1955. In *Studies in Linguistic Analysis*. Philological Society, Oxford. Reprinted in Palmer, F. (ed. 1968) Selected Papers of J. R. Firth, Longman, Harlow.

Wikimedia Foundation. 2023. Wikimedia downloads.

Louis Fournier and Ewan Dunbar. 2021. Paraphrases do not explain word analogies.

Louis Fournier, Emmanuel Dupoux, and Ewan Dunbar. 2020. Analogies minus analogy test: measuring regularities in word embeddings. In *Proceedings of the 24th Conference on Computational Natural Language Learning*, pages 365–375, Online. Association for Computational Linguistics.

Alex Gittens, Dimitris Achlioptas, and Michael W. Mahoney. 2017. Skip-gram - Zipf + uniform = vector additivity. In *Proceedings of the 55th Annual Meeting of the Association for Computational Linguistics (Volume 1: Long Papers)*, pages 69–76, Vancouver, Canada. Association for Computational Linguistics.

Anna Gladkova, Aleksandr Drozd, and Satoshi Matsuoka. 2016. Analogy-based detection of morphological and semantic relations with word embeddings: what works and what doesn't. In *Proceedings of the NAACL Student Research Workshop*, pages 8–15, San Diego, California. Association for Computational Linguistics.

Felix Hill, Roi Reichart, and Anna Korhonen. 2015. SimLex-999: Evaluating semantic models with (genuine) similarity estimation. *Computational Linguistics*, 41(4):665–695.

Omer Levy and Yoav Goldberg. 2014. Neural word embedding as implicit matrix factorization. In *Advances in Neural Information Processing Systems*, volume 27. Curran Associates, Inc.

Tal Linzen. 2016. Issues in evaluating semantic spaces using word analogies. In *Proceedings of the 1st Workshop on Evaluating Vector-Space Representations for NLP*, pages 13–18, Berlin, Germany. Association for Computational Linguistics.

Tomas Mikolov, Kai Chen, Gregory S. Corrado, and Jeffrey Dean. 2013a. Efficient estimation of word representations in vector space. In *International Conference on Learning Representations*.

Tomas Mikolov, Wen-tau Yih, and Geoffrey Zweig. 2013b. Linguistic regularities in continuous space word representations. In *Proceedings of the 2013 Conference of the North American Chapter of the Association for Computational Linguistics: Human Language Technologies*, pages 746–751, Atlanta, Georgia. Association for Computational Linguistics.

Jeffrey Pennington, Richard Socher, and Christopher Manning. 2014. GloVe: Global vectors for word representation. In *Proceedings of the 2014 Conference on Empirical Methods in Natural Language Processing (EMNLP)*, pages 1532–1543, Doha, Qatar. Association for Computational Linguistics.

Natalie Schluter. 2018. The word analogy testing caveat. In *Proceedings of the 2018 Conference of the North American Chapter of the Association for Computational Linguistics: Human Language Technologies, Volume 2 (Short Papers)*, pages 242–246, New Orleans, Louisiana. Association for Computational Linguistics.

Kilian Q Weinberger, John Blitzer, and Lawrence Saul. 2005. Distance metric learning for large margin nearest neighbor classification. In *Advances in Neural Information Processing Systems*, volume 18. MIT Press.

A Proofs

A.1 Derivation of Eq. (3)

Recall that the global objective of CWM for the vocabulary W and set of word vectors V can be written as:

$$\mathcal{L}(V) = \sum_{c \in W} \sum_{w \in W} \#(c,w) \sum_{w' \in D_{c,w}} \left[m - \hat{v}_c \cdot \hat{v}_w + \hat{v}_c \cdot \hat{v}_{w'} \right]_+ ,$$

where $D_{c,w} = \{w' | w' \sim U(W)\}, |D_{c,w}| = k$ denotes the set of k negative window words sampled uniformly from the vocabulary for each c, w word pair and $U(W)$ denotes the uniform distribution over the vocabulary.

For fixed c, w, w', consider the two cases where $m - \hat{v}_c \cdot \hat{v}_w + \hat{v}_c \cdot \hat{v}_{w'} > 0$ and $m - \hat{v}_c \cdot \hat{v}_w + \hat{v}_c \cdot \hat{v}_{w'} \le 0$. As the word vectors are not updated for the latter case, we examine the former by taking the partial derivative of $\mathcal{L}(V)$ with respect to v_c and setting it to 0:

$$\begin{aligned}
0 = &- \sum_{w \in W} \#(c,w) \\
&\sum_{w' \in D_{c,w}} \Bigg(\frac{v_w}{\|v_c\| \|v_w\|} - \frac{v_{w'}}{\|v_c\| \|v_{w'}\|} \\
&+ \left(\frac{\hat{v}_c \cdot \hat{v}_{w'}}{\|v_c\|^2} - \frac{(\hat{v}_c \cdot \hat{v}_w)}{\|v_c\|^2} \right) v_c \Bigg) \\
\Leftrightarrow &\sum_{w \in W} \#(c,w) \sum_{w' \in D_{c,w}} \frac{v_w}{\|v_c\| \|v_w\|} \\
&- \sum_{w \in W} \#(c,w) \sum_{w' \in D_{c,w}} \frac{v_{w'}}{\|v_c\| \|v_{w'}\|} \\
= &\sum_{w \in W} \#(c,w) \sum_{w' \in D_{c,w}} \Bigg(\frac{v_c v_w}{\|v_c\|^2 \|v_w\|} \\
&- \frac{v_c v_{w'}}{\|v_c\|^2 \|v_{w'}\|} \Bigg) \frac{v_c}{\|v_c\|}.
\end{aligned}$$

As $\sum_{w \in W} \#(c,w) \sum_{w' \in D_{c,w}} \frac{v_{w'}}{\|v_{w'}\|}$ represents $\sum_{w \in W} \#(c,w) \cdot k = k \cdot \#(c)$ uniform i.i.d. draws from the vocabulary, the following holds for sufficiently large values of $k \cdot \#(c)$:

$$\sum_{w \in W} \#(c,w) \sum_{w' \in D_{c,w}} \frac{v_{w'}}{\|v_{w'}\|} = k\#(c) \mathbb{E}_{w' \sim U(W)} \left[\frac{v_{w'}}{\|v_{w'}\|} \right].$$

Setting $\mathbb{E}_{w' \sim U(W)} \left[\frac{v_{w'}}{\|v_{w'}\|} \right] = v_p$ and dividing both sizes by $\frac{k\#(c)}{\|v\|}$,

$$\begin{aligned}
&\sum_{w \in W} \frac{\#(c,w)}{\#(c)} \frac{v_w}{\|v_w\|} - v_p \\
&= \left[\frac{v_c}{\|v_c\|} \left(\sum_{w \in W} \frac{\#(c,w)}{\#(c)} \frac{v_w}{\|v_w\|} - v_p \right) \right] \odot \frac{v_c}{\|v_c\|}.
\end{aligned}$$

Setting $\sum_{w \in W} \frac{\#(c,w)}{\#(c)} \frac{v_w}{\|v_w\|} = v_{p'}$ and $\gamma_c = \left\| \frac{v_c}{\|v_c\|} \left(\sum_{w \in W} \frac{\#(c,w)}{\#(c)} \frac{v_w}{\|v_w\|} - v_p \right) \right\|$, the above equation can be rewritten as:

$$\frac{v_c}{\|v_c\|} = \frac{v_{p'}}{\gamma_c} \cdot \frac{1}{\left\| \frac{v_c}{\|v_c\|} \right\|} \cdot \frac{1}{\cos\theta}.$$

where θ indicates the angle between $v_{p'}$ and $\frac{v_c}{\|v_c\|}$.

As $\left\| \frac{v_c}{\|v_c\|} \right\| = 1$,

$$v_c = \|v_c\| \cdot \frac{v_{p'}}{\gamma_c} \cdot \frac{1}{\cos\theta}$$

Notice that $v_c \parallel v_{p'}$ by the above construction , so $\cos\theta = 1$. Thus,

$$v_c = \|v_c\| \cdot \frac{v_{p'}}{\gamma_c} = \frac{\alpha \#(c)^{\frac{1}{\beta}}}{\gamma_c} \cdot v_{p'}. \quad \blacksquare$$

The second equality is derived from the empirically observed property $\|v_c\| \propto \#(c)^{\frac{1}{\beta}}$ for some constant $\beta \in \mathbb{R}$, which is verified below.

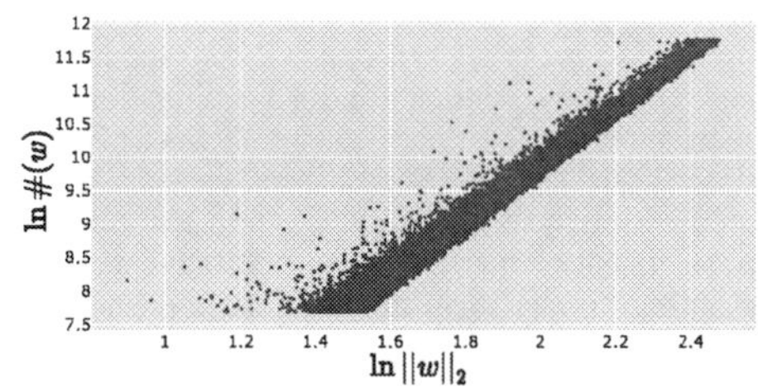

Interestingly, a similar linear relationship is also observed in existing word embedding models (Arora et al., 2016).

A.2 Proof for Theorem 1

Under the assumption that Eq. (3) holds, we can write the expressions for $\hat{v}_a - \hat{v}_b, \hat{v}_c - \hat{v}_d$ as follows.

$$\begin{aligned}
\hat{v}_a - \hat{v}_b = &\frac{1}{\gamma_a} \left(\sum_{w \in W} \left(\frac{\#(a,w)}{\#(a)} \frac{v_w}{\|v_w\|} \right) - v_p \right) \\
&- \frac{1}{\gamma_b} \left(\sum_{w \in W} \left(\frac{\#(b,w)}{\#(b)} \frac{v_w}{\|v_w\|} \right) - v_p \right).
\end{aligned}$$

Under the assumption that $\forall c \in W : \gamma_c = \gamma$ for some $\gamma \in \mathbb{R}$,

$$\hat{v}_a - \hat{v}_b = \frac{1}{\gamma} \sum_{w \in W} \left(\frac{\#(a,w)}{\#(a)} - \frac{\#(b,w)}{\#(b)} \right) \frac{v_w}{\|v_w\|}$$

Using Eq. (4),

$$\begin{aligned} \hat{v}_a - \hat{v}_b &= \frac{\zeta}{\gamma} \sum_{w \in W} \left(\frac{\#(c,w)}{\#(c)} - \frac{\#(d,w)}{\#(d)} \right) \frac{v_w}{\|v_w\|} \\ &= \zeta(\hat{v}_c - \hat{v}_d). \quad \blacksquare \end{aligned}$$

The invariance of the value γ_c can be verified through randomly sampling 5000 words c and computing the respectivve γ_c. The resulting mean and variance are respectively $\bar{\gamma_c} = 5.626$, $\mathrm{Var}(\gamma_c) = 0.033$, indicating a tight concentration around the mean.

A.3 Derivation of Eq. (1)

Here, we show that vanilla Skip-gram with the cross-entropy loss where the target distribution is represented as a one-hot vector induces an implicit pulling action on co-occuring words and pushes away other words.

For a given context word c, the cross-entropy loss is:

$$H(p(\cdot|c), \hat{p}(\cdot|c)) = -\sum_{w \in W} \hat{p}(w|c) \log p(w|c),$$

where $p(w|c) = \frac{e^{v_c^\intercal u_w}}{\sum_{w' \in W} e^{v_c^\intercal u_{w'}}}$ denotes the predicted distribution by Skip-gram. $\hat{p}(\cdot|c)$ denotes the target distribution where:

$$\forall w \in W : \hat{p}(w|c) = \begin{cases} 1 & \text{if } w \text{ is the target word} \\ 0 & \text{otherwise} \end{cases}$$

By construction of $\hat{p}(w|c)$, each term in the sum of the cross-entropy loss reduces to:

$$\hat{p}(w|c) \log p(w|c) = \begin{cases} -\log \frac{e^{v_c^\intercal u_w}}{\sum_{w' \in W} e^{v_c^\intercal u_{w'}}} & \text{if } w \text{ is the target word} \\ 0 & \text{otherwise} \end{cases}$$

Thus, for a fixed context word c and target word w, the loss of Skip-gram reduces to:

$$\mathcal{L}_{\text{SGNS}}(c, w) = -\log \frac{e^{v_c^\intercal u_w}}{\sum_{w' \in W} e^{v_c^\intercal u_{w'}}}.$$

Now, consider two words c, w that co-occur. Without loss of generality, if we assume w appears prior to c in the training corpus, Skip-gram first updates the context and target vectors of w and c respectively. Taking the gradient of $\mathcal{L}_{\text{SGNS}}$ with respect to v_a and u_b for two co-occurring words $a, b \in W$,

$$\frac{\partial \mathcal{L}_{\text{SGNS}}}{\partial v_a} = \sum_{w \in W} \left(\frac{e^{v_a^\intercal u_b}}{\sum_{w' \in W} e^{v_a^\intercal u_{w'}}} u_w \right) - u_b, \tag{5}$$

$$\frac{\partial \mathcal{L}_{\text{SGNS}}}{\partial u_b} = \left(\frac{e^{v_a^\intercal u_b}}{\sum_{w' \in W} e^{v_a^\intercal u_{w'}}} - 1 \right) v_a. \tag{6}$$

Observe that the gradients induce a pulling action between the vectors v_a and u_b.

Define the set of words that lie between c and w in the training corpus as C. Notice that c and w will co-occur with $\Delta - 1$ words. Hence, for each word $c' \in C = \{c_1, ..., c_{w-1}\}$, the gradient update in Eq. (5) and (6) is applied to all word pairs $(w, c_1), ..., (w, c_{w-1})$ and $(c, c_1), ..., (c, c_{w-1})$.

Consider the pulling action induced by the word pairs (w, c_i) and (b, c_i) for some $i \in [\Delta - 1]$. As we first update the context and target vectors for w and c_i, notice that

$$v_w^{\text{new}} = v_w + u_{c'} - \sum_{x \in W} \left(\frac{e^{v_w^\intercal u_{c'}}}{\sum_{w' \in W} e^{v_w^\intercal u_{w'}}} u_x \right),$$

$$u_{c'}^{\text{new}} = u_{c'} + \left(1 - \frac{e^{v_w^\intercal u_{c'}}}{\sum_{w' \in W} e^{v_w^\intercal u_{w'}}} \right) v_w. \tag{7}$$

Similarly, if we now update the context and target vectors for c and c_i,

$$v_c^{\text{new}} = v_c + u_{c'}^{\text{new}} - \sum_{x \in W} \left(\frac{e^{v_c^\intercal u_{c'}}}{\sum_{w' \in W} e^{v_c^\intercal u_{w'}}} u_x \right).$$

Plugging the expression for u_c^{new} in Eq. (7), we get

$$\begin{aligned} v_c^{\text{new}} =& v_c + \left(1 - \frac{e^{v_w^\intercal u_{c'}}}{\sum_{w' \in W} e^{v_w^\intercal u_{w'}}} \right) v_w + u_{c'} \\ & - \sum_{x \in W} \left(\frac{e^{v_w^\intercal u_c}}{\sum_{w' \in W} e^{v_w^\intercal u_{w'}}} u_x \right). \end{aligned}$$

The expression above indicates that v_c is pulled towards v_w implicitly and shifted closer to $u_{c'}$ explicitly in the update process while pushing away the weighted average of all word vectors. This update resembles the push-pull action in CWM.

A.4 Derivation of Eq. (2)

For a fixed word pair i, j, GloVe's local objective is:

$$\mathcal{L}_{\text{GloVe}}(i,j) = f(X_{ij})(v_i^\intercal u_j + b_i + \tilde{b}_j - \log X_{ij}),$$

where X_{ij} is the co-occurrence count of words i and j, $f(X_{ij})$ is a weighting term, $b_i, \tilde{b}_j$ are bias terms, and v_i, u_j denote the word vector and context word vectors respectively (cf. Pennington et al., 2014). Typically, $f(X_{ij})$ is set to $\min\{(X_i/X_{\max})^\alpha, 1\}$ where X_i denotes the occurrence count of word i and $X_{\max} = 100$. For the sake of demonstrating the pushing action in the gradient update, we consider a weighting function $f(X_{ij}) = \min\{(X_i/X_{\max})^\alpha + \epsilon, 1\}$ for a arbitrarily small $\epsilon > 0$.

The derivative of the local objective with respect to v_i and u_j are:

$$\frac{\partial \mathcal{L}_{\text{GloVe}}}{\partial v_i} = 2f(X_{ij})(v_i^\intercal u_j + b_i + \tilde{b}_j - \log X_{ij})u_j,$$
$$\frac{\partial \mathcal{L}_{\text{GloVe}}}{\partial u_j} = 2f(X_{ij})(v_i^\intercal u_j + b_i + \tilde{b}_j - \log X_{ij})v_i. \quad (8)$$

Consider two co-occurring words c, w and a word w' that co-occurs with neither. Then, there exists a word c' that co-occurrs with c and w but does not co-occur with w'. Define $X_{c'w'} = 0, X_{cc'} = \omega_c, X_{wc'} = \omega_w$ where $\omega_c, \omega_w \in \mathbb{N}$.

With Eq. (8), the updated vectors for c, w, w' can be written as:

$$v_c^{\text{new}} = v_c^{\text{old}} + 2f(\omega_c)(v_c^\intercal u_{c'} + b_c + \tilde{b}_{c'} - \log \omega_c)u_{c'},$$
$$v_w^{\text{new}} = v_w^{\text{old}} + 2f(\omega_w)(v_w^\intercal u_{c'} + b_w + \tilde{b}_{c'} - \log \omega_w)u_{c'},$$
$$v_{w'}^{\text{new}} = v_{w'}^{\text{old}} + 2f(\epsilon)(v_{w'}^\intercal u_{c'} + b_{w'} + \tilde{b}_{c'} - \log \epsilon)u_{c'}.$$

As $\forall i, j : f_{X_{ij}} > 0$, notice that

$$(v_c^\intercal u_{c'} + b_c + \tilde{b}_{c'} - \log \omega_c) < 0,$$
$$(v_w^\intercal u_{c'} + b_w + \tilde{b}_{c'} - \log \omega_w) < 0,$$
$$(v_{w'}^\intercal u_{c'} + b_{w'} + \tilde{b}_{c'} - \log \epsilon) > 0,$$

for sufficiently large ω_c and ω_w and for sufficiently small ϵ. Setting $2 \cdot |f(X_{ij})(v_i^\intercal u_j + b_i + \tilde{b}_j - \log X_{ij})| = g(i,j)$, we see that

$$v_c^{\text{new}} = v_c^{\text{old}} + g(c, c')v_{c'},$$
$$v_w^{\text{new}} = v_w^{\text{old}} + g(w, c')v_{c'},$$
$$v_{w'}^{\text{new}} = v_{w'}^{\text{old}} - g(w', c')v_{c'}.$$

Model	▱	WordSim	MEN	SimLex
CWM	0.27	0.66	0.73	0.34
SGNS	0.29	0.72	0.74	0.36
GloVe	0.29	0.61	0.75	0.37

Table 4: Performances for embedding models on parallelogram analogy recovery and word similarity tasks. ▱ refers to parallelogram recovery task. For word similarity, reported values are Spearman's rank correlation between word similarity rankings of human annotators and cosine similarites computed from word vectors.

This indicates that v_c and v_w will be pulled towards the context word vectors of words that c and w both co-occur with, while words that do not co-occur with c and w will be pushed away from v_c and v_w.

B Supplementary Experiments

B.1 Metric Details

Given a set of word pairs in an analogy $A = \{(a_1, b_1), (a_2, b_2), \dots\}$, PCS measures relative directional alignment by computing the separability of cosine similarities between true vector offsets $v_{a_i} - v_{b_i}$ and false offsets $v_{a_i} - v_{b_j}, i \neq j$. Concretely, denoting the set of true and false offsets as P and N respectively, PCS computes the expectation of the ROC-AUC score between P and a subset of the false vector offsets $N' \subset N$ where $|P| = |N'|$:

$$\text{PCS}(A) = \mathbb{E}_{N' \sim U(N)} \left[\text{AUC}(P, N')\right],$$

where $U(N)$ denotes the uniform distribution over all false vector offsets. Typically, the expectation is approximated by sampling $s = 50$ subsets.

In contrast, MSM represents the absolute alignment within analogies by computing the cosine similarities between all true vector offsets and the mean of the true offsets.

$$\text{MSM}(A) = \frac{1}{|P|} \sum_{v_p \in P} \cos\left(v_p, \frac{1}{|P|} \sum_{v_p \in P} v_p\right)$$

A high value of MSM indicates alignment between true vector offsets. However, note that MSM is susceptible to scoring undesirable vector structures with high values (e.g. when all vectors are collapsed onto one point in the embedding space, MSM = 1).

B.2 Word Similarity

While the analogy task is our primary focus, we evaluate CWM on other commonly used benchmarking tasks for completeness. To this end, we benchmark our model on WordSim353 (Finkelstein et al., 2002), the MEN Test Collection (Bruni et al., 2014), and SimLex999 (Hill et al., 2015).

On all tasks, CWM performs comparably with existing models (Table 4). We highlight that minor performance differences on word similarity tasks are negligible, as such benchmarks are built using human annotations and are subject to noise. Nevertheless, we believe further refinement of the CWM model is required to boost performance on various downstream tasks.

B.3 Analogies as Parallelograms

We also benchmark all models on the traditional parallelogram analogy recovery task using the BATS dataset.

Concretely, given an analogy pair $a : b = c : d$, we utilize the most common metric where we compute the x that satisfies:

$$x = \min_{x \in W \setminus \{a,b,c\}} \|v_b - v_a + v_c - v_x\|,$$

and compare whether $x = d$.

Results from Table 4 indicate that CWM recovers analogies as parallelograms comparably to existing models.

Syntax-Aware Graph-to-Graph Transformer for Semantic Role Labelling

Alireza Mohammadshahi
Idiap Research Institute & EPFL

James Henderson
Idiap Research Institute
{alireza.mohammadshahi, james.henderson}@idiap.ch

Abstract

Recent models have shown that incorporating syntactic knowledge into the semantic role labelling (SRL) task leads to a significant improvement. In this paper, we propose Syntax-aware Graph-to-Graph Transformer (SynG2G-Tr) model, which encodes the syntactic structure using a novel way to input graph relations as embeddings, directly into the self-attention mechanism of Transformer. This approach adds a soft bias towards attention patterns that follow the syntactic structure but also allows the model to use this information to learn alternative patterns. We evaluate our model on both span-based and dependency-based SRL datasets, and outperform previous alternative methods in both in-domain and out-of-domain settings, on CoNLL 2005 and CoNLL 2009 datasets.[1]

1 Introduction

The task of semantic role labelling (SRL) provides a shallow representation of the semantics in a sentence, and constructs event properties and relations among relevant words. Traditionally, a syntactic structure was considered a prerequisite for SRL models (Punyakanok et al., 2008; Gildea and Palmer, 2002), but, newer models that leverage deep neural network architectures (Cai et al., 2018; Tan et al., 2017; He et al., 2017; Marcheggiani et al., 2017) have outperformed syntax-aware architectures, without the need for explicit encoding of syntactic structure. However, recent studies (Zhou et al., 2020a; Strubell et al., 2018; He et al., 2017; Marcheggiani and Titov, 2017) have proposed that deep neural network models could benefit from using syntactic information, rather than disregarding it. These studies suggest that incorporating syntax into the model can improve SRL prediction by jointly learning both syntactic and semantic structures (Zhou et al., 2020a), training a self-attention head in Transformer (Vaswani et al., 2017a) to attend to each token's syntactic parent (Strubell et al., 2018), or encoding the syntactic structure using graph convolutional networks (Fei et al., 2021; Marcheggiani and Titov, 2017).

In this paper, we propose a novel method for encoding syntactic knowledge by introducing Syntax-aware Graph-to-Graph Transformer (SynG2G-Tr) architecture. The model conditions on the sentence's dependency structure and jointly predicts both span-based and dependency-based SRL structures. Inspired by Mohammadshahi and Henderson (2021, 2020), our model inputs graph relations as embeddings incorporated into the self-attention mechanism of Transformer (Vaswani et al., 2017b). Different from the original Graph-to-Graph Transformer, our self-attention function models the interaction of the graph relations with both the query and key vectors of self-attention mechanism, instead of just the query. We also find that excluding the interaction of graph structure with the value vectors of self-attention does not harm the performance. Furthermore, compared to the previous work on Graph-to-Graph Transformers (Mohammadshahi and Henderson, 2021, 2020), our architecture uses different types of graphs as the input and output. We show empirically that our model outperforms previous comparable models. In the in-domain setting, SynG2G-Tr model achieves 88.93 (87.57) F1 score on the CoNLL 2005 dataset, given the predicate (end-to-end), and 91.23 (88.05) F1 on the CoNLL 2009 dataset, given the predicate (end-to-end). In the out-of-domain setting, our model reaches 83.21 (80.53) F1 score on the CoNLL 2005 dataset, given predicate (end-to-end), and 86.43 (81.93) F1 scores on the CoNLL 2009 dataset, given predicate (end-to-end).

Our contributions are:

- We propose SynG2G-Tr model for encoding the dependency parsing graph in the SRL task.

[1]The implementation is publicly available at https://github.com/alirezamshi/SynG2GTr-SRL.

Proceedings of the 8th Workshop on Representation Learning for NLP (RepL4NLP 2023), pages 174–186
July 13, 2023 ©2023 Association for Computational Linguistics

Section	UAS	LAS	PoS
Development	96.72	94.83	96.81
Test	96.85	95.24	97.41

Table 1: Labelled and unlabelled attachment scores (LAS/UAS) and PoS accuracy. Sections 22&23 of WSJ Penn Treebanks (Marcus et al., 1993) are used as evaluation and test sets.

- We evaluate our model on CoNLL 2005 and CoNLL 2009 datasets and outperform previous comparable models in most cases of both in-domain and out-of-domain sets.

2 Syntax-aware Graph-to-Graph Transformer

The architecture of the SynG2G-Tr model is illustrated in Figure 1. The input to the model is the tokenised text ($W=(w_1,w_2,...,w_N)$), which are the nodes of the input and output graphs, and N is the length of tokenised input. The outputs are the dependency-based (G_{dep}) and span-based (G_{span}) SRL graphs. The SynG2G-Tr model can be formalised in terms of an encoder E^{sg2g} and decoder D^{sg2g}:

$$\begin{cases} Z=\mathrm{E}^{\mathrm{sg2g}}(W,P,G_{syn}) \\ G_{span},G_{dep}=\mathrm{D}^{\mathrm{sg2g}}(Z) \end{cases} \tag{1}$$

Initially, a syntactic parser predicts the dependency graph (G_{syn}), and Part-of-Speech (PoS) tags ($P=(p_1,p_2,...,p_N)$). Then the encoder of SynG2G-Tr (E^{sg2g}) encodes both sequences (W, P) and the dependency graph (G_{syn}) into contextualised representations of graph nodes (Z). This representation (Z) is then used by the decoder (D^{sg2g}) to jointly predict SRL graphs. For the decoder, we follow the same unified scorer and decoder as defined in Zhou et al. (2020a). Further explanation of SRL scorer and decoding mechanism is provided in Appendix A.

The encoder employs an enhanced way of inputting graph relations into the self-attention mechanism of Transformer (Vaswani et al., 2017b). Unlike the previously proposed version of Graph-to-Graph Transformer (Mohammadshahi and Henderson, 2021), we modify the self-attention mechanism to have a more comprehensive interaction between graph relations, queries and keys. We also find that excluding the interaction of graph relations with value vectors retains good performance.

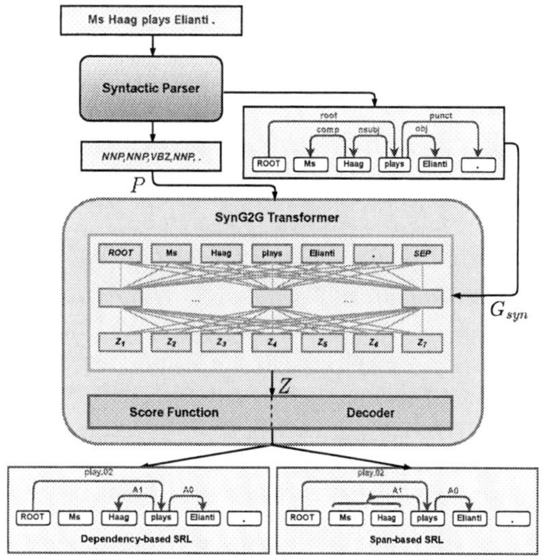

Figure 1: The architecture of SynG2G-Tr.

Specifically, given the output of an intermediate embedding layer $X=(x_1,...,x_N)$, we define the attention mechanism of each head in each layer to take the dependency graph as input. These attention scores (α_{ij}) are calculated as a Softmax function over e_{ij} values:

$$e_{ij}=\frac{1}{\sqrt{d}}\Big[x_i\boldsymbol{W^Q}(x_j\boldsymbol{W^K})^T+x_i\boldsymbol{W^Q}(r_{ij}\boldsymbol{W^R})^T +r_{ij}\boldsymbol{W^R}(x_j\boldsymbol{W^K})^T\Big] \tag{2}$$

where $\boldsymbol{W^Q},\boldsymbol{W^K}\in\mathbb{R}^{d_x\times d}$ are learned query and key matrices. $r_{ij}\in R$ is a one-hot vector specifying both the label and direction of the dependency relation between token i and token j. R is the matrix of graph relations, derived from the syntactic graph (G_{syn}). Figure 2 illustrates a sample computation of R matrix, where $r_{ij}=id_{label}$ if $i\rightarrow j$, $id_{label}+|L_{syn}|$ if $j\leftarrow i$, or NONE ($|L_{syn}|$ is the size of syntactic label set). $\boldsymbol{W^R}\in\mathbb{R}^{(2|L_{syn}|+1)\times d}$ is a matrix of learned relation embeddings. d is the attention head size, and d_x is the hidden size.

The second and third terms in Equation 2 incorporate the graph information into the self-attention mechanism of Transformer with a soft bias, while the model can still learn other structures, using this encoded graph information. For better efficiency, we share the relation embeddings across multiple attention heads in each layer. Additionally, the computation complexity of both the second and third terms is $O(N)$, as we ignore the NONE graph relation, and the syntactic dependency graph is a tree. The output of the attention function is the value embedding (v_i), which is calculated as:

$$v_i = \sum_j \alpha_{ij}(x_j \boldsymbol{W}^{\boldsymbol{V}}) \tag{3}$$

which, in our model, does not use the graph, and $\boldsymbol{W}^{\boldsymbol{V}} \in \mathbb{R}^{d_x \times d}$ is the learned value matrix.

Syntactic Parser. The parser jointly predicts PoS tags and the dependency graph. We apply the parser defined in Zhou et al. (2020a), which uses a joint scorer and decoder for dependency and constituency graphs based on Head-driven Phrase Structure Grammar (Zhou and Zhao, 2019). This method has achieved state-of-the-art results in the dependency parsing task.

3 Related Work

Several approaches have been proposed to use syntax for the SRL task. Roth and Lapata (2016) embed dependency paths, while some researchers (Fei et al., 2021; Munir et al., 2021; Marcheggiani and Titov, 2017) use graph convolutional networks to encode the syntactic structure. Strubell et al. (2018) incorporates a dependency graph by training one attention head of Transformer to attend to syntactic parents for each token, in a multi-task setting. He et al. (2019, 2018b) use syntactic information to guide the argument pruning. Xia et al. (2019) exploit different alternatives e.g. tree-structured GRU and graph features of dependency tree to encode syntactic knowledge. Kasai et al. (2019) apply BiLSTM to tag the text with supertags extracted from dependency parses and feed them into SRL models. Xia et al. (2020) showed that incorporating heterogeneous syntactic knowledge results in significant improvement. Some other work focus on joint learning of both SRL and syntax (Zhou et al., 2020a,b; Cai and Lapata, 2019a,b). Additionally, some approaches discarded the syntax, but achieve impressive results (Shi and Lin, 2019; Peters et al., 2018; He et al., 2018a; Marcheggiani et al., 2017; He et al., 2017; Tan et al., 2017; Zhou and Xu, 2015).

Our work is different from previous work since we encode the syntactic graph by directly inputting it as embeddings into the attention mechanism of Transformer, which provides a soft bias. Moreover, both sequences and syntactic graph can be encoded in one general model.

4 Results and Discussion

Experimental Setup. Our models are evaluated on CoNLL 2005 (Carreras and Màrquez, 2005)

Model	SA	WSJ (in-domain)			Brown (out-of-domain)		
		P	R	F1	P	R	F1
end-to-end							
He et al. (2017)	✗	85.0	84.3	84.6	74.9	72.4	73.6
He et al. (2018a)	✗	81.2	83.9	82.5	69.7	71.9	70.8
Strubell et al. (2018)	✓	85.53	84.45	84.99	75.8	73.54	74.66
Li et al. (2019)	✗	-	-	83.0	-	-	-
Xia et al. (2019)	✓	84.3	83.8	84.1	73.7	72.0	72.9
Xia et al. (2020)	✓	83.05	84.49	84.49	73.47	74.92	74.19
SynG2G-Tr (w/o BERT)	✓	84.48	86.46	**85.45**	73.92	76.65	**75.26**
+pre-training							
He et al. (2018a)	✗	84.8	87.2	86.0	73.9	78.4	76.1
Strubell et al. (2018)†	✓	87.13	86.67	86.9	79.02	77.49	78.25
Li et al. (2019)	✗	85.2	87.5	86.3	74.7	78.1	76.4
SynG2G-Tr	✓	86.86	88.3	**87.57**	80.01	81.07	**80.53**
given predicate							
Tan et al. (2017)	✗	84.5	85.2	84.8	73.5	74.6	74.1
He et al. (2018a)	✗	-	-	83.9	-	-	73.7
Strubell et al. (2018)†	✓	86.02	86.05	86.04	76.65	76.44	76.54
Ouchi et al. (2018)	✗	84.7	82.3	83.5	76.0	70.4	73.1
Xia et al. (2020)	✓	85.12	85.0	85.06	76.3	75.42	75.86
SynG2G-Tr (w/o BERT)	✓	86.46	86.56	**86.50**	77.73	77.18	**77.45**
+pre-training							
He et al. (2018a)	✗	-	-	87.4	-	-	80.4
Ouchi et al. (2018)	✗	88.2	87.0	87.6	79.9	77.5	78.7
Li et al. (2019)	✗	87.9	87.5	87.7	80.6	80.4	80.5
Jindal et al. (2020)	✗	87.70	88.15	87.93	81.52	81.36	81.44
Zhang et al. (2021)	✗	88.70	88.00	87.90	80.30	80.10	80.20
Jia et al. (2022)	✗	-	-	88.25	-	-	81.90
SynG2G-Tr	✓	89.11	88.74	**88.93**	83.93	82.50	**83.21**

Table 2: Comparing our SynG2G-Tr with previous comparable models on CoNLL 2005 test sets. 'SA' means a syntax-aware model. Scores being boldfaced means that they are significantly better than the second best model, specified by the underline marker.

and CoNLL 2009 (Hajič et al., 2009).[2] For predicate disambiguation, we follow previous work (Marcheggiani and Titov, 2017), and use an off-the-shelf disambiguator from Roth and Lapata (2016). As in previous work, we evaluate in both *end-to-end*, and *given predicate* settings. For a more accurate comparison, we train SynG2G-Tr both with and without BERT initialisation (SynG2G-Tr w/o BERT). The discrepancy between BERT tokenisation and the tokenisation used in the SRL corpora is handled as in Mohammadshahi and Henderson (2020). [3] For the syntactic parser, we use the same hyper-parameters as defined in Zhou et al. (2020a). The performance of the syntactic parser is shown in Table 1.

CoNLL 2005 Results.[4] The results for span-based SRL are shown in Table 2.[5] Without BERT

[2] Implementation details of datasets and SynG2G-Tr model are provided in Appendices B and C.

[3] For inputting the dependency graph, the relation between two sub-words of different words is defined as the same dependency relation between their corresponding words in the sentence. This means that the relation (i,j,l_{in}) is repeated for each sub-word of word x_i, and word x_j. The same strategy is applied to predicted PoS tags.

[4] Results are calculated with official evaluation scripts of CoNLL 2005 (`https://www.cs.upc.edu/~srlconll`).

[5] For a fair comparison, we excluded Li et al. (2021); Zhou et al. (2020a), as they use information from the constituency

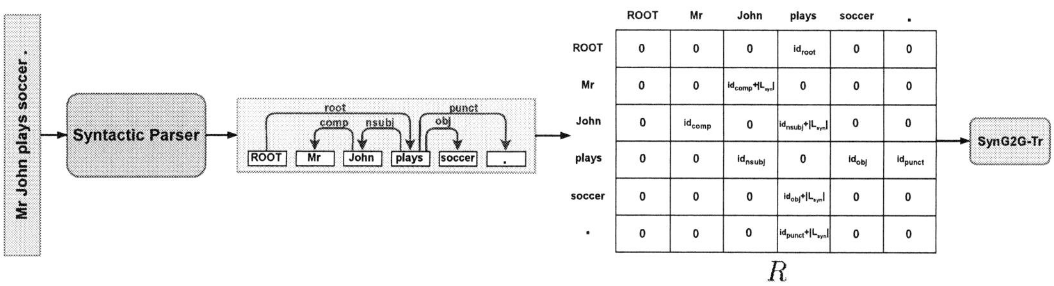

Figure 2: A sample computation of R matrix for the sentence "Mr John plays soccer.".

initialisation, our SynG2G-Tr model outperforms Strubell et al. (2018) (the second best model) in both *end-to-end* and *given-predicate* settings. This highlights the benefit of injecting the graph information into the self-attention mechanism using a soft bias, instead of hard-coding one attention head to attend to the syntactic parent of each token, as used in Strubell et al. (2018). The main reason for this improvement is that the model can still learn other attention patterns in combination with the graph information, which will be described later in this section. When adding BERT initialisation, our SynG2G-Tr model outperforms best previous work by 5.4%/8.8% F1 relative error reduction (RER) on average in both in-domain and out-of-domain evaluation sets, which demonstrates the compatibility of the modified self-attention mechanism of SynG2G-Tr with BERT (Devlin et al., 2019) initialisation.

CoNLL 2009 Results.[6] Table 3 illustrates the results of dependency-based SRL on the test set of CoNLL 2009 dataset. Without BERT initialisation, SynG2G-Tr significantly outperforms previous work in in-domain and out-of-domain settings. With BERT initialisation, our model significantly outperforms previous work in *end-to-end* setting with 3.2%/10.4% F1 RER in both in-domain and out-of-domain evaluation sets, while having competitive performance in *given-predicate* setting. For a better comparison with Fei et al. (2021) (last setting of Table 3), we also employ the gold dependency tree for training and use the predicted dependency graph at inference time. Our model significantly outperforms Fei et al. (2021), especially on the out-of-domain dataset. This shows the benefit of encoding the dependency graph by modifying the self-attention mechanism of Transformer (Vaswani et al., 2017b) compared to using graph convolutional network, as in Fei et al. (2021).

Model	SA	WSJ (in-domain)			Brown (out-of-domain)		
		P	R	F1	P	R	F1
end-to-end							
He et al. (2018b)	✓	83.9	82.7	83.3	-	-	-
Cai et al. (2018)	✗	84.7	85.2	85.0	-	-	72.5
Li et al. (2019)	✗	-	-	85.1	-	-	-
SynG2G-Tr (w/o BERT)	✓	84.10	87.07	**85.59**	73.66	72.56	**73.11**
+pre-training							
Li et al. (2019)	✗	84.5	86.1	85.3	74.6	73.8	74.2
SynG2G-Tr	✓	86.38	89.78	**88.05**	80.35	83.57	**81.93**
given predicate							
Marcheggiani et al. (2017)	✗	88.7	86.8	87.7	79.4	76.2	77.7
M&T(2017)	✓	89.1	86.8	88.0	78.5	75.9	77.2
He et al. (2018b)	✓	89.7	89.3	89.5	81.9	76.9	79.3
Cai et al. (2018)	✗	89.9	89.2	89.6	79.8	78.3	79.0
Cai and Lapata (2019c)	✓	90.5	88.6	89.6	80.5	78.2	79.4
Kasai et al. (2019)	✓	89.0	88.2	88.6	78.0	77.2	77.6
SynG2G-Tr (w/o BERT)	✓	89.78	90.28	**90.03**	81.32	82.15	**81.73**
+pre-training							
Li et al. (2019)	✗	89.6	91.2	90.4	81.7	81.4	81.5
Kasai et al. (2019)	✓	90.3	90.0	90.2	81.0	80.5	80.8
Lyu et al. (2019)	✗	-	-	90.99	-	-	82.18
Chen et al. (2019)	✗	90.74	91.38	**91.06**	82.66	82.78	82.72
He et al. (2019)	✓	90.41	91.32	90.86	86.15	86.70	**86.42**
Cai and Lapata (2019a)	✓	91.1	90.4	90.7	82.1	81.3	81.6
Munir et al. (2021)	✓	91.2	90.6	90.9	83.1	82.6	82.8
SynG2G-Tr	✓	91.31	91.16	**91.23**	86.40	86.47	**86.43**
gold syntax							
Fei et al. (2021)	✓	92.5	92.5	92.5	85.6	85.3	85.4
SynG2G-Tr+Gold	✓	92.71	93.37	**93.03**	88.27	88.31	**88.29**

Table 3: Comparing our SynG2G-Tr with previous comparable models on CoNLL 2009 test sets. 'SA' means a syntax-aware model. Scores being boldfaced means that they are significantly better than the second best model, specified by the underline marker.

Further Analysis. We also analyse the self-attention matrix of SynG2G-Tr model for different heads and layers. Figure 3 in Appendix D demonstrates that the self-attention mechanism of SynG2G-Tr ignores the dependency graph information in the first few layers, and only uses the context-dependent information. However, as it progresses to upper layers, it begins to utilise the graph relation information, as shown in the atten-

graph additional to the dependency tree. Also, to better understand the effect of syntactic information, we exclude Fernández-González (2023); Zhou et al. (2022); Conia and Navigli (2020), as they exploited different scorer and training mechanism for SRL graphs. However, the best setting of SynG2G-Tr model still shows competitive or better results when compared to aforementioned excluded works.

[6]Scores are calculated with CoNLL 2009 shared task script (`https://ufal.mff.cuni.cz/conll2009-st/`).

tion matrix. This highlights the benefit of encoding the dependency graph with a soft bias as the model can still learn different structures in different layers, given this encoded graph information. Furthermore, in Appendix E, we show that removing the interaction of graph embeddings with key vectors results in a performance drop. Additionally, ignoring the interaction of graph relations with both key and query vectors [7] results in a significant drop as well. However, integrating the graph information into Equation 3 as stated in Mohammadshahi and Henderson (2021) does not improve the performance, and we remove it for better efficiency.

5 Conclusion

In this paper, we propose the Syntax-aware Graph-to-Graph Transformer architecture, which effectively incorporates syntactic information by inputting the syntactic dependency graph into the self-attention mechanism of Transformer. Our mechanism for inputting graph relation embeddings differs from the original Graph-to-Graph Transformer in that it models the complete interaction between the dependency relation, query vector and key vector. It also excludes the graph interaction with value vectors while maintaining good performance. We have evaluated our model on CoNLL 2005 and CoNLL 2009 SRL datasets and outperformed previous comparable models. Future studies can apply our model to any NLP task which might benefit from conditioning on the syntactic structure or other graphs.

Limitations

SynG2G-Tr encodes the syntactic dependency graph because the nodes of input and output graphs should be similar. Future work could include investigating the use of constituency graphs in the self-attention mechanism of Transformer (Vaswani et al., 2017b), where the nodes of the input graph (constituency graph) are different from those of the SRL output graph. In this paper, we initialise our model with the pre-trained BERT (Devlin et al., 2019) model. As future study, larger and better pre-trained language models will be used for the initialisation of SynG2G-Tr models, to achieve better performance. Additionally, future studies can easily extend our work to multilingual SRL benchmarks.

[7]This leads to a BERT-based syntax-agnostic model, similar to Shi and Lin (2019).

Acknowledgement

We are grateful to the Swiss National Science Foundation (SNSF), grant CRSII5-180320, for funding this work. We also thank members of the IDIAP NLU group for helpful discussions and suggestions. We are grateful to anonymous reviewers for their fruitful comments and corrections.

References

Jimmy Lei Ba, Jamie Ryan Kiros, and Geoffrey E. Hinton. 2016. Layer normalization.

Jiaxun Cai, Shexia He, Zuchao Li, and Hai Zhao. 2018. A full end-to-end semantic role labeler, syntactic-agnostic over syntactic-aware? In *Proceedings of the 27th International Conference on Computational Linguistics*, pages 2753–2765, Santa Fe, New Mexico, USA. Association for Computational Linguistics.

Rui Cai and Mirella Lapata. 2019a. Semi-supervised semantic role labeling with cross-view training. In *Proceedings of the 2019 Conference on Empirical Methods in Natural Language Processing and the 9th International Joint Conference on Natural Language Processing (EMNLP-IJCNLP)*, pages 1018–1027, Hong Kong, China. Association for Computational Linguistics.

Rui Cai and Mirella Lapata. 2019b. Syntax-aware Semantic Role Labeling without Parsing. *Transactions of the Association for Computational Linguistics*, 7:343–356.

Rui Cai and Mirella Lapata. 2019c. Syntax-aware semantic role labeling without parsing. *Transactions of the Association for Computational Linguistics*, 7:343–356.

Xavier Carreras and Lluís Màrquez. 2005. Introduction to the CoNLL-2005 shared task: Semantic role labeling. In *Proceedings of the Ninth Conference on Computational Natural Language Learning (CoNLL-2005)*, pages 152–164, Ann Arbor, Michigan. Association for Computational Linguistics.

Xinchi Chen, Chunchuan Lyu, and Ivan Titov. 2019. Capturing argument interaction in semantic role labeling with capsule networks. In *Proceedings of the 2019 Conference on Empirical Methods in Natural Language Processing and the 9th International Joint Conference on Natural Language Processing (EMNLP-IJCNLP)*, pages 5415–5425, Hong Kong, China. Association for Computational Linguistics.

Simone Conia and Roberto Navigli. 2020. Bridging the gap in multilingual semantic role labeling: a language-agnostic approach. In *Proceedings of the 28th International Conference on Computational Linguistics*, pages 1396–1410, Barcelona, Spain (Online). International Committee on Computational Linguistics.

Jacob Devlin, Ming-Wei Chang, Kenton Lee, and Kristina Toutanova. 2019. BERT: Pre-training of deep bidirectional transformers for language understanding. In *Proceedings of the 2019 Conference of the North American Chapter of the Association for Computational Linguistics: Human Language Technologies, Volume 1 (Long and Short Papers)*, pages 4171–4186, Minneapolis, Minnesota. Association for Computational Linguistics.

Luis Espinosa Anke, Alexander Shvets, Alireza Mohammadshahi, James Henderson, and Leo Wanner. 2022. Multilingual extraction and categorization of lexical collocations with graph-aware transformers. In *Proceedings of the 11th Joint Conference on Lexical and Computational Semantics*, pages 89–100, Seattle, Washington. Association for Computational Linguistics.

Hao Fei, Fei Li, Bobo Li, and Donghong Ji. 2021. Encoder-decoder based unified semantic role labeling with label-aware syntax. *Proceedings of the AAAI Conference on Artificial Intelligence*, 35(14):12794–12802.

Daniel Fernández-González. 2023. Transition-based semantic role labeling with pointer networks. *Knowledge-Based Systems*, 260:110127.

Daniel Gildea and Martha Palmer. 2002. The necessity of parsing for predicate argument recognition. In *Proceedings of the 40th Annual Meeting of the Association for Computational Linguistics*, pages 239–246, Philadelphia, Pennsylvania, USA. Association for Computational Linguistics.

Jan Hajič, Massimiliano Ciaramita, Richard Johansson, Daisuke Kawahara, Maria Antònia Martí, Lluís Màrquez, Adam Meyers, Joakim Nivre, Sebastian Padó, Jan Štěpánek, Pavel Straňák, Mihai Surdeanu, Nianwen Xue, and Yi Zhang. 2009. The CoNLL-2009 shared task: Syntactic and semantic dependencies in multiple languages. In *Proceedings of the Thirteenth Conference on Computational Natural Language Learning (CoNLL 2009): Shared Task*, pages 1–18, Boulder, Colorado. Association for Computational Linguistics.

Luheng He, Kenton Lee, Omer Levy, and Luke Zettlemoyer. 2018a. Jointly predicting predicates and arguments in neural semantic role labeling. In *Proceedings of the 56th Annual Meeting of the Association for Computational Linguistics (Volume 2: Short Papers)*, pages 364–369, Melbourne, Australia. Association for Computational Linguistics.

Luheng He, Kenton Lee, Mike Lewis, and Luke Zettlemoyer. 2017. Deep semantic role labeling: What works and what's next. In *Proceedings of the 55th Annual Meeting of the Association for Computational Linguistics (Volume 1: Long Papers)*, pages 473–483, Vancouver, Canada. Association for Computational Linguistics.

Shexia He, Zuchao Li, and Hai Zhao. 2019. Syntax-aware multilingual semantic role labeling. In *Proceedings of the 2019 Conference on Empirical Methods in Natural Language Processing and the 9th International Joint Conference on Natural Language Processing (EMNLP-IJCNLP)*, pages 5350–5359, Hong Kong, China. Association for Computational Linguistics.

Shexia He, Zuchao Li, Hai Zhao, and Hongxiao Bai. 2018b. Syntax for semantic role labeling, to be, or not to be. In *Proceedings of the 56th Annual Meeting of the Association for Computational Linguistics (Volume 1: Long Papers)*, pages 2061–2071, Melbourne, Australia. Association for Computational Linguistics.

Zixia Jia, Zhaohui Yan, Haoyi Wu, and Kewei Tu. 2022. Span-based semantic role labeling with argument pruning and second-order inference. *Proceedings of the AAAI Conference on Artificial Intelligence*, 36(10):10822–10830.

Ishan Jindal, Ranit Aharonov, Siddhartha Brahma, Huaiyu Zhu, and Yunyao Li. 2020. Improved semantic role labeling using parameterized neighborhood memory adaptation. *ArXiv*, abs/2011.14459.

Jungo Kasai, Dan Friedman, Robert Frank, Dragomir Radev, and Owen Rambow. 2019. Syntax-aware neural semantic role labeling with supertags. In *Proceedings of the 2019 Conference of the North American Chapter of the Association for Computational Linguistics: Human Language Technologies, Volume 1 (Long and Short Papers)*, pages 701–709, Minneapolis, Minnesota. Association for Computational Linguistics.

Diederik P. Kingma and Jimmy Ba. 2014. Adam: A method for stochastic optimization.

Zuchao Li, Shexia He, Hai Zhao, Yiqing Zhang, Zhuosheng Zhang, Xi Zhou, and Xiang Zhou. 2019. Dependency or span, end-to-end uniform semantic role labeling.

Zuchao Li, Hai Zhao, Shexia He, and Jiaxun Cai. 2021. Syntax role for neural semantic role labeling. *Computational Linguistics*, 47(3):529–574.

Chunchuan Lyu, Shay B. Cohen, and Ivan Titov. 2019. Semantic role labeling with iterative structure refinement. In *Proceedings of the 2019 Conference on Empirical Methods in Natural Language Processing and the 9th International Joint Conference on Natural Language Processing (EMNLP-IJCNLP)*, pages 1071–1082, Hong Kong, China. Association for Computational Linguistics.

Diego Marcheggiani, Anton Frolov, and Ivan Titov. 2017. A simple and accurate syntax-agnostic neural model for dependency-based semantic role labeling. In *Proceedings of the 21st Conference on Computational Natural Language Learning (CoNLL 2017)*, pages 411–420, Vancouver, Canada. Association for Computational Linguistics.

Diego Marcheggiani and Ivan Titov. 2017. Encoding sentences with graph convolutional networks for semantic role labeling. In *Proceedings of the 2017 Conference on Empirical Methods in Natural Language Processing*, pages 1506–1515, Copenhagen, Denmark. Association for Computational Linguistics.

Mitchell P. Marcus, Beatrice Santorini, and Mary Ann Marcinkiewicz. 1993. Building a large annotated corpus of English: The Penn Treebank. *Computational Linguistics*, 19(2):313–330.

Alireza Mohammadshahi and James Henderson. 2020. Graph-to-graph transformer for transition-based dependency parsing. In *Findings of the Association for Computational Linguistics: EMNLP 2020*, pages 3278–3289, Online. Association for Computational Linguistics.

Alireza Mohammadshahi and James Henderson. 2021. Recursive Non-Autoregressive Graph-to-Graph Transformer for Dependency Parsing with Iterative Refinement. *Transactions of the Association for Computational Linguistics*, 9:120–138.

Alireza Mohammadshahi, Rémi Lebret, and Karl Aberer. 2019. Aligning multilingual word embeddings for cross-modal retrieval task. In *Proceedings of the Beyond Vision and LANguage: inTEgrating Real-world kNowledge (LANTERN)*, pages 11–17, Hong Kong, China. Association for Computational Linguistics.

Alireza Mohammadshahi, Vassilina Nikoulina, Alexandre Berard, Caroline Brun, James Henderson, and Laurent Besacier. 2022a. SMaLL-100: Introducing shallow multilingual machine translation model for low-resource languages. In *Proceedings of the 2022 Conference on Empirical Methods in Natural Language Processing*, pages 8348–8359, Abu Dhabi, United Arab Emirates. Association for Computational Linguistics.

Alireza Mohammadshahi, Thomas Scialom, Majid Yazdani, Pouya Yanki, Angela Fan, James Henderson, and Marzieh Saeidi. 2022b. Rquge: Reference-free metric for evaluating question generation by answering the question.

Kashif Munir, Hai Zhao, and Zuchao Li. 2021. Adaptive convolution for semantic role labeling. *IEEE/ACM Transactions on Audio, Speech, and Language Processing*, 29:782–791.

Vinod Nair and Geoffrey E. Hinton. 2010. Rectified linear units improve restricted boltzmann machines. In *Proceedings of the 27th International Conference on International Conference on Machine Learning*, ICML'10, page 807–814, Madison, WI, USA. Omnipress.

Hiroki Ouchi, Hiroyuki Shindo, and Yuji Matsumoto. 2018. A span selection model for semantic role labeling. In *Proceedings of the 2018 Conference on Empirical Methods in Natural Language Processing*, pages 1630–1642, Brussels, Belgium. Association for Computational Linguistics.

Matthew Peters, Mark Neumann, Mohit Iyyer, Matt Gardner, Christopher Clark, Kenton Lee, and Luke Zettlemoyer. 2018. Deep contextualized word representations. In *Proceedings of the 2018 Conference of the North American Chapter of the Association for Computational Linguistics: Human Language Technologies, Volume 1 (Long Papers)*, pages 2227–2237, New Orleans, Louisiana. Association for Computational Linguistics.

Vasin Punyakanok, Dan Roth, and Wen-tau Yih. 2008. The importance of syntactic parsing and inference in semantic role labeling. *Computational Linguistics*, 34(2):257–287.

Michael Roth and Mirella Lapata. 2016. Neural semantic role labeling with dependency path embeddings. In *Proceedings of the 54th Annual Meeting of the Association for Computational Linguistics (Volume 1: Long Papers)*, pages 1192–1202, Berlin, Germany. Association for Computational Linguistics.

Peng Shi and Jimmy Lin. 2019. Simple bert models for relation extraction and semantic role labeling.

Emma Strubell, Patrick Verga, Daniel Andor, David Weiss, and Andrew McCallum. 2018. Linguistically-informed self-attention for semantic role labeling. In *Proceedings of the 2018 Conference on Empirical Methods in Natural Language Processing*, pages 5027–5038, Brussels, Belgium. Association for Computational Linguistics.

Zhixing Tan, Mingxuan Wang, Jun Xie, Yidong Chen, and Xiaodong Shi. 2017. Deep semantic role labeling with self-attention.

Ashish Vaswani, Noam Shazeer, Niki Parmar, Jakob Uszkoreit, Llion Jones, Aidan N Gomez, Ł ukasz Kaiser, and Illia Polosukhin. 2017a. Attention is all you need. In *Advances in Neural Information Processing Systems*, volume 30. Curran Associates, Inc.

Ashish Vaswani, Noam Shazeer, Niki Parmar, Jakob Uszkoreit, Llion Jones, Aidan N Gomez, Ł ukasz Kaiser, and Illia Polosukhin. 2017b. Attention is all you need. In *Advances in Neural Information Processing Systems*, volume 30. Curran Associates, Inc.

Qingrong Xia, Zhenghua Li, Min Zhang, Meishan Zhang, Guohong Fu, Rui Wang, and Luo Si. 2019. Syntax-aware neural semantic role labeling. *Proceedings of the AAAI Conference on Artificial Intelligence*, 33(01):7305–7313.

Qingrong Xia, Rui Wang, Zhenghua Li, Yue Zhang, and Min Zhang. 2020. Semantic role labeling with heterogeneous syntactic knowledge. In *Proceedings of the 28th International Conference on Computational Linguistics*, pages 2979–2990, Barcelona, Spain (Online). International Committee on Computational Linguistics.

Zhisong Zhang, Emma Strubell, and Eduard H. Hovy. 2021. Comparing span extraction methods for semantic role labeling. In *SPNLP*.

Jie Zhou and Wei Xu. 2015. End-to-end learning of semantic role labeling using recurrent neural networks. In *Proceedings of the 53rd Annual Meeting of the Association for Computational Linguistics and the 7th International Joint Conference on Natural Language Processing (Volume 1: Long Papers)*, pages 1127–1137, Beijing, China. Association for Computational Linguistics.

Junru Zhou, Zuchao Li, and Hai Zhao. 2020a. Parsing all: Syntax and semantics, dependencies and spans. In *Findings of the Association for Computational Linguistics: EMNLP 2020*, pages 4438–4449, Online. Association for Computational Linguistics.

Junru Zhou, Zhuosheng Zhang, Hai Zhao, and Shuailiang Zhang. 2020b. LIMIT-BERT : Linguistics informed multi-task BERT. In *Findings of the Association for Computational Linguistics: EMNLP 2020*, pages 4450–4461, Online. Association for Computational Linguistics.

Junru Zhou and Hai Zhao. 2019. Head-driven phrase structure grammar parsing on Penn treebank. In *Proceedings of the 57th Annual Meeting of the Association for Computational Linguistics*, pages 2396–2408, Florence, Italy. Association for Computational Linguistics.

Shilin Zhou, Qingrong Xia, Zhenghua Li, Yu Zhang, Yu Hong, and Min Zhang. 2022. Fast and accurate end-to-end span-based semantic role labeling as word-based graph parsing. In *Proceedings of the 29th International Conference on Computational Linguistics*, pages 4160–4171, Gyeongju, Republic of Korea. International Committee on Computational Linguistics.

Appendix A SRL Scorer and Decoder Details

Scorer. Inspired by Zhou et al. (2020a), we first define span representation (s_{ij}) as the difference between right and left end-points of the span:

$$s_{ij} = \vec{sr}_j - \overleftarrow{sl}_i \tag{4}$$

where $\vec{sr}_j$ is defined as $[\vec{z_{j+1}};\vec{z_j}]$, and $\overleftarrow{sl}_i$ is calculated as $[\overleftarrow{z_i};\overleftarrow{z_{i+1}}]$. $\overleftrightarrow{z_i}$ is computed by dividing the output representation of Transformer (z_i) in half.
Argument (a_{ij}) and predicate (v_k) representations are defined as:

$$\begin{aligned} a_{ij} &= \text{ReLU}(\boldsymbol{W^1_{srl}} s_{ij} + b^1_{srl}) \\ v_k &= z_k \end{aligned} \tag{5}$$

where $\boldsymbol{W^1_{srl}}$ and b^1_{srl} are learned parameters and $\text{ReLU}(.)$ is the Rectified Linear Unit (Nair and Hinton, 2010) function.
We predict semantic roles as defined in Zhou et al. (2020a):

$$\Phi_l(v,a) = \boldsymbol{W^3_{srl}}(\text{LN}(\boldsymbol{W^2_{srl}}[a_{ij};v_k] + b^2_{srl})) + b^3_{srl} \tag{6}$$

where $\text{LN}(.)$ is the layer normalisation (Ba et al., 2016) function, and $\boldsymbol{W^2_{srl}}$, $\boldsymbol{W^3_{srl}}$, b^2_{srl}, and b^3_{srl} are learned parameters. The semantic role score for a specific label l_{out} is defined as:

$$\Phi_l(v,a,l_{out}) = [\Phi_l(v,a)]_{l_{out}} \tag{7}$$

Since the number of predicate-argument pairs is $O(n^3)$, we apply the pruning method proposed in Li et al. (2019); He et al. (2018a) by defining separate scorers for argument and predicate candidates (Φ_a and Φ_v), and pruning all but the top-ranked arguments and predicates based on their corresponding scores.

Training. The model is trained to optimise the probability $P(\hat{y}|W,P,G_{syn})$ of predicate-argument pairs, conditioned on input sequence (W), PoS tags (P), and predicated dependency graph (G_{syn}). This objective can be factorised as:

$$\begin{aligned} J(\theta) &= \sum_{y \in \Gamma} -log P_\theta(y|W,P,G_{syn}) \\ &= \sum_{\langle v,a,l_{out}\rangle \in \Gamma} -log \frac{\exp(\Phi(v,a,l_{out}))}{\sum_{\hat{l} \in L_{srl}} \exp(\Phi(v,a,\hat{l}))} \end{aligned} \tag{8}$$

where $\Phi(v,a,l_{out})$ is defined as $\Phi_v(v) + \Phi_a(a) + \Phi_l(v,a,l_{out})$, and θ is model parameters. Γ is the set of predicate-argument-relation tuples for all possible predicate-argument pairs and either the correct relation or NONE.

Decoders. Following Zhou et al. (2020a), we apply a single dynamic programming decoder according to the uniform score following the non-overlapping constraints (Punyakanok et al., 2008).

Appendix B Implementation Details and Pre-processing Steps

CoNLL 2005: In this shared task (Carreras and Màrquez, 2005) (under LDC license), the focus was on verbal predicates in English. The training data includes sections 2-21 of the Wall Street Journal (WSJ) dataset. Section 24 is considered as the development set, while section 23 is used as the in-domain test set. Three sections of the Brown corpus are used for the out-of-domain dataset. The dataset can be downloaded from here, and pre-processing steps are provided in here.

CoNLL 2009: This shared task (Hajič et al., 2009) (under LDC license) focused on dependency-based SRL and was created by merging PropBank and NomBank treebanks. We evaluate our models on the English dataset with the same split as the CoNLL 2005 dataset. The dataset and pre-processing steps can be found at here and here. The number of sentences in train and evaluation sets is as follows:

Train	Dev	Test-WSJ	Test-Brown
39'832	1'334	2'399	425

Table 4: The number of sentences for each split of CoNLL 2005 and CoNLL 2009 datasets.

Appendix C Hyper-parameters Setting

We use *bert-large-whole-word-masking*[8] (345M parameters) for the initialisation of encoder in SynG2G-Tr model. We use Adam optimiser (Kingma and Ba, 2014) and apply separate optimisers for pre-trained parameters and randomly initialised ones. We use bucket batching, grouping sentences by their lengths to the same batch to speed up the model. Early stopping is used to mitigate over-fitting, as in previous work (Mohammadshahi et al., 2022b,a, 2019). In a pre-defined predicate setting, we use different dynamic programming decoders to find SRL graphs, since predicates are not necessarily the same in dependency-based and span-based SRL graphs. For choosing the best hyper-parameters, we use manual tuning to find the base learning rate and BERT learning rate. For other hyper-parameters, we follow previous work (Zhou et al., 2020a). The base learning rate is selected from $\{1e-2,1e-3,1.5e-3\}$, and the BERT learning rate is chosen from $\{1e-5,1.5e-5,2e-5\}$. So, we train our models with 9 different learning rates to find the best performing model based on the summation of F1 scores of span-based and dependency-based SRL graphs. We use NVIDIA GeForce GTX 1080 Ti for training and evaluating our models. [9] For the dependency parser, we apply the same hyper-parameters as Zhou et al. (2020a). We use the base learning rate of $2e-3$, and the BERT learning rate of $1.5e-5$. Here is the list of hyper-parameters for the SynG2G-Tr model:

Component	Specification
Optimiser	Adam
Base Learning rate	1.5e-3
BERT Learning rate	1e-5
Adam Betas (b_1,b_2)	(0.9,0.999)
Adam Epsilon	1e-5
Weight Decay	0.01
Max-Grad-Norm	1
Warm-up	0.001
Self-Attention	
No. Layers	24
No. Heads	16
Embedding size	1024
Max Position Embedding	512

Component	Specification
Feed-Forward layers (SRL)	
Span Hidden size	512
Label Hidden size	250
Feed-Forward layers (PoS)	
Hidden size	250
Pruning (SRL)	
λ_{verb}	0.6
λ_{span}	0.6
Max No. Span	300
Max No. Verb	30
Epoch	100

Table 5: Hyper-parameters for training SynG2G-Tr.

Appendix D Attention Visualisation

Figure 3 shows the attention weights for different layers of self-attention in the SynG2G-Tr model (Figure 3b-3d), alongside the dependency relation matrix (Figure 3a). The self-attention matrix includes four patterns. The first layer of the SynG2G-Tr model (Figure 3b) ignores the graph relations and learns string-local context information. For the middle layer (Figure 3c), attention weights partially use the graph relation pattern. Then, in the last layer (Figure 3d), the dependency graph relations are evident in the attention pattern. This demonstrates the benefit of adding the graph information with a soft bias, allowing the model to learn different structures using both local context and graph information. Furthermore, it can be inferred that the last layers of the self-attention mechanism require a global view and between-edge information, while the first few layers learn local context information. More examples are provided in Figures 4-5-6.

[8] `https://github.com/google-research/bert`. Apache License 2.0.

[9] The training time of SynG2G-Tr model is 0h20m40s, and the evaluation time is 0h02m24s.

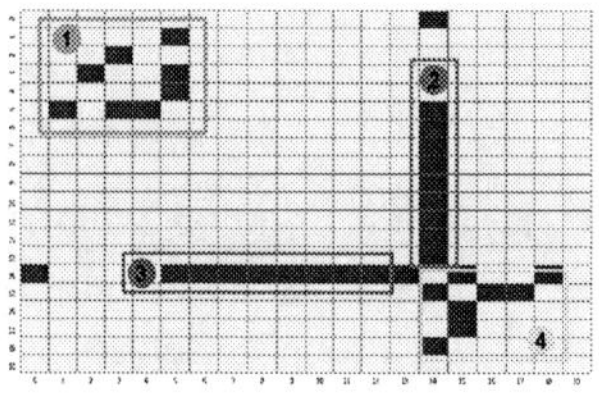

(a) Graph Relation Matrix

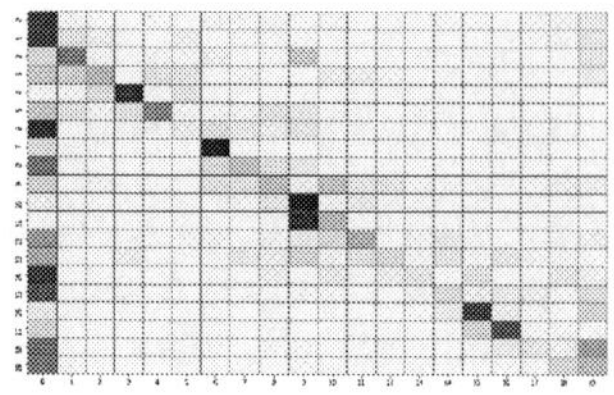

(b) First Layer

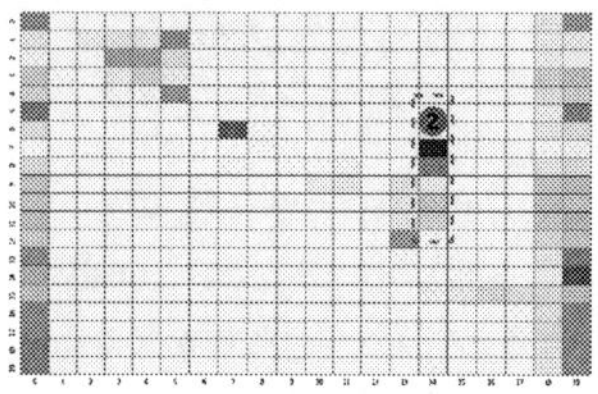

(c) Middle Layer

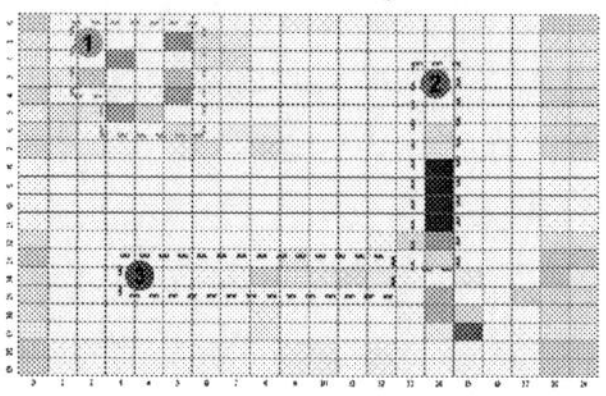

(d) Last Layer

Figure 3: The attention weights for the CoNLL 2009 example "[CLS] The most troublesome report may be the August merchandise trade deficit due out tomorrow . [SEP]". The first figure shows the dependency graph matrix.

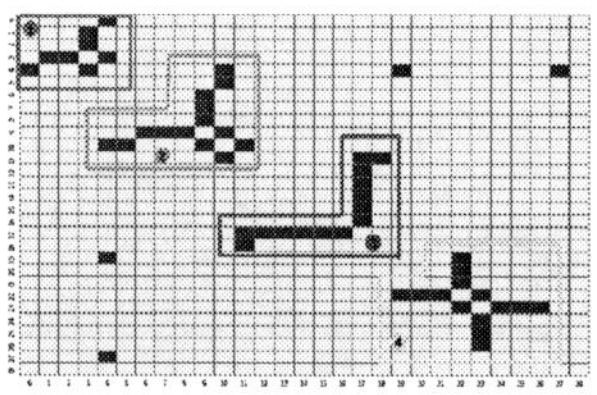

(a) Graph Relation Matrix

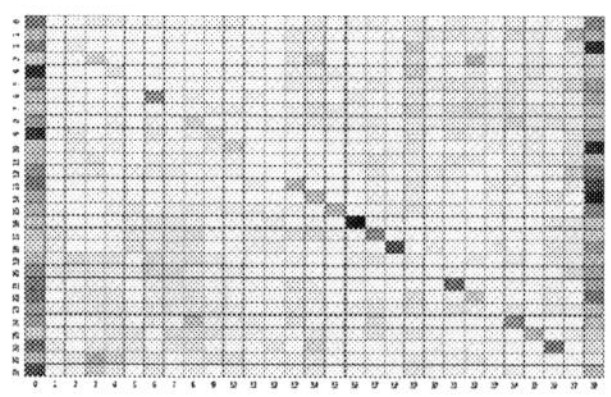

(b) First Layer

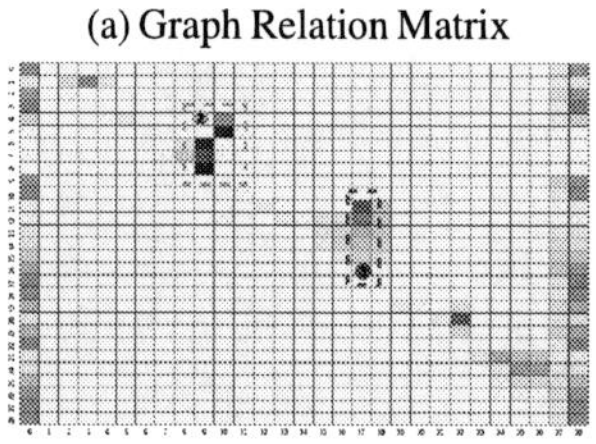

(c) Middle Layer

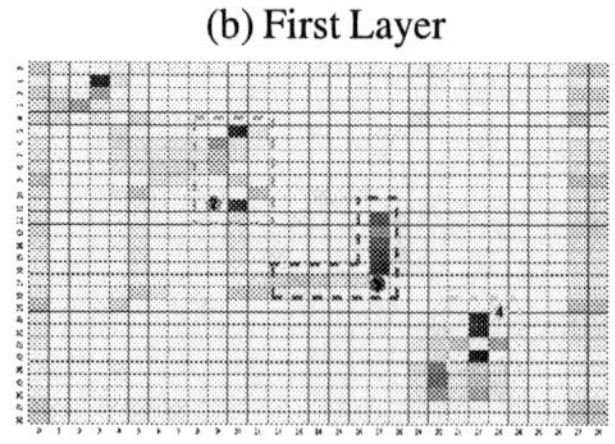

(d) Last Layer

Figure 4: The attention weights for a specific example "[CLS] The consensus view expects a 0.4 % increase in the September CPI after a flat reading in August . [SEP]" on CoNLL 2009 dataset. The first figure shows the dependency graph matrix.

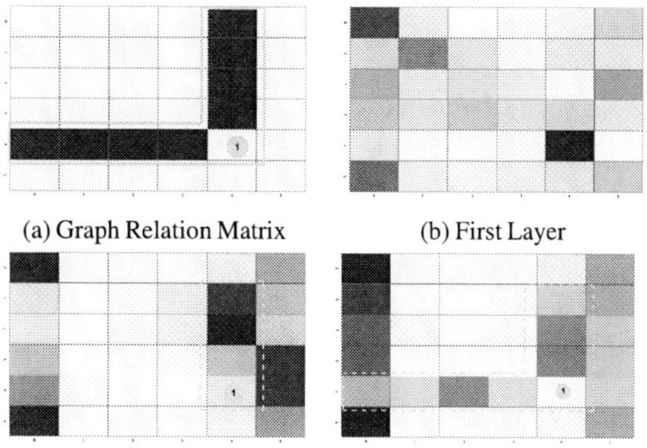

(a) Graph Relation Matrix (b) First Layer

(c) Middle Layer (d) Last Layer

Figure 5: The attention weights for a specific example "[CLS] Candid Comment [SEP]" on CoNLL 2009 dataset. The first figure shows the dependency graph matrix.

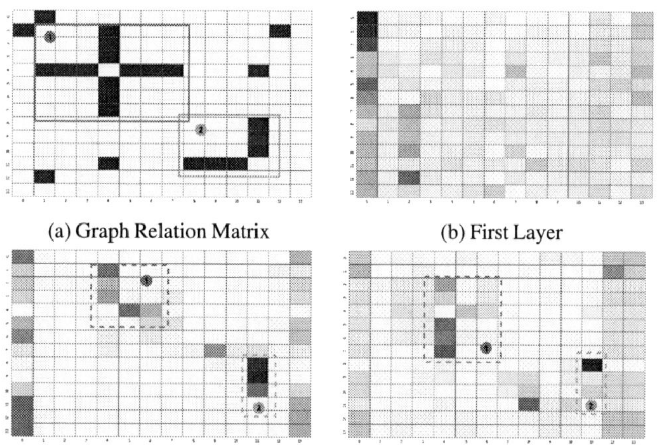

(a) Graph Relation Matrix (b) First Layer

(c) Middle Layer (d) Last Layer

Figure 6: The attention weights for a specific example "[CLS] Let 's make that 1929 , just to be sure . [SEP]" on CoNLL 2009 dataset. The first figure shows the dependency graph matrix.

Appendix E Ablation Study

In Table 6, we analyse the interaction of the dependency graph with key and query vectors in the attention mechanism, as defined in Equation 2. Excluding the key interaction results in a similar attention mechanism as defined in Mohammadshahi and Henderson (2021). This SynG2G-Tr-*key* model achieves similar results compared to the SynG2G-Tr model on the WSJ test dataset given the predicate, but the SynG2G-Tr model outperforms it on all other settings, including both types of out-of-domain datasets, confirming that key interaction is a critical part of the SynG2G-Tr model.

When both key and query interactions are excluded from the SynG2G-Tr model (SynG2G-Tr-*key-query*), it has significantly lower performance than the SynG2G-Tr model in all settings. This demonstrates the impact of encoding the graph relation embeddings in the self-attention mechanism of Transformer (Vaswani et al., 2017b) model.

We also evaluate adding the interaction of graph relations with value vectors to the SynG2G-Tr model, as defined in Espinosa Anke et al. (2022); Mohammadshahi and Henderson (2020). The SynG2G-Tr+*value* model achieves similar or worse results compared to the SynG2G-Tr model. So, we exclude this interaction to speed up the modified attention mechanism.

Model	CoNLL 2005			CoNLL 2009		
	Dev	WSJ	Brown	Dev	WSJ	Brown
end-to-end						
SynG2G-Tr *-key -query*	86.65	87.08	79.40	86.40	87.26	81.12
SynG2G-Tr *-key*	86.82	87.27	80.33	86.85	87.50	81.51
SynG2G-Tr	87.08	87.57	80.53	87.13	88.05	81.93
SynG2G-Tr *+value*	87.17	87.45	80.40	86.92	87.95	82.03
given predicate						
SynG2G-Tr *-key -query*	87.93	88.52	82.56	90.16	90.68	85.72
SynG2G-Tr *-key*	88.03	88.91	82.90	90.31	91.22	86.28
SynG2G-Tr	88.17	88.93	83.21	90.66	91.23	86.43
SynG2G-Tr *+value*	88.15	88.78	83.10	90.48	91.15	86.41

Table 6: Model comparison of SynG2G-Tr and other variants, by F1 score on CoNLL 2005 and CoNLL 2009 datasets. The SynG2G-Tr-*key-query* model is the same as the syntax-agnostic BERT model.

Improving Zero-shot Relation Classification via Automatically-acquired Entailment Templates

Mahdi Rahimi and **Mihai Surdeanu**
Department of Computer Science
University of Arizona, Tucson, Arizona, USA
{marahimi, msurdeanu}@arizona.edu

Abstract

While fully supervised relation classification (RC) models perform well on large-scale datasets, their performance drops drastically in low-resource settings. As generating annotated examples are expensive, recent zero-shot methods have been proposed that reformulate RC into other NLP tasks for which supervision exists such as textual entailment. However, these methods rely on templates that are manually created which is costly and requires domain expertise. In this paper, we present a novel strategy for template generation for relation classification, which is based on adapting Harris' distributional similarity principle to templates encoded using contextualized representations. Further, we perform empirical evaluation of different strategies for combining the automatically acquired templates with manual templates. The experimental results on TACRED show that our approach not only performs better than the zero-shot RC methods that only use manual templates, but also that it achieves state-of-the-art performance for zero-shot TACRED at 64.3 F1 score.

1 Introduction

Relation classification (RC) identifies the relation that holds between two entities that co-occur in the same text. For example, given the sentence: *Jane's White House desk has a sign "Home on the Range"*, the relation between *Jane* and *White House* is `employee_of`. Beyond this simple example, RC is a critical NLP task with important applications to many domains such as intelligence (Doddington et al., 2004) and biomedical (Nédellec et al., 2013; Krallinger et al., 2017).

Recent directions mitigate the amount of supervision necessary for RC by taking advantage of the knowledge stored in large language models (LLMs). For example, Sainz et al. (2021) reformulated RC as an entailment task based on templates that are manually created as the verbalizations of relation labels. Then they are used to formulate a hypothesis that can be verified with an off-the-shelf LLM entailment engine. Other directions feed prompts that capture the definition of the task and examples into encoder-decoder language models (Han et al., 2022b). However, most of these directions tend to rely on templates/prompts that are *manually-created* by domain experts. This strategy has a potential high cost, and also runs the risk of inserting undesired biases in the data. Directions that focus on automatically learning prompts often produce prompts that are nonsensical to humans (Shin et al., 2020)

Our work aims to limit the above drawbacks of template-based approaches for RC. In particular, we expand the approach of Sainz et al. (2021) with explainable templates that are automatically acquired from a large textual collection. For template acquisition, we modify the BERT-Informed Rule Discovery (BIRD) algorithm (Rahimi and Surdeanu, 2022), which, given a seed template, automatically generates templates with similar meaning. BIRD encodes templates using contextualized representations generated by a transformer network (Devlin et al., 2019), and then uses a similarity measure to acquire similar templates based on an extension of the distributional similarity principle (Harris, 1954) to templates. For example, given a manual template `{subj} was founded by {obj}`, the template `{subj} was created by {obj}` is automatically created.

We use these automatically-acquired templates to expand the pool of manual templates used for RC, and show that this expansion yields statistically significant performance improvements.

The key contributions of this paper are:

- We introduce a novel strategy for template generation for RC, which is based on adapting Harris' distributional similarity principle to templates encoded using contextualized representations.

Proceedings of the 8th Workshop on Representation Learning for NLP (RepL4NLP 2023), pages 187–195

- We perform an empirical analysis of different strategies for how to combine automatically-acquired templates with templates that were manually generated. The strategies include selection using entailment score, selection using BIRD's similarity score, and selection guided by the lowest entropy. All in all, our best combination obtains state-of-the-art performance for zero-shot TACRED, at 64.3 F1 score.

2 Related Work

Supervised Relation Classification. Most recent approaches for supervised relation classification use pre-trained language models such as models with self-supervised objectives, e.g., BERT (Devlin et al., 2019), RoBERTa (Liu et al., 2019) and GPT-3 (Brown et al., 2020), or adapt sequence-to-sequence models to the task, such as T5 (Raffel et al., 2020), BART (Lewis et al., 2020), and GLM (Du et al., 2021). Prior to the advent of large language models supervised models needed a large amount of labeled data for training models from scratch (Kambhatla, 2004, Zeng et al., 2014). Recent approaches outperform traditional approaches by finetuning language models (Wu and He, 2019, Joshi et al., 2020, Yamada et al., 2020, Wang et al., 2021b, Lyu and Chen, 2021, Paolini et al., 2021, Wang et al., 2022a) or prompting (Han et al., 2022b, Han et al., 2022a, Zhang et al., 2023).

Our work is different in that we focus on the zero-shot scenario, a common situation in the real world, where a RC system must be developed rapidly without the luxury of training data.

Zero-shot Relation Classification. Getting accurate annotations for RC can be expensive because it is challenging for annotators to identify and come to a consensus on the structural information required. This poses an obstacle for RC models, which have traditionally depended on direct supervision from a sufficient end-task training data. Standard supervised models often perform poorly when dealing with low-resource situations (Schick and Schütze, 2021), highlighting the importance of developing methods that perform well in low-resource settings. As a result, several approaches have been proposed for relation classification with few training examples (Han et al., 2018, Gao et al., 2019, Baldini Soares et al., 2019, Sabo et al., 2021, Sainz et al., 2021). For the problem of zero-shot relation classification, Rocktäschel et al. (2015) and Demeester et al. (2016) proposed the use of logic rules. Wang et al. (2022b) used silver standard data cleaned by a class-aware clean data detection mechanism to train a textual entailment engine. In the literature, zero-shot RC has been reformulated as other tasks such as reading comprehension (Levy et al., 2017), textual entailment (Obamuyide and Vlachos, 2018, Sainz et al., 2021, Wang et al., 2022b), summarization (Lu et al., 2022), span-prediction (Cohen et al., 2020), question answering (Cetoli, 2020), triple generation (Wang et al., 2022a, Wang et al., 2021a), and prompting (Gong and Eldardiry, 2021).

Our work fits within this latter group. However, our contribution is that it mixes manual seed templates with explainable templates automatically acquired using the distributional similarity principle tailored for templates. Our results indicate that this simple strategy yields state-of-the-art performance on a popular zero-shot RC task.

3 Background

As mentioned, our zero-shot approach for relation classification relies on an entailment engine that is fed automatically-generated templates. In this section we discuss the building blocks necessary for this idea.

3.1 The Relation Classification Task

In the relation classification task we intend to classify a sentence with two marked entities into a predefined set of relations, or indicate that none of the relations hold between them (none-of-the-above or NOTA). Each input is a triple $x_i = (s, e_1, e_2)_i$ which consists of a sentence s with an ordered pair of two entities e_1 and e_2 (each entity is a span over s). The output $r \in R \cup \{\text{NOTA}\}$ indicates the two entities conform to one of the relations defined in the target set of $R = \{r_1, r_2, ..., r_N\}$ or none of the relations hold.

3.2 Zero-shot RC as an Entailment Task

Since our work is based on the works of Sainz et al. (2021) that reformulated RC as an entailment task on TACRED dataset, we provide an overview of their work. In a zero-shot setup no training examples are provided to the model. Therefore, the RC model must make predictions on relation instances without seeing any related data prior to that. By reformulating RC as an entailment task, it is possible to take advantage of the existing off-the-shelf entailment engines and use them as-is. Fig-

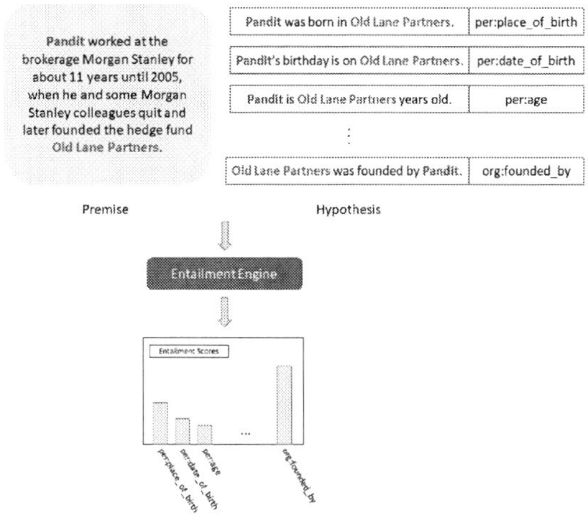

Figure 1: Overview of the entailment-based zero-shot relation classification approach via label verbalization.

ure 1 demonstrates the overview of the approach. First, a set of templates are manually created for each relation type in TACRED. The templates verbalize the relation types. For example, the relation `PER:DATE_OF_BIRTH` can be verbalized as `{subj}'s birthday is on {obj}`. Sainz et al. (2021) manually created 2 templates on average for each relation type. After that, an entailment engine is used to perform inference on each example in TACRED's test set. For each such example, the `{subj}` and `{obj}` placeholders of all the templates are replaced with the two marked entities of the example. After that, we use the TACRED example as premise and each template as hypothesis to feed them to an entailment engine. The entailment engine will produce an entailment score for each template. We pick the template with the highest score and return its corresponding relation type as the final prediction.

For the NOTA relation, however, creating templates does not produce good results. As a result, a threshold-based approach is used to detect NOTA. A threshold (between 0 and 1) is selected for the NOTA relation. If none of the entailment scores are above this threshold, the input example will be classified as NOTA. The treshold is selected by using 1% of TACRED's development set.

3.3 Rule Acquisition

BERT-Informed Rule Discovery or BIRD (Rahimi and Surdeanu, 2022) is a rule[1] acquisition algorithm. Informally, BIRD learns inferences from text such as *"X is the author of Y* $\approx$ *X writes Y"*. Some of these inferences are not exact paraphrases (but are still relevant and potentially useful) such as *"X is the author of Y* $\approx$ *X is known for Y"*. More formally, BIRD is initialized with a seed rule (e.g. *"X is the author of Y"*), which is implemented as a syntactic path connecting two concepts, and infers one or more possible matches (e.g. *"X writes Y"*) where each match is a syntactic path. BIRD generates the matches by implementing Harris' Distributional Hypothesis principle (Harris, 1954) to rules. It states that if two patterns tend to link the same sets of words, they tend to have similar meanings.

BIRD relies on contextualized representations generated by a transformer network (Devlin et al., 2019). In particular, a pattern has two slots (*X* and *Y*); BIRD computes contextualized embeddings for each slot. By doing so, a pattern will be represented by two embedding vectors. Then a (cosine) similarity score is calculated between each slot of any given two patterns, i.e., one similarity score is calculated for slot X and one similarity score is calculated for slot Y. Finally, the average of the two similarity scores is computed as the similarity score between the two patterns.

Given a corpus, BIRD extracts and stores all patterns from the corpus and then computes the contextualized embeddings for each slot of each pattern. Therefore, given a pattern, BIRD can search the extracted patterns space and find the most similar patterns to the input pattern.

3.4 TACRED Dataset

TACRED (Zhang et al., 2017) is a large-scale relation classification benchmark that is consisted of 106,264 examples and 42 relation types including the `no_relation (NOTA)` label. Each example contains the information about the entity type, among other linguistic information. TACRED examples include 68,124 for training, 22,631 for validation, and 15,509 for testing.

4 Approach

One limitation of (Sainz et al., 2021) is that they rely on *manually-generated* templates, which require effort to create and may prone to bias. Our work mitigates this limitation by automatically expanding the manual patterns using BIRD.

We utilize the manual templates as seed patterns to feed them into BIRD to generate new patterns that tend to have similar meanings to the

[1]Alternatively called patterns or syntactic paths.

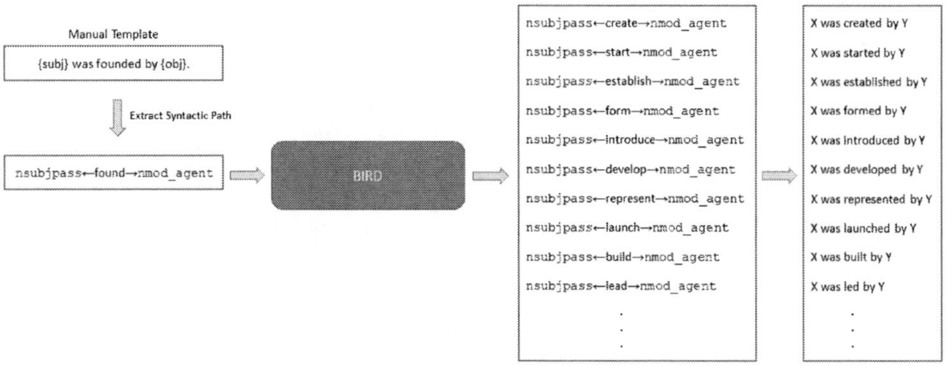

Figure 2: The process of using manual templates as seed pattern to generate similar patterns by BIRD.

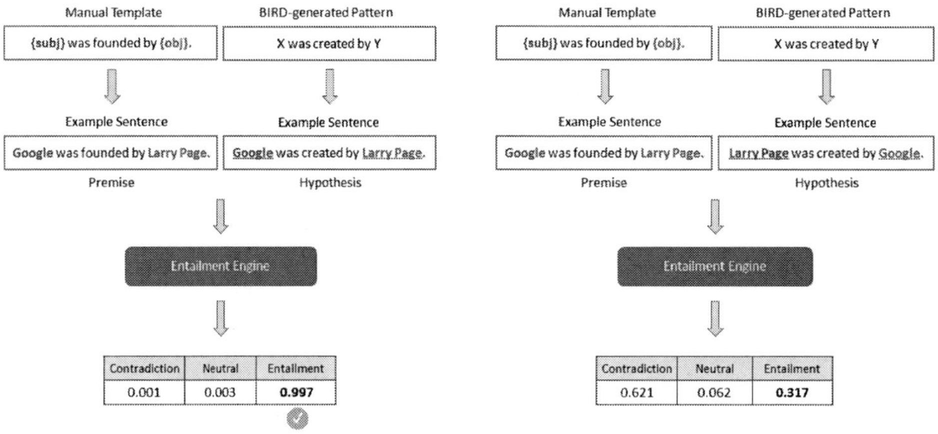

Figure 3: The process of determining the subject and object of a pattern generated by BIRD.

manual templates. Figure 2 shows this process. For each manual template, we extract its syntactic path. For example, for the template `{subj} was founded by {obj}`, we extract the syntactic path nsubjpass←found→nmod_agent (X was founded by Y). Then the syntactic path is fed to BIRD to generate new syntactic paths. We generate 40 patterns for each manual template. After the syntactic paths are generated, we generate their corresponding English text using a module we created. For example, for the syntactic path nsubjpass←create→nmod_agent, the English text "`X was created by Y`" is generated.

The corresponding patterns of 12 manual templates did not exist in BIRD's pattern collection. Therefore, it was not possible to use them as seed patterns. For these templates we manually selected an existing high-quality pattern that was very close in meaning. For example, the pattern *"X is spouse of Y"* did not exist in BIRD's pattern collection. We chose the pattern *"X married Y"* instead.

4.1 Determining Subject and Object of a Pattern

The manual templates have `{subj}` and `{obj}` placeholders which correspond to the subject and object of a relation, respectively. The patterns generated by BIRD do not contain this information. That is, it is unclear what the mapping is between the X and Y slots in a BIRD template and `{subj}` and `{obj}` in a relation template. Therefore, it is necessary to determine which slot of a pattern is the subject and which slot is the object. We use our off-the-shelf entailment engine to determine this information. Figure 3 demonstrates this procedure. For each generated pattern, we create an example sentence for its seed manual template. This example sentence will be used as premise. As for the hypothesis, we create two example sentences for the pattern by using the same words that filled the placeholders of the seed manual template to fill the slots of the pattern. The two example sentences are the same sentence except their slot-filler words are swapped. One of these two hypotheses is expected to have a similar meaning to the manual template's example sentence. Therefore, we expect the entailment engine to produce a high entailment score for it and to produce a low score for the other one. We pick the hypothesis with the highest entailment score to determine the subject and object of the pattern. If the entailment engine produces entailment scores below 0.5 for both of the hypotheses, we discard the pattern. By determining the subject and object of the patterns, they become fully functioning templates.

4.2 Selection of Patterns

After the templates are generated and set up, a selection mechanism is required to keep the most useful ones and discard the rest.[2] We always keep all of the manual templates and the selection mechanism is only applied on the BIRD-generated ones.

4.2.1 Selection using entailment score

In subsection 4.1, it was explained that an entailment score is obtained for each BIRD-generated pattern when the subject and object of the pattern is determined. We use this entailment score to sort the templates and keep the top ones.

4.2.2 Selection using BIRD's similarity score

For a seed pattern, BIRD generates similar patterns using a similarity measure. This yields a similarity score for each BIRD-generated pattern. We use this similarity score to sort the templates and keep the top ones.

4.2.3 Selection guided by lowest entropy

A low entropy for the prediction of a classifier means that the classifier was more confident when making the prediction. We use this idea to pick the templates that together result in the lowest entropy. For each TACRED test set example, we perform the following. For each relation $r_i \in R$, we pick the template (from the pool of templates for r_i) that produces the highest prediction score (entailment score when TACRED example is premise and the template is hypothesis). For all $r_j \in R - \{r_i\}$, we pick the template (from the pool of templates for r_j) that produces the lowest prediction score. The combination of these chosen templates create one candidate set of templates. This procedure is done for each $r_i \in R$. As a result, we will have 41 candidate sets. Each candidate set is expected to have a low entropy. We keep the candidate set with the lowest entropy. Note that during the candidate sets creation process, we never look at the gold labels and merely use the model prediction scores.

[2]Keeping all of the templates resulted in poor performance in our experiments.

4.3 Inference

After the final set of templates is selected, we perform the inference according to the method described in Sainz et al. (2021) as shown in Figure 1. During inference, they pick the template that produces the highest entailment score and return its corresponding relation type as the final prediction. In addition to using the "highest entailment score", we also experimented with two additional methods to perform the final prediction. Firstly, instead of choosing the relation type that has the highest entailment score, we computed the average of the top 3 highest entailment scores for each relation type, and then we pick the relation type that has the highest amount of this average. Secondly, we used a normalized unweighted voting mechanism. For each template, if its entailment score is more than its neutral and contradiction scores, we count this template as a positive vote. We count these positive votes for each relation type and then divide the count by the total number of templates for the relation type. The relation type with the highest normalized votes will be selected as the final prediction.

5 Experiments

5.1 Experimental Settings

We conducted our experiments on TACRED using the zero-shot RC setup from Sainz et al. (2021). For our experiments, we used DeBERTa which was the off-the-shelf entailment engine that produced the highest results in Sainz et al. (2021).

The set of templates that we used for our experiments included all of the manual templates as well as a small subset of the BIRD-generated templates. The subset was selected according to the pattern selection methods explained in subsection 4.2. Initially, we generate 40 patterns per each manual template. After that, we sort the generated patterns according to a scoring measure and keep the top k patterns with $k = \{1, 2, 3, 4\}$[3].

[3]Values of k higher than 4 did not yield better performance.

The no_relation threshold was selected using 1% of the validation set. Sainz et al. (2021) divided the validation set to 100 stratified folds, ran 100 experiments for each fold, and obtained 100 f1 scores. They reported the median f1 score along with f1 standard deviation. We do the same.

5.2 Results

Table 1 shows the zero-shot RC results including our best results which were obtained using "entailment score" as pattern selection method and "highest entailment score" as inference method. Third-party results are as reported by authors. The table indicates that our results match the current state-of-the-art for zero-shot TACRED (Zhang et al., 2017), and are 1.5 F1 points above Sainz et al. (2021)'s results. The improvement in F1 comes from both better precision and better recall. In order to confirm that the difference in F1 scores between our method and (Sainz et al., 2021) is statistically significant, we ran a significance test using bootstrap resampling experiment with 1000 samples. This test indicated that the difference in F1 scores between our method and (Sainz et al., 2021) is statistically significant with a p-value of 0.3. We find these results encouraging considering that the manual patterns in Sainz et al. (2021) were manually developed by domain experts, whereas the pattern acquisition method in BIRD was developed independently of the TACRED task and its distributional similarity statistics were acquired from a different dataset (a Wikipedia subset) (Rahimi and Surdeanu, 2022).

We experimented with different pattern selection methods as shown in Figure 4. We observed that entailment score performed better overall than the rest. We also observed that as the number of added templates increased, the performance of the models decreased indicating that increasing the number of templates had a negative effect on performance. In general, while BIRD's similarity score was more robust as more templates are considered, the best result was obtained with one added template. Furthermore, we experimented with different inference methods as shown in Figure 5 when the pattern selection method was entailment score (since it produced the highest results). We observed that highest entailment score performed better than the rest. We hypothesize that this is caused by the relatively noisy BIRD generated templates, which suggest that future work is needed to better align BIRD's output with the entailment-driven RC task.

Model	Pr.	Rec.	F1
SuRE	-	-	20.6
DEEPSTRUCT	-	-	36.1
DEEPEX	-	-	49.2
Zero-shot SQuAD	49.7	78.9	57.1
$NLI_{DeBERTa}$	66.3	59.7	62.8 ± 1.7
Wang et al. (2022b)	-	-	**64.3 ± 1.2**
NLI_{BIRD} (ours)	68.8	60.4	**64.3 ± 1.3**

Table 1: Zero-shot RC results. Our best results was obtained by using "entailment score" as pattern selection method and "highest entailment score" as inference method. Top six rows are from third-party zero-shot RC systems as reported by authors. Third party results are from SuRE (Lu et al., 2022), DEEPSTRUCT (Wang et al., 2022a), DEEPEX (Wang et al., 2021a), Zero-shot SQuAD (Cohen et al., 2020), $NLI_{DeBERTa}$ (Sainz et al., 2021), and Wang et al. (2022b).

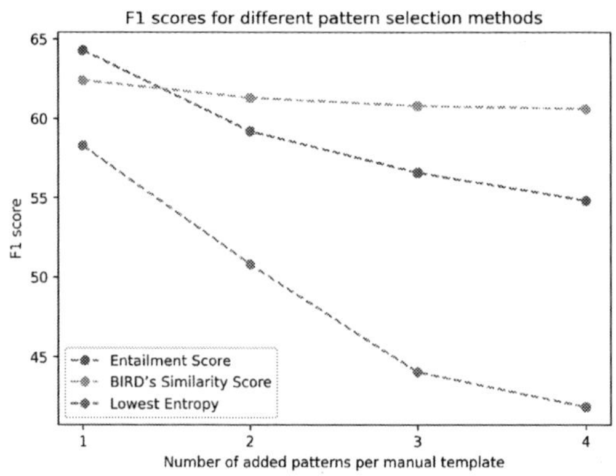

Figure 4: F1 scores for different pattern selection methods.

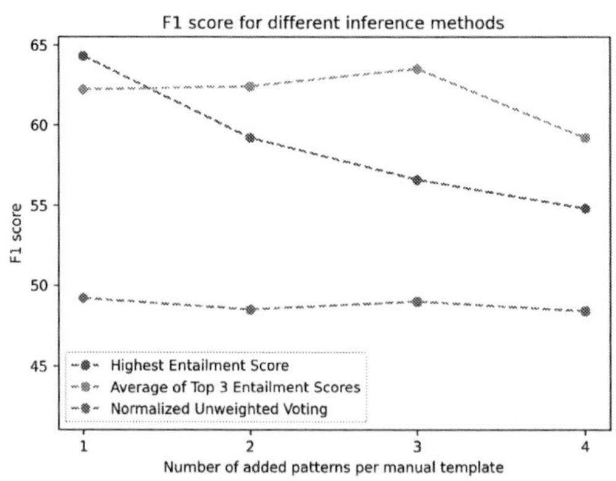

Figure 5: F1 scores for different inference methods when entailment score is used for pattern selection.

6 Conclusions

This paper introduces a zero-shot approach for relation classification. Our direction expands the method of Sainz et al. (2021), which converts the relation extraction task into textual entailment that is informed by manual templates that characterize the relations of interest. Unlike Sainz et al. (2021), we combine manual templates with templates that were automatically-acquired using an adaption of Harris' distributional similarity principle to templates encoded using contextualized representations.

We empirically evaluate our approach on a zero-shot setting of the TACRED relation classification task (Zhang et al., 2017). We investigated multiple strategies to rank the quality of the automatically-acquired templates. All in all, we found that a simple strategy, which considers the top template as ranked by a textual entailment engine, performs the best. Our results match the current state-of-the-art for zero-shot TACRED. We find this result exciting, especially considering that the template acquisition component is disconnected from the TACRED dataset. Beyond these results, this paper opens interesting questions for future work such as how to increase the relevance of the automatically-acquired templates for a specific task.

References

Livio Baldini Soares, Nicholas FitzGerald, Jeffrey Ling, and Tom Kwiatkowski. 2019. Matching the blanks: Distributional similarity for relation learning. In *Proceedings of the 57th Annual Meeting of the Association for Computational Linguistics*, pages 2895–2905, Florence, Italy. Association for Computational Linguistics.

Tom Brown, Benjamin Mann, Nick Ryder, Melanie Subbiah, Jared D Kaplan, Prafulla Dhariwal, Arvind Neelakantan, Pranav Shyam, Girish Sastry, Amanda Askell, et al. 2020. Language models are few-shot learners. *Advances in neural information processing systems*, 33:1877–1901.

Alberto Cetoli. 2020. Exploring the zero-shot limit of FewRel. In *Proceedings of the 28th International Conference on Computational Linguistics*, pages 1447–1451, Barcelona, Spain (Online). International Committee on Computational Linguistics.

Amir DN Cohen, Shachar Rosenman, and Yoav Goldberg. 2020. Relation classification as two-way span-prediction. *arXiv preprint arXiv:2010.04829*.

Thomas Demeester, Tim Rocktäschel, and Sebastian Riedel. 2016. Lifted rule injection for relation embeddings. In *Proceedings of the 2016 Conference on Empirical Methods in Natural Language Processing*, pages 1389–1399, Austin, Texas. Association for Computational Linguistics.

Jacob Devlin, Ming-Wei Chang, Kenton Lee, and Kristina Toutanova. 2019. BERT: Pre-training of deep bidirectional transformers for language understanding. In *Proceedings of the 2019 Conference of the North American Chapter of the Association for Computational Linguistics: Human Language Technologies, Volume 1 (Long and Short Papers)*, pages 4171–4186, Minneapolis, Minnesota. Association for Computational Linguistics.

George Doddington, Alexis Mitchell, Mark Przybocki, Lance Ramshaw, Stephanie Strassel, and Ralph Weischedel. 2004. The automatic content extraction (ACE) program – tasks, data, and evaluation. In *Proceedings of the Fourth International Conference on Language Resources and Evaluation (LREC'04)*, Lisbon, Portugal. European Language Resources Association (ELRA).

Zhengxiao Du, Yujie Qian, Xiao Liu, Ming Ding, Jiezhong Qiu, Zhilin Yang, and Jie Tang. 2021. All nlp tasks are generation tasks: A general pretraining framework. *arXiv preprint arXiv:2103.10360*.

Tianyu Gao, Xu Han, Hao Zhu, Zhiyuan Liu, Peng Li, Maosong Sun, and Jie Zhou. 2019. FewRel 2.0: Towards more challenging few-shot relation classification. In *Proceedings of the 2019 Conference on Empirical Methods in Natural Language Processing and the 9th International Joint Conference on Natural Language Processing (EMNLP-IJCNLP)*, pages 6250–6255, Hong Kong, China. Association for Computational Linguistics.

Jiaying Gong and Hoda Eldardiry. 2021. Prompt-based zero-shot relation classification with semantic knowledge augmentation. *arXiv preprint arXiv:2112.04539*.

Jiale Han, Shuai Zhao, Bo Cheng, Shengkun Ma, and Wei Lu. 2022a. Generative prompt tuning for relation classification. In *Findings of the Association for Computational Linguistics: EMNLP 2022*, pages 3170–3185, Abu Dhabi, United Arab Emirates. Association for Computational Linguistics.

Xu Han, Weilin Zhao, Ning Ding, Zhiyuan Liu, and Maosong Sun. 2022b. Ptr: Prompt tuning with rules for text classification. *AI Open*, 3:182–192.

Xu Han, Hao Zhu, Pengfei Yu, Ziyun Wang, Yuan Yao, Zhiyuan Liu, and Maosong Sun. 2018. FewRel: A large-scale supervised few-shot relation classification dataset with state-of-the-art evaluation. In *Proceedings of the 2018 Conference on Empirical Methods in Natural Language Processing*, pages 4803–4809, Brussels, Belgium. Association for Computational Linguistics.

Zellig S Harris. 1954. Distributional structure. *Word*, 10(2-3):146–162.

Mandar Joshi, Danqi Chen, Yinhan Liu, Daniel S. Weld, Luke Zettlemoyer, and Omer Levy. 2020. SpanBERT: Improving pre-training by representing and predicting spans. *Transactions of the Association for Computational Linguistics*, 8:64–77.

Nanda Kambhatla. 2004. Combining lexical, syntactic, and semantic features with maximum entropy models for information extraction. In *Proceedings of the ACL Interactive Poster and Demonstration Sessions*, pages 178–181, Barcelona, Spain. Association for Computational Linguistics.

Martin Krallinger, Martin Pérez-Pérez, Gael Pérez-Rodríguez, Aitor Blanco-Míguez, Florentino Fdez-Riverola, Salvador Capella-Gutierrez, Anália Lourenço, and Alfonso Valencia. 2017. The biocreative v. 5 evaluation workshop: tasks, organization, sessions and topics.

Omer Levy, Minjoon Seo, Eunsol Choi, and Luke Zettlemoyer. 2017. Zero-shot relation extraction via reading comprehension. In *Proceedings of the 21st Conference on Computational Natural Language Learning (CoNLL 2017)*, pages 333–342, Vancouver, Canada. Association for Computational Linguistics.

Mike Lewis, Yinhan Liu, Naman Goyal, Marjan Ghazvininejad, Abdelrahman Mohamed, Omer Levy, Veselin Stoyanov, and Luke Zettlemoyer. 2020. BART: Denoising sequence-to-sequence pre-training for natural language generation, translation, and comprehension. In *Proceedings of the 58th Annual Meeting of the Association for Computational Linguistics*, pages 7871–7880, Online. Association for Computational Linguistics.

Yinhan Liu, Myle Ott, Naman Goyal, Jingfei Du, Mandar Joshi, Danqi Chen, Omer Levy, Mike Lewis, Luke Zettlemoyer, and Veselin Stoyanov. 2019. Roberta: A robustly optimized bert pretraining approach. *arXiv preprint arXiv:1907.11692*.

Keming Lu, I-Hung Hsu, Wenxuan Zhou, Mingyu Derek Ma, and Muhao Chen. 2022. Summarization as indirect supervision for relation extraction. In *Findings of the Association for Computational Linguistics: EMNLP 2022*, pages 6575–6594, Abu Dhabi, United Arab Emirates. Association for Computational Linguistics.

Shengfei Lyu and Huanhuan Chen. 2021. Relation classification with entity type restriction. In *Findings of the Association for Computational Linguistics: ACL-IJCNLP 2021*, pages 390–395, Online. Association for Computational Linguistics.

Claire Nédellec, Robert Bossy, Jin-Dong Kim, Jung-jae Kim, Tomoko Ohta, Sampo Pyysalo, and Pierre Zweigenbaum. 2013. Overview of BioNLP shared task 2013. In *Proceedings of the BioNLP Shared Task 2013 Workshop*, pages 1–7, Sofia, Bulgaria. Association for Computational Linguistics.

Abiola Obamuyide and Andreas Vlachos. 2018. Zero-shot relation classification as textual entailment. In *Proceedings of the First Workshop on Fact Extraction and VERification (FEVER)*, pages 72–78, Brussels, Belgium. Association for Computational Linguistics.

Giovanni Paolini, Ben Athiwaratkun, Jason Krone, Jie Ma, Alessandro Achille, Rishita Anubhai, Cicero Nogueira dos Santos, Bing Xiang, and Stefano Soatto. 2021. Structured prediction as translation between augmented natural languages. In *9th International Conference on Learning Representations, ICLR 2021*.

Colin Raffel, Noam Shazeer, Adam Roberts, Katherine Lee, Sharan Narang, Michael Matena, Yanqi Zhou, Wei Li, and Peter J Liu. 2020. Exploring the limits of transfer learning with a unified text-to-text transformer. *The Journal of Machine Learning Research*, 21(1):5485–5551.

Mahdi Rahimi and Mihai Surdeanu. 2022. Do transformer networks improve the discovery of rules from text? In *Proceedings of the Thirteenth Language Resources and Evaluation Conference*, pages 3706–3714, Marseille, France. European Language Resources Association.

Tim Rocktäschel, Sameer Singh, and Sebastian Riedel. 2015. Injecting logical background knowledge into embeddings for relation extraction. In *Proceedings of the 2015 Conference of the North American Chapter of the Association for Computational Linguistics: Human Language Technologies*, pages 1119–1129, Denver, Colorado. Association for Computational Linguistics.

Ofer Sabo, Yanai Elazar, Yoav Goldberg, and Ido Dagan. 2021. Revisiting few-shot relation classification: Evaluation data and classification schemes. *Transactions of the Association for Computational Linguistics*, 9:691–706.

Oscar Sainz, Oier Lopez de Lacalle, Gorka Labaka, Ander Barrena, and Eneko Agirre. 2021. Label verbalization and entailment for effective zero and few-shot relation extraction. In *Proceedings of the 2021 Conference on Empirical Methods in Natural Language Processing*, pages 1199–1212, Online and Punta Cana, Dominican Republic. Association for Computational Linguistics.

Timo Schick and Hinrich Schütze. 2021. Exploiting cloze-questions for few-shot text classification and natural language inference. In *Proceedings of the 16th Conference of the European Chapter of the Association for Computational Linguistics: Main Volume*, pages 255–269, Online. Association for Computational Linguistics.

Taylor Shin, Yasaman Razeghi, Robert L Logan IV, Eric Wallace, and Sameer Singh. 2020. Autoprompt: Eliciting knowledge from language models with automatically generated prompts. *arXiv preprint arXiv:2010.15980*.

Chenguang Wang, Xiao Liu, Zui Chen, Haoyun Hong, Jie Tang, and Dawn Song. 2021a. Zero-shot information extraction as a unified text-to-triple translation. In *Proceedings of the 2021 Conference on Empirical Methods in Natural Language Processing*, pages 1225–1238, Online and Punta Cana, Dominican Republic. Association for Computational Linguistics.

Chenguang Wang, Xiao Liu, Zui Chen, Haoyun Hong, Jie Tang, and Dawn Song. 2022a. DeepStruct: Pretraining of language models for structure prediction. In *Findings of the Association for Computational Linguistics: ACL 2022*, pages 803–823, Dublin, Ireland. Association for Computational Linguistics.

Ruize Wang, Duyu Tang, Nan Duan, Zhongyu Wei, Xuanjing Huang, Jianshu Ji, Guihong Cao, Daxin Jiang, and Ming Zhou. 2021b. K-Adapter: Infusing Knowledge into Pre-Trained Models with Adapters. In *Findings of the Association for Computational Linguistics: ACL-IJCNLP 2021*, pages 1405–1418, Online. Association for Computational Linguistics.

Tianyin Wang, Jianwei Wang, and Ziqian Zeng. 2022b. Learning with silver standard data for zero-shot relation extraction. *arXiv preprint arXiv:2211.13883*.

Shanchan Wu and Yifan He. 2019. Enriching pretrained language model with entity information for relation classification. In *Proceedings of the 28th ACM international conference on information and knowledge management*, pages 2361–2364.

Ikuya Yamada, Akari Asai, Hiroyuki Shindo, Hideaki Takeda, and Yuji Matsumoto. 2020. LUKE: Deep contextualized entity representations with entity-aware self-attention. In *Proceedings of the 2020 Conference on Empirical Methods in Natural Language Processing (EMNLP)*, pages 6442–6454, Online. Association for Computational Linguistics.

Daojian Zeng, Kang Liu, Siwei Lai, Guangyou Zhou, and Jun Zhao. 2014. Relation classification via convolutional deep neural network. In *Proceedings of COLING 2014, the 25th International Conference on Computational Linguistics: Technical Papers*, pages 2335–2344, Dublin, Ireland. Dublin City University and Association for Computational Linguistics.

Wenjie Zhang, Xiaoning Song, Zhenhua Feng, Tianyang Xu, and Xiaojun Wu. 2023. Labelprompt: Effective prompt-based learning for relation classification. *arXiv preprint arXiv:2302.08068*.

Yuhao Zhang, Victor Zhong, Danqi Chen, Gabor Angeli, and Christopher D. Manning. 2017. Position-aware attention and supervised data improve slot filling. In *Proceedings of the 2017 Conference on Empirical Methods in Natural Language Processing*, pages 35–45, Copenhagen, Denmark. Association for Computational Linguistics.

MUX-PLMs: Data Multiplexing for High-throughput Language Models

Vishvak Murahari[1] **Ameet Deshpande**[1] **Carlos E. Jimenez**[1]
Izhak Shafran[2] **Mingqiu Wang**[2] **Yuan Cao**[2] **Karthik Narasimhan**[1]

[1]Princeton University [2] Google Brain
`muraharics.princeton.edu`

Abstract

The widespread adoption of large language models such as ChatGPT and Bard has led to unprecedented demand for these technologies. The burgeoning cost of inference for ever-increasing model sizes coupled with hardware shortages has limited affordable access and poses a pressing need for efficiency approaches geared towards high throughput and performance. Multi-input multi-output (MIMO) algorithms such as data multiplexing, offer a promising solution with a many-fold increase in throughput by performing inference for multiple inputs at the cost of a single input. Yet these approaches are not currently performant enough to be deployed in modern systems. We change that by developing MUX-PLMs, a class of high throughput pre-trained language models (PLMs) trained with data multiplexing, that can be fine-tuned for any downstream task to yield high-throughput high-performance. Our novel multiplexing and demultiplexing modules proficiently entangle and disentangle inputs, and enable high-performance high throughput MUX-PLMs that are competitive with vanilla PLMs while achieving 2x/5x inference speedup with only a $1-4\%$ drop on a broad suite of tasks. [1]

1 Introduction

Language models like ChatGPT (OpenAI, 2023), PaLM (Chowdhery et al., 2022), T5 (Raffel et al., 2020), and CM3 (Aghajanyan et al., 2022), have seen unprecedented adoption in diverse sectors ranging from education and healthcare to manufacturing and marketing. The proficiency of these tools has led to unprecedented demand for these models, with users facing frequent outages and capacity limits. Additionally, ever-increasing model sizes and hardware shortages have constrained models' ability to handle a very high load of requests, thus limiting large-scale affordable access to these models. These trends bring into focus the need for high-throughput, high-performance, efficient, and environmentally responsible models that can be deployed at scale to meet the quickly growing demand.

Multi-input Multi-output architectures (MIMO) (Havasi et al., 2021; Ramé et al., 2021; Murahari et al., 2022) are a promising hardware-agnostic and architecture-agnostic paradigm that perform inference for multiple inputs *simultaneously* at the cost of a single input. This efficiency paradigm is natively geared towards yielding high-throughput models, in addition to being complementary in approach and motivation to current efficiency methods such as pruning, quantization, and distillation. Interestingly, MIMO approaches are partly inspired by the human brain's extraordinary ability to process multiple inputs and propagate information at a high bandwidth with a few neural codes (Blumhagen et al., 2011; Akam and Kullmann, 2014; Pirschel and Kretzberg, 2016; Hong et al., 2016; Friedrich et al., 2004).

Murahari et al. (2022) introduced data multiplexing, a MIMO technique that can enable a many-fold increase in throughput. The method compresses N different instances into a single "multiplexed" hidden representation before decompressing it into N independent predictions. While they show the plausibility of MIMO training, their method leads to a significant drop in performance ($20-30\%$ points) compared to state-of-the-art models.

In this work, we introduce MUX-PLMs, a class of high-throughput pre-trained language models trained in a MIMO fashion with data multiplexing to process multiple inputs (2-10) simultaneously with a forward pass over a single instance. MUX-PLMs offer up to 400% improvement in throughput over baseline pre-trained models while only being ~ 4 points and ~ 2 points worse than baseline pre-trained language models for text classification and token classification tasks, respec-

[1]Code + Models: `https://github.com/princeton-nlp/datamux-pretraining/`.

Proceedings of the 8th Workshop on Representation Learning for NLP (RepL4NLP 2023), pages 196–211
July 13, 2023 ©2023 Association for Computational Linguistics

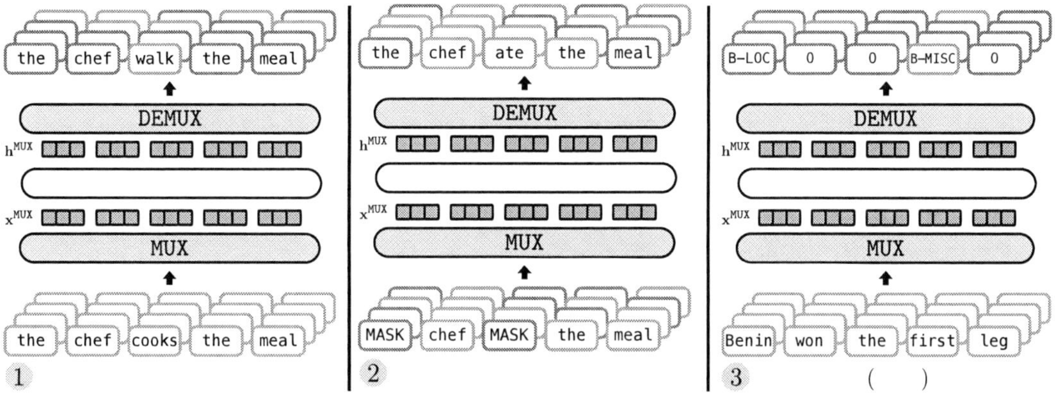

Figure 1: Illustrating the training process for MUX-PLMs. MUX-PLMs are first primed for MIMO style training with a token-retrieval auto-encoding task, where the model is trained to output the tokens in the N inputs. MUX-PLMs are then pre-trained by adapting standard pre-training objectives (BERT in this example), to MIMO style training with data multiplexing. The resulting MUX-BERT model, similar to standard PLMs, provides a general model initialization that can be fine-tuned on any downstream task (NER in this example). Output predictions are shown above the system head with highlighted predictions contributing to the gradient update; violet indicates a correct prediction while orange indicates an incorrect prediction. Red highlighted tokens in the input indicate a position that has been masked.

tively. MUX-PLMs, like other pre-trained language models, provide general model initialization that can be fine-tuned for *any* downstream task. We demonstrate the effectiveness and generality of our MUX-PLMs class of pre-trained models by training MUX-BERT and MUX-ELECTRA models, which are trained with pre-trained objectives adapted from BERT (Devlin et al., 2019) and ELECTRA (Clark et al., 2020) respectively, although in a MIMO fashion with data multiplexing.

Our work is the first to introduce MIMO architectures to PLMs. To enable this, we first develop a new demultiplexing module, RSA-demux (Figure 2), that randomly initializes and learns private key vectors to recover the multiple outputs from a multiplexed representation. Secondly, we introduce a new *Contextual Multiplexer* module (Figure 3) that uses a cross-instance attention-based mechanism to aggregate context across the set of multiplexed instances, which seems to be particularly effective for token-level tasks. Thirdly, our three-stage training algorithm (Figure 1) enables stable and efficient training of MUX-PLMs.

Importantly, MUX-PLMs are complementary to existing state-of-the-art model compression techniques. We hope our work validates MIMO architectures as a promising complementary direction to existing efficiency techniques. Consequently, we hope future research develops MIMO architectures in tandem with other efficiency approaches, leveraging the best of both paradigms. We publicly release our models and code to promote open-source research on the next generation of MIMO architectures for large language models.

2 Related Work

Efficient Inference with Transformers Recent methods in NLP rely heavily on transfer learning through Transformer-based (Vaswani et al., 2017) language models trained on large text corpora using self-supervised objectives, such as autoregressive (Radford and Narasimhan, 2018) or masked language modeling (Devlin et al., 2019). Prior analysis on pre-training language models has observed power-law scaling of model performance with respect to model size (Kaplan et al., 2020), leading the community to develop ever-larger language models. It is also generally recognized that pre-trained language models are significantly over-parameterized; effectively learning a *subnetwork* that utilizes only a relatively small number of their total parameters (Voita et al., 2019; Michel et al., 2019; Gordon et al., 2020; Prasanna et al., 2020).

The ubiquity of pre-trained language models, their growing size, and over-parameterization has inspired extensive research on improving inference efficiency. This includes methods such as structured pruning (Liu et al., 2019; Wang et al., 2020; Lagunas et al., 2021; Xia et al., 2022; Yang et al., 2022), knowledge distillation (Hinton et al., 2015;

Sanh et al., 2019; Sun et al., 2020; Jiao et al., 2020; Yin et al., 2021), quantization (Zafrir et al., 2019; Shen et al., 2020), and data multiplexing (Murahari et al., 2022). These approaches assume that PLMs are highly over-parametrized and attempt to approximate a large function by learning a smaller, compressed, version of the original model. Past work has also focused on unstructured pruning for both task finetuning (Chen et al., 2020; Sanh et al., 2020) and pre-trained (Zafrir et al., 2021; Jiang et al., 2022) language model settings, but don't increase model throughput due to hardware limits.

Multi-input Multi-output Models While pruning, quantization, and distillation seek to reduce overparameterization by reducing models' representational capacity, other lines of work seek to exploit overparameterization in other ways. Multi-input Multi-output (MIMO) architectures (Havasi et al., 2021; Ramé et al., 2021; Murahari et al., 2022) train models using mixed-instance representations, i.e. Zhang et al. (2018), in order to obtain predictions for multiple instances simultaneously. Unlike efficiency methods, Havasi et al. (2021) and Ramé et al. (2021) try to obtain better performance by inducing multiple subnetworks in a single convolutional model to perform "ensembling for free" during inference. Data multiplexing, introduced in DataMUX (Murahari et al., 2022), aims to improve model efficiency by training Transformer models with mixed-instance representations to perform simultaneous inference for language tasks, thereby improving inference throughput many-fold. Currently, MIMO architectures have only been used in a limited setting, achieving middling performance. Our work training PLMs with data multiplexing, dramatically improves inference throughput while preserving high accuracy for downstream tasks.

3 Methodology

We briefly introduce readers to the data multiplexing MIMO architecture (Murahari et al., 2022), which we denote T-MUX. We then detail our novel approach to train MUX-PLMs to yield high-throughput and performant language models.

3.1 T-MUX: Data multiplexing with Transformer

Data multiplexing allows parallel processing of multiple sequences with a single forward or backward pass through the model (M) and requires two crucial components, multiplexer, and demultiplexer.

Multiplexer The multiplexer module (MUX) combines an ordered set of multiple inputs – $X^{1:N} = \left(\mathbf{x}^1, \ldots, \mathbf{x}^N\right)$ into a single superimposed representation ($\mathbf{x}^{\text{MUX}}$). If $\mathbf{x}^i \in \mathbb{R}^d$, the multiplexer is a transformation (MUX: $\mathbb{R}^{N \times d} \to \mathbb{R}^d$) such that $\mathbf{x}^{\text{MUX}} = \text{MUX}\left(X^{1:N}\right)$.

To ensure MUX is an order-preserving transformation,T-MUX samples a vector ($\mathbf{v}^i \in \mathbb{R}^d$) from a standard multivariate Gaussian and applies the Hadamard product (element-wise multiplication) with the corresponding input representation ($\mathbf{x}^i$) before summing up vectors for all positions.

$$\begin{aligned} \mathbf{x}^{\text{MUX}} &= \text{MUX}\left(X^{1:N}\right) = \frac{1}{N}\sum_{i=1}^{N} \mathbf{x}^i \odot \mathbf{v}^i \\ \mathbf{v}^i &\in \mathbb{R}^d \sim \mathcal{N}\left(\mathbf{0}, \mathbf{I}\right) \end{aligned} \tag{1}$$

The model processes the multiplexed representation and emits a multiplexed hidden state – $\mathbf{h}^{\text{MUX}} = M\left(\mathbf{x}^{\text{MUX}}\right)$. To multiplex Transformers' sequenced inputs $\left(\mathbf{x}^i = \left(\mathbf{x}_1^i, \ldots, \mathbf{x}_L^i\right)\right)$ of length L, T-MUX applies the same $\mathbf{v}^i$ to all L positions of instance i.

$$\begin{aligned} &\mathbf{x}^{\text{MUX}} = \text{MUX}\left(X^{1:N}\right) = \\ &\left(\frac{1}{N}\sum_{i=1}^{N} \mathbf{x}_1^i \odot \mathbf{v}^i, \ldots, \frac{1}{N}\sum_{i=1}^{N} \mathbf{x}_L^i \odot \mathbf{v}^i\right) \end{aligned} \tag{2}$$

Demultiplexer A prediction needs to be made for each instance in $X^{1:N}$, and T-MUX's demultiplexer module (DeMUX) achieves this by separating the superimposed output ($\mathbf{h}^{\text{MUX}}$) into N output representations corresponding to the input ($\mathbf{h}^1, \ldots, \mathbf{h}^N$).

$$\begin{aligned} \mathbf{h}^i &= \text{DeMUX}\left(\mathbf{h}^{\text{MUX}}, \mathbf{p}^i\right) \\ \mathbf{h}_j^i &= \text{DeMUX}\left({\mathbf{h}^{\text{MUX}}}_j, \mathbf{p}^i\right) \end{aligned} \tag{3}$$

The vector $\mathbf{p}^i \in \mathbb{R}^d$ is dynamically generated for each instance (i) with the help of a prefix that is added to the input and re-used for all positions in the instance. They add a $\textit{prefix}_i$ to $\mathbf{x}^i$, represented by the following pattern, where ϵ^i is a special token, and $\mathbf{p}^i$ is set to be the output corresponding to token

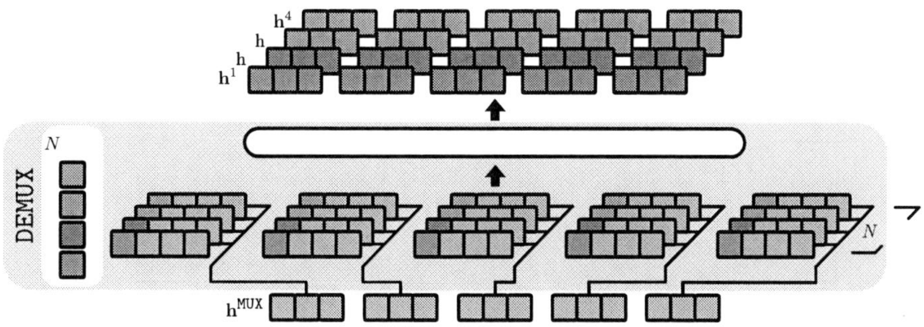

Figure 2: Illustrating our novel RSA-inspired demultiplexing module. The module is initialized with N key vectors which are used to demultiplex the transformed multiplexed representations (h^{MUX}). The keys are concatenated with h^{MUX} and are processed with an MLP to generate the demultiplexed output representations ($h_1 \cdots h_4$).

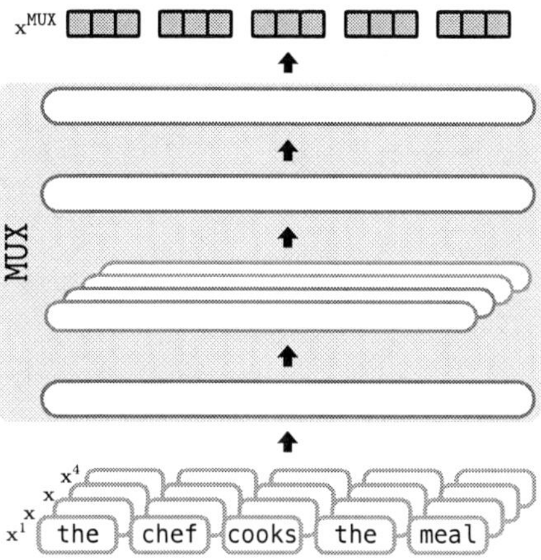

Figure 3: Illustrating our attention-based multiplexing module. The module generates contextual representations for instances $x_1 \cdots x_4$ with a Transformer layer and then applies a hadamard product between the contextual representations and the corresponding multivariate gaussian to generate instance-conditioned representations. The final multiplexed representations are generated by first applying another Transformer layer, which attends across the instances for all the positions in the sequence, and then averaging across the instances.

i in the prefix.

$$
\begin{aligned}
\textit{prefix}^1 &= [\epsilon^1, \epsilon^{\text{pad}}, \ldots, \epsilon^{\text{pad}}] \\
\textit{prefix}^2 &= [\epsilon^{\text{pad}}, \epsilon^2, \epsilon^{\text{pad}}, \ldots, \epsilon^{\text{pad}}] \\
& \ldots \\
\textit{prefix}^N &= [\epsilon^{\text{pad}}, \ldots, \epsilon^{\text{pad}}, \epsilon^N]
\end{aligned}
$$

3.2 MUX-PLMs: Data multiplexing for high-throughput language models

We propose MUX-PLMs, a class of high-throughput pre-trained Transformer-based language models trained in a MIMO fashion with data multiplexing. To demonstrate the viability and the generality of this class of models, we pre-train Transformer models with objectives based on BERT and ELECTRA, to get MUX-BERT and MUX-ELECTRA respectively. MUX-PLMs are trained with our three stage training algorithm (Figure 1). Firstly, MUX-PLMs are trained with the token retrieval task in T-MUX, which is an auto-encoding setup to decode all the tokens in the multiplexed input. This simple auto-encoding task is critical to prime the model for MIMO-style data multiplexing. The MUX-PLMs are then pre-trained with standard pre-training objectives but adapted to MIMO-fashioned training with data multiplexing. MUX-PLMs show significant throughput improvement over standard pre-trained LMs while matching their downstream task accuracies. Finally, MUX-PLMs, like other pre-trained language models, provide general model initialization that can be fine-tuned for *any* downstream task.

Contextual multiplexer T-MUX's multiplexer multiplexes tokens independent of 1) tokens in the same position in other instances and 2) other tokens in the instance, which could lead to suboptimal representations. We, therefore, explore a contextual multiplexing scheme that aggregates context both from tokens in the same instance and tokens in the same position of other instances (Figure 3). We first use a single transformer layer $\text{TRANS}_{\text{ctx}}$ to get contextual representations $\mathbf{h}^i_{\text{ctx}} = \text{TRANS}_{\text{ctx}}\left(\mathbf{x}^i_1, \ldots, \mathbf{x}^i_L\right)$ of length L. We apply a hadamard product with a multivariate gaussian $\mathbf{v}^i$ to all L positions.

$$\mathbf{g}^i_{\text{ctx}} = \mathbf{h}^i_{\text{ctx}} \odot \mathbf{v}^i \tag{4}$$

We generate multiplexed representations, $\mathbf{x}^{\text{MUX}}$, by applying another transformer layer $\text{TRANS}_{\text{inst}}$ across encoded representations from N instances at each position from 1 to L. This is done by transposing $\mathbf{g}_{\text{ctx}}$ and applying $\text{TRANS}_{\text{inst}}$.

$$\mathbf{x}^{\text{MUX}} = \text{TRANS}_{\text{inst}}\left(\mathbf{g}_{\text{ctx}}^{\top}\right) \tag{5}$$

RSA demultiplexer The *demultiplexer* in T-MUX requires a prefix whose length scales linearly with the number of instances (N), thus reducing the effective context length during pre-training, which degrades performance (Ainslie et al., 2020; Zaheer et al., 2020; Beltagy et al., 2020). Furthermore, it decreases throughput during inference for large N because the model must process an extra prefix of length N for each of the N instances. To address these issues, we draw inspiration from the RSA cryptosystem (Rivest et al., 1978) to randomly initialize and learn N (private) key vectors $(\mathbf{k}_1, \ldots, \mathbf{k}_N,\ \mathbf{k}_i \in \mathbb{R}^d)$ which are keys that can be used to demultiplex the output representation (Figure 2).

$$\begin{aligned} \mathbf{h}^i &= \text{DeMUX}\left(\mathbf{h}^{\text{MUX}}, \mathbf{k}^i\right) \\ \mathbf{h}^i_j &= \text{DeMUX}\left(\mathbf{h}^{\text{MUX}}{}_j, \mathbf{k}^i\right) \end{aligned} \tag{6}$$

Akin to RSA, $\mathbf{v_i}$ and $\mathbf{k_i}$ can be treated as the keys for multiplexing (encryption) and demultiplexing (decryption) while ensuring that, unlike T-MUX, the input sequence length does not change and thereby leading to an improvement in throughput. Importantly, this architecture ensures that the keys better transfer across the different stages of training as they are no longer conditioned on the input instances.

4 Experimental Setup

Datasets We pre-train all models on Wikipedia (Foundation) and Bookscorpus (Zhu et al., 2015). We evaluate on all datasets from the GLUE benchmark (Wang et al., 2018), which are CoLA (Warstadt et al., 2019), SST-2 (Socher et al., 2013), MRPC (Dolan and Brockett, 2005), QQP (qqp), STS-B (Cer et al., 2017), MNLI (Williams et al., 2018), QNLI (Wang et al., 2018), RTE (Wang et al., 2018), and WNLI (Levesque et al., 2012). We also evaluate on token classification tasks – named entity recognition (Sang and Meulder, 2003) and POS tagging (Grünewald et al., 2021). We don't report average over the two smallest tasks in GLUE, WNLI and CoLA, as we observe high variance across seeds. All numbers are reported on the dev split. We report scores for all tasks in Appendix E.

Model	N	GLUE		Token		↗
		Mean (std)	Max	Mean (std)	Max	
BERT	1	**85.4 (0.0)**	**85.4**	**95.8 (0.0)**	**95.8**	1.0×
ELECTRA		82.1 (0.0)	82.1	95.3 (0.0)	95.3	1.0×
T-MUX	2	60.4 (0.6)	61.8	81.4 (0.1)	81.5	1.9×
MUX-BERT‡		**82.5 (0.6)**	**83.4**	**95.2 (0.1)**	**95.4**	**2.0×**
MUX-ELEC‡		**82.5 (0.4)**	83.1	95.0 (0.0)	95.1	**2.0×**
T-MUX	5	59.7 (0.6)	60.6	81.3 (0.2)	81.5	4.4×
MUX-BERT‡		**80.3 (0.4)**	**80.9**	**93.6 (0.1)**	**93.6**	**4.9×**
MUX-ELEC‡		79.8 (0.6)	80.5	93.4 (0.0)	93.5	**4.9×**
T-MUX	10	58.1 (0.5)	59.1	79.7 (0.2)	80.0	8.4×
MUX-BERT‡		77.8 (0.6)	78.8	91.6 (0.1)	**91.8**	**9.8×**
MUX-ELEC‡		**78.2 (0.6)**	**79.0**	**91.7 (0.1)**	**91.8**	9.7×

Table 1: Average GLUE and token-level classification scores for the BASE (L=12, H=768) configuration, across ELECTRA, BERT, and MUX-PLMs for $N \in \{1, 2, 5, 10\}$. ‡ indicates our models and ↗ indicates throughput increase w.r.t. to a vanilla $\text{BERT}_{\text{BASE}}$ model. All models are evaluated on 5 seeds with mean and max scores reported.

Models We experiment with ELECTRA and BERT pre-training objectives and present the pre-trained multiplexed models **MUX-BERT** and **MUX-ELECTRA** for $N = 2, 5$ and 10. To simplify training, we use a random generator to train MUX-ELECTRA models, presented as an ablation in Clark et al. (2020), instead of using a smaller masked LM. Except where otherwise noted, we do not use the contextual MUX module, but instead, use the RSA demultiplexing module. Refer to Appendix B and C for implementation details.

Baselines We run experiments to compare our models against T-MUX, from Murahari et al. (2022) and baseline PLMs - ELECTRA and BERT, across three different model configurations (SMALL, BASE, and LARGE). We also provide a comparison to results reported in recent PLM pruning and distillation papers in Table 2.

Multi-run evaluation We evaluate all models across 5 random seeds to reduce variance for smaller datasets which is caused by the randomized order in which we multiplex instances in the batch. We report both the average and maximum scores across seeds in Table 1 to understand the importance of ordering the multiplexed instances and report average across seeds for all other results.

5 Results

5.1 Comparing MUX-PLMs with PLMs and T-MUX

Table 1 shows that both **MUX-BERT and MUX-ELECTRA outperform T-MUX at all levels of multiplexing** (N), with improvements between 12 and 20 points on GLUE and token-classification tasks respectively. Furthermore, MUX-PLMs' efficient RSA-inspired demultiplexing method allows it to achieve faster throughput than T-MUX, increasing it by over 16% for $N = 10$.

Moreover, **MUX-PLMs provide a significant boost in throughput (N times faster) when compared to PLMs, without a significant loss in performance.** For example, MUX-ELECTRA ($N = 2$) is 0.4 points better and only 0.3 points worse than ELECTRA for GLUE and TOKEN tasks respectively, while being 2× faster. Similarly, MUX-BERT ($N = 2$) is within 3 and 0.6 points of BERT for GLUE and TOKEN tasks respectively, while being significantly faster. We also observe that as N increases, MUX-PLMs' throughput is significantly better, though performance compared to PLMs can degrade. This is because a large N implies that MUX-PLMs must parallelly process more instances, thus having to share network parameters and activations with a larger number of instances, thus improving throughput and degrading performance. For example, the gap between ELECTRA and MUX-ELECTRA on TOKEN for $N = 2$ is 0.2 points and increases to 3.5 points for $N = 10$, which shows that N serves as a parameter to control the performance-throughput trade-off. We explore this further in Section 5.3 and Figure 4.

Model	↗	QNLI	QQP	SST2
BERT	1.0×	90.5	91.2	91.7
MUX-BERT (N=2)	2.0×	88.2	90.4	90.6
MUX-BERT (N=5)	4.9×	85.6	88.8	86.9
Use additional unlabelled or task-specific data				
DistilBERT$_6$	2.0×	89.2	88.5	91.3
Block Pruning	2.7×	89.7	-	91.2
Prune OFA	1.0×	90.3	91.2	91.5
Hybrid Approaches				
TinyBERT$_6$	2.0×	91.1	91.1	93.0
CoFi	2.7×	91.3	-	93.0
AutoTinyBERT	4.3×	89.7	89.9	91.4
MobileBERT	2.3×	91.0	-	92.1

Table 2: MUX-PLMs are complementary to existing efficiency methods, while being competitive standalone. Contrary to existing methods, MUX-PLMs *do not use additional unlabelled and task-specific data* and can be easily fine-tuned for *any* downstream task without architectural modifications. The inference speedups (↗) are reported against BERT$_{\text{BASE}}$.

Config	Model	GLUE	Token	↗
SMALL	BERT	80.6	94.0	5.9×
	T-MUX	59.5	81.8	8.7×
	MUX-BERT‡	79.0	93.3	11.5×
BASE	BERT	85.4	95.8	1.0×
	T-MUX	60.4	81.4	1.9×
	MUX-BERT‡	82.5	95.2	2.0×
LARGE	BERT	85.8	95.6	0.3×
	T-MUX	61.7	80.9	0.6×
	MUX-BERT‡	84.1	95.2	0.6×

Table 3: Changing the model size for MUX-BERT ($N = 2$) models. Across different model sizes, MUX-BERT outperforms T-MUX and achieve higher throughput (indicated under ↗ column). ‡ = our models.

5.2 Comparing MUX-PLMs with recent model compression methods

We compare our MUX-PLM models with other efficient learning methods, such as pruning and distillation, in Table 2. Contrary to other methods, our *vanilla* MUX-PLMs achieve competitive performance and significant throughput improvement without additional unlabeled and task-specific data, and can be easily fine-tuned to *any* downstream task without any architectural modifications. For instance, when compared to DistilBERT, MUX-BERT ($N = 2$) does 1 point worse on QNLI and 2 points better on QQP while being equally fast and not requiring any additional unlabeled data.

More broadly, methods like CoFi, AutoTinyBERT, and MobileBERT show that combining a wide range of paradigms (for example, CoFi combines structured pruning and knowledge distillation, AutoTinyBERT combines knowledge distillation and neural architecture search, and MobileBERT combines knowledge distillation with novel architectural innovations) is a promising approach towards efficient high-performance models.

Towards this end, MUX-PLMs are complementary in both approach and motivation to these methods, and can evolve in tandem with existing efficiency methods. MUX-PLMs demonstrate the viability of MIMO architectures for PLMs, in addition to being complementary to existing approaches, and we hope that MIMO architectures develop and evolve with other efficiency approaches while leveraging the best of all efficiency methods.

5.3 Effect of varying model size

In this section, we show that **our multiplexing techniques work on a host of model sizes** and report results for MUX-BERT on three models sizes, SMALL, BASE, and LARGE for $N = 2$ (Table 3). We report results for other values of N in the appendix. MUX-BERT's performance is close to that of BERT for all model sizes while having a significantly better throughput (the gap is less than 0.7 points for TOKEN tasks and 2.9 points for GLUE for close to twice the throughput). Multiplexing works effectively on all model sizes, with the drops with respect to BERT being 1.6 and 1.7 points on GLUE for SMALL and LARGE respectively. MUX-BERT's throughput is always $\approx 2\times$ that of BERT, which shows that a spectrum of MUX-PLM model sizes can be multiplexed during pre-training with competitive performance and with significantly higher throughput.

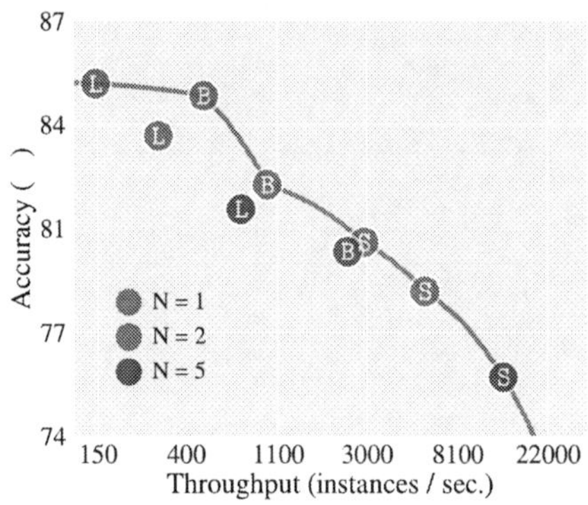

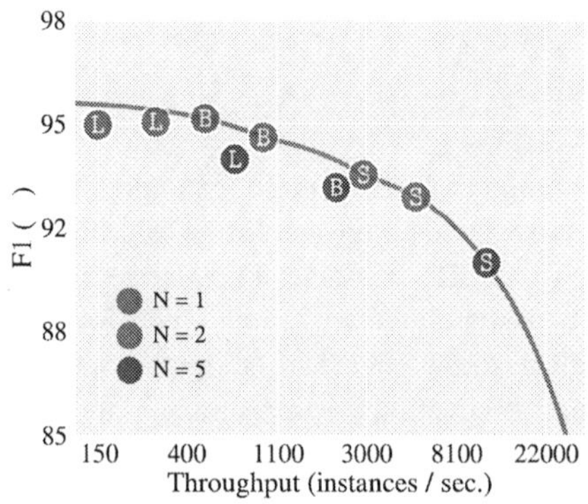

Figure 4: (Top) BERT GLUE performance and throughput and (Bottom) BERT Token task performance and throughput, for $N \in \{1, 2, 5, 10\}$ with the SMALL, BASE, and LARGE configurations (illustrated as S/B/L). All multiplexed models lie either on or very close to the Pareto frontier (shown in grey).

Pre-trained models typically have a performance-computational efficiency trade-off, with larger models having better performance but worse computational efficiency. MUX-PLMs offers a similar trade-off, with large N leading to better throughput but lower performance. To understand this trade-off, we plot the performance and throughput of BERT and MUX-BERT for different model sizes and draw the pareto-optimal envelope (Figure 4). For any model on the envelope, no model has both better accuracy and throughput. Users would only choose models on the envelope because for every model within the envelope, there always exists a model on the envelope which has *both* better performance *and* throughput. We note that **all multiplexed models lie either on or very close to the Pareto frontier**, for both TOKEN and GLUE tasks. This suggests that given an accuracy threshold, MUX-PLM models will usually be faster than PLMs. For instance, if we wanted the highest throughput model with a performance $\geq 77\%$ on GLUE, the optimal BERT model is the SMALL configuration with a throughput of 2815 (in/s), but for the MUX-BERT model would be the $N = 2$ with the SMALL configuration, achieving a significantly higher throughput of 5539 (in/s).

Model	Mux (N)	MNLI			QQP		
		No Ens	Ens	Δ	No Ens	Ens	Δ
MUX-BERT	**2**	80.6	**81.2**	+ 0.6	90.4	**90.8**	+ 0.4
	5	77.2	**78.8**	+ 1.6	88.8	**89.7**	+ 0.9
	10	73.6	**74.8**	+ 1.2	86.9	**87.7**	+ 0.8
MUX-ELEC	**2**	80.3	**80.8**	+ 0.5	90.6	**90.9**	+ 0.3
	5	77.0	**78.4**	+ 1.4	89.1	**89.9**	+ 0.8
	10	74.6	**76.0**	+ 1.4	87.6	**88.3**	+ 0.7

Table 4: Ensembling results for MUX-BERT and MUX-ELECTRA models for $N \in \{2, 5, 10\}$. *Ens* denotes Ensembling. Ensembling improves performance for all the models, with the gains increasing with increasing N. This suggests that the multiplexing approach can be naturally adapted to load-balancing applications, where the ensembling strategy can be changed based on demand.

5.4 Ensembling MUX-PLMs

As opposed to feeding N different instances to MUX-PLMs to improve throughput, we consider an alternate setting where we feed the same instance N times and build an ensemble by averaging the N class logits to make a single prediction. We randomly permute the batch, after duplicating the instance N times, to prevent distribution shift. We use the BASE size models for $N \in \{2, 5, 10\}$ for both MUX-BERT and MUX-ELECTRA (Table 4). **The ensemble model does significantly better than the non-ensemble variant** on both MNLI and QQP for all values of N (e.g., 1.6 and

Mux (N)	Model	Mux	Demux	GLUE	Token
2	MUX-BERT	Non-contextual	RSA-DeMUX	82.5	95.2
	Ablation 1	Non-contextual	Prefix	**83.2**	**95.3**
	Ablation 2	Contextual	RSA-DeMUX	82.3	95.3
5	MUX-BERT	Non-contextual	RSA-DeMUX	**80.3**	93.6
	Ablation 1	Non-contextual	Prefix	78.6	<u>38.9</u>
	Ablation 2	Contextual	RSA-DeMUX	76.8	**94.2**
10	MUX-BERT	Non-contextual	RSA-DeMUX	**77.8**	91.6
	Ablation 1	Non-contextual	Prefix	76.6	<u>25.6</u>
	Ablation 2	Contextual	RSA-DeMUX	76.0	**93.3**

Table 5: Ablation analysis for MUX-BERT (base configuration) for $N \in \{2, 5, 10\}$. Across most configurations, the prefix demultiplexing variant performs worse than our proposed approach and fails to converge for token-level tasks for $N \in \{5, 10\}$ (underlined numbers). The new contextual multiplexing variant (Contextual) outperforms Non-contextual on token-level tasks.

0.9 points on $N = 5$ MUX-BERT for the two tasks). We note that the improvement over the non-ensemble variant (Δ) is better for higher N, due to the larger ensemble size. This result shows that non-ensemble variants are faster but perform slightly worse, while the ensemble variant performs better but is slower. A spectrum of models lie between these two extremes, where only a fraction of the N multiplexed representations can be ensembled, allowing users to trade off performance and speed.

6 Analysis

6.1 Ablation study

We analyze multiplexing and demultiplexing components of MUX-PLMs and report the results in Table 5. We consider two variants, one which uses the prefix demultiplexing proposed in T-MUX instead of our proposed RSA-DeMUX and another which uses Contextual multiplexing instead of Non-contextual. We note that Variant 1, which uses prefix demultiplexing, performs worse than our MUX-BERT, other than for $N = 2$. In fact, Variant 1 does not converge for TOKEN tasks for $N = 5$ and $N = 10$ and performs 1.7 and 1.2 points worse on GLUE when compared to MUX-BERT.

Variant 2 uses Contextual multiplexing which takes into account other tokens present in the instance and also tokens present in the same position of other instances. This variant performs better than Non-contextual for TOKEN tasks (almost over 1.7 points on TOKEN for $N = 10$) but performs worse for GLUE tasks. We believe that Contextual multiplexing's better performance in TOKEN is because the model needs to make a prediction for every single position in the instance, which requires it to efficiently multiplex all token positions in the output. However, for GLUE tasks, the model needs to make a prediction only for the `[CLS]` token, for which Non-contextual multiplexing suffices.

6.2 Muxology: Analyzing hidden representations of multiplexed models

To understand the nature of representations being learned by MUX-BERT models, we analyze the absolute value of activations and entropy of the attention distribution across all the layers of the Transformer encoder, averaged over the evaluation split of WikiText-103 (Merity et al., 2016) (Figure 5). We report this analysis for different values of N and for different model sizes.

1. Activation norms spike for MUX-BERT in the last layer. Figure 5 (top) shows that activation norms spike in the last layer for multiplexed models. We believe this is because the model is preparing for demultiplexing and is packing information from all N instances, which makes the activations denser. We believe MUX-BERT has learned to efficiently encode multiple instances until the last layer where it needs to make independent predictions for them.

2. Entropy of the attention weights of MUX-BERT is lower than BERT for higher layers. Figure 5 (bottom) suggests that MUX-BERT tends to have lower entropy attention distributions on average as opposed to BERT for higher layers. This could be related to Deshpande and Narasimhan (2020)'s observation of pre-trained models having peaky attention distributions in the higher layers, with small irregularities. Since the model implicitly has to use the same attention distribution for all the multiplexed instances, the peaky distribution gets reinforced and is further corroborated by higher N having lower entropy in the final layer. We, therefore, believe that MUX-BERT has learned to create shared representations for multiple instances to effectively use the instance-independent attention distribution.

6.3 Effect of data sampling strategies during inference

During inference, our MUX-PLMs sample N instances uniformly at random from the evaluation set. However, other data-sampling strategies such as clustering similar instances based on word-overlap could improve performance. We explore the effect of composition of N instances on the performance of MUX-PLMs in Table 6. For each model variant, we consider 5 random seeds

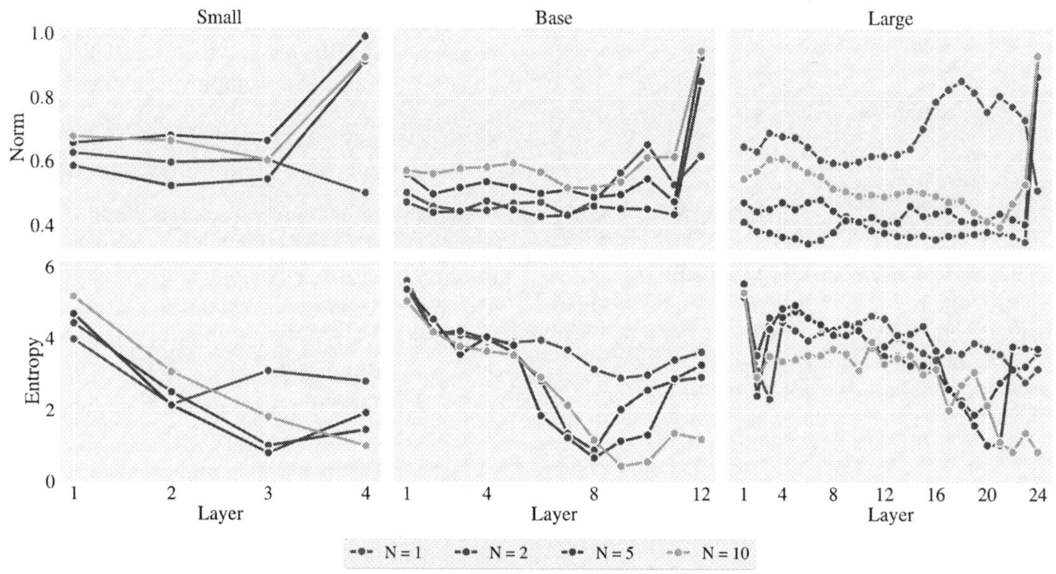

Figure 5: Comparing (Top) Layer-wise activation and (Bottom) attention entropy of MUX-BERT and BERT, for $N \in \{2, 5, 10\}$ across different configurations. Activation norms tend to spike for MUX-BERT in the last layer and entropy of MUX-BERT is lower than BERT for higher layers.

N	MUX-ELECTRA			MUX-BERT		
	Best ticket	Worst ticket	Δ	Best ticket	Worst ticket	Δ
2	83.1	82.0	1.1	83.4	81.8	1.6
5	80.5	78.9	1.6	80.9	79.7	1.2
10	79.0	77.3	1.7	78.8	77.0	1.8

Table 6: We consider 5 random seeds for every model variant, which can be viewed as lottery tickets as the seeds control the composition of N instances. We present the difference between the worst and the best-performing ticket across GLUE tasks and regularly see a ≥ 1 point difference.

which can be viewed as lottery tickets (Frankle and Carbin, 2018). Since the random seed controls the composition of N instances, we measure the difference (Δ) between the best-performing ticket and the worst-performing ticket and average the performance for all the GLUE tasks. Δ is consistently greater than 1 point for all values of N for both MUX-ELECTRA and MUX-BERT, and illustrates the importance of the composition of N instances. An improved data sampling strategy could lead to improvements and we leave this to future work.

7 Conclusion

We introduce MUX-PLMs, a class of high-throughput pre-trained language models trained with data multiplexing, a multi-input multi-output (MIMO) architecture. Our MUX-PLMs models, trained with novel MIMO modules, are competitive with state-of-the-art PLMs on several downstream tasks while achieving a many-fold increase in inference throughput. MUX-PLMs, similar to standard PLMs, can be fine-tuned on any downstream task to yield high-throughput, high-performance models. We hope our work inspires future research in MIMO architectures for PLMs as a complementary efficiency paradigm to existing approaches.

Acknowledgements

We gratefully acknowledge support from Google AI Princeton, where Vishvak Murahari was a student researcher for part of this work, and the Samsung GRO program. We thank Mengzhou Xia, Jens Tuyls, and Tianyu Gao, with special thanks to our espresso machine.

References

Quora. data.quora.com/First-Quora-Dataset-Release-Question-Pairs. Accessed: 2022-10-15.

Armen Aghajanyan, Bernie Huang, Candace Ross, Vladimir Karpukhin, Hu Xu, Naman Goyal, Dmytro Okhonko, Mandar Joshi, Gargi Ghosh, Mike Lewis, et al. 2022. Cm3: A causal masked multimodal model of the internet. arXiv preprint arXiv:2201.07520.

Joshua Ainslie, Santiago Ontañón, Chris Alberti, Philip Pham, Anirudh Ravula, and Sumit Sanghai. 2020.

ETC: encoding long and structured data in transformers. CoRR, abs/2004.08483.

Thomas Akam and Dimitri M Kullmann. 2014. Oscillatory multiplexing of population codes for selective communication in the mammalian brain. Nature Reviews Neuroscience, 15(2):111–122.

Iz Beltagy, Matthew E Peters, and Arman Cohan. 2020. Longformer: The long-document transformer. arXiv preprint arXiv:2004.05150.

Francisca Blumhagen, Peixin Zhu, Jennifer Shum, Yan-Ping Zhang Schärer, Emre Yaksi, Karl Deisseroth, and Rainer W Friedrich. 2011. Neuronal filtering of multiplexed odour representations. Nature, 479(7374):493–498.

Daniel Cer, Mona Diab, Eneko Agirre, Iñigo Lopez-Gazpio, and Lucia Specia. 2017. Semeval-2017 task 1: Semantic textual similarity multilingual and crosslingual focused evaluation. In Proceedings of the 11th International Workshop on Semantic Evaluation (SemEval-2017), pages 1–14.

Tianlong Chen, Jonathan Frankle, Shiyu Chang, Sijia Liu, Yang Zhang, Zhangyang Wang, and Michael Carbin. 2020. The lottery ticket hypothesis for pre-trained bert networks. In Advances in Neural Information Processing Systems, volume 33, pages 15834–15846. Curran Associates, Inc.

Aakanksha Chowdhery, Sharan Narang, Jacob Devlin, Maarten Bosma, Gaurav Mishra, Adam Roberts, Paul Barham, Hyung Won Chung, Charles Sutton, Sebastian Gehrmann, et al. 2022. Palm: Scaling language modeling with pathways. arXiv preprint arXiv:2204.02311.

Kevin Clark, Minh-Thang Luong, Quoc V Le, and Christopher D Manning. 2020. Electra: Pre-training text encoders as discriminators rather than generators. In International Conference on Learning Representations.

Ameet Deshpande and Karthik Narasimhan. 2020. Guiding attention for self-supervised learning with transformers. In Findings of the Association for Computational Linguistics: EMNLP 2020, pages 4676–4686.

Jacob Devlin, Ming-Wei Chang, Kenton Lee, and Kristina Toutanova. 2019. BERT: Pre-training of deep bidirectional transformers for language understanding. In Proceedings of the 2019 Conference of the North American Chapter of the Association for Computational Linguistics: Human Language Technologies, Volume 1 (Long and Short Papers), pages 4171–4186, Minneapolis, Minnesota. Association for Computational Linguistics.

William B Dolan and Chris Brockett. 2005. Automatically constructing a corpus of sentential paraphrases. In Proceedings of the Third International Workshop on Paraphrasing (IWP2005).

Wikimedia Foundation. Wikipedia.

Jonathan Frankle and Michael Carbin. 2018. The lottery ticket hypothesis: Finding sparse, trainable neural networks. In International Conference on Learning Representations.

Rainer W Friedrich, Christopher J Habermann, and Gilles Laurent. 2004. Multiplexing using synchrony in the zebrafish olfactory bulb. Nature neuroscience, 7(8):862–871.

Mitchell Gordon, Kevin Duh, and Nicholas Andrews. 2020. Compressing BERT: Studying the effects of weight pruning on transfer learning. In Proceedings of the 5th Workshop on Representation Learning for NLP, pages 143–155, Online. Association for Computational Linguistics.

Stefan Grünewald, Prisca Piccirilli, and Annemarie Friedrich. 2021. Coordinate constructions in english enhanced universal dependencies: Analysis and computational modeling. In Proceedings of the 16th Conference of the European Chapter of the Association for Computational Linguistics: Main Volume, pages 795–809.

Marton Havasi, Rodolphe Jenatton, Stanislav Fort, Jeremiah Zhe Liu, Jasper Snoek, Balaji Lakshminarayanan, Andrew Mingbo Dai, and Dustin Tran. 2021. Training independent subnetworks for robust prediction. In International Conference on Learning Representations.

Geoffrey E. Hinton, Oriol Vinyals, and Jeffrey Dean. 2015. Distilling the knowledge in a neural network. ArXiv, abs/1503.02531.

Sungho Hong, Mario Negrello, Marc Junker, Aleksandra Smilgin, Peter Thier, and Erik De Schutter. 2016. Multiplexed coding by cerebellar purkinje neurons. Elife, 5:e13810.

Ting Jiang, Deqing Wang, and Fuzhen Zhuang. 2022. Pruning pre-trained language models without fine-tuning.

Xiaoqi Jiao, Yichun Yin, Lifeng Shang, Xin Jiang, Xiao Chen, Linlin Li, Fang Wang, and Qun Liu. 2020. TinyBERT: Distilling BERT for natural language understanding. pages 4163–4174.

Jared Kaplan, Sam McCandlish, Tom Henighan, Tom B. Brown, Benjamin Chess, Rewon Child, Scott Gray, Alec Radford, Jeffrey Wu, and Dario Amodei. 2020. Scaling laws for neural language models.

François Lagunas, Ella Charlaix, Victor Sanh, and Alexander M Rush. 2021. Block pruning for faster transformers. arXiv preprint arXiv:2109.04838.

Hector Levesque, Ernest Davis, and Leora Morgenstern. 2012. The winograd schema challenge. In Thirteenth international conference on the principles of knowledge representation and reasoning.

Zhuang Liu, Mingjie Sun, Tinghui Zhou, Gao Huang, and Trevor Darrell. 2019. Rethinking the value of network pruning. In International Conference on Learning Representations.

Stephen Merity, Caiming Xiong, James Bradbury, and Richard Socher. 2016. Pointer sentinel mixture models.

Paul Michel, Omer Levy, and Graham Neubig. 2019. Are sixteen heads really better than one? In Advances in Neural Information Processing Systems, volume 32. Curran Associates, Inc.

Vishvak Murahari, Carlos E Jimenez, Runzhe Yang, and Karthik R Narasimhan. 2022. DataMUX: Data multiplexing for neural networks. In Thirty-Sixth Conference on Neural Information Processing Systems.

OpenAI. 2023. Introducing chatgpt.

Friederice Pirschel and Jutta Kretzberg. 2016. Multiplexed population coding of stimulus properties by leech mechanosensory cells. Journal of Neuroscience, 36(13):3636–3647.

Sai Prasanna, Anna Rogers, and Anna Rumshisky. 2020. When BERT Plays the Lottery, All Tickets Are Winning. In Proceedings of the 2020 Conference on Empirical Methods in Natural Language Processing (EMNLP), pages 3208–3229, Online. Association for Computational Linguistics.

Alec Radford and Karthik Narasimhan. 2018. Improving language understanding by generative pretraining.

Colin Raffel, Noam Shazeer, Adam Roberts, Katherine Lee, Sharan Narang, Michael Matena, Yanqi Zhou, Wei Li, and Peter J Liu. 2020. Exploring the limits of transfer learning with a unified text-to-text transformer. Journal of Machine Learning Research, 21:1–67.

Alexandre Ramé, Rémy Sun, and Matthieu Cord. 2021. Mixmo: Mixing multiple inputs for multiple outputs via deep subnetworks. In Proceedings of the IEEE/CVF International Conference on Computer Vision (ICCV), pages 823–833.

Ronald L Rivest, Adi Shamir, and Leonard Adleman. 1978. A method for obtaining digital signatures and public-key cryptosystems. Communications of the ACM, 21(2):120–126.

Erik Tjong Kim Sang and Fien De Meulder. 2003. Introduction to the conll-2003 shared task: Language-independent named entity recognition. In CoNLL.

Victor Sanh, Lysandre Debut, Julien Chaumond, and Thomas Wolf. 2019. DistilBERT, a distilled version of bert: smaller, faster, cheaper and lighter. arXiv preprint arXiv:1910.01108.

Victor Sanh, Thomas Wolf, and Alexander Rush. 2020. Movement pruning: Adaptive sparsity by fine-tuning. In Advances in Neural Information Processing Systems, volume 33, pages 20378–20389. Curran Associates, Inc.

Sheng Shen, Zhen Dong, Jiayu Ye, Linjian Ma, Zhewei Yao, Amir Gholami, Michael W. Mahoney, and Kurt Keutzer. 2020. Q-bert: Hessian based ultra low precision quantization of bert. In AAAI.

Richard Socher, Alex Perelygin, Jean Wu, Jason Chuang, Christopher D Manning, Andrew Y Ng, and Christopher Potts. 2013. Recursive deep models for semantic compositionality over a sentiment treebank. In Proceedings of the 2013 conference on empirical methods in natural language processing, pages 1631–1642.

Zhiqing Sun, Hongkun Yu, Xiaodan Song, Renjie Liu, Yiming Yang, and Denny Zhou. 2020. MobileBERT: a compact task-agnostic bert for resource-limited devices. pages 2158–2170.

Ashish Vaswani, Noam M. Shazeer, Niki Parmar, Jakob Uszkoreit, Llion Jones, Aidan N. Gomez, Lukasz Kaiser, and Illia Polosukhin. 2017. Attention is all you need. In NIPS.

Elena Voita, David Talbot, Fedor Moiseev, Rico Sennrich, and Ivan Titov. 2019. Analyzing multi-head self-attention: Specialized heads do the heavy lifting, the rest can be pruned. In Proceedings of the 57th Annual Meeting of the Association for Computational Linguistics, pages 5797–5808, Florence, Italy. Association for Computational Linguistics.

Alex Wang, Amanpreet Singh, Julian Michael, Felix Hill, Omer Levy, and Samuel R Bowman. 2018. Glue: A multi-task benchmark and analysis platform for natural language understanding. In International Conference on Learning Representations.

Ziheng Wang, Jeremy Wohlwend, and Tao Lei. 2020. Structured pruning of large language models. In Proceedings of the 2020 Conference on Empirical Methods in Natural Language Processing (EMNLP). Association for Computational Linguistics.

Alex Warstadt, Amanpreet Singh, and Samuel Bowman. 2019. Neural network acceptability judgments. Transactions of the Association for Computational Linguistics, 7:625–641.

Adina Williams, Nikita Nangia, and Samuel R Bowman. 2018. A broad-coverage challenge corpus for sentence understanding through inference. In NAACL-HLT.

Mengzhou Xia, Zexuan Zhong, and Danqi Chen. 2022. Structured pruning learns compact and accurate models. In Association for Computational Linguistics (ACL).

Ziqing Yang, Yiming Cui, and Zhigang Chen. 2022. TextPruner: A model pruning toolkit for pre-trained language models. In Proceedings of the 60th Annual Meeting of the Association for Computational Linguistics: System Demonstrations, pages 35–43, Dublin, Ireland. Association for Computational Linguistics.

Yichun Yin, Cheng Chen, Lifeng Shang, Xin Jiang, Xiao Chen, and Qun Liu. 2021. AutoTinyBERT: Automatic hyper-parameter optimization for efficient pre-trained language models. pages 5146–5157.

Ofir Zafrir, Guy Boudoukh, Peter Izsak, and Moshe Wasserblat. 2019. Q8bert: Quantized 8bit bert. 2019 Fifth Workshop on Energy Efficient Machine Learning and Cognitive Computing - NeurIPS Edition (EMC2-NIPS), pages 36–39.

Ofir Zafrir, Ariel Larey, Guy Boudoukh, Haihao Shen, and Moshe Wasserblat. 2021. Prune once for all: Sparse pre-trained language models. arXiv preprint arXiv:2111.05754.

Manzil Zaheer, Guru Guruganesh, Kumar Avinava Dubey, Joshua Ainslie, Chris Alberti, Santiago Ontanon, Philip Pham, Anirudh Ravula, Qifan Wang, Li Yang, et al. 2020. Big bird: Transformers for longer sequences. Advances in Neural Information Processing Systems, 33:17283–17297.

Hongyi Zhang, Moustapha Cisse, Yann N Dauphin, and David Lopez-Paz. 2018. mixup: Beyond empirical risk minimization. In International Conference on Learning Representations.

Yukun Zhu, Ryan Kiros, Rich Zemel, Ruslan Salakhutdinov, Raquel Urtasun, Antonio Torralba, and Sanja Fidler. 2015. Aligning books and movies: Towards story-like visual explanations by watching movies and reading books. In The IEEE International Conference on Computer Vision (ICCV).

Hyperparameter	MUX-BERT			MUX-ELECTRA
	SMALL	BASE	LARGE	BASE
Number of layers	4	12	24	12
Hidden Size	512	768	1024	768
FFN intermediate hidden size	2048	3072	4096	3072
Attention heads	8	12	16	12
Attention head size	64	64	64	64
Mask percent	15	15	15	N/A
Learning Rate Decay	Linear	Linear	Linear	Linear
Warmup steps	10000	10000	10000	10000
Learning Rate	[1e-4, 5e-5]	[1e-4, 5e-5]	[1e-4, 5e-5]	[1e-4, 5e-5]
Adam ϵ	1e-6	1e-6	1e-6	1e-6
Adam β_1	0.9	0.9	0.9	0.9
Adam β_2	0.999	0.999	0.999	0.999
Attention Dropout	0.1	0.1	0.1	0.1
Dropout	0.1	0.1	0.1	0.1
Batch Size	256	256	256	256
Sequence Length	512	512	512	512
Train Steps	1M	1M	1M	1M

Table 7: Pre-train hyper-parameters for MUX-BERT and MUX-ELECTRA models. We only report results for the Base configuration for MUX-ELECTRA models.

A Appendices

B Pre-training Details

We report all pre-training related hyper-parameters in Table 7. We primarily use the HuggingFace Transformers implementations for BERT and ELECTRA based models. All pre-training experiments were run on 8 A100 GPUs with distributed training. We run a small hyper-parameter search over over two learning rates. All pre-trained models are primed with the token retrieval task introduced in Murahari et al. (2022). We train on the Wikipedia and Bookscorpus datasets for up to 10000 training steps with a learning rate of $1e-4$, and with a sequence length of 512.

For MUX-ELECTRA models, we don't train a generator as in the original ELECTRA work, but only use uniform-random token replacement. This is similar to what was used in ablations in ELECTRA (Clark et al., 2020). The generator randomly replaces 15% of tokens in the input with other tokens in the vocabulary.

C Fine-tuning Details

We report all the fine-tuning related hyper-parameters in Table 8. We run a small hyper-parameter search on the learning rate, batch size and number of training steps for different tasks. All models were trained with half-precision. We report numbers on the validation split. For GLUE tasks, we use the default metrics in Wang et al. (2018) and use F1 for the token-level tasks. All fine-tuning experiments were trained on 1 V100 GPU.

Speedup calculation For all models, we calculate throughput (samples/second) on a single V100 GPU and report throughput gains with respect to the $\text{BERT}_{\text{BASE}}$ model. We calculate throughput by averaging across 3 different trials (1 trial = 200 mini-batches) and use a batch size of 128 and a sequence length of 128 following prior work (Xia et al., 2022). We measure throughput for sequence-classification tasks on QQP and measure throughput for token-level classification tasks on named entity recognition.

Hyperparameter	Value
Learning Rate	[2e-5, 5e-5]
Adam ϵ	1e-8
Adam β_1	0.9
Adam β_2	0.999
Learning rate decay	Linear
Warmup fraction	0.1
Attention Dropout	0.1
Dropout	0.1
Weight Decay	0
Batch Size	[32, 128] for SMALL/ BASE, [16, 64] for LARGE
Train Steps	2000 for RTE and WNLI
	10000 for MRPC, COLA and STSB
	20000 for NER, SST2, QNLI and POS
	[20000, 100000] for MNLI and QQP
Sequence Length	128

Table 8: Fine-tune hyperparameters

D Analysis details

D.1 Ensembling results setup

We find that multiplexing the same instance by duplicating the instance N times leads to worse performance. This is likely because this input configuration is very out of distribution from what the multiplexed models are trained on. To address this, we randomly permute the instances in the batch after duplicating the instances N times. This ensures that the input to the multiplexer lies in a similar distribution to what the model was trained on.

D.2 Muxology setup

To analyze the hidden states of pre-trained MUX-BERT models at different layers, we take the average absolute value of hidden states and every layer for both multiplexed and baseline models, across different configurations. To analyze the entropies of the attention distributions at different layers, we calculate the attention distribution across different attention heads for each position in the sequence length. To measure how peaky the attention distribution is likely to be, we calculate the entropies of the attention distributions at all positions and average across all the positions and across all the attention heads to get the average entropy for all layers. We conduct this analysis on WikiText-103 and average across all the samples in the evaluation split.

E Task performance breakdown for all variants

Model Size	N	MNLI	QQP	QNLI	MRPC	WNLI	STSB	RTE	SST2	COLA	GLUE	GLUE$_{-\text{WNLI, COLA}}$
SMALL	1	**77.86**$_{\pm 0.0}$	**88.99**$_{\pm 0.0}$	84.00$_{\pm 0.0}$	77.70$_{\pm 0.0}$	**56.34**$_{\pm 0.0}$	**84.25**$_{\pm 0.0}$	**62.45**$_{\pm 0.0}$	**88.88**$_{\pm 0.0}$	**43.48**$_{\pm 0.0}$	**73.77**	**80.59**
	2	75.09$_{\pm 0.1}$	88.88$_{\pm 0.1}$	**84.31**$_{\pm 0.2}$	**79.75**$_{\pm 0.7}$	50.99$_{\pm 8.1}$	82.65$_{\pm 0.3}$	55.52$_{\pm 1.5}$	87.04$_{\pm 0.7}$	30.64$_{\pm 1.7}$	70.54	79.03
	5	70.50$_{\pm 0.1}$	86.39$_{\pm 0.1}$	81.23$_{\pm 0.2}$	74.26$_{\pm 1.0}$	**54.65**$_{\pm 3.3}$	79.90$_{\pm 0.2}$	58.56$_{\pm 1.9}$	82.57$_{\pm 0.3}$	12.78$_{\pm 1.6}$	66.76	76.20
	10	61.98$_{\pm 0.1}$	80.85$_{\pm 0.1}$	63.47$_{\pm 0.3}$	70.69$_{\pm 0.9}$	**56.62**$_{\pm 4.3}$	36.93$_{\pm 1.0}$	53.57$_{\pm 1.8}$	80.39$_{\pm 0.4}$	1.10$_{\pm 2.2}$	56.18	63.98
BASE	1	**84.24**$_{\pm 0.0}$	**91.19**$_{\pm 0.0}$	**90.54**$_{\pm 0.0}$	**87.75**$_{\pm 0.0}$	**56.34**$_{\pm 0.0}$	**89.18**$_{\pm 0.0}$	**63.18**$_{\pm 0.0}$	**91.74**$_{\pm 0.0}$	**58.79**$_{\pm 0.0}$	**79.22**	**85.40**
	2	80.59$_{\pm 0.1}$	90.36$_{\pm 0.1}$	88.17$_{\pm 0.1}$	83.77$_{\pm 1.4}$	50.70$_{\pm 7.0}$	85.84$_{\pm 0.1}$	58.19$_{\pm 1.6}$	90.62$_{\pm 0.6}$	55.61$_{\pm 1.6}$	75.98	82.51
	5	77.18$_{\pm 0.2}$	88.79$_{\pm 0.1}$	85.58$_{\pm 0.1}$	80.10$_{\pm 0.6}$	53.52$_{\pm 2.5}$	84.28$_{\pm 0.2}$	59.13$_{\pm 1.2}$	86.88$_{\pm 0.4}$	12.33$_{\pm 2.4}$	69.75	80.28
	10	73.62$_{\pm 0.3}$	86.94$_{\pm 0.1}$	82.08$_{\pm 0.3}$	78.63$_{\pm 0.6}$	52.68$_{\pm 6.0}$	81.62$_{\pm 0.2}$	58.27$_{\pm 2.4}$	83.44$_{\pm 0.6}$	0.00$_{\pm 0.0}$	66.36	77.80
LARGE	1	**85.79**$_{\pm 0.0}$	**91.46**$_{\pm 0.0}$	**92.29**$_{\pm 0.0}$	83.82$_{\pm 0.0}$	**56.34**$_{\pm 0.0}$	**89.53**$_{\pm 0.0}$	**66.06**$_{\pm 0.0}$	**91.40**$_{\pm 0.0}$	**57.79**$_{\pm 0.0}$	**79.39**	**85.76**
	2	83.23$_{\pm 0.2}$	90.85$_{\pm 0.1}$	90.66$_{\pm 0.2}$	**84.90**$_{\pm 0.8}$	**56.34**$_{\pm 0.0}$	88.22$_{\pm 0.2}$	59.21$_{\pm 0.9}$	91.38$_{\pm 0.4}$	**57.89**$_{\pm 1.5}$	78.08	84.06
	5	79.55$_{\pm 0.2}$	89.37$_{\pm 0.1}$	87.41$_{\pm 0.2}$	83.77$_{\pm 1.1}$	**54.93**$_{\pm 0.0}$	85.86$_{\pm 0.3}$	57.26$_{\pm 2.0}$	88.65$_{\pm 0.7}$	46.66$_{\pm 0.9}$	74.83	81.70
	10	35.45$_{\pm 0.0}$	63.18$_{\pm 0.0}$	50.54$_{\pm 0.0}$	68.38$_{\pm 0.0}$	**56.90**$_{\pm 5.2}$	82.81$_{\pm 0.2}$	52.13$_{\pm 1.9}$	50.92$_{\pm 0.0}$	1.87$_{\pm 4.6}$	51.35	57.63

Table 9: We show the full GLUE results for MUX-BERT. We report the mean accuracy and standard deviation over 5 seeds. Extrema and values within their standard deviation are emphasized for each model size.

Model Size	N	MNLI	QQP	QNLI	MRPC	WNLI	STSB	RTE	SST2	COLA	GLUE	GLUE$_{-\text{WNLI, COLA}}$
SMALL	1	**77.86**	**88.99**	84.00	77.70	56.34	**84.25**	**62.45**	**88.88**	**43.48**	**73.77**	**80.59**
	2	75.21	**89.01**	**84.61**	**80.64**	61.97	82.97	58.12	87.84	33.08	72.61	79.77
	5	70.66	86.46	81.60	75.74	61.97	80.24	60.65	83.49	15.57	68.49	76.98
	10	62.17	80.93	63.85	71.81	**63.38**	38.20	55.96	80.96	2.63	57.77	64.84
BASE	1	**84.24**	**91.19**	**90.54**	**87.75**	56.34	**89.18**	**63.18**	**91.74**	**58.79**	**79.22**	**85.40**
	2	80.82	90.47	88.28	86.03	**66.20**	86.06	60.65	91.51	56.93	78.55	83.40
	5	77.66	88.89	85.70	81.13	59.15	84.47	60.65	87.50	15.79	71.22	80.86
	10	74.04	87.03	82.45	79.41	63.38	81.89	62.45	84.29	0.00	68.33	78.79
LARGE	1	**85.79**	**91.46**	**92.29**	83.82	56.34	**89.53**	**66.06**	91.40	57.79	**79.39**	**85.76**
	2	83.40	90.94	90.96	**86.27**	56.34	88.50	60.29	**91.86**	**60.50**	78.78	84.60
	5	79.69	89.43	87.81	84.80	57.75	86.49	60.65	89.45	47.56	75.96	82.62
	10	35.46	63.18	50.89	68.38	**61.97**	83.04	55.60	50.92	7.55	53.00	58.21

Table 10: We show the full GLUE results for MUX-BERT. We report the *maximum* accuracy over 5 seeds. Extrema are emphasized.

N	MNLI	QQP	QNLI	MRPC	WNLI	STSB	RTE	SST2	COLA	GLUE	GLUE$_{-\text{WNLI, COLA}}$
1	**81.49**$_{\pm 0.0}$	**90.73**$_{\pm 0.0}$	**89.73**$_{\pm 0.0}$	75.98$_{\pm 0.0}$	**56.34**$_{\pm 0.0}$	**87.73**$_{\pm 0.0}$	57.76$_{\pm 0.0}$	**91.51**$_{\pm 0.0}$	**56.79**$_{\pm 0.0}$	**76.45**	82.13
2	80.29$_{\pm 0.2}$	90.58$_{\pm 0.1}$	88.39$_{\pm 0.2}$	**83.73**$_{\pm 0.7}$	**57.18**$_{\pm 2.1}$	86.80$_{\pm 0.1}$	**58.77**$_{\pm 1.1}$	88.65$_{\pm 0.4}$	51.92$_{\pm 1.7}$	76.26	**82.46**
5	76.99$_{\pm 0.2}$	89.08$_{\pm 0.0}$	85.40$_{\pm 0.3}$	80.25$_{\pm 1.6}$	**56.90**$_{\pm 4.5}$	84.27$_{\pm 0.2}$	57.26$_{\pm 1.0}$	85.09$_{\pm 1.0}$	26.89$_{\pm 1.2}$	71.35	79.76
10	74.62$_{\pm 0.2}$	87.63$_{\pm 0.1}$	82.70$_{\pm 0.2}$	77.89$_{\pm 0.7}$	50.99$_{\pm 4.9}$	81.96$_{\pm 0.5}$	**59.86**$_{\pm 2.1}$	82.71$_{\pm 0.5}$	27.76$_{\pm 2.3}$	69.57	78.20

Table 11: We show the full GLUE results for MUX-ELECTRA$_{\text{BASE}}$. We report the mean accuracy and standard deviation over 5 seeds. Extrema and values within their standard deviation are emphasized for each model size.

N	Retreival Rate	MNLI	QQP	QNLI	MRPC	WNLI	STSB	RTE	SST2	COLA	GLUE	GLUE$_{-\text{WNLI, COLA}}$
2	0.0	83.23$_{\pm 0.2}$	90.85$_{\pm 0.1}$	**90.66**$_{\pm 0.2}$	**84.90**$_{\pm 0.8}$	**56.34**$_{\pm 0.0}$	**88.22**$_{\pm 0.2}$	**59.21**$_{\pm 0.9}$	**91.38**$_{\pm 0.4}$	**57.89**$_{\pm 1.5}$	**78.08**	**84.06**
	0.1	**83.55**$_{\pm 0.3}$	**90.90**$_{\pm 0.1}$	**90.58**$_{\pm 0.2}$	**85.49**$_{\pm 1.1}$	**56.34**$_{\pm 0.0}$	**88.28**$_{\pm 0.2}$	**57.76**$_{\pm 1.4}$	90.69$_{\pm 0.8}$	**59.36**$_{\pm 1.4}$	**78.11**	83.89
	0.2	**83.50**$_{\pm 0.1}$	**90.96**$_{\pm 0.1}$	**90.69**$_{\pm 0.2}$	**84.95**$_{\pm 0.5}$	**56.34**$_{\pm 0.0}$	**88.28**$_{\pm 0.2}$	**58.34**$_{\pm 1.6}$	90.69$_{\pm 0.5}$	**59.17**$_{\pm 1.5}$	**78.10**	83.92
	0.5	**83.41**$_{\pm 0.2}$	**90.91**$_{\pm 0.0}$	90.47$_{\pm 0.1}$	**85.25**$_{\pm 0.5}$	**56.34**$_{\pm 0.0}$	88.02$_{\pm 0.1}$	**59.35**$_{\pm 1.6}$	89.52$_{\pm 0.6}$	**59.41**$_{\pm 2.0}$	**78.08**	83.85
5	0.0	**79.55**$_{\pm 0.2}$	**89.37**$_{\pm 0.1}$	**87.41**$_{\pm 0.2}$	**83.77**$_{\pm 1.1}$	54.93$_{\pm 0.0}$	**85.86**$_{\pm 0.3}$	**57.26**$_{\pm 2.0}$	**88.65**$_{\pm 0.7}$	**46.66**$_{\pm 0.9}$	**74.83**	**81.70**
	0.1	**79.49**$_{\pm 0.1}$	**89.34**$_{\pm 0.1}$	**87.25**$_{\pm 0.3}$	81.81$_{\pm 1.3}$	53.24$_{\pm 1.6}$	**85.80**$_{\pm 0.2}$	**55.60**$_{\pm 2.4}$	**88.19**$_{\pm 0.7}$	**47.60**$_{\pm 1.0}$	74.26	81.07
	0.2	**79.37**$_{\pm 0.1}$	**89.42**$_{\pm 0.1}$	**87.23**$_{\pm 0.3}$	82.40$_{\pm 1.1}$	54.93$_{\pm 0.0}$	**85.85**$_{\pm 0.2}$	**55.38**$_{\pm 2.6}$	87.84$_{\pm 0.8}$	43.58$_{\pm 1.2}$	74.00	81.07
	0.5	79.24$_{\pm 0.1}$	89.30$_{\pm 0.1}$	87.21$_{\pm 0.3}$	82.06$_{\pm 1.7}$	**56.34**$_{\pm 0.0}$	**85.97**$_{\pm 0.2}$	52.27$_{\pm 4.0}$	**88.58**$_{\pm 0.6}$	**47.01**$_{\pm 2.3}$	74.22	80.66
10	0.0	**35.45**$_{\pm 0.0}$	**63.18**$_{\pm 0.0}$	**50.54**$_{\pm 0.0}$	**68.38**$_{\pm 0.0}$	**56.90**$_{\pm 5.2}$	**82.81**$_{\pm 0.2}$	52.13$_{\pm 1.9}$	50.92$_{\pm 0.0}$	**1.87**$_{\pm 4.6}$	**51.35**	**57.63**
	0.1	**35.45**$_{\pm 0.0}$	**63.18**$_{\pm 0.0}$	**50.65**$_{\pm 0.2}$	**68.38**$_{\pm 0.0}$	**54.93**$_{\pm 5.0}$	4.45$_{\pm 1.5}$	51.48$_{\pm 2.4}$	50.92$_{\pm 0.0}$	**1.34**$_{\pm 1.8}$	42.31	46.36
	0.2	**35.45**$_{\pm 0.0}$	**63.18**$_{\pm 0.0}$	50.21$_{\pm 0.5}$	**68.43**$_{\pm 0.8}$	**54.65**$_{\pm 4.2}$	0.23$_{\pm 1.5}$	52.35$_{\pm 2.0}$	**51.72**$_{\pm 0.4}$	**0.29**$_{\pm 2.7}$	41.83	45.94
	0.5	**35.45**$_{\pm 0.0}$	**63.18**$_{\pm 0.0}$	50.43$_{\pm 0.4}$	**68.38**$_{\pm 0.0}$	**56.06**$_{\pm 0.6}$	82.01$_{\pm 0.6}$	**52.71**$_{\pm 0.0}$	50.92$_{\pm 0.0}$	**1.51**$_{\pm 1.7}$	51.18	**57.58**

Table 12: GLUE results for MUX-BERT$_{\text{LARGE}}$ when using a retrieval auxiliary objective during MLM pretraining with different trade-off rates to the MLM objective. We report the average accuracy over 5 seeds. Extrema and values within their standard deviation are emphasized for each value of N.

N	Mux Strategy	MNLI	QQP	QNLI	MRPC	WNLI	STSB	RTE	SST2	COLA	GLUE	$\text{GLUE}_{\text{-WNLI, COLA}}$
	MUX-BERT	$80.59_{\pm 0.1}$	$90.36_{\pm 0.1}$	$88.17_{\pm 0.1}$	$83.77_{\pm 1.4}$	$50.70_{\pm 7.0}$	$85.84_{\pm 0.1}$	$58.19_{\pm 1.6}$	$90.62_{\pm 0.6}$	$\mathbf{55.61}_{\pm 1.6}$	75.98	82.51
2	DataMUX	$\mathbf{81.64}_{\pm 0.2}$	$\mathbf{90.67}_{\pm 0.1}$	$88.39_{\pm 0.2}$	$\mathbf{84.17}_{\pm 0.4}$	$\mathbf{56.34}_{\pm 0.0}$	$\mathbf{86.36}_{\pm 0.2}$	$\mathbf{60.87}_{\pm 0.7}$	$90.50_{\pm 0.4}$	$53.74_{\pm 1.0}$	**76.96**	**83.23**
	Attention	$81.32_{\pm 0.2}$	$\mathbf{90.65}_{\pm 0.0}$	$\mathbf{88.77}_{\pm 0.1}$	$80.88_{\pm 0.6}$	$\mathbf{56.34}_{\pm 0.0}$	$\mathbf{86.25}_{\pm 0.1}$	$56.90_{\pm 1.2}$	$\mathbf{91.06}_{\pm 0.2}$	$47.15_{\pm 1.1}$	75.48	82.26
	MUX-BERT	$\mathbf{77.18}_{\pm 0.2}$	$88.79_{\pm 0.1}$	$\mathbf{85.58}_{\pm 0.1}$	$\mathbf{80.10}_{\pm 0.6}$	$53.52_{\pm 2.5}$	$\mathbf{84.28}_{\pm 0.2}$	$\mathbf{59.13}_{\pm 1.2}$	$\mathbf{86.88}_{\pm 0.4}$	$12.33_{\pm 2.4}$	69.75	**80.28**
5	DataMUX	$76.32_{\pm 0.1}$	$\mathbf{89.13}_{\pm 0.1}$	$84.22_{\pm 0.3}$	$78.38_{\pm 0.9}$	$\mathbf{59.44}_{\pm 3.5}$	$81.78_{\pm 0.4}$	$54.15_{\pm 1.3}$	$86.17_{\pm 0.4}$	$28.32_{\pm 0.8}$	**70.88**	78.59
	Attention	$\mathbf{77.16}_{\pm 0.1}$	$88.71_{\pm 0.0}$	$84.33_{\pm 0.1}$	$70.49_{\pm 0.6}$	$54.08_{\pm 3.2}$	$80.37_{\pm 0.3}$	$54.44_{\pm 2.5}$	$81.95_{\pm 0.3}$	$\mathbf{34.67}_{\pm 1.2}$	69.58	76.78
	MUX-BERT	$\mathbf{73.62}_{\pm 0.3}$	$86.94_{\pm 0.1}$	$82.08_{\pm 0.3}$	$\mathbf{78.63}_{\pm 0.6}$	$52.68_{\pm 6.0}$	$81.62_{\pm 0.2}$	$\mathbf{58.27}_{\pm 2.4}$	$\mathbf{83.44}_{\pm 0.6}$	$0.00_{\pm 0.0}$	66.36	**77.80**
10	DataMUX	$72.74_{\pm 0.1}$	$87.88_{\pm 0.1}$	$\mathbf{82.28}_{\pm 0.2}$	$77.30_{\pm 0.5}$	$\mathbf{56.34}_{\pm 0.0}$	$78.07_{\pm 0.4}$	$55.31_{\pm 1.2}$	$82.36_{\pm 0.3}$	$13.56_{\pm 3.0}$	67.32	76.56
	Attention	$71.83_{\pm 0.2}$	$\mathbf{88.00}_{\pm 0.0}$	$81.46_{\pm 0.2}$	$73.53_{\pm 0.5}$	$53.24_{\pm 5.4}$	$\mathbf{82.95}_{\pm 0.2}$	$52.71_{\pm 0.0}$	$81.28_{\pm 0.4}$	$\mathbf{32.84}_{\pm 0.6}$	**68.65**	75.97

Table 13: GLUE results for $\text{MUX-BERT}_{\text{BASE}}$ using alternative multiplexing-demultiplexing strategies. We report the average accuracy over 5 seeds. Extrema and values within their standard deviation are emphasized for each value of N.

Model Size	N	MNLI	QQP	QNLI	MRPC	WNLI	STSB	RTE	SST2	COLA	GLUE	$\text{GLUE}_{\text{-WNLI, COLA}}$
	2	$\mathbf{61.48}_{\pm 0.2}$	$\mathbf{80.33}_{\pm 0.0}$	$\mathbf{60.05}_{\pm 0.2}$	$\mathbf{68.43}_{\pm 0.5}$	$\mathbf{56.34}_{\pm 0.0}$	$\mathbf{15.02}_{\pm 0.4}$	$\mathbf{51.12}_{\pm 0.6}$	$\mathbf{79.75}_{\pm 0.3}$	$\mathbf{8.22}_{\pm 0.7}$	**53.42**	**59.45**
SMALL	5	$58.35_{\pm 0.2}$	$77.50_{\pm 0.1}$	$57.17_{\pm 0.3}$	$\mathbf{68.38}_{\pm 0.0}$	$\mathbf{56.34}_{\pm 0.0}$	$11.31_{\pm 0.3}$	$\mathbf{51.70}_{\pm 1.3}$	$77.78_{\pm 0.3}$	$6.02_{\pm 0.7}$	51.62	57.46
	10	$53.63_{\pm 0.2}$	$77.03_{\pm 0.1}$	$51.22_{\pm 0.3}$	$\mathbf{68.38}_{\pm 0.0}$	$\mathbf{57.46}_{\pm 6.3}$	$12.40_{\pm 1.3}$	$\mathbf{52.35}_{\pm 2.7}$	$50.92_{\pm 0.0}$	$0.00_{\pm 0.0}$	47.04	52.28
	2	$\mathbf{63.29}_{\pm 0.3}$	$\mathbf{81.42}_{\pm 0.1}$	$\mathbf{60.35}_{\pm 0.4}$	$68.38_{\pm 0.2}$	$56.90_{\pm 5.8}$	$\mathbf{17.65}_{\pm 1.0}$	$51.19_{\pm 1.7}$	$\mathbf{80.78}_{\pm 0.5}$	$\mathbf{9.62}_{\pm 1.5}$	**54.40**	**60.44**
BASE	5	$60.67_{\pm 0.2}$	$79.42_{\pm 0.1}$	$59.77_{\pm 0.2}$	$\mathbf{69.61}_{\pm 0.8}$	$53.80_{\pm 7.3}$	$14.92_{\pm 1.8}$	$\mathbf{52.71}_{\pm 0.8}$	$\mathbf{81.15}_{\pm 0.6}$	$\mathbf{10.35}_{\pm 1.7}$	53.60	59.75
	10	$59.07_{\pm 0.2}$	$78.22_{\pm 0.1}$	$57.99_{\pm 0.5}$	$68.38_{\pm 0.0}$	$\mathbf{60.28}_{\pm 3.0}$	$11.83_{\pm 0.6}$	$\mathbf{53.07}_{\pm 1.1}$	$78.35_{\pm 1.1}$	$7.40_{\pm 1.7}$	52.73	58.13
	2	$\mathbf{64.64}_{\pm 0.2}$	$\mathbf{82.10}_{\pm 0.1}$	$\mathbf{60.21}_{\pm 0.2}$	$\mathbf{69.95}_{\pm 0.9}$	$\mathbf{56.34}_{\pm 0.0}$	$\mathbf{21.62}_{\pm 0.4}$	$52.71_{\pm 0.0}$	$\mathbf{80.34}_{\pm 0.9}$	$\mathbf{8.72}_{\pm 2.1}$	**55.18**	**61.65**
LARGE	5	$60.78_{\pm 0.3}$	$78.56_{\pm 0.1}$	$\mathbf{60.19}_{\pm 0.3}$	$\mathbf{69.51}_{\pm 0.5}$	$\mathbf{56.34}_{\pm 0.0}$	$17.33_{\pm 1.1}$	$52.71_{\pm 0.0}$	$78.28_{\pm 0.8}$	$\mathbf{10.63}_{\pm 2.7}$	53.81	59.62
	10	$48.79_{\pm 0.6}$	$68.41_{\pm 0.1}$	$55.76_{\pm 0.8}$	$68.58_{\pm 0.6}$	$\mathbf{58.59}_{\pm 3.3}$	$8.38_{\pm 1.1}$	$\mathbf{54.95}_{\pm 0.9}$	$64.82_{\pm 1.0}$	$3.48_{\pm 3.9}$	47.97	52.81

Table 14: GLUE results for T-MUX with the original training recipe and implementation from Murahari et al. (2022). We report the average accuracy and standard deviation over 5 seeds. Extrema and values within their standard deviation are emphasized for each model size.

Mixed Orthographic/Phonemic Language Modeling: Beyond Orthographically Restricted Transformers (BORT)

Robert C. Gale[†] galer@ohsu.edu
Alexandra C. Salem[†] salem@ohsu.edu
Gerasimos Fergadiotis[‡] gf3@pdx.edu
Steven Bedrick[†] bedrick@ohsu.edu

[†]Oregon Health & Science University
Portland, Oregon, USA

[‡]Portland State University
Portland, Oregon, USA

Abstract

Speech language pathologists rely on information spanning the layers of language, often drawing from multiple layers (e.g. phonology & semantics) at once. Recent innovations in large language models (LLMs) have been shown to build powerful representations for many complex language structures, especially syntax and semantics, unlocking the potential of large datasets through self-supervised learning techniques. However, these datasets are overwhelmingly orthographic, favoring writing systems like the English alphabet, a natural but phonetically imprecise choice. Meanwhile, LLM support for the international phonetic alphabet (IPA) ranges from poor to absent. Further, LLMs encode text at a word- or near-word level, and pre-training tasks have little to gain from phonetic/phonemic representations. In this paper, we introduce BORT, an LLM for mixed orthography/IPA meant to overcome these limitations. To this end, we extend the pre-training of an existing LLM with our own self-supervised pronunciation tasks. We then fine-tune for a clinical task that requires simultaneous phonological and semantic analysis. For an "easy" and "hard" version of these tasks, we show that fine-tuning from our models is more accurate by a relative 24% and 29%, and improves on character error rates by a relative 75% and 31%, respectively, than those starting from the original model.

1 Introduction

Recently, large language models (LLMs) have shown notable success in capturing information across several linguistic layers, developing rich representations of syntactic and semantic structures within their hidden layers (Rogers et al., 2020). This is accomplished through the use of self-supervised techniques, in which LLMs are pre-trained on large corpora to perform generic, contrived tasks. With a well-designed task, the model can make the most of vast quantities of unlabeled text, gleaning the structural patterns of the language(s). For example, in masked language modeling (MLM), a model is trained to restore partially obscured text to its original form. Following this relatively generic pre-training task, the resulting model can then be used as a starting point, and its weights fine-tuned (or its architecture augmented with additional output layers) in a task-specific manner. Crucially, the task-specific training can be accomplished using orders of magnitude less data than is required for the original pre-training step.

This approach is well-suited to many linguistic tasks, particularly those that rely on syntax and semantics. However, tasks that also depend on explicit representation of *phonology* are under-served by the current paradigm. Examples of such tasks include: analysis of code-switched language; processing ambiguous and noisy output from automated speech recognition systems; handling of names and neologisms; and analysis of clinical language samples in the context of communication disorders.

There are two underlying reasons for this issue, the first of which involves input representation. As with any computational model, LLMs require language to be encoded into a numerical form, and a model's choice of encoding technique has a profound impact on its functionality. Today's LLMs typically rely on sub-word representations such as WordPieces (Schuster and Nakajima, 2012) or Byte-Pair Encoding (BPE) (Gage, 1994; Sennrich et al., 2016), which strike a balance between vocabulary size and semantic precision while allowing unrestricted input and avoiding the limitations arising from a fixed word vocabulary. Such tokenization schemes are generally optimized for representing textual input for word-level processing, based on the distributional properties of a training corpus, and as such in practice the most prevalent segments in a tokenized input sentence represent entire words or large word fragments, with sub-word token fragment boundaries only incidentally co-occurring with morphological boundaries.

While it has long been known that neural language models are able to capture implicit information about phonology from orthography (Elman, 1990; Prince and Smolensky, 1997), the extent to which this occurs will depend on the degree to which the model's unit of representation maps to the writing system in question's representation of phonology. Furthermore, the self-supervised pre-training techniques at the foundation of LLM tend to work (roughly) at a word-level or word-fragment scope; a task like MLM has little to gain

Proceedings of the 8th Workshop on Representation Learning for NLP (RepL4NLP 2023), pages 212–225
July 13, 2023 ©2023 Association for Computational Linguistics

from learning the sound relationships between words, so we have no reason to expect these models to adapt to phonetic tasks as well as they do semantic ones.[1]

The second underlying reason for LLMs' phonological naïveté is data-related. Phonology is typically expressed in written form using a writing system such as the International Phonetic Alphabet (IPA) or ARPAbet. One advantage of the tokenization schemes used by LLMs is that they are, at a technical level, able to represent arbitrary character input sequences: sequences of previously-unseen characters (e.g., a sequence of IPA glyphs representing a phonemically-transcribed utterance) simply resolve to a sequence of single-character tokens (rather than lumping together into sub-word units as do more commonly-seen sequences of characters). More recently, new techniques have emerged for training "token-free" LLMs that operate at the character level (e.g. CANINE (Clark et al., 2022)) yet retain many of the semantic benefits of word-level models; however, their pre-training remains exclusively orthographic in nature, and thus will only learn phonology indirectly (and in a way that is mediated by the specifics of the writing system in question). Furthermore, and most importantly, the data used to pre-train an LLM incidentally contains little IPA content if any at all. As such, regardless of the modeling strategy used, the resulting embedding of these tokens is likely to be uninformative from the a phonological perspective.

Previous attempts to augment LLMs with phonemic information have focused on speech-centered applications, and have emphasized phonology at the expense of orthography (Jia et al., 2021; Sundararaman et al., 2021; Li et al., 2023; Zhang et al., 2022). For many applications however, particularly including clinical applications in speech-language pathology, *both* are crucial, as expressive and receptive language depend on both phonology and semantics. In this paper, we introduce BORT, an LLM that accepts a mixture of English pronunciations in IPA and English orthography, and demonstrate its use on a task motivated by a real-world clinical problem: analysis of speech errors made by individuals with aphasia following a stroke.

In §3, we create the BORT models by extending the pre-training of an existing LLM, BART (Lewis et al., 2020). Our self-supervised task focuses on a novel IPA-to-orthography translation task: given a document, we transform some words into IPA, then train the model to restore the orthography. Hypothesizing that we could bolster the pre-trained models with two additional transforms, we experiment with configurations that include spelling and noise transforms. In §4, we evaluate the utility of BORT by fine-tuning to two clinically-motivated tasks: a) an "easy" task, another mixed IPA/orthography to orthography translation task, but in the context of aphasic speech; and b) a "hard" task, in which the model must predict the intended word for several types of word errors, including phonologically and semantically related errors. We make our pre-trained models available for anyone to download and fine-tune.[2]

2 Background

2.1 Speech Language Pathology

Speech language pathologists (SLPs) work to diagnose and treat speech and language disorders. Language disorders typically include breakdowns in the linguistic system that supports the abilities to activate the semantic representation of a concept; retrieve its lexical/syntactical representation; and, encode its phonological or orthographic form. Speech disorders include deficits that may stem from underdeveloped or faulty perceptual representations of speech sounds; difficulties specifying a motor plan for the articulatory gestures required for producing a word; and/or executing the motor plan. Such disorders often co-exist, and may be developmental (affecting primarily pediatric populations, as in the case of Specific Language Impairment), or acquired and seen primarily in adult populations (e.g., dementia, aphasia, dysarthria). In addition, they might affect different modalities including spoken (e.g., anomia) or written output (e.g., agraphia).

The use case described in the present work focuses on aphasia, a disorder in which an individual has an impairment to one or both of their expressive or receptive language abilities. In expressive language, this may take the form of difficulties in word retrieval or production; these difficulties may involve the inability to produce a word, the production of an unintended word, or the mispronunciation of a produced word. Aphasia typically follows an injury to be brain (such as a stroke or a traumatic brain injury), though it may also be a sign of certain neurodegenerative conditions.

To arrive at a diagnosis, clinical professionals typically elicit productions from patients, and then, based on the relationship between the intended target and the realized unexpected or atypical production, they draw inferences regarding the nature of the cognitive-linguistic or motoric deficits of the patient. Inherent in this diagnostic process is identifying what was the intended word of a speaker. That requires a clinician to combine multiple sources of information including semantic, phonemic, and/or orthographic information.

Consider for example the response /bəgænə/ when

[1] Though we note that Itzhak and Levy (2022) have demonstrated that LLMs working at the word and sub-word level do implicitly learn a certain amount about the character-level contents of their tokens.

[2] https://github.com/rcgale/bort

a stroke patient is asked to name the picture of an apple. A clinician, naturally, will recognize the phonological similarity of the production to the candidate intended word /bənænə/ ("banana") and given the semantic similarity of "banana" and "apple," the clinician will arrive at the conclusion that most likely the speaker's intended target was "banana." This step is critical in the diagnostic process across clinical populations and disorders. Therefore, the development of a robust computational tool that can combine multiple sources of information to predict a speaker's intended words during a paraphasic speech event is of great clinical significance.

There exist several settings in which tools such these may find applications. There are a variety of highly accurate and informative assessment techniques that are regularly used in research settings but rarely used in clinical practice due to the large amount of effort they require for delivery and scoring (Edmonds and Kiran, 2006; Abel et al., 2007; Kendall et al., 2013; Minkina et al., 2015; Walker and Hickok, 2016); automation has the potential to streamline this process greatly, thereby enabling their clinical use. Additionally, automation of this sort would be a key part in many telemedicine and remote assessment scenarios, which is an area of great clinical interest (Van De Sandt-Koenderman, 2004; Kiran et al., 2014) as there exist major challenges around access to care for many individuals in need of speech and language services (Hou et al., 2023).

Use cases such as these currently are limited by two categories of technical barrier. The first is the need for robust automated speech recognition algorithms able to accurately process the disordered speech characteristic of individuals with speech and language disabilities, and produce detailed phonemic transcriptions; this is needed given the impracticality of detailed manual transcription in a fast-paced clinical setting. The second category is a lack of specialized algorithms designed to process the resulting data to identify features of clinical interest, for example in speech error classification (Casilio et al., 2023). Both types of technology are necessary, and neither on their own are sufficient, to leverage NLP in this clinical domain. The present work, by design, only addresses the second of these categories; however, it is important to note that the first is an area of very active research (Fraser et al., 2013; Le et al., 2017; Jacks et al., 2019; Perez et al., 2020; Torre et al., 2021; Gale et al., 2022), with major strides being made in recent years.

A second setting of use for automation in the analysis of language produced by people with aphasia (PWA) is that of aphasiological research. Standard research practice typically results in the creation of recorded sessions with participants (for example, in a discourse elicitation task), which are then transcribed to a very high degree of accuracy by specially-trained research staff, for use in analysis. Often, this transcription is done at a mixture of orthographic and phonemic levels, with particular phonemic attention paid to clinically-relevant phenomena such as neologisms (non-word productions), mis-pronunciations, etc. There exist large databases of such transcripts, for example TalkBank and its many sub-projects (see https://talkbank.org; MacWhinney, 2000), and automated analysis of these datasets is extremely valuable from a scientific perspective.

Notably, in this scenario, one need not assume the existence of an ASR system robust to disordered speech in order for automation to be useful, as the data are transcribed as part of their collection and data management process. However, the specifics of this transcription process tend to be very closely linked to the scientific needs of the research team conducting the study, and while the amounts of data generated tend to be far more than humans can conveniently analyze by hand, they tend to be relatively small in comparison to the datasets commonly used in natural language processing. As such, techniques such as transfer learning have become crucial tools in this space.

2.2 Automating Clinical Language Evaluation

There exists a long history of use of NLP techniques in clinical language evaluation, across a wide variety of disorders including Alzheimer's disease (Petti et al., 2020), Autism Spectrum Disorder (Vimes et al., 2015; MacFarlane et al., 2023), and various forms of aphasia (Fraser et al., 2014; Azevedo et al., 2023). From a computational perspective, this typically takes the form of a pipeline accepting language samples of some sort as input, and producing as output some sort of relevant analysis, such as a score on a validated assessment instrument. The language samples used may consist of spontaneous speech, a patient's responses to a structured interaction of some kind, or a mixture of the two, and may feature continuous speech, or single-word productions. The input may be actual audio recordings, or transcriptions thereof.

Recent work has taken advantage of LLMs for automating clinical language evaluation tasks. Balagopalan et al. (2020) fine-tuned BERT to detect Alzheimer's disease from transcribed spontaneous speech, and found that BERT performed better than a standard model based on hand-crafted features. Liu et al. (2022) evaluated transformer models for use in identifying relevant pragmatic features of transcribed speech from adults with Autism Spectrum Disorder; their analysis identified both advantages and limitations of an LLM-based approach over previous methods. Gale et al. (2021) described a system that scored tests for Specific Language Impairment in children, finding that the DistilBERT architecture was adaptable to clinical language evaluation spanning several linguistic layers. Salem et al. (2022) fine-tuned DistilBERT for the automatic determination of semantic similarity in an aphasia test with accuracy 95.3%, improving over earlier methods that relied on word2vec (Fergadiotis et al., 2016).

LLMs demonstrate improved performance at many of these tasks, and bring two additional benefits over earlier methods: they are much more flexible with regard to their input representation, and they are well-suited for transfer learning via fine-tuning. Both attributes are crucial for work in clinical language evaluation, given the heterogeneity and limited size of the datasets used in this space. However, we note that technical approaches in this space tend to "live" in either the orthographic or phonemic space; this distinction is logical from a technical standpoint, given the nature and history of language technologies, but quite contrary to the actual clinical manifestation of speech and language disorders (and, of course, the way in which clinicians make use of language sampleswhere). From this perspective, we see BORT bridging the gap between audio recordings of spoken language tests—transcribed manually or by an automatic speech recognizer—and downstream language evaluation tasks.

2.3 Considering alternative methods

Conceptually, BORT enhances BART with phoneme-to-grapheme functionality. Existing English grapheme-to-phoneme (G2P) systems are highly accurate, with recent transformer models achieving a 5.23% character error rate and a 22.1% word error rate on CMUDict (Yolchuyeva et al., 2019). These systems are trained and evaluated on word-length samples, so integration with a contextual language model would require novel architectural adapters, lest translation errors propagate through to downstream tasks. Explicit phoneme-to-grapheme (P2G) systems are uncommon by comparison; however, the hidden Markov model and Gaussian mixture model (HMM-GMM) architecture used in last-generation ASR systems (Mohri et al., 2001) might be described as an n-gram language model with a phoneme-to-grapheme component. This architecture assumes predefined mappings between words and its known pronunciations, and thus cannot capture the open-ended variability of disordered speech (in which a production might bear little or no phonological relationship to a target word). Further, considering the benefits of transfer learning for clinical (see §2.2), HMM-GMM models lack the flexibility and ergonomics of pre-trained transformer models.

3 BORT

3.1 Model Selection

Our models are a direct continuation of a pre-trained BART model as described by Lewis et al. (2020). We chose BART for several reasons. First, it uses a BPE tokenizer, which is able to encode arbitrary Unicode characters, including the entirety of the IPA. By contrast, BERT models use WordPiece tokenizers with finite token inventories. None of the pretrained BERT-like models we considered covered the IPA symbols used in English phonology, and expanding a WordPiece inventory is a non-trivial task. We were also motivated by the denoising task behind BART, since the synthesis of word errors is at least tangentially relevant to speech language pathology. Finally, unlike most models derived from the BERT architecture, BART features a left-to-right decoder ideal for generative tasks, and its pre-training task allows a mask token to represent one or more tokens, thus enabling us to overcome key limitations we encountered while revisiting our earlier work on analysis of connected speech from aphasic speakers (Adams et al., 2017) using techniques and models developed by Salem et al. (2022).

3.2 An IPA-to-Orthography Translation Task

Our self-supervised approach was formulated as a translation task, restoring partially-transformed documents back to the originals. We experimented with three word transforms: pronunciation, spelling, and noise. Ultimately, we were aiming for a system that could convert a mixture of IPA and orthography to its all-orthographic equivalent. However, despite an abundance of orthographic text, our pronunciation dictionary (described in more detail in §3.3) was limited to only 98K words during training. In an effort to avoid overfitting, we experimented with the other two less-constrained transforms.

Pronunciation transform. Our self-supervised approach was formulated as an IPA-to-orthography translation task. We used Wikipedia articles as a resource for orthographic text. Similar to masked language modeling, we randomly obscured words in each article, but instead of a special mask token, we replaced words with their pronunciations written in the IPA. Since the IPA includes letters from the English alphabet, which the tokenizer is likely to merge, we strategically inserted bullet symbols to maintain separation between phonemes (e.g. "shakedown" was transformed into "ʃe·k·d·aʊn"). We then trained the model to restore the text to its original orthographic form.

Spelling transform. Considering how English orthography is related to its phonology (however difficult a relationship it may be), we experimented with a spelling transform that could be formulated around any word, even those outside our pronunciation dictionary. For this task, for randomly selected words, we inserted a bullet symbol before each letter, forcing the tokenizer to treat each letter as a discrete token (e.g. "pizza" becomes "·P·I·Z·Z·A"). Note that we also used uppercase letters to avoid any overlap with the English

IPA symbols.

Noise transform. We also include a denoising task like the one used in pre-training the BART models (Lewis et al., 2020), wherein input tokens are inserted, deleted, and replaced at random. We used these same kinds of transforms, except we only apply noise to pronounced or spelled words. For these words, we randomly replace, insert, and delete tokens in the word. Insertions were limited to letters from the appropriate alphabet (either English or IPA).

Experimental configurations. We experimented with several variations of the above transforms, replacing 10% of pronounceable words with IPA, 10% of words with spellings, as well as a combined pronounced/spelled configuration (at 10% each). We repeated these configurations with noise added at a 5% probability. Table 1 summarizes the pre-training configurations used in this paper.

3.3 Data Preparation

Data sources. We based our pronunciation dictionary on version 0.7b of CMUDict (Carnegie Mellon University, 2014).[3] We converted their ARPABet entries to IPA using hard-coded rules, removing stress symbols. As carrier text for our self-supervised task, we used the 20220301.en version of Wikipedia provided by Huggingface Datasets.[4]

Word/article associations. For most purposes, the synthetic dataset was designed to be as open-ended as resources allowed, applying the transforms according to the word frequency distributions of Wikipedia. However, considering how the pronunciation dictionary was by far the data bottleneck (and thus the primary focus of our validation strategies), we needed a way to intentionally and efficiently find a high quality context for a given word. To this end, we paired each word in the pronunciation dictionary with a unique article based on an algorithm based on word frequencies. Tallying how many times our dictionary words appeared in each article, we assigned each dictionary word a unique article with a simple algorithm: beginning with the rarest word, we chose the next available article with the highest count for that word. We used a few simple rules to avoid specific types of low-quality articles.[5]

Data splits. We split the final list of 122K words and their associated Wikipedia articlesinto training, validation, and test sets (80%, 10%, and 10%, respectively). The remaining 6.5M Wikipedia articles with no associated word were added to the training set. Anticipating approximately 3100 target words that we would use to evaluate fine-tuning in §4, we placed these words in the test set. Three pairs of words were found only in overlapping articles; we placed these words in the training split.

Pronunciation transforms were only allowed for words which could be found in the split's dictionary. A spelling transform was only allowed for words which were *not* be found in *another* split's dictionary.

Training and validation inputs. We iterated over each Wikipedia article, transforming and noising pronounceable/spellable words at the rates specified in §3.2. Training inputs were limited 1000 BPE tokens to fit within BART's attention limit. If the article had an associated word, the sample was trimmed so the median-position occurrence of that word was at the center, otherwise a trim window was chosen at random. To minimize computation required for the validation set, each sample was limited to 100 tokens, with the median-position occurrence of that word at the center. If the experiment included a pronunciation transform, the associated dictionary word in the center was always pronounced.

Since the training set contained the most words, and the test set contained a number of high frequency words held out for fine-tuning evaluation, we found that the validation set only transformed at a word rate of 7–8% in practice, short of the 10% observed in the training inputs.

Test data. For evaluation purposes, only a single instance of the associated dictionary word was pronounced. Inputs were limited to 100 tokens, with the median-position occurrence of that word at the center. Neither the spelling nor the noise transforms were applied during testing.

3.4 Pre-training

Model weights were initialized from the 140M parameter BART-BASE pre-trained model found on the Fairseq website.[6] We based our hyperparameters on (Lewis et al., 2020), using the fairseq toolkit (Ott et al., 2019). Training targeted a categorical cross-entropy loss, with a learn rate of 10^{-5} and a maximum batch size of 12288 tokens, resulting in 317K batches per epoch. We computed the validation loss every 1K batches, and restored the best model after validation loss failed to improve for 63K batches (20% of the Wikipedia data).

3.5 Evaluation

We evaluated our pre-trained models in terms of accuracy and character error rate (CER) of the test set.

[3] https://github.com/Alexir/CMUdict/blob/7a37de7/cmudict-0.7b

[4] https://huggingface.co/datasets/wikipedia/

[5] We noticed our algorithm favored articles like "List of people with surname Carpenter" and "Mercury (disambiguation)," which have high word frequencies for "carpenter" and "mercury," respectively. In Wikipedia, these articles function only as lists of links to other articles, and we used them only as a last resort.

[6] https://github.com/facebookresearch/fairseq/tree/main/examples/bart

Pre-trained Model	Pron.	Spell.	Noise	Example of Transformed Text
BORT-PR	10%	—	—	he retaliates by s·pɹɛdɪŋ false rumours
BORT-SP	—	10%	—	he ·R·E·T·A·L·I·A·T·E·S by spreading false rumours
BORT-PR-SP	10%	10%	—	he ·R·E·T·A·L·I·A·T·E·S by s·pɹɛdɪŋ false rumours
BORT-PR-NOISY	10%	—	5%	he retaliates by ɔɪs·pɛdɪŋ false rumours
BORT-SP-NOISY	—	10%	5%	he ·E·T·A·K·I·A·T·E·S by spreading false rumours
BORT-PR-SP-NOISY	10%	10%	5%	he ·E·T·A·K·I·A·T·E·S by ɔɪs·pɛdɪŋ false rumours

Table 1: The various self-supervised training configurations for our models, indicating the percentage of words replaced with either pronunciations in the IPA or spelled, with or without noise added to the replacements. Example text from Wikipedia is shown to demonstrate the transformations. Bullet characters are inserted to enforce separation between those letters which would otherwise be merged during BPE text encoding.

Recall that in the test set we only applied the transform we were most interested in for this work: pronunciation. Considering how each correct output contains nearly a hundred words of text also found in the input—a trivial task to predict—we defined CER as the number of character errors divided by the length of *only the target word*. Text case and whitespace were ignored during evaluation. Only the models applying the pronunciation transform could be directly evaluated in this manner, so we do not include a baseline for this evaluation, and some models are only evaluated indirectly in §4.

3.6 Results

Configurations which included the noise transform did better overall than those without. The one with spelling (BORT-PR-SP-NOISY) was the overall best with a 15.1% CER, compared to BORT-PR-NOISY at 19.5%. To a lesser extent, spelling improved CER in the models without a noise transform: BORT-PR-SP and BORT-PR had a CER of 23.4% and 22.4%, respectively. Accuracy followed a similar pattern, with BORT-PR-SP-NOISY, BORT-PR-NOISY, BORT-PR-SP, BORT-PR showing accuracies of 64.5%, 61.8%, 51.6%, and 55.0%, respectively.

As for our overfitting concerns, most of our models showed an increase in validation loss (i.e. early stopping was triggered) before completing a full epoch of 6.5M Wikipedia articles. The pronunciation-only model BORT-PR after about 1.0M articles. Adding only the spelling transform for BORT-PR-SP nearly tripled the training duration to about 2.8M articles, while adding only the noise transform for BORT-PR-NOISY actually shortened training to about 0.6M articles. The combination of spelling and noise for BORT-PR-SP-NOISY trained for about 4.4M articles. The only models which completed a full epoch were those trained without the pronunciation transform, with BORT-SP and BORT-SP-NOISY training for about 6.9M and 7.9M articles, respectively.

Configuration	CER	Accuracy
BORT-PR	0.234	0.550
BORT-PR-SP	0.224	0.516
BORT-PR-NOISY	0.195	0.618
BORT-PR-SP-NOISY	0.151	0.645

Table 2: Character error rates (CER) and accuracies for the pre-training task, Only those configurations which applied the pronunciation transform are shown.

3.7 Discussion

Out of the pre-training configurations we evaluated with CER, the best performance was seen with BORT-PR-SP-NOISY, the model trained on all three transforms (phonology, spelling, and noise). This indicates that all three transforms were useful for the task of restoring a word from its pronunciation. Additionally, noise was clearly helpful for these models, since the next best configuration also used the noise transform (BORT-PR-NOISY).

The evaluation at this stage was lower than we expected, but this can largely be explained in terms of how the problem and its evaluation were formulated. Our hold-out rules were unusually strict to ensure the model could not memorize any of the words used during fine-tuning, heavily biasing the test data toward common English words. Second, CER is an imperfect evaluation measure for a model which operates on subword tokens, and one which isn't strictly a P2G translator. Additionally, as we emphasize in §4, evaluation on 1-best is a poor measure of the usefulness of a model intended for use in a complex pipeline.

4 Fine-tuning BORT

4.1 Data

Fine-tuning data consisted of 2,234 transcripts from 339 people with aphasia (PWA) from the English AphasiaBank database (MacWhinney et al., 2011), a widely-used repository of recorded and transcribed administrations of a standardized protocol consisting of a variety of tasks including discourse tasks, meant for use in studying language and cognitive sequelae of post-stroke aphasia.[7] Demographic characteristics of the participants are included in Appendix A. The transcripts used in this study were from one of nine tasks designed to elicit discourse; the tasks themselves are described in more detail in Appendix B. The tasks were transcribed by human annotators according to the CHAT transcription manual (Codes for the Human Analysis of Transcripts; MacWhinney 2000).

In the AphasiaBank transcripts, non-word paraphasias are transcribed in IPA, whereas lexical paraphasias are written in their orthographic form. For each paraphasia, whenever possible, the human annotator also identified the target word for that production (i.e., the word the person intended to say). Given the paraphasia-target pair, the annotator also categorized the paraphasia according to whether it was a real word, whether it was phonologically related to the target, and whether it was semantically related to the target.

We filtered the transcripts to just the PWA's language, and removed annotations irrelevant to the task (e.g., gestures). Then, we prepared the transcripts for training in two ways: an "easy" way and a "hard" way. In the "hard" task, the model learned the task that the human annotators performed in AphasiaBank: to predict the target word given the pronunciation of the paraphasia (and the surrounding context). In the "easy" task, we instead replaced the paraphasia pronunciation with the correct pronunciation for its associated target word. That is, in the "easy" task, we train the model to fill in correct pronunciations for words with their corresponding orthographic form, and in the "hard" task we train the model to fill in paraphasias (i.e., incorrect pronunciations) with the intended orthographic word.

For both the "easy" and "hard" tasks, we only considered paraphasias with a known target provided by the human annotator. For the "easy" task, we additionally removed paraphasias where there was not a known pronunciation of the orthographic form of the target in our pronunciation dictionary. This left us with 10,120 paraphasias. With the "hard" task, for the real word paraphasias, we instead removed paraphasias where there was not a known pronunciation of the orthographic form of the *paraphasia* in the pronunciation dictionary. This left us with 9,781 paraphasias for the "hard" task.

Each usable production was prepared with the full context of its transcript: all productions in the transcript were prepared as phonemes separated by bullets (as in §3.2), whether it be the target pronunciation or the paraphasia itself, and the production for the model to predict was marked with surrounding angle brackets. Some of these prepared samples were too long when tokenized, and thus trimmed to the maximum length (1024 tokens) in such a way that the maximum possible context on either side of the paraphasia was preserved. Part of a prepared example with the target "screwed" is shown below:

> **"Easy"**: and it <s·kɹu·d > up. but I went to to the hɑs·pɪtəl. and my brain s·kæn·d.
>
> **"Hard"**: and it <ʃkɹu·d > up. but I went to to the ɑs·pɪtəl. and my brain s·tæn·d.

For "easy," we substituted the correct pronunciation for screwed ("screwed"), while in "hard" we included the paraphasia ("shcrewed").

4.2 Training

Given either a correct ("easy") or incorrect ("hard") pronunciation, we fine-tuned each pre-trained BORT model to predict the intended word. As a baseline, we fine-tuned from the unmodified source model, BART-BASE. . As in pre-training, we adapted code from the fairseq sequence modeling toolkit (Ott et al., 2019). We used 10-fold cross validation with participant as the grouping factor, sequentially holding one fold out as valid set, a second fold as test set, and the remaining eight folds as the training set. We trained each model until early stopping occurred using loss on the validation set after 20 epochs without improvement. Training hyperparameters were the same as §3.4 but with an effective batch size of 4000 tokens.

4.3 Evaluation

We evaluated performance for the "easy" and "hard" tasks using CER and accuracy. As we did in §3.5, we calculated CER between the top model prediction and the human identified target for each paraphasia in the test set. We also calculated top 1 accuracy (the top model prediction matched the human identified target) and top 5 accuracy (the human identified target was within the top 5 model predictions) for each of the fine-tuned models' predictions on the test set. We determined whether disagreements between top 1 accuracy of the different models were significant using McNemar's test with continuity correction (McNemar, 1947) and Bonferroni correction (Haynes, 2013). We conducted this test for all six models versus the baseline, as well as the best performing model versus all other models, for both "easy" and "hard" tasks, leading to 24 comparisons in total. Accounting for multiple comparisons and using an alpha of 0.05, a p-value of < 0.00208 was retained as the level of statistical significance . Finally,

[7] Our snapshot of the transcripts was copied from AphasiaBank on March 8th, 2023, and the corresponding demographic metadata downloaded on April 23, 2023.

for the best configuration in the "hard" task, we also calculated top 1 accuracy stratified by AphasiaBank task and error type, presented in Appendix C.

4.4 Results

CER, top 1 accuracy, and top 5 accuracy on the test set is shown for the "easy" and "hard" tasks in Tables 3a and 3b respectively. For both "easy" and "hard" tasks, all of the BORT models had significantly higher performance than BART-BASE at top 1 accuracy according to McNemar's test with $p < 0.00208$ for all comparisons.

In the "easy" task, the baseline configuration (BART-BASE) led to top 1 accuracy 72.5%, and CER 22.8%. Out of the models trained with noise, best performance was seen in BORT-PR-SP-NOISY with top 1 accuracy 89.5%. However, BORT-PR-SP saw the best performance out of all models, with a 90.1% chance of correctly predicting the appropriate word for a given correct pronunciation and a CER of just 5.7%, improving on the baseline by a relative 24% and 75%, respectively. The accuracy was significantly higher than all other models with $p < 0.00208$ for all comparisons. Allowing for five chances to get the correct prediction, this model achieved 94.7% accuracy.

For the "hard" task, the baseline achieved 36.3% top 1 accuracy and 60.6% CER. Out of the configurations which did not apply noise, BORT-PR-SP achieved the highest top 1 accuracy of 45.6% and CER 44.7%. The best pre-training configuration was BORT-PR-SP-NOISY, which applied all three transforms. It achieved top 1 accuracy 46.7% and CER 42.0%, improving on the baseline by a relative 29% and 31%, respectively. The top 1 accuracy was significantly higher than most models with $p < 0.00208$, except for BORT-PR-SP ($p = 0.020$) and BORT-PR-NOISY ($p = 0.023$). BORT-PR-SP-NOISY also had 65.6% top 5 accuracy. Accuracy within top 1–20 predictions of the baseline and best performing models for the "easy" and "hard" tasks can be seen in Figure 1. Performance increases for all models as we allow more chances to find the correct target, but the order of performance remains the same. Additional results—namely those stratified by AphasiaBank task and error types—can be found in Appendix C.

4.5 Discussion

The fine-tuning configurations without the pronunciation transform (BORT-SP and BORT-SP-NOISY) were the lowest performing of the BORT models, but they still had significantly higher top 1 accuracy than the fine-tuned BART-BASE model. Moreover, for both "easy" and "hard" tasks, the best performing models were trained with both the pronunciation and spelling transforms, and either with or without noise. This pattern implies that there is enough overlap between

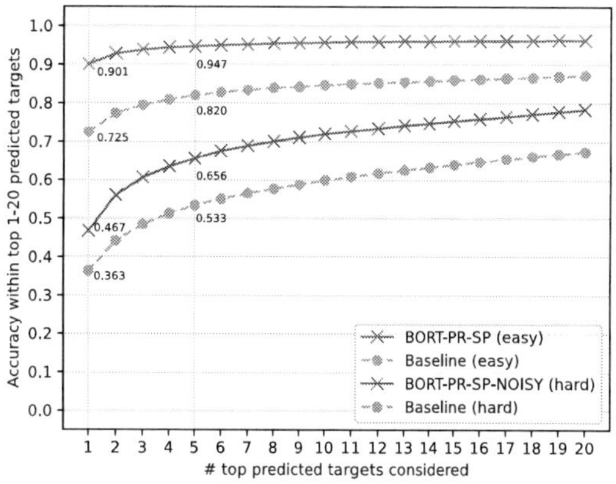

Figure 1: Accuracy within top 1-20 predictions of baseline and best performing models for "easy" and "hard" fine-tuning tasks.

orthography and phonology in the English language that pre-training the LLM to spell helped the model to perform the task at hand. Considering the G2P frame of reference—though we note again that this is a loose comparison (see §3.7)—a 5.7% CER is on par with what could be expected from a model strictly translating between phonemes and graphemes.

Aphasic speech is characterized by paraphasias, which can be considered "noisy" productions, so it stands to reason that learning to de-noise productions would help the model with the "hard" fine-tuning task. As we hypothesized, the "hard" task saw the best performance from the pre-training configuration with all three transforms (pronunciation, spelling, and noise), although its performance was not *significantly* different than the configuration without spelling (BORT-PR-NOISY) or without noise (BORT-PR-SP). Contrary to what we observed in §3.5, for the "easy" task, noise did not seem to help the models, and the best performing configuration was one that did not include noise in pre-training (BORT-PR-SP).

Moreover, the top 1 accuracy performance of this model was significantly different than all other "easy" models. This is surprising since the evaluation for pre-training and the "easy" task were quite similar, being a phoneme-to-grapheme translation task with and without context, respectively. This might be explained by the stricter hold-out rules during pre-training—we had no vocabulary restrictions during fine-tuning—or by the shift in data domain (Wikipedia vs. AphasiaBank). It is difficult to say with certainty why this discrepancy occurred, but perhaps noise was most helpful for language from a very diverse corpora (Wikipedia), while in the more constrained tasks from AphasiaBank, the more limited vocabulary did not benefit from synthetic variability.

Pre-training Configuration	CER Top 1	Accuracy Top 1	Accuracy Top 5
BORT-PR	0.083	0.869	0.931
BORT-SP	0.106	0.843	0.906
BORT-PR-SP	0.057	**0.901**	0.947
BORT-PR-NOISY	0.089	0.863	0.925
BORT-SP-NOISY	0.096	0.848	0.911
BORT-PR-SP-NOISY	0.060	0.895	0.947
BART-BASE	0.228	0.725	0.820

(a) "Easy" Task

Pre-training Configuration	CER Top 1	Accuracy Top 1	Accuracy Top 5
BORT-PR	0.462	0.451	0.634
BORT-SP	0.526	0.401	0.579
BORT-PR-SP	0.447	*0.456*	0.641
BORT-PR-NOISY	0.452	*0.458*	0.640
BORT-SP-NOISY	0.469	0.446	0.625
BORT-PR-SP-NOISY	0.420	**0.467**	0.656
BART-BASE	0.606	0.363	0.533

(b) "Hard" Task

Table 3: Accuracies for each pre-trained model after fine-tuning to our two tasks. Bold font indicates accuracy was significantly different from all other models, with the exception of those italicized, according to McNemar's test.

5 Conclusion

In §3, we pre-trained BORT to accept a mixture of orthography and IPA. During training and validation, we used one to three different transforms of words (pronunciation, spelling, noise) and trained the model to restore the words to their original form. We directly evaluated the four models trained on pronunciation using a test set of the Wikipedia data by testing the CER of their performance at restoring a word from its pronunciation. In §4, we evaluated all six models (and the baseline) by further fine-tuning them to restore words from productions in aphasic speech. This allowed us to evaluate the applicability of our mixed orthography/IPA LLM to a clinical task.

Our best BORT configurations achieved high accuracy and low CER rates for the "easy" fine-tuning task, with the fine-tuned accuracy as high as 90%. This indicates we were able to successfully produce a LLM that can accept both orthography and IPA. Moreover, observing differences between accuracy and CER revealed that even when our fine-tuned models incorrectly predicted the target word, they still may have found close-by words. For instance, considering the "easy" task, the best performing model picked the wrong target 10% of the time, but it achieved an average CER of just 5.7%. This indicates that there were likely instances where even though the LLM predicted the wrong target, it picked a similar word with overlapping letters with the target word.

Future work will improve on these pre-trained models. In §3.1 we hypothesized BART's generative architecture and denoising task were advantages for our use case. With model selection, though, we find certain tradeoffs, and we would like to test whether these advantages outweigh unique functionalities found in other models. In particular, models designed to operate at a character level (e.g. CANINE, Clark et al., 2022) could overcome other limitations of BORT (e.g. our explicit demarcation of phonemic and orthographic regions), and is perhaps generally well-suited for the task at hand.

An additional area of future work will consist of exploring alternative training strategies. In the present work, we were quite strict with regard to preparing the test split, withholding the most frequent English words because they appeared in our AphasiaBank evaluations. As our focus turns more toward downstream tasks, we will update our holdout methods to prioritize a stronger pre-trained model, holding out only as much data as needed for validation. Further, seeing how our models did not train for an entire pass through the Wikipedia data, we will adjust the training schedule (e.g. a ramp-up in the learning rate) and task configuration (e.g. word transform rates) to ensure we get the most out of the pre-training stage.

For our aphasia-specific application, we see room to improve the noise transform with more strategic approaches. Phoneme errors could be made more realistic with statistically or linguistically informed approaches (e.g. replacing phonemes with similar phonemes). To better prepare a model for semantic errors, whole-word replacements could be made with semantically similar words.

Limitations

The models presented here were trained with the basic inventory of English phonemes found in CMUDict. However, a more fine-grained phonetic analysis would require a pronunciation dictionary with more narrowly defined entries. Additionally, while this paper focused on models trained with English-only resources (pre-trained BART-BASE, English Wikipedia text, CMUDict, and the English AphasiaBank), the techniques should be applicable to non-English language models as well. Finally, from a clinical standpoint, the model we describe in this paper assumes the existence of transcribed input (from either a manual or automated source, discussed in detail in § 2.1); in its current form, this represents a limitation to its clinical implementation, though not to its use in research settings with archival or newly-transcribed datasets.

Ethics Statement

Our use of the AphasiaBank data was governed by the TalkBank consortium's data use agreement, and the underlying recordings were collected and shared with approval of the contributing sites' institutional review boards. Limitations exist regarding accents and dialect, which in turn would affect the scenarios in which a system based on our model could (and should) be used. It should also be noted that these models and any derived technology are not meant to be tools to diagnose medical conditions, a task best left to qualified clinicians.

Acknowledgements

We thank our anonymous reviewers for their helpful insights and detailed feedback. This work was supported by the National Institute on Deafness and Other Communication Disorders of the National Institutes of Health under award 5R01DC015999 (Principal Investigators: Bedrick & Fergadiotis). The content is solely the responsibility of the authors and does not necessarily represent the official views of the National Institutes of Health.

References

Stefanie Abel, Klaus Willmes, and Walter Huber. 2007. Model-oriented naming therapy: Testing predictions of a connectionist model. *Aphasiology*, 21(5):411–447.

Joel Adams, Steven Bedrick, Gerasimos Fergadiotis, Kyle Gorman, and Jan van Santen. 2017. Target word prediction and paraphasia classification in spoken discourse. In *BioNLP 2017*, pages 1–8, Vancouver, Canada,. Association for Computational Linguistics.

Nancy Azevedo, Eva Kehayia, Gonia Jarema, Guylaine Le Dorze, Christel Beaujard, and Marc Yvon. 2023. How artificial intelligence (AI) is used in aphasia rehabilitation: A scoping review. *Aphasiology*, pages 1–32.

Aparna Balagopalan, Benjamin Eyre, Frank Rudzicz, and Jekaterina Novikova. 2020. To BERT or not to BERT: Comparing speech and language-based approaches for Alzheimer's disease detection. In *Interspeech 2020*, pages 2167–2171. ISCA.

Carnegie Mellon University. 2014. Carnegie mellon university pronouncing dictionary (CMUDict), version 0.7b. http://www.speech.cs.cmu.edu/cgi-bin/cmudict.

Marianne Casilio, Gerasimos Fergadiotis, Alexandra C. Salem, Robert C. Gale, Katy McKinney-Bock, and Steven Bedrick. 2023. Paralg: A paraphasia algorithm for multinomial classification of picture naming errors. *Journal of Speech, Language, and Hearing Research*, pages 1–21.

Soojin Cho-Reyes and Cynthia K. Thompson. 2012. Verb and sentence production and comprehension in aphasia: Northwestern Assessment of Verbs and Sentences (NAVS). *Aphasiology*, 26(10):1250–1277.

Jonathan H. Clark, Dan Garrette, Iulia Turc, and John Wieting. 2022. Canine: Pre-training an efficient tokenization-free encoder for language representation. *Transactions of the Association for Computational Linguistics*, 10:73–91.

Lisa A. Edmonds and Swathi Kiran. 2006. Effect of Semantic Naming Treatment on Crosslinguistic Generalization in Bilingual Aphasia. *Journal of Speech, Language, and Hearing Research*, 49(4):729–748.

Jeffrey L. Elman. 1990. Finding structure in time. *Cognitive Science*, 14(2):179–211.

Gerasimos Fergadiotis, Kyle Gorman, and Steven Bedrick. 2016. Algorithmic classification of five characteristic types of paraphasias. *American Journal of Speech-Language Pathology*, 25(4S):S776–S787.

Kathleen Fraser, Frank Rudzicz, Naida Graham, and Elizabeth Rochon. 2013. Automatic speech recognition in the diagnosis of primary progressive aphasia. In *Proceedings of the Fourth Workshop on Speech and Language Processing for Assistive Technologies*, pages 47–54, Grenoble, France. Association for Computational Linguistics.

Kathleen C Fraser, Jed A Meltzer, Naida L Graham, Carol Leonard, Graeme Hirst, Sandra E Black, and Elizabeth Rochon. 2014. Automated classification of primary progressive aphasia subtypes from narrative speech transcripts. *Cortex*, 55:43–60.

Philip Gage. 1994. A new algorithm for data compression. *C Users Journal*, 12(2):23–38.

Robert Gale, Julie Bird, Yiyi Wang, Jan van Santen, Emily Prud'hommeaux, Jill Dolata, and Meysam Asgari. 2021. Automated scoring of tablet-administered expressive language tests. *Frontiers in Psychology*, 12.

Robert C. Gale, Mikala Fleegle, Gerasimos Fergadiotis, and Steven Bedrick. 2022. The post-stroke speech transcription (PSST) challenge. In *Proceedings of the RaPID Workshop - Resources and ProcessIng of linguistic, para-linguistic and extra-linguistic Data from people with various forms of cognitive/psychiatric/developmental impairments - within the 13th Language Resources and Evaluation Conference*, pages 41–55, Marseille, France. European Language Resources Association.

Winston Haynes. 2013. Bonferroni Correction. In Werner Dubitzky, Olaf Wolkenhauer, Kwang-Hyun Cho, and Hiroki Yokota, editors, *Encyclopedia of Systems Biology*, pages 154–154. Springer New York, New York, NY.

Yvette Hou, Aileen Zhou, Laura Brooks, Daniella Reid, Lyn Turkstra, and Sheila MacDonald. 2023. Rehabilitation access for individuals with cognitive-communication challenges after traumatic brain injury: A co-design study with persons with lived experience. *International Journal of Language & Communication Disorders*, pages 1460–6984.12895.

Itay Itzhak and Omer Levy. 2022. Models in a spelling bee: Language models implicitly learn the character composition of tokens. In *Proceedings of the 2022 Conference of the North American Chapter of the Association for Computational Linguistics: Human Language Technologies*, pages 5061–5068, Seattle, United States. Association for Computational Linguistics.

A Jacks, K L Haley, G Bishop, and T G Harmon. 2019. Automated speech recognition in adult stroke survivors: Comparing human and computer transcriptions. *Folia Phoniatrica et Logopaedica*, 71(5-6):286–296.

Ye Jia, Heiga Zen, Jonathan Shen, Yu Zhang, and Yonghui Wu. 2021. PnG BERT: Augmented BERT on Phonemes and Graphemes for Neural TTS. In *Proc. Interspeech 2021*, pages 151–155.

Edith Kaplan, Harold Goodglass, and Sandra Weintraub, editors. 2001. *Boston naming test*, 2. ed edition. Lippincott, Williams & Wilkins, Philadelphia.

Diane L Kendall, Rebecca Hunting Pompon, C Elizabeth Brookshire, Irene Minkina, and Lauren Bislick. 2013. An analysis of aphasic naming errors as an indicator of improved linguistic processing following phonomotor treatment. *American Journal of Speech-Language Pathology*, 22(2):S240–S249.

Andrew Kertesz. 2012. Western Aphasia Battery–Revised. Technical report, American Psychological Association. Type: dataset.

Swathi Kiran, Carrie Des Roches, Isabel Balachandran, and Elsa Ascenso. 2014. Development of an Impairment-Based Individualized Treatment Workflow Using an iPad-Based Software Platform. *Seminars in Speech and Language*, 35(01):038–050.

Duc Le, Keli Licata, and Emily Mower Provost. 2017. Automatic Paraphasia Detection from Aphasic Speech: A Preliminary Study. In *Proc. Interspeech 2017*, pages 294–298.

Mike Lewis, Yinhan Liu, Naman Goyal, Marjan Ghazvininejad, Abdelrahman Mohamed, Omer Levy, Veselin Stoyanov, and Luke Zettlemoyer. 2020. BART: Denoising sequence-to-sequence pre-training for natural language generation, translation, and comprehension. In *Proceedings of the 58th Annual Meeting of the Association for Computational Linguistics*, pages 7871–7880, Online. Association for Computational Linguistics.

Yinghao Aaron Li, Cong Han, Xilin Jiang, and Nima Mesgarani. 2023. Phoneme-level bert for enhanced prosody of text-to-speech with grapheme predictions.

Duanchen Liu, Zoey Liu, Qingyun Yang, Yujing Huang, and Emily Prud'hommeaux. 2022. Evaluating the performance of transformer-based language models for neuroatypical language. In *Proceedings of the 29th International Conference on Computational Linguistics*, pages 3412–3419, Gyeongju, Republic of Korea. International Committee on Computational Linguistics.

Heather MacFarlane, Alexandra C Salem, Steven Bedrick, Jill K Dolata, Jack Wiedrick, Grace O Lawley, Lizbeth H Finestack, Sara T Kover, Angela John Thurman, Leonard Abbeduto, and Eric Fombonne. 2023. Consistency and reliability of automated language measures across expressive language samples in autism. *Autism research : official journal of the International Society for Autism Research*, 16(4):802–816.

Brian MacWhinney. 2000. *The CHILDES project: Tools for analyzing talk*, 3rd edition. Lawrence Erlbaum Associates, Mahwah, NJ.

Brian MacWhinney, Davida Fromm, Margaret Forbes, and Audrey Holland. 2011. Aphasiabank: Methods for studying discourse. *Aphasiology*, 25(11):1286–1307.

Quinn McNemar. 1947. Note on the sampling error of the difference between correlated proportions or percentages. *Psychometrika*, 12(2):153–157.

Irene Minkina, Megan Oelke, Lauren P Bislick, C Elizabeth Brookshire, Rebecca Hunting Pompon, Joann P Silkes, and Diane L Kendall. 2015. An investigation of aphasic naming error evolution following phonomotor treatment. *Aphasiology*, pages 1–19.

Mehryar Mohri, Fernando Pereira, and Michael Riley. 2001. Weighted finite-state transducers in speech recognition. *Departmental Papers (CIS)*, page 11.

Myle Ott, Sergey Edunov, Alexei Baevski, Angela Fan, Sam Gross, Nathan Ng, David Grangier, and Michael Auli. 2019. fairseq: A fast, extensible toolkit for sequence modeling. In *Proceedings of the 2019 Conference of the North American Chapter of the Association for Computational Linguistics (Demonstrations)*, pages 48–53, Minneapolis, Minnesota. Association for Computational Linguistics.

Matthew Perez, Zakaria Aldeneh, and Emily Mower Provost. 2020. Aphasic Speech Recognition Using a Mixture of Speech Intelligibility Experts. In *Interspeech 2020*, pages 4986–4990. ISCA.

Ulla Petti, Simon Baker, and Anna Korhonen. 2020. A systematic literature review of automatic Alzheimer's disease detection from speech and language. *Journal of the American Medical Informatics Association : JAMIA*, 27(11):1784–1797.

Alan Prince and Paul Smolensky. 1997. Optimality: From neural networks to universal grammar. *Science*, 275(5306):1604–1610.

Anna Rogers, Olga Kovaleva, and Anna Rumshisky. 2020. A primer in BERTology: What we know about how BERT works. *Transactions of the Association for Computational Linguistics*, 8:842–866.

Alexandra C. Salem, Robert Gale, Marianne Casilio, Mikala Fleegle, Gerasimos Fergadiotis, and Steven Bedrick. 2022. Refining semantic similarity of paraphasias using a contextual language model. *Journal of Speech, Language, and Hearing Research*, pages 1–15.

Mike Schuster and Kaisuke Nakajima. 2012. Japanese and korean voice search. In *2012 IEEE International Conference on Acoustics, Speech and Signal Processing (ICASSP)*, pages 5149–5152.

Rico Sennrich, Barry Haddow, and Alexandra Birch. 2016. Neural machine translation of rare words with subword units. In *Proceedings of the 54th Annual Meeting of the Association for Computational Linguistics (Volume 1: Long Papers)*, pages 1715–1725, Berlin, Germany. Association for Computational Linguistics.

Mukuntha Narayanan Sundararaman, Ayush Kumar, and Jithendra Vepa. 2021. PhonemeBERT: Joint Language Modelling of Phoneme Sequence and ASR Transcript. In *Proc. Interspeech 2021*, pages 3236–3240.

Iván G. Torre, Mónica Romero, and Aitor Álvarez. 2021. Improving Aphasic Speech Recognition by Using Novel Semi-Supervised Learning Methods on AphasiaBank for English and Spanish. *Applied Sciences*, 11(19):8872.

Mieke Van De Sandt-Koenderman. 2004. High-tech AAC and aphasia: Widening horizons? *Aphasiology*, 18(3):245–263.

Marjo Virnes, Eija Kärnä, and Virpi Vellonen. 2015. Review of research on children with autism spectrum disorder and the use of technology. *Journal of Special Education Technology*, 30(1):13–27.

Grant M. Walker and Gregory Hickok. 2016. Bridging computational approaches to speech production: The semantic-lexical-auditory-motor model (SLAM). *Psychonomic Bulletin & Review*, 23(2):339–352.

Sevinj Yolchuyeva, Géza Németh, and Bálint Gyires-Tóth. 2019. Transformer Based Grapheme-to-Phoneme Conversion. In *Interspeech 2019*, pages 2095–2099. ISCA.

Guangyan Zhang, Kaitao Song, Xu Tan, Daxin Tan, Yuzi Yan, Yanqing Liu, Gang Wang, Wei Zhou, Tao Qin, Tan Lee, and Sheng Zhao. 2022. Mixed-phoneme bert: Improving bert with mixed phoneme and sup-phoneme representations for text to speech.

Appendix

A AphasiaBank Demographics

Demographic characteristics from the 339 participants are summarized in Table 4.

B Description of AphasiaBank Tasks

We used transcripts from nine tasks from AphasiaBank. Descriptions of each task are provided in Table 5. More information can be found on the AphasiaBank website.[8]

C Detailed Results

We calculated top 1 accuracy for our best performing model in the "hard" task, BORT-PR-SP-NOISY, stratified by AphasiaBank task type. These results are shown in Table 6. Performance was lowest for AphasiaBank's "Free Speech Samples" section with accuracies ranging from 33%–36%, followed by most of "Picture Descriptions" at 41.1%–44.5%, with the exception of Umbrella. The best performance was seen in the "Story Narrative" and "Procedural Discourse" sections with 53.3% and 52.2%, respectively, as well as the Umbrella picture description (61.8%). This pattern makes sense, since the fine-tuned models can use exposure to the task domain to learn what common vocabulary occurs in the tasks. Topics that are very open-ended, like the Free Speech Samples, instead could have a large range of possible targets for paraphasias.

[8] https://aphasia.talkbank.org/protocol/english/materials-aphasia

Characteristic	Value	Characteristic	Value
Age		**Aphasia Duration**	
M (*SD*)	61.8 (12.3)	*M* (*SD*)	5.4 (5.4)
Min - Max	25.6–90.7	Min - Max	0.08–44
Missing (*N*)	3	Missing (*N*)	16
Race			
White (*N*)	284	**WAB-R AQ**	
African American (*N*)	37	*M* (*SD*)	71.0 (19.6)
Asian (*N*)	2	Min - Max	10.8-99.6
Hispanic/Latino (*N*)	9	Missing (*N*)	37
Native Hawaiian / Pacific Islander (*N*)	2		
American Indian / Alaska Native (*N*)	1	**BNT-SF**	
Mixed (*N*)	2	*M* (*SD*)	7.1 (4.6)
Other (*N*)	1	Min - Max	0-15
Unavailable (*N*)	1	Missing (*N*)	69
Gender		**VNT**	
M (*N*)	199	*M* (*SD*)	14.3 (6.6)
F (*N*)	140	Min - Max	0-22
		Missing (*N*)	56
Years of Education			
M (*SD*)	15.4 (2.7)		
Min - Max	8–25		
Missing (*N*)	14		

Table 4: Demographic characteristics for the 339 participants at their first session, where available. WAB-R AQ is the Western Aphasia Battery-Revised Aphasia Quotient, and captures overall aphasia severity with higher values indicating lower severity (Kertesz, 2012). BNT-SF is the raw score from the Boston Naming Test-Short Form (Kaplan et al., 2001). VNT is the raw score from the Verb Naming Test (Cho-Reyes and Thompson, 2012). The BNT-SF and VNT are both confrontation picture naming tests, where the BNT-SF captures word retrieval deficits of object words and the VNT captures word retrieval deficits of action words.

Section	Task	Description
I: Free Speech Samples	Speech	The participant describes how their speech is currently.
	Stroke	The participant's story of his or her stroke.
	Important Event	A personal narrative with a wide range of possible topics.
II. Picture Descriptions	Window	A picture description task.
	Umbrella	A picture description task.
	Cat	A picture description task.
	Flood	A picture description task.
III. Story Narrative	Cinderella	The participant recounts a narrative of Cinderella, after reviewing pictures of central events of it.
IV. Procedural Discourse	Sandwich	The participant is asked to describe how to make a peanut butter & jelly sandwich.

Table 5: Descriptions of nine AphasiaBank tasks

AphasiaBank Task	N	Accuracy
I. Free Speech Samples		
Speech	265	0.340
Stroke	1620	0.357
Important Event	900	0.330
II. Picture Descriptions		
Window	711	0.414
Umbrella	1103	0.618
Cat	1197	0.445
Flood	180	0.411
III. Story Narrative		
Cinderella	3065	0.533
IV. Procedural Discourse		
Sandwich	740	0.522

Table 6: Number of samples (N) and top 1 accuracy for BORT-PR-SP-NOISY after fine-tuning to the "hard" task, stratified by AphasiaBank task.

Error Type	N	Accuracy
Phonological	4557	0.473
Semantic	3137	0.485
Neologism	1570	0.445
Morphological	417	0.350
Dysfluency	11	0.455
Multiple Types	82	0.488
Unknown Type	7	0.286

Table 7: Number of samples (N) and top 1 accuracy for BORT-PR-SP-NOISY after fine-tuning to the "hard" task, stratified by AphasiaBank error type annotations.

Effectiveness of Data Augmentation for Parameter Efficient Tuning with Limited Data

Stephen Obadinma[a] **, Hongyu Guo**[b,c]**, Xiaodan Zhu**[a]
[a]Department of Electrical and Computer Engineering, Queen's University,
[b]Digital Technologies Research Centre, National Research Council Canada,
[c]School of Electrical Engineering and Computer Science, University of Ottawa
[a] {16sco, xiaodan.zhu}@queensu.ca
[b,c] {Hongyu.Guo}@nrc-cnrc.gc.ca

Abstract

Recent work has demonstrated that using parameter efficient tuning techniques such as prefix tuning (or P-tuning) on pretrained language models can yield performance that is comparable or superior to fine-tuning while dramatically reducing trainable parameters. Nevertheless, the effectiveness of such methods under the context of data augmentation, a common strategy to improve learning under low data regimes, has not been fully explored. In this paper, we examine the effectiveness of several popular task-agnostic data augmentation techniques, i.e., EDA, Back Translation, and Mixup, when using two general parameter efficient tuning methods, P-tuning v2 and LoRA, under data scarcity. We show that data augmentation can be used to boost the performance of P-tuning and LoRA models, but the effectiveness of each technique varies and certain methods can lead to a notable degradation in performance, particularly when using larger models and on harder tasks. We further analyze the sentence representations of P-tuning compared to fine-tuning to help understand the above behaviour, and reveal how P-tuning generally presents a more limited ability to separate the sentence embeddings from different classes of augmented data. In addition, it displays poorer performance on heavily altered data. However, we demonstrate that by adding a simple contrastive loss function it can help mitigate such issues for prefix tuning, resulting in sizable improvements to augmented data performance.

1 Introduction

While large pretrained language models have achieved superior performance and widespread adoption across many NLP tasks (Zaheer et al., 2020; Bengio et al., 2021), they often contain hundreds of millions or even hundreds of billions of parameters, which significantly limits their application to tasks in which computation and storage resources are constrained.

To address this issue, an entire family of techniques called parameter efficient tuning (PET) methods have been developed. Most notably, deep prompt tuning (i.e., prefix tuning or P-tuning) (Li and Liang, 2021; Qin and Eisner, 2021; Liu et al., 2021) has attracted extensive attention, which, compared to fine-tuning, only tunes trainable continuous embeddings, resulting in a tiny percentage of tuned parameters for each task. Consequently, a single language model can be used for multiple tasks by swapping out the trained prompts on a task basis (Li and Liang, 2021). Such success has also been shown by the state-of-the-art P-tuning v2 model (Liu et al., 2021), which yields performance comparable to fine-tuning on various natural language understanding tasks. In addition, Low-Rank Adaptation (LoRA) (Hu et al., 2021) has also emerged as an alternative approach, whereby the weights of rank decomposition matrices that are injected into each layer are optimized in lieu of the full network weights, reducing trainable parameters while also achieving improvements in accuracy over fine-tuning and other PET methods.

When training data is scarce in a task, data augmentation (DA) is a widely used strategy that can boost the performance of deep learning models (see (Feng et al., 2021) for a survey on data augmentation in NLP). Then a basic question that needs to be answered is how effective is it when the above PET frameworks are applied in conjunction with data augmentation. To this end, we study three common task-agnostic DA methods, EDA (Wei and Zou, 2019), Back Translation (Sennrich et al., 2016), and Mixup (Guo et al., 2019a) with two common language models BERT (Devlin et al., 2019) and RoBERTa (Liu et al., 2019), trained using P-tuning v2 (Liu et al., 2021) and LoRA (Hu et al., 2021). We set up our study across five tasks, including 4 from SuperGLUE (Wang et al., 2019), in which the sizes of training data are small.

We show that data augmentation can increase

Proceedings of the 8th Workshop on Representation Learning for NLP (RepL4NLP 2023), pages 226–237
July 13, 2023 ©2023 Association for Computational Linguistics

the accuracy of prefix tuning models. However, the performance of each technique varies depending on the dataset and underlying pretrained model, and the effective techniques differ from fine-tuning. Certain methods can even lead to a notable degradation in performance, particularly when using larger models. To better understand the above phenomena, we visualize sentence representations of data under prefix tuning, a technique where many augmentation methods fail to get good results, to observe whether any limitations are present with how data is represented that are leading to poor performance in certain cases. Through this, we find that these models struggle more with separating the augmented embeddings from different classes. This observation is further supported by our additional experiments showing a lower robustness to heavily altered augmented data compared to fine-tuning, and an analysis of the cosine similarities between the sentence embeddings of augmented sentences and their original counterparts, where we see that prefix tuning produces highly similar embeddings irrespective of alterations. We seek to improve the performance when training on augmented data by adding a contrastive loss term (Oord et al., 2018) to minimize distances between intra-class embeddings in P-tuning v2, helping mitigate the above issues with sentence representations, and resulting in some improvements in accuracy. We hope this empirical study helps facilitate future work on leveraging data augmentation when training transformer-based models using parameter efficient tuning methods.

2 Related Work

A wide range of data augmentation techniques are used in NLP. Some general types of methods include rule-based techniques that use predetermined, rule-based transformations like synonym replacement that are not dependant on any model architecture (Feng et al., 2021). Example methods include EDA. Model-based techniques utilize language modelling to generate new data through means like seq2seq translation models as in back translation (Sennrich et al., 2016), masked language modelling using transformers on randomly masked inputs (Garg and Ramakrishnan, 2020), or using generative models like GPT-2 as in Anaby-Tavor et al. (2020) where a label-conditioned generation model is obtained by fine-tuning GPT-2 (Radford et al., 2019).

Despite widespread use in computer vision, DA is not as commonly used in the training of NLP models, largely due to the discrete nature of language making it difficult to apply perturbations without compromising the meaning, and the inconsistency in performance of different techniques (Feng et al., 2021). The effectiveness of DA on fine-tuned models has been studied previously. (Longpre et al., 2020) detail how BT and EDA could not generate consistent benefits on classification tasks with transformer-based models. Similarly, (Okimura et al., 2022) expand this previous study and test the impact of 12 different DA methods and find little benefit when training on datasets with thousands of examples, but that there is some improvement in performance with very limited data (only a few hundred training cases). Our study conducts a similar examination on the effectiveness of data augmentation with pretrained models, however we focus on prefix tuning and LoRA, and we inspect how the properties of prefix tuning under DA differ from fine-tuning and what practical effect this has, particularly in terms of sentence representations.

3 Data Augmentation with Parameter Efficient Tuning

Prefix Tuning Approach. We first experiment with prefix tuning, and base our approach on the P-tuning v2 (Liu et al., 2021) implementation. By optimizing prefix length, selectively applying reparameterization, and tuning a randomly-initialized classification head on top of the transformer sentence representations, P-tuning v2 can be applied to smaller language models and across many tasks, including classification, with no drop in performance compared to fine-tuning. P-tuning v2 works by adding prompts of length p tokens to all layers of the language model in the form of sequences of continuous prefix tokens. These continuous embeddings, represented by the vector $H_m = [h_0, ..., h_p]$ where each $h_i \in \mathbb{R}^d$ has the dimensionality of token embeddings d for each layer m in the transformer-based model, are prefixed to the embeddings of each transformer layer $E_m = [E_{CLS}, E_1, ..., E_n]$ where n is the max sequence length. Thus, each layer of the language model can attend over prompts independently. The overall language model parameters remain frozen during training, with only the parameters of the prefixes and linear head for the classification layer getting optimized. The prefixes can optionally be passed into a reparameterization encoder such as an MLP (Li and Liang, 2021), but this is not always effective and so we only selectively apply this in certain cases where we find it improves performance as in Liu et al. (2021).

LoRA. We test LoRA (Hu et al., 2021), which is a technique that similarly freezes the original transformer weights, but only tunes trainable pairs of rank-decomposition matrices that are inserted into each transformer layer to approximate the weight updates, greatly reducing the number of parameters needed by avoiding updating the full layer weights while not increasing inference costs. Instead of updating a pretrained weight matrix of a transformer $W_0 \in R^{d \times k}$ with a gradient-based weight update ΔW for time step t to get a new weight matrix as in $W_t = W_0 + \Delta W_t$, LoRA does a low-rank decomposition of the update into two matrices $W_B \in R^{d \times r}$ and $W_A \in R^{r \times k}$ that act as learnable parameters to represent the new update as $W_t = W_B W_A + W_0$, with W_0 being frozen and where r represents the rank of the decomposition. The authors find applying LoRA to the query and value projection matrices in the attention mechanism leads to the most optimal performance. LoRA often outperforms other PET methods, making it worthy of study in this context (He et al., 2022).

Data Augmentation Methods. In this study we focus on *task-agnostic* data augmentation, which are methods that are broadly applicable to a wide range of NLP tasks. Many popular DA methods exist and of these, we utilize: (1) *Easy Data Augmentation (EDA)* (Wei and Zou, 2019), a technique where augmented sentences are created by applying a number of rule-based text editing operations; (2) *Back Translation (BT)* (Sennrich et al., 2016) where augmented data is generated by translating text into a target language then translating it back into the original language; (3) *Mixup for Sentence Classification* (Guo et al., 2019a), where we take the senMixup approach by generating synthetic data through interpolation over the classification tokens of random pairs of sentences. All of these have shown an ability to improve model accuracy for limited data (Wei and Zou, 2019; Guo, 2020; Feng et al., 2021; Fabbri et al., 2020) while having a low cost of implementation.

4 Experimental Setup

We focus primarily on small datasets with less than a few thousand annotated data points, since limited data presents challenges in learning generalizable models and hence is a common use case for DA. Previous works have shown DA with pretrained language models tends to be largely ineffective for larger datasets (Okimura et al., 2022).

We test on five text classification datasets. Four are from the SuperGLUE benchmark (Wang et al., 2019), consisting of RTE (Dagan et al., 2006; Bar Haim et al., 2006; Giampiccolo et al., 2007; Bentivogli et al., 2009), CB (De Marneffe et al., 2019), COPA (Roemmele et al., 2011), and WSC (Levesque et al., 2011). These are the smallest datasets in the benchmark at only 2500, 250, 400, 554 training samples respectively. They capture a range of difficulty, and include diverse problems like textual entailment, commonsense-reasoning-based coreference resolution, determining cause or effect, and clause commitment. To capture performance on a simpler single sentence sentiment analysis task, we also use a downsampled subset of SST-2 (Socher et al., 2013), consisting of 400 training samples and 100 validation sentences. We experiment with BERT-base (Devlin et al., 2019) and RoBERTa-large (Liu et al., 2019), which have 110 million and 355 million parameters, respectively. Compared to larger models, their size makes them suitable when storage concerns are present. Each model is trained until convergence and we report results at the epoch where the highest validation accuracy is achieved. We provide the detailed training settings for our models in Appendix A. Below we describe the settings for each of the data augmentation methods:

EDA: We apply a combination of the synonym replacement, random swap, random insertion, and random deletion operations to a certain percentage of the words in a sentence to generate multiple augmented sentences per original sentence. For the amount of augmented sentences generated, and the percentage of words affected, we follow the recommended usage guidelines laid out by Wei and Zou (2019) which are dependant on the size of the training set. 16 augmented sentences per original are generated for the smallest datasets; CB, COPA, WSC, and SST-2 since they only contain a few hundred training samples samples. The percentage of words in the original text affected for each of the 4 operations is 5% ($\alpha = 0.05$). 8 sentences are generated per original for the RTE training set, with the same percentage of words being affected as the aforementioned datasets.

BT: For our implementation, we back-translate the sentences using a series of English to a target language and target language to English translation models for 4 common languages: French, Spanish, German, and Chinese. The specific models we use are the Helsinki NLP Opus translation modules (Tiedemann, 2020). These languages are chosen due to the substantial amount of parallel corpora available for training the respective language models, which yields higher quality translations that are better able preserve the semantics of the original sentence while still introducing some diversity.

Mixup: Inspired by Mixup in image classification (Zhang et al., 2018; Guo et al., 2019b), where random pairs of input images and their labels are linearly interpolated to help generated synthetic images, Mixup can be similarly applied over embeddings for text. As in Guo et al. (2019a), we adapt Mixup for text classification by interpolating on sentence embeddings (senMixup). In a mini batch of size N, we take the same number of random pairs of inputs texts, and interpolate over the d-dimensional (768 in the case of BERT-base and 1024 for RoBERTa-large) classification ([CLS]) tokens of the final hidden layer of the transformer encoder produced after each of the inputs is fed into transformer. The interpolated token is then passed into a fully connected later to generate the final softmax prediction vector. The interpolation for a given pair [CLS] token pair (x^i, x^j) with corresponding one hot label vectors (y^i, y^j), for inputs i and j is conducted as follows,

$$\tilde{x}^{ij} = \lambda x^i + (1 - \lambda)x^j, \quad (1)$$

$$\tilde{y}^{ij} = \lambda y^i + (1 - \lambda)y^j, \quad (2)$$

which results in interpolated vectors $\tilde{x}^{ij}$ and $\tilde{y}^{ij}$. Mixup is parameterized by mixing-ratio λ, which is different for every pair, and is obtained by sampling from the $Beta(\alpha, \alpha)$ distribution with the hyperparameter $\alpha = 1.0$, corresponding to a uniform distribution. This was the recommended setting in Guo et al. (2019a) and consequently we use this value as well. Mixup is done in a similar manner for prefix tuning, except we use the pooled version of the classification token (i.e. one that has gone through a linear layer and tanh activation).

Procedure for Augmentation: For simplicity, since most of the datasets use multiple input sentences/words per training sample (e.g. premise and hypothesis), we apply the static DA methods over the primary (first) input, which is the premise for RTE, CB, and COPA, though we use the full sentence for WSC and SST2.

Table 1: Accuracy of fine-tuning BERT and RoBERTa under various augmentation methods with the P-tuning and LoRA trained equivalents.

Model		Dataset				
		rte	cb	copa	wsc	sst2
Fine-tuned BERT	No Aug.	73.5	92.2	69.6	65.4	**91.1**
	EDA	67.4	**95.3**	**71.1**	63.5	88.4
	Mixup	**74.2**	92.9	68.8	**66.4**	89.3
	BT	71.8	93.8	70.5	63.5	**91.1**
P-tuning v2 BERT	No Aug.	69.4	90.6	72.3	**66.4**	89.3
	EDA	68.8	90.1	72.0	63.5	88.4
	Mixup	69.1	91.1	72.0	65.4	**90.2**
	BT	**71.2**	**94.8**	**75.0**	**66.4**	88.4
LoRA BERT	No Aug.	**74.2**	90.6	**72.7**	63.5	89.1
	EDA	69.1	90.6	65.2	63.5	86.6
	Mixup	66.0	89.6	68.0	62.5	**89.8**
	BT	70.4	**92.2**	67.0	**65.6**	87.5
Fine-tuned RoBERTa	No Aug.	**88.2**	98.2	**94.6**	63.5	**96.4**
	EDA	85.0	96.9	90.2	63.5	94.6
	Mixup	85.4	**98.4**	93.8	63.5	95.5
	BT	85.4	96.4	90.2	63.5	**96.4**
P-tuning v2 RoBERTa	No Aug.	**87.9**	**98.4**	**90.0**	63.5	**94.6**
	EDA	84.6	96.9	87.0	**64.4**	**94.6**
	Mixup	87.2	**98.4**	86.0	63.5	92.9
	BT	84.7	**98.4**	85.0	63.5	**94.6**
LoRA RoBERTa	No Aug.	86.5	**96.9**	**94.6**	63.5	95.5
	EDA	84.4	95.3	89.3	63.5	95.5
	Mixup	**88.2**	93.8	89.3	63.5	**96.4**
	BT	83.5	**96.9**	89.3	63.5	**96.4**

5 Experimental Results and Analyses

5.1 Data Augmentation with PET

Table 1 displays our primary results. The DA methods that achieve the best performance on each dataset and model type vary greatly. Some strong performance gains can be seen when using DA with P-tuning v2, most clearly seen when using BT with BERT on RTE, CB, and COPA. Similar cases exist with LoRA using Mixup on RTE with RoBERTa, and BT on BERT with CB. However, despite the cases of positive performance, frequent degradation to accuracy can be seen in most cases from using DA, particularly with the larger RoBERTa models, and on certain datasets like RTE with P-tuning v2 and COPA with LoRA. EDA in particular tends to perform poorly when paired with PET methods. WSC sees improvements with EDA, but these models are largely incapable of learning the data properly, so any benefits are likely spurious.

It is important to take notice of how the best performing method usually differs between fine-tuning, prefix tuning and LoRA, and that the per-

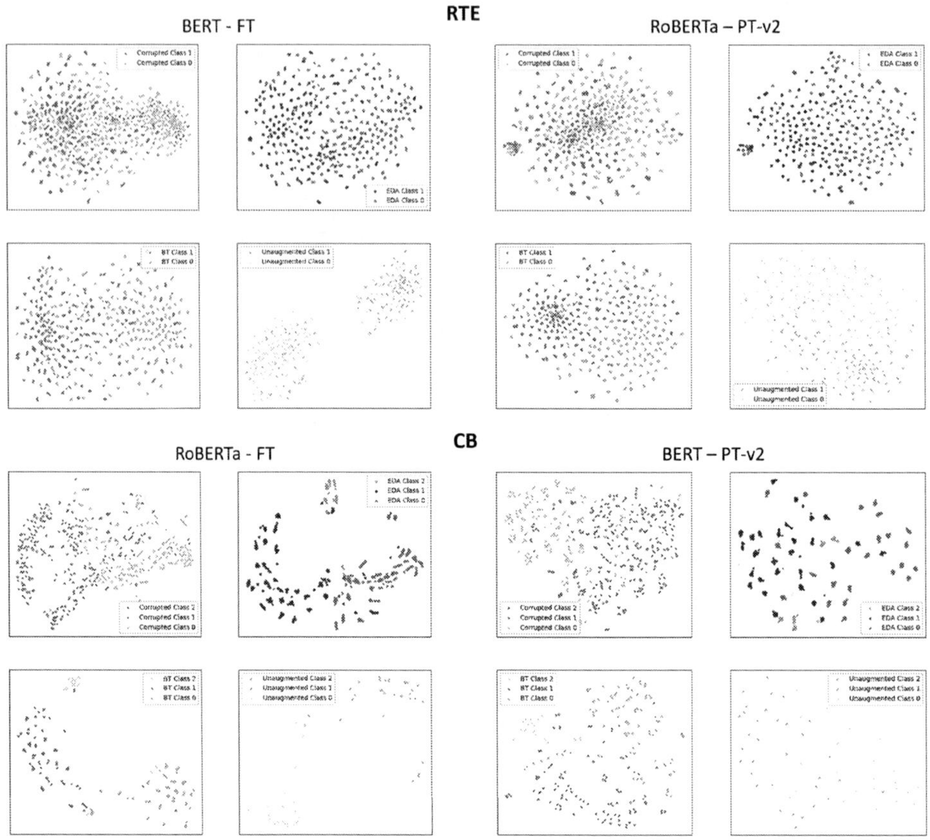

Figure 1: The t-SNE latent space for [CLS] token/sentence representation between BERT fine-tuning (top-left), BERT P-tuning v2 (bottom-right) and RoBERTa fine-tuning (bottom-left) and RoBERTa P-tuning v2 (top-right) on the RTE (top row) and CB (bottom row) datasets. Essentially, for each dataset we compare BERT and RoBERTa using either fine-tuning or P-tuning, while capturing all possible combinations across the two datasets. The resulting representations are obtained from training on clean data and testing on augmented validation data and the original validation data. Within each model scenario, each of the four boxes represents the results of testing that model on a different augmented dataset (blue for corrupted data, red for EDA, green for BT, and orange for the original data). The distribution of each individual class can be seen in these sub-boxes. Across each of the datasets and model types, the sentence representations of data for P-tuning v2 appear more jumbled and less separated across different classes.

formance of each DA method can change significantly between them as seen with BT on COPA between the the fine-tuned and prefix tuned versions of BERT, hence what works for fine-tuning cannot not be assumed to work for different PET methods. With these results we cannot universally recommend when using DA with prefix tuning or LoRA with limited data, although with careful selection, benefits can still be derived.

5.2 Embedding Analysis

The poor performance of EDA and BT across many scenarios, particularly with P-tuning v2 prompts

Table 2: Accuracy and average entropy of softmax predictions of P-tuning with fine-tuning when trained on heavily modified training data. P-tuning is generally less robust against the corruptions compared to fine-tuning.

Model	rte		cb		copa		sst2	
	acc	ent.	acc	ent.	acc	ent.	acc	ent.
FT BERT	67.7	11.6	84.4	19.3	65.2	70.2	88.4	59.9
PT-v2 BERT	66.6	63.5	84.4	14.0	73.0	21.4	87.5	39.2
FT RoBERTa	77.6	75.9	90.6	18.9	84.6	26.7	95.5	10.6
PT-v2 RoBERTa	70.6	27.3	89.1	11.4	76.9	19.9	91.1	9.4

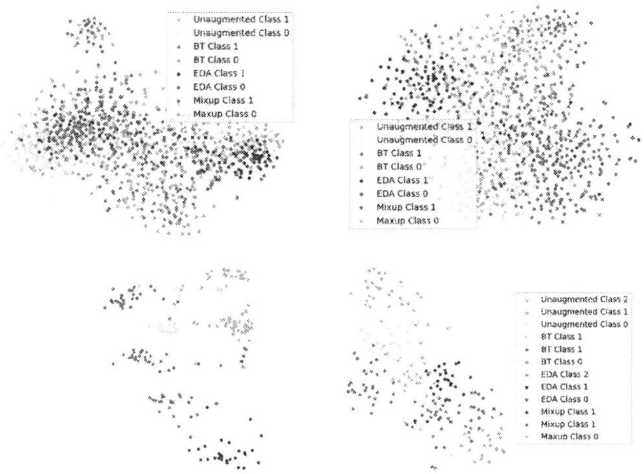

Figure 2: The t-SNE latent space for [CLS] token/sentence embeddings between fine-tuning BERT (top-left) and P-tuning RoBERTa (top-right) on RTE, and between fine-tuning (bottom-left) and P-tuning RoBERTa (bottom-right) on CB. The representations are the result of training on augmented data and testing on clean validation data (i.e. legend entries represent which training data was used).

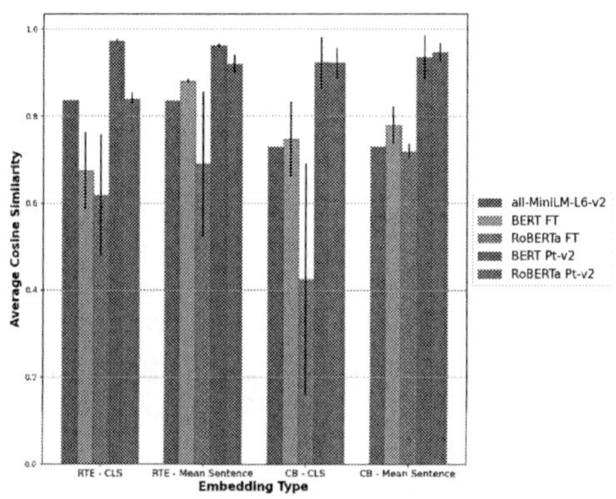

Figure 3: Comparison of average cosine similarity between the sentence representations of fine-tuned and P-tuning v2 versions of BERT and RoBERTa across the RTE and CB datasets. We compare the representations of the [CLS] token embeddings and the mean sentence embeddings. We also include a baseline using a Sentence Transformer for an ideal similarity measure.

further study on how prefix tuning learns sentence representations of and under augmented data to identify any potential issues leading to poor performance. To do this, we apply t-SNE (van der Maaten and Hinton, 2008) to visualize and understand the latent space sentence embeddings between fine-tuning and P-tuning v2 versions of BERT and RoBERTa across both the RTE and CB datasets where we originally observed stark differences in performance of DA, particularly on RTE since there was a major divide between where DA works well (fine-tuned BERT) versus not well (prefix tuned RoBERTa). We plot the 2-D representation of the [CLS] token in the final hidden layer. Figure 1 shows the visualizations where we show the representations learned when training on clean data and testing on augmented validation data that was augmented the same way as the training data. We use EDA, BT, and the heavy corruption method described below in Section 5.3, along with a baseline using no DA. Through this we can examine how well each method deals with unfamiliar augmented data, and whether the augmented data is represented similarly to the original data. Figure 2 displays a different style of representations that are generated from training on augmented data and testing on the clean validation data. This can show how training with DA influences how well the model learns representations between different types of data. In both figures, we observe the same general trends between fine-tuning and prefix tuning, irrespective of model type and dataset. Despite certain models such as P-tuning v2 RoBERTa having stronger predictive performance than their fine-tuned counterparts with BERT, there is a noticeable lack of distinct clustering between class samples of different classes. The sentence representations from different classes of augmented data are less separated. When trained on clean data, the representations of the augmented validation data are more jumbled and less separate in the representation space as well. Additionally, when trained using DA, the clustering in the BERT fine-tuned models is more distinct, especially for EDA and BT where P-tuning suffers. Even without augmentation and when using Mixup, the clustering differences remain. These visualizations demonstrate that there may be difficulties with how prefix tuning is able to process augmented data. Prefix tuning appears to be less robust against augmentation methods like EDA that can change the meaning of the original data, potentially presenting training challenges.

5.3 Influence of Heavily Perturbed Data

In view of the generally poor performance of prefix tuning with EDA, and how it has issues with separating the sentence representations, we run experiments to confirm that prefix tuning struggles more with augmented data that is highly perturbed compared to the original. To simulate this heavily altered data scenario, we use all four of the EDA operations to modify up to 50% of the sentence with each of the operations, and generate eight sentences per original on RTE, CB, COPA, and SST2, and we compare the best validation performance of each training method. A performance degradation can be expected since the model should have a more difficult time generalizing when learning from largely incoherent, noisy data as noted in (Wei and Zou, 2019). As Table 2 shows, prefix tuning is generally unable to cope as well as fine-tuning when trained on this data but is usually more confident. A possible explanation for this phenomena is that since the parameters of the language models are frozen, the lower number of trainable parameters may have an easier time overfitting to the noise in the augmented data, which explains the low softmax entropy/high prediction confidence. In effect, these results signal the importance of selecting data augmentation methods that can preserve the meaning and structure of the original training data but still provide lexical diversity.

5.4 Similarity Analysis

To formalize the qualitative analysis provided in Section 5.2 with quantitative results and to bring further insight on our results in Section 5.3, we run additional experiments comparing the average cosine similarities between the sentence embeddings produced by prefix tuning and fine-tuning.

Table 3: Accuracy with contrastive loss compared to original when training P-tuning v2 models with the static DA methods. There is usually an improvement when using the new loss (Cont.) compared to the original (OG) models.

		rte		cb		copa		sst2	
		OG	Cont.	OG	Cont.	OG	Cont.	OG	Cont.
BERT	EDA	68.8	72.0	90.1	90.6	72.0	73.2	88.4	89.8
	BT	71.2	73.2	94.8	93.8	75.0	75.8	88.4	90.6
RoBERTa	EDA	84.6	85.1	96.9	98.4	87.0	86.6	94.6	96.1
	BT	84.7	85.5	98.4	98.4	85.0	85.7	94.6	96.1

In particular, we compare the original and heavily corrupted versions of sentences. For this, we train fine-tuning and P-tuning v2 versions of BERT and RoBERTa on the clean data of the RTE and CB datasets, and evaluate on heavily corrupted validation constructed in the same manner as described in Section 5.3. We compute the cosine similarity between the sentence embeddings of the original and altered sentences and average across the whole dataset. We use both the [CLS] sentence embeddings as previously, and the mean sentence representation obtained by averaging all tokens in the final hidden state. To get an idea as to the ideal cosine similarities, we also include the average similarity obtained by using a model specifically tuned to measure sentence similarity; Sentence Transformer *all-MiniLM-L6-v2* (Reimers and Gurevych, 2019). We graph our results, which can be seen in Figure 3. We average our results over 3 runs and compute the standard deviation. We discover that prefix tuning outputs extremely high similarities despite the data being highly corrupted when compared to fine-tuning, across both types of representations. In most cases, fine-tuning is much closer to the Sentence Transformer, and hence shows a greatly ability to differentiate between the differences in semantics between the two inputs. This signals that prefix-tuning needs a greater ability to be able to differentiate between different data, which may be key to improving its performance on augmented data.

5.5 Benefits of Contrastive Loss

Given the results in Section 5.4, it is natural to ponder whether it is possible to improve the performance of DA with prefix tuning by using a method that can promote more defined clusters and greater dissimilarity between semantically different inputs. We study this by adding a contrastive loss term while training P-tuning v2. We generally adopt a version of NT-Xent loss proposed in

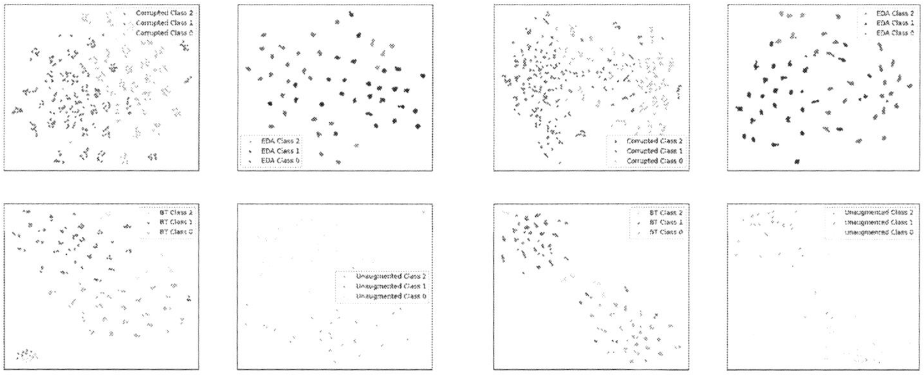

Figure 4: t-SNE latent space sentence embedding visualizations between P-tuning v2 RoBERTa with (right) and without (left) the contrastive loss term on the CB dataset. The representations shown are generated from training on EDA augmented data and then testing on various validation data (both augmented and unaugmented) similar to as described in Figure 1.

(Oord et al., 2018). We adapt their method to this task by creating positive samples in a batch via sampling pairs of inputs with the same class, and creating negative samples by sampling pairs of differing classes. More specifically, given a mini batch of size N, we generate an ith positive pair $A_i = (a_i, \hat{a}_i)$ out of N with class k, by randomly sampling two inputs with the same class label and using their [CLS] representations. We generate two negative pairs $B_i = (a_i, \hat{b}_i)$ and $C_i = (b_i, \hat{a}_i)$ in the same manner where the two randomly sampled inputs b and $\hat{b}$ do not have the same class label as the positive pair. These three pairs are used in the following equation for the contrastive loss, $\mathcal{L} = -\frac{1}{N}\sum_{i=1}^{N}\log\frac{e^{sim(a_i,\hat{a}_i)/\tau}}{e^{sim(a_i,\hat{a}_i)/\tau}+e^{sim(a_i,\hat{b}_i)/\tau}+e^{sim(\hat{a}_i,b_i)/\tau}}$, where $sim()$ is a similarity measure for the representations, for which we use cosine similarity. We find that using a high temperature parameter τ of 0.9 gives the best results. We also scale this additional loss by a parameter λ_{con} to avoid too much bias towards towards this loss, which we vary per model. In addition, we use the cosine similarity generated by Sentence Transformer *all-MiniLM-L6-v2* between the original and augmented training samples to weight the cross entropy loss values to prioritize learning more semantically similar inputs.

Table 3 shows the results when we applied these additional loss terms for the training of P-tuning v2 BERT and RoBERTa models across RTE, CB, COPA, and SST2 using both EDA and BT. We usually observe a rise in accuracy when adding the contrastive term to training with DA, especially with EDA, and in cases where there is no performance gain, the results still remain similar. This signals how contrastive methods may be key to getting good performance using DA with prefix tuning. We do see that in some cases the increase observed is not enough to increase accuracy beyond the model trained without DA, so in these cases these DA techniques are largely inherently too ineffective for that specific task.

5.6 Contrastive Loss Representations

As in Section 5.2, we qualitatively analyze the representations of the models trained using the contrastive loss when they are trained on augmented data. Figure 4 shows how adding the contrastive loss term not only helps the accuracy of augmenting P-tuning v2 RoBERTa on CB with EDA, but that it learns representations for augmented validation data that have more distinct clustering, especially with BT and the unaugmented validation data compared to only using regular cross entropy loss, showing how the method can help induce prefix tuning to learn more useful representations for augmented data. Our contrastive method is rather simple, and not particularly well suited for supervised learning. We do believe that exploring more suitable loss functions like Center Loss (Wen et al., 2016) might show even more promising results, which future work can explore.

6 Conclusion

We reveal how when limited training data is available, data augmentation can provide crucial improvements in accuracy when training classification models using PET methods, though the benefits are, however, not universal, and limitations exist when using certain methods. We also demonstrated how prefix tuning may have more difficulty learning sentence representations of augmented data. We further showed that contrastive learning can be a solution to these issues, and suggest that more work be done to find similar methods that can be more generalizable.

Limitations

Although we present our results across multiple datasets and models, we have largely adhered to natural language understanding tasks. How effective the augmentation methods are on generation-related tasks warrants further study.

In addition, another limitation is that we do not study the level of perturbations needed to have a negative effect on prefix tuning. Knowing this can shed light on what particular types of transformations are a problem for prefix tuning so that they can be avoided. Our hypothesis here is that such perturbation levels are sensitive to many factors during training, such as the difficulty of the task and the characteristics of the data augmentation approaches applied, which could be difficult to be quantified.

Ethics Statement

Any sort of technique where synthetic text data is generated in an automated fashion, especially with augmentation techniques like BT and EDA that can add or remove random words or completely rephrase sentences, can alter the original meaning or interpretation of a sentence. This has some potential to introduce additional unexpected biases into the training data, particularly when biased models are used to generate synthetic data (e.g. a racially biased translation model). Even with improved performance these biases can cause models to make unfair judgments, which can become a major concern in safety critical domains like in the legal or medical fields. As a consequence, before any data augmentation technique should be applied to PET techniques, there has to be a consideration of the underlying biases that can be introduced through the methods of producing synthetic data.

Acknowledgements

We would like to thank the anonymous reviewers for providing valuable feedback for polishing the paper. This work was supported by the Indigenous and Black Engineering and Technology (IBET) Momentum Fellowship and the NSERC Discovery Grants [RGPIN-2018-06415].

References

Ateret Anaby-Tavor, Boaz Carmeli, Esther Goldbraich, Amir Kantor, George Kour, Segev Shlomov, N. Tepper, and Naama Zwerdling. 2020. Do Not Have Enough Data? Deep Learning to the Rescue! In *AAAI*.

Roy Bar Haim, Ido Dagan, Bill Dolan, Lisa Ferro, Danilo Giampiccolo, Bernardo Magnini, and Idan Szpektor. 2006. The second PASCAL recognising textual entailment challenge.

Yoshua Bengio, Yann Lecun, and Geoffrey Hinton. 2021. Deep learning for ai. *Commun. ACM*, 64(7):58–65.

Luisa Bentivogli, Ido Dagan, Hoa Trang Dang, Danilo Giampiccolo, and Bernardo Magnini. 2009. The fifth PASCAL recognizing textual entailment challenge.

Ido Dagan, Oren Glickman, and Bernardo Magnini. 2006. The PASCAL recognising textual entailment challenge. In *Machine learning challenges. evaluating predictive uncertainty, visual object classification, and recognising tectual entailment*, pages 177–190.

Marie-Catherine De Marneffe, Mandy Simons, and Judith Tonhauser. 2019. The CommitmentBank: Investigating projection in naturally occurring discourse.

Jacob Devlin, Ming-Wei Chang, Kenton Lee, and Kristina Toutanova. 2019. BERT: Pre-training of deep bidirectional transformers for language understanding. In *Proceedings of the 2019 Conference of the North American Chapter of the Association for Computational Linguistics: Human Language Technologies, Volume 1 (Long and Short Papers)*, pages 4171–4186, Minneapolis, Minnesota. Association for Computational Linguistics.

Alexander R. Fabbri, Simeng Han, Haoyuan Li, Haoran Li, Marjan Ghazvininejad, Shafiq Joty, Dragomir Radev, and Yashar Mehdad. 2020. Improving Zero and Few-Shot Abstractive Summarization with Intermediate Fine-tuning and Data Augmentation.

Steven Y. Feng, Varun Gangal, Jason Wei, Sarath Chandar, Soroush Vosoughi, Teruko Mitamura, and Eduard H. Hovy. 2021. A Survey of Data Augmentation Approaches for NLP. In *ACL/IJCNLP (Findings)*, pages 968–988.

Siddhant Garg and Goutham Ramakrishnan. 2020. BAE: BERT-based adversarial examples for text classification. In *Proceedings of the 2020 Conference on Empirical Methods in Natural Language Processing (EMNLP)*. Association for Computational Linguistics.

Danilo Giampiccolo, Bernardo Magnini, Ido Dagan, and Bill Dolan. 2007. The third PASCAL recognizing textual entailment challenge. In *Proceedings of the ACL-PASCAL workshop on textual entailment and paraphrasing*, pages 1–9. Association for Computational Linguistics.

Hongyu Guo. 2020. Nonlinear Mixup: Out-Of-Manifold Data Augmentation for Text Classification. In *AAAI*.

Hongyu Guo, Yongyi Mao, and Richong Zhang. 2019a. Augmenting Data with Mixup for Sentence Classification: An Empirical Study. *ArXiv*, abs/1905.08941.

Hongyu Guo, Yongyi Mao, and Richong Zhang. 2019b. MixUp as Locally Linear Out-Of-Manifold Regularization. In *AAAI*.

Junxian He, Chunting Zhou, Xuezhe Ma, Taylor Berg-Kirkpatrick, and Graham Neubig. 2022. Towards a Unified View of Parameter-Efficient Transfer Learning. In *International Conference on Learning Representations*.

Edward Hu, Yelong Shen, Phil Wallis, Zeyuan Allen-Zhu, Yuanzhi Li, Lu Wang, and Weizhu Chen. 2021. LoRA: Low-Rank Adaptation of Large Language Models.

Hector J Levesque, Ernest Davis, and Leora Morgenstern. 2011. The Winograd schema challenge. In *AAAI Spring Symposium: Logical Formalizations of Commonsense Reasoning*, volume 46, page 47.

Xiang Lisa Li and Percy Liang. 2021. Prefix-Tuning: Optimizing Continuous Prompts for Generation.

Xiao Liu, Kaixuan Ji, Yicheng Fu, Zhengxiao Du, Zhilin Yang, and Jie Tang. 2021. P-Tuning v2: Prompt Tuning Can Be Comparable to Fine-tuning Universally Across Scales and Tasks. *CoRR*, abs/2110.07602.

Yinhan Liu, Myle Ott, Naman Goyal, Jingfei Du, Mandar Joshi, Danqi Chen, Omer Levy, Mike Lewis, Luke Zettlemoyer, and Veselin Stoyanov. 2019. RoBERTa: A Robustly Optimized BERT Pretraining Approach.

Shayne Longpre, Yu Wang, and Chris DuBois. 2020. How Effective is Task-Agnostic Data Augmentation for Pretrained Transformers? In *EMNLP (Findings)*, pages 4401–4411.

Ilya Loshchilov and Frank Hutter. 2019. Decoupled Weight Decay Regularization. In *International Conference on Learning Representations*.

Marius Mosbach, Maksym Andriushchenko, and Dietrich Klakow. 2021. On the stability of fine-tuning {bert}: Misconceptions, explanations, and strong baselines. In *International Conference on Learning Representations*.

Itsuki Okimura, Machel Reid, Makoto Kawano, and Yutaka Matsuo. 2022. On the impact of data augmentation on downstream performance in natural language processing. In *Proceedings of the Third Workshop on Insights from Negative Results in NLP*, pages 88–93, Dublin, Ireland. Association for Computational Linguistics.

Aaron van den Oord, Yazhe Li, and Oriol Vinyals. 2018. Representation Learning with Contrastive Predictive Coding.

Jonas Pfeiffer, Andreas Rücklé, Clifton Poth, Aishwarya Kamath, Ivan Vulić, Sebastian Ruder, Kyunghyun Cho, and Iryna Gurevych. 2020. AdapterHub: A Framework for Adapting Transformers. In *Proceedings of the 2020 Conference on Empirical Methods in Natural Language Processing: System Demonstrations*, pages 46–54.

Guanghui Qin and Jason Eisner. 2021. Learning How to Ask: Querying LMs with Mixtures of Soft Prompts.

Alec Radford, Jeff Wu, Rewon Child, David Luan, Dario Amodei, and Ilya Sutskever. 2019. Language Models are Unsupervised Multitask Learners.

Nils Reimers and Iryna Gurevych. 2019. Sentence-BERT: Sentence Embeddings using Siamese BERT-Networks. In *Proceedings of the 2019 Conference on Empirical Methods in Natural Language Processing*. Association for Computational Linguistics.

Melissa Roemmele, Cosmin Adrian Bejan, and Andrew S. Gordon. 2011. Choice of plausible alternatives: An evaluation of commonsense causal reasoning. In *2011 AAAI Spring Symposium Series*.

Rico Sennrich, Barry Haddow, and Alexandra Birch. 2016. Improving Neural Machine Translation Models with Monolingual Data. In *Proceedings of the 54th Annual Meeting of the Association for Computational Linguistics (Volume 1: Long Papers)*, pages 86–96, Berlin, Germany. Association for Computational Linguistics.

Richard Socher, Alex Perelygin, Jean Wu, Jason Chuang, Christopher Manning, Andrew Ng, and Christopher Potts. 2013. Parsing With Compositional Vector Grammars. In *EMNLP*.

Jörg Tiedemann. 2020. The tatoeba translation challenge – realistic data sets for low resource and multilingual MT. In *Proceedings of the Fifth Conference on Machine Translation*, pages 1174–1182, Online. Association for Computational Linguistics.

Laurens van der Maaten and Geoffrey Hinton. 2008. Visualizing Data using t-SNE. *Journal of Machine Learning Research*, 9(86):2579–2605.

Alex Wang, Yada Pruksachatkun, Nikita Nangia, Amanpreet Singh, Julian Michael, Felix Hill, Omer Levy, and Samuel R. Bowman. 2019. SuperGLUE: A stickier benchmark for general-purpose language understanding systems. *arXiv preprint 1905.00537*.

Jason Wei and Kai Zou. 2019. EDA: Easy data augmentation techniques for boosting performance on text classification tasks. In *Proceedings of the 2019 Conference on Empirical Methods in Natural Language Processing and the 9th International Joint Conference on Natural Language Processing (EMNLP-IJCNLP)*, pages 6382–6388, Hong Kong, China. Association for Computational Linguistics.

Yandong Wen, Kaipeng Zhang, Zhifeng Li, and Yu Qiao. 2016. A Discriminative Feature Learning Approach for Deep Face Recognition. In *ECCV*.

Thomas Wolf, Lysandre Debut, Victor Sanh, Julien Chaumond, Clement Delangue, Anthony Moi, Pierric Cistac, Tim Rault, Rémi Louf, Morgan Funtowicz, Joe Davison, Sam Shleifer, Patrick von Platen, Clara Ma, Yacine Jernite, Julien Plu, Canwen Xu, Teven Le Scao, Sylvain Gugger, Mariama Drame, Quentin Lhoest, and Alexander M. Rush. 2019. HuggingFace's Transformers: State-of-the-art Natural Language Processing.

Manzil Zaheer, Guru Guruganesh, Kumar Avinava Dubey, Joshua Ainslie, Chris Alberti, Santiago Ontanon, Philip Pham, Anirudh Ravula, Qifan Wang, Li Yang, and Amr Ahmed. 2020. Big Bird: Transformers for Longer Sequences. In *NeurIPS*, pages 17283–17297. Curran Associates, Inc.

Hongyi Zhang, Moustapha Cisse, Yann N. Dauphin, and David Lopez-Paz. 2018. mixup: Beyond Empirical Risk Minimization. In *International Conference on Learning Representations*.

A Training Settings and Hyperparameters

In this section, we provide details on the general training settings we use along with the hyperparameters. The ideal hyperparameters for each type of model were tuned very carefully by using random search with additional manual tuning, and by largely following the recommendations in Mosbach et al. (2021) to achieve stable, high performance with fine-tuning and LoRA. Likewise, we generally use similar hyperparameters settings as in Liu et al. (2021) for training P-tuning v2 on the SuperGLUE datasets, since the authors manage to achieve solid results with their settings, although our models still required additional tuning in most cases as our methods differ from their original scope since we incorporate DA.

The general settings across all the models and datasets include the tokenizer max sequence length being set to 128 tokens, with the exception of WSC and SST-2 which are capped at 64. We use an AdamW optimizer (Loshchilov and Hutter, 2019) for all experiments, with a linear scheduler with warmup. For the BERT models we use a gradient clipping value of 1.0. We generally choose batch sizes between 16 or 32. We train each of the models using NVIDIA RTX-3090 GPUs (24GB) with our implementation for the base models being based on HuggingFace Transformers (Wolf et al., 2019). We make use of the Sentence-Transformers library as well (Reimers and Gurevych, 2019).

Fine-tuning Settings: The settings specific to the fine-tuned models are as follows: across all fine-tuned models we use a warmup rate of 10%. For BERT we vary the learning rate from 1e-5 and 5e-5 depending on dataset. CB uses 5e-5 for example, though the ideal for the other datasets can vary with 2e-5 for SST-2. The best batch size varies between 16 and 32, though generally a value of 16 performs better. For RoBERTa we use learning rates of either 1e-5 or 2e-5 and a batch size of 16 to achieve stable performance across all datasets and augmentation methods. The number of training epochs we choose is dependant on when the model begins to converge. For EDA this generally falls within 2-4 epochs for all datasets, while for BT it is 4-8. For Mixup and regular training, training epochs are in the range of 8-12, though RTE generally only needs 5-7 epochs.

P-tuning v2 Settings: The ideal hyperparameters for P-tuning v2 strongly vary between the chosen dataset, augmentation method, and model-type, so to save space we only include the ranges over which tune the hyperparameters. We generally keep learning rates between 5e-3 to 5e-2, with the models trained with augmentation methods usually requiring lower rates from 7e-3 to 1e-2. The unaugmented models work best between 1e-2 to 5e-2. The ideal batch size is primarily 16 although 32 is more effective on datasets like RTE. The prefix sequence lengths are kept short, usually between 4 to 32 tokens. Prefix reparameterization is used across most of the datasets, and performs particularly well on CB and SST-2. The hidden dropout probability is consistently set at 0.1. Similarly, the prefix hidden size is kept consistent at 512. We do not use warmup for the prefix models. The number of training epochs to set generally falls within 10-25 for EDA, 20-40 for BT, and for Mixup and regular training 50-120, with the exact number depending on when the model converges to 100% training accuracy. The λ_{con} parameter we use when training with contrastive loss is set to be between 0.1 and 0.3, with most models using a value of 0.2.

LoRA settings: In many cases our settings for training the LoRA variations of the models are similar to those described for fine-tuning, though usually LoRA requires shorter training times. Regarding the LoRA specific parameters, rank r and LoRA reparametrization scaling parameter α , we mirror the settings for BERT-base and RoBERTa-large in the original paper by Hu et al. (2021) with $r = 8$, $\alpha = 8$ and $r = 8$, $\alpha = 16$ for each model type respectively. We use the adapter-transformers library (Pfeiffer et al., 2020) to implement LoRA.

Relational Sentence Embedding for Flexible Semantic Matching

Bin Wang[†], **Haizhou Li**[♮,§,†]
[†]National University of Singapore, Singapore
[♮]School of Data Science, The Chinese University of Hong Kong, Shenzhen, China
[§]Shenzhen Research Institute of Big Data
bwang28c@gmail.com

Abstract

We present Relational Sentence Embedding (RSE), a new paradigm to further discover the potential of sentence embeddings. Prior work mainly models the similarity between sentences based on their embedding distance. Because of the complex semantic meanings conveyed, sentence pairs can have various relation types, including but not limited to entailment, paraphrasing, and question-answer. It poses challenges to existing embedding methods to capture such relational information. We handle the problem by learning associated relational embeddings. Specifically, a relation-wise translation operation is applied to the source sentence to infer the corresponding target sentence with a pre-trained Siamese-based encoder. Later, the fine-grained relational similarity scores can be estimated with learned relational embeddings. We benchmark our method on 19 datasets covering a wide range of tasks, including semantic textual similarity, transfer, and domain-specific tasks. Experimental results show that our method is effective and flexible in modelling sentence relations and outperforms a series of state-of-the-art sentence embedding methods.[1]

Dataset	Relation	STS_avg
SNLI+MNLI	*Entailment	81.33
SNLI+MNLI	Entailment	77.67
QQP (149K)	Duplicate Question	75.96
Flicker (318K)	Same Caption	74.55
ParaNMT (5M)	Paraphrase	75.32
QNLI (55K)	Question Answer	72.21
All-Above	All 5 relations	74.62
RSE	***Mixed***	**82.17**
WIKI (1M)	Dropout	75.45

Table 1: Comparison of different supervised signals as positive sentence pairs. Averaged results on STS datasets are reported with $BERT_{base}$ model. * indicates the model is trained with hard negatives using contradiction pairs (Gao et al., 2021b). Experimental details can be found in Appendix A.

1 Introduction

Sentence representation learning is a long-standing topic in natural language understanding and has broad applications in many tasks, including retrieval, clustering, and classification (Cer et al., 2018). It has been studied extensively in existing literature (Kiros et al., 2015; Conneau et al., 2017; Reimers and Gurevych, 2019; Gao et al., 2021b) and the problem is defined as learning vector representation (e_i) for sentence (s_i) and the similarity between sentences (s_i, s_j) is inferred by their pairwise cosine similarity: $cos(e_i, e_j)$. Prior work found that the entailment relation in natural language inference (NLI) data aligns well with the semantic similarity concept defined in STS datasets (Conneau et al., 2017; Reimers and Gurevych, 2019; Gao et al., 2021b). However, the concept of similarity is vaguely defined, and the relationship between sentences is indeed multifaceted (Wang et al., 2022). One can only rely on experimental verification to determine what relation between sentences aligns well with human perception of "semantic similarity". The similarity intensity between sentences varies greatly based on the perspective of personal understanding.

In this work, we do not focus on discussing the detailed definition of semantic relations but focus on the explicit modelling of sentence relations. Instead of treating sentence pairs as either positive or negative samples in contrastive learning (Gao et al., 2021b; Yan et al., 2021; Wu et al., 2022), we treat sentence pairs as triples: (s_i, *relationship*, s_j), with relational information embedded. We learn a translational operation between sentence embeddings to contrastively model the relationship between sentences. Despite its simplicity, the re-

[1]Our code is available https://github.com/BinWang28/RSE

Proceedings of the 8th Workshop on Representation Learning for NLP (RepL4NLP 2023), pages 238–252
July 13, 2023 ©2023 Association for Computational Linguistics

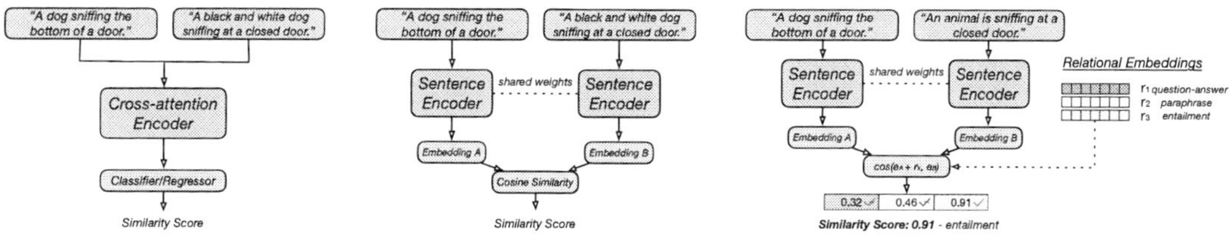

(a) Cross-Attention Matching (b) Sentence Encoder Matching (c) Relational Sentence Embedding

Figure 1: Comparison of different sentence-pair matching architectures. Relational sentence embedding adopts relation-specific embeddings for more flexible semantic matching with interpretable results. Meantime, the Siamese network allows much faster inference speech compared with cross-attention matching.

lational modelling component largely expands the concept of existing sentence embedding and introduces unique properties for more flexible semantic matching capabilities. Our method is called *Relational Sentence Embedding* (RSE).

First, with relation modelling, RSE can leverage multi-source relational data for improved generalizability. Earlier work mainly focuses on using NLI data for supervised sentence embedding learning, as the best performance is witnessed. It remains an under-explored problem to learn from multi-source relational data jointly for sentence representation learning. Table 1 shows our experimental study to combine multi-source relational data as the positive samples for contrastive sentence embedding learning (Gao et al., 2021b). Simply merging all relational data leads to performance down-gradation (ref. 'All-Above'). In contrast, with explicit relation modelling by translation operations, RSE can effectively leverage multi-source relational information into a shared sentence encoder while providing exceptional performance.

Second, unlike conventional SE, RSE can provide fine-grained relational similarity scores of sentence pairs. As shown in Figure 1b, conventional sentence embedding computes one unified similarity score for sentence pairs. It is less flexible and interpretable as no detailed information is provided about what aspects of sentences are similar. In contrast, as shown in Figure 1c, RSE can infer fine-grained sentence similarity scores according to the relation of interest, which are critical features for heterogeneous applications (e.g., retrieval and clustering). RSE can vastly extend the sentence embedding concept and has excellent potential in methodology development and applications.

We benchmark our approach on 19 datasets to verify the effectiveness and generalizability of our approach. For semantic textual similarity, we conduct experiment on seven standard STS (Agirre et al., 2012, 2013, 2014, 2015, 2016; Cer et al., 2017; Marelli et al., 2014) datasets and STR dataset (Abdalla et al., 2021). RSE achieves an averaged Spearsman's correlation of 82.18% with $\text{BERT}_{\texttt{base}}$ model on STS datasets. We also achieve SOTA performance on 7 transfer tasks (Conneau and Kiela, 2018), and 4 domain-specific tasks (Wang et al., 2021b). We also present the case study and in-depth discussions.

2 Related Work

Sentence embedding can be divided into unsupervised and supervised approaches. Even though unsupervised methods have greatly improved with effective data augmentation techniques for contrastive learning (Gao et al., 2021b; Wu et al., 2022; Chen et al., 2022), supervised methods still outperform their unsupervised counterparts. The success of supervised sentence embedding is mainly because of the availability of high-quality natural language inference (NLI) data (Bowman et al., 2015; Williams et al., 2018). InferSent (Conneau et al., 2017), SBERT (Reimers and Gurevych, 2019), and SimCSE (Gao et al., 2021b) are three milestones on sentence embedding that effectively leverage NLI data using LSTM, Pre-trained BERT and contrastive learning, respectively. The NLI data covers three sentence relations: entailment, contradiction and neutral. The relationships between sentences are manifold. However, prior work found that training with other supervised signals (Young et al., 2014; Wieting and Gimpel, 2018) does not achieve comparable performance as NLI data (Gao et al., 2021b). In this work, we focus on learning from multi-source relational signals for better sentence representation learning.

Knowledge graph embeddings are designed for relational data modelling on triples: (h, r, t). The

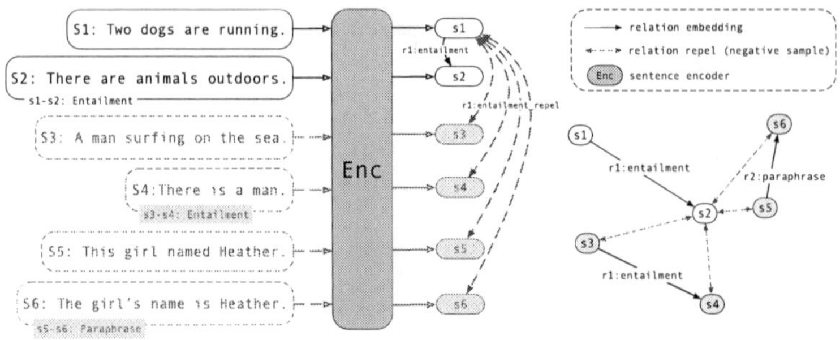

Figure 2: RSE takes the corresponding relation transformation as positive triples and treats other in-batch samples as negatives.

methods can be classified into structural-based models and semantic-enhanced models. The structural-based methods learn relational embedding and entity embedding jointly through scoring functions like TransE (Bordes et al., 2013), DistMult (Yang et al., 2015) and RotatE (Sun et al., 2019). Semantic-enhanced models incorporate additional information for entities, including entity types and textual descriptions, when learning embeddings. TEKE (Wang et al., 2016), InductivE (Wang et al., 2021a) and KG-BERT (Yao et al., 2019) belong to this type. For sentence representation learning from multi-source supervised signals, the sentence pairs can be viewed as triples: $(s_i, relationship, s_j)$. Therefore, we optimize the semantic representation of sentences and perform translation operations between them to model their respective relations. An analogy to the word-level relational graph as Word-Net (Miller, 1995), and Relational Word Embedding (Camacho-Collados et al., 2019), our work can also be viewed as a pioneering study on the sentence level.

3 Relational Sentence Embedding

Given n pre-defined relations $R = \{r_1, r_2, ..., r_n\}$, the multi-source relation sentence pair datasets are composed of triples: $D = \{(s_i, r_k, s_j)\}$, where s_i and s_j corresponds to the i_{th} and j_{th} sentence. The goal of relation sentence embedding is to learn sentence representations and relational embeddings jointly. The relational similarity intensity between sentences can be inferred from learned embeddings through either simple scoring functions or complex transformations. In this work, as a prototype of RSE, we use translation operation (Bordes et al., 2013) for sentence relation modelling.

3.1 Relational Contrastive Learning

Contrastive learning approaches have demonstrated their effectiveness in sentence embedding learning (Gao et al., 2021b; Janson et al., 2021). The core concept is learning representations that pull together close concepts and push away non-related ones. To build contrastive samples, we leverage the relational signal from sentence triples of supervised data. Assume we have relational triples (s_i, r_k, s_j), let $\mathbf{h_i}$ and $\mathbf{h_j}$ denote the representation of s_i and s_j obtained from sentence encoder $\mathbf{h_i} = f_\theta(s_i)$ and $\mathbf{h^r_k}$ denote the relational embedding of the k_{th} relation. We then treat $\mathbf{h_i} + \mathbf{h^r_k}$ and $\mathbf{h_j}$ as positive pair. Following the previous contrastive learning approach (Chen et al., 2020), other in-batch tail sentences are treated as negatives. Assuming we have N sentence triples in one mini-batch, the training objective can be written as follow:

$$\mathcal{L}_i = -\log \frac{e^{sim(\mathbf{h_i}+\mathbf{h^r_k},\mathbf{h_j})/\tau}}{\sum_{m=1}^{N} e^{sim(\mathbf{h_i}+\mathbf{h^r_k},\mathbf{h_m})/\tau}} \qquad (1)$$

where $sim(\cdot,\cdot)$ is the cosine similarity and τ is the temperature hyperparameter. The pre-trained BERT (Devlin et al., 2019) or RoBERTa (Liu et al., 2019) model $f_\theta(\cdot)$ is used to obtain sentence embedding. The relation embedding $\mathbf{h^r_k}$ is randomly initialized and jointly optimized with the pre-trained language model with the above relational contrastive objective.

Figure 2 is a graphical illustration of Eq. 1. The relational information is learned by relational embedding through translation operation. That is, for triple (s_i, r_k, s_j), we expect $\mathbf{h_i} + \mathbf{h^r_k} \approx \mathbf{h_j}$. The embedding property can further infer the relation intensity between sentences during inference.

In knowledge graph embedding, there are more diverse ways to model relations, including simple scoring functions (TransE (Bordes et al., 2013), TransR (Lin et al., 2015) and RotatE (Sun et al., 2019)), semantic matching methods (DistMult (Yang et al., 2015), TUCKER (Balazevic et al., 2019)) and neural network methods (ConvE (Dettmers et al., 2018)). In this work, we experiment with the simple translational operation for relation modeling for simplicity and interpretability. Other complex relation modeling methods can be explored in future work as they are more expressive in certain relation types, including symmetry, anti-symmetry, inversion, and composition (Sun et al., 2019).

3.2 Supervised Signals

The key to contrastive sentence embedding is building positive and negative samples. ConSERT (Yan et al., 2021) proposed to use adversarial attach, token shuffling, feature cutoff, and dropout as positive pair augmentation for unsupervised sentence embedding. SimCSE (Gao et al., 2021b) further explores the potential of dropout as positive-view augmentation. In this work, we collect multi-source relational data as positive samples and view the rest in-batch samples as negatives. In general, multi-source relational data can be either supervised or unsupervised. For unsupervised learning, we can view each data augmentation method as one relation and jointly learn from multiple data augmentation methods. In this work, we focus on artificial sentence triples and explore how to combine multiple human-labelled datasets with different relation types.

We deploy the following datasets for sentence triples (s_i, r_k, s_j). 1) SNLI (Bowman et al., 2015) + MNLI (Williams et al., 2018): contain natural language inference data. The relations are *entailment* (r_1), *contradiction* and *neutral*. We use *entailment* relation with *contradiction* relation as hard negatives. 2) QQP[2]: The Quora Question dataset. The label for each question pair is either *duplication-question* (r_2) or *non-duplicate-question*. We include the triples with *duplication-question* relation. 3) ParaNMT (Wieting and Gimpel, 2018): *paraphrase* (r_3) dataset generated by back-translation with filtering. 4) Flicker (Young et al., 2014): image captioning dataset. Each image is with 5 human-written captions. We treat the captions for the same image as relation *same-caption* (r_4). 5) QNLI (Wang et al., 2018): contains question-answer pairs. The label is *qa-entailment* (r_5) or *qa-not-entailment* based on whether the sentences contain the true answer to the question. We only use *qa-entailment* triples. 6) Dropout (Gao et al., 2021b): is constructed in an unsupervised way. We use the Wiki-1M dataset and treat the sentence with different random dropouts as one relation. We call this relation *same-sent* (r_6). We leverage all samples from the NLI dataset and at most 150K samples for other relations as the size of QQP for easy comparison.

[2]`https://data.quora.com/First-Quora-Dataset-Release-Question-Pairs`

3.3 Mining Hard Negatives

Contrastive learning commonly uses in-batch sentences as negative samples (Janson et al., 2021). However, the in-batch negatives are limited in relational sentence embeddings. It is because the in-batch samples are coming from different relation triples. The sentences from other relations are less likely to be confused with the current anchor triple. Therefore, we extend the (s_i, r_k, s_j) triple to (s_i, r_k, s_j, s_j^-) with an extra in-relation negative sample s_j^-. The s_j^- is one random sampled sentence from the triple of relation r_k. To better understand, the in-relation negative for relation *duplicate-question* will be a random question, a 'harder' negative than in-batch sentences. For the *entailment* relation, we use *contradiction* sentence as the hard negative. With the hard negative, the training objective can be written as follows (Ref. to Eq.1):

$$-\log \frac{e^{sim(\mathbf{h_i}+\mathbf{h_k^r},\mathbf{h_j})/\tau}}{\sum_{m=1}^{N}\left(e^{sim(\mathbf{h_i}+\mathbf{h_k^r},\mathbf{h_m})/\tau}+e^{sim(\mathbf{h_i}+\mathbf{h_k^r},\mathbf{h_m^-})/\tau}\right)} \quad (2)$$

As multiple relation triples are mixed in each batch during training, the batch size for each relation becomes smaller. Contrastive learning favors a relatively large batch size to reach good performance. Wu et al. (2022) incorporate momentum contrast (He et al., 2020) for better contrastive learning. However, we did not find its contribution to the supervised setting. As the GPU memory size constrains the batch size, we scale up the batch size of contrastive learning by decoupling back-propagation between contrastive learning and decoder using Gradient Cache (Gao et al., 2021a). As a result, we can train BERT`base` model with batch size 512 within an 11G GPU memory limit.

How can we use? As the relational information is

Model	STS12	STS13	STS14	STS15	STS16	STS-B	SICK-R	Avg.
				Unsupervised methods				
GloVe (avg.)	55.14	70.66	59.73	68.25	63.66	58.02	53.76	61.32
$\text{BERT}_{\texttt{base}}$ (first-last-avg)	39.70	59.38	49.67	66.03	66.19	53.87	62.06	56.70
CT - $\text{BERT}_{\texttt{base}}$	61.63	76.80	68.47	77.50	76.48	74.31	69.19	72.05
SimCSE - $\text{BERT}_{\texttt{base}}$	68.40	82.41	74.38	80.91	78.56	76.85	72.23	76.25
SimCSE - $\text{RoBERTa}_{\texttt{base}}$	70.16	81.77	73.24	81.36	80.65	80.22	68.56	76.57
				Supervised methods				
InferSent - GloVe	52.86	66.75	62.15	72.77	66.87	68.03	65.65	65.01
USE	64.49	67.80	64.61	76.83	73.18	74.92	76.69	71.22
$\text{SBERT}_{\texttt{base}}$	70.97	76.53	73.19	79.09	74.30	77.03	72.91	74.89
SimCSE - $\text{BERT}_{\texttt{base}}$	75.30	**84.67**	80.19	85.40	80.82	84.25	80.39	81.57
RSE - $\text{BERT}_{\texttt{base}}$	**76.27**$_{\pm.34}$	84.43$_{\pm.23}$	**80.60**$_{\pm.12}$	**86.03**$_{\pm.09}$	**81.86**$_{\pm.12}$	**84.34**$_{\pm.13}$	**81.73**$_{\pm.07}$	**82.18**$_{\pm.06}$
RSE - $\text{BERT}_{\texttt{large}}$	76.94$_{\pm.40}$	86.63$_{\pm.43}$	81.81$_{\pm.28}$	87.02$_{\pm.22}$	83.25$_{\pm.22}$	85.63$_{\pm.23}$	82.68$_{\pm.24}$	83.42$_{\pm.19}$
RSE - $\text{RoBERTa}_{\texttt{base}}$	76.71$_{\pm.47}$	84.38$_{\pm.34}$	80.87$_{\pm.56}$	87.12$_{\pm.42}$	83.33$_{\pm.19}$	84.62$_{\pm.18}$	81.97$_{\pm.32}$	82.71$_{\pm.20}$
RSE - $\text{RoBERTa}_{\texttt{large}}$	**77.81**$_{\pm.37}$	**87.04**$_{\pm.20}$	**82.73**$_{\pm.22}$	**87.92**$_{\pm.25}$	**85.44**$_{\pm.15}$	**86.79**$_{\pm.08}$	**83.13**$_{\pm.07}$	**84.41**$_{\pm.08}$

Table 2: Performance on STS tasks. Spearman's correlation is reported. For RSE approach, we also report the standard derivation of performance based on five runs with different random seeds. The best performance among all models and the best performance with $\text{BERT}_{\texttt{base}}$ backbone is displayed in **bold**.

Model	STR
Unsup. SimCSE - $\text{BERT}_{\texttt{base}}$	73.98
Sup. SimCSE - $\text{BERT}_{\texttt{base}}$	80.72
RSE - $\text{BERT}_{\texttt{base}}$	**81.23**$_{\pm.13}$
RSE - $\text{BERT}_{\texttt{large}}$	81.98$_{\pm.18}$
RSE - $\text{RoBERTa}_{\texttt{base}}$	82.57$_{\pm.30}$
RSE - $\text{RoBERTa}_{\texttt{large}}$	**84.10**$_{\pm.18}$

Table 3: Comparison of SimCSE and RSE performance on STR dataset.

explicitly embedded in RSE, it becomes very flexible for different applications. Given two sentence (s_i, s_j), we can infer their similarity score under relation r_k by $f(s_i, s_j, r_k) = sim(\mathbf{h_i} + \mathbf{h_k^r}, \mathbf{h_j})$. For retrieval and semantic similarity, we can use any relational similarity score or weighted sum of different relational scores as the final measure. We apply this in STS and USEB benchmarking tasks. As an additional classifier is trained, we use sentence embedding as the input for transfer tasks. We expect that with relational modelling capability, the result sentence embedding carries richer information.

4 Experiments on STS Tasks

We conduct experiment on 7 semantic textual similarity datasets including STS 12-16 (Agirre et al., 2012, 2013, 2014, 2015, 2016), STS-Benchmark (Cer et al., 2017) and SICK-Relatedness (Marelli et al., 2014). We also experiment with STR-2022 (Abdalla et al., 2021). A new STS dataset with improved label quality using comparative ranking. For a fair comparison, we report the result with the fully unsupervised setting, Spearman's correlation and 'all' for result aggregation following prior works (Reimers and Gurevych, 2019; Gao et al., 2021b).

4.1 Settings

We initialize our training checkpoint with pre-trained $\text{BERT}_{\texttt{base,large}}$ (Devlin et al., 2019) and $\text{RoBERTa}_{\texttt{base,large}}$ (Liu et al., 2019). The `[CLS]` token representation is taken as sentence representation ($\mathbf{h_i}$). We compare with both unsupervised and supervised sentence embedding methods, including 1) average GloVe embedding (Pennington et al., 2014), 2) average BERT embedding (Su et al., 2021), 3) CT-BERT (Janson et al., 2021), 4) InferSent (Conneau et al., 2017), 5) USE (Cer et al., 2018), 6) SBERT (Reimers and Gurevych, 2019) and 7) SimCSE (Gao et al., 2021b). For a fair comparison, we did not include T5-based methods to avoid the influence of pre-trained checkpoint (Ni et al., 2022; Chen et al., 2022). We use r_1 and r_2 as our labeled data with relational weights 1.0 and 0.5, respectively. We train our model for 3 epochs and evaluate every 125 training steps on the development set of STS-B to keep the best-performed checkpoint.

τ	0.001	0.01	0.05	0.1	1.0
Avg. STS	80.74	81.73	82.18	77.00	54.88

Table 4: Ablation study on temperature τ.

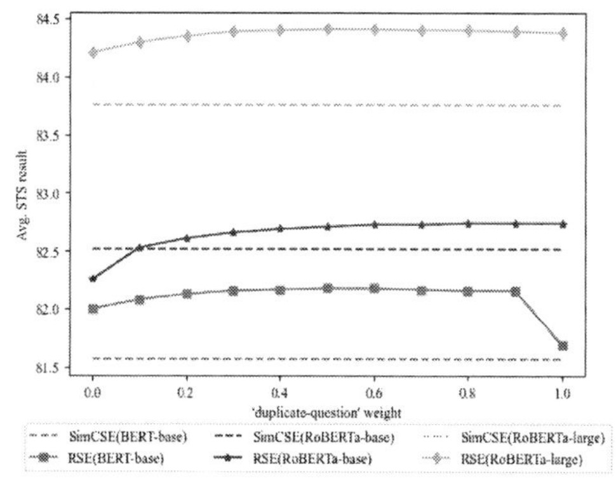

Figure 3: Performance comparison using different weights for 'duplicate-question' relation for STS tasks.

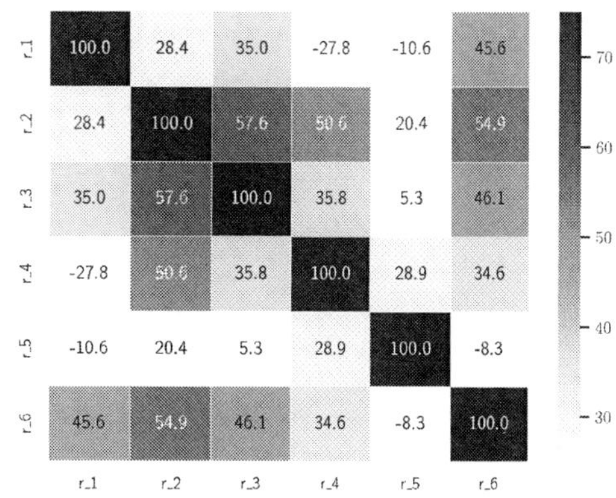

Figure 4: The similarity between relational embeddings. The relations $r_{1\sim 6}$ are *entailment, duplicate-question, paraphrase, same-caption, qa-entailment, same-sent.*

4.2 Main Results

Table 2 shows the evaluation results on 7 standard STS datasets. RSE can outperform all previous models in the supervised setting and improve the averaged STS result from 81.57% to 82.18% for Spearman's correlation with $\text{BERT}_{\texttt{base}}$ model. A further performance boost is witnessed with better pre-training checkpoints and larger model sizes. The averaged STS result with $\text{RoBERTa}_{\texttt{large}}$ model reaches 84.41%. We then experiment with five random seeds to test training stability and report the standard derivation. Results show that our method is robust against randomness. The performance on the STR-2022 dataset is shown in Table 3. We observe the same result patterns, and RSE can outperform the supervised SimCSE model.

Effect of Temperature. We study the influence of different τ values, and the result is shown in Table 4. $\tau = 0.05$ provides the best result, and we use the same setting for all experiments.

Effect of Relational Weight. We examine the performance by adjusting the weight of the relation 'duplication-question' and the results are shown in Figure 3. We witness that the avg. STS improved using the similarity score of both 'duplicate question' and 'entailment' relations. This phenomenon generalizes to different pre-trained models. For $\text{BERT}_{\texttt{base}}$ and $\text{RoBERTa}_{\texttt{large}}$ model, RSE can outperform others by only using the 'entailment' relation. The model can perform better when involving more relational scores, which we leave for future exploration.

5 Experiments on USEB Tasks

As there are some limitations in domain coverage of STS tasks (Wang et al., 2021b, 2022), we also experiment with Universal Sentence Embedding Benchmark (USEB) proposed in Wang et al. (2021b). It contains four tasks from heterogeneous domains, including Re-Ranking (RR), Information Retrieval (IR) and Paraphrase Identification (PI). The datasets are AskUbuntu (RR) (Lei et al., 2016), CQADupStack (IR) (Hoogeveen et al., 2015), TwitterPara (PI) (Xu et al., 2015; Lan et al., 2017), and SciDocs (RR) (Cohan et al., 2020).

5.1 Settings

Similarly, we experiment with four different pre-trained checkpoints $\text{BERT}_{\texttt{base, large}}$ and $\text{RoBERTa}_{\texttt{base, large}}$. We compare with different benchmarking including unsupervised methods: GloVe, Sent2Vec (Pagliardini et al., 2018), BM25 (Robertson et al., 1995), BERT, unsupervised SimCSE, and supervised methods: SBERT (Reimers and Gurevych, 2019), and SimCSE (Gao et al., 2021b). We did not compare with other in-domain adaption-based methods for fair comparison because RSE is an off-the-shelf method. For training, we include all relational data ($r_{1\sim 6}$ in Sec. 3.2) and use the similarity score from one specific relation for each task. We train our model for 3 epochs and evaluate every 1000 training steps on the development set of USEB to keep the best-performed checkpoint.

Model	AskU.	CQADup.	TwitterP. TURL	PIT	Avg.	SciDocs Cite	CC	CR	CV	Avg.	Avg.
GloVe (avg.)	51.0	10.0	70.1	52.1	61.1	58.8	60.6	64.2	65.4	62.2	46.1
Sent2Vec	49.0	3.2	47.5	39.9	43.7	61.6	66.0	66.1	66.7	65.1	40.2
BM25	53.4	13.3	71.9	70.5	71.2	58.9	61.3	67.3	66.9	63.6	50.4
$\text{BERT}_{\texttt{base}}$	48.5	6.5	69.1	61.7	65.4	59.4	65.1	65.4	68.6	64.6	46.3
*SimCSE - $\text{BERT}_{\texttt{base}}$	**55.9**	12.4	74.5	62.5	68.5	62.5	65.1	67.7	67.6	65.7	50.6
$\text{SBERT}_{\texttt{base}}$	53.4	11.8	75.4	69.9	72.7	66.8	70.0	70.7	72.8	70.1	52.0
SimCSE - $\text{BERT}_{\texttt{base}}$	53.5	12.2	76.1	69.7	72.9	66.8	69.5	**72.1**	70.7	69.8	52.1
RSE - $\text{BERT}_{\texttt{base}}$	54.8	**13.7**	**77.4**	**73.0**	**75.2**	**67.6**	**71.0**	71.8	**73.6**	**71.0**	**53.7**
RSE - $\text{BERT}_{\texttt{large}}$	56.2	13.9	76.7	76.8	76.7	68.6	71.9	72.5	74.5	71.9	54.7
RSE - $\text{RoBERTa}_{\texttt{base}}$	56.2	13.3	74.8	74.8	74.8	66.9	69.4	70.2	72.5	69.7	53.5
RSE - $\text{RoBERTa}_{\texttt{large}}$	**58.0**	**15.2**	76.2	**78.8**	**77.5**	**69.3**	**72.4**	**72.9**	**74.8**	**72.4**	**55.8**

Table 5: Results on domain-specific tasks. The out-of-the-box results of unsupervised and supervised approaches are shown. The first and second blocks show unsupervised and supervised methods, respectively. * refers to unsupervised SimCSE with dropout augmentation. Our proposed RSE outperforms all benchmarking approaches.

5.2 Main Results

Table 5 shows the evaluation result on 4 USEB tasks. Among the benchmarking methods, we found that unsupervised approaches outperform supervised approaches in AskUbuntu and CQADupStack tasks. The unsupervised SimCSE and BM25 achieve the best result on AskUbuntu and CQADupStack, respectively. It shows the heterogeneous character of USEB task and the previous supervised methods do not generalize well to various domains.

In contrast, RSE performs the best on 3 of the 4 tasks and achieves the best overall performance. The average result improves from 52.1 to 53.7 with $\text{BERT}_{\texttt{base}}$ model. For AskUbuntu and CQADupStack tasks, we find that the unsupervised SimCSE method achieves the best performance, even outperforming the supervised ones. RSE framework aligns with this finding that the best re-ranking and retrieval results are obtained by the similarity inferred from the 'same-sent' (r_6) relation. The TwitterPara dataset is for identifying whether two sentences are paraphrased or not. In RSE, we find the 'paraphrase' relation (r_3) trained on synthetic ParaNMT dataset works the best, which aligns with our intuition. Similarly, better performance is achieved with a larger pre-trained model as weight initialization. The USEB experiments verify the RSE's capability in modelling multi-source relational sentence-pair data. The relational-aware similarity scores can be flexibly applied to heterogeneous domain tasks.

Relation Similarity. We obtained 6 relation embeddings in our experiments after training with multi-source relational data. To study the similarity between relations, we compute the cosine similarity between pairwise relational embeddings, and the result is shown in Figure 4. From the results, we can witness the more similar relation pairs are *entailment* & *same-sent*, *duplicate-question* & *paraphrase*, *duplicate-question* & *same-caption*, *duplicate-question* & *same-sent*, and *paraphrase* & *same-sent*. The similar relations are more or less corresponding to sentence similarity, and we can see that the learned relational embeddings capture the relational information well. The *qa-entailment* relation models the relationship between question and answer pairs. Therefore, we can see it is indeed less similar to all other relations.

6 Experiments on Transfer Tasks

Besides the semantic similarity, ranking, and retrieval tasks, we also experiment with the following transfer tasks: MR (Pang and Lee, 2005), CR (Hu and Liu, 2004), SUBJ (Pang and Lee, 2004), MPQA (Wiebe et al., 2005), SST (Socher et al., 2013), TREC (Voorhees and Tice, 2000) and MRPC (Dolan and Brockett, 2005). Because the RSE model captures richer information by learning from multi-source relational data, we expect it generalizes better to different classification tasks.

6.1 Settings

Similarly, we experiment with four different initialization checkpoints. The averaged [CLS] token representation from the last five layers is taken as

Model	MR	CR	SUBJ	MPQA	SST	TREC	MRPC	Avg.
				Unsupervised methods				
GloVe (avg.)	55.14	70.66	59.73	68.25	63.66	58.02	53.76	61.32
$\text{BERT}_{\texttt{base}}$ (avg.)	78.66	86.25	94.37	88.66	84.40	92.80	69.54	84.94
SimCSE - $\text{BERT}_{\texttt{base}}$	81.18	86.46	94.45	88.88	85.50	89.80	74.43	85.81
SimCSE - $\text{RoBERTa}_{\texttt{base}}$	81.04	87.74	93.28	86.94	86.60	84.60	73.68	84.84
				Supervised methods				
InferSent - GloVe	81.57	86.54	92.50	90.38	84.18	88.20	75.77	85.59
USE	80.09	85.19	93.98	86.70	86.38	**93.20**	70.14	85.10
$\text{SBERT}_{\texttt{base}}$	**84.64**	**89.43**	94.39	89.86	**88.96**	89.60	76.00	87.41
SimCSE - $\text{BERT}_{\texttt{base}}$	82.69	89.25	94.81	89.59	87.31	88.40	73.51	86.51
w/ MLM	82.68	88.88	94.52	89.82	88.41	87.60	76.12	86.86
RSE - $\text{BERT}_{\texttt{base}}$	82.35	89.01	**95.33**	**90.56**	88.36	93.00	**77.39**	**88.00**
RSE - $\text{BERT}_{\texttt{large}}$	84.25	90.49	95.70	90.51	90.17	95.20	76.70	89.04
RSE - $\text{RoBERTa}_{\texttt{base}}$	84.52	**91.21**	94.39	90.21	**91.49**	91.40	77.10	88.62
RSE - $\text{RoBERTa}_{\texttt{large}}$	**86.29**	**91.21**	**95.17**	**91.16**	91.38	**95.40**	**78.20**	**89.83**

Table 6: Results on 7 transfer tasks. Both unsupervised and supervised methods are compared. Two versions of SimCSE are compared. The one with an additional mask language model (MLM) objective shows better performance. RSE outperforms other approaches on average.

the sentence representation ($\mathbf{h}_i$) (Wang and Kuo, 2020). The sentence encoder is used as a feature extractor. An MLP-based classifier is trained with sentence embeddings as the input. The default setting from the SentEval package is deployed (Conneau and Kiela, 2018).

We leverage the relations of *entailment* and *paraphrase* for training. As sentence embedding is used as the input to classifiers, relation embeddings are not incorporated in transfer task experiments. All models are trained for 3 epochs. We evaluate the model on the development set every 500 training steps and keep the best-performed checkpoint for final evaluation. We compare RSE with different competitive methods including InferSent (Conneau et al., 2017), USE (Cer et al., 2018), SBERT (Reimers and Gurevych, 2019), and SimCSE (Gao et al., 2021b).

6.2 Results and Analysis

Table 6 shows the evaluation results on 7 transfer tasks. The RSE model with $\text{BERT}_{\texttt{base}}$ architecture achieves an average score of 88.0, outperforming all benchmarked methods. SBERT outperforms SimCSE in 6 of 7 tasks. We infer that the classification-based training objective makes SBERT more transferable to transfer tasks. Even though the contrastive learning approach outperforms in semantic similarity tasks, it does not generalize well with additional trainable classifiers. In contrast, RSE is a contrastive-based approach, which already showed superior in semantic similarity tasks. Due to its learning capability from multi-source relational data, the learned sentence embeddings have better generalizability than single-source supervised learning. It leads to better transferability of the sentence embedding obtained from RSE models. Similar to previous findings, the performance of RSE improves with larger and better pre-trained checkpoints as initialization. Even though RSE is mainly designed for flexible semantic matching with multiple relational similarity scores, the learn sentence embedding captures richer semantic meanings for various transfer tasks.

7 Conclusion and Future Work

In this work, we propose RSE, a new sentence embedding paradigm with explicit relation modelling by translation operation. RSE can learn from multi-source relational data and provide interpretable relational similarity scores. Experiments on semantic similarity, domain-specific, and transfer tasks show that RSE can outperform SOTA approaches, verifying its flexibility and effectiveness. Relational sentence embedding can broaden the concept of conventional similarity-based sentence embedding and can be extended for different applications.

For future work, first, with more sentence relational data available, the relational sentence embedding can become more competitive and generalizable to different domains. The collection of sentence-level relational data has great potential. Second, more complex relation modelling methods can be incorporated into handling heterogeneous relations. Besides the translation operation in this work, other relation modelling functions, including rotation and semantic matching, can be further explored. Third, this work mainly focuses on supervised relation signals, and unsupervised relational sentence embedding still needs to be explored.

Limitations

The first limitation of RSE comes from data sparsity. Unlike word-level relational data, the variety of sentences is much larger than words. Therefore, even though we can collect more and more relational data on sentence pairs, it is generally hard to become densely connected between sentences. To alleviate this issue and generate sustainable sentence relational data, we should design automatic tools for sentence relation labelling with human-in-the-loop supervision.

Second, unsupervised sentence embedding also shows decent performance on semantic textual similarity tasks, and the focus is mainly on the design of unsupervised contrastive samples. Therefore, exploring different unsupervised view-augmentation techniques in relational sentence embedding remains an open question. In this work, we only study incorporate dropout augmentation without much discussion on other techniques like pseudo-labelling (Chen et al., 2022), word drop, word swap, and word repetition (Yan et al., 2021).

For relational data modelling, complex operations (Sun et al., 2019; Trouillon et al., 2016) for relation modelling are introduced and proven effective in knowledge graph completion. However, it is not straightforward to incorporate complex operations with pre-trained semantic representations. The study of RSE in complex space modelling remains unexplored.

Acknowledgement

This work is supported by the Agency for Science, Technology and Research (A*STAR) under its AME Programmatic Funding Scheme (Project No. A18A2b0046), Singapore, and by National Natural Science Foundation of China (Grant No. 62271432).

References

Mohamed Abdalla, Krishnapriya Vishnubhotla, and Saif M Mohammad. 2021. What makes sentences semantically related: A textual relatedness dataset and empirical study. *arXiv preprint arXiv:2110.04845*.

Eneko Agirre, Carmen Banea, Claire Cardie, Daniel Cer, Mona Diab, Aitor Gonzalez-Agirre, Weiwei Guo, Iñigo Lopez-Gazpio, Montse Maritxalar, Rada Mihalcea, German Rigau, Larraitz Uria, and Janyce Wiebe. 2015. SemEval-2015 task 2: Semantic textual similarity, English, Spanish and pilot on interpretability. In *Proceedings of the 9th International Workshop on Semantic Evaluation (SemEval 2015)*, pages 252–263, Denver, Colorado. Association for Computational Linguistics.

Eneko Agirre, Carmen Banea, Claire Cardie, Daniel Cer, Mona Diab, Aitor Gonzalez-Agirre, Weiwei Guo, Rada Mihalcea, German Rigau, and Janyce Wiebe. 2014. SemEval-2014 task 10: Multilingual semantic textual similarity. In *Proceedings of the 8th International Workshop on Semantic Evaluation (SemEval 2014)*, pages 81–91, Dublin, Ireland. Association for Computational Linguistics.

Eneko Agirre, Carmen Banea, Daniel Cer, Mona Diab, Aitor Gonzalez-Agirre, Rada Mihalcea, German Rigau, and Janyce Wiebe. 2016. SemEval-2016 task 1: Semantic textual similarity, monolingual and cross-lingual evaluation. In *Proceedings of the 10th International Workshop on Semantic Evaluation (SemEval-2016)*, pages 497–511, San Diego, California. Association for Computational Linguistics.

Eneko Agirre, Daniel Cer, Mona Diab, and Aitor Gonzalez-Agirre. 2012. SemEval-2012 task 6: A pilot on semantic textual similarity. In **SEM 2012: The First Joint Conference on Lexical and Computational Semantics – Volume 1: Proceedings of the main conference and the shared task, and Volume 2: Proceedings of the Sixth International Workshop on Semantic Evaluation (SemEval 2012)*, pages 385–393, Montréal, Canada. Association for Computational Linguistics.

Eneko Agirre, Daniel Cer, Mona Diab, Aitor Gonzalez-Agirre, and Weiwei Guo. 2013. *SEM 2013 shared task: Semantic textual similarity. In *Second Joint Conference on Lexical and Computational Semantics (*SEM), Volume 1: Proceedings of the Main Conference and the Shared Task: Semantic Textual Similarity*, pages 32–43, Atlanta, Georgia, USA. Association for Computational Linguistics.

Ivana Balazevic, Carl Allen, and Timothy Hospedales. 2019. TuckER: Tensor factorization for knowledge graph completion. In *Proceedings of the 2019 Conference on Empirical Methods in Natural Language Processing and the 9th International Joint Conference on Natural Language Processing (EMNLP-IJCNLP)*, pages 5185–5194, Hong Kong, China. Association for Computational Linguistics.

Antoine Bordes, Nicolas Usunier, Alberto Garcia-Duran, Jason Weston, and Oksana Yakhnenko. 2013. Translating embeddings for modeling multi-relational data. *Advances in neural information processing systems*, 26.

Samuel R. Bowman, Gabor Angeli, Christopher Potts, and Christopher D. Manning. 2015. A large annotated corpus for learning natural language inference. In *Proceedings of the 2015 Conference on Empirical Methods in Natural Language Processing*, pages 632–642, Lisbon, Portugal. Association for Computational Linguistics.

Jose Camacho-Collados, Luis Espinosa Anke, and Steven Schockaert. 2019. Relational word embeddings. In *Proceedings of the 57th Annual Meeting of the Association for Computational Linguistics*, pages 3286–3296, Florence, Italy. Association for Computational Linguistics.

Daniel Cer, Mona Diab, Eneko Agirre, Iñigo Lopez-Gazpio, and Lucia Specia. 2017. SemEval-2017 task 1: Semantic textual similarity multilingual and crosslingual focused evaluation. In *Proceedings of the 11th International Workshop on Semantic Evaluation (SemEval-2017)*, pages 1–14, Vancouver, Canada. Association for Computational Linguistics.

Daniel Cer, Yinfei Yang, Sheng-yi Kong, Nan Hua, Nicole Limtiaco, Rhomni St. John, Noah Constant, Mario Guajardo-Cespedes, Steve Yuan, Chris Tar, Brian Strope, and Ray Kurzweil. 2018. Universal sentence encoder for English. In *Proceedings of the 2018 Conference on Empirical Methods in Natural Language Processing: System Demonstrations*, pages 169–174, Brussels, Belgium. Association for Computational Linguistics.

Ting Chen, Simon Kornblith, Mohammad Norouzi, and Geoffrey Hinton. 2020. A simple framework for contrastive learning of visual representations. In *International conference on machine learning*, pages 1597–1607. PMLR.

Yiming Chen, Yan Zhang, Bin Wang, Zuozhu Liu, and Haizhou Li. 2022. Generate, discriminate and contrast: A semi-supervised sentence representation learning framework. In *Proceedings of the 2022 Conference on Empirical Methods in Natural Language Processing*, pages 8150–8161, Abu Dhabi, United Arab Emirates. Association for Computational Linguistics.

Arman Cohan, Sergey Feldman, Iz Beltagy, Doug Downey, and Daniel Weld. 2020. SPECTER: Document-level representation learning using citation-informed transformers. In *Proceedings of the 58th Annual Meeting of the Association for Computational Linguistics*, pages 2270–2282, Online. Association for Computational Linguistics.

Alexis Conneau and Douwe Kiela. 2018. SentEval: An evaluation toolkit for universal sentence representations. In *Proceedings of the Eleventh International Conference on Language Resources and Evaluation (LREC 2018)*, Miyazaki, Japan. European Language Resources Association (ELRA).

Alexis Conneau, Douwe Kiela, Holger Schwenk, Loïc Barrault, and Antoine Bordes. 2017. Supervised learning of universal sentence representations from natural language inference data. In *Proceedings of the 2017 Conference on Empirical Methods in Natural Language Processing*, pages 670–680, Copenhagen, Denmark. Association for Computational Linguistics.

Tim Dettmers, Pasquale Minervini, Pontus Stenetorp, and Sebastian Riedel. 2018. Convolutional 2d knowledge graph embeddings. In *Proceedings of the AAAI conference on artificial intelligence*, volume 32.

Jacob Devlin, Ming-Wei Chang, Kenton Lee, and Kristina Toutanova. 2019. BERT: Pre-training of deep bidirectional transformers for language understanding. In *Proceedings of the 2019 Conference of the North American Chapter of the Association for Computational Linguistics: Human Language Technologies, Volume 1 (Long and Short Papers)*, pages 4171–4186, Minneapolis, Minnesota. Association for Computational Linguistics.

William B. Dolan and Chris Brockett. 2005. Automatically constructing a corpus of sentential paraphrases. In *Proceedings of the Third International Workshop on Paraphrasing (IWP2005)*.

Luyu Gao, Yunyi Zhang, Jiawei Han, and Jamie Callan. 2021a. Scaling deep contrastive learning batch size under memory limited setup. In *Proceedings of the 6th Workshop on Representation Learning for NLP (RepL4NLP-2021)*, pages 316–321, Online. Association for Computational Linguistics.

Tianyu Gao, Xingcheng Yao, and Danqi Chen. 2021b. SimCSE: Simple contrastive learning of sentence embeddings. In *Proceedings of the 2021 Conference on Empirical Methods in Natural Language Processing*, pages 6894–6910, Online and Punta Cana, Dominican Republic. Association for Computational Linguistics.

Kaiming He, Haoqi Fan, Yuxin Wu, Saining Xie, and Ross Girshick. 2020. Momentum contrast for unsupervised visual representation learning. In *Proceedings of the IEEE/CVF conference on computer vision and pattern recognition*, pages 9729–9738.

Doris Hoogeveen, Karin M. Verspoor, and Timothy Baldwin. 2015. Cqadupstack: A benchmark data set for community question-answering research. In

Proceedings of the 20th Australasian Document Computing Symposium, ADCS '15, New York, NY, USA. Association for Computing Machinery.

Minqing Hu and Bing Liu. 2004. Mining and summarizing customer reviews. In *Proceedings of the tenth ACM SIGKDD international conference on Knowledge discovery and data mining*, pages 168–177.

Sverker Janson, Evangelina Gogoulou, Erik Ylipää, Amaru Cuba Gyllensten, and Magnus Sahlgren. 2021. Semantic re-tuning with contrastive tension. In *International Conference on Learning Representations, 2021*.

Ryan Kiros, Yukun Zhu, Russ R Salakhutdinov, Richard Zemel, Raquel Urtasun, Antonio Torralba, and Sanja Fidler. 2015. Skip-thought vectors. *Advances in neural information processing systems*, 28.

Wuwei Lan, Siyu Qiu, Hua He, and Wei Xu. 2017. A continuously growing dataset of sentential paraphrases. In *Proceedings of the 2017 Conference on Empirical Methods in Natural Language Processing*, pages 1224–1234, Copenhagen, Denmark. Association for Computational Linguistics.

Tao Lei, Hrishikesh Joshi, Regina Barzilay, Tommi Jaakkola, Kateryna Tymoshenko, Alessandro Moschitti, and Lluís Màrquez. 2016. Semi-supervised question retrieval with gated convolutions. In *Proceedings of the 2016 Conference of the North American Chapter of the Association for Computational Linguistics: Human Language Technologies*, pages 1279–1289, San Diego, California. Association for Computational Linguistics.

Yankai Lin, Zhiyuan Liu, Maosong Sun, Yang Liu, and Xuan Zhu. 2015. Learning entity and relation embeddings for knowledge graph completion. In *Twenty-ninth AAAI conference on artificial intelligence*.

Yinhan Liu, Myle Ott, Naman Goyal, Jingfei Du, Mandar Joshi, Danqi Chen, Omer Levy, Mike Lewis, Luke Zettlemoyer, and Veselin Stoyanov. 2019. Roberta: A robustly optimized bert pretraining approach. *arXiv preprint arXiv:1907.11692*.

Marco Marelli, Stefano Menini, Marco Baroni, Luisa Bentivogli, Raffaella Bernardi, and Roberto Zamparelli. 2014. A SICK cure for the evaluation of compositional distributional semantic models. In *Proceedings of the Ninth International Conference on Language Resources and Evaluation (LREC'14)*, pages 216–223, Reykjavik, Iceland. European Language Resources Association (ELRA).

George A Miller. 1995. Wordnet: a lexical database for english. *Communications of the ACM*, 38(11):39–41.

Jianmo Ni, Gustavo Hernandez Abrego, Noah Constant, Ji Ma, Keith Hall, Daniel Cer, and Yinfei Yang. 2022. Sentence-t5: Scalable sentence encoders from pretrained text-to-text models. In *Findings of the Association for Computational Linguistics: ACL 2022*, pages 1864–1874, Dublin, Ireland. Association for Computational Linguistics.

Matteo Pagliardini, Prakhar Gupta, and Martin Jaggi. 2018. Unsupervised learning of sentence embeddings using compositional n-gram features. In *Proceedings of the 2018 Conference of the North American Chapter of the Association for Computational Linguistics: Human Language Technologies, Volume 1 (Long Papers)*, pages 528–540, New Orleans, Louisiana. Association for Computational Linguistics.

Bo Pang and Lillian Lee. 2004. A sentimental education: Sentiment analysis using subjectivity summarization based on minimum cuts. In *Proceedings of the 42nd Annual Meeting of the Association for Computational Linguistics (ACL-04)*, pages 271–278, Barcelona, Spain.

Bo Pang and Lillian Lee. 2005. Seeing stars: Exploiting class relationships for sentiment categorization with respect to rating scales. In *Proceedings of the 43rd Annual Meeting of the Association for Computational Linguistics (ACL'05)*, pages 115–124, Ann Arbor, Michigan. Association for Computational Linguistics.

Jeffrey Pennington, Richard Socher, and Christopher Manning. 2014. GloVe: Global vectors for word representation. In *Proceedings of the 2014 Conference on Empirical Methods in Natural Language Processing (EMNLP)*, pages 1532–1543, Doha, Qatar. Association for Computational Linguistics.

Nils Reimers and Iryna Gurevych. 2019. Sentence-BERT: Sentence embeddings using Siamese BERT-networks. In *Proceedings of the 2019 Conference on Empirical Methods in Natural Language Processing and the 9th International Joint Conference on Natural Language Processing (EMNLP-IJCNLP)*, pages 3982–3992, Hong Kong, China. Association for Computational Linguistics.

Stephen E Robertson, Steve Walker, Susan Jones, Micheline M Hancock-Beaulieu, Mike Gatford, et al. 1995. Okapi at trec-3. *Nist Special Publication Sp*, 109:109.

Richard Socher, Alex Perelygin, Jean Wu, Jason Chuang, Christopher D. Manning, Andrew Ng, and Christopher Potts. 2013. Recursive deep models for semantic compositionality over a sentiment treebank. In *Proceedings of the 2013 Conference on Empirical Methods in Natural Language Processing*, pages 1631–1642, Seattle, Washington, USA. Association for Computational Linguistics.

Jianlin Su, Jiarun Cao, Weijie Liu, and Yangyiwen Ou. 2021. Whitening sentence representations for better semantics and faster retrieval. *arXiv preprint arXiv:2103.15316*.

Zhiqing Sun, Zhi-Hong Deng, Jian-Yun Nie, and Jian Tang. 2019. Rotate: Knowledge graph embedding by relational rotation in complex space. In *International Conference on Learning Representations*.

Théo Trouillon, Johannes Welbl, Sebastian Riedel, Éric Gaussier, and Guillaume Bouchard. 2016. Complex embeddings for simple link prediction. In *International conference on machine learning*, pages 2071–2080. PMLR.

Ellen M Voorhees and Dawn M Tice. 2000. Building a question answering test collection. In *Proceedings of the 23rd annual international ACM SIGIR conference on Research and development in information retrieval*, pages 200–207.

Alex Wang, Amanpreet Singh, Julian Michael, Felix Hill, Omer Levy, and Samuel Bowman. 2018. GLUE: A multi-task benchmark and analysis platform for natural language understanding. In *Proceedings of the 2018 EMNLP Workshop BlackboxNLP: Analyzing and Interpreting Neural Networks for NLP*, pages 353–355, Brussels, Belgium. Association for Computational Linguistics.

Bin Wang and C.-C. Jay Kuo. 2020. SBERT-WK: A sentence embedding method by dissecting bert-based word models. *IEEE/ACM Transactions on Audio, Speech, and Language Processing*, 28:2146–2157.

Bin Wang, C.-C. Jay Kuo, and Haizhou Li. 2022. Just rank: Rethinking evaluation with word and sentence similarities. In *Proceedings of the 60th Annual Meeting of the Association for Computational Linguistics (Volume 1: Long Papers)*, pages 6060–6077, Dublin, Ireland. Association for Computational Linguistics.

Bin Wang, Guangtao Wang, Jing Huang, Jiaxuan You, Jure Leskovec, and C.-C. Jay Kuo. 2021a. Inductive learning on commonsense knowledge graph completion. In *2021 International Joint Conference on Neural Networks (IJCNN)*, pages 1–8. IEEE.

Kexin Wang, Nils Reimers, and Iryna Gurevych. 2021b. TSDAE: Using transformer-based sequential denoising auto-encoderfor unsupervised sentence embedding learning. In *Findings of the Association for Computational Linguistics: EMNLP 2021*, pages 671–688, Punta Cana, Dominican Republic. Association for Computational Linguistics.

Zhigang Wang, Juanzi Li, Zhiyuan Liu, and Jie Tang. 2016. Text-enhanced representation learning for knowledge graph. In *Proceedings of International joint conference on artificial intelligent (IJCAI)*, pages 4–17.

Janyce Wiebe, Theresa Wilson, and Claire Cardie. 2005. Annotating expressions of opinions and emotions in language. *Language resources and evaluation*, 39(2):165–210.

John Wieting and Kevin Gimpel. 2018. ParaNMT-50M: Pushing the limits of paraphrastic sentence embeddings with millions of machine translations. In *Proceedings of the 56th Annual Meeting of the Association for Computational Linguistics (Volume 1: Long Papers)*, pages 451–462, Melbourne, Australia. Association for Computational Linguistics.

Adina Williams, Nikita Nangia, and Samuel Bowman. 2018. A broad-coverage challenge corpus for sentence understanding through inference. In *Proceedings of the 2018 Conference of the North American Chapter of the Association for Computational Linguistics: Human Language Technologies, Volume 1 (Long Papers)*, pages 1112–1122, New Orleans, Louisiana. Association for Computational Linguistics.

Xing Wu, Chaochen Gao, Liangjun Zang, Jizhong Han, Zhongyuan Wang, and Songlin Hu. 2022. ESimCSE: Enhanced sample building method for contrastive learning of unsupervised sentence embedding. In *Proceedings of the 29th International Conference on Computational Linguistics*, pages 3898–3907, Gyeongju, Republic of Korea. International Committee on Computational Linguistics.

Wei Xu, Chris Callison-Burch, and Bill Dolan. 2015. SemEval-2015 task 1: Paraphrase and semantic similarity in Twitter (PIT). In *Proceedings of the 9th International Workshop on Semantic Evaluation (SemEval 2015)*, pages 1–11, Denver, Colorado. Association for Computational Linguistics.

Yuanmeng Yan, Rumei Li, Sirui Wang, Fuzheng Zhang, Wei Wu, and Weiran Xu. 2021. ConSERT: A contrastive framework for self-supervised sentence representation transfer. In *Proceedings of the 59th Annual Meeting of the Association for Computational Linguistics and the 11th International Joint Conference on Natural Language Processing (Volume 1: Long Papers)*, pages 5065–5075, Online. Association for Computational Linguistics.

Bishan Yang, Wen-tau Yih, Xiaodong He, Jianfeng Gao, and Li Deng. 2015. Embedding entities and relations for learning and inference in knowledge bases. *International Conference on Learning Representations*.

Liang Yao, Chengsheng Mao, and Yuan Luo. 2019. KG-BERT: BERT for knowledge graph completion. *arXiv preprint arXiv:1909.03193*.

Peter Young, Alice Lai, Micah Hodosh, and Julia Hockenmaier. 2014. From image descriptions to visual denotations: New similarity metrics for semantic inference over event descriptions. *Transactions of the Association for Computational Linguistics*, 2:67–78.

A Joint-Learning with Multiple Datasets

SimCSE (Gao et al., 2021b) found that the positive sentence pairs extracted from *entailment* relation are the most effective supervision signals in contrastive sentence representation learning. We first experiment with different supervision as positive sentence pairs. The averaged STS result is reported in Table 1. The result shows that using *entailment* for positive and *contrastive* for negatives provides the best performance. It outperforms all other supervision, including QQP, Flicker, ParaNMT, and

QNLI datasets. This explains why only NLI dataset is widely used in previous work for supervised sentence representation learning (Conneau et al., 2017; Reimers and Gurevych, 2019; Gao et al., 2021b).

Another question comes to the stage: Can we simultaneously leverage the supervision from the above-mentioned datasets for better-supervised representation learning? An intuitive way to learn from multi-source relational data is to treat all supervised signals as positive samples in contrastive learning. Therefore, we experiment with merging all supervision data and performing contrastive sentence representation learning following Gao et al. (2021b). The result is shown in Table 1. We can tell that merging all sentence pairs for joint training will hurt the performance (77.67 -> 74.62) of STS datasets compared with a single source for positive sentence pairs.

Based on the above experimental results, we conclude it is not a trivial task to leverage multi-source supervision signals in supervised sentence representation learning. With explicit relation modeling techniques proposed in RSE, we can effectively learn from multi-source relational data and achieve better flexibility and performance in various tasks.

Relation	MRR	Hits@1	Hits@3	Hits@10
Entailment	0.80	0.74	0.85	0.93
Duplicate Question	0.83	0.76	0.88	0.97
Paraphrase	0.97	0.95	0.98	1.00
QA Entailment	0.85	0.80	0.90	0.95
Same Caption	0.56	0.45	0.63	0.79
All	0.81	0.74	0.84	0.92

Table 7: Performance on in-domain relation prediction. We follow the evaluation protocol of link prediction in knowledge graph completion literature.

B In-domain Relation Prediction

As the relation sentence embedding is trained in a contrastive manner, the trained model can also be used to predict the validity of new triples. Therefore, we did further experiments to test the model's performance on link prediction.

For dataset creation, we use data from five different relations, including *entailment*, *duplicate-question*, *paraphrase*, *same-caption*, and *qa-entailment*. We did not include the prediction for *same-sent* relation as the prediction for the same sentence is a trivial task. We use all available data for training. For validation and testing, we randomly sampled 2,000 sentence triples each.

We perform link prediction experiments following the literature of knowledge graph completion (Sun et al., 2019). The task is to predict the tail entity (sentence) given the head entity (sentence) and relation. It is a retrieval-based task, and performance is measured by the rank of the valid positive samples. Our experimental result is shown in Table 7. From the result, we can see that the *paraphrase* relation is the easiest to predict. It is understandable because the sentences from the paraphrased data are very similar. In contrast, we see that the *same-caption* relation is the hardest to be retrieved. It is because the sentence pairs are collected from the descriptions for the same image. The captions for each image can be generated based on various aspects. The relationship between large number sentence pairs is not very strong. It poses challenges on *same-caption* relations in link prediction.

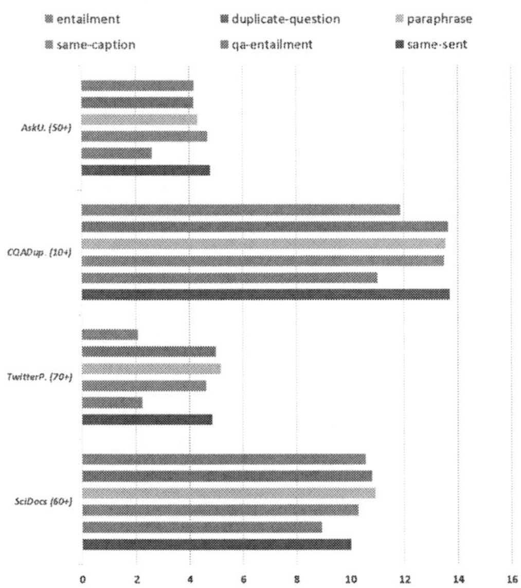

Figure 5: Performance on the USEB benchmark (4 datasets) using different relational similarity scores. The model is $\text{BERT}_{\texttt{base}}$.

C Comparison of Relational Score Selection on USEB Tasks

In Section 5, we report the best result on four tasks with the best relational similarity score. We found that different dataset favors different relational similarity score. We look into the detailed performance with all relational similarity scores to further study the effect. The result is shown in Figure 5.

For AskU. dataset, the unsupervised SimCSE shows the best performance. Similarly, we also found that the unsupervised relation (*same-sent*) demonstrated to be the best relation similarity score to be used in AskU. and CQADup. datasets. TwitterP. dataset is a paraphrase identification task and the similarity score under *paraphrase* relation in RSE shows the best result. In contrast, as no dataset in USEB focuses on question-answer pair retrieval or ranking, the similarity score from *qa-entailment* relation does not lead to a good performance. From the above discussion, we can see that different relational similarity scores will apply to different applications. A wise choice of relational score can lead to better performance, proving that our proposed RSE model can be flexible to various tasks with explicit relation modeling capability.

D Hyperparameter Settings

Table 8 shows the datasets, relations, examples and their applied tasks in our experiments. We train our model for 3 epochs in all experiments and evaluate every 125, 1000, and 500 steps for best checkpoint selection on STS, USEB, and Transfer tasks, respectively. We select the best model based on its performance on the development set. Due to resource limitations, we perform a small-scale grid search for the model hyperparameter settings. The grid search is on batch size $\in \{128, 256, 512\}$ and learning rate $\in \{1e-5, 3e-5, 5e-5\}$. The learning rate for relation embedding is set to $1e-2$ in all experiments because they are randomly initialized parameters without pre-training. All experiments take the representation for `[CLS]` token as sentence representation. The temperature hyperparameter is set to 0.05, and the maximum sentence length is set to 32. We did not use warm-up or weight decay in all experiments.

E Case Study

To better understand the property of RSE, we present the case study of four sentence pairs and their inferred relational scores in Table 9. The results show that the RSE model can estimate the most likely relationship between sentence pairs. Because the QA entailment relation is very distinct from other relation types, the question-answering pairs are easily distinguished. The QA sentences show the highest score in QA entailment relation, as indicated by the first two cases. Meantime, because of the similar property between relations of *'duplicate question'*, *'paraphrase'* and *'same sent'*, from the third case, we can see highly similar sentence pairs have high relational scores in all three relations. It also aligns with our relation study in Figure 4. The last case shows two entailment sentence pairs, and we can see that RSE successfully presents the highest score as an entailment relation.

Dataset	Relationship	Example Sentence Pair	Tasks
MNLI & SNLI	Entailment (r_1)	(s_1) He mostly hangs out with a group of older, Southern black men, who call him Jumper and Black Cat. (s_2) The group of guys he tends to hang out with gave him the nickname Jumper.	STS, USEB, Transfer
QQP	Duplicate Question (r_2)	(s_1) How can I be a good geologist? (s_2) What should I do to be a great geologist?	STS, USEB
ParaNMT	Paraphrase (r_3)	(s_1) he loved that little man , by the way . (s_2) he liked the little boy .	USEB, Transfer
Flicker	Same Caption (r_4)	(s_1) Two men in green shirts are standing in a yard. (s_2) Two friends enjoy time spent together.	USEB
QNLI	QA entailment (r_5)	(s_1) How many alumni does Olin Business School have worldwide? (s_2) Olin has a network of more than 16,000 alumni worldwide.	USEB
WIKI	Same Sent (r_6)	(s_1) A meeting of promoters was also held at Presbyterian Church. (s_2) A meeting of promoters was also held at Presbyterian Church.	USEB

Table 8: Example sentence triples for different relations and their applied tasks.

Sentences	Entailment	Duplicate question	Paraphrase	Same caption	QA entailment	Same sent
"Where is ACL 2023 hold?" *"The 61st Annual Meeting of the Association for Computational Linguistics (ACL23) will take place in Toronto, Canada from July 9th to July 14th, 2023."*	0.1639	0.3204	0.3037	0.3468	0.4470	0.3078
"Is Singapore a city or state?" *"Singapore is a sunny, tropical island in South-east Asia, off the southern tip of the Malay Peninsula."*	0.4220	0.5640	0.5605	0.5774	0.6599	0.5451
"Giraffes can consume 75 pounds of food a day." *"Giraffes can eat up to 75 pounds of food in a day.*	0.8622	0.9596	0.9546	0.9434	0.9021	0.9569
"Young man breakdancing on a sidewalk in front of many people." *"A man dancing outside."*	0.6680	0.6126	0.6176	0.5606	0.5062	0.6396

Table 9: Case study on sentence pairs and the relation scores inferred by our RSE model.

Tucker Decomposition with Frequency Attention for Temporal Knowledge Graph Completion

Likang Xiao[1,3], **Richong Zhang**[1], **Zijie Chen**[2], **Junfan Chen**[1]
[1]SKLSDE, School of Computer Science and Engineering, Beihang University, Beijing, China
[2]School of Electrical and Computer Engineering, University of Toronto, Toronto, Canada
[3]Shen Yuan Honors College, Beihang University, Beijing, China
{xiaolk, zhangrc, chenjf}@buaa.edu.cn
chenzijie162@gmail.com

Abstract

Temporal Knowledge Graph Completion aims to complete missing entities or relations under temporal constraints. Previous tensor decomposition-based models for TKGC only independently consider the combination of one single relation with one single timestamp, ignoring the global nature of the embedding. We propose a Frequency Attention (FA) model to capture the global temporal dependencies between one relation and the entire timestamp. Specifically, we use Discrete Cosine Transform (DCT) to capture the frequency of the timestamp embedding and further compute the frequency attention weight to scale embedding. Meanwhile, the previous temporal tucker decomposition method uses a simple norm regularization to constrain the core tensor, which limits the optimization performance. Thus, we propose Orthogonal Regularization (OR) variants for the core tensor, which can limit the non-superdiagonal elements of the 3-rd core tensor. Experiments on three standard TKGC datasets demonstrate that our method outperforms the state-of-the-art results on several metrics. The results suggest that the direct-current component is not the best feature for TKG representation learning. Additional analysis shows the effectiveness of our FA and OR models, even with smaller embedding dimensions.

1 Introduction

Knowledge graph (KG) contains a number of structured facts (h, r, t), where a fact expresses a directed relation r from a head entity h to a tail entity t. The complex KGs, such as FreeBase (Berant et al., 2013), DBPedia (Auer et al., 2007), and Wikidata (Vrandečić and Krötzsch, 2014), are collected manually or automatically from structured or unstructured data on the web. Such KGs are successfully applied to several downstream tasks, e.g., Question Answering (Berant et al., 2013) and Recommender System (Wang et al., 2018). However, those works ignore that many facts in the

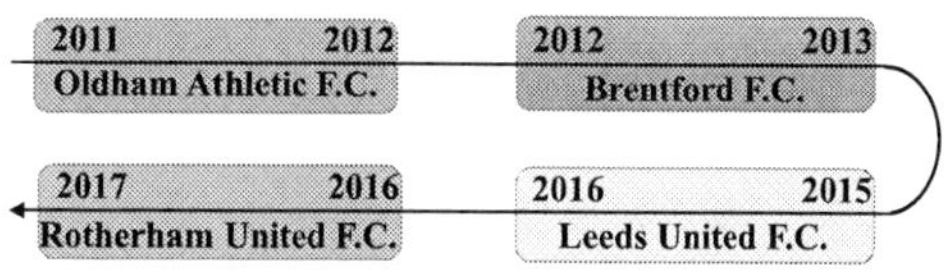

Figure 1: A toy example from the temporal knowledge graph shows an athlete's career. This example illustrates the temporal dependencies of facts that Tom Adeyemi plays for four teams from 2011 to 2017. Toy example scores calculated by TuckER-FA are in the appendix C.

KGs change over time. Temporal facts can be expressed as a quadruplet (h, r, t, τ), with τ being the timestamp. The temporal Knowledge graphs (TKGs), such as ICEWS (Lautenschlager et al., 2015), GDELT (Leetaru and Schrodt, 2013) and YAGO (Mahdisoltani et al., 2015), are then built to handle these facts coupled with timestamps.

One problem that hinders the application of TKGs in downstream tasks is the inevitable incompleteness or knowledge scarcity problem caused by missing entities or relations. Thus, Temporal Knowledge Graph Completion (TKGC) aiming to complete the missing entities or relations over time has become an essential task in the research community. The previous methods for TKGC can be divided into four branches, in which the critical challenge is how to integrate timestamps into KGC modeling. Time-dependent Embedding method (Trivedi et al., 2017; Goel et al., 2020; Dasgupta et al., 2018) considers the temporal information as a transformation or an activation function for entities or relations. Timestamp Embedding method (Han et al., 2021b; Lacroix et al., 2020; Shao et al., 2022) treats timestamps as additional learnable embeddings of the score function. Experimental experience (Han et al., 2021b) suggests that timestamp embeddings generally perform better than time-dependent embeddings. Knowledge Graph Snapshots method (Liao et al., 2021; Li et al.,

Proceedings of the 8th Workshop on Representation Learning for NLP (RepL4NLP 2023), pages 253–265
July 13, 2023 ©2023 Association for Computational Linguistics

2021) aggregates multi-relational interactions of cropped subgraph to achieve more precise representations. Historical Context method (Jung et al., 2021; Zhu et al., 2021) model n-hop facts chain or repeat facts to increase the interpretability.

The previous timestamp embedding methods model each quadruplet independently, which only captures the *local* temporal dependencies, ignoring the *global* temporal dependencies between one relation and entire timestamp. As shown in Figure 1, an athlete plays for different teams in different periods. We treat such events as a continuous line of events rather than as separate events. We propose a Frequency Attention (FA) model to address this issue. Specifically, we treat each dimension in the timestamp embedding as a long-term signal and use Discrete Cosine Transform (DCT) to capture the frequency of the signal. Furthermore, we take the frequency and part of the relation embedding as input to calculate attention weights for each timestamp. The proposed frequency attention model can easily apply to exist tensor decomposition methods.

The previous tucker decomposition method is interpreted as a high-dimensional linear classifier to distinguish facts. TuckERTNT (Shao et al., 2022), uses a simple L2 norm as the core tensor regularization. However, this regularization may be overstrict, leading the embedding to change sharply and risk vanishing or explosion. Inspired by orthogonal regularization in (Brock et al., 2019), we propose two variants of orthogonal regularization (OR) for the core tensor, i.e., excluding superdiagonal elements or diagonal elements of each slice matrix of the core tensor. This way, we achieve a balanced core tensor regularization, preventing the embedding norm from vanishing or exploding.

In summary, our work makes the following contributions:

(1) we propose a frequency attention model using DCT to capture the global temporal dependency between relations and entire timestamp.

(2) we introduce two variants of core tensor orthogonal regularization for the tucker decomposition, which can prevent the embedding norm from vanishing or explosion.

(3) Experiment results on three standard datasets show that our model outperforms the SOTA models on several metrics. The additional analysis demonstrates the effectiveness of our frequency attention model and orthogonal regularization.

2 Related Works

2.1 Static KG Embedding

There has been ample research on static knowledge graph embedding. We grouped all mainstream models into four main categories. Tensor decomposition-based models RESCAL (Nickel et al., 2011), Distmult(Yang et al., 2015), ComplEx (Trouillon et al., 2016), and TuckER (Balazevic et al., 2019) compute triplet score in real or complex domain. Distance-based models are built upon euclidean or hyperbolic distance as shown in TransE (Bordes et al., 2013), mainfoldE (Xiao et al., 2016) and RotatE (Sun et al., 2019). DURA (Zhang et al., 2020) figure out that distance-based method can be viewed as decomposition method with a L_2 regularization. Neural-based models use a convolutional network to capture the KG structure information, as shown in ConvE (Dettmers et al., 2018). Other models learn from a variety of experiences from fields. Inspired by reinforcement learning, MultiHopKG (Lin et al., 2018) sample n-hop triplets chain to compute the fact triplet scores and re-rank candidates.

2.2 Temporal KG Embedding

There are two scenarios for integrating temporal information into existing static embedding models, timestamp embedding and time-dependent entity embedding. Time-dependent entity embedding can explicitly model dynamic changes of entities, such as periodicity and trending. A well-known time-dependent entity embedding is diachronic embedding (Goel et al., 2020), which uses the sine function to represent the frequency of entity evolution over different time granularity. (Han et al., 2021b) compares six KG embedding models, and figures out that timestamp embedding can achieve similar or even better performance with significantly fewer parameters. Although timestamp embedding might suffer from the growing number of timestamps, the time granularity can also be controlled within an appropriate range by enlarging. Further analysis in TNTComplEx (Lacroix et al., 2020) points out that time-dependent relation embedding can obtain comparable results to time-dependent entity embedding with smaller computational costs.

From the viewpoint of the subgraph, there are a series of knowledge graph snapshots/subgraphs over time, which contain potential multi-relational interactions. (Liao et al., 2021) adopt probabilistic entity representations based on variational

Bayesian inference to jointly model the entity features and the uncertainty. (Li et al., 2021) employs a multi-layer graph convolutional network on each subgraph to capture the dependencies of adjacent facts. From another contextual perspective, the relevance between the query and its historical context can be used as evidence for reasoning. (Jung et al., 2021) proposes a multi-hop reasoning model using a graph attention layer and finds that temporal displacements are more indicative for inference than timestamps. (Zhu et al., 2021) notice more than 80% of events from 1995 to 2019 in the ICEWS repository are repeated events. In this case, they introduce a copy mechanism to re-rank the candidates.

3 Preliminaries

3.1 Problem Definition

To formally define the problem and describe the solution, we use consistent notations in the rest of the paper. We represent scalars with the lower case letters, e.g., d_r, represent sets with the flower letters, e.g., $\mathcal{E}$, represent vectors with the bold lower case letters, e.g., $\boldsymbol{h}_i$, denoting the ith entity embedding. We use bold upper letters $\boldsymbol{H}$ to denote the embedding matrix and represent the high order tensor with bold flower letters $\boldsymbol{\mathcal{W}}$.

We use $\boldsymbol{a} \odot \boldsymbol{b}$ to denote Hadamard (element-wise) product of two vectors or matrix, $\boldsymbol{a} \otimes \boldsymbol{b}$ to denote the tensor outer product, $[\boldsymbol{A}|\boldsymbol{B}]$ to denote the vector or matrix concatenation operator, $||\cdot||_p$ to denote the p-norm of a vector or tensor.

A temporal knowledge graph $\mathcal{G}$ consists of a set of facts $\{(h_i, r_j, t_k, \tau_l)\} \subseteq \mathcal{E} \times \mathcal{R} \times \mathcal{E} \times \mathcal{T}$, where $\mathcal{E}$ is a finite entity set, $\mathcal{R}$ is a finite relation set and $\mathcal{T}$ is a finite timestamp set. Each quadruplet (h_i, r_j, t_k, τ_l) respectively denotes a relation r_j from the head entity h_i to tail entity t_k at a specific time τ_l. A temporal knowledge graph uses a binary tensor $\mathcal{X} = \{0,1\}^{|\mathcal{E}|\times|\mathcal{R}|\times|\mathcal{E}|\times|\mathcal{T}|}$ to indicate whether the corresponding quadruplets occurs in the KG data set. $|\mathcal{E}|$, $|\mathcal{R}|$ and $|\mathcal{T}|$ denote the number of entities, relations, and timestamps, respectively.

Although knowledge graphs contain large numbers of facts, they are still incomplete due to the complex nature of the real world. TKGC aims to predict the missing entity. We focus on the link prediction problem, aiming to predict the tail entity or head entity through the query $(h_i, r_j, ?, \tau_l)$ or $(?, r_j, t_k, \tau_l)$. The problem reduces to ranking a set of candidate entities to select the most likely entity that makes the partial quadruplet factual. The problem can be formulated as a ranking problem to learn a quadruplet score function $\hat{\mathcal{X}}(\mathcal{E}, \mathcal{R}, \mathcal{E}, \mathcal{T}) \in \mathbb{R}$ to sort all candidate entities.

3.2 Tucker Decomposition for TKG Embedding

Many tensor decomposition methods apply to the KG embeddings, such as bilinear decomposition, canonical decomposition, and tucker decomposition. Among these methods, tucker decomposition, a kind of principal component analysis approach for high-order tensors, is viewed as the general one. In particular, when the super-diagonal elements in the core tensor of Tucker equal 1 and other elements equal 0, tucker decomposition degrades into canonical decomposition. TuckER (Balazevic et al., 2019) has proved that Dismult (Yang et al., 2015) and ComplEx (Trouillon et al., 2016) can be included into the framework of TuckER. In KGC task, An 3-order tensor $\boldsymbol{\mathcal{X}}$ can be decomposed into a core tensor $\boldsymbol{\mathcal{W}} \in \mathbb{R}^{D_e \times D_r \times D_e}$ and entity/relation embedding matrix $\boldsymbol{E}/\boldsymbol{R}$ as factor matrix. The formula of the tucker decomposition is as follows.

$$\begin{aligned}\mathcal{X} &= \boldsymbol{\mathcal{W}} \times_1 \boldsymbol{E} \times_2 \boldsymbol{R} \times_3 \boldsymbol{E} = <\boldsymbol{\mathcal{W}}; \boldsymbol{E}, \boldsymbol{R}, \boldsymbol{E}> \\ &= \sum_{d_1=1}^{D_e} \sum_{d_2=1}^{D_r} \sum_{d_3=1}^{D_e} W_{d_1 d_2 d_3} \boldsymbol{h}_{:d_1} \otimes \boldsymbol{r}_{:d_2} \otimes \boldsymbol{t}_{:d_3}\end{aligned}$$

$\times_n$ denotes the n-mode product of the tensor, which can be explained as the core tensor expanding into a matrix along the n-th dimension.

To obtain proper timestamp embedding $\boldsymbol{T}$, TuckERTNT (Shao et al., 2022) use two relation embeddings $\boldsymbol{R}$ and $\boldsymbol{R}^t$ to separately capture time-variant information and time-invariant information as follows.

$$\mathcal{X} = <\boldsymbol{\mathcal{W}}; \boldsymbol{E}, \boldsymbol{R}^t \odot \boldsymbol{T} + \boldsymbol{R}, \boldsymbol{E}>$$

Although previous works have achieved good results in the TKGC task, they may still encounter many problems. First, the learnable parameters representing the frequency of DE-SimplE may be clustered around 0, affecting the model performance (as shown in Appendix D). Second, TuckERTNT constrains the core tensor with the fourth power of L_4 norm. However, it is not guaranteed that the n-mode product of the core tensor is well-perform. Therefore, there is still space to improve the temporal tucker decomposition for the TKGC task.

4 Model

We propose a new framework, TuckER-FA, combining the FA and OR with the temporal tucker decomposition method. We input the timestamp embedding and relation embedding to the FA model to compute frequency attention weights, then weighted-sum the timestamp embedding and combine it with the relation embedding. The timestamp-enhanced relation feature and head/tail entity embedding compose the factor matrix of tucker decomposition. In learning progress, we include several regularization losses and the orthogonal regularization of the core tensor into the overall objective.

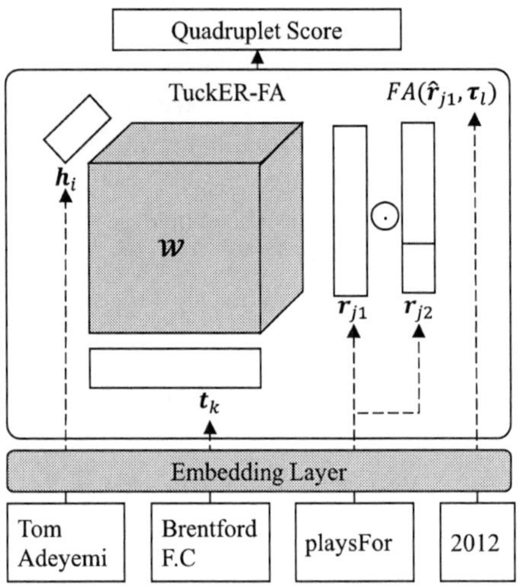

Figure 2: The score function of TuckER-FA, which can measure how likely the quadruplet is to be true. The gray part contains the learnable parameters.

4.1 Score Function

We propose a score function for TKGC based on tucker decomposition shown in Figure 2. Specifically, the formula of the score function is.

$$\mathcal{X}_{ijkl} = <\mathcal{W}; \boldsymbol{h}_i, \boldsymbol{r}_{j1} \odot [\boldsymbol{r}_{j2} | FA(\hat{\boldsymbol{r}}_{j1}, \boldsymbol{t}_l)], \boldsymbol{t}_k>$$

We use $\rho = \frac{d_\tau}{d_r}$ to control the embedding dimension ratio between timestamps and relations. $r_{j1} \in \mathbb{R}^{d_r}$ and $r_{j2} \in \mathbb{R}^{d_r - d_\tau}$ respectively denote two relation embeddings. $\tau_l \in \mathbb{R}^{d_\tau}$ is the timestamp embedding. FA represents the Frequency Attention model. The input $\hat{\boldsymbol{r}}_{j1}$ denote the part of relation embedding which aligns with τ_l. The main amount of computation is concentrated on tucker decomposition rather than the FA model.

4.2 Frequency Attention

To capture the crucial temporal features of TKG, we propose a Frequency Attention (FA) model shown in Figure 3. We treat the evolution of timestamp embedding over time as a combination of periodic functions with different frequencies. Inspired by FcaNet (Qin et al., 2021), we use Discrete Cosine Transform (DCT) to capture the different frequency components of timestamp embeddings. In this way, we can capture the global temporal dependency of one relation and the entire timestamp.

The chronologically arranged timestamp embedding $\boldsymbol{T} \in \mathbb{R}^{N_\tau \times d_\tau}$ is viewed as d_τ different temporal signals. The direct-current (DC) component f_0 and frequency component f_k of DCT are respectively formulated as follows.

$$f_0 = \sum_{i=0}^{N_\tau - 1} T_i = GAP(T) N_\tau$$

$$f_k = \sum_{i=0}^{N_\tau - 1} T_i cos(\frac{\pi k}{N_\tau}(i + \frac{1}{2})) \quad k \in \{0, ..., N_\tau - 1\}$$

GAP represents the global average pooling operation, which always use to calculate the channel attention weight in the computer vision domain. In the TKGC task, the main calculation procedure of direct-current component frequency attention is as follows.

$$FA(\boldsymbol{\tau}_l) = \sigma(FC(GAP(T_{:d})N_\tau)) \odot \tau_{:d}$$

The FC block represents a fully-connected layer, and σ denotes sigmoid function. It is natural to include more frequency components to calculate attention weight. Considering the limitation of computing resources, we optionally select part of the frequency components. We divide the time embedding dimension d_τ into n parts and assign a set of selected frequencies $f_0, ... f_n$ to each part. We also introduce $\hat{\boldsymbol{r}}_{j1}$, part of relation embedding aligned with τ_l, into the FA model.

$$FA(\hat{\boldsymbol{r}}_j, \boldsymbol{\tau}_l) = \sigma(FC(\hat{\boldsymbol{r}}_{j1} \odot [f_0 | f_1 | ... | f_n])) \odot \boldsymbol{\tau}_l$$

In addition, the computation complexity of the operation with finite orthogonal function bases is linear. The cost of computation of the frequency attention model is negligible compared to the cost of computation in tucker decomposition. The frequency attention weight determines how much timestamp embedding information for the corresponding dimension is retained. The FA model considers the evolution of a single relation over the entire timestamp.

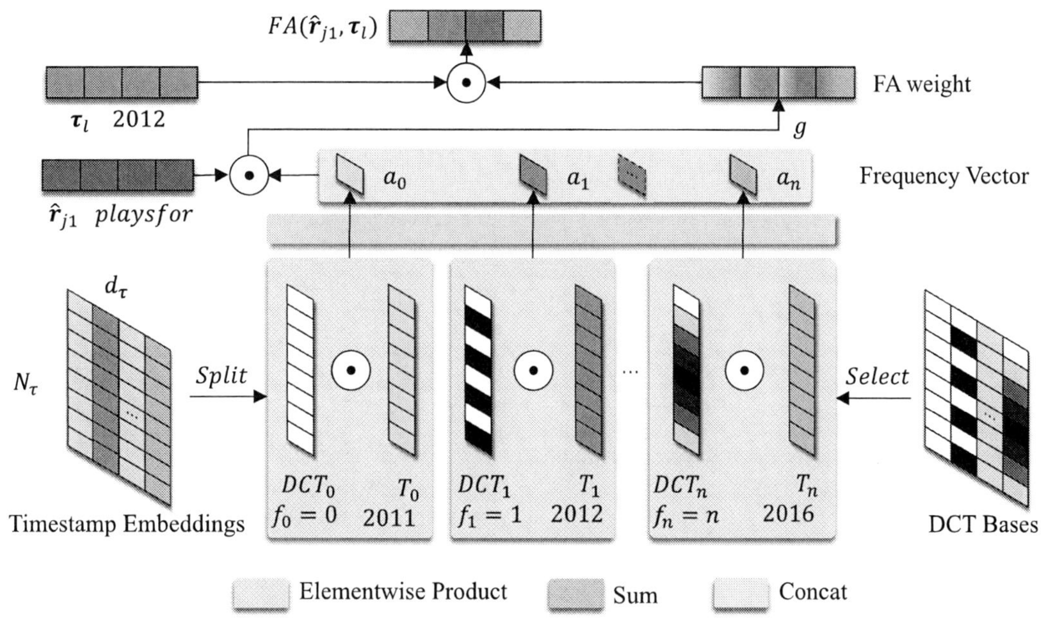

Figure 3: The framework of the Frequency Attention model, which can capture the global temporal dependency of one relation and entire timestamp. Here g is a simple two-layer MLP plus sigmoid function.

4.3 Orthogonal Regularization for Core Tensor

There have been many research results on orthogonal regularization of the matrix, such as (Miyato et al., 2018). In summary, the orthogonal regularization allows the parameter matrix to be closer to the diagonal-dominant non-singular matrix. A non-singular matrix prevents abrupt truncation changes of the feature map during matrix multiplication. Furthermore, tucker decomposition can be viewed as matrix multiplication for factor matrix with the arbitrary slice of core tensor. In other words, orthogonal regularization could be applied to core tensor multiplication.

Inspired by BigGAN (Brock et al., 2019), we heuristically propose two variants of core tensor orthogonal regularization Φ_1 and Φ_2. The baseline is the simple norm regularization Φ_0 used in TuckERTNT.

$$\Phi_0(\theta) = ||\mathcal{W}||_4^4$$
$$\Phi_1(\theta) = ||\mathcal{W} \odot (\mathbf{1} - \mathcal{I})||_4^4$$
$$\Phi_2(\theta) = ||\mathcal{W} \odot (\mathbf{1} - Proj(\mathcal{I}))||_4^4$$

$\mathbf{1}, \mathcal{I}, Proj(\mathcal{I})$ is tensors with the same shape as $\mathcal{W}$. All the elements of $\mathbf{1}$ are 1. The superdiagonal elements of $\mathcal{I}$ are 1, and the other elements are 0. The diagonal elements of the arbitrary slice matrix of $Proj(\mathcal{I})$ are 1, and the other elements are 0. The tucker decomposition degenerates to the CP decomposition when the super-diagonal elements of the core tensor are 1, and the rest are 0. Φ_1 regularization can restrict the result of the tucker decomposition to the neighborhood of the weighted CP decomposition. (the super-diagonal elements of the core tensor are weights, and the rest elements indicate a slight difference from weighted CP decomposition.

4.4 Other Regularization

Researchers have investigated many different kinds of embedding regularization to alleviate the overfitting problem. TNTComplex uses the third power of Nuclear-3 norm twice for temporal or non-temporal quadruplets. TIMEPLEX (Jain et al., 2020) use sampled weighted L2 regularization to avoid the overfitting problem. In our model, we use embedding regularization as ChronoR (Sadeghian et al., 2021) does, using the fourth power of $L4$ norm as embedding regularization.

$$\Omega_4(\theta) = ||\boldsymbol{h}||_4^4 + ||\boldsymbol{t}||_4^4 + ||\boldsymbol{r}_1||_4^4 + ||[\boldsymbol{r}_2|FA(\boldsymbol{\tau})]||_4^4$$

Because of the real-world time continuity, it is natural to guarantee adjacent timestamp embeddings or repeat timestamp embeddings closer in the embedding space. TuckERTNT (Shao et al., 2022) proposes several temporal regularization to smooth the timestamp embedding. Notice that YAGO15K has many quadruplets without any timestamp, in which we artificially add a unique timestamp. This unique timestamp is excluded when computing temporal regularization terms. To be consistent with the embedding regularization, the adjacent timestamp differential regularization is as follow.

$$\Lambda_4(\theta) = \frac{1}{|\mathcal{T}|-1} \sum_{i=1}^{|\mathcal{T}|-1} ||\boldsymbol{\tau}_{i+1} - \boldsymbol{\tau}_i||_4^4$$

4.5 Loss Function

For each training data, we use instantaneous multi-class loss.

$$\mathcal{L}(\mathcal{X}_{ijkl}) = -\mathcal{X}_{ijkl} + log(\sum_{k'} exp(\mathcal{X}_{ijk'l}))$$

Considering instantaneous multi-class loss and the above three regularization term jointly, we train our model by minimizing the following loss function.

$$\mathcal{L}(\mathcal{X};\theta) = \frac{1}{|S|} \sum_{(i,j,k,l)\in S} [\mathcal{L}(\mathcal{X};\theta) + \lambda\Phi_n(\mathcal{X};\theta) + \lambda_1\Omega_4(\mathcal{X};\theta) + \lambda_2\Lambda_4(\mathcal{X};\theta))] \quad n = 1,2,3$$

where λ_1, λ_2 and λ is importance hyperparameter for tuning.

5 Experiments

5.1 Datasets and Evaluation Metrics

We choose three of the most commonly-used datasets to evaluate our model, including ICEWS14, GDELT, and YAGO15K. The detailed statistics of each dataset are shown in Table 1.

ICEWS14 is extracted from the Integrated Crisis Early Warning System (Lautenschlager et al., 2015) repository, which contains political events with daily timestamp points. This dataset, for the most part, is time-sensitive and accurate in descriptions.

GDELT is extracted from the Global Database of Events, Language, and Tone (Leetaru and Schrodt, 2013), which covers news data from 1979 to the present by automatically crawling. GDELT is a complicated dataset because of its abstract entity, such as government and organization.

YAGO15K (Friedland and Lim, 2018) augmented events of FB15K (Bordes et al., 2013) with time interval. YAGO15K is worst-perform in TKGC tasks because it requires the model to handle both temporal and non-temporal knowledge.

We follow the standard evaluation set in previous work, and report two standard metrics, Hit@k ($k \in \{1, 3, 10\}$) and filtered Mean Reciprocal Rank (MRR). They can evaluate the rank of the correct entity in the filtered candidate set. Hit@k reflects the percentage of the query whose correct tail entities are ranked within the top k candidates. Mean Reciprocal Rank, which computes the average of the reciprocal of mean rank, reflects the correct fact rank of the model. We follow the time-aware filtering (Han et al., 2021a), which means entities that cause ambiguity are removed from the candidate list for a query. We using reciprocal setting to add $(t_k, r_j^{-1}, h_i, \tau_l)$ into train set for each quadruplet (h_i, r_j, t_k, τ_l). The detailed hyperparameters of our model are shown in Appendix B.

Table 1: The statistics of the benchmark datasets.

	ICEWS14	GDELT	YAGO15K
#Entity	7128	500	15403
#Relation	230	20	34
#Timestamp	365	366	198
#Facts	90730	3419607	138056
Timespan	2014	2015-2016	1513-2017
Granularity	Daily	Daily	Annually
Type	Point	Point	Interval

5.2 Main Results

Table 2 shows the main temporal knowledge graph completion results. The results of other models come from the original paper. We use the bold number to indicate the existing best results. Our model slightly outperforms or ties with previous SOTA results on several metrics of ICEWS14 and YAGO3-10. On GDELT, our model achieves significant improvement results on all metrics. Compared with TuckERTNT, our model TuckER-FA has $d[(1-\rho)|\mathcal{T}| + (2+\rho)|\mathcal{R}|]$ fewer parameters and 1.1% higher MRR performance when using the same embedding dimensionality. Compared with 2500+ dimensions of entity and relation of TNTComplex and ChronoR, our model gets better results using only 400 dimensions of entity and relation.

Increasing the number of model parameters substantially improves MRR performance on the GDELT, but the improvement on the other two

Table 2: The evaluation results on ICEWS14, GDELT, and YAGO15K. For the other works, we report the best results reported in their original paper.

Model	ICEWS14				GDELT				YAGO15K			
Metric	MRR	H@1	H@3	H@10	MRR	H@1	H@3	H@10	MRR	H@1	H@3	H@10
TransE	28.0	9.4	-	63.7	15.5	6.0	17.8	33.5	29.6	22.8	-	46.8
SimplE	45.8	34.1	51.6	68.7	20.6	12.4	22.0	36.6	-	-	-	-
ComplEx	47.0	35.0	54.0	71.0	21.3	13.3	22.5	36.6	36.0	29.0	36.0	45.0
TTransE	25.5	7.4	-	60.1	11.5	0.0	16.0	31.8	32.1	23.0	-	51.0
TA-DistMult	47.7	36.3	-	68.6	20.6	12.4	21.9	36.5	29.1	21.6	-	47.6
DE-SimplE	52.6	41.8	59.2	72.5	23.0	14.1	24.8	40.3	-	-	-	-
TeMP	60.7	54.5	67.3	77.4	-	-	-	-	27.5	19.1	29.7	43.7
TNTComplex	62.0	52.0	66.0	76.0	22.4	14.4	23.9	38.1	36.0	28.4	37.0	53.7
ChronoR	62.5	**54.7**	66.9	77.3	-	-	-	-	**36.6**	**29.1**	37.9	53.8
BoxTE	61.5	53.2	66.7	76.4	35.2	26.9	37.7	51.1	-	-	-	-
TuckERTNT	62.5	54.4	67.3	77.3	44.8	35.2	49.2	63.0	-	-	-	-
TuckER-FA	**62.7**	54.4	**67.7**	**78.0**	**48.6**	**39.3**	**53.2**	**66.0**	36.5	28.2	**39.2**	**54.3**

Table 3: Ablation study of FA and OR TuckER-FA.

MRR	ICEWS14	GDELT	YAGO15K
ALL	62.7	48.6	36.5
w/o FA	62.0(-0.7)	47.3(-1.3)	34.8 (-1.7)
w/o OR	60.6(-2.1)	46.1(-2.5)	33.4 (-3.1)
w/o Both	58.4(-4.3)	44.9(-3.7)	32.6 (-3.9)

models is slight. Compared with ICEWS14, the GDELT dataset has nearly 38 times the number of facts, and fewer entities/relations, within the same time span. The corresponding graph of GDELT is spatially denser, with many more recurring facts. As a result, GDELT greatly enhances the global temporal dependency of relations, which is exactly our FA model focus on. Complex global temporal dependency explains TuckER-FA outstanding advantage on GDELT compared with its counterparts.

5.3 Ablation Study

Table 3 shows the ablation study of the Frequency Attention(FA) model and core tensor Orthogonal Regularization(OR) model. It can be observed that both models are valuable when working individually, and the combination of them performs even better. We can point out that the OR model is more effective than the FA model.

The single FA model increases the accuracy significantly in ICEWS14 compared with the vanilla model, which is probably because this dataset has the shortest time span and the minimal data. The improvement of the single OR model is slight in YAGO15K, and it may be attributed to the presence of facts without timestamps.

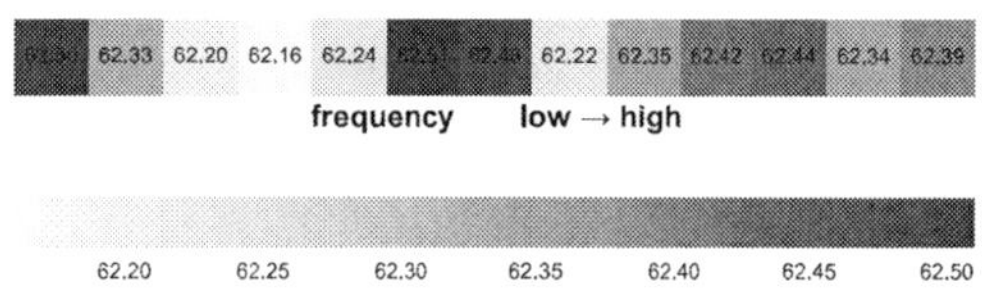

(a) ICEWS14

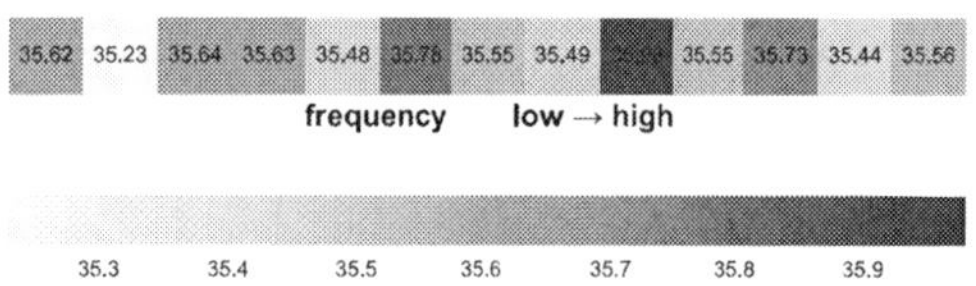

(b) YAGO15K

Figure 4: The MRR performance using different single frequency in the FA model. The darker colors indicate better results. Knowledge graph has inherent frequencies based on its own data distribution.

5.4 Frequency of Temporal Knowledge Graph

From the result of FcaNet (Qin et al., 2021) in the Appendix E, we can notice frequency attention model with a single direct-current component always reach the best result in the Image Classi-

Table 4: MRR Results for different test set divisions on ICEWS14 and YAGO15k.

Dataset	Total	DC	HF
ICEWS14	62.5	61.3	64.2
YAGO15k	36.5	35.1	39.4

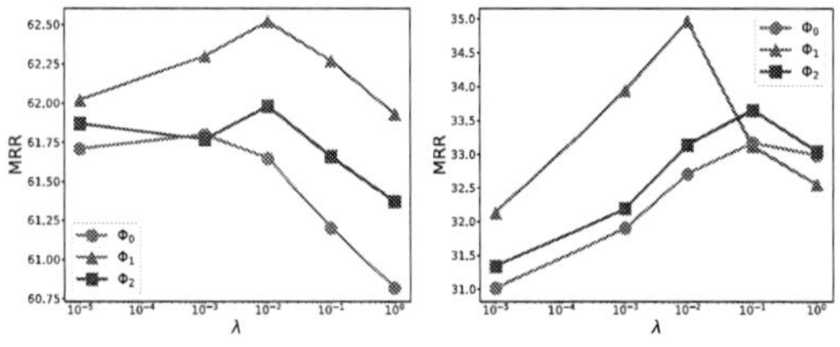

(a) ICEWS14 (b) YAGO15K

Figure 5: The MRR performance of norm regularization and two variants of orthogonal regularization. The Φ_1 regularization without the superdiagonal elements of the core tensor performs best.

fication task. The low-frequency component is more critical than the high-frequency component because the low-frequency signal of the images provides information such as shape or size, while the high-frequency signal provides information such as edge details. However, this phenomenon does not occur in the TKGC task. Usually, it is difficult to have many repeated details in a naturally captured image. In contrast, many facts, such as the toy example, continuously change over time in TKGC. These facts determine that there exist some inherent frequencies in timestamp embedding.

Figure 4 shows the results of the frequency attention model with different single DCT bases. We use a combination of frequencies from the top six results to achieve our best results. The difference between the frequencies was insignificant, meaning the global temporal dependency spread over all frequencies. In detail, the direct-current component is the second-high result in ICEWS14 but the sixth-high in YAGO15K. The reason may be that the facts without a timestamp in YAGO15K disturb the estimation of the intrinsic frequency. The above results show that finding a suitable frequency feature with FA is helpful for the TKGC task.

To study why TuckER-FA performs differently on different datasets compared to other baselines, we count the number of the query $(h, r, ?, ?)$ occurrences over the entire timestamp. The average number of occurrences per query in GDELT is 284.7, and queries that occur more than once account for 98.8% of the training set. The statistics are 7.33, 40.8% in ICEWS14, and 4.51, 54.9% in YAGO15k, respectively. Thus, TuckER-FA gains better results on GDELT because the FA module is good at capturing the global temporal dependencies between one relation over the entire timestamp.

Table 4 show the MRR Results for two test set divisions on ICEWS14 and YAGO15k. We split the test set into two subsets, one consisting of queries that occur only once (direct-currency component, DC) and the other consisting of queries that appear multiple times (high-frequency component, HF). In conclusion, our model works much better on the high-frequency component test set. Because the GDELT dataset is almost exclusively high-frequency components, it boosts most significantly.

5.5 Orthogonal Regularization

Figure 5 shows the detailed comparison of three regularizations for the core tensor. In this experiment, we fix the λ_1 and λ_2 and only use the direct-current component for the frequency attention model. The Φ_2 regularization without the diagonal elements of the arbitrary slice matrix of the core tensor performs slightly better than the Φ_0 norm regularization. The Φ_1 regularization without the superdiagonal elements of the core tensor performs best.

The Φ_1 regularization increase MRR by 0.7 points on ICEWS14 and 1.8 points on YAGO15K. Top Performing Φ_1 can increase MRR to 2.1 points on ICEWS14 and 3.1 points on YAGO15K. We can point out that the relaxation of the core tensor constraint is effective.

5.6 Effect of Parameter Complexity

To compare model results more fairly, we add two experiments controlling the number of parameters or entity dimensionality between TNTcomplEx, TeLM, and TuckER-FA. A complete parameter comparison between baseline models and TuckER-FA is in Appendix A.

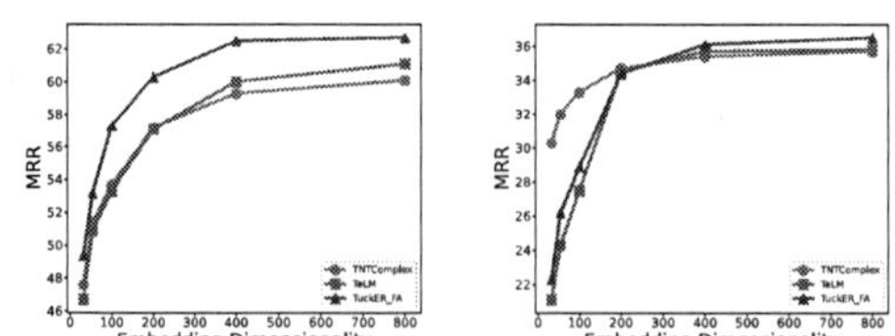

(a) ICEWS14 (b) YAGO15K

Figure 6: The MRR performance of different models with different embedding dimensionality. With the same embedding dimensionality, our model consistently outperforms TeLM.

Figure 6 shows our TuckER-FA consistently outperforms the baseline TNTComplEx and TeLM with the same dimensionality on ICEWS14. TNTComplEx uses a specialized matrix to represent non-timestamp embedding, which allows it to perform best in low dimensionality on YAGO15K. Our TuckER-FA can overtake in high dimensionality. The upper limit of TeLM is not as high as TuckER-FA. In summary, our model has the highest performance ceiling for TKGC.

Table 5 shows the comparison with the same parameters and 50 epochs training on ICEWS14. We limit the size of the learnable parameters to approximately 67M, which means 2110 embedding dimensions for TeLM, 4000 for TNTComplEX, and 400 for our TuckER-FA. We can point out that our TuckER-FA model achieves a significant improvement in MRR and Hit@3 and a weak improvement in the other two metrics.

Table 5: Results with approximately 67M parameters of TNTComplEx, TeLM, and TuckER-FA on ICEWS14.

Model	MRR	Hit@1	Hit@3	Hit@10
TuckER-FA	62.5	54.3	67.5	77.2
TNTComplEx	61.2	52.4	66.3	77.4
TeLM	62.1	54.2	66.7	77.0

6 Conclusion

In our work, we propose a DCT-based Frequency Attention model and two variants of Orthogonal Regularization for the core tensor of tucker decomposition. The FA model considers the global temporal dependency between one relation and the entire timestamp. Each KG has its unique inherent frequency. The OR term relaxes the constraint on the superdiagonal of the core tensor and improves the performance of tucker decomposition. TuckER-FA achieves SOTA results on three standard datasets of temporal knowledge graph completion task. There might be further discussions on an efficient frequency selection strategy or a theoretical assumption for tensor regularization.

7 Limitation

Although our method has been shown effective, it has two limitations that may be improved in the future. First, the FA model has advantages in computation but relies on an effective frequency selection strategy, which is difficult to design. We just simply select some manual frequencies for different datasets by experience. The more effective frequency selection strategy needs further exploration. Second, there is no theoretical guarantee that the orthogonal regularization can generalize to a 3-order tensor. Our OR terms are only formally consistent with matrix orthogonal regularization, which has been empirically shown effective.

Acknowledgements

This work is supported partly by the National Key R&D Program of China under Grant 2021ZD0110700, partly by the Fundamental Research Funds for the Central Universities, and partly by the State Key Laboratory of Software Development Environment.

References

Sören Auer, Christian Bizer, Georgi Kobilarov, Jens Lehmann, Richard Cyganiak, and Zachary Ives. 2007. Dbpedia: A nucleus for a web of open data. In *The Semantic Web*, pages 722–735, Berlin, Heidelberg. Springer Berlin Heidelberg.

Ivana Balazevic, Carl Allen, and Timothy M. Hospedales. 2019. Tucker: Tensor factorization for knowledge graph completion. In *Proceedings of the 2019 Conference on Empirical Methods in Natural Language Processing and the 9th International Joint Conference on Natural Language Processing, EMNLP-IJCNLP 2019, Hong Kong, China, November 3-7, 2019*, pages 5184–5193. Association for Computational Linguistics.

Jonathan Berant, Andrew Chou, Roy Frostig, and Percy Liang. 2013. Semantic parsing on freebase from question-answer pairs. In *Proceedings of the 2013 conference on empirical methods in natural language processing*, pages 1533–1544, Seattle, USA. Association for Computational Linguistics.

Antoine Bordes, Nicolas Usunier, Alberto García-Durán, Jason Weston, and Oksana Yakhnenko. 2013. Translating embeddings for modeling multi-relational data. In *Advances in Neural Information Processing Systems 26: 27th Annual Conference on Neural Information Processing Systems 2013. Proceedings of a meeting held December 5-8, 2013, Lake Tahoe, Nevada, United States*, pages 2787–2795.

Andrew Brock, Jeff Donahue, and Karen Simonyan. 2019. Large scale GAN training for high fidelity natural image synthesis. In *7th International Conference on Learning Representations, ICLR 2019, New Orleans, LA, USA, May 6-9, 2019*. OpenReview.net.

Shib Sankar Dasgupta, Swayambhu Nath Ray, and Partha Pratim Talukdar. 2018. Hyte: Hyperplane-based temporally aware knowledge graph embedding. In *EMNLP*.

Tim Dettmers, Pasquale Minervini, Pontus Stenetorp, and Sebastian Riedel. 2018. Convolutional 2d knowledge graph embeddings. In *Proceedings of the Thirty-Second AAAI Conference on Artificial Intelligence, (AAAI-18), the 30th innovative Applications of Artificial Intelligence (IAAI-18), and the 8th AAAI Symposium on Educational Advances in Artificial Intelligence (EAAI-18), New Orleans, Louisiana, USA, February 2-7, 2018*, pages 1811–1818. AAAI Press.

Shmuel Friedland and Lek-Heng Lim. 2018. Nuclear norm of higher-order tensors. *Math. Comput.*, 87(311):1255–1281.

Rishab Goel, Seyed Mehran Kazemi, Marcus A. Brubaker, and Pascal Poupart. 2020. Diachronic embedding for temporal knowledge graph completion. In *AAAI*.

Zhen Han, Zifeng Ding, Yunpu Ma, Yujia Gu, and Volker Tresp. 2021a. Learning neural ordinary equations for forecasting future links on temporal knowledge graphs. In *Proceedings of the 2021 Conference on Empirical Methods in Natural Language Processing, EMNLP 2021, Virtual Event / Punta Cana, Dominican Republic, 7-11 November, 2021*, pages 8352–8364. Association for Computational Linguistics.

Zhen Han, Gengyuan Zhang, Yunpu Ma, and Volker Tresp. 2021b. Time-dependent entity embedding is not all you need: A re-evaluation of temporal knowledge graph completion models under a unified framework. In *Proceedings of the 2021 Conference on Empirical Methods in Natural Language Processing, EMNLP 2021, Virtual Event / Punta Cana, Dominican Republic, 7-11 November, 2021*, pages 8104–8118. Association for Computational Linguistics.

Prachi Jain, Sushant Rathi, Mausam, and Soumen Chakrabarti. 2020. Temporal knowledge base completion: New algorithms and evaluation protocols. In *Proceedings of the 2020 Conference on Empirical Methods in Natural Language Processing, EMNLP 2020, Online, November 16-20, 2020*, pages 3733–3747. Association for Computational Linguistics.

Jaehun Jung, Jinhong Jung, and U. Kang. 2021. Learning to walk across time for interpretable temporal knowledge graph completion. *Proceedings of the 27th ACM SIGKDD Conference on Knowledge Discovery & Data Mining*.

Timothée Lacroix, Guillaume Obozinski, and Nicolas Usunier. 2020. Tensor decompositions for temporal knowledge base completion. In *8th International Conference on Learning Representations, ICLR 2020, Addis Ababa, Ethiopia, April 26-30, 2020*. OpenReview.net.

Jennifer Lautenschlager, Steve Shellman, and Michael Ward. 2015. ICEWS Event Aggregations.

Kalev Leetaru and Philip A Schrodt. 2013. Gdelt: Global data on events, location and tone, 1979-2012.

Zixuan Li, Xiaolong Jin, Wei Li, Saiping Guan, Jiafeng Guo, Huawei Shen, Yuanzhuo Wang, and Xueqi Cheng. 2021. Temporal knowledge graph reasoning based on evolutional representation learning. *Proceedings of the 44th International ACM SIGIR Conference on Research and Development in Information Retrieval*.

Siyuan Liao, Shangsong Liang, Zaiqiao Meng, and Qiang Zhang. 2021. Learning dynamic embeddings for temporal knowledge graphs. *Proceedings of the 14th ACM International Conference on Web Search and Data Mining*.

Xi Victoria Lin, Richard Socher, and Caiming Xiong. 2018. Multi-hop knowledge graph reasoning with reward shaping. In *Proceedings of the 2018 Conference on Empirical Methods in Natural Language Processing, Brussels, Belgium, October 31 - November 4, 2018*, pages 3243–3253. Association for Computational Linguistics.

Farzaneh Mahdisoltani, Joanna Biega, and Fabian M. Suchanek. 2015. YAGO3: A knowledge base from multilingual wikipedias. In *Seventh Biennial Conference on Innovative Data Systems Research, CIDR 2015, Asilomar, CA, USA, January 4-7, 2015, Online Proceedings*. www.cidrdb.org.

Takeru Miyato, Toshiki Kataoka, Masanori Koyama, and Yuichi Yoshida. 2018. Spectral normalization for generative adversarial networks. In *6th International Conference on Learning Representations, ICLR 2018, Vancouver, BC, Canada, April 30 - May 3, 2018, Conference Track Proceedings*. OpenReview.net.

Maximilian Nickel, Volker Tresp, and Hans-Peter Kriegel. 2011. A three-way model for collective learning on multi-relational data. In *Proceedings of the 28th International Conference on Machine Learning, ICML 2011, Bellevue, Washington, USA, June 28 - July 2, 2011*, pages 809–816. Omnipress.

Zequn Qin, Pengyi Zhang, Fei Wu, and Xi Li. 2021. Fcanet: Frequency channel attention networks. In *2021 IEEE/CVF International Conference on Computer Vision, ICCV 2021, Montreal, QC, Canada, October 10-17, 2021*, pages 763–772. IEEE.

Ali Sadeghian, Mohammadreza Armandpour, Anthony Colas, and Daisy Zhe Wang. 2021. Chronor: Rotation based temporal knowledge graph embedding. In *Thirty-Fifth AAAI Conference on Artificial Intelligence, AAAI 2021, Thirty-Third Conference on Innovative Applications of Artificial Intelligence, IAAI 2021, The Eleventh Symposium on Educational Advances in Artificial Intelligence, EAAI 2021, Virtual Event, February 2-9, 2021*, pages 6471–6479. AAAI Press.

Pengpeng Shao, Dawei Zhang, Guohua Yang, Jianhua Tao, Feihu Che, and Tong Liu. 2022. Tucker decomposition-based temporal knowledge graph completion. *Knowl. Based Syst.*, 238:107841.

Zhiqing Sun, Zhi-Hong Deng, Jian-Yun Nie, and Jian Tang. 2019. Rotate: Knowledge graph embedding by relational rotation in complex space. In *7th International Conference on Learning Representations, ICLR 2019, New Orleans, LA, USA, May 6-9, 2019*. OpenReview.net.

Rakshit S. Trivedi, Hanjun Dai, Yichen Wang, and Le Song. 2017. Know-evolve: Deep temporal reasoning for dynamic knowledge graphs. In *ICML*.

Théo Trouillon, Johannes Welbl, Sebastian Riedel, Éric Gaussier, and Guillaume Bouchard. 2016. Complex embeddings for simple link prediction. In *Proceedings of the 33nd International Conference on Machine Learning, ICML 2016, New York City, NY, USA, June 19-24, 2016*, volume 48 of *JMLR Workshop and Conference Proceedings*, pages 2071–2080. JMLR.org.

Denny Vrandečić and Markus Krötzsch. 2014. Wikidata: A free collaborative knowledgebase. *Commun. ACM*, 57(10):78–85.

Hongwei Wang, Fuzheng Zhang, Jialin Wang, Miao Zhao, Wenjie Li, Xing Xie, and Minyi Guo. 2018. Ripplenet: Propagating user preferences on the knowledge graph for recommender systems. In *Proceedings of the 27th ACM International Conference on Information and Knowledge Management*, pages 417–426.

Han Xiao, Minlie Huang, and Xiaoyan Zhu. 2016. From one point to a manifold: Knowledge graph embedding for precise link prediction. In *Proceedings of the Twenty-Fifth International Joint Conference on Artificial Intelligence, IJCAI 2016, New York, NY, USA, 9-15 July 2016*, pages 1315–1321. IJCAI/AAAI Press.

Chenjin Xu, Mojtaba Nayyeri, Fouad Alkhoury, Hamed Shariat Yazdi, and Jens Lehmann. 2020. Temporal knowledge graph completion based on time series gaussian embedding. In *The Semantic Web - ISWC 2020 - 19th International Semantic Web Conference, Athens, Greece, November 2-6, 2020, Proceedings, Part I*, volume 12506 of *Lecture Notes in Computer Science*, pages 654–671. Springer.

Bishan Yang, Wen-tau Yih, Xiaodong He, Jianfeng Gao, and Li Deng. 2015. Embedding entities and relations for learning and inference in knowledge bases. In *3rd International Conference on Learning Representations, ICLR 2015, San Diego, CA, USA, May 7-9, 2015, Conference Track Proceedings*.

Zhanqiu Zhang, Jianyu Cai, and Jie Wang. 2020. Duality-induced regularizer for tensor factorization based knowledge graph completion. *CoRR*, abs/2011.05816.

Cunchao Zhu, Muhao Chen, Changjun Fan, Guangquan Cheng, and Yan Zhan. 2021. Learning from history: Modeling temporal knowledge graphs with sequential copy-generation networks. In *AAAI*.

A Parameter Complexity

Table 6: Parameter complexity of different models. Here d denotes the embedding dimensionality.

DE-SimplE	$d((1+2\rho)\vert\mathcal{E}\vert+\vert\mathcal{R}\vert)$
TNTComplEx	$2d(\vert\mathcal{E}\vert+\vert\mathcal{T}\vert+4\vert\mathcal{R}\vert)$
TeLM	$4d(\vert\mathcal{E}\vert+\vert\mathcal{T}\vert+\vert\mathcal{R}\vert+1)$
TuckERTNT	$d(\vert\mathcal{E}\vert+\vert\mathcal{T}\vert+4\vert\mathcal{R}\vert)+d^3$
TuckER-FA	$d(\vert\mathcal{E}\vert+\rho\vert\mathcal{T}\vert+(2-\rho)\vert\mathcal{R}\vert)+d^3$

When d is smaller the number of entity/relation/timestamp collection, tucker decomposition has considerable parameter advantage. Compared with TuckERTNT of the same type, our TuckER-FA gets better results with parameter advantage in modeling relation embedding.

B Hyperparameters

Table 7: Obtained best hyperparameters.

	ICEWS14	GDELT	YAGO15K
ρ	0.75	0.90	0.75
λ_1	1e-2	1e-1	1e-4
λ_2	1e0	1e0	1e-2
λ	1e-2	1e-4	1e-3

We implement our model based on two previous models, TuckER and TNTcomplex. Other baseline models mentioned above have yet to provide publicly available code. During the pre-processing data phase, we convert all time intervals into two different time points and consider them independent. The time intervals in YAGO15K look like "OccursUntil/OccurSince 1994". The time interval is split into two parts, "OccursSince" or "OccursUntil" merged into a relation, and the time point transforms the timestamp. Note that quadruplet without timestamps in YAGO15K also own a unique timestamp.

Although the dimensionality of entity and relation can be different, we use the same dimensionality in our experiments. For general learning settings, we set the dimensionality of entity and relation to 800, batch size to 1000, learning rate to 0.1, and dropout probability to 0.3. Each embedding initializes from 0.01 times the Standard Gaussian distribution. Moreover, the learnable parameters of the core tensor initialize from the uniform distribution from -1 to 1. The frequency attention model uses a single frequency component from f_0 to f_{12} input. We choose ratio ρ form {0.45, 0.6, 0.75, 0.9}, embedding regularization balance term λ_1 from {1e-1, 1e-2, 1e-3, 1e-4}, temporal regularization balance term λ_2 from {1e0, 1e-1, 1e-2, 1e-3}, and core tensor regularization balance term λ from {1e-2, 1e-3, 1e-4, 1e-5}. Note that the timestamp embedding dimensionality should be divisible by n, the number of the selected frequency components. We repeats the experiment three times and reported the average results.

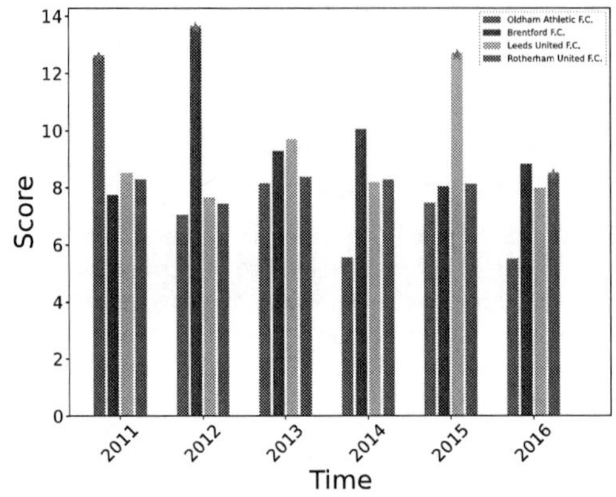

Figure 7: Scores for a set of facts (Tom Adeyemi, playsFor, {Oldham Athletic F.C.|Brentford F.C.|Leeds United F.C.|Rotherham United F.C.}, [2011-2017]) sampled from YAGO15K. The red star indicates that the tail entity is the ground truth at the corresponding timestamps.

C Visualization of Toy Example

To illustrate whether our frequency attention model captures the temporal dependencies between a relation and the entire timestamp, we visualize the scores of a selected set of facts. Figure 7 show the scores change of the toy example. The factual tail entity can consistently score high by TuckER-FA. The gray entity's score changes very little because its ground truth belongs to the test set. The ground truth of the other three color entities belongs to the train set. The facts in the same category (Tom Adeyemi, playsFor,?) change quickly, which reflects a high intrinsic frequency of global temporal dependency. The scores of ground truth are very high on timestamps where facts exist, while all entities achieve a low score on timestamps where facts do not exist. Our model can capture the fast-changing temporal dependency of facts in the same category.

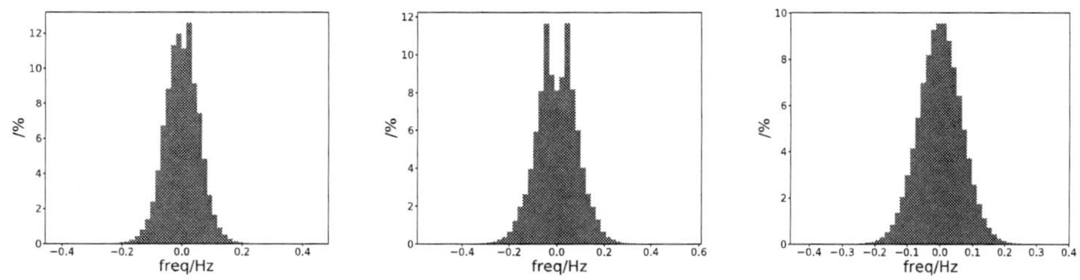

(a) Year (b) Month (c) Day

Figure 8: Histogram of frequency parameters in DE-SimplE. These learnable parameters are concentrated around 0, which means that only low-frequency information about entities over time is captured.

D The Frequency of DE-SimplE

DE-SimplE divides the timestamp 2014-01-31 into three numbers representing the year, month, and day. Then, these time numbers are fed into the sine function along with the frequency and phase parameters. Figure 8 shows the histogram of learned frequency parameters of DE-SimplE on the ICEWS14 dataset. These learned parameters concentrate around 0, meaning only low-frequency information about entities over time is captured.

In previous work (Xu et al., 2020), the evolution process is divided into four different components: static component, periodicity component, trend component, and randomness component. In our opinion, the random component focuses on model robustness, and the static component focuses on the static entity or relation rather than the timestamp. The periodicity and trend components mean the temporal dependency of relations and timestamps, which can be captured by a periodic function such as cosine. If the period of the function is greater than the entire time span, then the cosine function captures the trend component. Similarly, if the period of the function is less than the entire time span, the cosine function captures the periodicity component.

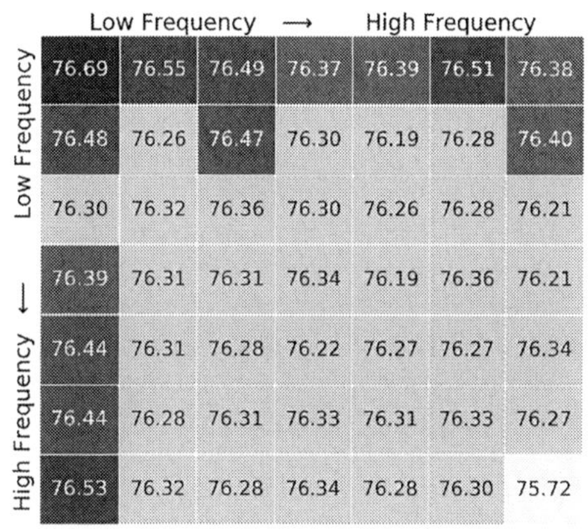

Figure 9: Top-1 accuracies of FcaNet (Qin et al., 2021) in Image Classification Results. The low-pass filtering of the spectrum has strong applicability to images. The DC component performs best.

E Frequency Attention for Image

The image uses 2-dimensional DCT as Figure 9, while the KG uses only one-dimensional DCT. Frequency is an essential characteristic of DCT and indicates how many repetitive structures there are in the data. The main body of the image is composed of low-frequency features, while the TKG body has high-frequency features due to repeated quadruplets.

CLIP-based image captioning via unsupervised cycle-consistency in the latent space

Romain Bielawski
ANITI
Université de Toulouse, France
rom.bielawski@gmail.com

Rufin VanRullen
CerCo
CNRS UMR5549, Toulouse
rufin.vanrullen@cnrs.fr

Abstract

Image captioning typically involves an image encoder to extract meaningful image features, and a text decoder to generate appropriate sentences. Powerful pretrained models can be used for both image encoding and text decoding; but in this case, a separate multimodal translation stage between image-encoder output features and text-decoder input features must be learned. One exception is when image and text features are already aligned by construction, as in the CLIP model (Contrastive Language and Image Pretraining – a bimodal network pretrained on 400M image-text pairs). Pretrained CLIP-image features can be directly fed to a text-decoder trained to reconstruct captions from their pretrained CLIP-text features. Here we show that this direct captioning method is in fact sub-optimal. Instead, we propose an alternative method to translate CLIP-image features into CLIP-text features in a strictly unsupervised way, using the CycleGAN architecture – originally designed for unpaired image-to-image translation. Our Latent CycleGAN, optimized solely for an unsupervised cycle-consistency objective, generates CLIP-text latent features conditioned on CLIP-image latent features and vice-versa. Using these CLIP-text latent features as input to the text decoder, our method largely outperforms the direct captioning method that uses CLIP-image features – despite the fact that CLIP's large-scale pretraining should have already aligned the two feature spaces. This implies that cycle-consistency on unmatched multimodal data can be efficiently implemented in a bimodal latent space, and that CLIP-based image captioning can be improved without additional supervised training.

1 Introduction

Multimodality is gaining popularity due to the recently available online resources that make the creation of huge visio-linguistic datasets possible (Jia et al., 2021). Many models have been created to perform specific bimodal tasks such as Visual Question Answering or Image Captioning (Anderson et al., 2017; Lu et al., 2019; Li et al., 2019; Singh et al., 2019), but some have been designed with a more general objective: producing a multimodal latent vectorial space where images and text can be represented and compared. Among these models, CLIP – an algorithm trained with a multimodal contrastive objective on a large dataset (400M samples) of image-caption pairs – has shown impressive zero-shot learning abilities (Radford et al., 2021). This model has recently been tested on tasks for which it was not initially trained, such as transfer learning and few-shot learning on unimodal and multimodal datasets, or image captioning, establishing new SOTA results on some tasks (Bielawski et al., 2022; Mokady et al., 2021).

In the specific case of image captioning, many studies use pretrained models for image feature encoding as well as for text generation. An end-to-end image-to-caption fine-tuning stage is typically required, however, to align visual and linguistic representations in a supervised way on a matched image-caption dataset (Chen et al., 2021; Fang et al., 2021; Zhou et al., 2019). There is an obvious exception to this rule: when the pretraining of the model already aligned text and image features – as in the case of CLIP. Therefore, here we aim at leveraging this property by implementing a captioning pipeline that does not use matched image-caption data.

We first train a "CLIP-text decoder" to reconstruct captions based on their textual features in CLIP's latent space (a unimodal, linguistic objective); this text decoder is subsequently frozen. Hence, we compare a direct captioning pipeline – feeding the text-decoder with CLIP image features in order to generate a caption – with a pipeline where a CycleGAN (Zhu et al., 2017) inspired translator – trained with only unpaired visual and textual features – is used to convert image features

Proceedings of the 8th Workshop on Representation Learning for NLP (RepL4NLP 2023), pages 266–275

into text features before feeding them to the text-decoder. Even though CLIP's latent space was already pretrained with a brute-force approach to align its visual and linguistic representations on 400M image-caption pairs, we demonstrate that our feature conversion model trained using cycle-consistency in the CLIP latent space significantly improves captioning performance, compared with the direct method.

2 Dataset

To train our algorithms, we use the COCO (Lin et al., 2014) train 2014 dataset, composed of images representing complex scenes, along with their descriptions. We simply use the captions and the images independently, as two sets of unpaired unimodal data from each modality.

For the evaluation, we use the COCO validation 2014 dataset.

3 Models

3.1 Pretrained models

We use CLIP ViT-B/32, a pretrained Vision-Transformer-based (Dosovitskiy et al., 2020) CLIP checkpoint, as image and text encoder. CLIP's vision encoder will be therafter referred to as just CLIP, and CLIP's text encoder will be called CLIP-T.

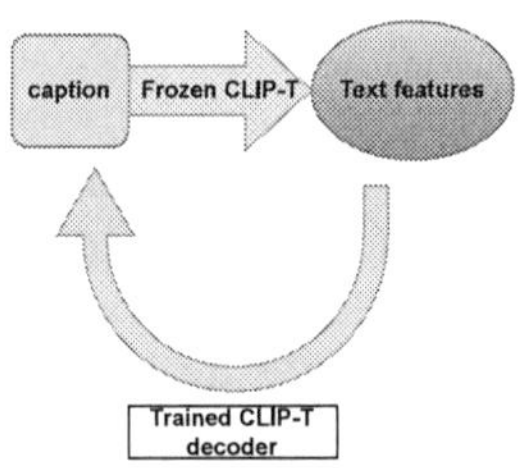

Figure 1: The text decoder is trained to reconstruct COCO train captions from their textual embedding in CLIP's latent space. It learns a mapping from CLIP-T features to prefixes that condition the generation of text with a pretrained (frozen) GPT-2. Note that the text-decoder is trained only with (unimodal) linguistic data.

In order to create our CLIP-T decoder (see Figure 1) we rely on the code provided by Mokady et al. (2021), inspired from Li and Liang (2021). Their decoder was originally trained on the CLIP image features of COCO images, with the objective to reconstruct their corresponding captions (therefore using paired vision-language data to align the text decoder training with pretrained image features). Instead, our text decoder is trained in a unimodal setting on the CLIP-T textual features of captions from the COCO train set (414K captions), with the objective of regenerating the original text. This decoder uses GPT-2 (Radford et al., 2019) as a frozen language generator, and learns to produce prefixes that condition the generation of text. The parameters of the text decoder are shown in Table 1. Once trained, our text decoder is frozen and used as such in the two captioning pipelines that we compare.

3.2 Architecture

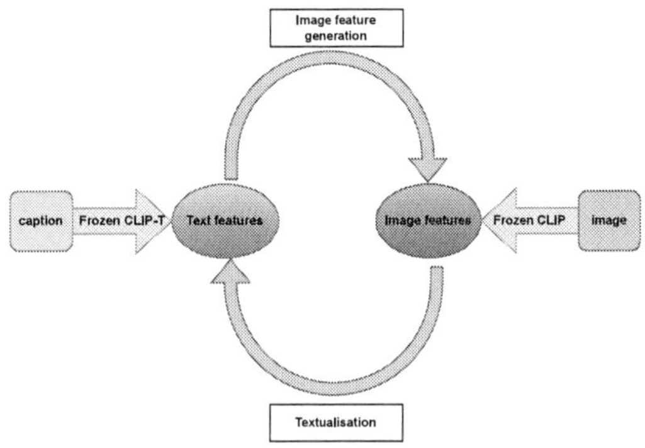

Figure 2: The full architecture of the latent CycleGAN. The generators (purple arrows) are trained with unmatched multimodal data from the COCO dataset. One is trained to generate latent image features given a CLIP-T embedding, the other is trained to produce latent text features given the image features, i.e. to "textualize" them. Discriminators are not shown here.

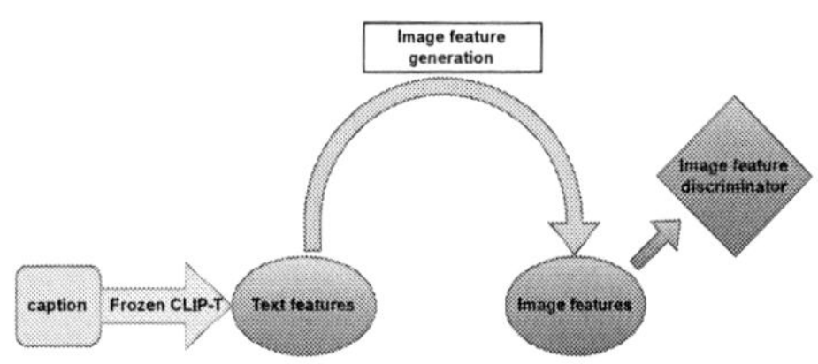

Figure 3: The GAN objective for Image feature generation: the generator must fool the discriminator, which must distinguish between real and fake inputs (here, between real image features and those translated from text features). A similar training objective and discriminator network exists for the other "textualisation" generator (not shown here).

The architecture and training procedure of the Latent CycleGAN are shown in Figure 2 to 4, the parameters of the architecture are displayed in Table 2. It is trained as a CycleGAN on unpaired data

Parameter	# of epochs	prefix length	CLIP prefix length	mapping type	batch size	fine-tune GPT-2	# of layers	CLIP version
Value	20	40	40	Transformer	64	False	8	ViT-B/32

Table 1: Parameters used for the training of the text decoder. For details see Mokady et al. (2021).

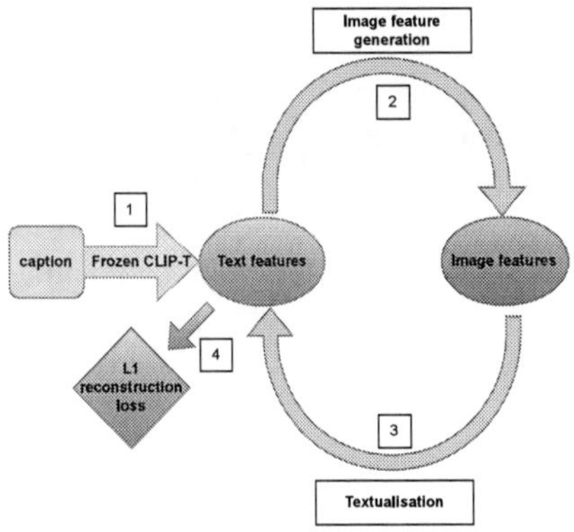

Figure 4: The cycle consistency objective consists in minimizing the L1 loss between a feature vector and its reconstruction after passing successively through both generators (here the translation of text features to and back from image features). The same cycle-consistency objective is also applied with cycles starting from the other (image) modality (not shown here).

Parameter	# of epochs	batch size	# of layers	Latent space dimensions
Value	20	64	8	512

Table 2: Parameters used for the Cycle-consistent architecture.

from the image and text modalities of the COCO train dataset (83K images and 414K captions). The training takes two generators – one of text features, one of image features – and two discriminators – to discriminate between real image (resp. text) features and fake/generated ones (Figure 2).

Just as in any GAN, the objective of each generator is to fool the corresponding discriminator. This is done by generating a fake latent vector in one modality, given a real latent vector from the other (this source vector can thus be considered as the noise that conditions the generation). The discriminator's objective is to guess whether any latent feature vector is real or generated (Figure 3). The generators of a CycleGAN (Zhu et al., 2017) also have specific extra objectives. The cycle consistency objective (Figure 4) minimizes the L1 loss between a feature vector and its reconstruction when passed successively through the two generators (e.g. an image feature vector is passed through the text feature generator, then this vector is passed though the image feature generator: the result of this operation is a reconstructed image feature vector). The identity objective aims at learning the identity function when the image (resp. the text) generator is fed with an image (resp. text) feature vector.

Each generator is composed of 4 dense layers of dimension 512x512 with Tanh activation; the discriminators are composed of two dense layers, one of dimension 512x256, the other of 256x1, with LeakyReLU activation.

After having trained the Latent Cycle-GAN to convergence, we can then compare the two captioning pipelines illustrated in Figure 5.

The first one uses the fact that in CLIP's latent space, the features extracted from an image are intended to be as close as possible to the features computed by CLIP-T for a matching caption. This similarity was enforced by extensive contrastive training over 400M paired image-captions. Therefore, we may simply feed our CLIP-T decoder (trained on text features) with image features, and generate a corresponding caption.

The second pipeline uses the image-to-text-feature generator (the rest of the Latent CycleGAN was only required during training, i.e. to compute and optimize cycle-consistency). The image-to-text-feature generator is used for what we call here "textualisation", i.e. it generates a text feature vector conditioned on an input image feature vector. After the textualisation of an image vector, the textualised vector is fed to the CLIP-T decoder to generate the caption.

4 Task

Given an image from the COCO dataset, the model's task is to reconstruct one of the corresponding captions. Several scores can be used to evaluate the quality of the reconstruction. Here we dispay the BLEU-1 to BLEU-4 (Papineni et al., 2002) (BLEU-n counts matching n-grams in the model output to n-grams in the reference text), the ROUGE_L (Lin, 2004) (measuring the longest common subsequence between the model output and the reference), the CIDEr (Vedantam et al., 2014) (computing the average n-gram cosine similarity between the model output and several descrip-

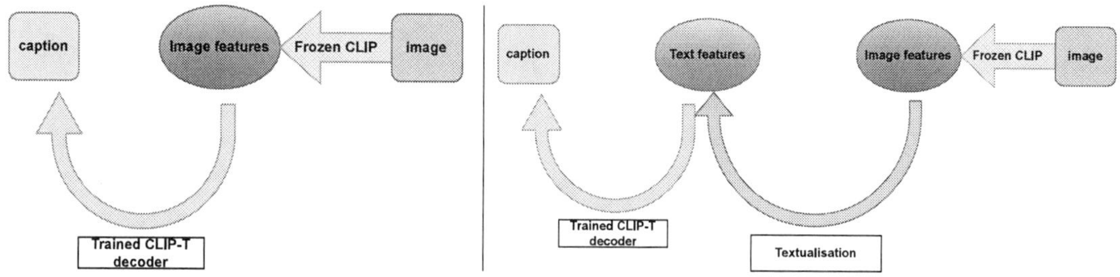

Figure 5: The two pipelines compared here for generating a caption. Our baseline (left) relies on the fact that CLIP was trained to project an image and its caption as close as possible in the latent multimodal space: the text decoder can thus generate a caption when given image features. The second one uses our generator, trained in an unsupervised way with unpaired multimodal data, to textualise the image features before feeding them to the text decoder.

Scoring method	Image features as input	Textualised image features as input
BLEU-1	0.281	0.407
BLEU-2	0.120	0.231
BLEU-3	0.047	0.121
BLEU-4	0.020	0.062
ROUGE_L	0.239	0.341
METEOR	0.098	0.161
CIDEr	0.064	0.247

Table 3: Scores for image captioning on the COCO validation set, for the two pipelines displayed in Figure 5. Higher scores indicate better captioning. The captioning pipeline with image features as input to the text decoder underperforms, compared to the one with features textualised using the text feature generator.

tions of reference and several n) and the METEOR (Denkowski and Lavie, 2014) (a variation of BLEU that aligns the reference and the output differently by incorporating semantic knowledge) scores.

5 Results

Results for the captioning task are displayed in Table 3. Despite the fact that CLIP's latent space was specifically designed and trained so that the encoding of an image and its description are as similar as possible, the strategy of directly using image latent features as input to the CLIP-T decoder does not perform well (for all scoring methods).

By simply training a Latent CycleGAN on unmatched COCO images and description (i.e. training in an unsupervised way on 82K images and their 500K descriptions, compared to the 400M image-text pairs of CLIP's initial training set) the improvement in score can go up to more than a factor 3.

Some uncurated examples of images and output captions from the COCO validation set can be seen in Appendix A.

6 Discussion and conclusion

CLIP's bimodal alignment can allow image captioning at a SOTA level, but this requires a fine-tuning with paired image-caption data (Mokady et al., 2021). Since image and text are projected in the same latent space, it is also possible to use a direct captioning method with a trained CLIP-T decoder, without requiring any bimodal training; however, as we show here, this method is sub-optimal. We show how, using only unpaired images and captions, it is possible to significantly improve performance, while still taking advantage of CLIP's latent space multimodal alignment. Nonetheless, the results of the unpaired translation method implemented here remain far from the SOTA reached with supervised image captioning. Moreover, in our experiment, each caption implicitly matched an image from the training dataset, even though the matching was not given to the model. In future work, one might try enlarging the training domain of each modality, and incorporating data from separate, potentially larger unimodal datasets.

Our work suggests that the geometries of the representation of the vision and language modalities differ in CLIP's latent space. That is, CLIP's training has not properly brought together the two modalities. If it had, the image features would be directly usable by the text decoder, and our unsupervised "textualisation" training would not help the caption generation. This means that CLIP can represent vision and language in the same space, but vectors extracted from one domain are not fully multimodal in the sense that they are not indistinguishable from vectors from the other domain – in other words, modality-specific information appears to interfere with full multimodality. Our Latent CycleGAN helps bridge the gap between the two latent representations, by enabling a unimodal text decoder to better understand image features, once they have been "textualised" by the text feature generator.

The recently proposed DALL-E2 (Ramesh et al., 2022) model, which uses a diffusion process to generate images from a caption, appears to have been based on a similar realization. Their diffusion image generator was trained to reconstruct an image given its CLIP image feature vector; however, for text-to-image generation, they did not directly feed the CLIP-T embedding into the diffusion generator, but first "translated" it into a suitable image-feature latent vector, exactly as we propose here.

Acknowledgments

This research was funded by an ANITI Research Grant ANR-19-PI3A-0004 to RV. Some of the reported work was performed using HPC resources from CALMIP (Grant 2016-P20032)

References

Peter Anderson, Xiaodong He, Chris Buehler, Damien Teney, Mark Johnson, Stephen Gould, and Lei Zhang. 2017. Bottom-up and top-down attention for image captioning and VQA. *CoRR*, abs/1707.07998.

Romain Bielawski, Benjamin Devillers, Tim Van De Cruys, and Rufin Vanrullen. 2022. When does CLIP generalize better than unimodal models? when judging human-centric concepts. In *Proceedings of the 7th Workshop on Representation Learning for NLP*, pages 29–38, Dublin, Ireland. Association for Computational Linguistics.

Jun Chen, Han Guo, Kai Yi, Boyang Li, and Mohamed Elhoseiny. 2021. Visualgpt: Data-efficient image captioning by balancing visual input and linguistic knowledge from pretraining. *CoRR*, abs/2102.10407.

Michael Denkowski and Alon Lavie. 2014. Meteor universal: Language specific translation evaluation for any target language. In *Proceedings of the EACL 2014 Workshop on Statistical Machine Translation.*

Alexey Dosovitskiy, Lucas Beyer, Alexander Kolesnikov, Dirk Weissenborn, Xiaohua Zhai, Thomas Unterthiner, Mostafa Dehghani, Matthias Minderer, Georg Heigold, Sylvain Gelly, Jakob Uszkoreit, and Neil Houlsby. 2020. An image is worth 16x16 words: Transformers for image recognition at scale. *CoRR*, abs/2010.11929.

Zhiyuan Fang, Jianfeng Wang, Xiaowei Hu, Lin Liang, Zhe Gan, Lijuan Wang, Yezhou Yang, and Zicheng Liu. 2021. Injecting semantic concepts into end-to-end image captioning. *CoRR*, abs/2112.05230.

Chao Jia, Yinfei Yang, Ye Xia, Yi-Ting Chen, Zarana Parekh, Hieu Pham, Quoc V. Le, Yun-Hsuan Sung, Zhen Li, and Tom Duerig. 2021. Scaling up visual and vision-language representation learning with noisy text supervision. *CoRR*, abs/2102.05918.

Liunian Harold Li, Mark Yatskar, Da Yin, Cho-Jui Hsieh, and Kai-Wei Chang. 2019. Visualbert: A simple and performant baseline for vision and language. *CoRR*, abs/1908.03557.

Xiang Lisa Li and Percy Liang. 2021. Prefix-tuning: Optimizing continuous prompts for generation. *CoRR*, abs/2101.00190.

Chin-Yew Lin. 2004. ROUGE: A package for automatic evaluation of summaries. In *Text Summarization Branches Out*, pages 74–81, Barcelona, Spain. Association for Computational Linguistics.

Tsung-Yi Lin, Michael Maire, Serge J. Belongie, Lubomir D. Bourdev, Ross B. Girshick, James Hays, Pietro Perona, Deva Ramanan, Piotr Dollár, and C. Lawrence Zitnick. 2014. Microsoft COCO: common objects in context. *CoRR*, abs/1405.0312.

Jiasen Lu, Dhruv Batra, Devi Parikh, and Stefan Lee. 2019. Vilbert: Pretraining task-agnostic visiolinguistic representations for vision-and-language tasks. *CoRR*, abs/1908.02265.

Ron Mokady, Amir Hertz, and Amit H. Bermano. 2021. Clipcap: CLIP prefix for image captioning. *CoRR*, abs/2111.09734.

Kishore Papineni, Salim Roukos, Todd Ward, and Wei Jing Zhu. 2002. Bleu: a method for automatic evaluation of machine translation.

Alec Radford, Jong Wook Kim, Chris Hallacy, Aditya Ramesh, Gabriel Goh, Sandhini Agarwal, Girish Sastry, Amanda Askell, Pamela Mishkin, Jack Clark, Gretchen Krueger, and Ilya Sutskever. 2021. Learning transferable visual models from natural language supervision. *CoRR*, abs/2103.00020.

Alec Radford, Jeff Wu, Rewon Child, David Luan, Dario Amodei, and Ilya Sutskever. 2019. Language models are unsupervised multitask learners.

Aditya Ramesh, Prafulla Dhariwal, Alex Nichol, Casey Chu, and Mark Chen. 2022. Hierarchical text-conditional image generation with clip latents.

Amanpreet Singh, Vivek Natarajan, Meet Shah, Yu Jiang, Xinlei Chen, Dhruv Batra, Devi Parikh, and Marcus Rohrbach. 2019. Towards VQA models that can read. *CoRR*, abs/1904.08920.

Ramakrishna Vedantam, C. Lawrence Zitnick, and Devi Parikh. 2014. Cider: Consensus-based image description evaluation. *CoRR*, abs/1411.5726.

Luowei Zhou, Hamid Palangi, Lei Zhang, Houdong Hu, Jason J. Corso, and Jianfeng Gao. 2019. Unified vision-language pre-training for image captioning and VQA. *CoRR*, abs/1909.11059.

Jun-Yan Zhu, Taesung Park, Phillip Isola, and Alexei A. Efros. 2017. Unpaired image-to-image translation using cycle-consistent adversarial networks. *CoRR*, abs/1703.10593.

A Appendix: Uncurated captioning examples

Ground truth	Pair of commodes side by side in unfinished bathroom area. A torn apart bathroom with some toilets inside of it. A demolished bathroom with two toilets and a window The floor and wall of the bathroom are coming apart. A toilet and bidet sit in a bathroom that is under construction.
Direct method	Damaged CCTV image of restaurant staff posing as uncanny and uncanny people.
Textualised input	A view of a rough and dingy bathroom with many objects in it.

Ground truth	A group of people are standing on the sandy beach. Several people on the beach with their surf boards. Three men and three women posing on a beach in front of surf boards. A group of young people standing next to each other on a beach. A group of people pose for a picture near surfboards.
Direct method	A photograph of a young Irish kitty with a sun-dappled beach, and her friends at the bottom of the ocean.
Textualised input	The group of people posing and holding surfboards and a surf board.

Ground truth	A cheesy pizza with red peppers is in a box. A meal from japan or china on a tray. A cheesy casserole covered with toppings is depicted. A pizza with cheese and vegetables in a box. A large square shaped pizza covered in melted cheese and veggies.
Direct method	A quick chili sauce knife cut in the background, and green beans, muffin, and muffin
Textualised input	A bunch of cheese, ready to go and baked in a cheesy tortilla

Ground truth	A man stands beside his black and red motorcycle near a park. A man in black jacket next to a red motorcycle. An older man is standing beside a red motorcycle. A man standing by a motor cycle on a street. A man riding on the side of a red motorcycle.
Direct method	A Frank Miller Fun Road shot taken from the time I was born in 2006.
Textualised input	This person is showing on the road with some fresh motorcycle parts on the horizon.

Token-level Fitting Issues of Seq2seq Models

Guangsheng Bao[1,2], Zhiyang Teng[3], and Yue Zhang[*,2,4],
[1] Zhejiang University
[2] School of Engineering, Westlake University
[3] Nanyang Technological University
[4] Institute of Advanced Technology, Westlake Institute for Advanced Study
[2] {baoguangsheng, zhangyue}@westlake.edu.cn
[3] zhiyang.teng@ntu.edu.sg

Abstract

Sequence-to-sequence (seq2seq) models have been widely used for natural language processing, computer vision, and other deep learning tasks. We find that seq2seq models trained with early-stopping suffer from issues at the token level. In particular, while some tokens in the vocabulary demonstrate overfitting, others underfit when training is stopped. Experiments show that the phenomena are pervasive in different models, even in fine-tuned large pretrained-models. We identify three major factors that influence token-level fitting, which include token frequency, parts-of-speech, and prediction discrepancy. Further, we find that external factors such as language, model size, domain, data scale, and pretraining can also influence the fitting of tokens.

1 Introduction

Deep learning models tend to overfit on relatively small datasets because of their strong capacity and a massive number of parameters (Brownlee, 2018; Li et al., 2019; Rice et al., 2020; Bejani and Ghatee, 2021). Studies suggest regularization and early stopping to control the generalization error caused by overfitting (Hastie et al., 2009; Zhang et al., 2017; Chatterjee and Zielinski, 2022). Previous studies mainly analyze the generalization issue on image classification task (Arpit et al., 2017; Zhang et al., 2021), where the learning target is relatively simple. In contrast, NLP task such as machine translation (Zhang et al., 2015; Singh et al., 2017) is more complex with regard to the learning targets, which involve a sequence of tokens.

Natural languages exhibit a long-tailed distribution of tokens (Powers, 1998). The long-tail phenomena have been associated with performance degradation of NLP tasks (Gong et al., 2018; Raunak et al., 2020; Yu et al., 2022), where the rare (low frequency) tokens are ascribed as hard learning targets and popular (high frequency) tokens as easy learning targets. These criteria of easiness of learning targets are intuitive but coarse-grained, which are not associated with the training dynamics. In this paper, we study the easiness of tokens as learning targets from the perspective of overfitting and underfitting. Intuitively, the learning on hard tokens will be slower than that on easy tokens, which may result in underfitting on hard tokens and overfitting on easy tokens, as illustrated by Figure 1. We propose two measures to quantify fitting – *fitting-offset* and *potential-gain*. Fitting-offset measures the offset of the best fit from the early-stopping point, which reflects the degree of overfitting or underfitting. Potential-gain measures the accuracy gap between the early-stopping checkpoint and the best fit, which also estimates the accuracy decrease caused by overfitting or underfitting.

We use machine translation as our test bed, training models on English-German benchmark datasets, including News and Europarl domains. Our extensive experiments reveal novel findings: 1) Both overfitting and underfitting occur in a trained seq2seq model. 2) High-frequency tokens are expected to overfit, but some are found underfitted, and low-frequency tokens are expected to underfit, but some are found overfitted. 3) Large pretrained models reduce underfitting effectively during finetuning but are less effective on overfitting. Besides, we propose a direct indicator of easiness – prediction discrepancy, using the probability difference of predictions made by full context and local context as a criterion to group tokens.

In addition to tokens, sentences have also been considered as learning targets, where curriculum learning methods distinguish sentences as easy or hard (Kocmi and Bojar, 2017; Platanios et al., 2019; Xu et al., 2020). For example, the length of a sentence is used as a criterion to identify easy sentences from hard ones, where the easy (short) sen-

* Corresponding author.

Proceedings of the 8th Workshop on Representation Learning for NLP (RepL4NLP 2023), pages 276–288
July 13, 2023 ©2023 Association for Computational Linguistics

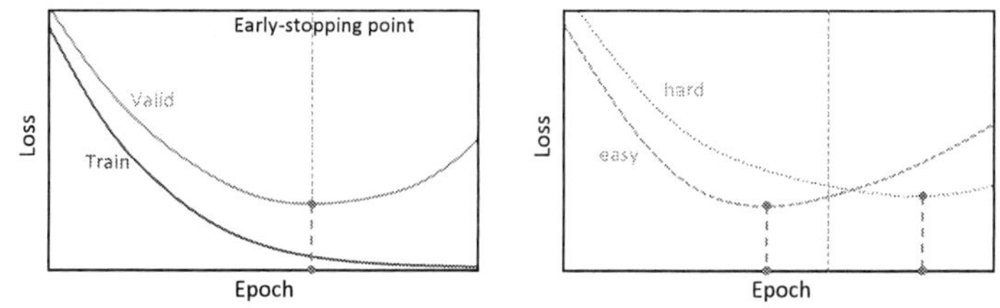

(a) Idealized training and validation loss curves, where the model is selected by early stopping.

(b) Easy tokens overfit at the early-stopping point, while hard tokens underfit.

Figure 1: Seq2seq models trained with early stopping may suffer from overfitting or underfitting.

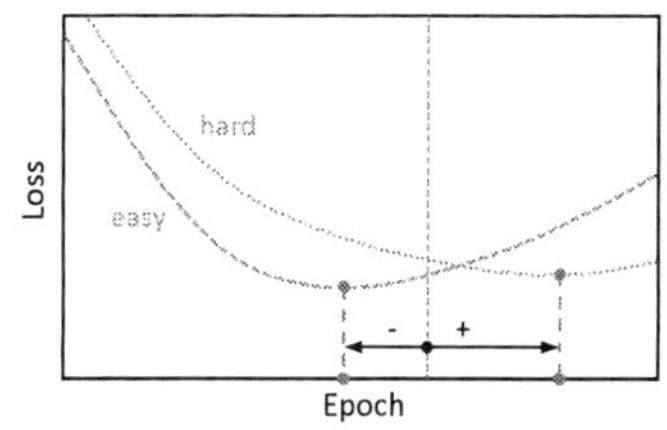

Figure 2: Fitting-offset measures the relative distance of the best fit from the early-stopping point, which is negative for the left side and positive for the right side.

tences are first learned and then the hard (long) sentences. Using our metrics, we find that the length of a sentence is not a good indicator of easy or hard sentences from the perspective of overfitting and underfitting.

2 Related Work

Previous studies compare the fitting of real data and noise data, demonstrating that real data is easier to learn and has a faster convergence speed than noise data (Zhang et al., 2017; Arpit et al., 2017; Chatterjee and Zielinski, 2022). The different convergence speeds also provide an explanation of how early stopping prevents the memorization of noise data. However, these works do not compare the fitting among different learning targets inside the real data, neither between different samples nor between different parts of each sample. In this paper, we conduct experiments on a more complex seq2seq task instead of simple classification. We study the fitting of token-level learning targets, demonstrating that both overfitting and underfitting occur when training seq2seq models.

There are few works studying overfitting and underfitting in NLP. Sun et al. (2017) report that complex structure leads to overfitting in structured prediction. Wolfe and Caliskan (2021) demonstrate that low-frequency names exhibit bias and overfitting in the language model. Varis and Bojar (2021) illustrate that machine translation models generalize poorly on the test set with unseen sentence length. These works discuss overfitting issues on specific conditions, such as complex structure, frequent names, and unseen length. In comparison, we conduct a systematic analysis of the general phenomena of overfitting and underfitting in language. Specifically, we propose quantitative measures, identify major factors, and conduct statistical hypothesis testing on the phenomena.

3 Experimental Settings

3.1 Datasets

We use the News corpus as a major dataset for our experiments and analysis, and we further use the Europarl corpus for the comparison of different domains and data scales.

News We use News Commentary v11 for training, newstest2015 for validation, and newstest2016 for testing. The English-German machine translation dataset contains $236,287$ sentence pairs for training, $2,169$ pairs for validation, and $2,999$ pairs for testing.

Europarl We use English-German Europarl v7, following Maruf et al. (2019) to split the train, validation, and test sets. The dataset contains $1,666,904$ sentence pairs for training, $3,587$ pairs for validation, and $5,134$ pairs for testing.

We tokenize the sentences using MOSES (Koehn et al., 2007), followed by truecase and a BPE (Sennrich et al., 2015) with $30,000$ merging operations. We use separate embedding tables for source and target languages in the model.

3.2 Model Configurations

We study the overfitting and underfitting issues on three model configurations. We use the base model in section 4 and 5, the pre-trained model in section 6, and the big model for the model-size evaluation in section 7.

Base Model We use the standard Transformer base model (Vaswani et al., 2017), which has 6 layers, 8 heads, 512 output dimensions, and 2048 hidden dimensions. We train the model with a learning rate of 5×10^{-4}, a dropout of 0.3, a label smoothing of 0.1, and an Adam optimizer (Kingma and Ba, 2014).

Big Model Following the standard Transformer big model (Vaswani et al., 2017), we use 6 layers, 16 heads, 1024 output dimensions, and 4096 hidden dimensions. We train the model with a learning rate of 3×10^{-4}, a dropout of 0.3, a label smoothing of 0.1, and an Adam optimizer.

Pretrained Large Model We use mBART25 (Liu et al., 2020), which has the similar setting as BART large model (Lewis et al., 2020), using 12 layers, 16 heads, 1024 output dimensions, and 4096 hidden dimensions. We fine-tune the model with a learning rate of 3×10^{-5}, a dropout of 0.3, an attention-dropout of 0.1, a label smoothing of 0.2, and an Adam optimizer.

For each experiment, we train 40 models using random seeds from 1 to 40, obtaining 40 samples for the significance test. During the training of the base or big model, we keep the last 20 checkpoints for analysis, where the checkpoint of early-stopping is the 10-th of the 20 checkpoints. For mBART25, we keep the last 10 checkpoints, and the early-stopping checkpoint is at the 5-th of the checkpoints.

3.3 Evaluation Metric

Measures We propose two measures: fitting-offset and potential-gain.

Fitting-offset represents how far (i.e., number of epochs) the best fit of a group of tokens diverges from the point of early stopping. In this paper, we use epoch as its unit because we evaluate the model using the validation set at the end of each training epoch. As Figure 2 shows, for the easy tokens, the fitting-offset is negative, denoting overfitting, where the best fit is before the early-stopping epoch. For the hard tokens, the fitting-offset is positive, denoting an underfitting, where the best fit is after the early-stopping epoch. Using fitting-offset, we can quantify the degree of overfitting and underfitting.

Potential-gain represents the potential accuracy increase if we move the best fit to the early-stopping epoch. We calculate the measure by subtracting the accuracy of the early-stopping checkpoint from the accuracy of the best fit. Using this measure, we can quantitatively estimate the potential benefits by fixing the overfitting or underfitting issue.

Significance Test Since the distribution of fitting-offset is unknown, we use a non-parametric sign-test (Dixon and Mood, 1946; Hodges, 1955) to test our hypothesis. We train the model N times

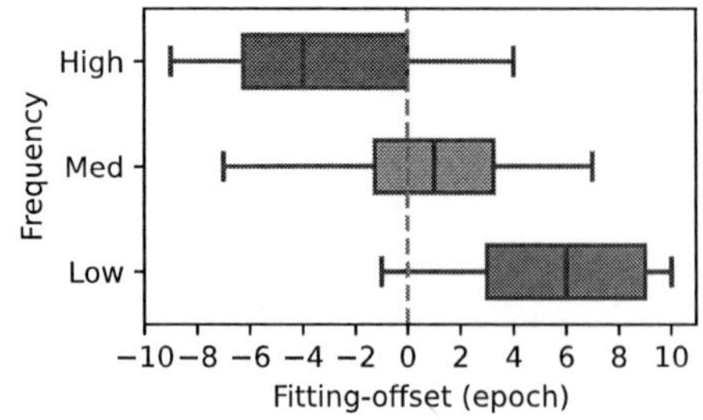

Figure 3: Fitting-offset of tokens grouped by token *frequency*.

to obtain N observations on the fitting-offset. The hypothesis about the overfitting and underfitting can be expressed by

$$\begin{cases} H_0 : \text{fitting-offset} = 0, & \text{no fitting issue,} \\ H_1 : \text{fitting-offset} \neq 0, & \text{has fitting issue.} \end{cases} \tag{1}$$

If H_0 is true, the N observations are expected to be half positive and half negative. The total number of positive observations N_+ follows a binomial distribution, through which we decide the rejection region according to a significance level α.

Grouping Ideally, we can calculate the two measures on each token to tell which tokens are overfitted and which tokens are underfitted at the early-stopping epoch. However, direct observation of each token is noisy and does not show obvious patterns. We group the tokens and average the valid losses to reduce the noise, through which the pattern emerges, and we obtain stable measures.

4 Token-level Results

4.1 Fitting of Rare Tokens in Seq2seq Model Training

Previous studies suggest that long-tail token distribution affects the performance of NLP tasks (Gong et al., 2018; Raunak et al., 2020; Yu et al., 2022). We hypothesize that the low-frequency tokens underfit during training and conduct verification experiments as follows.

Settings We experiment on the News dataset, using a Transformer base model (Vaswani et al., 2017). We categorize the target tokens into high/medium/low-frequency according to their distribution in the training set, with balanced probability mass on the three buckets.

Hypothesis Testing For each group of high/medium/low-frequency tokens, we measure

Group	Parts-of-speech (POS)
Noun	NOUN, PRON, PROPN
Verb	VERB, AUX
Adj	ADJ, ADV
Num	NUM
Func	ADP, CONJ, CCONJ, DET, PART, SCONJ
Symb	PUNCT, SYM

Table 1: Groups aggregating parts of speech.

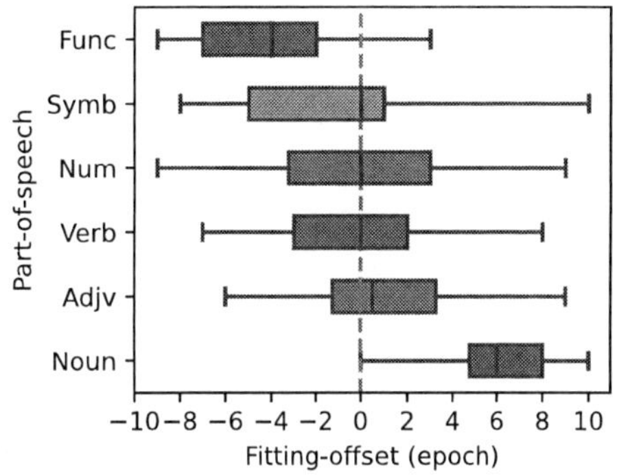

Figure 4: Fitting-offset of tokens grouped by *parts-of-speech*.

the fitting-offset using the checkpoints of each model, obtaining 40 samples for each group. We test our hypothesis on each group using a sign-test (Eq. 1). As a result, we obtain a p-value of 1.9×10^{-5} for high-frequency and 7.5×10^{-11} for low-frequency, which strongly supports the hypothesis that the high/low-frequency tokens either overfit or underfit.

Further as Figure 3 shows, the average fitting-offset for high-frequency tokens is -3.7 with a standard deviation of 3.4. The negative value of the fitting-offset indicates that the high-frequency tokens overfit, where the best fit happens at an average of 3.7 epochs, before the early-stopping point. The average fitting-offset for low-frequency tokens is 5.8 with a standard deviation of 3.3. The positive value of the fitting-offset indicates underfitting, where the best fit happens at 5.8 epochs, after the early-stopping point on average. Based on this evidence, we conclude that *Both overfitting and underfitting at the token level occur when training seq2seq models.*

Analysis The significant divergence of fitting-offset between the high/low-frequency tokens suggests that the frequency of tokens has a significant influence on their fitting. We quantify the influence using the potential-gain. In particular, take the low-frequency tokens as an example. The potential-gain is 0.73, which means that the average accuracy is expected to be increased from 45.61 to 46.34 if we move the best fit to the early-stopping epoch. The potential-gain of the high-frequency tokens is 0.05, and that of the medium-frequency tokens is 0.23, which is relatively smaller than that of the low-frequency tokens, suggesting underfitting of the low-frequency tokens is the major issue.

4.2 Linguistic Factors to Token-level Fitting

In section 4.1, we find that the high-frequency tokens tend to overfit and the low-frequency tokens tend to underfit in the seq2seq model as a group. In order to further understand a fine-grained correlation between the frequency and the fitting of a token, we further split the high/low-frequency tokens into smaller groups and conduct experiments on the specific categories. Linguistic factors are considered in the detailed experiments.

Parts-of-speech (POS) We speculate that parts-of-speech, as an important linguistic feature, may provide a different perspective to study the overfitting and underfitting issues. We group tokens according to their parts-of-speech as listed in Table 1. Specifically, we first obtain POS tagging on each word using spaCy [1]. Then we map the POS of words to tokens by labeling all the tokens of a word with the same POS. Last, we group these tokens according to their POS. Take the group Noun as an example. We group tokens with the POS of NOUN, PRON, and PROPN into one category, naming Noun. We aggregate the major parts of speech into six groups according to their functional similarity, as shown in the Table.

As Figure 4 shows, parts-of-speech has a significant influence on the fitting of tokens. The function words are most likely to overfit, which is likely because they are close-set and easier to learn from the linguistic perspective. On the contrary, nouns are most likely to underfit, which can be due to the openness of the set and the challenging context dependencies.

The potential-gain of nouns is 0.69, increasing the accuracy from 52.38 to 53.07. The potential-

[1] https://spacy.io/

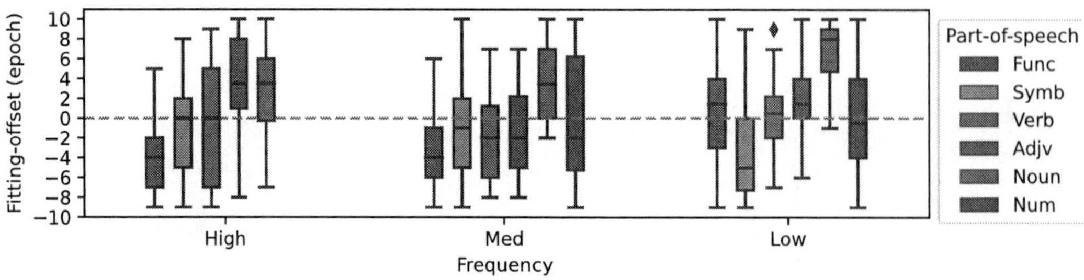

Figure 5: Fitting-offset of tokens grouped by *frequency* and *parts-of-speech*.

Frequency	Function	Symbol	Number	Verb	Adj/Adv	Noun
High	56.82 +0.15	84.77 **+0.59**	nan +nan	59.13 **+1.09**	71.02 **+1.67**	60.87 **+0.89**
Med	49.59 +0.16	69.63 **+3.41**	73.47 **+1.50**	47.64 +0.12	44.56 +0.24	59.21 **+0.76**
Low	43.76 **+1.38**	72.24 **+3.55**	74.84 **+1.20**	36.25 **+0.51**	41.18 +0.43	48.03 **+0.88**

Table 2: Potential-gain for each category grouped by *frequency* and *parts-of-speech*. The column is in a format of "averaged-accuracy potential-gain", where the "+" in the potential-gain indicates an increase in the accuracy and the "-" indicates a decrease in the accuracy. We mark potential-gains bigger than 0.5 with the bold font to indicate their significance.

gains of numbers, symbols, verbs, and adj/adv words are 1.09, 0.58, 0.26, and 0.22, respectively. Surprisingly, the potential-gain of function words is negligible, even though they obviously overfit. We attribute it to the overall high frequency of function words because sufficient training samples reduce the negative impact of overfitting. It is confirmed by the detailed potential-gains shown in Table 2, where the function words with low frequency have a much higher potential-gain of 1.38.

It is worth noting that we use sub-word tokens in the experiments, where we assign the POS of a word to all its sub-words. We also tried words as tokens, which give a similar distribution of fitting offset, and the conclusions hold.

Frequency and Parts-of-speech We combine frequency and POS to make a detailed analysis of the high/low-frequency tokens. As Figure 5 shows, frequency and POS work independently. Among the high-frequency tokens, the function words tend to overfit, while adjectives and nouns tend to underfit. Among the low-frequency tokens, the symbols tend to overfit, while the adjectives and nouns tend to underfit. Based on this evidence, we arrive at a counter-intuitive conclusion that *in a seq2seq model, the high-frequency tokens (popular tokens) mostly overfit but can also underfit, and the low-frequency tokens (rare tokens) mostly underfit but can also overfit.*

When we look into the potential-gains, as shown in Table 2, we see higher potential-gains than in the previous section. The potential-gain of low-frequency function words, symbols, and numbers are 1.38, 3.55, and 1.20, respectively. The potential-gains on med-frequency symbols and numbers are 3.41 and 1.50, respectively. Overall the high-frequency tokens have low potential-gains, and the verbs and adjectives have potential-gains of 1.09 and 1.67, respectively. These results demonstrate that combining the frequency and linguistic factors reveals stronger overfitting and underfitting, forecasting higher potential-gains in specific categories.

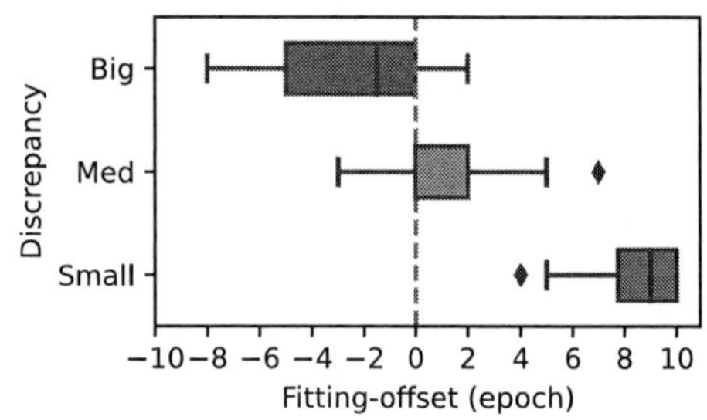

Figure 6: Fitting-offset of tokens grouped by prediction *discrepancy*.

4.3 Prediction Discrepancy as A Factor to Token-level Fitting

Given that neither frequency nor parts of speech are decisive factors, we propose a new factor – prediction discrepancy, which measures the degree of dependence on long context for predicting each token in a text sequence. The intuition behind this factor is that some tokens may require more infor-

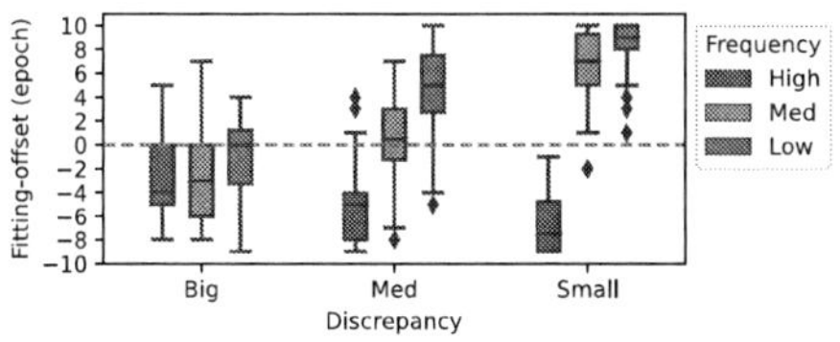

Figure 7: Fitting-offset of tokens grouped by *discrepancy* and *frequency*.

Discrepancy	Frequency High	Med	Low
Big	63.91 +0.09	26.88 -0.22	10.57 +0.11
Med	66.96 +0.09	47.77 +0.31	20.22 **+0.86**
Small	72.49 +0.09	80.95 **+0.62**	73.19 **+0.85**

Table 3: Potential-gain for each category grouped by *discrepancy* and *frequency*.

mation from the surrounding context to be correctly predicted, while others may be more independent and rely more on their local context. Specifically, consider a sentence, "*I was quoted about 12 months .*" the word "*months*" could most likely be told according to its local context "*12*". In comparison, in a German sentence "*es war schwer , ihn zu kennen .*", where the word-by-word translation is "*it was hard , him to know .*" the word "*kennen*" requires much longer context to predict.

The prediction discrepancy is calculated as

$$D_j = |P(Y_j|Y_{<j}, X) - P(Y_j|Y_{j-1}, X)|, \quad (2)$$

where X is the source sequence, and Y is the target. For each token Y_j, we predict it using its full context $Y_{<j}$ and its local context Y_j. We use the discrepancy between these two predictions to indicate its dependence on long context. We train an altered Transformer model to do the predictions using two decoders, where one decoder uses the full context of a target while another decoder uses the local context. The two decoders share the same token embedding table and encoder. According to the value of discrepancy, we categorize the tokens into three groups, with big, medium, and small discrepancy, respectively.

Results As Figure 6 shows, the big-discrepancy tokens have an average fitting-offset of -2.7 with a standard deviation of 3.0. The medium-discrepancy tokens have an average fitting-offset of 1.0 with a standard deviation of 2.1. The small-discrepancy tokens have an average fitting-offset of 8.2 with a standard deviation of 1.8, showing a trend to exceed the boundary of 10. In comparison with frequency, the bigger range of the average fitting-offsets and the smaller standard deviations suggest that discrepancy is a better indicator than frequency. This indicates that the discrepancy is a good indicator of overfitting and underfitting.

The potential-gain of the small-discrepancy tokens is 0.63, increasing the average accuracy of the tokens from 75.85 to 76.48. In comparison with the potential-gain of 0.75 for the low-frequency tokens, which increases the average accuracy from 45.61 to 46.34, the baseline accuracy of small-discrepancy is much higher, suggesting the effectiveness of discrepancy in discovering fitting issues among high accuracy predictions.

Discrepancy and Frequency Intuitively, discrepancy and frequency are two independent factors, given that discrepancy relies on context and frequency relies on the token itself. As Figure 7 shows, the most significant difference between high-frequency and med/low-frequency tokens is that med/small discrepancy tokens with high frequencies tend to overfit, while the med/small discrepancy tokens with med/low frequencies tend to underfit. In addition, as shown in Table 3, when frequency and discrepancy are combined to predict the overfitting and underfitting, the biggest potential-gain of low-frequency tokens increases from 0.73 to 0.86, suggesting that frequency and discrepancy are two independent factors.

Discrepancy and Parts-of-speech (POS) As Figure 8 shows, discrepancy and POS also work orthogonally. Overall, tokens with a smaller discrepancy have a larger fitting-offset, which consistently appears on numbers, verbs, adjectives, and nouns. Function words and symbols show a different pattern that the med-discrepancy tokens tend to have smaller fitting-offset than high-discrepancy.

As shown in Table 4, small-discrepancy tokens have potential gains of 1.63 and 1.15 on symbols and numbers, respectively. The potential gain on numbers with big/med-discrepancy are 2.72 and 2.02, respectively, suggesting the effectiveness of combining the two factors.

Summary We have identified three independent factors that affect token-level fitting in seq2seq model training, including frequency, parts-of-speech, and discrepancy. While the former two are internal to the token, the third is external and context-dependent. These indicate that the fitting of tokens results from interestingly complex factors.

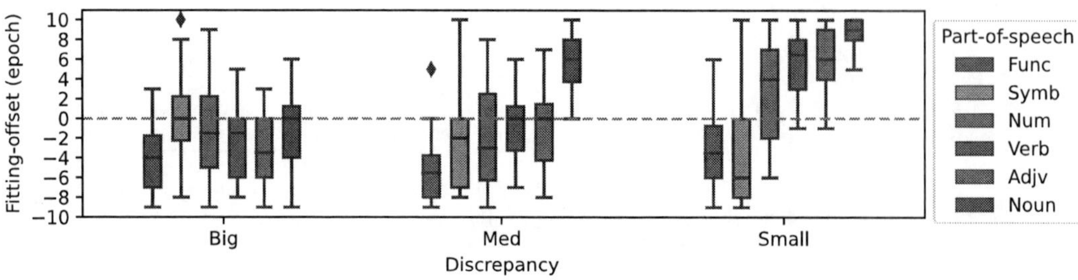

Figure 8: Fitting-offset of tokens grouped by *discrepancy* and *parts-of-speech*.

Discrepancy	Function	Symbol	Number	Verb	Adj/Adv	Noun
Big	45.43 -0.07	83.38 **+0.51**	31.58 **+2.72**	20.31 +0.12	13.38 -0.10	20.58 -0.06
Med	58.33 +0.08	78.79 **+0.96**	36.49 **+2.02**	39.69 +0.25	29.51 +0.14	33.30 **+0.93**
Small	77.06 +0.44	77.98 **+1.63**	89.20 **+1.15**	69.90 **+0.84**	71.93 **+0.75**	77.08 **+0.85**

Table 4: Potential-gain for each category grouped by *discrepancy* and *parts-of-speech*.

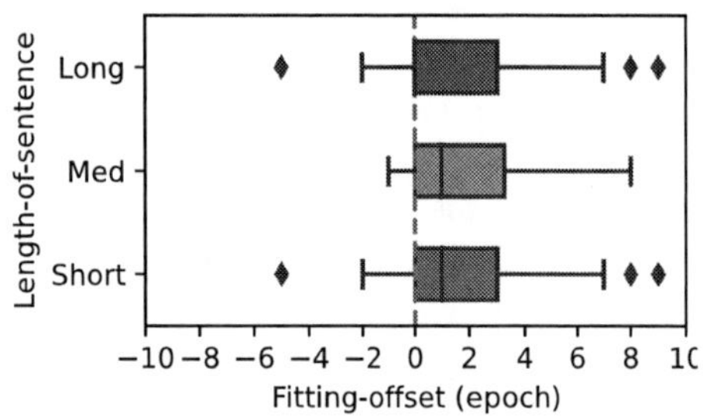

Figure 9: Fitting-offset of tokens grouped by *length-of-sentence*.

5 Easy Sentences vs Hard Sentences

Curriculum learning starts with easy sentences and then with hard sentences (Kocmi and Bojar, 2017; Zhang et al., 2018; Platanios et al., 2019; Xu et al., 2020; Zhou et al., 2020), whereas different criteria are used to measure the difficulty of sentences. Among these criteria, the length-of-sentence is the simplest and most popular one, which hypothesizes that short sentences will be easy to learn and long sentences will be hard to learn. We test the hypothesis by evaluating whether short sentences overfit and long sentences underfit in a trained seq2seq model.

Length-of-sentence We categorize sentences into short/medium/long sentences according to the sentence length that each bucket is allocated with almost the same number of sentences. On the News dataset, the length of short sentences is between 1 and 18 tokens, the length of medium sentences between 19 and 31, and the length of long sentences between 32 and 792.

Hypothesis Testing. We test our hypothesis using sign-test on News English-German dataset, obtaining a p-value of 3.6×10^{-5} for short-sentence, 2.1×10^{-5} for medium-sentence, and 2.6×10^{-3} for long-sentence, which indicates overfitting or underfitting. The fitting-offset has an average of 1.95, 2.0, and 1.38 for short/medium/long-sentences, respectively. The positive fitting-offsets suggest that they overfit in the trained models. However, as Figure 9 shows, the degree of overfitting and underfitting is less than that of frequency (Figure 3) and discrepancy (Figure 6).

Summary The above experiments suggest that although the length-of-sentence can differentiate easy sentences from hard sentences, its effectiveness may not be as significant as other factors such as frequency, discrepancy, and parts-of-speech. More surprisingly, short sentences are more likely to underfit than long sentences, which is also confirmed by experiments on pretraining settings in section 6, suggesting that we could not simply judge the short-sentences as easy and long-sentences as hard.

6 Fine-tuning of Pretrained Language Models

Fine-tuning on a large pretrained model has become the dominant setting for NLP tasks (Kenton and Toutanova, 2019; Lewis et al., 2020; Brown et al., 2020; Liu et al., 2020). We investigate the overfitting and underfitting issues, particularly in the pretraining setting.

Hypothesis Testing We first test whether the overfitting and underfitting issues exist under the pretraining setting. We experiment by fine-tuning

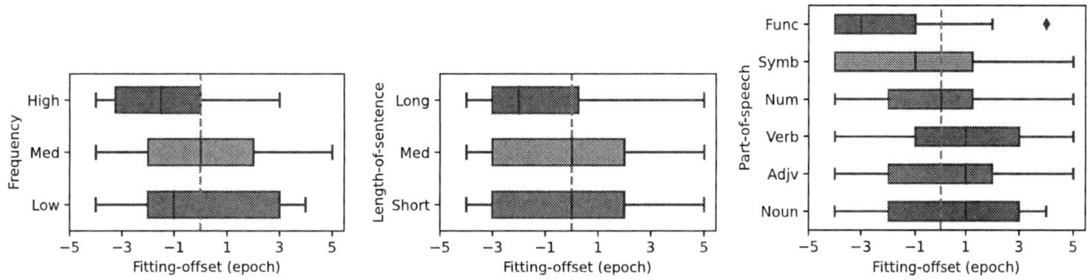

(a) Fitting-offset of tokens grouped by *frequency*. (b) Fitting-offset of tokens grouped by *length-of-sentence*. (c) Fitting-offset of tokens grouped by *parts-of-speech*.

Figure 10: The distribution of fitting-offset on *pretraining* setting.

mBART25 on the News English-German dataset.

First, we evaluate frequency as an indicator of overfitting and underfitting. As Figure 10a shows, we obtain a p-value of 1.2×10^{-3} and an average fitting-offset of -1.48 on high-frequency tokens, suggesting the tendency of overfitting on high-frequency tokens. Results on medium/low-frequency tokens do not show significance, although the average fitting-offsets of 0.08 on medium-frequency tokens suggest slight underfitting.

Next, we consider length-of-sentence. As Figure 10b shows, the fine-tuning tends to overfit for long-sentence and we obtain a p-value of 1.1×10^{-2} and an average fitting-offset of -1.2 on long-sentences. It suggests obvious overfitting of long sentences, which is counter-intuitive because it is widely assumed that long-sentence is harder to learn than short-sentence.

Last, we examine parts of speech. As Figure 10c shows, fine-tuning on function words tends to overfit and that on nouns underfit, which is consistent with the result on non-pretraining setting (Figure 4). A difference is that the fine-tuning of verbs shows underfitting, which is not significantly observed in the non-pretraining settings. We obtain a p-value of 5.8×10^{-2} and an average fitting-offset of 0.8 on verbs, suggesting an observable underfitting on verbs. The issue on function words is more significant than on verbs, on which we obtain a p-value of 4.3×10^{-6} and an average fitting-offset of -2.3, suggesting significant overfitting on function words.

The experiments above confirm that the overfitting and underfitting issues exist in the pretraining setting, although it is not as significant as that in the non-pretraining settings. In addition, it shows that overfitting is the major issue in comparison with underfitting. We attribute it to the effectiveness of large pretraining to prevent underfitting.

It is worth noting that the vocabulary used by the pre-trained model is different from other non-pretraining settings, which may affect the statistical figures but the conclusions hold.

7 Additional Factors to the Fitting Issue

Most of the figures and tables for this section are placed in Appendix A.

The Language As a comparison of languages, we study the issues on the News dataset but with a reversed direction of languages, translating German to English instead of English to German. As Figure 11 shows, our observations on target English tokens are consistent with previous observations on target German tokens. First, the high-frequency tokens tend to overfit, while the low-frequency tokens tend to underfit. Second, the big-discrepancy tokens tend to overfit, while the small-discrepancy tokens tend to underfit. Third, the function words tend to overfit, while the nouns tend to underfit. Last, we also obtain bigger potential-gains by combining the factors and the most significant potential-gains happen on the consistent categories, such as low-frequency symbols, high-frequency adj/advs, and big/med-discrepancy numbers, as the bold numbers in Table 5, 6, and 7 show.

The Model Size To evaluate the influence of model size, we conduct experiments with a big model on the News English-German dataset. As Figure 15 shows, the distribution of fitting-offset on each category is very close to that of the base model but with a smaller range. We attribute it to the faster convergence of bigger model (Li et al., 2020). One significant difference between the big model and the base model is that the fitting-offset of symbols moves toward the negative region, suggesting overfitting for symbols in the big model. We attribute it to the stronger memorization ability of the bigger model.

The Domain Previous experiments are done on the News dataset. To justify that the phenomena are not domain specific, we conduct the same experiments on the Europarl English-German dataset, which is from the Europarl domain. We randomly sample $250,000$ sentence pairs from the Europarl training set for a fair comparison with the News dataset, which contains $236,287$ samples.

As Figure 16 shows, the observations described in "The Language" block hold but with slight differences in the distribution of fitting-offset of tokens grouped by parts-of-speech, in comparison with Figure 4 evaluated on News dataset. The major difference happens in verbs, adjectives, and nouns, reflecting a different distribution of topics of Europarl in comparison with News.

The Data Scale Intuitively, overfitting and underfitting should be more severe on small datasets. For comparison, we test on a bigger dataset from Europarl. We sample $500,000$ sentence pairs from the Europarl training set in comparison with the model trained using $250,000$ samples.

As Figure 17 shows, the observations described in "The Language" block still hold but the range of the distribution increases. Looking into the potential-gains, we see that they decrease by about $1/4$ compared to that of the experiments with $250,000$ samples. The results suggest that the fitting-offset is more challenging to measure, and the potential-gain decreases when the model is trained on a larger dataset, which is expected due to the larger dataset reducing overfitting and underfitting.

8 Discussion on Possible Solutions

Our observation and insights are based on *general language phenomena*: long-tail distribution, uneven context dependencies, and different parts of speech, which are general among different NLP tasks, and may deserve further study on possible solutions.

Intuitively, the model training or fine-tuning process could be improved by reducing learning on overfitting tokens and increasing learning on underfitting tokens. One example is the previous work on abstractive summarization (Shi et al., 2018), which uses focal loss to give high-freq tokens smaller weights and low-freq tokens larger weights, achieved 1.5 points improvement on ROUGE-2 on the abstractive summarization task. Such *dynamic token-specific weights* can partially address the underfitting and overfitting from the perspective of the frequency factor. However, the issue is far from being solved, given that a combination of the frequency and discrepancy factors (Figure 7) reveals more severe fitting issues than the frequency only (Figure 3). We could expect more gains by designing more appropriate methods to consider the combined factors.

9 Conclusion

We study overfitting and underfitting issues of learning targets in the context of neural machine translation. Our experiments demonstrate that overall rare tokens tend to underfit and frequent tokens overfit. We explored detailed factors related to the overfitting and underfitting issues and identified three major influencing factors, which include frequency, parts-of-speech, and discrepancy. This shows that fitting is the result of a complex interaction between multiple factors. Further experiments demonstrate that the issues exist as a general problem for both non-pretraining and pretraining settings. Future work includes the investigation of strategies to alleviate the overfitting and underfitting issues.

Limitations

This paper hypothesizes that seq2seq models have token-level overfitting and underfitting issues, and provides direct evidence to support the hypothesis in various settings, raising a valuable problem for NLP modeling. However, this paper does not provide a solution to the problem due to the theoretical and practical challenges of measuring the convergence speed of each token. We leave the exploration of this topic to future work.

Acknowledgements

We would like to thank the anonymous reviewers for their valuable feedback. This work is funded by the China Strategic Scientific and Technological Innovation Cooperation Project (grant No. SQ2022YFE020038) and the National Natural Science Foundation of China (grant NSFC No. 62161160339). Zhiyang Teng is partially supported by CAAI-Huawei MindSpore Open Fund (CAAIXSJLJJ-2021-046A).

References

Devansh Arpit, Stanisław Jastrzębski, Nicolas Ballas, David Krueger, Emmanuel Bengio, Maxinder S. Kanwal, Tegan Maharaj, Asja Fischer, Aaron Courville, Yoshua Bengio, and Simon Lacoste-Julien. 2017. A closer look at memorization in deep networks. In *Proceedings of the 34th International Conference on Machine Learning*, volume 70 of *Proceedings of Machine Learning Research*, pages 233–242. PMLR.

Mohammad Mahdi Bejani and Mehdi Ghatee. 2021. A systematic review on overfitting control in shallow and deep neural networks. *Artificial Intelligence Review*, 54(8):6391–6438.

Tom Brown, Benjamin Mann, Nick Ryder, Melanie Subbiah, Jared D Kaplan, Prafulla Dhariwal, Arvind Neelakantan, Pranav Shyam, Girish Sastry, Amanda Askell, et al. 2020. Language models are few-shot learners. *Advances in neural information processing systems*, 33:1877–1901.

Jason Brownlee. 2018. *Better deep learning: train faster, reduce overfitting, and make better predictions*. Machine Learning Mastery.

Satrajit Chatterjee and Piotr Zielinski. 2022. On the generalization mystery in deep learning. *arXiv preprint arXiv:2203.10036*.

Wilfrid J Dixon and Alexander M Mood. 1946. The statistical sign test. *Journal of the American Statistical Association*, 41(236):557–566.

Chengyue Gong, Di He, Xu Tan, Tao Qin, Liwei Wang, and Tie-Yan Liu. 2018. Frage: Frequency-agnostic word representation. *Advances in neural information processing systems*, 31.

Trevor Hastie, Robert Tibshirani, Jerome H Friedman, and Jerome H Friedman. 2009. *The elements of statistical learning: data mining, inference, and prediction*, volume 2. Springer.

Joseph L Hodges. 1955. A bivariate sign test. *The Annals of Mathematical Statistics*, 26(3):523–527.

Jacob Devlin Ming-Wei Chang Kenton and Lee Kristina Toutanova. 2019. Bert: Pre-training of deep bidirectional transformers for language understanding. In *Proceedings of NAACL-HLT*, pages 4171–4186.

Diederik P Kingma and Jimmy Ba. 2014. Adam: A method for stochastic optimization. *arXiv preprint arXiv:1412.6980*.

Tom Kocmi and Ondřej Bojar. 2017. Curriculum learning and minibatch bucketing in neural machine translation. In *Proceedings of the International Conference Recent Advances in Natural Language Processing, RANLP 2017*, pages 379–386.

Philipp Koehn, Hieu Hoang, Alexandra Birch, Chris Callison-Burch, Marcello Federico, Nicola Bertoldi, Brooke Cowan, Wade Shen, Christine Moran, Richard Zens, et al. 2007. Moses: Open source toolkit for statistical machine translation. In *Proceedings of the 45th annual meeting of the association for computational linguistics companion volume proceedings of the demo and poster sessions*, pages 177–180.

Mike Lewis, Yinhan Liu, Naman Goyal, Marjan Ghazvininejad, Abdelrahman Mohamed, Omer Levy, Veselin Stoyanov, and Luke Zettlemoyer. 2020. Bart: Denoising sequence-to-sequence pre-training for natural language generation, translation, and comprehension. In *Proceedings of the 58th Annual Meeting of the Association for Computational Linguistics*, pages 7871–7880.

Haidong Li, Jiongcheng Li, Xiaoming Guan, Binghao Liang, Yuting Lai, and Xinglong Luo. 2019. Research on overfitting of deep learning. In *2019 15th International Conference on Computational Intelligence and Security (CIS)*, pages 78–81. IEEE.

Zhuohan Li, Eric Wallace, Sheng Shen, Kevin Lin, Kurt Keutzer, Dan Klein, and Joey Gonzalez. 2020. Train big, then compress: Rethinking model size for efficient training and inference of transformers. In *International Conference on Machine Learning*, pages 5958–5968. PMLR.

Yinhan Liu, Jiatao Gu, Naman Goyal, Xian Li, Sergey Edunov, Marjan Ghazvininejad, Mike Lewis, and Luke Zettlemoyer. 2020. Multilingual denoising pretraining for neural machine translation. *Transactions of the Association for Computational Linguistics*, 8:726–742.

Sameen Maruf, André FT Martins, and Gholamreza Haffari. 2019. Selective attention for context-aware neural machine translation. In *Proceedings of the 2019 Conference of the North American Chapter of the Association for Computational Linguistics: Human Language Technologies, Volume 1 (Long and Short Papers)*, pages 3092–3102.

Emmanouil Antonios Platanios, Otilia Stretcu, Graham Neubig, Barnabas Poczos, and Tom M Mitchell. 2019. Competence-based curriculum learning for neural machine translation. In *Proceedings of NAACL-HLT*, pages 1162–1172.

David MW Powers. 1998. Applications and explanations of zipf's law. In *New methods in language processing and computational natural language learning*.

Vikas Raunak, Siddharth Dalmia, Vivek Gupta, and Florian Metze. 2020. On long-tailed phenomena in neural machine translation. In *Findings of the Association for Computational Linguistics: EMNLP 2020*, pages 3088–3095.

Leslie Rice, Eric Wong, and Zico Kolter. 2020. Overfitting in adversarially robust deep learning. In *International Conference on Machine Learning*, pages 8093–8104. PMLR.

Rico Sennrich, Barry Haddow, and Alexandra Birch. 2015. Neural machine translation of rare words with subword units. *arXiv preprint arXiv:1508.07909*.

Yunsheng Shi, Jun Meng, Jian Wang, Hongfei Lin, and Yumeng Li. 2018. A normalized encoder-decoder model for abstractive summarization using focal loss. In *Natural Language Processing and Chinese Computing: 7th CCF International Conference, NLPCC 2018, Hohhot, China, August 26–30, 2018, Proceedings, Part II 7*, pages 383–392. Springer.

Shashi Pal Singh, Ajai Kumar, Hemant Darbari, Lenali Singh, Anshika Rastogi, and Shikha Jain. 2017. Machine translation using deep learning: An overview. In *2017 international conference on computer, communications and electronics (comptelix)*, pages 162–167. IEEE.

Xu Sun, Weiwei Sun, Shuming Ma, Xuancheng Ren, Yi Zhang, Wenjie Li, and Houfeng Wang. 2017. Complex structure leads to overfitting: A structure regularization decoding method for natural language processing. *arXiv preprint arXiv:1711.10331*.

Dusan Varis and Ondřej Bojar. 2021. Sequence length is a domain: Length-based overfitting in transformer models. In *Proceedings of the 2021 Conference on Empirical Methods in Natural Language Processing*, pages 8246–8257.

Ashish Vaswani, Noam Shazeer, Niki Parmar, Jakob Uszkoreit, Llion Jones, Aidan N Gomez, Łukasz Kaiser, and Illia Polosukhin. 2017. Attention is all you need. *Advances in neural information processing systems*, 30.

Robert Wolfe and Aylin Caliskan. 2021. Low frequency names exhibit bias and overfitting in contextualizing language models. In *Proceedings of the 2021 Conference on Empirical Methods in Natural Language Processing*, pages 518–532.

Chen Xu, Bojie Hu, Yufan Jiang, Kai Feng, Zeyang Wang, Shen Huang, Qi Ju, Tong Xiao, and Jingbo Zhu. 2020. Dynamic curriculum learning for low-resource neural machine translation. In *Proceedings of the 28th International Conference on Computational Linguistics*, pages 3977–3989.

Sangwon Yu, Jongyoon Song, Heeseung Kim, Seongmin Lee, Woo-Jong Ryu, and Sungroh Yoon. 2022. Rare tokens degenerate all tokens: Improving neural text generation via adaptive gradient gating for rare token embeddings. In *Proceedings of the 60th Annual Meeting of the Association for Computational Linguistics (Volume 1: Long Papers)*, pages 29–45.

Chiyuan Zhang, Samy Bengio, Moritz Hardt, Benjamin Recht, and Oriol Vinyals. 2017. Understanding deep learning requires rethinking generalization. In *International Conference on Learning Representations*.

Chiyuan Zhang, Samy Bengio, Moritz Hardt, Benjamin Recht, and Oriol Vinyals. 2021. Understanding deep learning (still) requires rethinking generalization. *Communications of the ACM*, 64(3):107–115.

Jiajun Zhang, Chengqing Zong, et al. 2015. Deep neural networks in machine translation: An overview. *IEEE Intell. Syst.*, 30(5):16–25.

Xuan Zhang, Gaurav Kumar, Huda Khayrallah, Kenton Murray, Jeremy Gwinnup, Marianna J Martindale, Paul McNamee, Kevin Duh, and Marine Carpuat. 2018. An empirical exploration of curriculum learning for neural machine translation. *arXiv preprint arXiv:1811.00739*.

Yikai Zhou, Baosong Yang, Derek F Wong, Yu Wan, and Lidia S Chao. 2020. Uncertainty-aware curriculum learning for neural machine translation. In *Proceedings of the 58th Annual Meeting of the Association for Computational Linguistics*, pages 6934–6944.

A Appendix

We present the experimental results of the additional factors here, prefixing the name of each factor on the caption.

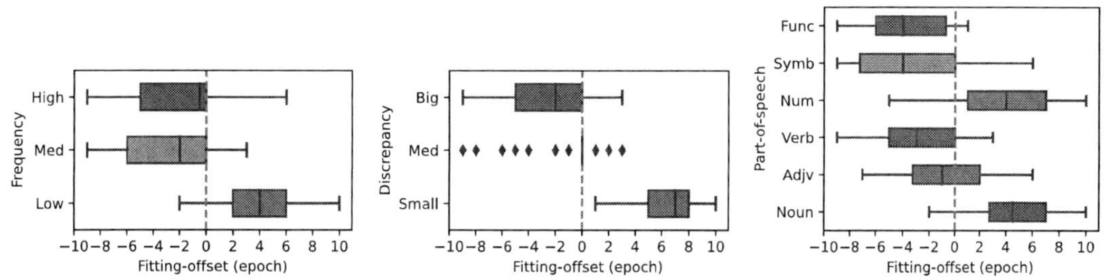

(a) Fitting-offset of tokens grouped by *frequency*.

(b) Fitting-offset of tokens grouped by *discrepancy*.

(c) Fitting-offset of tokens grouped by *parts-of-speech*.

Figure 11: The Language: Fitting-offset of English tokens evaluated on News *German-English* dataset.

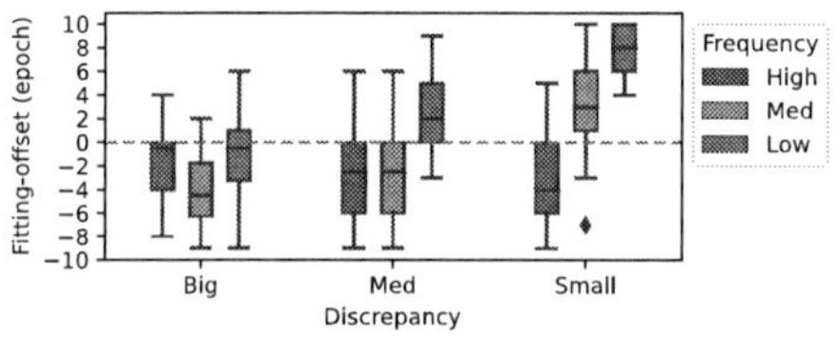

Figure 12: The Language: Fitting-offset of tokens grouped by *discrepancy* and *frequency*.

Discrepancy	Frequency High	Frequency Med	Frequency Low
Big	67.14 +0.21	27.14 -0.27	9.90 +0.20
Med	69.91 +0.07	47.08 -0.08	14.67 **+0.78**
Small	62.99 +0.33	81.85 +0.33	66.38 **+1.35**

Table 5: The Language: Potential-gain for each category grouped by *frequency* and *discrepancy*.

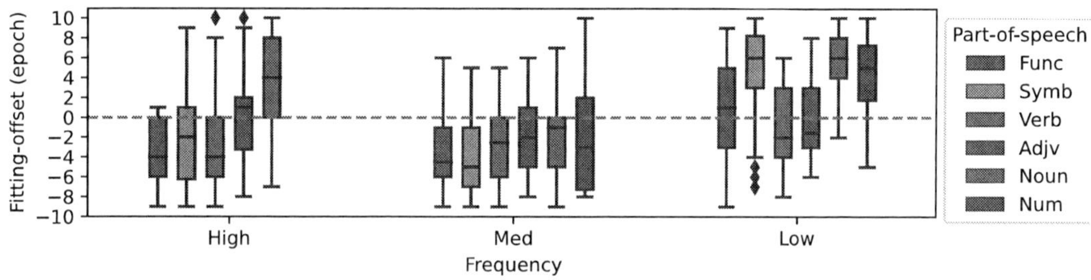

Figure 13: The Language: Fitting-offset of tokens grouped by *frequency* and *POS*.

Frequency	Function	Symbol	Number	Verb	Adj/Adv	Noun
High	64.8 +0.15	80.08 **+0.86**	nan +nan	64.51 **+1.20**	38.24 **+1.93**	49.15 **+4.01**
Med	49.82 +0.13	66.23 **+1.67**	69.43 **+1.29**	47.03 +0.38	55.78 +0.34	61.54 +0.21
Low	11.12 **+1.75**	36.09 **+5.98**	72.28 **+1.29**	30.92 **+0.57**	37.76 **+0.78**	42.13 **+1.20**

Table 6: The Language: Potential-gain for tokens grouped by *frequency* and *POS*.

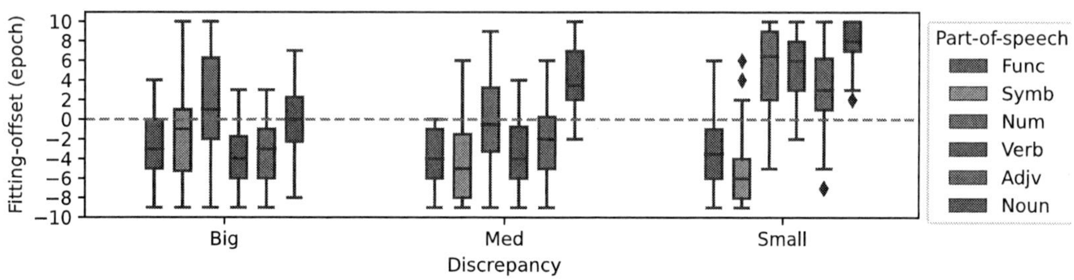

Figure 14: The Language: Fitting-offset of tokens grouped by *discrepancy* and *POS*.

Discrepancy	Function	Symbol	Number	Verb	Adj/Adv	Noun
Big	55.19 +0.10	77.67 **+0.58**	28.34 **+1.78**	20.76 +0.04	15.50 -0.20	16.61 +0.19
Med	63.84 +0.03	75.72 **+1.05**	38.57 **+2.92**	32.44 -0.10	29.21 +0.35	26.49 **+0.92**
Small	71.99 +0.20	75.22 **+1.32**	86.89 **+1.08**	65.93 **+1.14**	72.88 **+0.81**	72.12 **+1.20**

Table 7: The Language: Potential-gain for tokens grouped by *discrepancy* and *POS*.

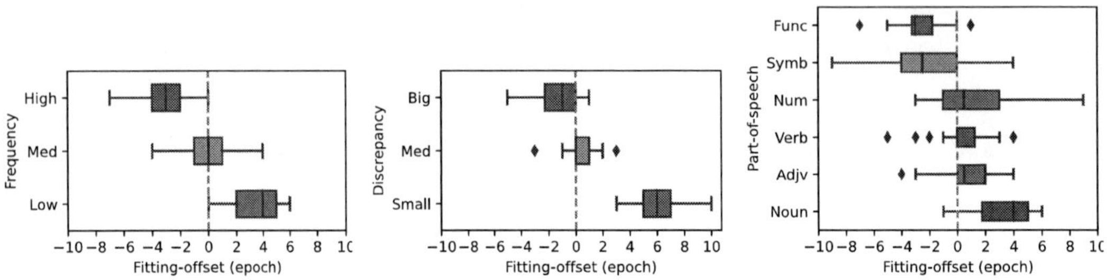

(a) Fitting-offset of tokens grouped by *frequency*. (b) Fitting-offset of tokens grouped by discrepancy. (c) Fitting-offset of tokens grouped by *parts-of-speech*.

Figure 15: The Model Size: Fitting-offset of German tokens evaluated on News English-German with *big* model.

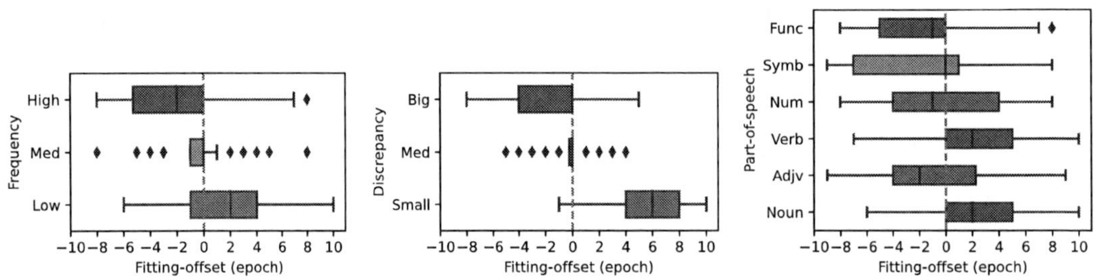

(a) Fitting-offset of tokens grouped by *frequency*. (b) Fitting-offset of tokens grouped by *discrepancy*. (c) Fitting-offset of tokens grouped by *parts-of-speech*.

Figure 16: The Domain: Fitting-offset of tokens evaluated on *Europarl* English-German (250, 000 samples).

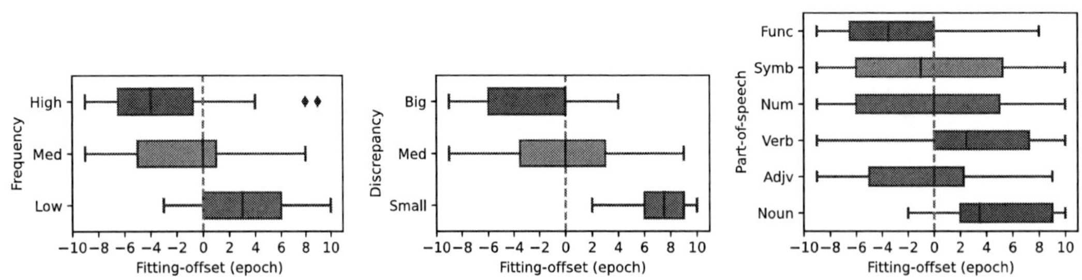

(a) Fitting-offset of tokens grouped by *frequency*. (b) Fitting-offset of tokens grouped by *discrepancy*. (c) Fitting-offset of tokens grouped by *parts-of-speech*.

Figure 17: The Data Scale: Fitting-offset of tokens evaluated on Europarl English-German (500, 000 *samples*)..

Revealing the Blind Spot of Sentence Encoder Evaluation by HEROS

Cheng-Han Chiang[†] **Yung-Sung Chuang**[‡] **James Glass**[‡] **Hung-yi Lee**[†]
dcml0714@gmail.com yungsung@mit.edu
National Taiwan University[†] Massachusetts Institute of Technology[‡]

Abstract

Existing sentence textual similarity benchmark datasets only use a single number to summarize how similar the sentence encoder's decision is to humans'. However, it is unclear what kind of sentence pairs a sentence encoder (SE) would consider similar. Moreover, existing SE benchmarks mainly consider sentence pairs with low lexical overlap, so it is unclear how the SEs behave when two sentences have high lexical overlap. We introduce a high-quality SE diagnostic dataset, HEROS. HEROS is constructed by transforming an original sentence into a new sentence based on certain rules to form a *minimal pair*, and the minimal pair has high lexical overlaps. The rules include replacing a word with a synonym, an antonym, a typo, a random word, and converting the original sentence into its negation. Different rules yield different subsets of HEROS. By systematically comparing the performance of over 60 supervised and unsupervised SEs on HEROS, we reveal that most unsupervised sentence encoders are insensitive to negation. We find the datasets used to train the SE are the main determinants of what kind of sentence pairs an SE considers similar. We also show that even if two SEs have similar performance on STS benchmarks, they can have very different behavior on HEROS. Our result reveals the blind spot of traditional STS benchmarks when evaluating SEs.[1]

1 Introduction

Sentence encoders (SEs) are fundamental building blocks in miscellaneous natural language processing (NLP) tasks, including natural language inference, paraphrase identification, and retrieval (Gillick et al., 2018; Lan and Xu, 2018). SEs are mostly evaluated with the semantic textual similarity (STS) datasets (Agirre et al., 2016; Cer et al., 2017) and SICK-R (Marelli et al., 2014), which consist of sentence pairs with human-labeled similarity scores. The performance of the SEs is summarized using Spearman's correlation coefficient between the human-labeled similarity and the cosine similarity obtained from the SE.

	R1	R2	RL	Lev	Len
STS-b	55.8	32.5	53.2	0.54	12.2
SICK-R	61.2	37.4	56.2	0.53	10.0
HEROS	92.9	84.8	92.9	0.10	13.8

Table 1: We use the ROUGE F1 scores (R1, R2, RL) and the normalized Levenshtein distance (Lev) between sentence pairs to evaluate the degree of lexical overlaps in HEROS and another two widely used STS benchmarks. A higher ROUGE score and a lower normalized Levenshtein distance imply higher lexical overlaps. Len is the average sentence length. Please find details about the metrics used here in Appendix B.

While the STS benchmarks are widely adopted, there are two problems with these benchmarks. First, the performance on the STS dataset does not reveal much about what kind of sentence pairs would the SE deem *similar*. Spearman's correlation coefficient only tells us how correlated the sentence embedding cosine similarity and the ground truth similarity are. However, the idea of what is similar can vary among different people and depend on the task at hand. Therefore, just because the sentence embedding cosine similarity is strongly correlated to the ground truth similarity, it does not provide much information about the specific type of similarity that the SE captures. Prior works mostly resort to a few hand-picked examples to illustrate what kind of sentence pairs an SE would consider similar or dissimilar (Gao et al., 2021; Chuang et al., 2022; Wang et al., 2022). But it is hard to fully understand the traits of an SE by using only a few hand-picked samples.

The second issue is that sentence pairs in the STS-related benchmarks often have low lexical

[1]We release the dataset on https://huggingface.co/datasets/dcml0714/Heros.

Proceedings of the 8th Workshop on Representation Learning for NLP (RepL4NLP 2023), pages 289–302
July 13, 2023 ©2023 Association for Computational Linguistics

overlaps, as shown in Table 1, making it unclear how the SEs will perform on sentence pairs with high lexical overlaps, which exist in real-world applications such as adversarial attacks in NLP. Adversarial samples in NLP are constructed by replacing some words in an original sentence with some other words (Alzantot et al., 2018), and the original sentence and the adversarial sample will have high lexical overlaps. SEs are often adopted to check the semantic similarity between the original sentence and the adversarial sample (Garg and Ramakrishnan, 2020; Li et al., 2020b). If we do not know how SEs perform on high lexical overlap sentences, using them to check semantic similarity is meaningless.

To address the above issues, we construct and release a new dataset, HEROS: **H**igh-l**e**xical ove**r**lap diagn**o**stic dataset for **s**entence encoders, for evaluating SEs. HEROS is composed of six subsets, and each subset includes 1000 sentence pairs with very high lexical overlaps. For the two sentences in a sentence pair, one of them is created by modifying the other sentence based on certain rules, and each subset adopts a different rule. These rules are (1) replacing a word with a synonym, (2) replacing a word with an antonym, (3) replacing a word with a random word, (4) replacing a word with its typo, and (5,6) negating the sentence. By comparing the sentence embedding cosine similarity of sentence pairs in different subsets, we can understand what kind of sentence pairs, when they have high lexical overlaps, would be considered similar by an SE. We evaluate 60 sentence embedding models on HEROS and reveal many intriguing and unreported observations on these SEs.

While some prior works also crafted sentence pairs to understand the performance of SEs, they either do not make the datasets publicly available (Zhu et al., 2018; Zhu and de Melo, 2020) or do not consider so many SEs as our paper does (Barancikova and Bojar, 2020), especially unsupervised SEs. Our contribution is relevant and significant as it provides a detailed understanding of SEs using a new dataset. The contribution and findings of this paper are summarized as follows:

- We release HEROS, a high-quality dataset consisting of 6000 sentence pairs with high lexical overlaps. HEROS allows researchers to systematically evaluate what sentence pairs would be considered similar by SEs when the lexical overlap is high.
- We evaluate 60 SEs on HEROS and reveal several facts that were never reported before or only studied using a few hand-picked examples.
- We show that supervised SEs trained for different downstream tasks behave differently on different subsets of HEROS, indicating that the SEs for different tasks encode different concepts of similarity.
- We find that all unsupervised SEs are considerably insensitive to negation, and further fine-tuning on NLI datasets makes them acquire the concept of negation.
- We observe that SEs can have very different performances on different subsets of HEROS even if their average STS benchmark performance difference is less than 0.2 points.

2 HEROS

HEROS consists of six subsets, and each subset consists of 1000 sentence pairs. The six subsets are **Synonym**, **Antonym**, **Typo**, **Random MLM**, and two types of **Negation** subsets. In all subsets, each pair of sentences have high lexical overlap, and the two sentences only differ in at most one content word; we call these paired sentences *minimal pairs*.

The dataset is constructed from the GoEmotions dataset (Demszky et al., 2020), a dataset for emotion classification collected from Reddit comments. We select one thousand sentences from GoEmotions and replace *one word* in the original sentences with its synonym, antonym, a typo of the replaced word, and a random word obtained from BERT (Devlin et al., 2019) mask-infilling. Last, we convert the original sentence into its negation using two different rules. After this process, we obtain six sentences for each of the 1000 selected sentences. We pair the **original sentence** and a **converted sentence** to form a minimal pair, which has high lexical overlaps. We will explain the above process in detail in Section 2.2. Samples from HEROS are shown in Table 2.

2.1 Motivation and Intended Usage

Unlike traditional STS benchmark datasets that asked humans to assign a similarity score as the ground truth similarity, HEROS does not provide a ground truth similarity score for sentence pairs. This is because it is difficult to define how similar two sentences should be for them to be given a certain similarity score. Moreover, the concept of similarity differs in downstream tasks. For example, in paraphrase tasks, a Negation minimal pair is considered semantically different; but for a retrieval task, we might consider them similar.

Thus, instead of providing a ground truth label for each sentence pair and letting future researchers pursue state-of-the-art results on HEROS, we hope this dataset is used for diagnosing the characteristics of an SE. Specifically, one can compare the average sentence embedding cosine similarity of sentence pairs in different subsets to understand what kind of similarity is captured by the sentence embedding model.

Different subsets in HEROS capture various aspects of semantics. Comparing the average cosine similarity between minimal pairs in Synonym and Antonym allows one to understand whether replacing a word with an antonym is more dissimilar to the original semantics than replacing a word with a synonym. The average cosine similarity between minimal pairs in Negation can tell us how negation affects sentence embedding similarity. Typos are realistic and happen every day. While humans can infer the original word from a typo and get the original meaning of the sentence, it will be interesting to see how the typos affect the sentences' similarity with the original sentences. The Random MLM subset can tell us how similar the sentence embedding can be when two sentences are semantically different but with high lexical overlaps. By comparing the performance of different SEs on different subsets in HEROS, we can further understand the trait of different SEs.

2.2 Dataset construction

2.2.1 Raw dataset preprocessing

HEROS are constructed from GoEmotions. For the sentences in GoEmotions, we only select sentences whose lengths are more than 8 words and less than 25 words. We filter out sentences with cursing, and we use language-tool to filter out sentences that language-tool find ungrammatical. We manually remove the sentences that we find offensive or harmful. The selected sentences are called **original sentences** in our paper. More details on preprocessing are presented in Appendix A.1.

2.2.2 Selecting which word to replace

The next step is to determine which word to replace in the original sentences obtained from preprocessing. The selected word must be (1) semantically significant to the original sentence so that when it is replaced with a non-synonym word, the two sentences will have vastly different meanings and would be considered contradictory in an NLI task. (2) The selected word must have synonyms and antonyms at the same time since it will be replaced with its synonyms and antonyms. We only select verbs and adjectives for replacement because changing them greatly alters the semantics of a sentence. Sentences that do not contain a word that satisfies the two criteria are dropped.

2.2.3 Synonym and Antonym Subsets

The first subset in HEROS includes the minimal pairs formed by replacing a word in the original sentence with its synonym; the second subset includes the minimal pairs formed by replacing a word with its antonym. After selecting the word to be replaced, we determine what synonym and antonym should be used for replacement. There are three principles for replacement: (1) the replacement should fit in the context, (2) the synonym should match the word sense of the original word in the sentence[2], and (3) the collocating words (e.g., prepositions, definite articles) may also need to be modified. The three guiding principles make this process require high proficiency in English and this process is impossible to be done using an automatic process. Thus, this process is performed by the authors ourselves. We use our proficiency in English and four online dictionaries to select the replacement words. The four resources are thesaurus.com, thesaurus of Merriam-Webster, Online Oxford Collocation Dictionary, and Cambridge Dictionary. This step takes 72 hours.

2.2.4 Random MLM

The third subset in HEROS is obtained by replacing the word to be replaced with a random word predicted by a masked language model. We mask the word to be replaced by `[MASK]` token and use `bert-large-uncased` to fill in the masked position. We filter out the synonym, antonym, and their derivational forms[3] from the masked prediction using WordNet and LemmInflect. Additionally, we filter out punctuations and subword tokens that are not complete words. Moreover, we manually filter out mask predictions that are very similar in mean-

[2]A word can have different word senses, and each word sense has its own synonym sets. Synonym sets of different word senses might be different.

[3]For example, different tenses of a verb.

Subset	Example (adjective)	Example (verb)
Original	*And that is why it is (or was) illegal.*	*You do not know how much that boosted my self-esteem right now.*
Synonym	*And that is why it is (or was) illegitimate.*	*You do not know how much that increased my self-esteem right now.*
Antonym	*And that is why it is (or was) legal.*	*You do not know how much that lowered my self-esteem right now.*
Random MLM	*And that is why it is (or was) here.*	*You do not know how much that affects my self-esteem right now.*
Typo	*And that is why it is (or was) illiegal.*	*You do not know how much that booste my self-esteem right now.*
Negation (Main)	*And that is not why it is (or was) illegal.*	*You do know how much that boosted my self-esteem right now.*
Negation (Antonym)	*And that is why it is (or was) not illegal.*	*You do not know how much that did not boost my self-esteem right now.*

Table 2: Two examples from HEROS. One example selects a verb while the other selects an adjective for replacement. The first row shows the original sentences in the GoEmotions, and the words highlighted in blue are the words to be replaced. Starting from the second rows are the corresponding sentences obtained from the original sentence for different subsets, and the changes compared with the original sentence are highlighted in green.

ing to the original word when used in the same context. This is because even if a word is not a synonym of the word to be replaced, it may still express the same meaning when used in the same context. For example, "great" is not a synonym of "good" according to WordNet, but their meaning is very similar. The resulting sentences can be ungrammatical in very few cases, but we leave them as is.

2.2.5 Typos

The fourth subset in HEROS is constructed by swapping the word to be replaced with its typo. Typos are spelling or typing errors that occur in real life. If the word to be typoed is in the Wikipedia lists of common misspellings, we replace the word with its typo in the list. If the word is not in the common misspelling list, we create a typo by randomly deleting or replacing one character or swapping two different characters in the word (He et al., 2021).

2.2.6 Negation

The last subset in HEROS is constructed by negating the original sentence. Negation can happen at different levels in a sentence, and we create two different types of negation datasets based on where the negation happens. The first one is negating the main verb, which is the action performed by the subject, in the sentence.[4] If the main verb is not negated, we negate it by adding appropriate auxiliary verbs and the word "not". If the main verb is already negated, we directly remove the word "not" and do not remove the auxiliary verb. We call this type of negation dataset the **Negation (Main)**.

The other type of negation dataset is related to the Antonym subset. A minimal pair in the Antonym subset is formed by replacing a word in a sentence with its antonym. This *implicitly* negates the meaning of the original sentence. Here, we construct another subset called **Negation (Antonym)**, which *explicitly* negates the word that is replaced with an antonym in the Antonym subset. Given a sentence pair in the Antonym dataset, there is a verb or adjective in the original sentence that is replaced by its antonym in the converted sentence. We directly negate that word in the original sentence by adding "not" in front of an adjective or adding "not" and an auxiliary verb for verbs.[5]. If the word is already negated, we remove the "not". These sentences might sound a bit strange, but

[4]When selecting the original sentences, we do not consider interrogative sentences, so we will not create a negative interrogative sentence. An interrogative sentence and its negation ask the same question and are not semantically different.

[5]If the negation of the minimal pair in the Antonym dataset happens at the main verb, the sentence pair in Negation (Main) and Negation (Antonym) will be the same.

they are still understandable. This type of negation dataset is called Negation (Antonym) because the negation is in the same place as the antonym replacement in the Antonym subset.

3 Comparing 60 Sentence Embedding Models

In this section, we compare the behavior of 60 SEs on HEROS. Detailed information about the SEs, including training data and model size, is listed in Appendix C. We calculate the cosine similarity between each minimal pair in HEROS and normalize it by a baseline cosine similarity to remove the effect of anisotropic embedding space (Ethayarajh, 2019; Li et al., 2020a). The baseline cosine similarity is calculated by averaging the similarity between 250K random sentence pairs (details in Appendix D). We report the average normalized similarity of different subsets in HEROS for each SE. For simplicity, we will use "similarity" to refer to the normalized cosine similarity.

3.1 Supervised SEs

We use 30 supervised transformer-based SEs in the SentenceTransformers toolkit (Reimers and Gurevych, 2019, 2020). These SEs are trained supervisedly using different datasets for specific downstream tasks. The results are presented in Figure 1. In Figure 1, we group SEs into groups based on what training dataset they used. We denote the datasets used to fine-tune the SEs in the parentheses in Figure 1. There are a lot of interesting observations one can obtain from Figure 1, and we are just listing some of those observations.

SEs fine-tuned only on QA datasets are insensitive to negation: The first and second blocks in Figure 1 include different SEs obtained from fine-tuning on QA datasets using contrastive learning (Hadsell et al., 2006). In the fine-tuning stage, a positive pair for contrastive learning is a pair of question and the answer to the question. The high similarity of the two Negation subsets can be explained by the dataset type used for fine-tuning: whether the answer is negated or not, it may still be considered a valid answer to the question. Hence, it is reasonable that a sentence and its negation have high similarity. We also find that replacing a word with a typo will cause the resulting sentence to have lower similarity with the original sentence compared with replacing the word with a synonym. While humans can understand the real meaning of a typo word, this is not the case for the SEs.

SEs fine-tuned from T5 are less sensitive to typos when the model size scales up: The GTR models (Ni et al., 2021) in the second block of Figure 1 and the ST5 models (Ni et al., 2022) in the fourth block are SEs fine-tuned from T5 (Raffel et al., 2020). Although the two types of models are trained using different datasets, we find that their performance on the Typo subset shares an interesting trend when the model size scales up from the smallest base-size model to the largest xxl-size model: The similarity on the Typo subset grows higher as the model gets larger and can be as high as or higher than the similarity of the Synonym subset; meanwhile, the similarity on the Synonym subset is almost unchanged when the model size gets larger. This shows that deeper model can better mitigate the negative impact of typos on sentence embeddings.

SEs fine-tuned on paraphrase datasets are extremely sensitive to negations and antonyms: The third block in Figure 1 includes the results of SEs fine-tuned on paraphrase datasets using contrastive learning. Paraphrase datasets include a combination of different datasets such as premise-hypothesis pairs in NLI datasets and duplicate question pairs. Contrary to the previous paragraph which shows fine-tuning only using question-answer pairs makes the model insensitive to negation, we see a completely different result in the third block of Figure 1. We infer that this is mainly due to the NLI datasets used for fine-tuning: negating the original sentence results in a sentence that semantically contradicts the original sentence, and will be considered as a hard negative in contrastive learning. Hence, SEs fine-tuned on NLI will be very sensitive negation. For the same reason, these SEs are also sensitive to replacing words with antonyms. The only exception is the `MiniLM L3 (para)` model (Wang et al., 2020), which has very high similarity on the Negation subsets and is even higher than the Synonym subset. We hypothesize that this is because the number of parameters of the model and the sentence embedding dimension are too small, thus limiting the expressiveness of the sentence embeddings.

SEs fine-tuned on all available sentence pair datasets are again insensitive to negations: The models in the last block in Figure 1 are fine-tuned on all available sentence-pair training data, denoted as *(all)*. The training data consist of 32 datasets

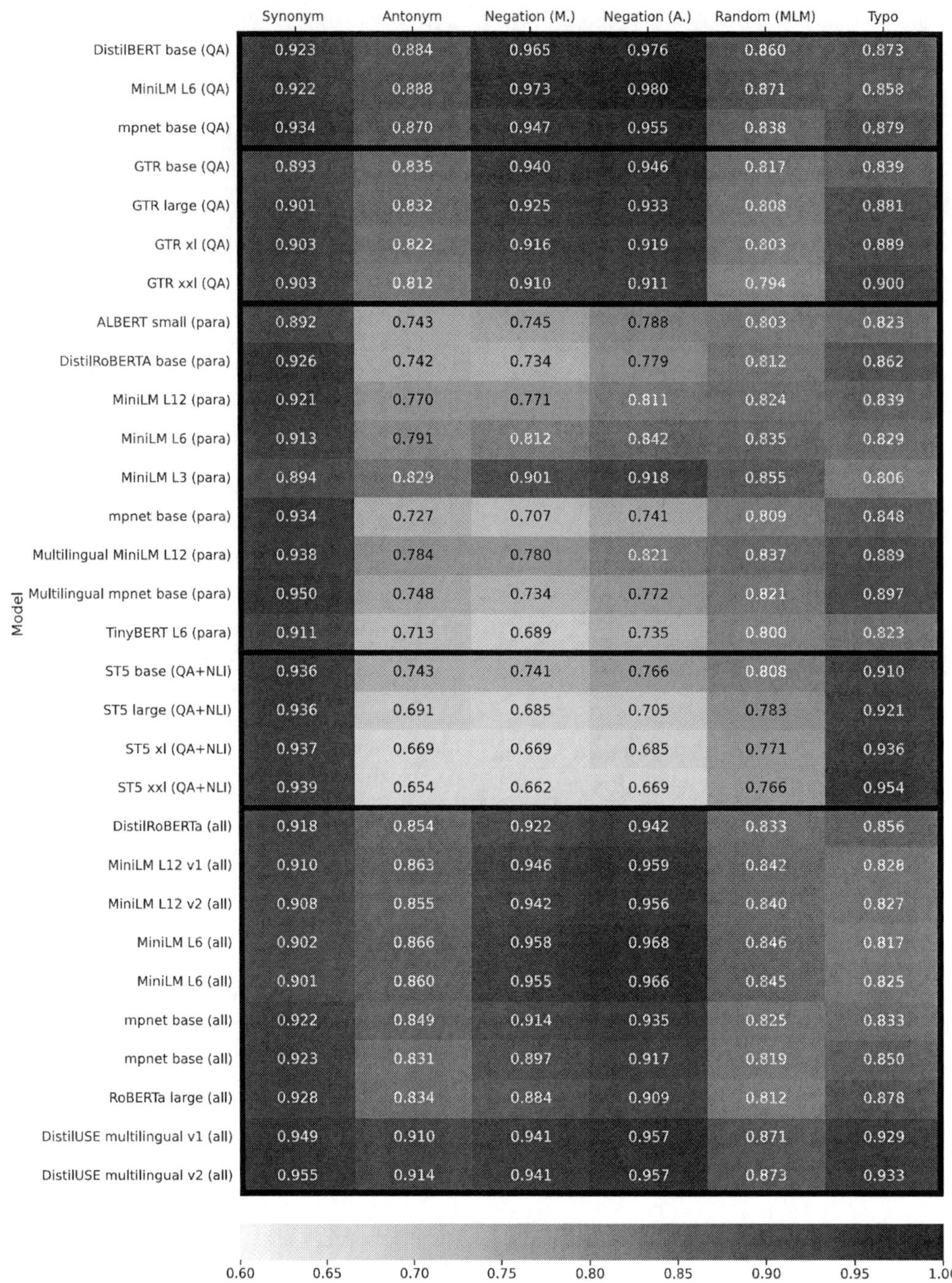

Figure 1: Normalized cosine similarity of supervised SEs. We group SEs that use different training datasets or training procedures together. We denote the datasets used to train the SEs in parentheses.

and have a total of 1.17B sentence pairs, including question-answer pairs in QA datasets, premise-hypothesis pairs in NLI dataset, and context-passage pairs in retrieval datasets. In the fifth block, the similarity between sentence pairs from the two Negation subsets is very high and is even higher than the similarity of the Synonym subset for most models. This means that when using these models for retrieval, given a source sentence, it is more likely to retrieve the negation of the source sentence, instead of another sentence that only differs from the source sentence by a synonym. While

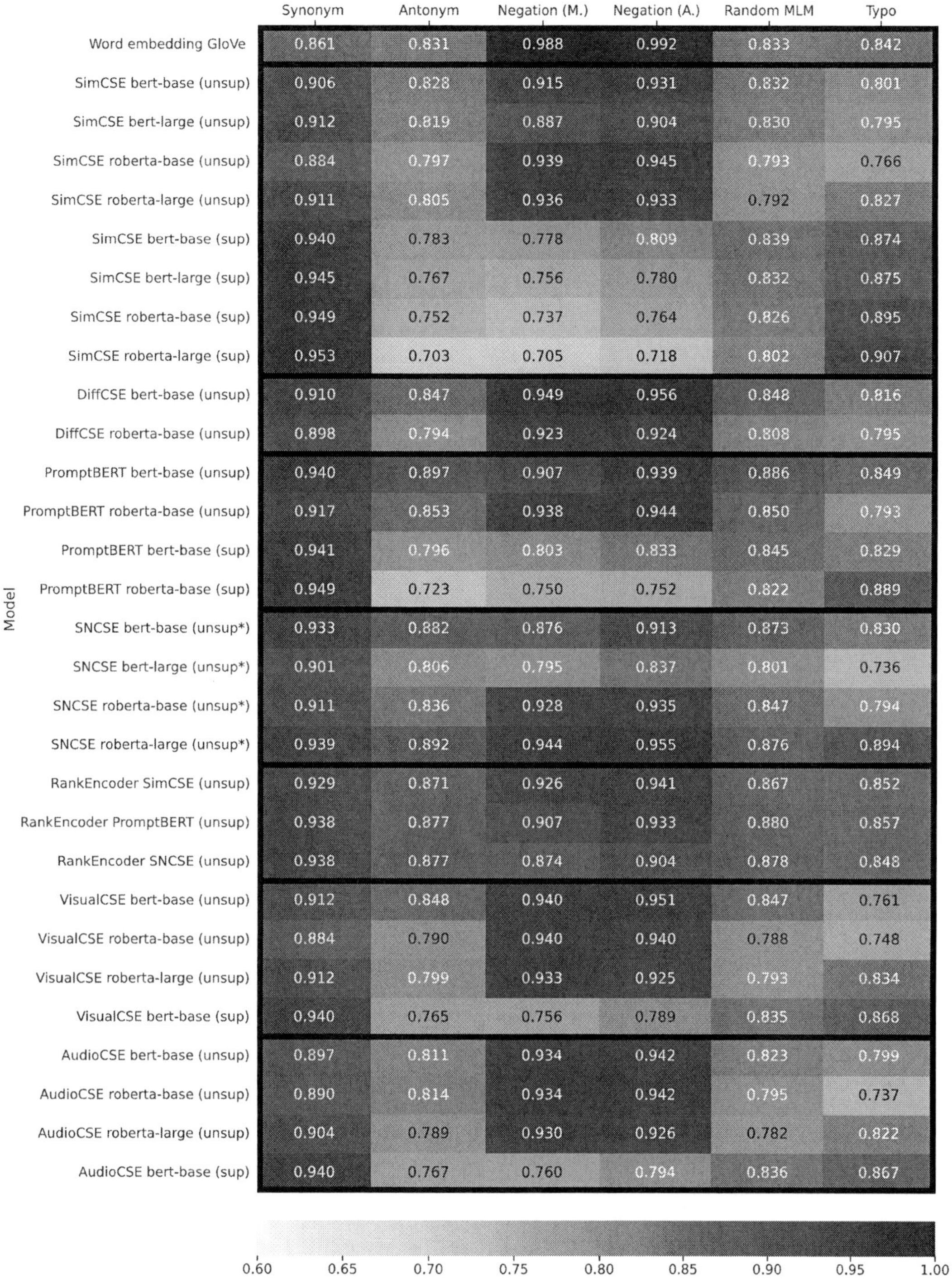

Figure 2: Normalized cosine similarity of unsupervised SEs and their derived supervised SEs. We group the SEs based on the unsupervised fine-tuning method.

these models are also fine-tuned on NLI datasets, the NLI datasets only compose 0.24% of the whole training data. This makes the models in this block much less sensitive to negations, compared with models fine-tuned mainly with NLI datasets (e.g., ST5) and models fine-tuned on paraphrase datasets.

HEROS reveal different characteristics of different SEs: Overall, we see that even if the sentences in HEROS all have high lexical overlaps, the similarity score can still be very different among HEROS subsets for the same SE. HEROS also shows that how the concept of similarity is encoded by an SE is highly related to what the SE is trained on. This further allows us to understand what kind of similarity is required by the task related to the training dataset. For example, NLI tasks consider negation pairs as dissimilar while question-answer pair retrieval task considers negation to be similar. Such interesting observations are not revealed by any prior SE benchmarks, making HEROS very valuable. It will also be interesting to see if there is any correlation between an SE's performance on different subsets in HEROS and different downstream tasks in SentEval (Conneau and Kiela, 2018); we save this in future work.

3.2 Unsupervised SEs

Next, we turn our attention to unsupervised SEs. Unlike supervised SEs that are fine-tuned on labeled pairs of sentences, unsupervised SEs are trained using specially designed methods that do not use labeled sentence pairs. Most of these unsupervised SEs can be further fine-tuned on NLI datasets to further improve the performance on the STS benchmarks (Gao et al., 2021; Jiang et al., 2022; Jian et al., 2022). We show the result on HEROS of 7 different types of unsupervised SEs and their derived supervised SEs in Figure 2.

For the completeness of the result, we also report the performance of sentence embeddings calculated by averaging the GLoVe embeddings (Pennington et al., 2014) in the sentence. The result is presented in the first row in Figure 2. We observe that the sentence before and after negation have very high similarity, and the similarity is much higher than replacing one word with its synonym or antonym. This shows that negation words have a very small contribution to the sentence embedding obtained from averaging the GLoVe embeddings.

Unsupervised SEs are insensitive to negation: Unsupervised SEs, denoted with *unsup* in Figure 2, have high similarity on Negation subsets, sometimes even higher than Synonym subsets. SNCSE (Wang et al., 2022) models are an exception, where Negation subsets may have a lower similarity. SNCSE uses the dependency tree of a sentence to convert it into its negation as a "soft-negative" in contrastive learning, but it needs a dependency parser, making it not truly unsupervised. Hence, we use *unsup** to denote SNCSE models in Figure 2. The lower similarity on Negation datasets is not consistent for different SNCSE models, possibly due to a poor negation method in the implementation of SNCSE that does not consider negative contractions, resulting in low-quality augmented data.

Further supervised fine-tuning on NLI datasets significantly change the model's behavior on HEROS: Fine-tuning unsupervised SEs on NLI datasets (denoted with *sup* in Figure 2) leads to a significant drop in similarity on Negation and Antonym and an increase in similarity on the Synonym subset. This show that supervised fine-tuning greatly changes how SEs encode similarity. An interesting trend is that after fine-tuning, similarity on the Typo subset increases for most models, likely because the SE better captures semantic similarity and pays less attention to superficial lexical form.

Almost all SEs rate Negation (Main) to be less similar compared with Negation (Antonym) Recall that the Negation (Main) subsets are created by negating the **main** verb while the Negation (Antonym) subset does not always negate the main verb. The lower similarity on the Negation (Main) subset shows that SEs consider negating the main verb to be less similar to the original sentence, compared with negating other positions in the original sentence. This implies that the SEs can capture the level of the verb in the dependency tree of the sentence, and it considers negating the main verb to be more influential to sentence embeddings.

Close performance on STS benchmarks can have different behaviors on HEROS: We find that two SEs that achieve similar average performance on STS benchmarks (STS 12-17, STS-b, and SICK-R) can perform very differently on HEROS. For example, `RoBERTa large (all)` and `DistilRoBERTa base (para)` in Figure 1 have similar average STS scores (81.07 and 81.12, respectively), but the former have very high similarity on the Negation subsets while the latter does not. This is also the case for `SNCSE roberta-large` in Figure 2 and `mpnet base (para)` in Figure 1, which have average scores of 81.77 and 81.57 on the STS benchmarks, respectively. This shows that HEROS can reveal some traits of the SEs that the traditional STS benchmarks cannot identify.

4 Conclusion

We introduce HEROS, a new dataset of 6000 human-constructed sentence pairs with high lexical overlaps. It is composed of 6 subsets that capture different linguistic phenomena. Evaluating an SE on HEROS can reveal what kind of sentence pairs the SE considers similar. HEROS fills a void in current SE evaluation methods, which only use correlation coefficients with human ratings or performance on downstream tasks to summarize an SE, and mainly use sentence pairs with low lexical overlaps. We use HEROS to evaluate 60 models and reveal numerous new observations. We believe that HEROS can aid in interpreting SE behavior and comparing the performance of different SEs.

Limitations

The SEs in this paper are mainly transformer-based SEs, and we are not sure whether the observations hold for other SEs. However, considering that transformer-based SEs dominate the current NLP community, we think it is fine to only evaluate 59 transformer-based SEs. Another limitation is that the sentences in HEROS are converted from Reddit, which is an online forum and the texts on Reddit may be more casual and informal. This makes the sentence pairs in HEROS tend to be more informal. Users should note such a characteristic of the sentence pairs of HEROS and beware that the results obtained using HEROS may be different from the results obtained using more formal texts. An additional limitation is that there can be more diverse rules to create different sentence pairs other than the six subsets included in HEROS, and our paper cannot include them all. As a last limitation, during the construction of HEROS, we remove sentences that are ungrammatical based on language-tool, so our results may not generalize to ungrammatical sentences.

Ethics Statement

The main ethical concern in this paper is our dataset, HEROS. HEROS is constructed from an existing dataset, GoEmotion. As listed in the model card of GoEmotion, GoEmotion contains biases in Reddit and some offensive contents. As stated in Section 2.2.1, the authors have tried our best to remove all content that we find to be possibly offensive to users. We cannot guarantee that our standard of unbiased and unharmful fits everyone. Thus, we also remind future users of HEROS to be aware of such possible harms. To make sure the accessibility of our paper, we have used an online resource to carefully check that the figures in the paper are interpretable for readers of different backgrounds.

References

Eneko Agirre, Carmen Banea, Daniel Cer, Mona Diab, Aitor Gonzalez-Agirre, Rada Mihalcea, German Rigau, and Janyce Wiebe. 2016. SemEval-2016 task 1: Semantic textual similarity, monolingual and cross-lingual evaluation. In *Proceedings of the 10th International Workshop on Semantic Evaluation (SemEval-2016)*, pages 497–511, San Diego, California. Association for Computational Linguistics.

Moustafa Alzantot, Yash Sharma, Ahmed Elgohary, Bo-Jhang Ho, Mani Srivastava, and Kai-Wei Chang. 2018. Generating natural language adversarial examples. In *Proceedings of the 2018 Conference on Empirical Methods in Natural Language Processing*, pages 2890–2896, Brussels, Belgium. Association for Computational Linguistics.

Petra Barancikova and Ondřej Bojar. 2020. COSTRA 1.0: A dataset of complex sentence transformations. In *Proceedings of the Twelfth Language Resources and Evaluation Conference*, pages 3535–3541, Marseille, France. European Language Resources Association.

Samuel R. Bowman, Gabor Angeli, Christopher Potts, and Christopher D. Manning. 2015. A large annotated corpus for learning natural language inference. In *Proceedings of the 2015 Conference on Empirical Methods in Natural Language Processing*, pages 632–642, Lisbon, Portugal. Association for Computational Linguistics.

Daniel Cer, Mona Diab, Eneko Agirre, Iñigo Lopez-Gazpio, and Lucia Specia. 2017. SemEval-2017 task 1: Semantic textual similarity multilingual and crosslingual focused evaluation. In *Proceedings of the 11th International Workshop on Semantic Evaluation (SemEval-2017)*, pages 1–14, Vancouver, Canada. Association for Computational Linguistics.

Yung-Sung Chuang, Rumen Dangovski, Hongyin Luo, Yang Zhang, Shiyu Chang, Marin Soljacic, Shang-Wen Li, Scott Yih, Yoon Kim, and James Glass. 2022. DiffCSE: Difference-based contrastive learning for sentence embeddings. In *Proceedings of the 2022 Conference of the North American Chapter of the Association for Computational Linguistics: Human Language Technologies*, pages 4207–4218, Seattle, United States. Association for Computational Linguistics.

Arman Cohan, Sergey Feldman, Iz Beltagy, Doug Downey, and Daniel Weld. 2020. SPECTER: Document-level representation learning using citation-informed transformers. In *Proceedings of the 58th Annual Meeting of the Association for Computational Linguistics*, pages 2270–2282, Online. Association for Computational Linguistics.

Alexis Conneau and Douwe Kiela. 2018. SentEval: An evaluation toolkit for universal sentence representations. In *Proceedings of the Eleventh International Conference on Language Resources and Evaluation (LREC 2018)*, Miyazaki, Japan. European Language Resources Association (ELRA).

William Coster and David Kauchak. 2011. Simple English Wikipedia: A new text simplification task. In *Proceedings of the 49th Annual Meeting of the Association for Computational Linguistics: Human Language Technologies*, pages 665–669, Portland, Oregon, USA. Association for Computational Linguistics.

Nick Craswell, Bhaskar Mitra, Emine Yilmaz, Daniel Campos, and Jimmy Lin. 2021. Ms marco: Benchmarking ranking models in the large-data regime. In *Proceedings of the 44th International ACM SIGIR Conference on Research and Development in Information Retrieval*, SIGIR '21, page 1566–1576, New York, NY, USA. Association for Computing Machinery.

Dorottya Demszky, Dana Movshovitz-Attias, Jeongwoo Ko, Alan Cowen, Gaurav Nemade, and Sujith Ravi. 2020. GoEmotions: A Dataset of Fine-Grained Emotions. In *58th Annual Meeting of the Association for Computational Linguistics (ACL)*.

Jacob Devlin, Ming-Wei Chang, Kenton Lee, and Kristina Toutanova. 2019. BERT: Pre-training of deep bidirectional transformers for language understanding. In *Proceedings of the 2019 Conference of the North American Chapter of the Association for Computational Linguistics: Human Language Technologies, Volume 1 (Long and Short Papers)*, pages 4171–4186, Minneapolis, Minnesota. Association for Computational Linguistics.

Matthew Dunn, Levent Sagun, Mike Higgins, V Ugur Guney, Volkan Cirik, and Kyunghyun Cho. 2017. Searchqa: A new q&a dataset augmented with context from a search engine. *arXiv preprint arXiv:1704.05179*.

Kawin Ethayarajh. 2019. How contextual are contextualized word representations? Comparing the geometry of BERT, ELMo, and GPT-2 embeddings. In *Proceedings of the 2019 Conference on Empirical Methods in Natural Language Processing and the 9th International Joint Conference on Natural Language Processing (EMNLP-IJCNLP)*, pages 55–65, Hong Kong, China. Association for Computational Linguistics.

Anthony Fader, Luke Zettlemoyer, and Oren Etzioni. 2014. Open question answering over curated and extracted knowledge bases. In *Proceedings of the 20th ACM SIGKDD International Conference on Knowledge Discovery and Data Mining*, KDD '14, page 1156–1165, New York, NY, USA. Association for Computing Machinery.

Angela Fan, Yacine Jernite, Ethan Perez, David Grangier, Jason Weston, and Michael Auli. 2019. ELI5: Long form question answering. In *Proceedings of the 57th Annual Meeting of the Association for Computational Linguistics*, pages 3558–3567, Florence, Italy. Association for Computational Linguistics.

Manaal Faruqui, Ellie Pavlick, Ian Tenney, and Dipanjan Das. 2018. WikiAtomicEdits: A multilingual corpus of Wikipedia edits for modeling language and discourse. In *Proceedings of the 2018 Conference on Empirical Methods in Natural Language Processing*, pages 305–315, Brussels, Belgium. Association for Computational Linguistics.

Katja Filippova and Yasemin Altun. 2013. Overcoming the lack of parallel data in sentence compression. In *Proceedings of the 2013 Conference on Empirical Methods in Natural Language Processing*, pages 1481–1491, Seattle, Washington, USA. Association for Computational Linguistics.

Tianyu Gao, Xingcheng Yao, and Danqi Chen. 2021. Simcse: Simple contrastive learning of sentence embeddings. In *Proceedings of the 2021 Conference on Empirical Methods in Natural Language Processing*, pages 6894–6910.

Siddhant Garg and Goutham Ramakrishnan. 2020. BAE: BERT-based adversarial examples for text classification. In *Proceedings of the 2020 Conference on Empirical Methods in Natural Language Processing (EMNLP)*, pages 6174–6181, Online. Association for Computational Linguistics.

Daniel Gillick, Alessandro Presta, and Gaurav Singh Tomar. 2018. End-to-end retrieval in continuous space. *arXiv preprint arXiv:1811.08008*.

Raia Hadsell, Sumit Chopra, and Yann LeCun. 2006. Dimensionality reduction by learning an invariant mapping. In *2006 IEEE Computer Society Conference on Computer Vision and Pattern Recognition (CVPR'06)*, volume 2, pages 1735–1742. IEEE.

Xuanli He, Lingjuan Lyu, Lichao Sun, and Qiongkai Xu. 2021. Model extraction and adversarial transferability, your bert is vulnerable! In *Proceedings of the 2021 Conference of the North American Chapter of the Association for Computational Linguistics: Human Language Technologies*, pages 2006–2012.

Matthew Henderson, Paweł Budzianowski, Iñigo Casanueva, Sam Coope, Daniela Gerz, Girish Kumar, Nikola Mrkšić, Georgios Spithourakis, Pei-Hao Su, Ivan Vulić, and Tsung-Hsien Wen. 2019. A repository of conversational datasets. In *Proceedings of the First Workshop on NLP for Conversational AI*, pages 1–10, Florence, Italy. Association for Computational Linguistics.

Christopher Hidey and Kathy McKeown. 2016. Identifying causal relations using parallel Wikipedia articles. In *Proceedings of the 54th Annual Meeting of the Association for Computational Linguistics (Volume 1: Long Papers)*, pages 1424–1433, Berlin, Germany. Association for Computational Linguistics.

Yiren Jian, Chongyang Gao, and Soroush Vosoughi. 2022. Non-linguistic supervision for contrastive learning of sentence embeddings. In *Advances in Neural Information Processing Systems*.

Ting Jiang, Shaohan Huang, Zihan Zhang, Deqing Wang, Fuzhen Zhuang, Furu Wei, Haizhen Huang, Liangjie Zhang, and Qi Zhang. 2022. Promptbert: Improving bert sentence embeddings with prompts. *arXiv preprint arXiv:2201.04337*.

Daniel Khashabi, Amos Ng, Tushar Khot, Ashish Sabharwal, Hannaneh Hajishirzi, and Chris Callison-Burch. 2021. Gooaq: Open question answering with diverse answer types. *arXiv preprint*.

Mahnaz Koupaee and William Yang Wang. 2018. Wikihow: A large scale text summarization dataset. *arXiv preprint arXiv:1810.09305*.

Tom Kwiatkowski, Jennimaria Palomaki, Olivia Redfield, Michael Collins, Ankur Parikh, Chris Alberti, Danielle Epstein, Illia Polosukhin, Jacob Devlin, Kenton Lee, et al. 2019. Natural questions: a benchmark for question answering research. *Transactions of the Association for Computational Linguistics*, 7:453–466.

Wuwei Lan and Wei Xu. 2018. Neural network models for paraphrase identification, semantic textual similarity, natural language inference, and question answering. In *Proceedings of the 27th International Conference on Computational Linguistics*, pages 3890–3902.

Patrick Lewis, Yuxiang Wu, Linqing Liu, Pasquale Minervini, Heinrich Küttler, Aleksandra Piktus, Pontus Stenetorp, and Sebastian Riedel. 2021. PAQ: 65 million probably-asked questions and what you can do with them. *Transactions of the Association for Computational Linguistics*, 9:1098–1115.

Bohan Li, Hao Zhou, Junxian He, Mingxuan Wang, Yiming Yang, and Lei Li. 2020a. On the sentence embeddings from pre-trained language models. In *Proceedings of the 2020 Conference on Empirical Methods in Natural Language Processing (EMNLP)*, pages 9119–9130, Online. Association for Computational Linguistics.

Linyang Li, Ruotian Ma, Qipeng Guo, Xiangyang Xue, and Xipeng Qiu. 2020b. BERT-ATTACK: Adversarial attack against BERT using BERT. In *Proceedings of the 2020 Conference on Empirical Methods in Natural Language Processing (EMNLP)*, pages 6193–6202, Online. Association for Computational Linguistics.

Tsung-Yi Lin, Michael Maire, Serge J Belongie, James Hays, Pietro Perona, Deva Ramanan, Piotr Dollár, and C Lawrence Zitnick. 2014. Microsoft coco: Common objects in context. In *ECCV (5)*.

Kyle Lo, Lucy Lu Wang, Mark Neumann, Rodney Kinney, and Daniel Weld. 2020. S2ORC: The semantic scholar open research corpus. In *Proceedings of the 58th Annual Meeting of the Association for Computational Linguistics*, pages 4969–4983, Online. Association for Computational Linguistics.

Marco Marelli, Stefano Menini, Marco Baroni, Luisa Bentivogli, Raffaella Bernardi, and Roberto Zamparelli. 2014. A sick cure for the evaluation of compositional distributional semantic models. In *Proceedings of the Ninth International Conference on Language Resources and Evaluation (LREC'14)*, pages 216–223.

Jianmo Ni, Gustavo Hernandez Abrego, Noah Constant, Ji Ma, Keith Hall, Daniel Cer, and Yinfei Yang. 2022. Sentence-t5: Scalable sentence encoders from pretrained text-to-text models. In *Findings of the Association for Computational Linguistics: ACL 2022*, pages 1864–1874, Dublin, Ireland. Association for Computational Linguistics.

Jianmo Ni, Chen Qu, Jing Lu, Zhuyun Dai, Gustavo Hernández Ábrego, Ji Ma, Vincent Y Zhao, Yi Luan, Keith B Hall, Ming-Wei Chang, et al. 2021. Large dual encoders are generalizable retrievers. *arXiv preprint arXiv:2112.07899*.

Jeffrey Pennington, Richard Socher, and Christopher Manning. 2014. GloVe: Global vectors for word representation. In *Proceedings of the 2014 Conference on Empirical Methods in Natural Language Processing (EMNLP)*, pages 1532–1543, Doha, Qatar. Association for Computational Linguistics.

Colin Raffel, Noam Shazeer, Adam Roberts, Katherine Lee, Sharan Narang, Michael Matena, Yanqi Zhou, Wei Li, Peter J Liu, et al. 2020. Exploring the limits of transfer learning with a unified text-to-text transformer. *J. Mach. Learn. Res.*, 21(140):1–67.

Pranav Rajpurkar, Jian Zhang, Konstantin Lopyrev, and Percy Liang. 2016. SQuAD: 100,000+ questions for machine comprehension of text. In *Proceedings of the 2016 Conference on Empirical Methods in Natural Language Processing*, pages 2383–2392, Austin, Texas. Association for Computational Linguistics.

Nils Reimers and Iryna Gurevych. 2019. Sentence-bert: Sentence embeddings using siamese bert-networks. In *Proceedings of the 2019 Conference on Empirical Methods in Natural Language Processing*. Association for Computational Linguistics.

Nils Reimers and Iryna Gurevych. 2020. Making monolingual sentence embeddings multilingual using knowledge distillation. In *Proceedings of the 2020 Conference on Empirical Methods in Natural Language Processing*. Association for Computational Linguistics.

Yeon Seonwoo, Guoyin Wang, Sajal Choudhary, Changmin Seo, Jiwei Li, Xiang Li, Puyang Xu, Sunghyun Park, and Alice Oh. 2022. Ranking-enhanced unsupervised sentence representation learning. *arXiv preprint arXiv:2209.04333*.

Alex Wang, Amanpreet Singh, Julian Michael, Felix Hill, Omer Levy, and Samuel R. Bowman. 2019. GLUE: A multi-task benchmark and analysis platform for natural language understanding. In *International Conference on Learning Representations*.

Hao Wang, Yangguang Li, Zhen Huang, Yong Dou, Lingpeng Kong, and Jing Shao. 2022. Sncse: Contrastive learning for unsupervised sentence embedding with soft negative samples. *arXiv preprint arXiv:2201.05979*.

Wenhui Wang, Furu Wei, Li Dong, Hangbo Bao, Nan Yang, and Ming Zhou. 2020. Minilm: Deep self-attention distillation for task-agnostic compression of pre-trained transformers.

Adina Williams, Nikita Nangia, and Samuel Bowman. 2018. A broad-coverage challenge corpus for sentence understanding through inference. In *Proceedings of the 2018 Conference of the North American Chapter of the Association for Computational Linguistics: Human Language Technologies, Volume 1 (Long Papers)*, pages 1112–1122, New Orleans, Louisiana. Association for Computational Linguistics.

Peter Young, Alice Lai, Micah Hodosh, and Julia Hockenmaier. 2014. From image descriptions to visual denotations: New similarity metrics for semantic inference over event descriptions. *Transactions of the Association for Computational Linguistics*, 2:67–78.

Xiang Zhang, Junbo Zhao, and Yann LeCun. 2015. Character-level convolutional networks for text classification. *Advances in neural information processing systems*, 28.

Xunjie Zhu and Gerard de Melo. 2020. Sentence analogies: Linguistic regularities in sentence embeddings. In *Proceedings of the 28th International Conference on Computational Linguistics*, pages 3389–3400, Barcelona, Spain (Online). International Committee on Computational Linguistics.

Xunjie Zhu, Tingfeng Li, and Gerard De Melo. 2018. Exploring semantic properties of sentence embeddings. In *Proceedings of the 56th Annual Meeting of the Association for Computational Linguistics (Volume 2: Short Papers)*, pages 632–637.

A Further Details of HEROS

A.1 Dataset Preprocess

The sentences in GoEmotions are already anonymized, where the names of people are replaced with a special `[NAME]` token, so we do not need to further perform anonymization. We filter out all sentences that have more than one `[NAME]` token and replace all `[NAME]` with a gender-neutral name "Jackie".

A.2 Dataset License

HEROS is constructed based on the GoEmotion dataset (Demszky et al., 2020). GoEmotion is released under the Apache 2.0 license, so our modification and redistribution to GoEmotion are granted by the dataset license. **Our dataset, HEROS is also released under the Apache 2.0 license.**

B Comparing the Lexical Overlaps of Different Datasets

In Table 1, we show the basic statistics of three different datasets. We use the ROUGE F1 and Levenshtein distance to quantify the lexical overlap between sentence pairs of a dataset. The statistics of HEROS is averaged over different subsets, and those of STS-b and SICK-R are calculated based on the test set.

R1, R2, and RL: ROUGE F1 score between the sentence pairs. (R1 and R2: unigram and bigram overlap; RL: longest common subsequence.) We use the implementation of python rouge 1.0.1 to calculate the ROUGE score.

Lev is the average normalized **token-level** Levenshtein distance among the sentence pairs, and the normalized Levenshtein distance is the Levenshtein distance between two sentences divided by the length of the longer sequence of the sentence pairs. We first tokenize the sentence using the tokenizer of `bert-base-uncased` and calculate the Levenshtein distance between the token ids of the sentence pairs. We normalize the Levenshtein distance to make it falls in the range of $[0, 1]$.

The average sentence length is the average number of tokens per sentence, and the tokens are obtained by using the tokenizer of `bert-base-uncased`.

C Supplementary Materials for Sentence Encoders

C.1 Supervised Sentence Encoders

Table 3 shows the number of parameters and the sentence embedding dimension of the SEs used in this paper.

C.1.1 Datasets Used to Train Supervised SEs

The datasets indicated in Figure 1 is listed as follows:

all Reddit comments (2015-2018) (Henderson et al., 2019), S2ORC Citation pairs (Abstracts) (Lo et al., 2020), WikiAnswers Duplicate question pairs (Fader et al., 2014), PAQ (Question, Answer) pairs (Lewis et al., 2021), S2ORC Citation pairs (Titles) (Lo et al., 2020), S2ORC (Title, Abstract) (Lo et al., 2020), Stack Exchange (Title, Body) pairs, MS MARCO triplets (Craswell et al., 2021), GOOAQ: Open Question Answering with Diverse Answer Types (Khashabi et al., 2021), Yahoo Answers (Title, Answer) (Zhang et al., 2015), Code Search, COCO Image captions (Lin et al., 2014), SPECTER citation triplets (Cohan et al., 2020), Yahoo Answers (Question, Answer) (Zhang et al., 2015), Yahoo Answers (Title, Question) (Zhang et al., 2015), SearchQA (Dunn et al., 2017), Eli5 (Fan et al., 2019), Flickr 30k (Young et al., 2014), Stack Exchange Duplicate questions (titles), SNLI (Bowman et al., 2015), MNLI (Williams et al., 2018), Stack Exchange Duplicate questions (bodies), Stack Exchange Duplicate questions (titles+bodies), Sentence Compression (Filippova and Altun, 2013), Wikihow (Koupaee and Wang, 2018), Altlex (Hidey and McKeown, 2016), Quora Question Triplets (Wang et al., 2019), Simple Wikipedia (Coster and Kauchak, 2011), Natural Questions (NQ) (Kwiatkowski et al., 2019), SQuAD2.0 (Rajpurkar et al., 2016), and TriviaQA.

QA All the QA datasets in ***all***.

paraphrase SNLI (Bowman et al., 2015), MNLI (Williams et al., 2018), Simple Wikipedia (Coster and Kauchak, 2011), Altlex (Hidey and McKeown, 2016), MS MARCO triplets (Craswell et al., 2021), Quora Question Triplets (Wang et al., 2019), COCO Image captions (Lin et al., 2014), Flickr 30k (Young et al., 2014), Yahoo Answers (Title, Question) (Zhang et al., 2015), Stack Exchange Duplicate questions (titles+bodies) and WikiAtomicEdits (Faruqui et al., 2018).

GTR fine-tuning data: QA+MRC Natural Questions (NQ) (Kwiatkowski et al., 2019), MS MARCO triplets (Craswell et al., 2021), input-response pairs and question-answer pairs from online forums and QA websites including Reddit, Stack-Overflow, etc.[6]

ST5 fine-tuning data: QA+NLI SNLI (Bowman et al., 2015) and question-answer pairs from community QA websites.

C.2 Unsupervised Sentence Encoders

The full list of unsupervised SEs and their supervised derivations we compared are: SimCSE (Gao et al., 2021), DiffCSE (Chuang et al., 2022), PromptBERT (Jiang et al., 2022), SNCSE (Wang et al., 2022), RankEncoder (Seonwoo et al., 2022), AudioCSE and VisualCSE (Jian et al., 2022). For all the unsupervised SEs shown in Figure 2, if it is a base-size model, its number of parameters is roughly 110M; if it is a large-size model, its number of parameters is roughly 335M. The `bert` models shown in Figure 2 are all `uncased` models.

D Normalization

For each SE, we first calculate the cosine similarity between each minimal pair in HEROS. However, if the embedding space is highly anisotropic (Ethayarajh, 2019; Li et al., 2020a), the cosine similarity between two random sentences is expected to be rather high. To remove the effect of anisotropic embedding space and better interpret the result, we normalize the cosine similarity by a baseline cosine similarity. The baseline cosine similarity is calculated by the following procedure: We split the 1000 original sentences into the first 500 and the last 500 sentences, and calculate the average cosine similarity between the sentence embeddings of these 500 × 500 random sentence pairs. This average cosine similarity, $\cos_{avg}$, gives us an idea of how similar sentence embedding can be for two randomly selected sentences. Last, we normalize the cosine similarity of the minimal pairs to lessen the effect of anisotropy by the following formula:

$$\cos_{normalized} = \frac{\cos_{orig} - \cos_{avg}}{1 - \cos_{avg}}, \quad (1)$$

where $\cos_{orig}$ is the original cosine similarity of a sentence pair and $\cos_{normalized}$ is the similarity after normalization.

E Runtime and Computation Resource

The experiments on Section 3, except T5 xl and xxl, are conducted on an NVIDIA 1080 Ti, and it takes less than one hour to run all the experiments. The T5 xxl and xl models cannot be loaded on a 1080 Ti, and we use V100 to conduct the experiment of the SEs whose base models are T5 xl and xxl, which takes less than 15 minutes.

[6]Ni et al. (2021) does not specify the exact online forums.

Model and Link	#Param	d_{emb}
Word embedding GloVe	120M	300
DistilBERT base (multi-QA)	66M	768
MiniLM L6 (multi-QA)	22M	384
mpnet base (multiQA)	110M	768
ALBERT small (paraphrase)	11M	768
DistilRoBERTA base v2 (paraphrase)	82M	768
MiniLM L12 v2 (paraphrase)	33M	384
MiniLM L3 v2 (paraphrase)	17M	384
MiniLM L6 v2 (paraphrase)	22M	384
mpnet base v2 (paraphrase)	110M	768
Multilingual MiniLM L12 v2 (paraphrase)	33M	384
Multilingual mpnet base v2 (paraphrase)	110M	768
TinyBERT L6 v2 (paraphrase)	14.5M	768
GTR base	110M	768
GTR large	335M	768
GTR xl	1,24B	768
GTR xxl	4.8B	768
Sentence-T5 base	110M	768
Sentence-T5 large	335M	768
Sentence-t5 xl	1,24B	768
Sentence-T5 xxl	4.8B	768
DistilRoBERTa v1 (all)	82M	768
MiniLM L12 v1 (all)	33M	384
MiniLM L12 v2 (all)	33M	384
MiniLM L6 v1 (all)	22M	384
MiniLM L6 v2 (all)	22M	384
mpnet base v1 (all)	110M	768
mpnet base v2 (all)	110M	768
RoBERTa large v1 (all)	355M	1024
DistilUSE base multilingual v1 (all)	134M	512
DistilUSE base multilingual v2 (all)	134M	512

Table 3: The model sizes and embedding dimensions of the supervised SEs shown in Figure 1. The model names are clickable links. # is the number of parameters of the SE, and d_{emb} is the dimension of the sentence embedding.

One-Shot Exemplification Modeling via Latent Sense Representations

John Harvill[1], **Hee Suk Yoon**[2], **Eunseop Yoon**[2], **Mark Hasegawa-Johnson**[1], **Chang D. Yoo**[2]
[1]University of Illinois Urbana-Champaign,
[2]Korea Advanced Institute of Science and Technology,
{harvill2, jhasegaw}@illinois.edu, {hskyoon, esyoon97, cd_yoo}@kaist.ac.kr

Abstract

Exemplification modeling is a recently proposed task that aims to produce a viable sentence using a target word that takes on a specific meaning. This task can be particularly challenging for polysemous words since they can have multiple meanings. In this paper, we propose a one-shot variant of the exemplification modeling task such that labeled data is not needed during training, making it possible to train our system using a raw text corpus. Given one example at test time, our proposed approach can generate diverse and fluent examples where the target word accurately matches its intended meaning. We compare our approach to a fully-supervised baseline trained with different amounts of data and focus our evaluation on polysemous words. We use both automatic and human evaluations to demonstrate how each model performs on both seen and unseen words. Our proposed approach performs similarly to the fully-supervised baseline despite not using labeled data during training.

1 Introduction

Many vocabulary words can represent different meanings depending on the contexts in which they are placed. This inherent semantic ambiguity has led to two types of NLP tasks: **1**) Determining the correct meaning (sense) of a word in context and **2**) Generating a sentence where a target word takes on a desired meaning. Word Sense Disambiguation (WSD) and Definition Modeling (DM) are both tasks in the first category. WSD is a classification task where the correct sense must be chosen for a word in context from a predefined sense inventory (Navigli, 2009; Barba et al., 2021c,a; Raganato et al., 2017), and DM is a related task where the goal is to produce a string representing the definition for a word in context (Bevilacqua et al., 2020). Exemplification modeling (EM), recently proposed by Barba et al. (2021b), falls under the second category. EM can be seen as the reverse problem of DM where the desired inputs and outputs are inverted. Given a target word, DM seeks to produce a definition given the sentence, while EM seeks to produce a sentence given the desired definition. EM is useful for generating example sentences for specific word senses when constructing dictionaries (He and Yiu, 2022) and data augmentation for training a WSD system (Barba et al., 2021b).

The two prominent works on EM thus far are ExMaker (Barba et al., 2021b), where the task is first introduced, and Controllable Dictionary Example Generation (CDEG) (He and Yiu, 2022), where generated example sentences are controlled in terms of length and lexical complexity. Both methods require a corpus consisting of (lemma, definition, example sentence) tuples where each example sentence uses the target lemma with the given definition. An autoregressive neural model is trained via minimization of the cross-entropy loss such that inputting the lemma and definition encourages the production of the corresponding example sentence. We corroborate the finding from He and Yiu (2022) that the performance of these supervised approaches depends on the amount of training data available, where the full dataset (Oxford Dictionary) contains 1.3M examples. Collecting such a large dataset can be difficult and may not be feasible for other languages. This difficulty is the main motivation for the approach we propose in this paper. We demonstrate that it is possible to perform exemplification modeling in a one-shot setting, where (lemma, definition, example sentence) tuples are no longer necessary for training. Only a raw, unlabeled text corpus is required.

In this paper, we make the following contributions: **1**) Propose a one-shot format for EM where one example sentence using the target word correctly is provided at inference time, instead of giving the target word and its definition. **2**) Propose a neural architecture that can accurately perform our one-shot format of EM without requiring la-

Proceedings of the 8th Workshop on Representation Learning for NLP (RepL4NLP 2023), pages 303–314
July 13, 2023

beled data for training. **3**) Evaluate our proposed approach in terms of target word semantic match, sentence diversity, and sentence fluency against a variety of baseline settings that provide deeper insight into the strengths and limitations of both methods. **4**) Provide extensive examples of generated data from our proposed approach that demonstrate its ability to create fluent sentences using the target word with its intended meaning. **5**) Provide a qualitative analysis of how reference example sentence length affects generation length and example diversity.

2 Related Work

Constrained Text Generation. EM falls under constrained text generation, where generated text must satisfy a given set of requirements. There already exists a multitude of constrained text generation tasks, including sentiment transfer (Luo et al., 2019), style transfer (Fu et al., 2018), lexically-constrained decoding (Dinu et al., 2019; Lin et al., 2020; Lu et al., 2022), word ordering (Zhang and Clark, 2015), storytelling (Fan et al., 2018; Yao et al., 2019), essay generation (Yang et al., 2019), paraphrasing (Zhou and Bhat, 2021), and definition modeling (Bevilacqua et al., 2020). These approaches vary in whether finetuning is necessary or decoding is constrained in some way. Approaches involving finetuning require training datasets but are faster at inference time. In contrast, constrained decoding can be applied to a pre-trained model but requires much more computational power during generation. Our proposed work falls under the first category; we require a training dataset of raw text but do not interfere with the decoding process (i.e. nucleus sampling).

Definition Modeling. EM is most similar to DM, since the input of one task is the output of the other. Generationary (Bevilacqua et al., 2020) is a recent DM approach that learns to create definitions for an arbitrary text span within a sentence. Similar to ExMaker (Barba et al., 2021b), it uses a neural encoder-decoder architecture. During training, Generationary takes as input a sentence where the target word or phrase has been enclosed in the `<define>` token and is encouraged to generate the gold definition via the cross-entropy loss. At inference time, Generationary can produce a high-quality contextual definition of an arbitrary text span, generalizing to words or phrases not seen during training.

3 One-Shot Sentence Generation

Exemplification Modeling (EM) was first proposed by Barba et al. (2021b). The goal of EM is to produce a sentence containing a target word, where the word represents a specific meaning. The proposed system, ExMaker (Barba et al., 2021b), uses as input a (lemma, definition) pair. A proper input/output example is given below:

Input	Output
contract: be stricken by an illness	He might contract pneumonia.

Training of ExMaker (Barba et al., 2021b) requires paired data where the sense of the target word is known in the example sentence. Such paired data is not abundant and can be difficult to collect. We propose a one-shot variant of EM that allows us to train a system without paired data in both a self-supervised and semi-supervised fashion, requiring only one reference example at inference time. Instead of using a (lemma, definition) pair as input, we use as input an example sentence where the target word has a desired meaning. We then produce a new sentence where the target word has the same meaning. An example is given below:

Input	Output
contract: The athlete signed the contract.	They agreed to the terms of the contract.

As we will show in the following section, this form of EM has the advantage that it does not require sense inventories for training nor generation.

Training. We can use a neural autoencoder to solve our proposed format of EM. Given a sentence, we want to reconstruct it by conditioning on a latent vector representation of the target word meaning extracted from the sentence itself. We denote these vectors as Latent Sense Representations (LSR) and call our overall approach Sense2Sentence (S2S). We denote the LSR as l, the target word as w, and the sentence as s. During training, we select w uniformly from a word-level tokenization of s and maximize the following:

$$p(s|l, w) = \prod_{i=2}^{|s|} p(s_i|s_{1:i-1}, l, w) \quad (1)$$

We model the conditional distribution in Equation 1 by finetuning a pretrained BART (Lewis et al., 2020) model. The representation of w is extracted

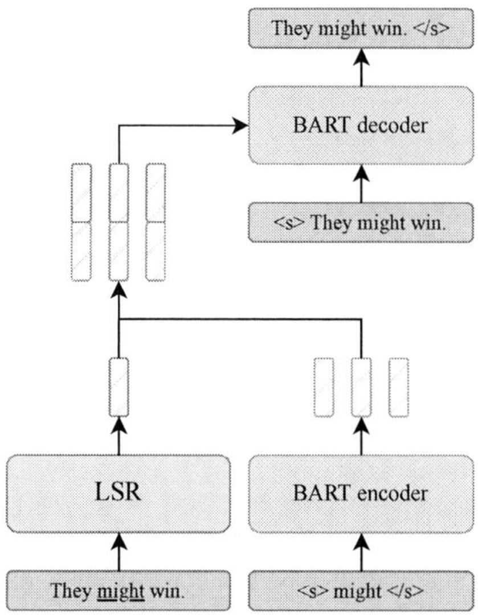

Figure 1: Training approach for S2S. LSR is kept frozen and produces a single fixed-length embedding of the target word sense that is concatenated to all timesteps of the BART encoder output.

from the BART encoder by passing the target word in isolation. The vector l is then concatenated to all timesteps of the BART encoder output. This joint representation is then passed to the BART decoder as conditioning input (see Figure 1). We use cross-entropy loss with teacher-forcing to train the model on BookCorpus (Zhu et al., 2015), an unlabeled dataset of English sentences taken from novels.

Latent Sense Representations. The choice of LSR is critical to the success of the S2S approach. We propose two techniques: **1**) contextual word embedding of target word w and **2**) sentence embedding of s. The contextual word embedding uses a local context to represent target sense information, whereas the sentence embedding uses the entire sentence as context (see Figure 2).

1. Contextual Word Embedding. Pretrained language models have been shown to create high-quality contextual representations of words (Vulić et al., 2020b), which are extracted by averaging the embeddings of the target word tokens at the output of the model. We initially experimented with this approach for computing l using pretrained BERT (Devlin et al., 2019) as the language model. Due to the BERT pretraining objective, we found empirically that the contextual word embedding contains too much information about its surrounding context such that prediction of the next token in the training sentence becomes trivial. The model does not learn

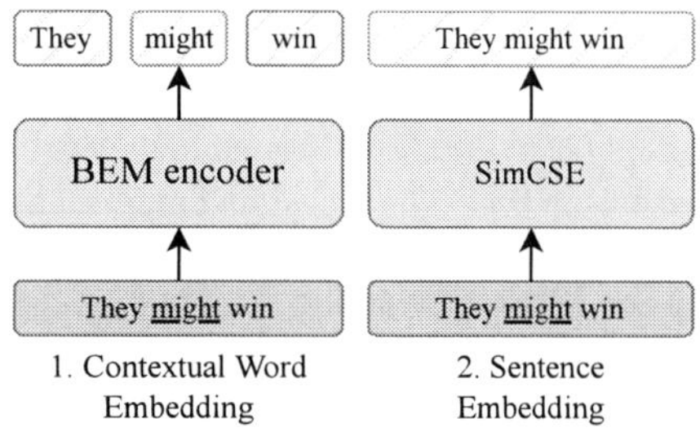

Figure 2: Depiction of both proposed types of LSR. Orange blocks represent the LSR for each method.

the intended task, because generated sentences are almost identical copies of the input. To restrict the information in l only to that of the intended target meaning of w, we use the contextual encoder of a pretrained Bi-Encoder Model (BEM) (Blevins and Zettlemoyer, 2020). BEM is a BERT model fine-tuned on Word Sense Disambiguation (WSD) and thus tries to encode a representation of the contextual meaning of each word in a given sentence. We find empirically that conditioning on this representation produces a training loss that plateaus slightly beneath that of the same model trained without any conditional input, indicating that little information about the surrounding context leaks through and the embedding contains mostly word sense information. To produce the LSR during training, we extract the contextual embedding of w when passing s through BEM. Note that this approach is semi-supervised, because it requires WSD training data[1] during pretraining of BEM. For this reason, we denote our approach using contextual word embeddings for the LSR as S2S_{semi}.

2. Sentence Embedding. We want to explore a fully self-supervised solution to our one-shot format of EM. Since word senses often appear in specific contexts, a semantic representation of the input sentence can be useful for determining the target sense for w in the generated sentence. To encode the sentence-level semantics into a vector that serves as the LSR, we use the unsupervised variant of SimCSE (Gao et al., 2021) to embed s. Since neither our training approach nor the pretraining process of SimCSE or BART require any labeled data, we denote this approach as S2S_{self}.

Generating Examples. To generate a new example sentence with a specific word sense, we provide

[1] The pretrained BEM we use for our experiments is taken from the original paper (Blevins and Zettlemoyer, 2020) and was pretrained using SemCor (Miller et al., 1993), one of the datasets used for training a baseline EM model in this paper.

one source sentence s containing the target word w with the desired sense to our system. The LSR is extracted from s, and w is passed to the BART encoder in isolation. The embedded representations are then concatenated and passed to the BART decoder, where we decode using nucleus sampling (Holtzman et al., 2019), setting $p = 0.5$.

4 Baseline

We reimplement ExMaker (Barba et al., 2021b) ourselves and train it to produce example sentences using one (lemma, definition) pair as input. For comparison to a sense-agnostic system, we additionally train a vanilla version of ExMaker where the input definition is replaced with the empty string. Validation is performed using the same approach proposed in ExMaker (Barba et al., 2021b). The final model chosen is the one that produces target words that match their intended meaning best according to ExMaker's automatic semantic match validation method (see Section 7 for details). For both ExMaker and S2S, we finetune the same pretrained BART[2] model (Lewis et al., 2020).

5 Data

Given that S2S requires no labeled EM data for training, but rather raw text only, we compare to the baseline in settings where evaluation words are either included or held out from training. For the "seen" baseline setting, all validation and test words are included in the training data. For the "unseen" baseline setting, all validation and test words are excluded. We discuss construction of the validation and test word sets in the following sections.

Training. We use the Huggingface version of BookCorpus[3] (Zhu et al., 2015) to train S2S, which consists of 74M sentences. We use SemCor (Miller et al., 1993) and Oxford Dictionary[4] to train ExMaker. SemCor is much smaller than Oxford Dictionary, containing only 33k unique sentences and 200k labeled instances; Oxford Dictionary contains 1.3M examples.

[2]`https://huggingface.co/facebook/bart-base`

[3]`https://huggingface.co/datasets/bookcorpus` - This version of BookCorpus is uncased, which is critical to the success of S2S. When training with cased data, target polysemous words in generated sentences often do not match their intended meaning well. Cased examples in this paper have been truecased using the NLTK and StanfordNLP toolkits.

[4]We use the dataset prepared by He and Yiu (2022), available at `https://github.com/NLPCode/CDEG`.

Validation. We use the automatic target word semantic match validation scheme (see Section 7) from ExMaker (Barba et al., 2021b) and thus need to generate text using each saved model checkpoint for a small set of validation words. We randomly choose 100 polysemous words disjoint from our test set for validation and evaluate on all word senses for each validation word.

Test Set. EM is most difficult for words that take on two or more meanings. For this reason, we choose to evaluate words that are known to have more than one distinct meaning, i.e. homographs. For a set of ground truth homographs, we use the Wikipedia Homograph Dataset (Gorman et al., 2018) and choose only those homographs that have the "Lexical" homograph type label. We evaluate only on those word senses that appear in SemCor such that S2S and ExMaker are evaluated on the same set of word senses. This gives us a total of 78 unique words with 334 total senses for our automatic evaluations. We use a manually-curated subset of these words for human evaluations (see Section 8).

6 Experimental Setup

Training and Validation Hyperparameters. We train all S2S and ExMaker models for 500k steps. For S2S, we train with a batch size of 64 and use the 500k model checkpoint ($\sim$one half epoch for BookCorpus). For ExMaker, we train with a batch size of 32 and validate models every 25k steps when training with Oxford Dictionary and every 10k steps when training with SemCor. These baseline hyperparameters were chosen to balance the risk of overfitting (especially with SemCor) and computation time for the validation process. Final baseline models are chosen based on the best validation score. See Appendix A for further details.

Generation. For ExMaker, we provide each (lemma, definition) pair for each word sense in our test set and generate 50 examples per pair. For S2S, we choose one SemCor example sentence per test word sense from which we generate 50 new examples for that word sense (one-shot evaluation).[5]

[5]For a fair evaluation of S2S, we want the single input example sentence for a given word sense to be of reasonable quality. We found empirically that short input sentences tend to produce less diverse examples (see Section 10), so we first sort example sentences for a given word sense by length. Then, if there is at least one example sentence with length in the range of 70-180 characters, we randomly choose one sentence from the example sentences satisfying that requirement. Otherwise, we randomly choose the example input sentence from whatever is available.

	Training Data	Diversity SB4↓	B4↓	Sem. Match SM↑	SM_H ↑	Fluency F_H ↑
$S2S_{semi}$	BookCorpus	0.62	0.51	0.44	8.41	8.06
$S2S_{self}$	BookCorpus	0.70	0.57	0.39	6.49	7.15
ExMaker (unseen)	SemCor	0.62	0.41	0.32	-	-
ExMaker (seen)	SemCor	0.91	0.89	**0.52**	-	-
ExMaker (unseen)	Oxford Dict.	0.52	0.41	0.35	**8.67**	**8.70**
ExMaker (seen)	Oxford Dict.	0.52	0.40	0.36	-	-
$ExMaker_V$ (unseen)	Oxford Dict.	**0.48**	0.40	0.26	-	-
$ExMaker_V$ (seen)	Oxford Dict.	**0.48**	**0.39**	0.27	-	-
Gold (SemCor)	NA	0.51	1.00	0.52	9.59	8.74

Table 1: Automatic and human evaluation of semantic match, diversity, and fluency of generated sentences. Columns with missing values are human evaluations (we evaluated on the most interesting subset of approaches (based on automatic evaluations) to make the workload reasonable for our volunteer annotators). Abbreviations are as follows: $ExMaker_V$: ExMaker vanilla (no conditioning on definition), SB4: Self-BLEU-4, B4: BLEU-4, SM: Sense Match, SM_H: Semantic Match (human), F_H: Fluency (human). Human evaluation values are the mean of scores on a scale from 0-10 where results are statistically significant at $p < 0.05$ between all shown methods except gold/ExMaker for F_H and ExMaker/$S2S_{semi}$ for SM_H. Best score is bolded and worst score is underlined (excluding gold data).

Evaluations. We perform both automatic and human evaluations of text generation quality. For automatic analysis, we examine the target word semantic match and the diversity of generated sentences. For human evaluations, we examine overall fluency and target word semantic match.

7 Automatic Evaluations

Semantic Match. We use one automatic analysis technique to evaluate target word semantic match quality, which we call Sense Match (SM). This technique is identical to the ExMaker validation method (Barba et al., 2021b). Explicitly, we extract the contextual embedding of the target word from a pretrained BERT-large[6] model and compute cosine similarity with respect to its word sense embedding from ARES (Scarlini et al., 2020). ARES uses the same BERT-large model when extracting word sense embeddings, so both the target word contextual embeddings and sense embeddings are directly comparable.

Diversity. We want to explore how diverse the generated sentences are across two dimensions: **1)** similarity to other generated sentences, and **2)** similarity to SemCor data.[7] To analyze the diversity of generated sentences from themselves, we use Self-BLEU (Zhu et al., 2018). To analyze the diversity of generated sentences with respect to gold data (SemCor), we compute the BLEU score (Papineni et al., 2002) using generated sentences as hypotheses and SemCor sentences as references. Note that unlike in machine translation, we want BLEU scores (including Self-BLEU) to be as low as possible because we want diverse outputs.

Self-BLEU. For each word sense, we compute the Self-BLEU (Zhu et al., 2018) score using only sentences generated for that particular word sense. For a fair comparison to the gold Self-BLEU score, we limit the number of generated sentences per word sense to the number of SemCor examples for each given sense. The overall Self-BLEU score for a given model is the mean of all word sense Self-BLEU scores.

BLEU. We use this metric to gauge how much the generated sentences are partial copies of SemCor data. For each word sense, we compute the average BLEU score between the generated sentences for that word sense and the SemCor sentences containing that word sense (each generated sentence is a hypothesis and the SemCor sentences are the references). The overall score is the mean of the BLEU scores for each word sense.

8 Human Evaluations

We want to compare the quality of generated sentences from S2S and ExMaker, and gold sentences from SemCor. To evaluate the quality as judged by humans, we recruit five volunteer native-speaker annotators (see Appendix B) to judge both the fluency and target word semantic match of the example sentences. We ask annotators to assign each example sentence a score from zero to ten for each evaluation criterion where ten is the best score.

Dataset Construction. For human evaluations,

[6] `https://huggingface.co/bert-large-cased`

[7] SemCor is used as training data for ExMaker and as conditioning input for S2S, so it is important to check how different the generated sentences are from those already in SemCor.

Word Sense Information	Generated Sentences
Word: object **Definition**: A tangible and visible entity; an entity that can cast a shadow **Input**: Science is fully competent to deal with any element of experience which arises from an object in space and time.	1. But we can only think of such things as being in any dimension in relation to an object in a higher plane. 2. They could see things that no other person could, as if they were connected to an object in space. 3. We are given the most complete understanding of the existence of space and time by an object in a hologram.
Word: object **Definition**: Express or raise an objection or protest or criticism or express dissent **Input**: Most of these former churches are now used as warehouses, but "neither Anglicans nor nonconformists object to selling churches to Roman Catholics", and have done so.	1. "I have no interest in making a whole town, and none of my parents or any of my grandparents object to creating a new town, but we have no business doing that." 2. "I've worked in the mines for over a year, but no members of the nile nor of the mayan or christian nation object to using the power of the indian sea."
Word: contract **Definition**: A binding agreement between two or more persons that is enforceable by law **Input**: Enter into contracts with educational institutions, scientific organizations, and industrial and engineering firms;	1. They have joint contracts with firms in various departments of government and the defense industry. 2. You have formal contracts with academic and business organizations? 3. You have joint contracts with scientists, directors, managers, scientists, and teachers.
Word: contract **Definition**: Become smaller or draw together **Input**: Dr. Bonnor supports the idea that the universe both expands and contracts, that in several billion years the expansion will slow up and reverse itself and that the contraction will set in.	1. And then, when the universe has become so vast that it contracts, the universe will be able to pick up the energy in a way that isn't so obvious to the eye. 2. We are one hundred percent sure that the cosmos is larger and contracts, but the universe is still the same, and the theory is that the core is not.

Table 2: Examples of generated sentences using S2S_{semi} for distinct senses of the words "object" and "contract."

we use a subset of word senses from our test set. This subset is chosen by hand such that senses are noticeably distinct in meaning for a given word, resulting in a set of 40 word senses.[8] For each model, we generate one sentence per word sense. Each of our five annotators rates the fluency and target word semantic match of every sentence, giving us a total of 200 annotations per evaluation criterion per model.

Fluency and Semantic Match. We ask annotators to rate the fluency of each sentence, i.e. how well it adheres to proper grammar rules on a scale from zero to ten. For the semantic match judgment, we provide annotators with an example sentence, target word, and target definition. We then ask annotators to rate how well the contextual meaning of the target word in the example sentence matches the target definition on a scale from zero to ten.

Inter-Annotator Agreement. We use the Average Mean Inter-Annotator Agreement (AMIAA) metric (Vulić et al., 2020a) to judge how well annotators agree. AMIAA is written explicitly as:

$$\text{AMIAA} = \frac{\sum_i \rho(s_i, \mu_i)}{K}, \text{ where } \mu_{i,n} = \frac{\sum_{j \neq i} s_{j,n}}{K-1} \tag{2}$$

[8] https://github.com/jharvill23/LatentSenseRepresentationsEM

K is the number of annotators and $\rho(s_i, \mu_i)$ is the Spearman's rank correlation between the scores for annotator i and the mean scores from all other annotators. The mean score $\mu_{i,n}$ for each datapoint n is the average of each annotator's score $s_{j,n}$ when leaving out annotator i. For our human evaluations, the AMIAA for fluency and semantic match are 0.55 and 0.56, respectively, indicating moderate agreement.

9 Results

The results for automatic and human evaluations are in Table 1. We discuss the key takeaways below.

Baseline overfits on SemCor. All three automatic evaluation metrics (Self-BLEU, BLEU, Sense Match) indicate that the baseline severely overfits under the seen setting when trained with SemCor, generating only slight modifications of the sentences it was trained on. This results in an unrealistically good Sense Match score and unrealistically poor Self-BLEU and BLEU scores.

Baseline improves with more data. There is noticeable improvement in both Sense Match and Self-BLEU scores for the unseen setting when training with Oxford Dictionary compared to training with SemCor. Also, the baseline seems to generalize better with more data and not suffer from overfitting when training with Oxford Dictionary,

Word: project	Definition: A planned undertaking
	Input: They worked on the group project together.
Generated:	1. During the creative project, we worked together.
	2. We spent the day working on the group project.
	Input: It had been months since the two engineers started working on the project together, but unfortunately they had not made much progress.
Generated:	1. The crew was busy working on the preliminary design of the project in the back of the rover.
	2. I hadn't really paid much attention to the project in the past couple of years, so I had no idea how much effort it took to construct the model.
Word: project	**Definition**: Cause to be heard
	Input: The singer knew how to project her voice.
Generated:	1. I was able to manage to project my voice.
	2. She was the perfect person to project her voice.
	Input: The crowd was too large, and he knew if he was going to get help he would need to project his voice all the way up to security personnel at the front of the stage.
Generated:	1. The new bartender in the bar wasn't about to back down, but he was going to project his voice out to the crowd in a way that would get people to listen.
	2. We were just going to talk about the police and how they'd come in, but I was ready to project my voice out of the audience and into the crowd.

Table 3: Comparison of generated sentences using input sentences with different lengths for $S2S_{semi}$.

because the seen setting shows only the slightest improvement over the unseen setting in this case.

Semi-supervised approach performs similarly to baseline. $S2S_{semi}$ demonstrates impressive performance across all automatic and human evaluations, coming close to the baseline for some metrics and surpassing it for others. $S2S_{semi}$ only slightly underperforms the baseline for diversity and fluency metrics, while surpassing the baseline (not including overfit seen setting) for the automatic Sense Match evaluation and performing the same[9] as the baseline for the human semantic match evaluation.

Self-supervised approach underperforms semi-supervised approach. As expected, we see a reduction in performance across all metrics for $S2S_{self}$ compared to $S2S_{semi}$. The differences are relatively small for the automatic evaluations, but are more noticeable for the human evaluations. We see the largest relative drop in performance for the human evaluation of semantic match, indicating that $S2S_{self}$ frequently produces incorrect or vague meanings of target words in its generated sentences. This demonstrates that sentence-level semantics can often indicate the meaning of a target word but that representations of the immediate context are more reliable for one-shot EM.

10 Generation Examples

We provide example sentences generated using our best[10] proposed approach, $S2S_{semi}$, in Tables 2 and 3. Table 2 shows generated examples for two distinct senses each for the words "object" and "contract." Table 3 shows generated examples for two distinct senses of the word "project" using a short and long sentence as input. While the generated examples are fluent, diverse, and use the target word with its intended definition, there are several notable qualitative properties that we hypothesize are a result of information leakage in the contextual word embedding LSR. It appears that some information related to the input sentence's vocabulary, syntax and length is encoded in the LSR, in addition to the desired target word sense information.

Vocabulary, Topical and Syntactical Overlap. There is noticeable overlap between vocabulary and topics between input and output sentences. For example, all three generated sentences for the first sense of "object" in Table 2 revolve around themes present in the input like "science" and "outer space." This is evident through the use of words or phrases like "dimension," "higher plane," "space," and "hologram" that appear in the output. Beyond simple topical or vocabulary overlap, we see longer stretches of identical text with the presence of the 3-gram "space and time" in both the input and the third generated sentence. We also find syntactical overlap between input and output sentences. For example, the third generated sentence for the first sense of "contract" in Table 2 lists entities with which a contract may be held just as the input sentence does.

Dependence on Input Length. The examples in

[9]Difference between $S2S_{semi}$ and ExMaker is not statistically significant for SM_H, see Table 1.

[10]See Appendix C for examples generated by $S2S_{self}$.

Table 3 demonstrate that the length of each generated sentence is similar to that of its respective input sentence. Further, we see that the relative location of the target word in the generated sentence is similar to that in the input sentence, indicating that input sentence length and target word location information is encoded in the LSR.

Increased Diversity with Input Length. When comparing the outputs generated by short and long sentences in Table 3, we see that longer input sentences produce more diverse outputs. This makes sense given the previous observation about the output's dependence on input length, because there are more possible outputs that satisfy the EM constraints when the output is encouraged to be longer. This property is why we choose to use input sentences of length 70-180 characters, when available, for our one-shot evaluations (see Section 6).

11 Future Work

There are several avenues of future work including potential improvements to our proposed one-shot EM approach as well as applications of our technique to downstream tasks.

Self-Supervised Disentanglement of Sense Information. While we demonstrate that it is possible to perform EM in a self-supervised fashion by using sentence embeddings as the LSR, the quality is much lower than the semi-supervised approach that uses the contextual word embedding extracted from the BEM (Blevins and Zettlemoyer, 2020). We believe future research efforts should strive to create disentangled sense representations in a self-supervised fashion that are of similar quality to that of the BEM, instead of relying on WSD training data. One possible approach is to use product quantization as is done in Wav2Vec2.0 (Baevski et al., 2020) on top of the contextual word embedding output by a pretrained BERT model (Devlin et al., 2019). By mapping the continuous representation output by BERT to a set of discrete codebook vectors, it may be possible to create representations that resemble synsets and thus disentangle contextual information unrelated to the target word sense.

Optimizing One-Shot EM for Downstream Tasks via Filtering. Our proposed one-shot approach to EM slightly underperforms the baseline, but only in a statistical sense. We are still able to generate high-quality examples, and generation is fast and computationally cheap. Thus, a dedicated filtering scheme that picks out good examples may prove useful when applying our approach to downstream tasks like data augmentation for WSD or automatic dictionary construction in low-resource languages.

Improving Diversity via Feedback Loop. The generated examples in Tables 2 and 3 demonstrate topical overlap with their respective inputs while still being unique sentences. It may be possible to create more diverse examples starting from one input sentence by feeding the outputs back in as input in a feedback loop. It is likely that target word meaning would drift from its desired definition, but such a tradeoff could be explored in future work.

12 Conclusions

In this paper, we proposed a variant of Exemplification Modeling (EM) that uses an example sentence as input instead of the lemma and target definition. We demonstrated empirically that this format of EM can be performed in a one-shot setting, requiring no labeled data for training. Our approach, S2S, uses a Latent Sense Representation (LSR) as a conditional variable that encourages the generated sentence to use the target word with the intended definition. We proposed two types of LSR and performed extensive evaluation of fluency, diversity, and semantic match in the generated sentences. Additionally, we performed a thorough qualitative analysis that highlights properties such as topical and vocabulary overlap that appear in sentences generated by S2S.

This work is the first paper to analyze the ability of a system to perform EM by conditioning on a latent variable derived from contextual use of the target word instead of a string indicating its definition. While both proposed LSRs have drawbacks, the contextual word embedding LSR leads to impressive results and inspires future improvement. Optimization of the LSR to encode only word sense information in a self-supervised way could lead to improved performance while requiring no labeled data at any point in the LSR pretraining or S2S training process. Given the ability of S2S models to be trained with only raw text, it may be possible to improve performance beyond that of the fully-supervised baseline for a larger set of word senses than those in Oxford Dictionary when conditioning on an LSR that completely disentangles word sense information in a self-supervised fashion.

13 Limitations

Our initial work on one-shot EM shows promising results but comes with several limitations. By inspecting generated examples, we find evidence of information leakage in the LSR that causes generated sentences to be similar in topic and length to the input sentence. We also require one example at inference time in order to generate a new example for a specific word sense. We demonstrated empirically that the baseline does not have this restriction, because the baseline method generalizes well to words that were unseen during training (see Table 1). Additionally, our best approach, $S2S_{semi}$, still requires WSD training data for pretraining of the BEM, which is used for LSR extraction. Finally, the S2S models in this paper have the limitation that the target word looks identical in both the input and output sentence, whereas the baseline is capable of generating examples with various target word forms for a given target lemma. This could be fixed in the future by lemmatizing the target word before passing it to the S2S BART encoder during training and generation, but we did not run this experiment due to our initial focus on using as little supervision as possible to perform EM.

14 Ethics Statement

In this paper, we have focused on exemplification modeling using data (SemCor, Oxford Dictionary, BookCorpus) and models (BART) that may contain biases related to attributes like gender, race, or disability. It is possible that these biases surface in sentences generated using the techniques proposed in this paper (Nadeem et al., 2021; Liang et al., 2021), because we do not actively focus our efforts on the removal of such biases. For this reason, sentences generated by our proposed models or the baseline should be used with caution in order to prevent perpetuation of harmful stereotypes.

References

Alexei Baevski, Yuhao Zhou, Abdelrahman Mohamed, and Michael Auli. 2020. wav2vec 2.0: A framework for self-supervised learning of speech representations. *Advances in Neural Information Processing Systems*, 33:12449–12460.

Edoardo Barba, Tommaso Pasini, and Roberto Navigli. 2021a. Esc: Redesigning wsd with extractive sense comprehension. In *Proceedings of the 2021 Conference of the North American Chapter of the Association for Computational Linguistics: Human Language Technologies*, pages 4661–4672.

Edoardo Barba, Luigi Procopio, Caterina Lacerra, Tommaso Pasini, and Roberto Navigli. 2021b. Exemplification modeling: Can you give me an example, please? In *IJCAI*, pages 3779–3785.

Edoardo Barba, Luigi Procopio, and Roberto Navigli. 2021c. Consec: Word sense disambiguation as continuous sense comprehension. In *Proceedings of the 2021 Conference on Empirical Methods in Natural Language Processing*, pages 1492–1503.

Michele Bevilacqua, Marco Maru, and Roberto Navigli. 2020. Generationary or "how we went beyond word sense inventories and learned to gloss". In *Proceedings of the 2020 Conference on Empirical Methods in Natural Language Processing (EMNLP)*, pages 7207–7221, Online. Association for Computational Linguistics.

Terra Blevins and Luke Zettlemoyer. 2020. Moving down the long tail of word sense disambiguation with gloss informed bi-encoders. In *Proceedings of the 58th Annual Meeting of the Association for Computational Linguistics*, pages 1006–1017, Online. Association for Computational Linguistics.

Jacob Devlin, Ming-Wei Chang, Kenton Lee, and Kristina Toutanova. 2019. BERT: Pre-training of deep bidirectional transformers for language understanding. In *Proceedings of the 2019 Conference of the North American Chapter of the Association for Computational Linguistics: Human Language Technologies, Volume 1 (Long and Short Papers)*, pages 4171–4186, Minneapolis, Minnesota. Association for Computational Linguistics.

Georgiana Dinu, Prashant Mathur, Marcello Federico, and Yaser Al-Onaizan. 2019. Training neural machine translation to apply terminology constraints. In *Proceedings of the 57th Annual Meeting of the Association for Computational Linguistics*, pages 3063–3068, Florence, Italy. Association for Computational Linguistics.

Angela Fan, Mike Lewis, and Yann Dauphin. 2018. Hierarchical neural story generation. In *Proceedings of the 56th Annual Meeting of the Association for Computational Linguistics (Volume 1: Long Papers)*, pages 889–898, Melbourne, Australia. Association for Computational Linguistics.

Zhenxin Fu, Xiaoye Tan, Nanyun Peng, Dongyan Zhao, and Rui Yan. 2018. Style transfer in text: Exploration and evaluation. In *Proceedings of the AAAI Conference on Artificial Intelligence*, volume 32.

Tianyu Gao, Xingcheng Yao, and Danqi Chen. 2021. SimCSE: Simple contrastive learning of sentence embeddings. In *Proceedings of the 2021 Conference on Empirical Methods in Natural Language Processing*, pages 6894–6910, Online and Punta Cana, Dominican Republic. Association for Computational Linguistics.

Kyle Gorman, Gleb Mazovetskiy, and Vitaly Nikolaev. 2018. Improving homograph disambiguation with supervised machine learning. In *Proceedings of the Eleventh International Conference on Language Resources and Evaluation (LREC 2018)*, Miyazaki, Japan. European Language Resources Association (ELRA).

Xingwei He and Siu Ming Yiu. 2022. Controllable dictionary example generation: Generating example sentences for specific targeted audiences. In *Proceedings of the 60th Annual Meeting of the Association for Computational Linguistics (Volume 1: Long Papers)*, pages 610–627.

Ari Holtzman, Jan Buys, Li Du, Maxwell Forbes, and Yejin Choi. 2019. The curious case of neural text degeneration. *arXiv e-prints*, pages arXiv–1904.

Mike Lewis, Yinhan Liu, Naman Goyal, Marjan Ghazvininejad, Abdelrahman Mohamed, Omer Levy, Veselin Stoyanov, and Luke Zettlemoyer. 2020. BART: Denoising sequence-to-sequence pre-training for natural language generation, translation, and comprehension. In *Proceedings of the 58th Annual Meeting of the Association for Computational Linguistics*, pages 7871–7880, Online. Association for Computational Linguistics.

Paul Pu Liang, Chiyu Wu, Louis-Philippe Morency, and Ruslan Salakhutdinov. 2021. Towards understanding and mitigating social biases in language models. In *International Conference on Machine Learning*, pages 6565–6576. PMLR.

Bill Yuchen Lin, Wangchunshu Zhou, Ming Shen, Pei Zhou, Chandra Bhagavatula, Yejin Choi, and Xiang Ren. 2020. CommonGen: A constrained text generation challenge for generative commonsense reasoning. In *Findings of the Association for Computational Linguistics: EMNLP 2020*, pages 1823–1840, Online. Association for Computational Linguistics.

Ximing Lu, Sean Welleck, Peter West, Liwei Jiang, Jungo Kasai, Daniel Khashabi, Ronan Le Bras, Lianhui Qin, Youngjae Yu, Rowan Zellers, Noah A. Smith, and Yejin Choi. 2022. NeuroLogic a*esque decoding: Constrained text generation with lookahead heuristics. In *Proceedings of the 2022 Conference of the North American Chapter of the Association for Computational Linguistics: Human Language Technologies*, pages 780–799, Seattle, United States. Association for Computational Linguistics.

Fuli Luo, Peng Li, Pengcheng Yang, Jie Zhou, Yutong Tan, Baobao Chang, Zhifang Sui, and Xu Sun. 2019. Towards fine-grained text sentiment transfer. In *Proceedings of the 57th Annual Meeting of the Association for Computational Linguistics*, pages 2013–2022.

George A. Miller, Claudia Leacock, Randee Tengi, and Ross T. Bunker. 1993. A semantic concordance. In *Human Language Technology: Proceedings of a Workshop Held at Plainsboro, New Jersey, March 21-24, 1993.*

Moin Nadeem, Anna Bethke, and Siva Reddy. 2021. StereoSet: Measuring stereotypical bias in pretrained language models. In *Proceedings of the 59th Annual Meeting of the Association for Computational Linguistics and the 11th International Joint Conference on Natural Language Processing (Volume 1: Long Papers)*, pages 5356–5371, Online. Association for Computational Linguistics.

Roberto Navigli. 2009. Word sense disambiguation: A survey. *ACM computing surveys (CSUR)*, 41(2):1–69.

Kishore Papineni, Salim Roukos, Todd Ward, and Wei-Jing Zhu. 2002. Bleu: a method for automatic evaluation of machine translation. In *Proceedings of the 40th annual meeting of the Association for Computational Linguistics*, pages 311–318.

Alessandro Raganato, Jose Camacho-Collados, and Roberto Navigli. 2017. Word sense disambiguation: A unified evaluation framework and empirical comparison. In *Proceedings of the 15th Conference of the European Chapter of the Association for Computational Linguistics: Volume 1, Long Papers*, pages 99–110.

Bianca Scarlini, Tommaso Pasini, and Roberto Navigli. 2020. With more contexts comes better performance: Contextualized sense embeddings for all-round word sense disambiguation. In *Proceedings of the 2020 Conference on Empirical Methods in Natural Language Processing (EMNLP)*, pages 3528–3539.

Ivan Vulić, Simon Baker, Edoardo Maria Ponti, Ulla Petti, Ira Leviant, Kelly Wing, Olga Majewska, Eden Bar, Matt Malone, Thierry Poibeau, Roi Reichart, and Anna Korhonen. 2020a. Multi-SimLex: A large-scale evaluation of multilingual and crosslingual lexical semantic similarity. *Computational Linguistics*, 46(4):847–897.

Ivan Vulić, Edoardo Maria Ponti, Robert Litschko, Goran Glavaš, and Anna Korhonen. 2020b. Probing pretrained language models for lexical semantics. In *Proceedings of the 2020 Conference on Empirical Methods in Natural Language Processing (EMNLP)*, pages 7222–7240, Online. Association for Computational Linguistics.

Pengcheng Yang, Lei Li, Fuli Luo, Tianyu Liu, and Xu Sun. 2019. Enhancing topic-to-essay generation with external commonsense knowledge. In *Proceedings of the 57th Annual Meeting of the Association for Computational Linguistics*, pages 2002–2012.

Lili Yao, Nanyun Peng, Ralph Weischedel, Kevin Knight, Dongyan Zhao, and Rui Yan. 2019. Plan-and-write: Towards better automatic storytelling. In *Proceedings of the AAAI Conference on Artificial Intelligence*, volume 33, pages 7378–7385.

Yue Zhang and Stephen Clark. 2015. Discriminative syntax-based word ordering for text generation. *Computational linguistics*, 41(3):503–538.

Jianing Zhou and Suma Bhat. 2021. Paraphrase generation: A survey of the state of the art. In *Proceedings of the 2021 Conference on Empirical Methods in Natural Language Processing*, pages 5075–5086.

Yaoming Zhu, Sidi Lu, Lei Zheng, Jiaxian Guo, Weinan Zhang, Jun Wang, and Yong Yu. 2018. Texygen: A benchmarking platform for text generation models. In *The 41st International ACM SIGIR Conference on Research & Development in Information Retrieval*, pages 1097–1100.

Yukun Zhu, Ryan Kiros, Rich Zemel, Ruslan Salakhutdinov, Raquel Urtasun, Antonio Torralba, and Sanja Fidler. 2015. Aligning books and movies: Towards story-like visual explanations by watching movies and reading books. In *The IEEE International Conference on Computer Vision (ICCV)*.

A Computational Details

We run experiments across two NVIDIA RTX 3090 Ti GPUs, but each individual experiment runs on one GPU (we train two models simultaneously, one on each GPU). The pretrained BART, BEM context encoder, and SimCSE models have 141M, 109M, and 109M parameters, respectively. It takes approximately 1.5 days to train each S2S or ExMaker model.

B Human Evaluations

The annotators are from the United States and are acquaintances of the authors, but are not from the same research group. Consent was obtained via email, and annotators were made fully aware that annotations would only be used for this paper to demonstrate differences in model performance (see Table 1).

C Generation Examples for Self-Supervised Approach

We provide examples of generated sentences from $S2S_{self}$ in Table 4. There appears to be information leakage in the sentence embedding LSR, with some slight differences compared to the contextual word embedding LSR. We discuss the key qualitative takeaways below.

Vocabulary and Topical Overlap. We notice the same trend of overlapping vocabulary and topics that we observe in sentences generated by $S2S_{semi}$, although the overlap appears more pronounced for $S2S_{self}$. For example, for the first sense of "object" in Table 4, the subject of the input sentence, "science", appears as the subject in both generated sentences. In Table 2 ($S2S_{semi}$), we see for the same respective sense that the generated sentences revolve around scientific themes, but do not explicitly make use of the word "science" itself.

Dependence on Input Length. The length of generated sentences for $S2S_{self}$ are similar to that of their respective input sentences, as is the case for sentences generated by $S2S_{semi}$. The key distinction between $S2S_{self}$ and $S2S_{semi}$ in this respect is that the target word location does not appear to be encoded in the LSR for $S2S_{self}$. For example, the two sentences generated for the first sense of "object" in Table 4 use the target word in the first half and the very end of the sentence, respectively, while the target word appeared towards the end of the input sentence.

Incorrect Target Word Meaning. We see two examples of the target word adopting the wrong meaning in Table 4 (incorrect target word usages are italicized). In both cases, the intended part-of-speech is verb, but the example sentences have used the target word as a noun. We hypothesize such mistakes are due to imperfect representation of the target word sense via sentence-level semantics, but further analysis is needed to confirm this. In cases where the target word meaning is unclear based on sentence-level semantics, the model may produce a sentence exemplifying the most frequent sense of the target word.

Word Sense Information	Generated Sentences
Word: object **Definition**: A tangible and visible entity; an entity that can cast a shadow **Input**: Science is fully competent to deal with any element of experience which arises from an object in space and time.	1. Science itself requires a scientific object to take practical, practical, and comprehending knowledge of the worlds that arise from it. 2. The field of science requires a great deal of experience to approach the subject matter as it exists in any form or object.
Word: object **Definition**: Express or raise an objection or protest or criticism or express dissent **Input**: Most of these former churches are now used as warehouses, but "neither Anglicans nor nonconformists object to selling churches to Roman Catholics", and have done so.	1. "However some of the latter have been converted into churches, and are now used as storage areas for goods or goods only, although most object to the practices of the church." 2. "Some of the churches remain empty or have not been converted into warehouses, although they are generally in use as auction boxes as a tourist *object*."
Word: contract **Definition**: A binding agreement between two or more persons that is enforceable by law **Input**: Enter into contracts with educational institutions, scientific organizations, and industrial and engineering firms;	1. Open up; engage in the creation of scientific and technical contracts; engage in various academic and industrial programs; employ engineers and teachers; obtain federal and state grants; and so forth. 2. Industrial companies must engage in employment, through partnership contracts, in private laboratories, and so forth.
Word: contract **Definition**: Become smaller or draw together **Input**: Dr. Bonnor supports the idea that the universe both expands and contracts, that in several billion years the expansion will slow up and reverse itself and that the contraction will set in.	1. He argues that the natural climate theory, which will take effect over the next two decades, creates massive gravitational pulls and contracts with time, expanding and expanding in a way that we both know will be so. 2. He explained that the general theory believes that the natural process of expansion will grow between decades, if not centuries, and that the economic climate will squeeze out both forces in a heartbeat and collapse out of the shrinking spaces between *contracts*.

Table 4: Examples of generated sentences using $S2S_{self}$ for distinct senses of the words "object" and "contract." The target word is italicized in examples where it takes on a different meaning from what was intended.

Sen2Pro: A Probabilistic Perspective to Sentence Embedding from Pre-trained Language Model

Lingfeng Shen, Haiyun Jiang, Lemao Liu, Shuming Shi
Natural Language Processing Center
Tencent AI Lab

Abstract

Sentence embedding is one of the most fundamental tasks in Natural Language Processing and plays an important role in various tasks. The recent breakthrough in sentence embedding is achieved by pre-trained language models (PLMs). Despite its success, an embedded vector (Sen2Vec) representing a point estimate does not naturally express uncertainty in a task-agnostic way. This paper thereby proposes an efficient framework on probabilistic sentence embedding (Sen2Pro) from PLMs, and it represents a sentence as a probability density distribution in an embedding space to reflect both model uncertainty and data uncertainty (i.e., many-to-one nature) in the sentence representation. The proposed framework performs in a plug-and-play way without retraining PLMs anymore, and it is easy to implement and generally applied on top of any PLM. The superiority of Sen2Pro over Sen2Vec has been theoretically verified and practically illustrated on different NLP tasks.

1 Introduction

Sentence embedding, which maps an input sentence to a point (i.e., a vector) in an embedded space, is one of the most fundamental tasks in Natural Language Processing (NLP), and it plays an important role in various downstream tasks such as sentiment analysis, text classification, and natural language inference (Howard and Ruder, 2018; Reimers and Gurevych, 2019; Gao et al., 2021). There is a surge of interest in learning sentence embedding. The early work resorts to word embedding (Bengio et al., 2003; Mikolov et al., 2013; Pennington et al., 2014) and represents an input sentence by a pooling vector (mean or weighted mean) over all embeddings of its words (Kiros et al., 2015; Wieting et al., 2015a). More recently, sentence embedding obtained from pre-trained language models (PLMs) made a breakthrough thanks to PLM's powerful ability in modeling global context (Peters et al., 2018; Devlin et al., 2019; Liu et al., 2019), and it quickly became the standard practice for sentence embedding.

Despite the success of sentence embedding from PLMs, an embedded vector (Sen2Vec) representing a point estimate does not naturally express uncertainty about the target concepts associated with the input sentence (Vilnis and McCallum, 2015). In essence, this uncertainty originates from many-to-one nature in language representation: (1) **model uncertainty**: model uncertainty refers to the notion of randomness caused by inherently random effects within the model. (i.e. one sentence may have many representations according to different representations within the same model (e.g., dropout)) Considering that these representation are from the same sentence, they should remain close to each other; (2) **data uncertainty**: many sentences with different linguistic structure (e.g., paraphrase) may have the same meaning in semantics. Considering the identical semantics, their corresponding representation should get close with each other.

When quantifying uncertainty, we assume that close-semantic sentences' representation follows the same probability distribution. Given a sentence, since the model only observes one sample, it is natural to ask how much a language model can capture such a rich distribution.

A natural solution to this issue is to merge such a probabilistic perspective into sentence embedding, which represents a sentence as a distribution $P(\mu, \Sigma)$, where μ is the mean and covariance Σ intuitively portrays the uncertainty of the distribution P. Unfortunately, there is a critical challenge to putting this idea into practice: previous works (Bamler and Mandt, 2017; Camacho-Collados and Pilehvar, 2018; Zhou et al., 2019) are only plausible on word embedding and require retraining word embedding with probabilistic embedding on large-scale data to advance SOTA. It is costly even for training a PLM without probabilistic embed-

Proceedings of the 8th Workshop on Representation Learning for NLP (RepL4NLP 2023), pages 315–333
July 13, 2023 ©2023 Association for Computational Linguistics

ding (Devlin et al., 2019; Radford et al., 2019; He et al., 2020; Clark et al., 2019; Raffel et al., 2020), which typically consumes considerable GPU computations for weeks.

In this paper, we propose an efficient framework for probabilistic sentence embedding (Sen2Pro) from PLMs that represents a sentence as a probability density in an embedding space to reflect the uncertainty in the sentence representation.

Concerning **model uncertainty** and **data uncertainty**, we propose two simple methods to quantify both on top of a PLM. Specifically, to measure model uncertainty, we assume a sentence vector is drawn from a distribution $P(\mu^m, \Sigma^m)$, which can be estimated by many representations of the targeted sentence using a set of stochastic PLMs obtained from Monte Carlo dropout (Gal and Ghahramani, 2016).

Similarly, we apply the data augmentation technique to generate many semantically equivalent sentences to the targeted sentence for measuring data uncertainty. Then we assume a sentence vector is drawn from a distribution $P(\mu^d, \Sigma^d)$, which the representations of the augmented sentences from the PLM can estimate. In addition, we also introduce some ways to utilize both μ^m (μ^d) and Σ^m (Σ^d) as the final sentence representation for different downstream tasks.

Moreover, drawing from previous works (Chen et al., 2016; Li and Chen, 2019; Gao et al., 2019; Tschannen et al., 2019; Grohs et al., 2021) that explored the relationships between deep learning representation and relative entropy, we present theoretical explanations of why our probabilistic sentence embedding (Sen2Pro) is superior to point vector-based sentence embedding (Sen2Vec). Meanwhile, extensive experiments demonstrate the practical effectiveness of Sen2Pro on text classification, semantic similarity match, dialogue generation evaluation, and machine translation evaluation. Besides, Sen2Pro demonstrates its superiority in capturing sentence-level linguistic analogy over Sen2Vec.

2 Related Work

2.1 Sentence Embedding

Methods for sentence embedding learning have been extensively explored, and all these methods represent a sentence as a point embedding. Early works use the weighted sum of word embedding to represent a sentence. Then some methods based on the distributional hypothesis have been done. Hill (Hill et al., 2016) learned sentence representations with the internal structure of each sentence, and Kiros (Kiros et al., 2015) followed the idea of Word2Vec (Mikolov et al., 2013) to represent a sentence by predicting its surrounding sentences. In recent years, the pre-trained language model (Devlin et al., 2019) has become the standard sentence paradigm because of its strong ability to capture syntactic and semantic features of sentences by learning from the large-scale corpus. Furthermore, several researchers used contrastive learning to augment sentence representation (Zhang et al., 2020; Yan et al., 2021; Meng et al., 2021; Gao et al., 2021; Wang et al., 2021), based on the assumption that a high-quality representation method should bring similar sentences closer while pushing away dissimilar ones. They belong to Sen2Vec and thus fail to model uncertainty. This paper goes beyond point sentence embedding and explores probabilistic sentence embedding.

2.2 Probabilistic Word Embedding

In NLP, probabilistic embedding originated from word embedding (Bengio et al., 2003; Mikolov et al., 2013), and existing probabilistic embedding methods work only on words, where a word from the vocabulary is represented as a density distribution in an embedding space. Although variants of probabilistic word embedding have been developed (Vilnis and McCallum, 2015; Bamler and Mandt, 2017; Camacho-Collados and Pilehvar, 2018; Zhou et al., 2019), they used a similar paradigm, which adapts the Skip-gram model (Mikolov et al., 2013) with a non-parametric approach. Specifically, a Skip-gram model is retrained as the density distribution with a specific word sampling (e.g., synonym) method and a specific loss function (e.g., a margin loss). Therefore, existing probabilistic embedding needs an extremely time-consuming retraining stage and can not be applied to PLMs (e.g., BERT). Different from them, this paper contributes to the literature by developing probabilistic embedding for sentences that serves as a plug-and-play method on pre-trained language models (Devlin et al., 2019) without any time-consuming retraining stage.

3 Methodology: Sen2Pro

Because of the many-to-one nature of sentence embedding, we model the uncertainty from two perspectives, i.e., model uncertainty and data uncertainty. Accordingly, we assume that the representation of one sentence follows a distribution $P(\mu, \Sigma)$, which measures either model uncertainty or data uncertainty. The goal of our Sen2Pro framework is to estimate the two distributions $P(\mu, \Sigma)$ for a sentence embedding based on a pre-trained language model f_θ (e.g., BERT), where θ denotes its parameters. In general, there are two steps in Sen2Pro: the sampling stage and the estimation stage. The sampling stage generates embedding instances to capture two kinds of uncertainties: model uncertainty and data uncertainty (§3.1). The estimation stage aims to estimate the parameters in the density distributions (i.e., mean vector and covariance matrix) based on the embedding instances (§3.2). After both distributions are estimated, the general idea to apply them to specific tasks is presented (§3.3).

3.1 Sampling Stage

Model Uncertainty Model uncertainty originates from the fact that one sentence may have different representations due to inherent randomness within models. In this paper, we use a pre-trained language model f_θ and try to quantify *model uncertainty*. Considering that the key ingredient of model uncertainty is to vary the model while keeping the sentence s unchanged, we utilize MC dropout to create embedding instances for quantifying model uncertainty. Specifically, for each sentence s, we utilize MC Dropout (Gal and Ghahramani, 2016; Lakshminarayanan et al., 2017) over the parameters θ as sampling, and repeat sampling N times to obtain different subsets of the parameters θ: $\{\widehat{\theta}_i \mid i = 1, \ldots, N\}$. In this way, we generate a set of embeddings as follows:

$$\mathcal{S}^m = \left\{x_i = f_{\widehat{\theta}_i}(s) \mid i = 1, \ldots, N\right\} \quad (1)$$

As shown in Eq. 1, each subset of model's parameters represent a sub-structure of the model, which naturally matches with the definition of model uncertainty.

Data Uncertainty Data uncertainty corresponds to the many-to-one nature of sentence embedding. In other words, sentences that are semantically similar but slightly different should have close representations. Data uncertainty exists in universal real-world scenarios: since the model requires lots of training data to perform well, it is common to augment high-quality labeled sentences with lower-quality web-crawled data to save time and effort. To naturally imitate such uncertainty, in this paper, a simple data augmentation method, word-level operation, is applied to the input sentence, which adds proper noise to an input sentence. After repeating data augmentation N times (i.e., randomly dropping a word in s, swapping two words, replacing or inserting a word in s with any word from vocabulary) for the input sentence s, a set of new sentences, $s_1, s_2, \ldots, s_N$ are obtained. Then, the sentences are fed to the pre-trained model f_θ to get N embeddings. In this way, we can obtain a set of embeddings as follows:

$$\mathcal{S}^d = \left\{x_i = f_\theta(s_i) \mid i = 1, \ldots, N\right\} \quad (2)$$

3.2 Estimation Stage

After obtaining the required embedding instances for model and data uncertainty, we can estimate the probability distributions on them, respectively. Similar to cases of (Kendall and Gal, 2017; Maddox et al., 2019; Ovadia et al., 2019; Abdar et al., 2021; Hüllermeier and Waegeman, 2021), we do estimation towards two uncertainty individually rather than unifying, which is also empirically verified in Appendix D. Suppose $\mathcal{S}$ denotes either $\mathcal{S}^m$ or $\mathcal{S}^d$, it is natural to estimate its mean and covariance as follows:

$$\mu = \frac{1}{|\mathcal{S}|} \sum_{x \in \mathcal{S}} x \quad (3)$$

$$\Sigma = \frac{1}{|\mathcal{S}|} \sum_{x \in \mathcal{S}} (x - \mu)(x - \mu)^\top \quad (4)$$

where $|\mathcal{S}|$ means the size of the set $\mathcal{S}$ and $(.)^\top$ is an transpose operation. We use μ^m and Σ^m respectively to denote the statistics estimated from model uncertainty (i.e., $\mathcal{S} = \mathcal{S}_m$), and μ^d and Σ^d denote those estimated through data uncertainty (i.e., $\mathcal{S} = \mathcal{S}_d$).

However, such a simple covariance matrix estimator (SCE) owns severe problems on both theoretical (Xiao and Wu, 2012) and practical sides: it is known to degrade rapidly as an estimator as the number of variables increases, thus performing badly in a high-dimensional case (e.g., 768 dimensions in BERT). To address this issue, inspired by Bien et al. (2016), we instead employ the banding estimator, which uses an off-diagonal entry removal operation on the covariance matrix.

Specifically, for a covariance matrix $\Sigma = (\Sigma_{ij})_{k \times k}$ where k is the dimension of Σ, we use

$B(\Sigma)$ as the estimation of Σ as follows:

$$\hat{\Sigma} = B(\Sigma) = \text{Diag}(\Sigma) \quad (5)$$

Besides, Theorem 1 provides an estimation error bound for our banding estimator, whose proof is presented in Appendix A.

Theorem 1. *Suppose Σ is the covariance matrix of the ground truth distribution $P(\mu, \Sigma)$, and $\hat{\Sigma}$ denote $B(\Sigma)$, then we have*

$$\left\|\hat{\Sigma} - \Sigma\right\|_2 = O_p\left(\left(\frac{\log k}{n}\right)^M\right) \quad (6)$$

where k is the dimension of Σ, and M is a positive constant satisfying $M < \frac{1}{2}$. O_p and n means $\frac{\log k}{n})^M$ is stochastically bounded as $n \to \infty$.

Besides, SCE also in practicability problems compared to the banding estimator. SCE owns a significantly worse performance-efficiency trade-off than our banding estimator, which will be empirically verified in Sec 5. Moreover, theoretical analyses for comparison between Sen2Vec and Sen2Pro are deferred to Appendix B.

3.3 Usage of Sen2Pro

Unlike previous works on probabilistic embedding that drop $\hat{\Sigma}$ in tasks, in Sen2Pro, both mean vector μ (i.e., μ^m and μ^d) and covariance vector $\hat{\Sigma}$ (i.e., $\hat{\Sigma}^m$ and $\hat{\Sigma}^d$) are used for sentence embedding. In the next section, we illustrate our strategies to use μ and $\hat{\Sigma}$, more details are presented in Sec 4.1.

4 Experiment

This section comprehensively evaluates the effectiveness of our Sen2Pro framework on the following various tasks. The results consistently show that Sen2Pro outperforms Sen2Vec. Specifically, we choose two sets of tasks for evaluation: Fine-tune-need Task and Fine-tune-free Task.

4.1 Basic Setting

Recall that μ^m and $\hat{\Sigma}^m$ (μ^d and $\hat{\Sigma}^d$) denote the estimated mean and covariance from model (data) uncertainty. Then we present how to use them for different tasks.

Fine-tune-need Task: Text Classification After estimation stage in data and model uncertainty, each sentence is represented as the concatenation of $\frac{\mu^m+\mu^d}{2}$ and (diagonal entries of) $\frac{\hat{\Sigma}^m+\hat{\Sigma}^d}{2}$. Specifically, we use reparameterization to handle the non-differentiable issue of the sampling process.

Fine-tune-free Task: Sentence Similarity, Dialogue Evaluation, Neural Machine Translation Evaluation For such NLP tasks, the distance between two representations is needed. Although KL divergence is natural to measure the distance between two distributions, it has practical drawbacks. For example, in BERT-base case where $\mu \in \mathcal{R}^{768\times 1}$, $\hat{\Sigma} \in \mathcal{R}^{768\times 768}$, KL divergence not only is time-consuming but also results in numerical errors, considering that KL divergence includes operations $det(\hat{\Sigma})$ and $\hat{\Sigma}^{-1}$. In practice, most entries of $\hat{\Sigma}$ are between 0 and 0.5, so the determinant becomes extremely small, which leads to numerical errors. Moreover, the computation of $\hat{\Sigma}^{-1}$ will be unstable when the dimension is high.

Therefore, a simple function is taken to measure the distance between two probabilistic sentence embeddings (μ_a, Σ_a) and (μ_b, Σ_b) as follows:

$$\begin{aligned} & d(\mathcal{N}(\mu_a, \Sigma_a), \mathcal{N}(\mu_b, \Sigma_b)) \quad (7) \\ & = (1-\alpha) l_1(\mu_a - \mu_b) + \alpha l_1(\Sigma_a - \Sigma_b) \end{aligned}$$

where l_1 represents the l_1-norm and α is to balance the two terms. For α, we consider it as a balance factor for different magnitudes of μ and Σ, defined as follows:

$$\alpha = \frac{l_1(\mu_a - \mu_b)}{l_1(\Sigma_a - \Sigma_b)} \quad (8)$$

In most cases, α ranges from 0.01 to 0.05. Besides, we will try to apply Sen2Pro on other evaluation tasks (Shen et al., 2022a,b) like paraphrase, data-to-text, and summarization.

4.2 Text Classification

Benchmarks and Setting We choose four widely-used text classification benchmarks: AG News (Zhang et al., 2015), DBpedia (Maas et al., 2011), Yahoo! Answers (Chang et al., 2008) and IMDB (Maas et al., 2011). The evaluation metric is the test accuracy, and the best performance is selected based on validation set accuracy. The baseline is Sen2Vec, with 15 data augmentation samples per sentence. In Sen2Pro, we choose the BERT-base model as the PLM and use the 'first-last-avg'(a pooling way that average first and last layer representation). The sampling number is 15 for the model uncertainty and data uncertainty. Moreover, we use two settings for model evaluation: few-shot and full-dataset. In the few-shot setting, models are trained with randomly selected 10 and 200 labeled sentences per class. In the full-dataset setting, models are trained with the whole training set.

Dataset	Model	10	200	Full	Dataset	Model	10	200	Full
AGNews	BERT-base	69.5	87.5	95.2	DBPedia	BERT-base	95.2	98.5	99.3
	BERT-base-G	74.4(1.1)	90.2(0.3)	95.6(0.1)		BERT-base-G	96.5(0.2)	99.1(0.1)	99.3(*)
Yahoo	BERT-base	56.2	69.3	77.6	IMDB	BERT-base	67.5	86.9	95.6
	BERT-base-G	60.5(1.8)	72.9(0.6)	78.2(0.2)		BERT-base-G	70.4(0.6)	88.5(0.3)	95.7(*)

Table 1: Test accuracy(%) comparison between Sen2Pro and Sen2Vec for text classification. The results on each dataset are the mean of three runs; the standard derivation (i.e., the values in brackets) is given for PLM-G, where * means the derivation is smaller than 0.1%.

Baseline	STS-12	STS-13	STS-14	STS-15	STS-16	Avg
BERT	57.86→59.55	61.97→66.20	62.49→65.19	70.96→73.50	69.76→72.10	63.69→66.70(+3.01)
BERT$_l$	57.74→59.90	61.16→66.20	61.18→65.62	68.06→73.01	70.30→74.72	62.62→67.47(+4.85)
W-BERT	63.62→64.50	73.02→73.69	69.23→69.69	74.52→74.69	72.15→76.11	69.21→70.39 (+1.18)
W-BERT	64.02→64.90	73.27→73.94	69.58→70.04	74.77→74.94	72.50→76.44	69.58→70.69 (+1.26)
C-BERT	64.09→65.01	78.21→78.54	68.68→69.04	79.56→79.90	75.41→75.74	72.27→72.69 (+0.42)
C-BERT$_l$	70.23→70.70	82.13→82.54	73.60→74.12	81.72→82.01	77.01→77.58	76.03→76.48 (+0.45)
Sim-BERT	68.93→69.33	78.68→78.93	73.57→73.95	79.68→80.01	79.11→79.29	75.11→75.44 (+0.33)
Sim-BERT$_l$	69.25→69.60	78.96→79.30	73.64→73.92	80.06→80.31	79.08→79.42	75.31→75.61 (+0.30)

Table 2: The experimental results of adding our Sen2Pro on widely used sentence embedding methods. Specifically, BERT$_l$ means BERT$_{large}$.

Sentence Embedding	MRR	Hits@1	Hits@3
BERT	68.01	51.70	81.91
BERT+Ours	68.69	52.24	82.63
BERT-whitening	66.58	46.54	84.22
BERT-whitening+Ours	67.49	48.23	84.56
Sentence-BERT	64.12	47.07	79.05
Sentence-BERT+Ours	66.10	48.55	80.34
SimCSE	69.50	52.34	84.43
SimCSE+Ours	70.01	52.68	84.69

Table 3: Performances on EvalRank (Wang et al., 2022) using Sen2Vec and Sen2Pro. '+Ours' means Sen2Pro, and the results are the mean of five runs to show the statistical significance with p value <0.05.

Performances The results are listed in Table 1. Our Sen2Pro consistently performs better than Sen2Vec under few-shot settings because Sen2Pro contains more semantic information about a sentence due to its probabilistic characteristic. Moreover, Sen2Pro achieves comparable or better performances in the full training setting than Sen2Vec.

4.3 Sentence Similarity

Benchmarks and Setting We use seven commonly-used STS datasets (Agirre et al., 2012, 2013, 2014, 2015, 2016) for evaluation. Besides, considering the limitation of traditional intrinsic evaluation (Wang et al., 2022), we choose EvalRank (Wang et al., 2022) for linguistic analogy evaluation, which overcomes the previous limitation. In Sen2Pro, we use several state-of-the-art pre-trained language models, including BERT-base (Devlin et al., 2019), BERT-whitening (Su et al., 2021; Huang et al., 2021), Sentence-BERT (Reimers and Gurevych, 2019), and SimCSE (Gao et al., 2021). Specifically, EvalRank uses the mean reciprocal rank (MRR) and Hits@k scores for evaluation, and a higher score indicates a better embedding model. The sampling number for each uncertainty is set as 15.

Performances The results of Sen2Pro are reported in Table 2 and 3, which illustrate that Sen2Pro outperforms Sen2Vec with a substantial gap under all settings. Moreover, Sen2Pro using the'base' PLMs can achieve better or comparable performance than Sen2Vec using 'large' PLMs.

4.4 Dialogue Evaluation

Benchmark and Setting We choose three widely-used dialogue benchmarks: Daily(H) (Lowe et al., 2017), Convai2 (Dinan et al., 2020), and Empathetic (Rashkin et al., 2019). Each benchmark consists of dialogue queries, the corresponding responses, and human-annotated responses. For baseline metrics, we choose BLEU (Papineni et al., 2002), ROUGE (Lin, 2004), METEOR (Denkowski and Lavie, 2014), Greedy Matching (Rus and Lintean, 2012), Embedding Average (Wieting et al., 2015b), Vector Extrema (Forgues et al., 2014) and BERTScore (Zhang et al., 2019). For

Metric	Daily(H)		Convai2		Empathetic	
	Spr	Pr	Spr	Pr	Spr	Pr
BLEU	44.5	44.4	80.0	80.1	13.6	33.1
METEOR	1.8	5.0	80.0	76.7	38.2	13.3
ROUGE-L	54.5	41.7	20.0	6.1	39.1	47.2
Greedy	85.5	76.4	60.0	79.4	73.6	86.4
Average	20.9	20.9	60.0	87.9	66.4	72.5
Extrema	74.5	76.1	80.0	76.6	61.8	72.2
B-SCORE	85.5	85.7	80.0	93.9	60.0	69.7
Sen2Vec	69.9	76.1	60.0	63.9	55.2	60.3
Sen2Pro	87.3	81.4	100	85.9	80.9	81.6

Table 4: Correlations of the evaluation metrics on the dialogue corpora. 'Spr.' and 'Pr.' refer to Spearman and Pearson correlation coefficients, respectively; B-SCORE represents BERTScore.

Sen2Pro, we use the BERT-base model and the 'first-last-avg' representation and set the sampling number of uncertainty to 15.

Performances The performances of various evaluation metrics are reported in Table 4. Sen2Pro performs best in most cases, demonstrating its good generalization ability and robustness for the dialogue evaluation task.

4.5 NMT Evaluation

Benchmark and Setting We work on the WMT-17 machine translation benchmark (Bojar et al., 2017). Moreover, BLEU (Papineni et al., 2002), CDER (Leusch et al., 2006), BLEND (Ma et al., 2017), Sen2Vec, and BERTScore (Zhang et al., 2019) are chosen as baseline metrics. The setting of Sen2Pro is the same as the one of dialogue evaluation.

Performances The results are shown in Table 5. Our Sen2Pro achieves comparable performance towards a top metric (i.e., BERTScore) and significantly outperforms Sen2Vec, which demonstrates the effectiveness of Sen2Pro in the NMT evaluation task. Segment-level results are shown in Appendix H. The results indicate that our Sen2Pro can yield competitive performance to SOTA as an automatic metric to evaluate dialogue generation.

5 Analysis and Discussion

This section presents analyses of Sen2Pro, and the BERT model is used as the PLM in the analyses. Specifically, the representation uncertainty analysis is made on the STS task, and detailed results are deferred to Appendix E and F. Moreover, we choose the BERT model as our pre-trained sentence encoder in the analysis.

Feature with higher model uncertainty is more important We investigate the relation between the model uncertainty and the **feature importance** on the STS task. In Sen2Pro, a sentence is represented as $\mu^m \in \mathcal{R}^{768\times1}$ and diagonal entries of $\hat{\Sigma}^m \in \mathcal{R}^{768\times768}$. From another perspective, a sentence is represented by 768 features in μ^m, and $\hat{\Sigma}^m$ reflects the corresponding model uncertainties of such features. Let T be the feature set, and $t \in T$ is a feature subset. We define the **feature importance** as follows:

$$score(t) = |\rho(T) - \rho(T/t)| \quad (9)$$

where ρ represents Spearman's correlation in STS evaluation, and $score(t)$ describes the performance change after removing the feature subset t from T. Then we separate the 768 features into five groups according to their uncertainty $\hat{\Sigma}^m$, and name them as 'I' to 'V', as shown in Figure 1. When a group of features is removed from T, these features are set to 0 in μ^m and $\hat{\Sigma}^m$, respectively. Figure 1 lists the results on STS-12. In Figure 1, as the feature's uncertainty decreases, the importance score drops, indicating that features with higher uncertainty are more important in the STS task.

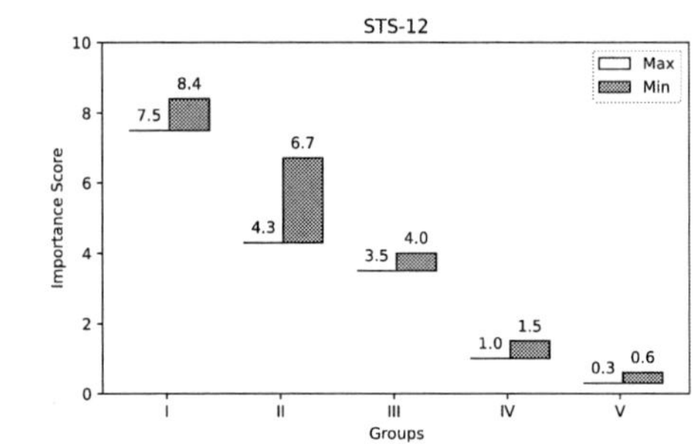

Figure 1: The importance score of five groups of features. 'I' represents the features with top 20% highest uncertainty; 'V' indicates the features with bottom 20% lowest uncertainty; 'Min' and 'Max' mean the lowest and highest importance score under three runs.

Sen2Pro brings more benefits when model uncertainty are higher We also investigate the relation between the model uncertainty and the performance improvement of Sen2Pro over Sen2Vec on the STS task. Firstly, we define a metric called

Metric	cs-en	de-en	fi-en	lv-en	ru-en	tr-en	zh-en	Avg
BLEU	97.1	92.3	90.3	97.9	91.2	97.6	86.4	93.3
CDER	98.9	93.0	92.7	98.5	92.2	97.3	90.4	94.7
BLEND	96.8	97.6	95.8	97.9	96.4	98.4	89.4	96.0
BERTScore	99.6	98.2	94.7	97.9	956	98.6	98.4	97.6
Sen2Vec	97.3	92.5	93.1	98.6	90.1	98.0	92.1	94.5
Sen2Pro	99.8	96.2	99.0	99.5	96.5	99.0	97.9	97.8

Table 5: Pearson correlations with system-level machine translation evaluation on WMT17.

Model	STS-12	STS-13	STS-14	STS-15	STS-16	STS-B	SICK-R	Average
BERT-base	57.84	61.95	62.48	70.95	69.81	59.04	63.75	63.69
BERT-base-G_{m+d}	59.40	63.03	64.18	71.97	70.73	62.59	64.69	65.23 (+1.54)
BERT-base-G_m	58.86	62.66	63.77	71.48	70.56	61.89	64.28	64.79 (+1.10)
BERT-base-G_d	58.14	62.20	62.83	71.00	70.36	59.30	64.10	63.99 (+0.30)

Table 6: Ablation studies on the two uncertainties in STS. BERT-base-G_m and BERT-base-G_d represent Sen2Pro with only model uncertainty or data uncertainty, respectively.

Dataset	Model	10	200	Full	Dataset	Model	10	200	Full
AGNews	BERT-base	69.5	87.5	95.2	DBPedia	BERT-base	95.2	98.5	99.3
	BERT-base-G	73.4(0.5)	89.2(0.3)	95.4(0.1)		BERT-base-G	96.3(0.2)	99.1(0.1)	99.3(*)
	BERT-base-G_m	71.6(1.0)	88.3(0.4)	95.2(0.2)		BERT-base-G_m	95.8(0.2)	98.8(*)	99.3(*)
	BERT-base-G_d	73.0(0.4)	89.0(0.3)	95.4(0.1)		BERT-base-G_d	96.3(0.3)	99.1(0.1)	99.3(*)
Yahoo	BERT-base	56.2	69.3	77.6	IMDB	BERT-base	67.5	86.9	95.6
	BERT-base-G	60.1(0.8)	72.4(0.6)	78.0(0.1)		BERT-base-G	70.3(0.6)	88.2(0.3)	95.7(*)
	BERT-base-G_m	58.1(1.0)	70.3(0.5)	77.9(*)		BERT-base-G_m	69.2(0.6)	87.5(0.2)	95.6(*)
	BERT-base-G_d	59.9(0.7)	71.7(0.3)	78.0(0.1)		BERT-base-G_d	69.8(0.4)	88.2(0.1)	95.7(*)

Table 7: Ablation studies on the two uncertainties in text classification.

Fluctuation Rate Q as follows:

$$Q(f, D) = \frac{\Sigma_{i=1}^{|D|}(\Sigma_{j=1}^{k}\sigma_{ij})}{k \times |D|} \quad (10)$$

where[1] f and D represent the PLM and benchmark, and σ_{ij} is j-th element of the covariance matrix for i-th sentence in D, and k denotes the dimension of model f. Such a metric can generally reflect the uncertainty of a specific model towards a specific benchmark. Based on $Q(f, D)$, we define the improvement score I reflecting the improvement of Sen2Pro over Sen2Vec as follows:

$$I = P_{Sen2Pro}(f, D) - P_{Sen2Vec}(f, D) \quad (11)$$

where $P_{Sen2Pro}(f, D)$ and $P_{Sen2Vec}(f, D)$ represent the performance of model f on D under Sen2Pro and Sen2Vec, respectively. Besides, we add the result of [CLS] representation into experiments since the [CLS] representation owns a significantly higher fluctuation rate than the 'first-last-avg' representation. The results on STS-12 are illustrated in Figure 2. As the fluctuation rate increases, the improvement score becomes more significant. Such empirical results demonstrate that the effectiveness of Sen2Pro is highly correlated to the model uncertainty and show Sen2Pro's superiority over Sen2Vec owns a positive correlation to model uncertainty.

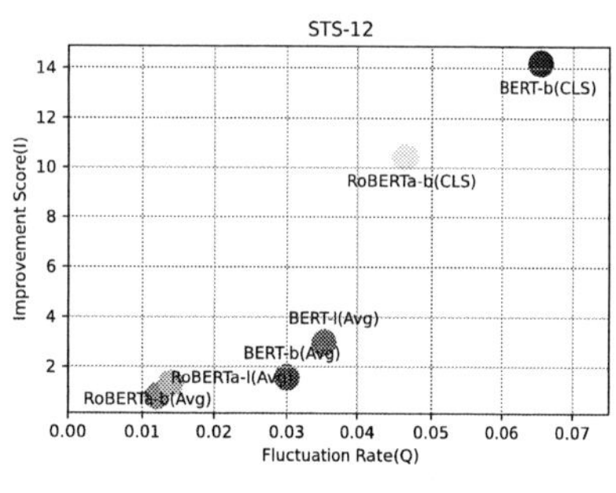

Figure 2: The relation between fluctuation rate (Q) and improvement score (I). '-b' and '-l' indicate 'base' and 'large', and 'Avg' and 'CLS' represent the 'first-last-avg' and '[CLS]' representation.

Effectiveness of Two Uncertainties We verify the effect of model and data uncertainty on

[1]Note that σ corresponds to $\hat{\Sigma}^m$, we change the notation here to avoid repeating with the sum operation Σ.

Sen2Pro's performances. Specifically, Sen2Pro is evaluated on one intrinsic evaluation (STS) and one downstream task (text classification), and the results are demonstrated in Table 6 and Table 7, respectively. As shown in Table 6, the performance decreases when the data uncertainty is applied alone for the STS task since sentences' semantics may be changed due to the data augmentation. In contrast, the model uncertainty consistently brings benefits to the sentence representation. For text classification, both uncertainties improve the representation's generalization. Specifically, the contribution of the data uncertainty is higher than the model uncertainty. These empirical results also illustrate the usage of Sen2Pro (§3.3).

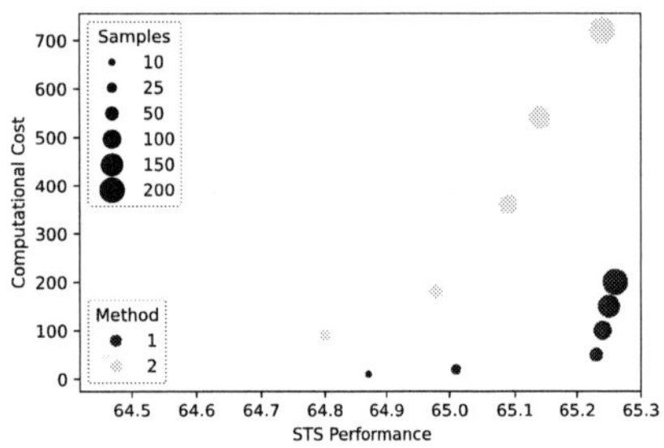

Figure 3: The performance-efficiency trade-off between SCE and our banding estimator, where '1' represents our estimation and '2' represents 'SCE'.

Method	STS	TC	Dialog	NMT
SCE	64.98	75.11	87.5	97.0
Ours	65.23	75.45	89.4	97.8

Table 8: Comparisons between SCE and banding estimator. The number is the average performance.

Effect of the Banding Estimator As mentioned in Sec 3.2, we use the banding estimator for covariance estimation. This part compares SCE (the usual estimator) and the banding estimator in two aspects: performance and efficiency. We choose BERT-base as the PLM, and the results are presented in Table 8, and the efficiency is shown in Figure 3. As shown in Figure 3, our estimator achieves a significantly better performance-efficiency trade-off than SCE, demonstrating the banding estimator's effectiveness.

Embedding	x	Embedding	x
BERT	21.3	SBERT	15.6
BERT+Ours	14.7	SBERT+Ours	11.0
whitening	18.8	SimCSE	12.0
whitening+Ours	12.9	SimCSE+Ours	10.1

Table 9: Results on the analogy task. Smaller x means better. We can observe that our methods bring improvements to baselines.

6 Linguistic Case Study

We conduct case studies following the famous analogy from Word2Vec (Mikolov et al., 2013). The widely used analogy takes the following form: Knowing that A is to B as C is to D, given l_2 normalized embeddings $\vec{v}_A, \vec{v}_B, \vec{v}_C, \vec{v}_D$ for sentences A, B, C, D for an analogy of the above form, the task compare the embedding distance $dis(A, B)$ and $dis(C, D)$, which is defined as follows:

$$x = |\vec{v}_A - \vec{v}_B|_2 - |\vec{v}_C - \vec{v}_D|_2 \quad (12)$$

Then we use the sentence analogy set created from (Zhu and de Melo, 2020), which is specifically for this test. Here is a quadruple example:

A: A man is not singing.

B: A man is singing.

C: A girl is not playing the piano.

D: A girl is playing the piano.

We can see that the relation between A(C) and B(D) is negation; ideally, x in this quadruple should be small. We list the performance of the sentence embedding method w/ and w/o Sen2Pro in Table 9.

7 Conclusion and Future Work

This paper investigates the probabilistic representation for sentences and proposes Sen2Pro, which portrays the representation uncertainty from model and data uncertainty. The effectiveness of Sen2Pro is theoretically explained and empirically verified through extensive experiments, which show the great potential of probabilistic sentence embedding. In the future, we will investigate several aspects of Sen2Pro, like how to pre-train language models from an uncertainty perspective since existing pre-training models are based on Sen2Vec. Also, we expect to design more natural schemes that utilize Sen2Pro instead of concatenating the mean and variance vectors. Such directions can further enhance Sen2Pro's performance and efficiency.

Limitation

This major limitation of Sen2Pro lies in the computational cost due to the generation of several samples. Thus, improving the efficiency of Sen2Pro is a future direction. Besides, since we choose to concat the representation of different samples, there may be more natural ways to merge information from samples.

References

Moloud Abdar, Farhad Pourpanah, Sadiq Hussain, Dana Rezazadegan, Li Liu, Mohammad Ghavamzadeh, Paul Fieguth, Xiaochun Cao, Abbas Khosravi, U Rajendra Acharya, et al. 2021. A review of uncertainty quantification in deep learning: Techniques, applications and challenges. *Information Fusion*, 76:243–297.

Eneko Agirre, Carmen Banea, Claire Cardie, Daniel Cer, Mona Diab, Aitor Gonzalez-Agirre, Weiwei Guo, Inigo Lopez-Gazpio, Montse Maritxalar, Rada Mihalcea, et al. 2015. Semeval-2015 task 2: Semantic textual similarity, english, spanish and pilot on interpretability. In *Proceedings of the 9th international workshop on semantic evaluation (SemEval 2015)*, pages 252–263.

Eneko Agirre, Carmen Banea, Claire Cardie, Daniel Cer, Mona Diab, Aitor Gonzalez-Agirre, Weiwei Guo, Rada Mihalcea, German Rigau, and Janyce Wiebe. 2014. Semeval-2014 task 10: Multilingual semantic textual similarity. In *Proceedings of the 8th international workshop on semantic evaluation (SemEval 2014)*, pages 81–91.

Eneko Agirre, Carmen Banea, Daniel Cer, Mona Diab, Aitor Gonzalez Agirre, Rada Mihalcea, German Rigau Claramunt, and Janyce Wiebe. 2016. Semeval-2016 task 1: Semantic textual similarity, monolingual and cross-lingual evaluation. In *SemEval-2016. 10th International Workshop on Semantic Evaluation; 2016 Jun 16-17; San Diego, CA. Stroudsburg (PA): ACL; 2016. p. 497-511.* ACL (Association for Computational Linguistics).

Eneko Agirre, Daniel Cer, Mona Diab, and Aitor Gonzalez-Agirre. 2012. Semeval-2012 task 6: A pilot on semantic textual similarity. In * *SEM 2012: The First Joint Conference on Lexical and Computational Semantics–Volume 1: Proceedings of the main conference and the shared task, and Volume 2: Proceedings of the Sixth International Workshop on Semantic Evaluation (SemEval 2012)*, pages 385–393.

Eneko Agirre, Daniel Cer, Mona Diab, Aitor Gonzalez-Agirre, and Weiwei Guo. 2013. * sem 2013 shared task: Semantic textual similarity. In *Second joint conference on lexical and computational semantics (* SEM), volume 1: proceedings of the Main conference and the shared task: semantic textual similarity*, pages 32–43.

Robert Bamler and Stephan Mandt. 2017. Dynamic word embeddings. In *International conference on Machine learning*, pages 380–389. PMLR.

Yoshua Bengio, Réjean Ducharme, Pascal Vincent, and Christian Janvin. 2003. A neural probabilistic language model. *The journal of machine learning research*, 3:1137–1155.

Peter J Bickel and Elizaveta Levina. 2008. Regularized estimation of large covariance matrices. *The Annals of Statistics*, 36(1):199–227.

Jacob Bien, Florentina Bunea, and Luo Xiao. 2016. Convex banding of the covariance matrix. *Journal of the American Statistical Association*, 111(514):834–845.

Ondřej Bojar, Jindřich Helcl, Tom Kocmi, Jindřich Libovický, and Tomáš Musil. 2017. Results of the wmt17 neural mt training task. In *Proceedings of the second conference on machine translation*, pages 525–533.

Jose Camacho-Collados and Mohammad Taher Pilehvar. 2018. From word to sense embeddings: A survey on vector representations of meaning. *Journal of Artificial Intelligence Research*, 63:743–788.

Ming-Wei Chang, Lev-Arie Ratinov, Dan Roth, and Vivek Srikumar. 2008. Importance of semantic representation: Dataless classification. In *Aaai*, volume 2, pages 830–835.

Xi Chen, Yan Duan, Rein Houthooft, John Schulman, Ilya Sutskever, and Pieter Abbeel. 2016. Infogan: Interpretable representation learning by information maximizing generative adversarial nets. In *Proceedings of the 30th International Conference on Neural Information Processing Systems*, pages 2180–2188.

Kevin Clark, Minh-Thang Luong, Quoc V Le, and Christopher D Manning. 2019. Electra: Pre-training text encoders as discriminators rather than generators. In *International Conference on Learning Representations*.

Thomas M Cover. 1999. *Elements of information theory*. John Wiley & Sons.

Michael Denkowski and Alon Lavie. 2014. Meteor universal: Language specific translation evaluation for any target language. In *Proceedings of the ninth workshop on statistical machine translation*, pages 376–380.

Jacob Devlin, Ming-Wei Chang, Kenton Lee, and Kristina Toutanova. 2019. Bert: Pre-training of deep bidirectional transformers for language understanding. In *Proceedings of the 2019 Conference of the North American Chapter of the Association for Computational Linguistics: Human Language Technologies, Volume 1 (Long and Short Papers)*, pages 4171–4186.

Emily Dinan, Varvara Logacheva, Valentin Malykh, Alexander Miller, Kurt Shuster, Jack Urbanek, Douwe Kiela, Arthur Szlam, Iulian Serban, Ryan Lowe, et al. 2020. The second conversational intelligence challenge (convai2). In *The NeurIPS'18 Competition*, pages 187–208. Springer.

Gabriel Forgues, Joelle Pineau, Jean-Marie Larchevêque, and Réal Tremblay. 2014. Bootstrapping dialog systems with word embeddings. In *Nips, modern machine learning and natural language processing workshop*, volume 2.

Yarin Gal and Zoubin Ghahramani. 2016. Dropout as a bayesian approximation: Representing model uncertainty in deep learning. In *international conference on machine learning*, pages 1050–1059. PMLR.

Tianyu Gao, Xingcheng Yao, and Danqi Chen. 2021. Simcse: Simple contrastive learning of sentence embeddings. *arXiv preprint arXiv:2104.08821*.

Weihao Gao, Yu-Han Liu, Chong Wang, and Sewoong Oh. 2019. Rate distortion for model compression: From theory to practice. In *International Conference on Machine Learning*, pages 2102–2111. PMLR.

Philipp Grohs, Andreas Klotz, and Felix Voigtlaender. 2021. Phase transitions in rate distortion theory and deep learning. *Foundations of Computational Mathematics*, pages 1–64.

Pengcheng He, Xiaodong Liu, Jianfeng Gao, and Weizhu Chen. 2020. Deberta: Decoding-enhanced bert with disentangled attention. In *International Conference on Learning Representations*.

Felix Hill, Kyunghyun Cho, and Anna Korhonen. 2016. Learning distributed representations of sentences from unlabelled data. In *Proceedings of the 2016 Conference of the North American Chapter of the Association for Computational Linguistics: Human Language Technologies*, pages 1367–1377.

Jeremy Howard and Sebastian Ruder. 2018. Universal language model fine-tuning for text classification. In *Proceedings of the 56th Annual Meeting of the Association for Computational Linguistics (Volume 1: Long Papers)*, pages 328–339.

Junjie Huang, Duyu Tang, Wanjun Zhong, Shuai Lu, Linjun Shou, Ming Gong, Daxin Jiang, and Nan Duan. 2021. Whiteningbert: An easy unsupervised sentence embedding approach. *arXiv preprint arXiv:2104.01767*.

Eyke Hüllermeier and Willem Waegeman. 2021. Aleatoric and epistemic uncertainty in machine learning: An introduction to concepts and methods. *Machine Learning*, 110(3):457–506.

Alex Kendall and Yarin Gal. 2017. What uncertainties do we need in bayesian deep learning for computer vision? *Advances in neural information processing systems*, 30.

Ryan Kiros, Yukun Zhu, Russ R Salakhutdinov, Richard Zemel, Raquel Urtasun, Antonio Torralba, and Sanja Fidler. 2015. Skip-thought vectors. In *Advances in neural information processing systems*, pages 3294–3302.

Balaji Lakshminarayanan, Alexander Pritzel, and Charles Blundell. 2017. Simple and scalable predictive uncertainty estimation using deep ensembles. *Advances in neural information processing systems*, 30.

Gregor Leusch, Nicola Ueffing, and Hermann Ney. 2006. Cder: Efficient mt evaluation using block movements. In *11th Conference of the European Chapter of the Association for Computational Linguistics*.

Qing Li and Yang Chen. 2019. Rate distortion via deep learning. *IEEE Transactions on Communications*, 68(1):456–465.

Chin-Yew Lin. 2004. Rouge: A package for automatic evaluation of summaries. In *Text summarization branches out*, pages 74–81.

Yinhan Liu, Myle Ott, Naman Goyal, Jingfei Du, Mandar Joshi, Danqi Chen, Omer Levy, Mike Lewis, Luke Zettlemoyer, and Veselin Stoyanov. 2019. Roberta: A robustly optimized bert pretraining approach.

Ryan Lowe, Michael Noseworthy, Iulian Vlad Serban, Nicolas Angelard-Gontier, Yoshua Bengio, and Joelle Pineau. 2017. Towards an automatic turing test: Learning to evaluate dialogue responses. In *Proceedings of the 55th Annual Meeting of the Association for Computational Linguistics (Volume 1: Long Papers)*, pages 1116–1126.

Qingsong Ma, Yvette Graham, Shugen Wang, and Qun Liu. 2017. Blend: a novel combined mt metric based on direct assessment—casict-dcu submission to wmt17 metrics task. In *Proceedings of the second conference on machine translation*, pages 598–603.

Andrew Maas, Raymond E Daly, Peter T Pham, Dan Huang, Andrew Y Ng, and Christopher Potts. 2011. Learning word vectors for sentiment analysis. In *Proceedings of the 49th annual meeting of the association for computational linguistics: Human language technologies*, pages 142–150.

Wesley J Maddox, Pavel Izmailov, Timur Garipov, Dmitry P Vetrov, and Andrew Gordon Wilson. 2019. A simple baseline for bayesian uncertainty in deep learning. *Advances in Neural Information Processing Systems*, 32.

Yu Meng, Chenyan Xiong, Payal Bajaj, Saurabh Tiwary, Paul Bennett, Jiawei Han, and Xia Song. 2021. Coco-lm: Correcting and contrasting text sequences for language model pretraining.

Tomas Mikolov, Ilya Sutskever, Kai Chen, Greg S Corrado, and Jeff Dean. 2013. Distributed representations of words and phrases and their compositionality. In *Advances in neural information processing systems*, pages 3111–3119.

Yaniv Ovadia, Emily Fertig, Jie Ren, Zachary Nado, David Sculley, Sebastian Nowozin, Joshua Dillon, Balaji Lakshminarayanan, and Jasper Snoek. 2019. Can you trust your model's uncertainty? evaluating predictive uncertainty under dataset shift. *Advances in neural information processing systems*, 32.

Kishore Papineni, Salim Roukos, Todd Ward, and Wei-Jing Zhu. 2002. Bleu: a method for automatic evaluation of machine translation. In *Proceedings of the 40th annual meeting of the Association for Computational Linguistics*, pages 311–318.

Jeffrey Pennington, Richard Socher, and Christopher D Manning. 2014. Glove: Global vectors for word representation. In *Proceedings of the 2014 conference on empirical methods in natural language processing (EMNLP)*, pages 1532–1543.

Matthew E. Peters, Mark Neumann, Mohit Iyyer, Matt Gardner, Christopher Clark, Kenton Lee, and Luke Zettlemoyer. 2018. Deep contextualized word representations. In *Proceedings of the 2018 Conference of the North American Chapter of the Association for Computational Linguistics: Human Language Technologies, Volume 1 (Long Papers)*, pages 2227–2237, New Orleans, Louisiana. Association for Computational Linguistics.

Alec Radford, Jeffrey Wu, Rewon Child, David Luan, Dario Amodei, Ilya Sutskever, et al. 2019. Language models are unsupervised multitask learners. *OpenAI blog*, 1(8):9.

Colin Raffel, Noam Shazeer, Adam Roberts, Katherine Lee, Sharan Narang, Michael Matena, Yanqi Zhou, Wei Li, and Peter J Liu. 2020. Exploring the limits of transfer learning with a unified text-to-text transformer. *Journal of Machine Learning Research*, 21(140):1–67.

Hannah Rashkin, Eric Michael Smith, Margaret Li, and Y-Lan Boureau. 2019. Towards empathetic open-domain conversation models: A new benchmark and dataset. In *Proceedings of the 57th Annual Meeting of the Association for Computational Linguistics*, pages 5370–5381.

Nils Reimers and Iryna Gurevych. 2019. Sentence-bert: Sentence embeddings using siamese bert-networks. In *Proceedings of the 2019 Conference on Empirical Methods in Natural Language Processing and the 9th International Joint Conference on Natural Language Processing (EMNLP-IJCNLP)*, pages 3982–3992.

Vasile Rus and Mihai Lintean. 2012. An optimal assessment of natural language student input using word-to-word similarity metrics. In *International Conference on Intelligent Tutoring Systems*, pages 675–676. Springer.

Lingfeng Shen, Haiyun Jiang, Lemao Liu, and Shuming Shi. 2022a. Revisiting the evaluation metrics of paraphrase generation. *arXiv preprint arXiv:2202.08479*.

Lingfeng Shen, Lemao Liu, Haiyun Jiang, and Shuming Shi. 2022b. On the evaluation metrics for paraphrase generation. In *Proceedings of the 2022 Conference on Empirical Methods in Natural Language Processing*, pages 3178–3190.

Jianlin Su, Jiarun Cao, Weijie Liu, and Yangyiwen Ou. 2021. Whitening sentence representations for better semantics and faster retrieval. *arXiv preprint arXiv:2103.15316*.

Michael Tschannen, Josip Djolonga, Paul K Rubenstein, Sylvain Gelly, and Mario Lucic. 2019. On mutual information maximization for representation learning. In *International Conference on Learning Representations*.

Luke Vilnis and Andrew McCallum. 2015. Word representations via gaussian embedding. In *ICLR*.

Bin Wang, C-c Kuo, and Haizhou Li. 2022. Just rank: Rethinking evaluation with word and sentence similarities. In *Proceedings of the 60th Annual Meeting of the Association for Computational Linguistics (Volume 1: Long Papers)*, pages 6060–6077.

Dong Wang, Ning Ding, Piji Li, and Haitao Zheng. 2021. Cline: Contrastive learning with semantic negative examples for natural language understanding. In *Proceedings of the 59th Annual Meeting of the Association for Computational Linguistics and the 11th International Joint Conference on Natural Language Processing (Volume 1: Long Papers)*, pages 2332–2342.

John Wieting, Mohit Bansal, Kevin Gimpel, and Karen Livescu. 2015a. From paraphrase database to compositional paraphrase model and back. *Transactions of the Association for Computational Linguistics*, 3:345–358.

John Wieting, Mohit Bansal, Kevin Gimpel, and Karen Livescu. 2015b. Towards universal paraphrastic sentence embeddings. *arXiv preprint arXiv:1511.08198*.

Han Xiao and Wei Biao Wu. 2012. Covariance matrix estimation for stationary time series. *The Annals of Statistics*, 40(1):466–493.

Yuanmeng Yan, Rumei Li, Sirui Wang, Fuzheng Zhang, Wei Wu, and Weiran Xu. 2021. Consert: A contrastive framework for self-supervised sentence representation transfer. *arXiv preprint arXiv:2105.11741*.

Tianyi Zhang, Varsha Kishore, Felix Wu, Kilian Q Weinberger, and Yoav Artzi. 2019. Bertscore: Evaluating text generation with bert. In *International Conference on Learning Representations*.

Xiang Zhang, Junbo Zhao, and Yann LeCun. 2015. Character-level convolutional networks for text classification. *Advances in neural information processing systems*, 28:649–657.

Yan Zhang, Ruidan He, Zuozhu Liu, Kwan Hui Lim, and Lidong Bing. 2020. An unsupervised sentence embedding method by mutual information maximization. In *Proceedings of the 2020 Conference on Empirical Methods in Natural Language Processing (EMNLP)*, pages 1601–1610.

Chunting Zhou, Xuezhe Ma, Di Wang, and Graham Neubig. 2019. Density matching for bilingual word embedding. In *Proceedings of the 2019 Conference of the North American Chapter of the Association for Computational Linguistics: Human Language Technologies, Volume 1 (Long and Short Papers)*, pages 1588–1598.

Xunjie Zhu and Gerard de Melo. 2020. Sentence analogies: Linguistic regularities in sentence embeddings. In *Proceedings of the 28th International Conference on Computational Linguistics*, pages 3389–3400.

A Proof of Theorem 1

To accomplish further derivation on theorem 1. we first present a lemma from (Bickel and Levina, 2008; Bien et al., 2016).

Lemma 1. *Let X_i be i.i.d. $N(0, \Sigma)$ and $\lambda_{\max}(\Sigma) \leq \epsilon$, where ϵ is a positive constant. Also, let σ denote Σ, then we have*

$$P\left(\left|\sum_{i=1}^{n}(X_{ij}X_{ik} - \sigma_{jk})\right| \geq nh\right) \leq C_1 e^{-C_2 n v^2}$$

for $|h| \leq \delta$, where C_1, C_2 and threshold δ depend on ϵ only, and n is the sample number for X_i.

Proof 1. *We firstly denote the maximum element of a matrix A as $|A|_{max}$, we have*

$$\begin{aligned}
&\left\|B\left(\hat{\Sigma}\right) - B(\Sigma)\right\|_2 \\
&= O_p\left(\left\|B\left(\hat{\Sigma}\right) - B(\Sigma)\right\|_\infty\right) \\
&= O_p\left(\left|B\left(\hat{\Sigma}\right) - B(\Sigma)\right|_{max}\right)
\end{aligned}$$

Naturally, based on Lemma 2, we can know that

$$P\left(\left|B\left(\hat{\Sigma}\right) - B(\Sigma)\right|_{max} \geq t\right) \leq 3ke^{-nt^2\gamma(\epsilon,\lambda)}$$

for $|t| \leq \lambda(\epsilon)$. By choosing $t = M(\log(k)/n)^{1/2}$, we conclude that

$$\left|B\left(\hat{\Sigma}\right) - \Sigma\right|_{max} = O_p\left(\left(n^{-1}\log k\right)^{1/2}\right)$$

Putting them together, we have the result that completes the proof for Theorem 1.

B Theoretical Analysis

This section presents theoretical explanations why Sen2Pro is better than Sen2Vec. Our framework is built on comparisons through distribution distances, which is inspired from representation learning based on KL divergence (relative entropy) (Chen et al., 2016; Li and Chen, 2019; Gao et al., 2019; Tschannen et al., 2019).

B.1 Problem Formulation

We present the formulation of sentence representation: for a representation X (with dimension k) of a sentence s, we assume that $X \sim P(\mu, \Sigma)$, where $P(\mu, \Sigma)$ is the ground-truth but unknown probability distribution.

Recall that both Sen2Pro and Sen2Vec methods adopt the following representations:

- Sen2Pro: sentence s is represented as $(\hat{\mu}, \hat{\Sigma})$, where $\hat{\mu} \in \mathcal{R}^{k\times 1}$ and $\hat{\Sigma} \in \mathcal{R}^{k\times 1}$ are estimated through i.i.d. samples $X_1, X_2, \cdots, X_N$. Therefore, Sen2Pro corresponds to a random variable $\hat{X} \sim P(\hat{\mu}, \hat{\Sigma})$.

- Sen2Vec: sentence s is represented as $v \in \mathcal{R}^{k\times 1}$, where v may be a sample X_i from Sen2Pro.

Probabilistic Viewpoint Accordingly, from the viewpoint of probability, both Sen2Pro and Sen2Vec can be considered as the following random variables whose density functions are unknown but mean and covariance are known:

- Sen2Pro: $X_{\text{P}} \sim P(\hat{\mu}, \hat{\Sigma})$.

- Sen2Vec: $X_{\text{V}} \sim P(v, \epsilon I)$.

where ϵ is a constant as a smoothing operator which makes a deterministic quantity v like a random variable X_{V}. Note that since ϵI is constant for any sentence s, $(v, \epsilon I)$ as sentence embedding is equivalent to v as sentence embedding for downstream tasks.

Then our goal is to show whether the $P(\hat{\mu}, \hat{\Sigma})$ is closer to $P(\mu, \Sigma)$ than $P(v, \epsilon I)$, which is defined as follows:

$$D(X_{\mathrm{P}}, X) < D(X_{\mathrm{V}}, X) \tag{13}$$

Specifically, we use the KL divergence D as the distance measurement.

B.2 Superiority of Sen2Pro

In this part, we conduct derivations based on distribution distance to answer the above question. Unfortunately, since the density distributions of all three random variables X, X_{P}, X_{V} are unknown, it is intractable to derive the equations on KL divergence. To this end, we make the following assumption about their density functions.

Gaussian Distribution Assumption Intuitively, an exponential family is suitable for the density function of Sen2Pro, such as Gaussian, Poisson, and Bernoulli. In this paper, we assume all three random variables X, X_{P}, X_{V} are from Gaussian distribution, because non-Gaussian random variables possess smaller entropy (i.e., less uncertainty) than Gaussian random variables (Cover, 1999). In this way, the ground-truth random variable X contains the maximal uncertainty.

Based on the above assumption, we have: $X \sim \mathcal{N}(\mu, \Sigma)$, $X_{\mathrm{P}} \sim \mathcal{N}(\hat{\mu}, \hat{\Sigma})$, and $X_{\mathrm{V}} \sim \mathcal{N}(\hat{v}, \epsilon I)$. Then, we provide the following theoretical guarantee to show the superiority of Sen2Pro, which indicates that $\mathcal{N}(\hat{\mu}, \hat{\Sigma})$ is closer to $\mathcal{N}(\mu, \Sigma)$ than $\mathcal{N}(v, \epsilon I)$:

Theorem 2. *If $\epsilon < \frac{\sqrt[k]{|\hat{\Sigma}|}}{e}$ with e as the natural number, then the following inequality holds:*

$$D(X_P, X) < D(X_V, X) \tag{14}$$

C Proof of Theorem 2

Before we start to prove the theorem, we provide some definitions that will be useful for further derivation:

Definition 1. *For a random variable X with mean μ, the moment generating function is*

$$M_{X-\mu}(\lambda) = \mathbb{E}\exp(\lambda(X - \mathbb{E}X)) \tag{15}$$

the cumulant-generating function is

$$\Gamma_{X-\mu}(\lambda) = \log M_{X-\mu}(\lambda) \tag{16}$$

We denote $D(X_{\mathrm{P}}, X)$ and $D(X_{\mathrm{V}}, X)$ as D_a and D_b, and rewrite $D(X_{\mathrm{P}}, X)$ and $D(X_{\mathrm{V}}, X)$ as follows:

$$D(\mathcal{N}(\mu, \Sigma)||\mathcal{N}(\hat{\mu}, \hat{\Sigma})) = \frac{1}{2}[\log(\frac{|\Sigma|}{|\epsilon I|}) + \mathrm{tr}\left(\epsilon I \Sigma^{-1}\right) - k] \tag{17}$$

$$D(\mathcal{N}(\mu, \Sigma)||\mathcal{N}(\hat{v}, \epsilon I)) = \frac{1}{2}[\log(\frac{|\Sigma|}{|\hat{\Sigma}|}) + \mathrm{tr}\left(\Sigma\hat{\Sigma}^{-1}\right) - k + (\mu - \hat{\mu})^{\top}\hat{\Sigma}^{-1}(\mu - \hat{\mu})] \tag{18}$$

Proof 2. *As defined in the main paper, we have $D_a = D(\mathcal{N}(\mu, \Sigma)||\mathcal{N}(\hat{\mu}, \hat{\Sigma})) = \frac{1}{2}[\log(\frac{|\Sigma|}{|\epsilon I|}) + \mathrm{tr}\left(\epsilon I \Sigma^{-1}\right) - p]$ and $D_b = D(\mathcal{N}(\mu, \Sigma)||\mathcal{N}(\hat{v}, \epsilon I)) = \frac{1}{2}[\log(\frac{|\Sigma|}{|\hat{\Sigma}|}) + \mathrm{tr}\left(\Sigma\hat{\Sigma}^{-1}\right) - p + (\mu - \hat{\mu})^{\top}\hat{\Sigma}^{-1}(\mu - \hat{\mu})]$. As illustrated in the methodology of Sen2Pro, we have the following derivation:*

$$|\Sigma^{-1}| = \prod_{i=1}^{n} \frac{1}{\Sigma_{ii}} \tag{19}$$

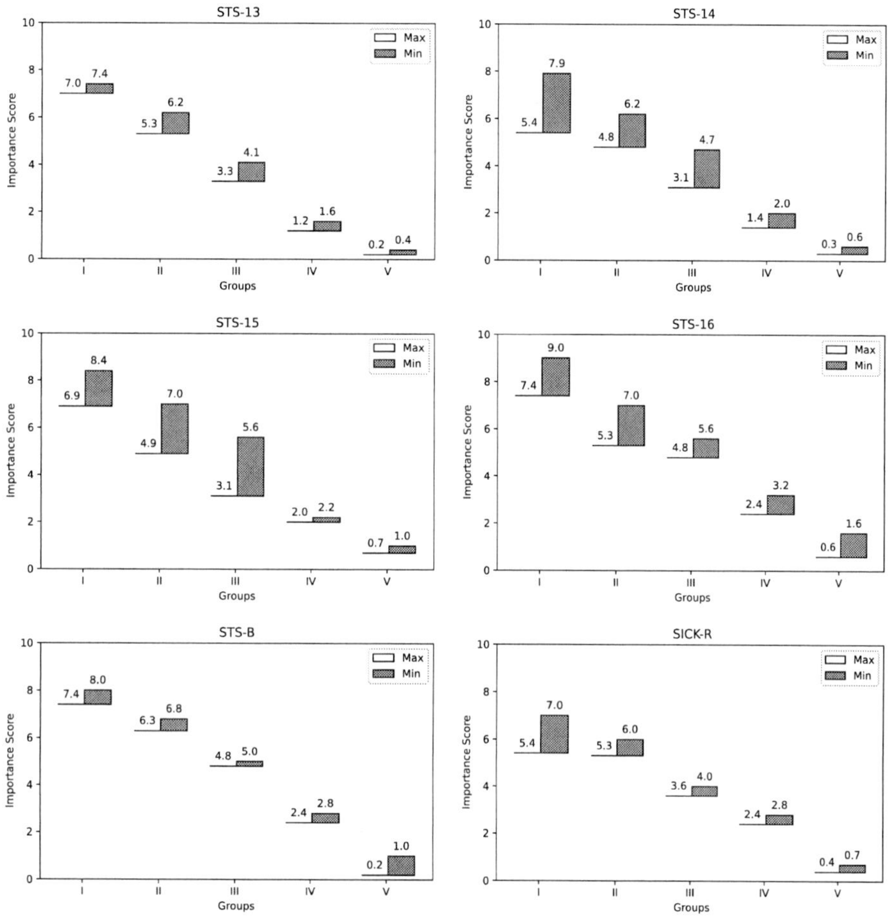

Figure 4: The importance score of five groups of features on STS benchmarks.

$$|\Sigma| = \prod_{i=1}^{n} \Sigma_{ii} \tag{20}$$

Then we focus on the term:

$$\begin{aligned} D_a &= D(\mathcal{N}(\mu, \Sigma) \| \mathcal{N}(\hat{\mu}, \hat{\Sigma})) \\ &= \frac{1}{2}[\log(\frac{|\Sigma|}{|\epsilon I|}) + \operatorname{tr}\left(\epsilon I \Sigma^{-1}\right) - p] \\ &\approx \frac{1}{2}[\log(\frac{|\Sigma|}{|\epsilon I|}) - p] \end{aligned} \tag{21}$$

since ϵ is an extremely small number. Besides, we also make derivation on D_b:

$$\begin{aligned} D_a &= D(\mathcal{N}(\mu, \Sigma) \| \mathcal{N}(\hat{\mu}, \hat{\Sigma})) \\ &= \frac{1}{2}[\log(\frac{|\Sigma|}{|\hat{\Sigma}|}) + \operatorname{tr}\left(\Sigma \hat{\Sigma}^{-1}\right) - p \\ &+ (\mu - \hat{\mu})^\top \hat{\Sigma}^{-1} (\mu - \hat{\mu})] \\ &= \frac{1}{2}[\log(\frac{|\Sigma|}{|\hat{\Sigma}|}) + (\mu - \hat{\mu})^\top \hat{\Sigma}^{-1} (\mu - \hat{\mu})] \end{aligned} \tag{22}$$

To better analyze the $(\mu - \hat{\mu})^\top \hat{\Sigma}^{-1} (\mu - \hat{\mu})$ term of D_a, we present the following lemma:

Lemma 2. *For $X \sim N\left(\mu, \sigma^2\right)$, where X is a single Gaussian variable,*

$$\Gamma_{X-\mu}(\lambda) = \frac{\lambda^2 \sigma^2}{2}, \qquad \Gamma^*_{X-\mu}(\epsilon) = \frac{\epsilon^2}{2\sigma^2}.$$

For $X_1, \ldots, X_n \sim N\left(\mu, \sigma^2\right)$, it's easy to check that the bound is tight:

$$\lim_{n \to \infty} \frac{1}{n} \ln P\left(\bar{X}_n - \mu \geq \epsilon\right) = -\frac{\epsilon^2}{2\sigma^2}.$$

Therefore, we can represent $|\mu - \hat{\mu}|_2$ as $O(\epsilon)$ and we have the following:

$$\begin{aligned} &(\mu - \hat{\mu})^\top \hat{\Sigma}^{-1} (\mu - \hat{\mu}) \\ &= D(\mathcal{N}(\mu, \Sigma) \| \mathcal{N}(\hat{\mu}, \hat{\Sigma})) \\ &= O(\epsilon^2) \end{aligned} \tag{23}$$

Naturally, we drop all $O(\epsilon^2)$ term and formulate D_a as follows:

$$D_a = \frac{1}{2}[\log(\frac{|\Sigma|}{|\hat{\Sigma}|}) + \operatorname{tr}\left(\Sigma \hat{\Sigma}^{-1}\right) - p] \tag{24}$$

$$= \frac{1}{2}[\log(\frac{|\Sigma|}{|\hat{\Sigma}|})] \tag{25}$$

Then we insert the condition to the equality $D_a < D_b$, and we can complete the proof.

D Comparisons between individual estimation and unified estimation

This section conducts comparisons between individual estimation and unified estimation.

- Concretely, individual estimation refers to estimate $\mu^m, \hat{\Sigma}^m$ and $\mu^d, \hat{\Sigma}^d$ based on $\mathcal{S}^m$ and $\mathcal{S}^d$, respectively. Then we use $\frac{\mu^m + \mu^d}{2}$ and $\frac{\hat{\Sigma}^m + \hat{\Sigma}^d}{2}$ for sentence representation.

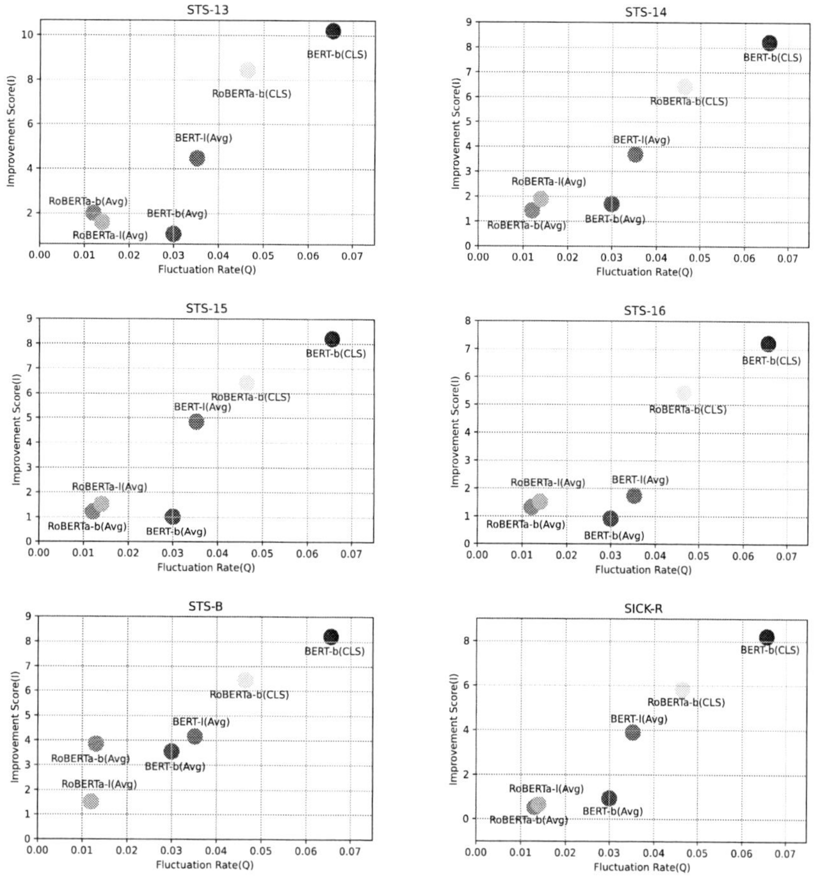

Figure 5: The relation between fluctuation rate (Q) and improvement score (I) on STS benchmarks.

- Correspondingly, unified estimation refers to estimate $\mu^u, \hat{\Sigma}^u$ based on $\mathcal{S}^m \cap \mathcal{S}^d$. Then use $\mu^u, \hat{\Sigma}^u$ for sentence representation.

The experimental settings follow the Sec 4, and the results are shown in Table 10. We can observe that unified estimation under-performs individual estimation. Thus, we choose to estimate uncertainty in an individual way.

Model	STS-12	STS-13	STS-14	STS-15	STS-16	STS-B	SICK-R	Average
BERT-base	57.84	61.95	62.48	70.95	69.81	59.04	63.75	63.69
BERT-base-G_{m+d}	59.40	63.03	64.18	71.97	70.73	62.59	64.69	65.23 (+1.54)
BERT-base-G_u	58.86	62.66	63.77	71.48	70.56	61.89	64.28	64.79 (+1.02)

Table 10: BERT-base-G_{m+d} and BERT-base-G_u represent Sen2Pro with individual and unified estimation, respectively.

E Relation between model uncertainty and feature importance

This section serves as a complementary material for demonstrating the relation between the model uncertainty and feature importance, and the results on the STS task are illustrated in the Figure **??** **??** 4.

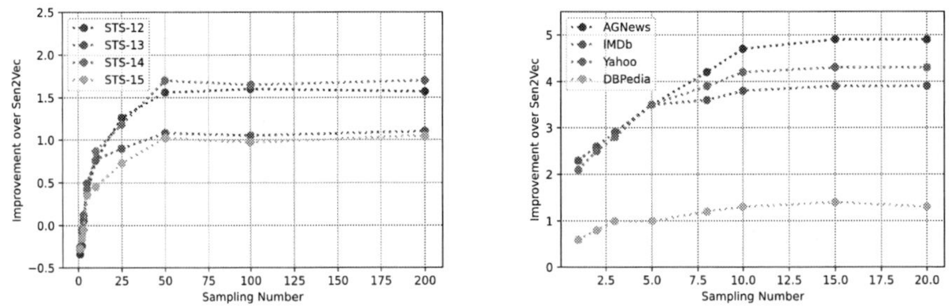

Figure 6: Results as the sampling number n_1 changes with 'BERT-base-G'. The text classification task uses the '10-shot' setting.

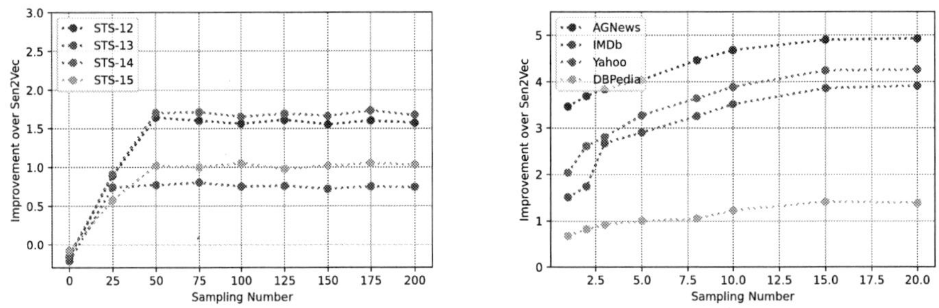

Figure 7: Results as sampling number n_2 changes with 'BERT-base-G'. The text classification task uses the '10-shot' setting.

F Relation between model uncertainty and performance improvements

This section serves as a complementary material for demonstrating the relation between the model uncertainty and performance improvements, and the results on the STS task are illustrated in the Figures 5.

G Influence of the Sampling Number

This section examines the effect of the sampling number n_1 in the model uncertainty and the sampling number n_2. To examine the effect of n_1, an experiment is run, where n_1 varies and n_2 is set 30. The results of the STS and text classification task are illustrated in Figure 6. From Figure 6, we select $n_1 = 50$ and $n_1 = 15$ for the STS and text classification task, respectively, since smaller n_1 result in imprecise sentence representation and larger n_1 brings significant computational burden with little improvements. To examine the effect of the sampling number n_2, we change n_2 and keep the optimal n_1, and show the results in Figure 7. Overall, when n_2 is greater than 30, Sen2Pro achieves a stable performance.

H Results of Segment-level Evaluation of Neural Machine Translation

In the main paper, we make the evaluations on the system-level NMT. Here, we present the results of segment-level Evaluation of Neural Machine Translation. The experimental settings are kept the same as the ones in our main paper. The results are listed in Table 11. As the results demonstrate, Sen2Pro outperforms Sen2Vec and achieves comparable performances to BERTScore.

Metric	cs-en	de-en	fi-en	lv-en	ru-en	tr-en	zh-en	Avg
BLEU	23.3	41.5	28.5	15.4	22.8	14.5	17.8	21.2
ITER	19.8	39.6	23.5	12.8	13.9	2.9	14.4	18.1
RUSE	34.7	49.8	36.8	27.3	31.1	25.9	21.8	32.5
Sen2Vec	33.8	48.6	35.9	26.0	29.0	22.4	21.0	31.0
BERTScore	36.5	51.4	37.2	26.8	31.7	27.2	22.9	33.4
Sen2Pro	38.7	54.1	38.9	28.3	34.5	28.0	24.8	35.3

Table 11: Pearson correlations with segment-level machine translation evaluation on WMT17.

Visual Coherence Loss for Coherent and Visually Grounded Story Generation

Xudong Hong[124], **Vera Demberg**[24], **Asad Sayeed**[3], **Qiankun Zheng**[24] **and Bernt Schiele**[14]

[1]Dept. of Computer Vision and Machine Learning, MPI Informatics
[2]Dept. of Language Science and Technology and Dept. of Computer Science, Saarland University
[3]Dept. of Philosophy, Linguistics, and Theory of Science, University of Gothenburg
[4]Saarland Informatics Campus, Saarbrücken
`{xhong,vera,qzheng}@coli.uni-saarland.de`
`schiele@mpi-inf.mpg.de, asad.sayeed@gu.se`

Abstract

Local coherence is essential for text generation models. We identify two important aspects of local coherence within the visual storytelling task: (1) the model needs to represent re-occurrences of characters within the image sequence in order to mention them correctly in the story; (2) character representations should enable us to find instances of the same characters and distinguish different characters. In this paper, we propose a loss function inspired by a linguistic theory of coherence for learning image sequence representations. We further propose combining features from an object detector and a face detector to construct stronger character features. To evaluate visual grounding that current reference-based metrics do not measure, we propose a character matching metric to check whether the models generate referring expressions correctly for characters in input image sequences. Experiments on a visual story generation dataset show that our proposed features and loss function are effective for generating more coherent and visually grounded stories. Our code is available at `https://github.com/vwprompt/vcl`.

1 Introduction

Storytelling is humans using language to convey stories to audiences, which is one of the oldest human activities of language use (Lucarevschi, 2016). In this paper, we focus on the visual storytelling task of generating stories from visual narratives, i.e., a sequence of images with a plot (Park and Kim, 2015; Huang et al., 2016; Hong et al., 2023). Stories, unlike image captions, contain several characters and events involving recurrent characters and their interactions with each other and the environment. Especially, *characters* are among the most important aspects of story writing (Goldfarb-Tarrant et al., 2020).

However, the current state-of-the-art (SOTA) visual storytelling models often fail to generate correct referring expressions for characters (Modi and Parde, 2019). To confirm this, we generate 50 stories using a SOTA model (TAPM; Yu et al., 2021) and annotate different types of errors.[1] The most prevalent error that appears in 60% of the generated stories is *lacking local coherence* which manifests as the characters appearing in the image not being mentioned correctly in the stories. For instance, in the first two rows of Figure 1, the character Jeremy appears across all images. The SOTA model TAPM first mentions him as *Jeremy* in the first sentence but misses him in the second sentence and inconsistently misnames him as *Adam* in the last sentence.

We identify two fundamental causes of this problem: 1) Most previous models do not represent the recurrence of characters in the image sequence explicitly. In particular, it is not clear whether the parameters in the model can capture character recurrence such that the *visual coherence*, local coherence in image sequences, can be reflected in textual coherence by repeated mentions of the recurrent characters in the story. We argue that a model that captures and represents the visual coherence better would also lead to more coherent stories.

2) Previous models mostly consider visual features without a focus on human characters, such as features extracted with a general vision backbone model. These features lack enough power to represent properties such as age, gender, face, or body shape. As a result, models using these features cannot distinguish between different instances of the same human character, which introduces wrong character mentions in generated stories.

Our **contributions** for tackling these limitations:

(a) To tackle limitation 1), we propose a new ranking loss function, *Visual Coherence Loss (VCL)*, which is inspired by models of cohesion in language (see section 4.1). VCL punishes standalone instances and rewards instances that appear

[1]TAPM is the only SOTA model that has publically available source code. See Appendix A for the details of annotation.

Proceedings of the 8th Workshop on Representation Learning for NLP (RepL4NLP 2023), pages 334–346
July 13, 2023

Model	  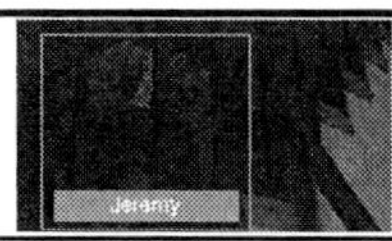	CM	METEOR
TAPM (SOTA)	Jeremy was hiding behind the wall . ??? Adam was able to get up and leave the building . Adam was able to escape .	0.5	22.67
VCL	Jeremy was in the middle of a fight with a gun . ??? Jeremy was hiding behind the wall . Jeremy is still in the room and he is trying to get out .	0.83	38.6
VCL + Insightface	Jeremy was hiding behind the wall . Jeremy and Adam were hiding behind the wall . Jeremy was hiding behind a wall .	1	22.74
Oracle	Jeremy was the one who was hiding in the room . ??? Adam was not happy with the plan . Jeremy was hiding behind the stairs .	0.83	27.16
Human	Jeremy was trying to escape with a gun and bullets around his neck. Adam found Jeremy sitting on the stairs. Jeremy started weeping and begging for his forgiveness.	1	-

Figure 1: Case study of generated/human-written stories given an example image sequence. ??? denotes the error of Too Few REs defined in 5.2. The Wrong Referring Expression error is marked with a red background. We also report the CM scores together with METEOR scores.

consecutively in visual narratives. Experiments show that the proposed loss function increases the coherence of the generated stories (see section 5.1).

(b) To obtain better character representations and tackle limitation 2), we experiment with different features that have proven useful for person re-identification tasks (see section 6). We then add the resulting features separately to visual story generation models. Experiments show that the representation from the face detector is most effective for character representation.

(c) When evaluating the stories generated by the models, we find that reference-based metrics cannot capture referring expression errors, so we propose a new evaluation metric *character matching (CM)* for image-text relevance in visual stories (see section 3). This metric is based on a weighted bipartite matching graph between the instances in the images and the co-referring expressions in the stories. We compute a coefficient from the weighted bipartite matching that measures local coherence. We apply our metric to prove the effectiveness of our loss function.

2 Related Work

Visually-grounded Story Generation. Modelling visual grounding is essential for vision-based language generation tasks like image captioning (Pont-Tuset et al., 2020), paragraph generation (Ilinykh and Dobnik, 2022) and visual dialog (Yu et al., 2022). However, previous work in visual story generation conducted experiments only on the Visual Storytelling dataset (VIST, Huang et al., 2016), which doesn't have annotations for visual grounding. Parallel to our research, Liu and Keller (2023) annotate recurring characters in the VIST dataset which enable further exploration of grounding human characters in visual narratives.

Most of the previous models for visual storytelling only use *global features*, full image features extracted with a general vision backbone model trained on the image classification task (Yu et al., 2017; Wang et al., 2018; Huang et al., 2019). Some recent researches use *local features*, which are features of a specific part of the image such as objects, to generate visually grounded stories (Wang et al., 2020; Hong et al., 2020; Yu et al., 2021; Qi et al., 2021; Braude et al., 2022). Only a few works make use of human-related features like emotions (Li et al., 2019), sentiments (Chen et al., 2022) or persona (Chandu et al., 2019). One work that focuses on recurrences of characters is Dong et al. (2019), which employs a Bi-LSTM to encode conference chains in texts. However, their model requires textual features from the corresponding conference chains as input in the test time. On the contrary, our model only requires visual features from the images.

Coherent Story Generation. Coherence is one of the major properties that people would like to achieve in story generation (Alabdulkarim et al., 2021). Previous work generates a story conditioned on a prompt such as keywords (Yao et al., 2019), story plot (Rashkin et al., 2020), cue phrases (Xu et al., 2020), or scripts (Pu et al., 2022). Training data for story generation includes the STORIUM dataset (Akoury et al., 2020). Its collaboratively-written long stories contain rich annotations such as narrator prompts, character goals, and other attributes to guide story generation. Previous models based on these datasets require access to character labels which are expensive to obtain and not always available in real-world settings. In contrast, our model only needs an additional loss function during model training.

Character Representations for NLG. Characters are essential to stories written and read by humans. Unfortunately, only a limited amount of work has been done on constructing explicit character representations. In story generation, Clark et al. (2018) represent characters with separate trainable parameters and integrate them with the latent representations of the language decoder using max pooling. But they only apply their method to referring expression generation instead of end-to-end story generation. In movie description, Rohrbach et al. (2017) extract head and body representations for characters and train the model for character re-identification and movie description jointly. However, all these methods integrate character features into RNN language decoders. Our model is the first attempt to encode character explicitly in Transformer-based models.

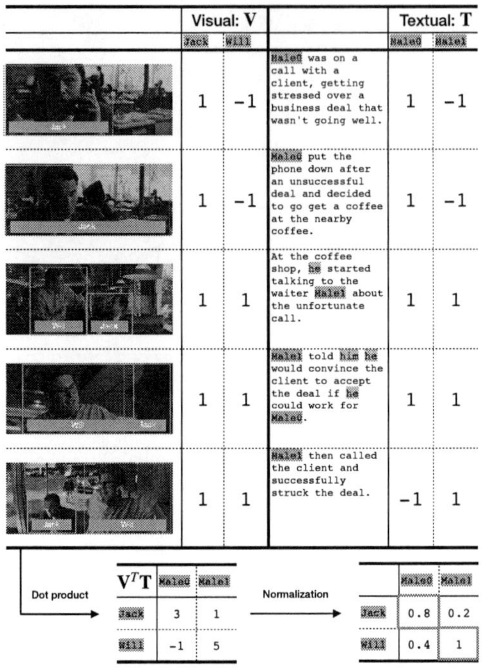

Figure 2: Computation process of character matching metric demonstrated with an example pair of image sequence and text. We show the corresponding Visual appearance matrices (**V**) and textual appearance matrices (**T**) of characters. The resulting maximum weighted bipartite match is in red boxes.

3 Image-Text Relevance Metric

In previous visually-grounded story generation work, models are evaluated with reference-based metrics like METEOR. However, the reference-based metrics only measure similarities between reference texts and generated stories such that the actual relevance of input images to output text is not evaluated. Specifically, we design a character-matching metric (CM) to determine whether expressions referring to human characters in image sequences are generated correctly.

The computation process of CM is in Figure 2. For each pair of image sequence and story, we first construct the appearance matrices $\mathbf{V} \in \{1, -1\}^{m \times n_v}$ and $\mathbf{T} \in \{1, -1\}^{m \times n_t}$, which indicate for each character whether it is present (1) vs. absent (-1) in an image or a sentence, where n_v is the number of characters in the image sequence, n_t is the number of referring expressions in generated stories and m is the number of images/texts. We then compute the matrix of matching scores of each pair as: $\mathbf{M} = \mathbf{V}^T\mathbf{T}$. We normalize the matching scores to the domain $[0, 1]$ and obtain the matrix $\mathbf{M}' = (\mathbf{M}/m + \mathbf{1})/2$. To obtain the optimal match between the images and sentences by the occurrences of characters, we compute the maximum weighted bipartite matching by applying the Hopcroft-Karp algorithm (Hopcroft and Karp, 1973) implemented in SciPy (Virtanen et al., 2020). The final overall character matching score is obtained by averaging the scores of the maximum matches across all characters (e.g. 0.9 in Figure 2).

3.1 Analysis of Baselines

We apply our CM metric to show the limitation of current models, which requires the labels of characters in image sequences. We use Visual Writing Prompts (VWP; Hong et al., 2023), a vision-based dataset that contains image sequences aligned with human-written stories in English[2]. In VWP, each image is corresponding to a piece of text. Instances of each main character are annotated with the name of the character (see Figure 1). Our baselines are:

Seq2Seq. (Seq2Seq; Huang et al., 2016) is a

[2] https://vwprompt.github.io/

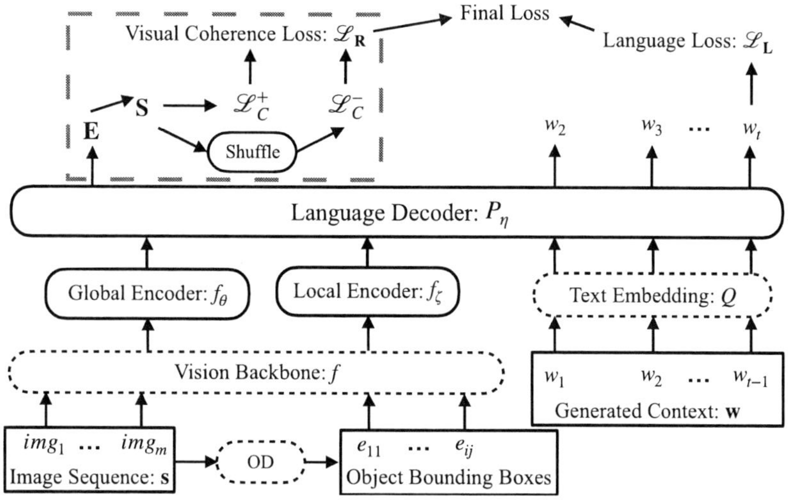

Figure 3: Architecture of visual story generation model with visual coherence loss. Our contributions are in the blue box. Components in dash lines are frozen during training. OD is the pre-trained object detector.

Model	LF	CM	std
Lower bound	-	32.04	-
Seq2Seq		68.03	1.27
Seq2Seq	obj	67.41	0.88
TAPM		67.33	1.13
TAPM	obj	67.99	0.97
Human	-	73.65	-
Upper bound	-	100	-

Table 1: Comparison of baseline models using different local features (LF) on the test set of VWP using character matching metric (CM). All numbers of models are an average of three runs with different random seeds.

seq2seq model with an encoder-decoder architecture. Visual features are first projected with an encoder which is a feed-forward neural network, then fed to the decoder which is a pre-trained GPT-2 model.

TAPM. (TAPM; Yu et al., 2021) is a Transformer-based model which adapts the visual features with pre-trained GPT-2. This is the current state-of-the-art model for visual story generation.

For generated text, we run a coreference resolution model (Lee et al., 2018) to capture all referring expressions. We compute the CM metric for the generated stories of two baseline models as well as the human-written stories. We compute the CM upper bound (100) by treating gold annotations of characters in image sequences as referring expressions in texts, i.e., using **V** as the textual appearance matrix. We also estimate the lower bound (32.04) by randomly shuffling the appearance matrices and then calculating the CM metric using the shuffled matrices.

Results in Table 1 show that humans outperform the baselines significantly, which indicates that human-written stories match better with input image sequences in terms of characters. We believe that the gap between current SOTA models and the human stories stems from the models' lack of representations for the recurrence of characters in the image sequence.

4 Visually Grounded Story Generation

In this section, we describe the visually grounded story generation model with a new loss function for self-supervised learning of image sequences. In the visual story generation task, given a sequence of images $\mathrm{s} = (img_1, img_2, ..., img_m), \mathrm{s} \in \mathbb{D}^m$, the model needs to generate a story $\mathbf{w}_o = (w_1, w_2, ..., w_{t-1}, w_t), \mathbf{w}_o \in \mathbb{D}^t$.

Encoder-decoder architecture Figure 3 represents our whole architecture, which is based on an encoder-decoder architecture that is also used in most previous work; our architectural changes are represented in the dashed blue box.

The first input to the model is the image sequence s. For the image $img_i \in \mathrm{s}$, we extract global features $f(img_i) \in \mathbb{R}^d$ from the output of the last fully-connected layer of a pre-trained vision backbone model f. We then obtain n_i bounding boxes of object $e_{ij}, j \in [1, n_i]$ predicted by an object detector using the image encoder f as the backbone. We crop each detected object e_{ij} and feed the cropped image region to f to get the local features $f(e_{ij}) \in \mathbb{R}^d$.

The global and local features are first fed to the global encoder f_θ and the local encoder f_ζ correspondingly in order to project them to the same hidden dimensions as the transformer-based language decoder P_η, to which the hidden representations are fed. To generate tokens auto-regressively, the context $\mathbf{w}$ consisting of previously generated tokens $(w_1, w_2, ..., w_{t-1})$ are fed into a pre-trained text embedding layer Q and then to P_η. Given the input sequence $(\mathbf{s}, \mathbf{w})$, the model represents the probability distribution of the next token w_t as:

$$P(w_t|\mathbf{s}, \mathbf{w}) = P_\eta(f_\theta(f(img_i)), f_\zeta(f(e_{ij})), Q(\mathbf{w}))$$

The major limitation of the encoder-decoder architecture is that there are no representations in both global and local encoders for recurring characters in the input image sequence which we believe are essential to visual coherence in image sequences. The parameters η in the language generator P_η are not sufficient to capture character re-occurrence among the local representations $\mathbf{L_{ij}} = f_\zeta(f(e_{ij}))$. So the visual coherence present in the image sequence is not reflected in textual coherence. We hypothesize that a model that captures and represents the visual coherence better would lead to more coherent stories.

4.1 Visual Coherence Loss

We propose Visual Coherence Loss (VCL, in the blue box of Figure 3) as an auxiliary loss to enable the model to capture the visual coherence of image sequences. Our goal is to measure visual coherence in terms of the recurrence of characters.

Centering theory (Grosz et al., 1995) is one way to explain the relationship between character recurrence and narrative coherence. This theory holds that if a pair of adjacent sentences contain the same discourse entities (here: characters), readers are more likely to find the transition between this sentence pair to be coherent. Character recurrence is very common in visual as well as textual narratives. In addition, images in visual narratives can be considered sentences in textual narratives. Inspired by these, we apply centering theory on measuring coherence in visual narratives.

Character instance similarities. To apply centering theory, we first need to find the same-character recurrences, but we do not have labels for characters at test time. Instead, we can take advantage of the similarities between character instances (as bounding boxes of *person* objects) of the same character across different images. We use the similarities as soft labels to capture different instances of that one character without any manual labels.

To compute similarities between character instances, the first step is to obtain their representations. We identify the objects depicting people automatically and use their local representations $\mathbf{L} = f_\zeta(f(e))$. The representations must be in the latent space of the language decoder P_η. So we pass the local representations through the language decoder to get the contextualized local representations as $\mathbf{E} = P_\eta(\mathbf{L})$. The next step is to compute similarities of character instances across all images. We calculate an instance similarity matrix, consisting of dot products of contextualized local representations, as: $\mathbf{S}' = (s_{ijkl}) = (\mathbf{E}_{ik}^{\mathrm{T}}\mathbf{E}_{jl})$, where $k \in [1, n_i], l \in [1, n_j]$.

Character re-occurrence. Another condition of applying centering theory is to be able to identify where the characters actually recur or not in two adjacent images. We first need to identify occurrences of each character instance in each image. We, therefore, compute a matrix of image-instance similarity. We group elements by image along one dimension indexed by k in $\mathbf{S}'$ and compute the average as: $\mathbf{S} = \text{mean}_{k=1}^{k=n_i}(s_{ijkl}) = (s_{ijl})$ where $i \in [1, m], j \in [1, m], l \in [1, n_j]$. Each element s_{ijl} is the similarity between image i and character instance e_{jl} in image j.

We measure visual coherence in terms of the squared difference between similarities of character instances in the two adjacent images. For an illustration of this idea, consider the following three cases: 1) if the similarity between a character in the present and the previous image is high and the similarity between a character in the present and the next image is low, it implies a sharp transition, the difference is high; 2) if both of them are high, it implies a smooth transition, the difference is low; 3) if both of them are low, it suggests that this character does not appear in either of the two images, the difference is also low. We can thus use the squared difference to measure the level of recurrence of characters across images. Finally, we can compute the average squared difference for all character instances in all pairs of adjacent images as the visual coherence coefficient. We let $\mathbf{S}_{a...b}$ be the

Model	LF	CM	B-1	B-2	B-3	B-4	M	R-L	C
Baseline									
Seq2Seq		68.03	38.65	20.28	9.78	4.68	31.64	24.24	1.66
Seq2Seq	obj	67.41	40.65	21.35	10.20	4.87	31.69	24.05	1.85
TAPM		67.33	39.85	21.70	10.72	5.19	32.38	**25.09**	1.48
TAPM	obj	67.99	40.86	22.13	10.83	5.25	32.34	24.91	1.82
ObjGrid	obj	70.65	47.66	25.26	11.95	5.42	32.83	24.42	4.68
Ours									
VCL	obj	71.18	46.50	24.71	11.85	5.60	33.12	24.58	3.67
Oracle									
CharGrid	oracle	69.33	47.72	25.34	11.94	5.43	33.03	25.02	**4.82**
Seq2Seq	oracle	**74.00**	**48.23**	**26.26**	**12.69**	**6.01**	**33.23**	24.94	4.26

Table 2: Comparison of all models using different local features (LF) on the test set of VWP using reference-based metrics including BLEU (B), METEOR (M), ROUGE-L (R-L), and CIDEr (C) and our character matching metric (CM). All numbers are an average of three runs with different random seeds.

rows from a to b indexed by i of S. We can define the coefficient as $\mathcal{L}_\mathbf{C} = ||\mathbf{S}_{2...m} - \mathbf{S}_{1...(m-1)}||_2$.

Loss function. The lack of local coherence in the visual embeddings is detrimental to the ability of the latent representations in the language to produce coherent stories. We address this by defining a visual coherence loss to encourage the latent representations to be coherent and maintain the coherence structures in the visual narratives.

We design a ranking loss function to punish stand-alone instances and reward instances that appear consecutively in image visual narratives. To do so, we first construct negative samples by randomly shuffling images in the visual narratives which breaks existing coherent groups of recurrent characters. Then we compute the visual coherence coefficient for negative samples as $\mathcal{L}_C^-$. Lastly, we define the visual coherence loss as a ranking loss: $\mathcal{L}_\mathbf{R} = max\{0, 1 - \mathcal{L}_C^+ + \mathcal{L}_C^-\}$ where $\mathcal{L}_C^+$ is the visual coherence coefficient for positive samples. The final loss function is $\mathcal{L} = \mathcal{L}_\mathbf{L} + \alpha\mathcal{L}_\mathbf{R}$ where $\mathcal{L}_\mathbf{L}$ is the cross-entropy loss for language modeling and α is the weight of ranking loss.

Model training. To better adapt the latent space of model parameters to fit the image sequence, we pre-train our model to optimize the visual coherence loss with image sequences only. We can do so because both terms in the visual coherence loss can be computed with images only. After pre-training, we fine-tune our model with paired image sequences and stories to optimize the final loss.

5 Experiment and Evaluation

In this section, we experiment with the Visual Writing Prompt (VWP; Hong et al., 2023) dataset to demonstrate the effectiveness of our loss function (see Section 3.1). We follow their settings to separate the data into train, validation and test split. We extract global features for all images using the Swin Transformer (Liu et al., 2021), a state-of-the-art supervised vision backbone model. We use the *base* model pre-trained on the ImageNet-21K dataset released on Hugging Face Models. For local features, object features are obtained using a Cascade Mask R-CNN object detector (Cai and Vasconcelos, 2019) with the same Swin Transformer backbone. We crop the bounding boxes of the top 20 objects that the detector predicts for each image. Then we extract the object features (*obj*) similarly as how we extract the global features. We also construct the oracle (*oracle*) features by passing the IDs of the characters to the language decoder. We encode the character IDs via the positions of the feature vectors. For example, character #1 takes the 1st position of the character feature matrix. Because the positional encodings in the language decoder are sensitive to the positions, the character IDs are also encoded in the input.

We use GPT-2 (Radford et al., 2019), a Transformer-based language model pre-trained on large-scale text as the language decoder. We use the small version which is widely used in previous works of story generation. We compare baseline models using the visual coherence loss combined with different character features against the two baseline models defined in Section 3.1.

Model	LF	F	M	W	Sum
TAPM	obj	9	26	40	75
VCL (ours)	obj	5	24	31	60
Seq2Seq	oracle	5	19	28	52

Table 3: Number of the three types of character errors in the 50 annotated stories. F, M and W denote Too Few REs, Too Many REs and Wrong REs respectively, as defined in Section 5.2.

5.1 Automatic Metrics

To check whether referring expressions of human characters in stories are generated correctly, we apply our character-matching (CM) metric defined in Section 3. To compare with previous baselines, we also evaluate our models with reference-based metrics including unigram (B-1), bigram (B-2), trigram (B-3), and 4-gram (B-4) BLEU scores (B; Papineni et al., 2002), METEOR (M; Banerjee and Lavie, 2005), ROUGE-L (R; Lin, 2004), and CIDEr (C; Vedantam et al., 2015), which were used in the visual storytelling shared task (Mitchell et al., 2018).

Results in Table 2 show that our model trained with visual coherence loss (VCL) substantially outperforms previous baselines like Seq2Seq and TAPM on the CM metric. This supports the hypothesis that the visual coherence loss is an effective means to make the texts better reflect the visual coherence of recurrent characters in the image sequence. We also observe that the model outperforms the baseline on most reference-based metrics except ROUGE-L. The Seq2Seq model with oracle features performs best which again shows the importance of character information.

5.2 Human Evaluation

As we mention in Section 1, we find that most errors are related to lack of local coherence (60% of stories). To get a better understanding of how model fails, we subdivide these errors into three types based on character consistency between images and stories:

Wrong Referring Expressions (REs): Consistent number of characters in the images and stories, but incorrect reference.

Too Few REs: The number of characters in the stories is smaller than the number in the images.

Too Many REs: The number of characters in the stories is more than the number in the images.

We ask three graduate students with a sufficient level of English to annotate these three types of errors. The annotation was preceded by a training phase, during which annotators were instructed to familiarize themselves with the error types and to perform trial annotations. Then, we collected their annotations and gave them feedback to correct for misunderstandings and biases. Formal annotations started after the completion of the training phase, and was blind to condition, i.e., annotators did not know which story was generated by which model. We collected 50 annotated stories for each model.

For each generated story, we counted the occurrence of the three types of character errors and then calculated the mean inter-annotator agreement (IAA) using Pearson's r and Cohen's κ. IAA on this task is moderate $r(48) = 0.45$, $p < 0.01$ and Cohen's kappa coefficient $\kappa = 0.42$.

Results in Table 3 show that compared with the state-of-the-art models, our model makes much fewer character errors. On the other hand, there is still a large gap between our model and one with oracle features, both in Table 2 and Table 3. The global/obj features are not sufficient to represent characters. We thus explore different character features in the next section.

Feature	Diff↓	Same↑	Δ↑
Swin Transformer			
body	16.41	79	<u>62.59</u>
head ← body	<u>15.41</u>	74.95	59.54
upper body ← body	16.44	78.24	61.8
face	17.85	**<u>79.47</u>**	61.63
body ← face	15.44	77.66	62.22
upper body ← face	16.44	78.29	61.84
head ← face	15.84	77.71	61.87
insightface	**1.07**	67.73	**66.65**
ID	0	100	100

Table 4: Comparison of different vision models for character representations. Diff is the average cosine similarities (%) of different instances of the same character. Same is the average similarities between different characters. Underlined numbers are the best using the same backbone and bold numbers are the best over all.

6 Character Representation

Another possible cause of local incoherence is that previous models mostly consider only the global or local visual features without a specific focus on human characters. The only local features that are related to human characters are object features, i.e., the bounding boxes or masks around the *person* objects from the object detector. Object features

LF	CM	B	M	R-L	C
obj	70.12	**22.66**	32.90	**24.88**	**4.19**
obj, body	70.11	22.16	**32.92**	24.64	3.65
obj, insightface	**71.52**	21.34	32.86	24.36	2.48

Table 5: Results of VCL model with different local features (LF) on the test set of VWP using reference-based metrics including BLEU (B), METEOR (M), ROUGE-L (R-L), and CIDEr (C) and our character matching metric (CM).

are effective and widely used in visual story generation. However, these features are either extracted using a general vision backbone model trained on the ImageNet dataset or directly from the output of the last hidden layer of the object detector. These features do not represent human age, gender, face, or body shape. These features can thus not distinguish between different instances of the same human character, which introduces wrong mentions of characters in generated stories.

To improve character representations, we need the following: **1.** distinguishing different characters; **2.** identifying different instances of the same characters. We claim that with these two properties, the visual encoder can represent the characters effectively, and the language decoder can capture these characteristics and generate more coherent and visually-grounded stories.

6.1 Types of Features

To identify characters, the use of facial features seems most promising, as face detectors have been shown to achieve highly accurate results (Deng et al., 2020). To avoid problems due to covered or invisible faces, we also consider features from other body parts. For visual narratives, it is often safe to assume that clothing over other body parts doesn't change between the images of a narrative. Joon Oh et al. (2015) employs the full body features and also inferred upper body features and head features to help person re-identification in photo albums. Body features have been proven to be effective on other similar tasks like character re-identification (Yu et al., 2020), social relation recognition (Sun et al., 2017), and movie description (Rohrbach et al., 2017).

Inferred Features. In our case, we cannot guarantee that our gold labels of human characters cover full bodies, because our annotations are based on the movie shots which often only contain half bodies or heads of the characters.

For each person bounding box, we first pass it to the face detector to get the face bounding box. We propose to use the top boundary of the character bounding box and the other three boundaries of the detected face from face detection to infer a head bounding box. Then we crop the images to get the head features (*head←face*). We follow Joon Oh et al. (2015) to compute body (*body←face*) and upper body (*upper body←face*) features using the inferred head features.

6.2 Analysis of Properties

After obtaining the face and body features, the first question that we would like to investigate is whether these features can distinguish different instances of the same character and also can distinguish different characters. Therefore, we compute the average similarities of different instances of the same character (**Same**) and the average similarities between different characters (**Diff**). We further compute differences between these two similarities (Δ) to show their ability on representing characters.

The results in Table 4 show that general vision backbone models like Swin Transformer are insufficient for differentiating different characters because the Diff scores of Swin-based features are much higher than the insightface features. The most effective method is to use the hidden representations directly extracted from the insightface Face detection system[3].

6.3 Ablation Study

To further compare the best-performing features extracted with Swin Transformer (body) and features based on insightface, we conduct experiments on VWP dataset. We apply different character features one-by-one together with object features to VCL model in visual story generation. We evaluate the models with the same metric as Section 5.1 except we report the BLEU score (B) as the average of BLEU-1 to BLEU-4 scores.

The results in Table 5 show that the model with *body* features performs on par with the model that only uses *obj* on all metrics. However, insightface features improve the character matching score significantly (t-test, $p < 0.05$), proving face features to be effective.

[3]https://insightface.ai/

6.4 Case Studies

To better illustrate the effectiveness of our CM metric, we present a case study in Figure 1. According to the error types defined in Section 5.2, we can see that the Oracle, TAPM and VCL model all make the *Too Few REs* error and additionally the TAPM model makes an *Wrong REs* error, while our proposed VCL model with the insightface feature avoids these problems. Furthermore, comparing the results of METEOR and our proposed CM, we find that METEOR does not reflect the errors in referring expressions: although the VCL model makes one reference error, its METEOR score is higher than the VCL model with the insightface feature, even though it does not make any error in referring expressions. In contrast, our proposed CM can faithfully reflect such errors.

7 Conclusions

We identified a major important problem of current vision-based story generation models, lack of local coherence (characters are not mentioned correctly). We dissect this problem into two aspects: 1) whether the latent visual representations fed to the language decoder are sensitive to the coherent structure in the visual narratives; 2) whether the visual features can distinguish different characters or identify instances of the same character. We then propose a visual coherence loss to constrain the latent visual representations together with the parameters in the language decoder such that they can represent recurrences of characters. Our model trained with visual coherence loss generates more coherent stories and obtains superior performance on both automatic metrics and human judgments. We also find that using the visual features of characters allows us to produce stories with better identification of recurring characters, which are as a result more locally coherent.

8 Limitations

One limitation is that the importance and visual salience of character instances are not measured directly. We plan to settle these in future work.

9 Ethics Statement

The VWP dataset we used is publicly accessible. It is described in a paper (Hong et al., 2023) that is published in TACL under the CC-BY license.

The potential risk of this work is that it can be used to generate harmful content. There could be potentially offensive images in VWP dataset because it is based on movies. Our model might suffer from the risk of learning unwanted correlations between these images and offensive words in the underlying language model GPT-2 because it has been found that there is a significant amount of unreliable or toxic content in the training data of GPT-2 (Gehman et al., 2020). Although we have not seen any generated in our human evaluations, our proposed model and code are for research purposes only.

Acknowledgements

This research was funded in part by the German Research Foundation (DFG) as part of SFB 1102 "Information Density and Linguistic Encoding" and a Swedish Research Council (VR) grant (2014-39) for the Centre for Linguistic Theory and Studies in Probability (CLASP). Xudong Hong is supported by International Max Planck Research School for Computer Science (IMPRS-CS) of Max-Planck Institute for Informatics (MPI-INF). We sincerely thank the anonymous reviewers for their insightful comments that helped us to improve this paper. We thank the students who help us to evaluate the generated stories: Mattes Alexander Warning, Sijie Wu and Trevor Atkins.

References

Nader Akoury, Shufan Wang, Josh Whiting, Stephen Hood, Nanyun Peng, and Mohit Iyyer. 2020. Storium: A dataset and evaluation platform for machine-in-the-loop story generation. In *Proceedings of the 2020 Conference on Empirical Methods in Natural Language Processing (EMNLP)*, pages 6470–6484.

Amal Alabdulkarim, Siyan Li, and Xiangyu Peng. 2021. Automatic story generation: Challenges and attempts. In *Proceedings of the Third Workshop on Narrative Understanding*, pages 72–83, Virtual. Association for Computational Linguistics.

Satanjeev Banerjee and Alon Lavie. 2005. METEOR: An automatic metric for MT evaluation with improved correlation with human judgments. In *Proceedings of the ACL Workshop on Intrinsic and Extrinsic Evaluation Measures for Machine Translation and/or Summarization*, pages 65–72, Ann Arbor, Michigan. Association for Computational Linguistics.

Tom Braude, Idan Schwartz, Alex Schwing, and Ariel Shamir. 2022. Ordered attention for coherent visual storytelling. In *Proceedings of the 30th ACM International Conference on Multimedia*, pages 3310–3318.

Zhaowei Cai and Nuno Vasconcelos. 2019. Cascade r-cnn: high quality object detection and instance segmentation. *IEEE transactions on pattern analysis and machine intelligence*, 43(5):1483–1498.

Khyathi Chandu, Shrimai Prabhumoye, Ruslan Salakhutdinov, and Alan W Black. 2019. "my way of telling a story": Persona based grounded story generation. In *Proceedings of the Second Workshop on Storytelling*, pages 11–21, Florence, Italy. Association for Computational Linguistics.

Wei Chen, Xuefeng Liu, and Jianwei Niu. 2022. Sentistory: A multi-layered sentiment-aware generative model for visual storytelling. *IEEE Transactions on Circuits and Systems for Video Technology*, 32(11):8051–8064.

Elizabeth Clark, Yangfeng Ji, and Noah A. Smith. 2018. Neural text generation in stories using entity representations as context. In *Proceedings of the 2018 Conference of the North American Chapter of the Association for Computational Linguistics: Human Language Technologies, Volume 1 (Long Papers)*, pages 2250–2260, New Orleans, Louisiana. Association for Computational Linguistics.

Jiankang Deng, Jia Guo, Evangelos Ververas, Irene Kotsia, and Stefanos Zafeiriou. 2020. Retinaface: Single-shot multi-level face localisation in the wild. In *Proceedings of the IEEE/CVF Conference on Computer Vision and Pattern Recognition (CVPR)*.

Ruo-Ping Dong, Khyathi Raghavi Chandu, and Alan W Black. 2019. Induction and Reference of Entities in a Visual Story.

Samuel Gehman, Suchin Gururangan, Maarten Sap, Yejin Choi, and Noah A. Smith. 2020. RealToxicityPrompts: Evaluating neural toxic degeneration in language models. In *Findings of the Association for Computational Linguistics: EMNLP 2020*, pages 3356–3369, Online. Association for Computational Linguistics.

Seraphina Goldfarb-Tarrant, Tuhin Chakrabarty, Ralph Weischedel, and Nanyun Peng. 2020. Content planning for neural story generation with aristotelian rescoring. In *Proceedings of the 2020 Conference on Empirical Methods in Natural Language Processing (EMNLP)*, pages 4319–4338.

Barbara J. Grosz, Aravind K. Joshi, and Scott Weinstein. 1995. Centering: A framework for modeling the local coherence of discourse. *Computational Linguistics*, 21(2):203–225.

Xudong Hong, Asad Sayeed, Khushboo Mehra, Vera Demberg, and Bernt Schiele. 2023. Visual writing prompts: Character-grounded story generation with curated image sequences. *Transactions of the Association for Computational Linguistics*, 11.

Xudong Hong, Rakshith Shetty, Asad Sayeed, Khushboo Mehra, Vera Demberg, and Bernt Schiele. 2020. Diverse and relevant visual storytelling with scene graph embeddings. In *Proceedings of the 24th Conference on Computational Natural Language Learning*, pages 420–430, Online. Association for Computational Linguistics.

John E Hopcroft and Richard M Karp. 1973. An n^5/2 algorithm for maximum matchings in bipartite graphs. *SIAM Journal on computing*, 2(4):225–231.

Qiuyuan Huang, Zhe Gan, Asli Celikyilmaz, Dapeng Wu, Jianfeng Wang, and Xiaodong He. 2019. Hierarchically structured reinforcement learning for topically coherent visual story generation. In *Proceedings of the AAAI Conference on Artificial Intelligence*, volume 33, pages 8465–8472.

Ting-Hao Kenneth Huang, Francis Ferraro, Nasrin Mostafazadeh, Ishan Misra, Aishwarya Agrawal, Jacob Devlin, Ross Girshick, Xiaodong He, Pushmeet Kohli, Dhruv Batra, C. Lawrence Zitnick, Devi Parikh, Lucy Vanderwende, Michel Galley, and Margaret Mitchell. 2016. Visual storytelling. In *Proceedings of the 2016 Conference of the North American Chapter of the Association for Computational Linguistics: Human Language Technologies*, pages 1233–1239, San Diego, California. Association for Computational Linguistics.

Nikolai Ilinykh and Simon Dobnik. 2022. Attention as grounding: Exploring textual and cross-modal attention on entities and relations in language-and-vision transformer. In *Findings of the Association for Computational Linguistics: ACL 2022*, pages 4062–4073, Dublin, Ireland. Association for Computational Linguistics.

Seong Joon Oh, Rodrigo Benenson, Mario Fritz, and Bernt Schiele. 2015. Person recognition in personal photo collections. In *Proceedings of the IEEE international conference on computer vision*, pages 3862–3870.

Kenton Lee, Luheng He, and Luke Zettlemoyer. 2018. Higher-order coreference resolution with coarse-to-fine inference. In *Proceedings of the 2018 Conference of the North American Chapter of the Association for Computational Linguistics: Human Language Technologies, Volume 2 (Short Papers)*, pages 687–692, New Orleans, Louisiana. Association for Computational Linguistics.

Nanxing Li, Bei Liu, Zhizhong Han, Yu Shen Liu, and Jianlong Fu. 2019. Emotion reinforced visual storytelling. *ICMR 2019 - Proceedings of the 2019 ACM International Conference on Multimedia Retrieval*, pages 297–305.

Chin-Yew Lin. 2004. ROUGE: A package for automatic evaluation of summaries. In *Text Summarization Branches Out*, pages 74–81, Barcelona, Spain. Association for Computational Linguistics.

Danyang Liu and Frank Keller. 2023. Detecting and grounding important characters in visual stories. In *37th AAAI Conference on Artificial Intelligence*. AAAI Press.

Ze Liu, Yutong Lin, Yue Cao, Han Hu, Yixuan Wei, Zheng Zhang, Stephen Lin, and Baining Guo. 2021. Swin transformer: Hierarchical vision transformer using shifted windows. In *Proceedings of the IEEE/CVF International Conference on Computer Vision (ICCV)*, pages 10012–10022.

Claudio Rezende Lucarevschi. 2016. The role of storytelling on language learning: A literature review. *Working Papers of the Linguistics Circle*, 26(1):24–44.

Margaret Mitchell, Ting-Hao 'Kenneth' Huang, Francis Ferraro, and Ishan Misra, editors. 2018. *Proceedings of the First Workshop on Storytelling*. Association for Computational Linguistics, New Orleans, Louisiana.

Yatri Modi and Natalie Parde. 2019. The steep road to happily ever after: an analysis of current visual storytelling models. In *Proceedings of the Second Workshop on Shortcomings in Vision and Language*, pages 47–57, Minneapolis, Minnesota. Association for Computational Linguistics.

Kishore Papineni, Salim Roukos, Todd Ward, and Wei-Jing Zhu. 2002. Bleu: a method for automatic evaluation of machine translation. In *Proceedings of the 40th Annual Meeting of the Association for Computational Linguistics*, pages 311–318, Philadelphia, Pennsylvania, USA. Association for Computational Linguistics.

Cesc C Park and Gunhee Kim. 2015. Expressing an image stream with a sequence of natural sentences. *Advances in neural information processing systems*, 28:73–81.

Jordi Pont-Tuset, Jasper Uijlings, Soravit Changpinyo, Radu Soricut, and Vittorio Ferrari. 2020. Connecting vision and language with localized narratives. In *Computer Vision–ECCV 2020: 16th European Conference, Glasgow, UK, August 23–28, 2020, Proceedings, Part V 16*, pages 647–664. Springer.

Dongqi Pu, Xudong Hong, Pin-Jie Lin, Ernie Chang, and Vera Demberg. 2022. Two-stage movie script summarization: An efficient method for low-resource long document summarization. In *Proceedings of The Workshop on Automatic Summarization for Creative Writing*, pages 57–66, Gyeongju, Republic of Korea. Association for Computational Linguistics.

Mengshi Qi, Jie Qin, Di Huang, Zhiqiang Shen, Yi Yang, and Jiebo Luo. 2021. Latent memory-augmented graph transformer for visual storytelling. In *Proceedings of the 29th ACM International Conference on Multimedia*, pages 4892–4901.

Alec Radford, Jeffrey Wu, Rewon Child, David Luan, Dario Amodei, Ilya Sutskever, et al. 2019. Language models are unsupervised multitask learners. *OpenAI blog*, 1(8):9.

Hannah Rashkin, Asli Celikyilmaz, Yejin Choi, and Jianfeng Gao. 2020. PlotMachines: Outline-conditioned generation with dynamic plot state tracking. In *Proceedings of the 2020 Conference on Empirical Methods in Natural Language Processing (EMNLP)*, pages 4274–4295, Online. Association for Computational Linguistics.

Anna Rohrbach, Marcus Rohrbach, Siyu Tang, Seong Joon Oh, and Bernt Schiele. 2017. Generating descriptions with grounded and co-referenced people. In *Proceedings of the IEEE Conference on Computer Vision and Pattern Recognition*, pages 4979–4989.

Qianru Sun, Bernt Schiele, and Mario Fritz. 2017. A domain based approach to social relation recognition. In *Proceedings of the IEEE conference on computer vision and pattern recognition*, pages 3481–3490.

Ramakrishna Vedantam, C Lawrence Zitnick, and Devi Parikh. 2015. Cider: Consensus-based image description evaluation. In *Proceedings of the IEEE Conference on Computer Vision and Pattern Recognition*, pages 4566–4575.

Pauli Virtanen, Ralf Gommers, Travis E. Oliphant, Matt Haberland, Tyler Reddy, David Cournapeau, Evgeni Burovski, Pearu Peterson, Warren Weckesser, Jonathan Bright, Stéfan J. van der Walt, Matthew Brett, Joshua Wilson, K. Jarrod Millman, Nikolay Mayorov, Andrew R. J. Nelson, Eric Jones, Robert Kern, Eric Larson, C J Carey, İlhan Polat, Yu Feng, Eric W. Moore, Jake VanderPlas, Denis Laxalde, Josef Perktold, Robert Cimrman, Ian Henriksen, E. A. Quintero, Charles R. Harris, Anne M. Archibald, Antônio H. Ribeiro, Fabian Pedregosa, Paul van Mulbregt, and SciPy 1.0 Contributors. 2020. SciPy 1.0: Fundamental Algorithms for Scientific Computing in Python. *Nature Methods*, 17:261–272.

Ruize Wang, Zhongyu Wei, Piji Li, Qi Zhang, and Xuanjing Huang. 2020. Storytelling from an image stream using scene graphs. In *The Thirty-Fourth AAAI Conference on Artificial Intelligence, AAAI 2020, New York, NY, USA, February 7-12, 2020*, pages 9185–9192. AAAI Press.

Xin Wang, Wenhu Chen, Yuan-Fang Wang, and William Yang Wang. 2018. No metrics are perfect: Adversarial reward learning for visual storytelling. In *Proceedings of the 56th Annual Meeting of the Association for Computational Linguistics (Volume 1: Long Papers)*, pages 899–909, Melbourne, Australia. Association for Computational Linguistics.

Peng Xu, Mostofa Patwary, Mohammad Shoeybi, Raul Puri, Pascale Fung, Anima Anandkumar, and Bryan Catanzaro. 2020. MEGATRON-CNTRL: Controllable story generation with external knowledge using large-scale language models. In *Proceedings of the 2020 Conference on Empirical Methods in Natural Language Processing (EMNLP)*, pages 2831–2845, Online. Association for Computational Linguistics.

Lili Yao, Nanyun Peng, Ralph Weischedel, Kevin Knight, Dongyan Zhao, and Rui Yan. 2019. Plan-and-write: Towards better automatic storytelling. In *Proceedings of the AAAI Conference on Artificial Intelligence*, volume 33, pages 7378–7385.

Licheng Yu, Mohit Bansal, and Tamara Berg. 2017. Hierarchically-attentive RNN for album summarization and storytelling. In *Proceedings of the 2017 Conference on Empirical Methods in Natural Language Processing*, pages 966–971, Copenhagen, Denmark. Association for Computational Linguistics.

Xintong Yu, Hongming Zhang, Ruixin Hong, Yangqiu Song, and Changshui Zhang. 2022. Vd-pcr: Improving visual dialog with pronoun coreference resolution. *Pattern Recognition*, 125:108540.

Youngjae Yu, Jiwan Chung, Heeseung Yun, Jongseok Kim, and Gunhee Kim. 2021. Transitional adaptation of pretrained models for visual storytelling. In *Proceedings of the IEEE/CVF Conference on Computer Vision and Pattern Recognition*, pages 12658–12668.

Youngjae Yu, Jongseok Kim, Heeseung Yun, Jiwan Chung, and Gunhee Kim. 2020. Character grounding and re-identification in story of videos and text descriptions. In *European Conference on Computer Vision*, pages 543–559. Springer.

A Settings of Human Evaluation

For the self-assessment in Section 1, we first adopt the list of common errors from Modi and Parde (2019). Then we add additional errors that we identified. We also merge errors that are too similar for simplicity. Finally, we define nine error types which are described in Table 6. After that, one author annotated 50 stories generated by the SOTA model TAPM.

For the human evaluation in Section 5.2, the annotation guideline is in Figure 4. We process all the data we collect to delete the unique identities of annotators. One annotator is paid by the funding source under a student assistant contract. The other two are student volunteers. One annotator is a native speaker of English and the other two are graduate school students of Saarland University who speak proficient English.

B Settings of Experiments

For the analysis in Section 3.1, We use this implementation of a coreference resolution system[4] from AllenNLP. We use this version[5] of Scipy.

For the experiments in Section 5.2, We build our system based on the code[6] by Yu et al. (2021). We follow their settings for hyper-parameters as the initial setting. Then we tune our hyper-parameters based on evaluation results on the validation split. We use the Huggingface transformer for Transformer-based models: Swin Transformers[7] and GPT-2[8]. Due to our limited computing resources, we use the *base* versions of both Swin Transformers and GPT-2. E.g. our maximum batch size is 6 on a GPU with 32GB memory. The total computation time is about 6 hours for 20 training epochs on one Nvidia V100 32GB GPU. Our code is in the Supplemental, which is unlicensed and for review only. All hyperparameters are in *config.py*. We will publish our code on GitHub after the review process of this submission.

C Experiments on VIST and VIST-Character

We also evaluate our visual coherence loss on the VIST dataset (Huang et al., 2016) and the VIST-Character dataset (Liu and Keller, 2023). We first train all the models on VIST. Then we evaluate them on the test split of VIST and the VIST-Character dataset. We use the same set of metrics described in Section 5.1 but we only report BLEU-1 and BLEU-4 for BLEU scores here for a better format. The results in Figure 7 show that model with our VCL only outperforms the Seq2Seq baseline significantly on BLEU-1 scores. The differences between VCL and all other models in all metrics are not significant. The reason is that the VIST dataset is collected in a way to exhibit less visual coherence (lower rates of recurring characters). It contains fewer human characters per story than VWP. Also, some of the features we are using for character re-identification may not be suitable to other datasets to the same extent (for instance, if the clothing of characters changes more often between album photos). We also show that the results on VIST-Character are much lower than the results on the VIST test set, which indicates that modelling character in visual stories is still very challenging.

[4] `https://demo.allennlp.org/coreference-resolution`

[5] `https://docs.scipy.org/doc/scipy/reference/generated/scipy.sparse.csgraph.maximum_bipartite_matching.html`

[6] `https://github.com/JiwanChung/tapm/`

[7] `https://huggingface.co/microsoft/swin-base-patch4-window12-384-in22k`

[8] `https://huggingface.co/gpt2`

Error Type	Description
Too generic	Lack of semantic variations. E.g. too many "good/great time", "happy".There are biases in the dataset.
Wrong event	Incorrect recognition of the event: due to the context
Wrong object	Incorrect recognition of the event participant
Grammatical error	Syntactic error: using noun phrases (NPs), missing function words, and others...
Repetition	Duplicated: a later utterance has almost the same meaning with an earlier utterance
Semantically inconsistent	Semantically inconsistent: 1) Violation of selectional preferences 2) Missing entity
Wrong character	Discourse coherence: incorrect use of anaphora
Lack of script knowledge	The connections between events contradict commonsense knowledge
Lack of narrativity	The text doesn't not contain a plot

Table 6: Error types of human evaluation and results of a SOTA model.

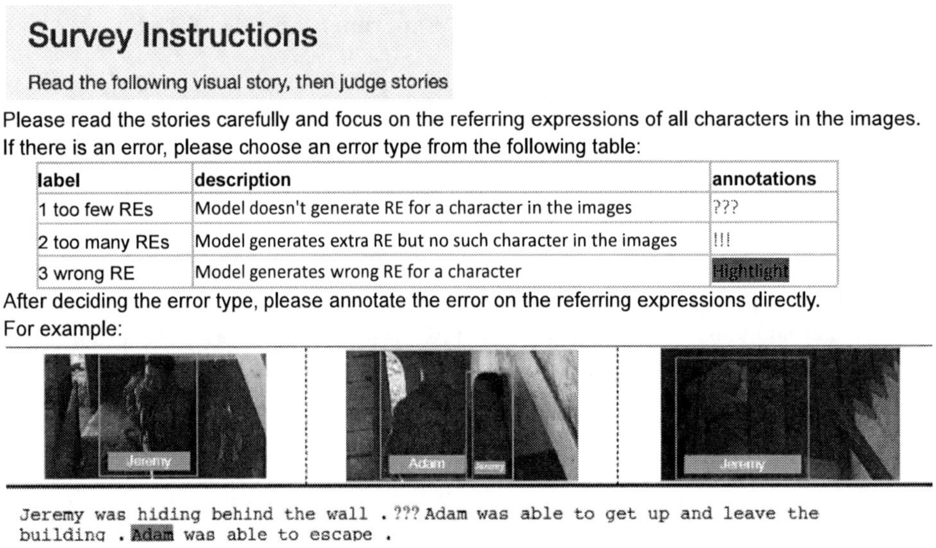

Figure 4: Survey instructions.

Model	LF	VIST B-1	VIST B-4	VIST M	VIST R-L	VIST C	VIST-Character B-1	VIST-Character B-4	VIST-Character M	VIST-Character R-L	VIST-Character C	VIST-Character CM
Baseline												
Seq2Seq		58.82**	10.45+	33.71+	29.84	7.39+	25.24	2.48	26.97+	21.58+	3.99	74.05
Seq2Seq	obj	60.23	10.84	34.08	29.91	8.24	26.47	2.67	27.52	21.83	5.21	73.66
TAPM		61.65	11.67	34.59	30.53	8.84	27.13	3.04	27.98	22.37	5.45	72.39
TAPM	obj	60.99	11.73	34.79	30.49	8.37	26.32	2.77	27.67	22.05	5.05	72.23
Ours												
VCL	obj	60.46	10.69	33.99	29.64	7.73	26.45	2.66	27.39	21.71	4.65	73.96

Table 7: Comparison of all models on the VIST test set using BLEU (B), METEOR (M), ROUGE-L (R-L), and CIDEr (C). All numbers are an average of three runs with different random seeds. +, * and ** represent that the number is one, two or three standard deviations away from the mean of the VCL model.